BIOLOGICAL WEAPONS AND TERRORISM

BIOLOGICAL WEAPONS AND TERRORISM

(In Two Volumes)

Volume-1

Dr. G.C. Satpathy

Publications

KALPAZ PUBLICATIONS

DELHI-110052

Biological Weapons and Terrorism

(Terrorism)

Rs. 1800 (Set)

ISBN: 81-7835-168-4 (Set)
81-7835-169-2 (Vol. 1)

Published in 2004 in India by
Kalpaz Publications
C-30, Satyawati Nagar
Delhi-110052
E-mail : kalpaz@hotmail.com

Laser Typesetting at: Sharma Graphic, Delhi
Printed at: Mehra Offset Press, Delhi

Contents

Foreword

Biological weapons and terrorism are a challenge to the peace and prosperity of the civilized world. Though, they are in existence from time immemorial, yet the events in USA of September 11, 2001 has shocked every human being more than ever before. It has been able to draw the attention of the super-power to the dangers of terrorism. Technology to develop weapons of mass destruction, biological and toxins warfare agents does not require huge financial resources. Its application to the target can produce devastation beyond imagination. It has the capacity to wipe out entire living world. Therefore, biological weapons of mass destruction in the hands of terrorists and fanatics have been the greatest concern of mankind.

It calls for urgent steps to sensitize the society to the dangers of bioterrrorism. It also calls for immediate review of international law and its enforcement all throughout the globe for identification of terrorist group, biological weapons and other weapons of mass destruction. It calls for co-ordination and co-operation amongst the countries of the world for immediate demolition of biological weapons of mass destruction. In the interest of future of humanity, it has been more important to resolve existing conflicts between nations and different religious and ethnic groups through a time bound agenda. Collectively, the entire world need to ensure that no conflict leads to terrorism and development of biological weapons of mass destruction.

The book on "Biological Weapons and Terrorism" by Dr G.C. Satpathy is a milcstonc on the subject. There cannot be a more appropriate time for a book on a topic of such importance than where we all are in today. Dr. Satpathy is a prolific writer. He has been able to present a complex scientific and social issue in a very simple and lucid way to the readers. His depth of knowledge on the subject is impressive. His command over language and style of presentation can mesmerize any reader. I compliment Dr Satpathy for his hard work. I hope the book will fulfil the very objective for which it has been written and published.

Dr. N.C. Borah

Chairman GNRC & Health Care Foundation of North East

Dispur, Guwahati, Assam Pin-781 -006

Introduction

Germs as Arms : Old Dogs, New Tricks

Suddenly, everyone is talking about biological warfare, that is the deliberate employment of microbes to attack and affect military forces, civil population, crops and livestocks. This is being designated as the ugly face of global terrorism. There is nothing new about biological warfare. Biological agents, chemicals and toxins are used in wars along with conventional weapons often enough. Even in the most-ancient civilizations methods like poisoning of food and drinking water meant for public consumption were employed. It was known to Hindu civilization as back as 500 BC. The ancient Romans who knew a thing or two about warfare may be considered the pioneer in the field. They use to throw animal carcasses into the water sources, contaminating it. In around 1346 AD, the Tartars replicated the Roman tactics (using cadavns of plague victims) with resounding success. Not only did the city of Kaffa (seaport on the Black Sea) fall, but also it was speculated that the bubonic plague epidemic that swept through medieval Europe between 1347 and 1331 was a result of this.

If biological terrorism is a nightmare for civilizations, it is a challenge for the diplomatic, technical, military, medical and intelligence communities. The dangers of nuclear holocaust are wellknown. But people are generally less aware of equally potent threat to the survival of mankind, is the biological weapons, compared to the effects of nuclear missiles and bombs, the bio-weapons have greater impact by their long term effects on humans, animals and plant life systems of the planet. A wide range of microbes and viruses capable of causing small pox, bubonic plague, cholera, typhoid, diphtheria, anthrax, malaria, dengue fever, encephalitis, botulism, tularaemia, viral haemorrhage fever etc. may serve as devastating biological bomb and can be deployed much more easily at a much lower cost.

The scenario becomes scary, if we realise that these weapons can reach the hands of terrorists. They are easy to conceal and carry. Besides, they have prolonged effect. For example, Anthrax, which kills by destroying the membranes of lungs and intestines of human beings, remains active and lethal for more than 40 years. There are self perpetuations, mutations and creation of new variants by these germs and viruses. Certain biological agents only incapacitate, others kill. The Ebola virus, for example, can kill 90 per cent of the infected people in little over a week. Victims die thrashing about a convulsive fits, bleeding from every orifice. Pathorenesis of Ebola still poorly understood, and yet no cure.

The production of biological weapons, their storage for long period, transportation and deployment in destruction of enemy power involves considerable intricacies. These have been mastered through systematic research in what may be called as areas of "military genetics". For example, anthrax germs can be transformed into a bread like form that is stable in extreme conditions of temperature and atmosphere. Such developments mark the transition of dangerous biological agents into biological weapons. Reportedly, more than a dozen countries have stocks of biological weapons including some developed countries. Delivery of plague and anthrax microbes through ballistic missiles was said to be the plan of some powerful European countries, as preparation of World War III. This is inspite of the fact that a Biological Weapons Convention (BWC) was drafted as far back in 1972 and came into force in 1975, to prevent development, production, stockpiling of such weapons, Despite it was signed by 159 countries, there is no agreement in how to enforce it. In fact, there is no definitive information on existing stocks of these weapons or facilities that exist for their production and storage in different countries. Publicly, of course, every country denies possession of such weapons.

All said and done, we have already entered the brightening new era of biological warfare. It goes without saying that the world is not prepared to face "bioterrorism". Defensive measures based on prevention, detection, treatment and decontamination may work in case of potential individual targets, but are grossly inadequate in cases of mass attacks, specially surprised terrorist attacks. Such attacks, apart from inflicting damage on the immediate target may start chain-reactions that may be beyond human control. Again, preventive steps, like vaccination are of little use against genetically engineered variants of known germs. Unless there is absolute moratorium on this madrace, the effects will be somewhat like "global suicide".

In the contemporary international scenario, the terrorist attacks on Sept. 11, 2001 that destroyed the world famous World Trade Centre at New York, left American wondering, "What next? The retaliation by US Government; the military action in Afghanistan to punish Osama-bin-Laden further raised the fears of Americans. Most of them anticipated a terrorist attack using chemical or biological weapons.

What later followed was the anthrax attack; less real but more in the shape of putting fear in people's mind. Many letters were received by various people that carried a powder and a warning that pointed to anthrax fear. Most of them turned out to be bogies but they succeeded in putting fear in people's mind. As the threat wore on, some real ones came and shook the Americans. Anthrax is a disease that is spread by aerosods. It causes respiratory failure and death. Antibiotics can save life if given in an early stage.

The fear of use of biological weapons by terrorists has given rise to many a question. Use of biological weapons or its likelihood was always there. But recent developments have made the world sit up and take serious note of it. Biological weapons have certain features which are not there in other kinds of weapons. To begin with, very small capital is needed to build these weapons. Next, there is not much equipment needed for this. These can be created in a small laboratory. Thirdly, no highly-skilled professionals are needed to create these weapons. Fourthly, these weapons are very easy to transport. An individual can carry these weapons of mass destruction on his person, capable of killing lakhs of people without being detected. Also, the strike capability of these weapons is enormous. Additionally, there is time lapse between the spreading of germs and people falling victim to them. This time allows the persons responsible for spreading them reach thousands of miles away before the strike becomes known.

This book goes deep into the various aspects of biological weapons, anthrax in particular. It also deals with the actions mooted to control them and the various acts and laws created to deal with terrorism linked to biological weapons. The first chapter of the book depicts the post-September 11 scenario which played on the psyche of Americans. It tells us about the anthrax cases that took place in various parts of the US. And warns us that criminals and terrorists are a step ahead of us. What is their next step is never known. Just when 19 men turned planes into bombs, authorities tightened the airport security. This was when they started sending anthrax through mail. It is futile to fight the previous battle, instead of concentrating on the next.

Chapter number two concentrates on discussing the disease, that is known as anthrax. It tells us about its symptoms, infectious agents, preventive measures, etc. It also takes up the issue of bioterrorism as linked to anthrax. It explains to us that we are always ill-equipped to deal with a terrorist attack that makes use of biological weapons. A chemical release or a major explosion is far easier to manage in comparison to the biological challanges posed by the biological agents like small pox or anthrax. In case of a chemical or explosive weapon, the worst effects are quickly over. Efforts are thus, directed towards stabilization and recovery. Same is not the case with a biological attack. Day after day, new cases keep coming into light and in new areas.

The next chapter deals with the biological and toxin warfare agents. In the past, biological weapons or BWs as they are known in short, were regarded as being of little military importance. But in the recent past, military has started showing interest in such weapons. It is because, with the advances in genetic engineering, they have become far more potent as compared to the chemical weapons. Also, they have the capability to multiply. They also have the same advantage as the chemical weapons and neutron bombs—killing people without destroying the equipment.

Fourth chapter brings us face-to-face with the bio-terrorism. This chapter describes the terrorist act carried out by the members of a religious sect Aum Shinrikyo. Bioterrorism is a threat that can harm the mankind by destroying food and agriculture also. Bioterrorism is effective even in its crude form also. Bioweapons need not perform efficiently to bring about the desired result. A little of technical skill and some knowledge of biology is all that is needed to develop a bioweapon.

Fifth chapter makes an attempt to define terrorism. It tells us that Indian government has made several laws to deal with terrorism. But in most of these laws, the term 'terrorism' has not been defined. The Terrorist-Affected Areas (Special Courts) Act 1984 is the first Act where an attempt is made to define who a terrorist is. A terrorist under this Act is defined as, 'any person who indulges in wanton killing of persons or in violence or in the disruption of services or means of communications necessary to the community or in damaging property with a view to -

(a) putting the public or any section of the public in fear,

(b) adversely affecting the harmony between various religious racial, language or regional groups or castes or communities,

(c) coercing or overawing the government established by law,

(d) endangering the sovereignty and integrity of India.

The later definition as given in the Terrorist and Disruptive Activities Act (TADA) was only a slight modification over the above definition. The main difference between TADA and earlier laws was the inclusion of the element of 'motive' leading up to a terrorist attack. The same provides the basic thrust to the definition of terrorism as laid down in the Prevention of Terrorism Ordinance 2001, now passed by Parliament to be an Act.

Chapter six looks at the different laws formulated internationally to plug the evil of terrorism countries around the world have turned, at one point of time or another, to international law.

The first time that the international communities grouped together against terrorism was, in the League of Nations' after the assassination of King Alexander I and Louis Barthou in Marseilles, France. This led to the first United Nations Convention against terrorism. Since then, many important developments have taken place. There have been many ghastly acts of terrorism and each such act has highlighted the need for an effective mechanism to deal with terrorism. There have been some UN conventions but only partly successful in restraining the countries from harbouring the terrorists. The 'third party' route is also gaining popularity where dealing with terrorists involves a third party acceptable to both the parties.

Role of the *Interpol* is also considered important in tracking down of terrorists. But there is a stumbling block in the form of Article 3 of Interpol Constitution. It informs the member states that they are 'prohibited to undertake any intervention or activities of a political, military, religious or racial character.' This was used as an excuse by the US to protect a group of Czech 'refugees' who hijacked an aeroplane and then sought political asylum. The US argue that the hijacking was simply political and any action against them would be violative of Article 3 of the Interpol Constitution. This served as a death blow to the effectiveness of Interpol against terrorist attacks.

International Criminal Court can be a worthy legal remedy for all those seeking it against global terrorism.

The next chapter, i.e., chapter seven deals on terrorism, ideology and law. Modern day terrorism has much to do with ideology. This phenomenon began with the left wing student movements in Europe in the third quarter of twentieth century. It was the first time then that one came across the highly motivated groups with radical views against the establishment using violence as a means to make their point. These groups made targetted attacks initially but later also exploited the soft underbelly of the state. This represented terrorism backed by ideology.

Another thing associated with terrorism is that no act of terrorism is on impulse or accidental. There is quite often a pronounced political slant to it.

To tackle the madness called terrorism, there is a need to have an independent national Centre for Counter-terrorism. To involve the whole political spectrum of the country in the anti-terrorist initiative is perhaps the best way to end the air of cussedness that has generally marked the executive-judiciary relationship over the issue of special powers. For this the government of the day needs to show greater generosity in involving others than it has so far done.

Chapter eight deals with efforts of Indian government to create a special law to deal with terrorism. After scrapping of TADA, a kind of vacuum existed, to deal effectively with terrorism. Hence, the need for a new law. At the root of it lies the hijacking of Indian Airlines flight IC 814 en route Kathmandu to Delhi. Three reasons can be cited that are behind the developing of a new law. One, the terrorism went up unabatedly; two, terrorism was not being combated well enough; three, the curice laws, were soft in dealing with fanatics like terrorists.

Next chapter is devoted to the botulinum toxin which is a major BW agent much under speculation in recent years. Kinds of this organism, its natural habitat, symptoms of disease caused by it in man, outbreak of botulinum in human population; its symptoms and outbreak in animals, pathogenicity of difference types of botulinum-toxin etc. are discussed in this chapter. Botulinum toxin is an important possible BW agent for various reasons. It is the most potent poison known so far. It can affect man and also animals; and its effect is deadly.

Chapter number ten introduces us to a new generation of BW agents having suitability for operational use against humans. Possibility of new arms race has dawned on the horizon due to use of advancement in the genetic engineering methods and likelihood of their use for development of novel BW agents.

Efforts to control biological weapons began as early as in 1925 with the Geneva Protocol. This protocol was a continuation of efforts to ameliorate the calamities of war. More recent Biological Weapon Convention, 1972 and the five yearly reviews of it form part of a continuing chain efforts aimed at controlling the biological weapons by the international community. Biological weapons control through the international control regime form part of the eleventh chapter. The next chapter brings us to the British experience in trying to tackle terrorism legally.

There are more lessons to be learnt from this than one can, from the Law Commission of India. The British experience is important in the Indian context because it has the Irish insurgency at the core of problems like our own problem in the Jammu and Kashmir. The two acts—NI (EP) AC and the PTA—formed the basis of British anti-terrorist legislation for several years.

The last chapter describes us the various laws and Acts in place to tackle with different aspects of terrorism. It includes laws like Disturbed Areas (Special Courts Act), 1976, the National Security Act, 1980, Terrorism Affected Areas (Special Courts) Act, 1984, the Terrorist and Disruption Activities (Prevention) Act, 1987, the SAARC Convention (Suppression of Terrorism) Act, 1993, the Prevention of Terrorism Ordinance, 2001, etc.

The book also includes 'Bibliography' recommending relevant literature for further reading and the index making it a worthy book for its readers. This book would not only appeal to those concerned with it from the point of view of their research and study but also to general public as it is a timely and thought provoking work on the burning topic of Anthrax and related biological weapons.

This compilation will be of immense utility for knowledge, research and planning in army and semi-army organisations besides in police and parapolice units. The institutions engaged in biomedical research, corporate hospitals, medical colleges and pharmaceutical companies will be benefited in fields like anti-microbial and vaccine research. It will be informative to city planners and health administrators.

The author is highly grateful to Dr. N.C. Borah, an eminent neurologist and a pioneer in corporate health sector in India for going through the entire draft of the book and given his valuable comments recorded as "Foreword" in this book. He also thanks the large number of reference providers and encouragers, without which the work would not have been completed.

Dr. G.C. Satpathy

1

Anthrax Scare : Aftermath of September 11

The September 11 strike on the WTC in NY left the world wondering about what else can happen. What followed was the scare of Anthrax. Anthrax has the lethal capabilities and is a likely future biological weapon of mass destruction.

Initially, the anthrax scares seen everywhere could be dismissed as the products of overactive imaginations. In Florida, where residents were already spooked by reports that September 11 skyjackers had inquired about renting crop-dusters, authorities had received more than 100 calls about suspicious powders following the WTC incident; they all turned out to be innocuous substances such as plaster dust. In Trenton, N.J., two office buildings were evacuated after employees reported opening packages containing a white powder. Tests were conducted and no traces of any pathogens were found. An Internal Revenue office in Covington, Ky., was sealed off and 200 employees briefly quarantined after powder was found in an envelope. It, too, was harmless and so was the brown powder found in an envelope sent to a state agency in Ohio, the powder in a Halloween card sent to The Columbus Dispatch and the yellow powder in an envelope that an Ohio couple opened exactly a month after the September 2001, terrorist attacks. That one also contained a note. "You are now infected with anthrax." They weren't. Nor was the divorce lawyer of a woman to whom a bitter husband sent a letter that, according to him was impregnated with anthrax, the FBI told Newsweek.

Anthrax Panic

Although anthrax is not contagious, fear of it was epidemic. But if the FBI, intelligence officials, local police and—most of all—Americans who had vowed not to live in terror were tempted to dismiss these scares as hoaxes or hysteria, they were quickly proved wrong. By midweek eight employees at American Media Inc. in Boca Raton, Fla., had been exposed to Bacillus anthracis; one, photo editor Robert Stevens, died as the result of inhaling thousands of deadly spores. On October 12 in New York City, NBC News assistant Erin O'Connor tested positive for cutaneous anthrax, apparently the result of exposure to a powder in an envelope she had opened three weeks before. And the next day a letter received at a Microsoft office in Reno, Nev., tested positive for anthrax : the envelope, in which Microsoft had sent a check to a vendor in Malaysia, had been returned, with the check intact. It also had pornographic pictues cut from a magazine, and dusted with anthrax spores. Suddenly, a hypothetical threat became all too real, and fears that had been bubbling under the surface for the past month burst into the open. In New York, Celeste Sharpe, a mother of two and former assistant district attorney in the Bronx, found out about the NBC anthrax through NYPD friends. Anxiously withdrawing cash from an ATM, she told a friend by cell phone, "I'm getting the hell out of the city." President George W. Bush implored all Americans to live their lives as normally as possible. "Our government is doing everything we can to make our country as safe as possible," he said. But while everyone agreed that panic wasn't called for, prudence was.

The U.S. Postal Service advised all Americans to monitor their mail carefully and to be wary of any envelopes without return addresses, with stains or odours or with too much postage (a hint that the sender really, really doesn't want it returned for insufficient postage). The State Department ordered all U.S. Embassies to purchase and keep ready three days' supplies of the antibiotic ciprofloxacin—as a precaution. Bayer, the German pharmaceutical giant, announced that it would raise production of Cipro, its trademark ciprofloxacin, by 25 per cent beginning Nov. 1: wholesalers were running low on the drug throughout the United States.

The panic was understandable: people are much more afraid of exotic, seemingly uncontrollable risks like anthrax than they are of more familiar ones like flu (which kills more than 20,000 Americans each year). Anthrax is nothing if not exotic, at least in America. It is caused by a bacterium, Bacillus anthracis. This rod-shaped microbe develops in soil, where it can be ingested by sheep, cows, horses and goat. That's why anthrax is labeled a veterinary disease, and why those most likely to contract it work with animals or animal products (such as wool). If growing conditions are bad, the bacteria form microscopic spores, which can remain dormant (and lethal) for decades. In the worst-known anthrax outbreak, at least 66 people died when spores were released from a bioweapons plant in Sverdlovsk, Russia, in 1979. At every step in the anthrax investigations, officials were quick to minimize the threat.

Yet those reassurances were eclipsed by other cases or by evidence that authorities are ill-equipped for a bioterror attack. When Bob Stevens was diagnosed with inhalation anthrax, his was an "isolated' case, Florida and federal health officals insisted, and almost certainly the result of accidental, natural exposure—even though anthrax has never been reported in animals or soil east of the Mississippi River and even though the United States recorded just 18 cases of inhalation anthrax in the 20th century and none since 1978. But when alert doctors found anthrax spores in the nose of AMI mailroom supervisor Ernesto Blanco, 73, who was hospitalized with pneumonia, "isolated" looked like it had company. FBI agents sealed the building two days after the death of Stevens, and agents in airtight jumpers and oxygen masks swarmed through AMI's offices, scouring it for traces of anthrax. The next day, October 8, AMI's 700 employees and recent visitors lined up at the white annex building of the county Health Department in Delray Beach to have nasal swabs taken. By midweek AMI mailroom worker Stephanie Dailey, 36, had also tested positive for the presence of anthrax spores in her nose. Although hardly an official statement went by without the assurance that anthrax is not contagious, the message was not getting through in south Florida. In Boca Raton, when 3-year-old Alexander de Jesus got ready to climb into a barber's chair, the hair stylist showed him and his mother the door.

Panic, and perhaps copycats, spread like a nasty flu. St. Petersburg Times columnist Howard Troxler got a letter warning, in unsteady handwriting, "Howard Troxler ....1st case of disease now blow away this dust so you see how the real thing flys." "This" was a white, sugarlike substance. Later, it tested negative for the presence of anthrax and other pathogens. Although seemingly every sicko with a grudge had decided that there's nothing like an anthrax threat to strike terror in the heart of your target, the copycat threats that followed the Florida case seemed empty—until October 12.

Before dawn that morning the FBI learned that the anthrax bug had hit New York. NBC, the FBI reported, had received a suspicious business letter addressed to "Nightly News" anchor Tom Brokaw. Postmarked St. Petersburg, Fla., it arrived September 25, with no return address. When Brokaw's assistant, Erin O'Connor, opened it, she found white powder and a note: "The unthinkable. See what happens next." NBC's security office called the FBI, which picked up the letter the next day. Within days O'Connor, 38, developed a rash below her left collarbone. After it became more irritated, ulcerous and necrotic (filled with dead tissue), she consulted a doctor. The Cipro he prescribed on Oct. 1 cleared the lesion. But a call from one of O'Connor's doctors to the city Health Department, reporting a possible case of anthrax, and a call from the city to the FBI, alerted the bureau. The FBI ordered tests on the powder in the letter O'Connor opened , as well as a skin biopsy from O' Connor, at the U.S. Centers for Disease Control and Prevention in Atlanta. O' Connor tested positive for cutaneous anthrax. But the powder tested negative.

When the FBI interviewed O'Connor more extensively, she recalled that she had got another letter, postmarked Sept. 18. She hadn't thought anything of it. But, she finally remembered, it did contain some kind of dark, sandlike powder. That letter, postmarked Trenton, N.J., contained traces of anthrax, the FBI reported. The delay in identifying the powder, and O'Connor's lesions, confirmed fears that neither public-health officials nor law-enforcement agencies will be able to trace bioterrorism quickly. That would be especially horrific if the bug were a contagious microbe such as smallpox. On the same day that O'Connor was diagnosed with cutaneous anthrax, The New York Times received a letter, postmarked St. Petersburg, on the same date as the letter sent to Troxler. It was addressed to Judith Miller, coauthor with three Times colleagues of the new best-seller "Germs: Biological Weapons and America's Secret War," and filled with white powder. There were "some similarities" in the handwriting on the letters to NBC and the Times, said Barry Mawn, head of the FBI's New York office.

Although the substance contained no anthrax, the Times assured readers in a front-page box in its Saturday edition "that no copies of the newspaper are printed in (oru) Manhattan headquarters."

To trace the postal anthrax, investigators kept trying to identify the strain in the Florida, Nevada and New York cases. To do that they first grew the suspected anthrax spores in a nutrient medium, such as beef broth, until they germinate into live, roddshaped bacterial cells, says Calvin Chue, research scientist at the Center for Civilian Biodefense Studies at Johns Hopkins University. If anthrax is present, antibodies in a test kit bind to antigens on its surface. If they do—the test takes half an hour - the antibodies fluoresce. In Reno, however, the state lab tested directly for anthrax spores and got a hit. In the current criminal investigations, the FBI hopes to find out which of the hundred-plus genetically distinct strains of anthrax were sent to AMI, NBC and Microsoft. They have not yet succeeded and it's not clear that doing so is going to help much. Many types of anthrax can be found at microbiology labs across the world. The Ames strain, for example, named after an lowa lab where it was first isolated half a century ago, "is a very common virulent strain that's used in every antibiotic and vaccine" study, says Martin Hugh-Jones of Louisiana State University.

If the science offers few leads, old-fashioned police work might. In Florida, investigators focuses on a one-page, handwritten love letter addressed to Jennifer Lopez. It was sent to The Sun, says a source, in Lantana, Fla. It reportedly arrived sometime after September 17. Staffers laughed over it and passed it around the third-floor editorial personnel. Enclosed was a small Star of David and a tablespoon or so of a bluish substance that resembled dishwashing powder. Bob Stevens was among those who handled the letter. As one staffer later recalled, "The only difference between Bob and those who watched him open it was that Bob [who had poor eyesight] held it up to his face. "Stevens's spartan workstation-Macintosh computer, a mousepad decorated with photos of his friends, crayon drawings from a colleague's young son—was a hot spot of anthrax. So was a receptacle in the mailroom, where Blanco and Dailey worked. But how five additional employees were exposed (their blood tests came back positive) is a mystery: some work for The National Enquirer, whose offices are "way the heck down the hall and around the corner," says The Sun's Carla Chadick.

Even if anthrax reached AMI through a letter, it wasn't much to go on. "I'm not sure the FBI is prepared to handle the amount of weird mail we get," says Grant Balfour, a Sun writer. When you write about alien abductions, celebrity brawls and the size of Osama bin Laden's private parts, you're not surprised when letters arrive with dirty underwear, human feces, claims to being a Romanov heir and other rants.

FBI officials do not accept that the anthrax at NBC, Microsoft and American Media Inc. came from Osama bin Laden or any other known terrorist. The connections so far are circumstantial. Last summer Mohamed Atta and Marwan Al-shehhi, who piloted the planes that hit the World Trade Center, rented an apartment in Delray Beach, a few miles from the AMI building, and underwent flying lessons nearby. The White House was calling the FBI every two hours one night after getting a report that the two skyjackers had asked a Delray Beach pharmacist for an antibiotic to fight anthrax. Rather than antibiotics, in fact, Atta asked for something to soothe an inflammation of his hands. The redness resembled the irritation caused by detergent or bleach. The pharmacist gave him a cream called acid mantle. The incident gave rise to fears that Atta had been using caustic chemicals in a bioterror experiment: detergent effectively breaks up clumps of anthrax spores into smaller, deadlier particles. Although the FBI did not rule out a connection to Al Qaeda, one senior U.S. Official said "my instinct says it's a nut case." One death, one easily treated rash and seven symptom-free people with anthrax spores in their noses or antibodies in their blood are hardly what experts expected from terrorists wielding a bioweapon. Every scenario until now was envisioned anthrax spores being aerosolized—dried and turned into a powder—and then disseminated widely in the air, probably into an enclosed space like a building or airplane. The goal would be to spread the spores like an invisible, lethal fog, keeping the particles small enough so that they get inhaled before settling to the ground. Additionally, many bioweapons experts thought terrorists intent on mass murder rather than just mass panic would use an antibiotic-resistant strain. The Russians engineered anthrax strains resistant to penicillin, doxycycline and other antibiotics by splicing in genes from naturally resistant strains of, say, the common intestinal bacterium E. coli. The Florida strain was not genetically engineered, and is vulnerable to antibiotics.

But there is another reason law—enforcement officials have been at pains to stress that the anthrax cases have not been linked to Al Qaeda or any other terrorist group. "Biological-weapons agents can easily be obtained," Ron Atlas, president of the American Society of Microbiology, wrote recently. "A survey of nearly 1,500 U.S. academic institutions suggests that 22 per cent work with pathogenic micro organisms and toxins that could be used in biological-weapons development." You can't just walk into a lab and swipe a vial of anthrax, but researchers agree that nothing would stop a determined individual from hiring on at a lab, as a student or technician, and obtaining a starter culture. "We all use student workers who are 18 or 19," says LSU's Hugh-Jones. "Most of them don't even have any background you can check."

Pathogens Market

Until the Feds cracked down in the late 1990s, pathogens could also be bought. In 1995, white supremacist Larry Wayne Harris ordered three vials of freeze-dried bubonic-plague bacteria from the non-profit American Type Culture Collection, for $240. The germs in this were an innocuous vaccine strain (weakened, or attenuated, so they don't give you the disease itself rather than trigger immunity to it). In 1986 ATCC sold three types of anthrax to the University of Baghdad, and in 1988 sold four strains to the Iraqi Ministry of Trade. All these ATCC's sales were legal. During the gulf war, however, American intelligence agencies were sure that ATCC's strains were among those that Iraq used in its biological-weapons programme. A 1996 law restricts sales of the most deadly microbes, including anthrax and Ebola, but if scientists are denied access to the bugs, research on vaccines and cures will end. The current anthrax cases have not changed one crucial reality: turning pathogens into weapons of mass destruction is hugely difficult.

As far as intelligence agencies know, the group that put the greatest effort into bioterror was Japan's Aum Shinrikyo cult. In April 1990, memebers drove an automobile outfitted to disseminate botulinum toxin around Japas's Parliament building. In June 1993, they made an effort to disrupt the wedding of Japan's crown prince by spreading botulinum toxin the same way. They also attempted, for four straight days to spread anthrax from a rooftop in Tokyo.

"Nine failures in nine attempts attest to the difficulty of actually deploying biological weapons to cause mass casualties," says Atlas. And Aum Shinrikyo had a war chest estimated at more than $ 300 million, and also half a dozen labs and experienced biologists. Growing anthracis is no more difficult than growing sourdough starter. But turning bacteria into spores, the only form haldy and stable enough to be spread, needs the tricky step of shocking the bacteria with heat or chemicals without killing them. Perhaps the greatest problem is getting particles of the right size. Spores tend to clump. Yet particles must be between one and five microns to enter the lungs and trigger inhalation anthrax; it's not easy to get a sprayer to dispense such a fine mist, as Aum Shinrikyo came to know. Assassination by microbe, however, is a different story. In 1978 the Bulgarian secret police killed dissident Georgi Markov by injecting deadly ricin (derived from castor beans) into his thigh with a pellet shot from an umbrella. And someone killed Bob Stevens. It all appeared like a bad movie. "What are the chances?" asked Penny Robbins, who works in the Microsoft building. "Reno and anthrax?"

It would be foolish to think we can imagine what criminals and terrorists will try next. But we might observe that, after 19 men turned planes into bombs, we ramped up airport security—just when people began sending anthrax through the mail. Now we treat our mail like toxic waste, planes with "mysterious powders" on bathroom counters get impounded and doctors bone up on anthrax. Perhaps, instead of fighting the last battle, we need to concentrate to anticipate the next. "If we just focus on anthrax," says Ken Alibek, a top scientist in the Soiviet bioweapons programme who defected to the United states, "we're going to be surprised." We saw the effects of surprise, all too horrifically, on September 11.

2

Anthrax and Bioterrorism

Anthrax is an acute bacterial desease that is now theratis to be used as a biological weapon. Its symptoms, infectious agent, preventive measures, bioterrorism measures etc. are discussed here.

I Anthrax

Symptoms

An acute bacterial disease that normally affects the skin, but which may very rarely involve the oropharynx, mediastinum or intestinal tract. In cutaneous anthrax, itching of an exposed skin surface occurs first, and this is followed by a lesion that becomes papular, then vesicular and in 2-6 days develops into a depressed black eschar. The eschar is often surrounded by moderate to severe and very extensive edema, sometimes with small secondary vesicles. Pain is unusual and, if present, is because of edema or secondary infection. The head, forearms and hands are common sites of infection. The lesion has been confused with human orf. Untreated infections may spread to regional lymph nodes and also to the bloodstream with an overwhelming septicemia. The meninges can become involved. Untreated cutaneous anthrax has a case-fatality rate between five to twenty per cent, but with effective antibiotic therapy few deaths occur. The lesion evolves through typical local changes even after the intiation of antibiotic therapy. Initial symptoms of inhalation anthrax are mild and nonspecific and may involve fever, malaise and mild cough or chest pain, acute symptoms of respiratory distress, X-ray evidence of mediastinal widening, fever and shock follow in 3-5 days, with death shortly thereafter. Intestinal anthrax is not common and more difficult to recognize, except that it tends to occur in explosive food poisoning outbreaks; abdominal distress is followed by fever, signs of septicemia and death in the typical case.

An oropharyngeal form of primary disease has been described. Laboratory confirmation is made by demonstration of the causative organism in blood, lesions or discharges by direct polychrome methylene blue (M' Fadyean)-stained smears or by culture or inoculation of mice, guinea pigs or rabbits. Rapid identification of the organism with the help of immunodiagnostic testing, ELISA and PCR may be available in certain reference laboratories.

Infectious Agent

Bacillus anthracis, a Gram-positive, encapsulated, spore forming, nonmotile rod.

Occurrence

Basically a disease of herbivores; humans and carnivores are incidental hosts. Anthrax is an infrequent and sporadic human infection in most industrialized countries. It is an occupational hazard for those workers who process hides, hair (especially from goats), bone and bone products and wool; and of veterinarians and agriculture and wildlife workers who may handle infected animals. Human anthrax is endemic in those agricultural regions of the world where anthrax in animals is common; these include countries in South and Central America, southern and eastern Europe, Asia and Africa. New areas of infection in livestock may develop through introduction of contaminated animal feed. Environmental events such as floods may provoke epizootics. Anthrax is regarded a major potential agent in bioterrorism or biowarfare and, as such, could present in epidemiologicaily unusual circumstances.

Mode of Transmission

Cutaneous infection is through contact with tissues of animals (cattle, sheep, goats, horses, pigs and others) dying of the disease; possibly by biting flies that had partially fed on such animals; through contact with contaminated hair, wool, hides or products made from them, such as drums, brushes or rugs; or by contact with soil linked to infected animals or contaminated bone meal used in gardening. Inhalation anthrax results from inhalation of spores in risky industrial processes—like tanning hides and processing wool or bone—where aerosols of B. anthracis spores may be produced. Intestinal and oropharyngeal anthrax is caused by ingestion of contaminated undercooked meat; there is no evidence that milk from infected animals transmits anthrax. The disease spreads among grazing animals through contaminated soil and feed; among omnivorous and carnivorous animals through contaminated meat, bone meal or other feeds, and among wildlife from feeding on infected carcasses. Accidental infections may occur among laboratory workers.

An outbreak of inhalation anthrax occurred in 1979 in Yekaterinburg (Sverdlovsk), Russia, in which 66 individuals were documented to have died of anthrax and 11 infected persons were known to have survived; several other cases are presumed to have occurred, investigations revealed that the cases occurred as the result of a plume emanating from a biological research institute and led to the conclusion that the outbreak had resulted from an accidental aerosol generated in work linked to biological warfare studies.

Incubation Period

From 1 to 7 days, although incubation periods up to 60 days are possible. (In the Sverdlovsk outbreak, incubation periods extended up to 43 days.) Transmission from person to person does not usually occur. Articles and soil contaminated with spores may remain infective for decades.

Preventive Measures

(i) Immunize high risk persons with a cell-free vaccine made from a culture filtrate containing the protective antigen (available in the USA from the Bioport Corporation, 3500 N. Martin Luther King, Jr., Boulevard, Lansing MI 48909). Evidence suggests that this vaccine is effective in preventing cutaneous and inhalational anthrax, it is recommended for laboratory workers who regularly work with B. anthracis and workers who handle potentially contaminated industrial raw materials. It may also be used to protect military personnel against likely exposure to anthrax used as a biological warfare agent. Annual booster injections should be taken if the risk of exposure continues.

(ii) Educate employees who handle potentially contaminated articles about modes of anthrax transmission, care of skin abrasions and personal cleanliness.

(iii) Properly ventilate work areas and control dust in hazardous industries, especially those that handle raw animal materials. Maintain continuing medical supervision of employees and provide prompt medical care of all suspicious skin lesions. Workers should use protective clothing and have enough facilities for washing and changing clothes after work. Locate eating facilities away from places of work.

(iv) Wash, disinfect or sterilize hair, wool and bone meal or other feed of animal origin prior to processing.

(v) So not sell the hides of animals, that have been exposed to anthrax or use their carcasses as food or feed supplements (i.e., as bone or blood meal).

(vi) In case anthrax is suspected, do not necropsy the animal but aseptically collect a blood sample for culture. Avoid contamination of the area. If a necropsy is inadvertently performed, autoclave, incinerate or chemically disinfect/fumigate all instruments or materials. Since the anthrax spores may survive for decades if the carcasses are buried, the preferred disposal technique is to incinerate the carcasses at the site of death or to remove them to a rendering plant, ensure no contamination en route to the plant. If these methods cannot be applied deeply bury carcasses at the site of death, if possible; do not burn them on open fields. Decontaminate soil seeded by carcasses or discharges with five per cent lye or anhydrous calcium oxide (quicklime). Carcasses buried deep should be covered with quicklime.

(vii) Control effluents and trade wastes from rendering plants that handle potentially infected animals and those from factories that make products from hair, wool, bones or hides exposed to contamination.

(viii) Annually immunize and reimmunize all animals at risk. Treat symptomatic animals with penicillin or tetracyclines; immunize these animals after cessation of therapy. They should not be used for food for some months. Treatment in lieu of immunization may be used for animals exposed to a discrete source of infection, such as contaminated commercial feed.

Controlling the Immediate Environment, Patient and Contacts

(i) Report to local health authority, Also report to the appropriate livestock or agriculture authority. Even a single case of human anthrax, especially of the inhalational variety, is so unusual that it should be at once reported to both public health and law enforcement authorities for consideration of a bioterrorist source.

(ii) Isolation: Standard precautions to be followed for the duration of illness for cutaneous and inhalation anthrax. Antibiotic therapy sterilizes a skin lesion within 24 hours, but the lesion progresses through its typical cycle of ulceration, sloughing and resolution.

(iii) Concurrent disinfection: Of discharges from lesions and articles soiled by these Hypochlorite is sporicidal and good when organic matter is not overwhelming and the item is not corrodable; hydrogen peroxide, peracetic acid or glutaraldehyde may be alternatives; formaldehyde, ethylene oxide and cobalt irradiation have been used. Sopres need steam sterilization, autoclaving or burning to make sure total destruction. Fumigation and chemical disinfection may be used for valuable equipment. Terminal cleaning.

(iv) Quarantine: None.

(v) Immunization of contacts: None.

(vi) Investigation of contacts and source of infection: Try to find out history of exposure to infected animals or animal products and trace to place of origin. In a manufacturing plant, inspect for adequacy of preventive measures as outlined in 9A, above. As mentioned in 9B1, a potential bioterrorist source may require ruling out for all human cases of anthrax, especially for those cases with no obvious occupational source of infection.

(vii) Specific treatment: Penicillin is the drug of choice for cutaneous anthrax and this needs to be given for 5-7 days. Tetracyclines, erythromycin and chloramphenicol are also effective. The U.S. military recommends parenteral infusion of ciprofloxacin or doxycycline for inhalational anthrax; but the duration of therapy is not well defined.

Epidemic Nature

Outbreaks may be an occupational hazard of animal husbandry. The occasional epidemics in the USA are local industrial outbreaks among employees who work with animal products, especially goat hair. Outbreaks related to handling and consuming meat from infected cattle have occurred in Asia, Africa and the former Soviet Union.

International Measures

Sterilize imported bone meal before use as animal feed. Disinfect wool, hair and other products when indicated and practical.

Bioterrorism Measures

During 1998, there were more than two dozen anthrax threats made in the USA. None of these threats was real. The general procedures in the USA for dealing with these civilian threats is as given below:

(i) Anyone who receives a threat about dissemination of anthrax organisms should notify the local office of the Federal Bureau of investigation (FBI) immediately.

(ii) In the USA, the FBI is basically responsible for the investigation of such biological threats, and all other agencies are to cooperate and provide assistance as requested by the FBI.

(iii) Local and state health departments should also be notified and be prepared to provide any public health management and follow-up that may be needed.

(iv) Persons who may have been exposed to anthrax are not contagious, so quarantine is not necessary.

(v) Persons who may have been exposed should be advised to wait for laboratory results and need not be placed on chemoprophylaxis. If they become ill before laboratory results are available, they should contact their local health department at once and proceed to a predetermined emergency care unit, where they should inform the attending staff of their potential exposure.

(vi) In case the threat of exposure to aerosolized anthrax is credible or confirmed, persons at risk should begin postexposure prophylaxis with both an appropriate antibiotic (fluoroquinolones are the drugs of choice and doxycycline is a substitute) and vaccine. Postexposure immunization with an inactivated, cell-free anthrax vaccine is indicated together with chemoprophylaxis following a proven biologic incident. Immunization is recommended due to the uncertainty of when or if inhaled spores may germinate. Postexposure immunization consists of three injections: as early as possible after exposure and at 2 and 4 weeks after exposure. This vaccine has not been evaluated for safety and efficacy in children less than 18 years of age or adults below 60 years of age or older .

(vii) All first responders should follow local protocols for incidents of biological hazards.

(viii) Responders can be saved from anthrax spores by donning splash protection, gloves and a full face respirator with high-efficiency particle air (HEPA) filters (Level C) or self-contained breathing appraratus (SCBA) (Level B).

(ix) Those who may have been exposed and are potentially contaminated should be decontaminated with soap and lots of water in a shower. Usually no bleach solutions are required. A 1:10 dilution of household bleach (i.e., a final hypochlorite concentration of 0.5 per cent) should be used only in case there is gross contamination with the agent and an inability to remove the materials through soap and water decontamination. The use of bleach decontamination is recommended only after soap and water decontamination, and the solution should be rinsed off after 10 to 15 minutes.

(x) All persons to be docontaminated should remove their clothing and other personal belongings and place all items in plastic bags, which should be labeled clearly with the owner's name, contact telephone number and inventory of the bag's contents. Personal items may be kept as evidence in a criminal trial or returned to the owner in case the threat is unsubstantiated.

(xi) If the suspect envelope or package linked to an anthrax threat remains sealed (not opened), then first responders should take no other action than notifying the FBI and packaging the evidence. Quarantine, evacuation, decontamination and chemoprophylaxis efforts are not indicated if the envelope or package remains sealed. For incidents involving possibly contaminated letters, the environment in direct touch with the letter or its contents should be decontaminated with a 0.5 per cent hypochlorite solution following a crime scene investigation. Personal items may be decontaminated in the same fashion.

(xii) Technical help can be given immediately by contacting the National Response Center at 800-424-8802 or the local Weapons of Mass Destruction Coordinator of the FBI.

II Bioterrorism

The long ignored and denied threat of bioterrorism has increased over the past few years. Recent events in Iraq, Japan, and Russia cast an ominous shadow. Two candidate agents are of special concern: smallpox and anthrax. The magnitude of the problems and the gravity of the scenarios linked to release of these organisms have been vividly portrayed by two epidemics of smallpox in Europe during the 1970s and by an accidental discharge of aerosolized anthrax from a Russian bioweapons facility in 1979. Attempts in the United States to deal with possible incidents involving bioweapons in the civilian sector have only recently begun and have made only limited progress. Only with substantial additional resources at the federal, state, and local levels can a credible and meaningful response be mounted. For longer-term solutions, the medical community must educate both the public as well as the policy makers about bioterrorism and create a global consensus condemning its use.

Recent Rise

In the recent past, biological terrorism had been little discussed or written about. Until recently, I had doubts about publicizing the subject due to concern that it might entice some to undertake dangerous, perhaps catastrophic experiments. However, events of the past year or two have made it clear that likely perpetrators already envisage every possible scenario.

The following points of view prevalent among national policy circles and the academic community at various times have served to dismiss biological terrorism as simply a theoretical possibility:

(1) Biological weapons have so seldom been deployed that precedent would suggest they will not be used.

(2) Their use is so morally repugnant that no one would deign to use them.

(3) The science of producing enough organisms and dispersing them is so difficult that it is within the reach of only the most sophisticated laboratories.

(4) Like the concept of a "nuclear winter," the potential destructiveness of bioweapons is essentially unthinkable and so to be dismissed. Each of these arguments is without validity.

There are nations and dissident groups that have both the motivation and access to skills to selectively cultivate some of the most dangerous pathogens and to use them as agents in acts of terrorism or war. After the Gulf War, Iraq was found to have a large biological weapons programme. In 1995, Iraq acknowledged that it had produced, filled, and deployed bombs, rockets, and aircraft spray tanks containing Bacillus anthracis and botulinum toxin[1,2]; its work force and technologic infrastructure are still wholly intact. Also in 1995, the Japanese cult, Aum Shinrikyo, released the nerve gas Sarin in the Tokyo subway. The cult also had plans for biological terrorism[3]; its arsenal included large quantities of nutrient media, botulinum toxin, anthrax cultures, and drone aircraft equipped with spray tanks. Members of this group had gone to Zaire in 1992 to get samples of Ebola virus for weapons development.

A concern that has recently come up, is the status of one of Russia's largest and most sophisticated former bioweapons facilities, called Vector, in Koltsovo, Novosibirsk. Through the early 1990s, this was a 4,000-person, 30-building facility with enough biosafety level 4 laboratory facilities, used for the isolation of both specimens and human cases. Situated on an open plain surrounded by electric fences and protected by an elite guard, the facility housed the smallpox virus as also work on Ebola, Marburg, and the hemorrhagic fever viruses (e.g., Machupo and Crimean-Congo). A visit in the autumn of 1997 found a half-empty facility protected by a handful of guards who were not paid for months. The number of countries engaged in biological weapons experimentation rose from 4 in the

1960s to 11 in the 1990s[4]. Meanwhile, the bombing of the World Trade Center and the Oklahoma City Federal Building have dramatized the serious problems even small dissident groups can cause. A comprehensive review of the problems posed by biological terrorism and warfare has been published[5]. Four observations deserve special mention. First, biological terrorism is now possible more than ever before and much more threatening than either explosives or chemicals. Second, official actions directed at the threat to the civilian population (less than 2 years in the making) have been only marginally funded and minimally supported[6]. Third, stopping or countering bioterrorism will be extremely difficult. Recipes for making biological weapons are now openly floating on the Internet, and even groups with modest finances and basic training in biology and engineering could develop, should they wish, an effective weapon[7] at little cost. Fourth, detection or interdiction of those intending to use biological weapons is next to impossible. Thus, the first evidence of such weapons will almost certainly be cases in hospital emergency rooms. Specialists in infectious diseases thus constitute the front line of defence.

The speed with which they and emergency room personnel reach a proper diagnosis and the rapidity with which they apply preventive and therapeutic measures could spell the difference between thousands and perhaps tens of thousands of casualties. Of course, the survival of physicians and health-care staff caring for the patients may be at stake. However, today few have ever seen so much as a single case of smallpox, plague, or anthrax, or, for that matter, would recall the features of such cases. Few, if any, diagnostic laboratories are prepared to confirm promptly such diagnoses. Only a small number of pothogens are reasonably easy to prepare and disperse and can inflict sufficiently severe disease to paralyze a city and perhaps a nation. In April 1994, Antoliy Vorobyou, a Russian bioweapons expert, provided to a working group of the National Academy of Sciences the conclusions of Russian experts as to the agents most likely to be used[8]. Smallpox headed the list followed closely by anthrax and plague. None of these agents has so far effectively been deployed as a biological weapon, and thus no real world events exist to provide likely scenarios. However, we have had several well-documented smallpox importations into Europe over recent decades; two bear recounting. Smallpox is caused by a virus that spreads from person to person; infected persons have a characteristic fever and rash. Virus infection invariably results in symptomatic disease. There are no mild, subclinical infections among unvaccinated persons.

After an incubation period of 10 to 12 days, the patient has high fever and pain. Then a rash starts with small papules developing into pustules on day 7 to 8 and finally changing to scabs around day 12. Between 25 per cent and 30 per cent of all unvaccinated patients die of the disease. There was, no specific treatment; nor there is. Until 1980, essentially all countries carried on vaccination programmes of some kind, whether or not they had endemic disease[9]. Until 1972, the United States mandated smallpox vaccination for all children at school entry, although the last cases had occurred in 1949, 23 years before. In the United Kingdom, four standby hospitals were to be opened only if smallpox cases were imported, and in Germany, two state-of-the-art isolation hospitals were built in the 1960s specifically for the isolation of smallpox cases should they may come to light. In 1962, the initial response of U.S. officials to the occurrence of a single case of smallpox illustrated extreme concern. That year, a yound Canadian boy came back from Brazil, travelling by air to New York and by train to Toronto by way of Albany and Buffalo[10]. Soon after arrival in Toronto, he developed a rash and was hospitalized.

In response to this single case, senior U.S. government officials seriouly considered a plan of action that called for the border with Canada to be closed, for mass vaccination campaigns to be carried out in all cities along the route from New York through Albany, Syracuse, Rochester, and Buffalo, and for vaccination of all who had been in Grand Central Station on the day the Canadian boy was there. Sensibly, this plan was soon done away with, for more modest measures, albeit not without considerable debate.

Great Potential

The potential of aerosolized smallpox to spread over a considerable distance and to infect at low doses was vividly exposed in an outbreak in Germany in 1970[11]. That year, a German electrician returning from Pakistan became ill with high fever and diarrhoea. On January 11, he was admitted to a local hospital and was isolated in a separate room on the ground floor as it was feared he might have typhoid fever. He had contact with only two nurses over the next 3 days. On January 14 a rash developed, and on January 16 the diagnosis of smallpox was confirmed. He was immediately taken to one of Germany's special isolation hospitals, and more than 100,000 persons were promptly vaccinated.

The hospital had been closed to visitors due to an influenza outbreak for several days before the patient was admitted. After the diagnosis of smallpox, other hospital patients and staff were quarantined for 4 weeks and were vaccinated; acutely ill patients received vaccinia-immune globulin first. However, the smallpox patient had had a cough, a symptom nor normally seen with smallpox; coughing can produce a large-volume, small-particle aerosol like what might occur after its use as a terrorist weapon. Later, 19 cases occurred in the hospital, including four in other rooms on the patent's floor, eitht on the floor above, and nine on the third floor. Two were contact cases. One of the cases was in a visitor who had spent less than 15 minutes in the hospital and had only briefly opened a corridor door, easily 30 feet from the patient's room, to ask directions. Three of the patients were nurses, one of whom died. This outbreak took place in a well-vaccinated population. An outbreak in Yugoslavia in February 1972 also demonstrates the havoc created even by a small number of cases. Yugoslavia's last case of smallpox had occurred in 1927. Nevertheless, Yugoslavia, like many other countries, had continued population-wide vaccination to protect against imported cases. In 1972, a pilgrim coming back from Mecca became ill with an undiagnosed febrile disease.

Friends and relatives visited from a number of different areas; 2 weeks later, 11 of them became ill with high fever and rash. The patients were not aware of each other's illness, and their physicians (few of whom had ever seen a case of smallpox) failed to diagnose correctly. One of the 11 patients was a 30-year-old teacher who soon became critically ill with the hemorrhagic form, a form not readily diagnosed even by experts. The teacher was first given penicillin at a local clinic, but as he became increasingly ill, he was shifted to a dermatology ward in a city hospital, then to a similar ward in the capital city, and finally to a critical care unit because he was bleeding profusely and was in the state of shock. He died before a definitive diagnosis was made. He was buried 2 days before the first case of smallpox was recognized.

The initial cases were rightly diagnosed 4 weeks after the first patient became ill, but by then, 150 persons were already infected; of these, 38 (including two physicians, two nurses, and four other hospital staff) were infected by the yound teacher. The cases took place in widely separated areas of the country. By the time of diagnosis, the 150 secondary cases had already begun to expose yet another generation, and, inevitably, questions arose as to how many other yet undetected cases there might be. Health authorities launched a nationwide vaccination campaign. Mass vaccination clinics were held, and checkpoints along roads were set up to examine vaccination certificates. Twinty million persons were vaccinated. Hotels and residential apartments were taken over, cordoned off by the military, and all known contacts of cases were forced into these centres under military guard. Some 10,000 persons spent nearly 2 weeks or more in isolation. Meanwhile, neighbouring countries closed their borders. Nine weeks after the first patient became ill, the outbreak stopped. In all, 175 patients contracted smallpox, and 35 passed away. What might happen if smallpox were released today in a U.S. city? First, routine vaccination stopped in the United States in 1972. Some travellers, many military recruits, and a handful of laboratory workers were vaccinated over the following 8 years.

Overall, however, it is not clearly known that more than 10 per cent to 15 per cent of the population today has residual smallpox immunity. If some modest volume of virus were to be released (perhaps by exploding a light bulb containing virus in a Washington subway), the event would definitely go unnoticed until the first cases with rash began to appear 9 or 10 days later. With patients seen by different physicians (who almost certainly had never before seen a smallpox case) in different clinics, many days would probably elapse before the diagnosis of smallpox was confirmed and an alarm was sounded. Even if only 100 persons were infected and needed hospitalization, a group of patients many times larger would become ill with fever and rash and receive an uncertain diagnosis. Some would be reported from other cities and other states.

Where would all of these patients be admitted? In the Washington, D.C., metropolitan area, only about 100 hospital beds provide adequate isolation. Who would care for the patients? Few hospital staff have any smallpox immunity. Moreover, one or two patients with severe hemorrhagic cases (which typically have very short incubation periods), who would have been hospitalized before smallpox was suspected, would have been attended by a large, unprotected intensive care team. What of contacts? In past outbreaks, contacts of confirmed or suspected cases were found to be in the thousands, if not tens of thousands. What measures should or could be taken to deal with such numbers? Would patients be isolated as in Yugoslavia, and if so, where? Logistics could be simplified if fast, easily used laboratory tests could confirm or rule out smallpox among suspected cases. Curently, however, such tests are known only to scientists in two government laboratories. An immediate clamour for mass vaccination (as in the outbreaks in Germany and Yugoslavia) can be predicted and is under standable. U.S. stocks of small pox vaccine are nominally listed at 15 million doses, but with packaging, the useful number of doses is perhaps half that number.

How widely and quickly should this vaccine be used? Were vaccine to be given strictly to close contacts of confirmed cases, comparatively few doses would be needed. However, the realities of dealing with even a small epidemic would most probably preclude such a cautious, measured vaccination effort. Vaccine reserves would disappear fast, and there is, at present, no manufacturing capacity to produce additional quantities of vaccine. If an emergency effort were made to produce new stocks of smallpox vaccine, many months to a year or more would be needed. What of anthrax, which has been so enthusiastically embraced by both Iraq and the Aum Shinrikyo?

The organism is not difficult to produce in large quantities. In its dried form, it is highly stable. The effect of aerosolized anthrax on humans once had to be inferred from animal experiments and the occasional human infection among workers in factories processing sheep and goat hides [12]. It was evident that inhalation of anthrax is highly lethal. Just how lethal became clear in the 1979 Sverdlovsk epidemic. In all, 77 cases were identified with certainty; 66 patients died. The actual total number of cases was probably considerably more than one hundred.

The persons affected lived or worked somewhere within a narrow zone extending about four kilometres south and east of a military bioweapons facility. An accidental airborne release of anthrax spores took place during a single day and may well have lasted no more than minutes. Further investigations showed anthrax deaths among sheep and cows in six different villages up to 50 km southeast of the military compound along the same axis as the human cases. Of the 58 patients with known dates of disease onset, only nine revealed symptoms within a week after exposure; some became ill as late as 6 weeks after exposure. Whether the onset of illness occurred sooner or later, death almost invariably followed within 1 to 4 days after onset. However, there appeared to be a somewhat higher proportion of survivors after the fourth week. This near certainty resulted from the widespread application of penicillin prophylaxis and anthrax vaccine, both of which were distributed in mid-April throughout a population of 59,000. Meselson and his colleagues, who documented this outbreak, found that the weight of spores released as an aerosol could have been as little as a few milligrams or as much as "nearly a gram." Iraq acknowledged producing at least 8,000 L of solution with an anthrax spore and cell count of 109/ml. The ramifications of even a modest-sized release of anthrax spores in a city are profound. Emergency rooms would start seeing a few patients with high fever and some difficulty breathing perhaps 3 to 4 days after exposure.

By the time the patients were seen, it is nearly certain that it would be too late for antibiotic therapy. All patients would die within 24 to 48 hours. No emergency room physicians or infectious disease specialists have ever come across a case of inhalation anthrax; medical laboratories have had virtually no experience in its diagnosis. Thus, at least 3 to 5 days would pass before a definitive diagnosis would be made. Once anthrax was diagnosed, one would be faced with the dilemna of what to do over the succeeding 6 to 8 weeks. Should vaccine be given to those who might have been exposed? At present, little vaccine is available, and no plan exists to produce any for civilian use. Should antibiotics be administered prophylactically? If so, which antibiotics, and what should be the criteria for exposure? What quantity would be needed to treat an exposed population of perhaps 500,000 over a 6-week period? Should one be concerned about additional infections resulting from anthrax spores later resuspended and inhaled by others?

Should everyone who has been anywhere near the city report to a local physician for treatment at the first occurrence of fever or cough, however mild? Undoubtedly, many would have such symptoms, more so in the winter, how can such symptoms be distinguished from the premonitory symptoms of anthrax that may proceed to death within 24 to 48 hours? We are ill-equipped to deal with a terrorist attack that makes use of biological weapons. In countering civilian terrorism, the focus (a modest extension of existing protocols to deal with a hazard materials incident) has been almost wholly on chemical and explosive weapons.

A chemical release or a major explosion is far more manageble than the biological challenges posed by smallpox or anthrax. After an explosion or a chemical attack, the worst effects are quickly over, the dimensions of the catastrophe can be defined, the toll of injuries and deaths can be ascertained, and attempts can be directed to stabilization and recovery. Same is not the case following the use of smallpox or anthrax. Day after relentless day, additional cases could be expected, and in different areas.

Long Term Response

The spectre of biological weapons use is an ugly one with every bit as grim and foreboding as that of a nuclear winter. As was done while responding to the nuclear threat, the medical community should educate the public and policy makers about the threat. We need to develop on lines of the 1972 Biological and Toxin Weapons Convention to strengthen measures preventing the development and production of biological weapons and to ensure compliance with existing agreements. In a broader sense, we need a strong moral consensus condemning biological weapons. But this is not enough.

In the longer term, we need to be as prepared to detect, diagnose, characterize epidemiologically, and respond appropriately to biological weapons use as to the threat of new and reemerging infections. In fact, the needs are convergent. We need at international, state, and local levels a greater capacity for surveillance; a far superior network of laboratories and better diagnostic instruments; and a bigger cadre of trained epidemiologists, clinicians, and researchers. On the immediate horizon, we cannot delay the development and implementation of strategic plans for coping with civilian bioterrorism.

The needed stocking of vaccines and drugs as well as the training and mobilization of health workers, both public and private, at state, city, and local levels will need time. Knowing fully well what little has been done, one can only say that a great task lies before us.

References

1. Ekeus R. Iraq's biological weapons programme: UNSCOM's experience. Memorandum report to the United Nations Security Council; 1996 20 Nov; New York.

2. Zalinskas R.A. *Iraq's biological weapons: the past as future?* JAMA 1997; 278: 418-24.

3. Daplan E, Marchell A . The cult at the end of the world. New York: Crown Publishing Group; 1996.

4. Roberts B. New challenges and new policy priorities for the 1990s. In : Biologic weapons: weapons of the future. Washington: Center for Strategic and International Studies; 1993.

5. Bioweapons and bioterrorism. JAMA 1997; 278:351-70, 389-436.

6. Tucker JB. *National health and medical services response to incidents of chemical and biological terrorism.* JAMA 1997; 285:362-8.

7. Danzig R, Berkowsky PB. Why should we be concerned about biological warfare? JAMA 1997;285: 431-2.

8. Vorobyov A. Criterion rating as a measure of probable use of bio agents as biological weapons. In: Papers presented to the Working Group on Biological Weapons Control of the Committee on International Security and Arms Control, National Academy of Sciences; 1994 April; Washington.

9. Fenner F, Henderson DA, Arita I, Jezek Z, Ladnyi I. Smallpox and its eradication. Geneva: World Health Organisation; 1988.

10. Epidemiologic report. Smallpox, Canada. MMWR Morb Mortal Wkly Rep 1962; 11:258.

11. Wehrle PF, Posch J, Richter KH, Henderson DA. *An airborne outbreak of smallpox in a German hospital and its significance with respect to other recent outbreaks in Europe.* Bull World Health Organ 1970; 4:669-79.

12. Brachman PS, Friedlander AM. Anthrax In: Plotkin SA, Mortimer EA, editors. Vaccines. Philadelphia: WB Saunders; 1994.

13. Further Reading—Resurgence of Anthrax-T.K. Dutta, R. Kanungo, L.H. Ghatekar, Post Graduate Medicine (API) 2001.

3

Biological and Toxin Warfare Agents

Biological and toxin warfare agents are considered poor man's atomic bomb. A renewed interest is shown by the military in recent times though then were considered of little military importance in the past. BW agents are advantageous militarily in that they kill people without destroying the materials.

In the recent past the military has shown a growing interest in biological warfare (BW) and toxin warfare (TW) agents. Until the 1970s BW agents had been regarded as being of little military importance. They are far more potent than chemical weapons because of their capability to multiply. For example, one single organism of Coxiella burnetii, a putative BW agent inhaled or injected intraperitoneally, is enough to initiate Q fever[1]. In 1974 Fred C. Ikle, then Director of the US Arms Control and Disarmament Agency (ACDA), declared that 'the military utility of these weapons is dubious at best, the effects are unpredictable and potentially uncontrollable, and there exists no military experience concerning them'. Biological warfare agents are particularly uncontrollable and unpredictable if they are dispersed by living vectors which might set up reservoirs in the local animal population.

In addition, BW agents were considered as not being effective battlefield weapons since they act more slowly than chemical agents. Instead they were considered to be suitable weapons for damaging whole populations as well as crops and farm animals. It has been said, however, that BW agents offer the same 'advantages' as chemical weapons and neutron bombs—killing people without destroying equipment. Thus, the Committee on Science and Astronautics of the US House of Representatives held 'CBR ('the shorthand for chemical, biological and radiological warfare) as a weapon which is not competitive with nuclear weapons, but complementary to them, designed to do a different job'. The Committee also opined that 'it is granted that some forms of CBR offer the prospect and the hope of winning battles without taking human life or destroying houses and factories'. It envisaged, however, that 'Their real potential lies in the future. They can conceivably become the most potent and the most selective weapons available'.

The view was held that BW agents might be considered as 'the poor man's atomic bomb'[2] or the terrorists' bomb. G.W. Merck, in 1946, special consultant for biological warfare, in a report to the Secretary of War stated: 'It is important to note that, unlike the development of the atomic bomb and other secret weapons during the war, the development of agents for biological warfare is possible in many countries, large and small, without vast expenditures of money or the construction of huge production facilities.

It is clear that the development of biological warfare could very well proceed in many countries, perhaps under the guise of legitimate medical or bacteriological research'. President James E. Carter stated more than three decades later that 'the production of biological weapons does not always require elaborate or highly specialized installations.... and small research facilities....can make significant contributions to the achievement of a biological capability.' In this connection it is also worth mentioning that about 50 per cent of the developing and poor countries are not yet States Parties to the Biological Weapons Convention[3], while the 'Plame Report' describes 'the Third World (as) the scene of most of the world's violence since 1945' (independent Commission, 1982, p. 11) and mentions that 'the horrors of chemical and biological warfare appear to be peculiarly reserved for the peoples of the developing world'.

Correspondingly, the former Indian Ambassador to Sweden, A.K. Damodaran, suggests that 'the world has grown used to the idea that chemical and biological means can be used to achieve military purposes in remote parts of the world difficult to monitor'[4]. Chemical warfare agents have undoubtedly been used by Iraq in the Gulf War, although Iraq is a state party to the Geneva Protocol of

1925 which forbids CW and BW. This raises the question—why then should the developing countries hold back from using BW agents as well? A member of the US Army Science Board, in a report on 'The Challenge of Terrorism' mentions that the terrorist Baader-Meinhf group had threatened to use mustard gas against cities fo FR Germany, and that in 1972 'two college youths were charged with conspiracy to commit murder in a plot to poison Chicago's water supply with "typhoid and other deadly bacteria". Later, West German authorities received similar threats of the introduction of anthrax into the country's water supply'. In October 1981, protesters had deposited soil infected with spores of Bacillus anthracis, taken from Gruinard Island where experiments using anthrax spores as a potential BW agent were done during World War II, at the Chemical Defence Establishment at Porton Down, Wiltshire, and at Blackpool Tower only a few hundred yards from the Conservative Party conference in the Winter Gardens[5]. Releasing an anonymous statement to newspapers, the protesters said the 'seeds of death' were being sent back to where they came from.

The protesters were accused by Mr Gray, MP for Ross and Cromarty, of gross irresponsibility. 'These people have put the whole country at danger by such a silly action' Hurwitz points out for a long time now essentially anyone has been able to order quantities of Clostridium botulinum at the American Type Culture Collection in Rockville, Maryland, for a fee of $34. 'All that the collection requires is that the request be made on a business letterhead or requisition form from a suitable research facility or laboratory...There is even an 800 (i.e., free) number provided for easier service! 'Botulinum toxin was said to be used in murdering Reinhard Heydrich, the then Nazi Reichsprotektor of Bohemia and Moravia, on 23 May 1942. 'The predecessor organisation—the Organization of Strategic Services— of the Central Intelligence Agency (CIA) appears also to have been involved in the use of BW materials against enemy leaders as the CIA informed Senator Edward M. Kennedy in 1977 (USA.1977a, p. 243). Referring primarily to actions of its predecessor organisation (the Organisation of Strategic Services), the CIA mentioned 'an instance involving a Nazi leader during a period of the war to prevent his appearance at a major economic conference during the war. They used food poisoning, which was rather successful'. (The symptoms of food poisoning are induced by, among other things, staphylococcal enterotoxin, a TW agent which has been stockpiled at least until 1970 by the CIA (USA, 1970b). Even the introduction of genetic engineering did not immediately alter the view that BW agents have only limited military importance: as late as 1978 President Carter felt 'that such agents can only create serious problems for the user, that they will be indiscriminate in their application, ineffective as weapons of combat, and they cannot be controlled. Under these conditions there is a very strong chance that they might cause as much harm to the user as the intended adversaries' (USA, 1978a, p. 220). Some experts questioned whether recombinant DNA techniques and other biotechnological methods which emerged in the 1970s; would contribute significantly to biological warfare purposes. In their background paper prepared for the States Parties to the Biological Weapons Convention before the first Review Conference, the three depositary governments (the UK, the USA and the USSR) stressed that 'modifying an organism by recombinant DNA techniques is similar in effect to modifying it by llassical genetic techniques' (UN, 1980a, p.7). An expert panel formed by the US Department of State expressed the opinion that 'genetic engineering will not yield pathogens that are any more lethal than some that already exist (e.g., anthrax)' (USA, 1981b, p. 4).

Over past few years this opinion has changed. According to former Prime Minister Margaret Thatcher, chemical and biological weapons are as devastating as nuclear weapons (UK, 1985). And Caspar Weinberger, US Secretary of Defense, explained that 'for biological warfare purposes, genetic engineering could open a large number of possibilities. Harmless in general , non-disease-producing organisms could be devised to become highly toxic or produce diseases for which an opponent has no known treatment or cure. Other agents, now considered too unstable for storage or biological warfare applications, could be changed sufficiently to be an effective agent.

Biological Warfare Agents

Biological weapons, are 'living organisms', whatever their nature, or infective material derived from them, which are intended to cause disease or death in man, animals and plants, and which depend for their effects on their ability to multiply in the person, animal, or plant attacked'. This definition, given in the report of the UN Secretary-General (UN, 1969, p. 6), more or less corresponds to that used by the World Health Organisation (WHO) in its 1970 report, although WHO lays stress that BW agents are 'intended for use in war' (WHO, 1970, p. 12). BW agents, however, might be used not only in wars, but also in acts of terrorism. One should therefore refer to living organisms 'used for hostile purposes[7]. It should further be noted that the pathogenic effects of some biological agents do not depend on the ability to multiply in the infected host. Some viruses, for instance, are cytotoxic and kill their host cells by adsorbing to them.

Furthermore, in advance of the first Review Conference on the Biological Weapons Convention the Swedish representatives made suggestion that 'pure nucleic acids containing information for synthesis of toxic material may in the future possibly be introduced into exposed organisms and then through gene action induce damage in the host' and which 'do not need a proliferation stage in the host before induction of damage' (UN, 1980c, p. 3). Therefore, the definition of BW agents should normally refer to agents usually depending on their ability to multiply in the infected host. The UN Secretary-General also makes clear that many different organisms including viruses and fungi, can be used as BW agents, and emphasizes, that 'in the context of warfare all these are generally recognized as "bacteriological weapons"' (UN, 1969, p. 6). In his report, therefore, the phrase 'bacteriological (biological) weapons' is used 'to comprehend all forms of biological warfare' and to eliminate any possible ambiguity.

By specifying that BW agents are able to multiply, it becomes clear that toxin warfare agents must be distinguished from BW agents. The use of a definition of BW agents which specifies that these are able to multiply makes clear that toxin warfare agents do not come under this category.

Toxin and other Chemical Warfare Agents

Toxins are substances usually produced by living organisms which are poisonous in nature. Toxin warfare (TW) agents, or toxin weapons, are toxins used for hostile purposes. TW agent unequivocally are types of chemical warfare (CW) agent. CW agents, or chemical weapons, are those chemical substances whether gaseous, liquid, or solid, which are used for hostile purposes to cause disease or death in humans, animals or plants and which depend on their direct toxicity for their primary effect (UN, 1969, p. 6). TW agents, like all other CW agents, are inanimate and thus they are incapable of multiplying. They are CW agents without regard to whether they are produced by a living organism or by chemical synthesis or even whether they are responsible for the qualification of that organism as a BW agent. Their juxtaposition in the text of the Biological Weapons Convention makes it clear that the States Parties to the Covention recognise TW agents as different from BW agents.

And yet, TW agents are often mistakenly considered to be biological weapons, and definitions of biological warfare (BW) occasionally include TW agents. An important example of such a fault appears in Protocol III of the Revised Brussels Treaty, Annex II, Section III, issued in 1954. There a BW agent is defined as 'any equipment or apparatus expressly designated to use, for military purposes, harmful insects or other living or dead organisms, or their toxic products [8]. A similar description is used by FR Germany in a law issued in 1955 (FRG, 1955, p. 270). Identical standpoints were revealed by representatives of the United States several times since 1946. In 1946, G.W. Merck, in his report to the Secretary of War defined biological warfare 'as the use of bacteria, fungi, viruses, rickettsies, and toxic agents from living organisms (as different from synthetic chemicals used as gases or poison) to produce death or disease in men, animals, or plants' (emphasis added) (USA, 1946, p. 65). In 1959, the US Department of Health, Education and Welfare also included herbicides when defining biological warfare as 'the intentional emloyment of living organisms, toxic biological products and chemical plant growth regulators to produce death or casualties in man, animals, or plants' (emphasis added) (USA, 1959b, p.24).

In 1976 'the United States considers biological toxins to be biological weapons[9], and in 1977, the US Army defined biological warfare much in the same way as Merck's definition of 30 years before 'as the use of microorganisms ("germs"), such as bacteria, fungi, viruses, rickettsiae, and substances (toxins) derived form living organisms (as distinguished from synthetic chemicals used as gases or poisons) to produce death or disease in humans, animals, or plants' (emphasis added) (USA, 1977b, p. 24). Again in 1985 BW is defined as 'the use of living organisms (such as bacteria and viruses), toxic agents derived from dead microorganisms, and plant growth regulators to produce lethal or non-lethal casualties among human's, animals and or plants; defenses against sucn action' (emphasis added) (Collins & Cronin, 1985, p. 303). Interestingly enough, not toxins alone (although only those 'derived from dead microorganisms') are regarded as BW agents but plant growth regulators as well as we come across in the 1959 definition made by the US Department of Health, Education and Welfare. A tendency is also seen to differentiate between 'true toxins' and other poisonous substances, because 'traditionally, the toxicologist has used the word toxin to indicate a toxic protein. Thus, in an Emergency Manual Guide issued by the US Department of Health, Education and Welfare it is clearly stated that 'true toxins are of a protein-like nature' (USA, 1959b, p. 28). In one of the technical manuals of the US Army dealing with BW and TW agents, two definitions for toxins are supplied : Toxin—generally, any poisonous substance of microorganism, vegetable, or animal origin. True toxins are of a protein-like nature....' (emphasis added)(USA, 1964, p. 88). In the introductory chapter of the manual, toxins are defined as 'poisonous substances chemically allied to proteins' (USA, 1964, p. 14).

Consequently, saxitoxin, a non-proteinaceous low-molecular-weight toxin produced by algae (Dinoflagellatae) (see table 3.1) is included in the list of 'super-toxic lethal chemicals' proposed in annex III, schedule A , of the draft Chemical Weapons Convention submitted by the USA on 18 April 1984.

Table 3.1
Diseases and their Agents as Studied by Japanese during 1935-45

Agent	*Disease*
Anthrax	Plant Diseases
Botulism	Salmonella
Brucellosis	Typhus
Cholera	Songo[d]
Dysentery	Smallpox
Fugu Toxin[b]	Streptococcus
Gas Gangrene	Tetanus

Contd.

Agent	Disease
Glanders	Tick Encephalitis
Influenza	Tuberculosis
Meningococcus	Tularemia
Mucin[c]	Tsutsugamushi
Plague	Typhoid

At others place TW agents between CW and BW agents; for instance, in 1983 P. Ricaud, then director of France's chemical warfare analysis and development programme stated: "The well-defined chemical structure of these mycotoxins.... puts them between the chemical toxins and the biological warfare agents. Further, during the process of repeated revision of the 'Recombinant DNA Research Guidelines' issued by the National Institutes of Health of the USA the term 'toxins' as used in the first issue of the Guidelines (USA, 1976, p. 27915) was later changed by use of expressions 'toxic molecules lethal for vertebrates' and 'molecules toxic for vertebrates' (USA, 1982b, pp. 38050, 38060). Phrases such as 'genes coding for the biosynthesis of molecules toxic for vertebrates' or 'toxic molecule genes' (emphasis added clarify that within the scope of the Recombinant DNA Research Guidelines toxins were referred to. Nevertheless such terms remove the borderline between toxins and synthetic poisons. One must not be surprised to find that even a critic of military biology research, S. Murphy (1985, p. 35) refers to 'natural poisons' when comparing toxins with some 'chemical agents'.

History of Warfare Agents

Concerning the development and possible use of BW and TW agents, three major stages can be distinguished whose boundaries correspond roughly to periods in the development of modern genetics.

The Classical Stage of BW and TW Agents

The classical stage of BW and TW is marked by the direct use of biological agents and toxins and by attempts to develop their use as weapons. Lack of knowledge about the existence of bacteria and viruses or of their genetics hindered attempts to develop strains more suitable as BW agents. This stage extended from ancient times—when primitive forms of BW were used, as described in the early Persian, Greek and Roman literature—through World War II. The Mongols practised biological warfare as early as in the 14th century. In 1346 after a three-year unsuccessful siege they hurled plague-infected cadavers over the walls of the essentially impregnable Crimean seaport Caffa (the present-day Feodosija) which had been constructed by the Genoese. De Mussis, an eyewitness, writes: 'The Tatars, stung by such a plague and pestiferous disease, stupefied and amazed, saw themselves dying without hope of health, and ordered cadavers placed on their hurling machines and thrown into the city of Caffa, so that by means of these intolerable passengers the defenders died widely. Thus there were projected mountains of dead, nor could the Christians hide or flee, or be freed from such disaster[12]. Finally the Genoese left the city and fled by water. De, Mussis then reports of the further dissemination of plague by those who fled from Caffa. His ship had plague victims aboard of whom only 10 of 1000 survived. His ship and undoubtedly many others carrying refugees from Caffa carried the disease to a number of islands, including Sicily, Sardinia, Corsica, and finally to Genoa. From there it spread across Italy and over Europe, destroying large parts of the population. In addition, it induced large-scale massacres of Jews who were accused of being responsible for the 'Black Death'. Every second inhabitant of a plague stricken city met his end. An estimated 30 per cent of the European population, nearly 25 millions became victims of the 'Black Death'.

The US Department of Defense considers 'the "Black Death" example (as) one which demonstrates that pathogens as military agents have their place in a military arsenal' (USA, 1964, p. 2). Characteristic features of BW agents were seen 600 years ago: they are clearly the weapons of mass destruction, whose effects are unpredictable and uncontrollable and which are capable of destroying not only specific target populations but other populations also. The US Committee on Science and Astronautics, which investigated research on chemical, biological and radiological warfare, referred to an Italian tactical manual which by the 16th century described how to make artillery shells for delivery of disease to the enemy. Around that time, however, at least one monarch refused to use BW agents. It is reported that Louis XIV (1643-1715) 'when an Italian chemist offered him the first bacteriological weapon, ...gave him a pension on condition that he never divulge his invention' (Encyclopaedia, 1985a, p. 501).

British forces used smallpox virus against the Amerindians two centuries later. During an Indian uprising, in 1763, Sir Jeffrey Amherst, commander-in-chief of the British forces, suggested to Colonel Bouquet: 'Could it not be considered to send the small pox among those disaffected tribes of Indians? We must on this occasion use every strategy in our power to reduce them' (Parkman, 1901, p. 44). Bouquet, in a letter dated Carlisle, 13 July 1763, replied thus : 'I will try to inoculate the .....with some blankets that may fall in their hands, and take care not to get the disesae myself[13]. This should have favoured the execution of the plan, similar to the situation 400 years ago when the Mongols used the cadavers of their plague-infected population. Amherst replied: 'You will do well to try to inoculate the Indians by means of blankets, as well as to try every other method that can serve to extirbate this execrable race[14]. And on 24 June 1763, Captain Ecuyer wrote in his journal : 'Out of regard for them (i.e., two Indian chiefs) we gave them two blankets and a handkerchief out of the smallpox hospital. I hope it will have desired effect[15]. Following this, smallpox spread among the tribes of the Ohio, and even during the following spring a hundred Mingoes and Delawares and some Shawanoes died of it[16].

Trials of Bacillus anthracis as a potential agent of BW were carried out in 1941 and 1942 on Gruinard Island off the west coast of Scotland (57°56' N, 5°35′ W). Small bombs carrying spores of B. anthracis were suspended from a gantry and detonated, producing widespread contamination of the island's surface. The result was a heavy contamination of this island with persistent spores of a virulent micro-organism. A survey conducted by members of the British Chemical Defence Establishment, Porton Down (scientists of its predecessor, the Microbiological Research Establishment in Porton, Wiltshire, did the experiment), revealed that viable spores of B. anthracis could still be found in 1979 in at least a small area of the isle[17]. Experiments to check, whether decontamination is possible were started in 1983[18]. As nearly two hectares are contaminated, decontamination would require the application of at least 10-million litres of disinfectant (Staff of Nature, 1983).

Anthrax

Contradictory opinions have been expressed about certain Allied BW contingency plans to use the anthrax weapon, code-named N, against Nazi Germany. Harris and Paxman (1982, p. 129) claim that Winston Churchill had thought about the use of anthrax for retaliation in case of a German BW attack. Lewis (1982, p. 27), however, claims that only on one brief occasion the feasibility of using anthrax was considering by the Chiefs of Staff organisation, only to be immediately dismissed as impracticable'. (In any case, there is little reason to believe that the Germans intended to use BW agents on a larger scale against humans, although Lt Col Robert P. McQuail reported from a 1947 meeting of experts from the USA and the USSR interrogating Japanese BW activities, that 'at Nuremberg trials, a German expert witness said spreading typhus by fleas was regarded best method of BW' (USA, 1947a, p. 271). As late as in July 1943 it was decided at a secret meeting of the Oberkommando der Wehrmacht to begin work on BW agents suitable for use against farm animals and crops[19].

Nevertheless, more than 500 prisoners were misused in Nazi concentration camps such as Buchenwald for inhuman medical research including infections with biological agents and treatment with vaccines and drugs under development. Human beings were infected with Rickettsia prowazeki mainly, as well as with R. mooseri, Hepatitis A virus, and Plasmodium in attempts to develop vaccines against spotted fever and for studies on the pathogenesis and etiology of Hepatitis epidemica and malaria, and to facilitate the development of sulphonamides. Whether the Allied had considered the use of anthrax in World War II or not, the Gruinard experiment shows the potency of at least one special type of BW agent. With the experience of Gruinard, the director of Porton Down, Dr R. G. H. Watson, during a television interview shown on BBC-2 Newsnight, 1 May 1981, concurred in the view, that, if the plans had been put into effect, the cities of Aachen, Berlin, Frankfurt am Main, Hamburg, Stuttgart and Wilhelmshafen would probably even now be uninhabitable due to anthrax contamination[20].

While the experiments conducting on Gruinard Island were publicized in 1967 by the British Broadcasting Corporation (BBC)[21] and later by two books.[22] Imperial Japanese BW activities became public only after ratification of the Biological Weapons Convention.

They had, however, been previously disclosed in 1949 during a Soviet trial of 12 Japanese prisoners accused of preparing and employing BW agents during the war (USSR, 1950). Official US sources as also numerous influential newspapers, however, categorized the Japanese biological warfare programme with remarkable success as a 'dead issue' and as a 'smoke screen' launched by 'extensive Russian propaganda'. Although the US committee studying CBR felt that 'limited biological warfare may have been tested by Japan in China during the period of World War II' (USA, 1959a, p. 5), as late as in 1979'. Dr Mortimer A. Rothenberg, Scientific Director of the US Army's biological warfare proving ground at Dugway, Utah, told J.W. Powell (1980, p. 15), that the Soviet summary of the Khabarovsk trial was 'a lot of baloney' and 'just propaganda'. In the meantime, however, largely due to efforts of J. W. Powell, former editor of the Shanghai-based *China Weekly Review*, numerous top-secret documents, some 8000 pages worth, have been secured under the US Freedom of Information Act (Powell, 1980; 1981). Tsuneishi (1985a) has selected and released about 350 pages of this material. More information, including statements by scientists then involved, as well as by victims who have survived, was provided by a British TV report on 'Unit 731-Did The Emperor Know? (TVS, 1985) which was broadcast in the UK and in Sweden and gained much public attention.

Such reports and other records reveal that at least 11 Chinese cities were subjected to Japanese BW attacks between 1940 and 1944. Thousands of people were hospitalized and approximately 700 persons fell victims to artificially disseminated plague alone. In addition, 130 kilos of anthrax and paratyphiod were spread in Central China (TVS, 1985). Japan was not at that time a party to the 1925 Geneva Protocol which bans the use of BW agents; it did not ratify it until 1970[23]. Japan, however, signed the 1969 report of the UN Secretary-General on CBW which includes the statement that there is no concrete evidence that these agents have ever been used as modern military weapons' (UN, 1969, p. 2). These attacks obviously were 'field trials' directed by the Imperial Army's No. 731 Unit within a programme to develop BW agents. Unit 731, the Japanese major biological warfare unit, was set up around 1930 at the small village Pingfan near Harbin and was headed by Lt General Shiro Ishii, who simultaneously headed a laboratory of the Army Medical College in Tokyo [24].

At least 3000 prisoners of war—Chinese, Koreans, Mongolians, Soviets, Americans, British, Australians and others—were misused in Unit 731 as human guinea pigs, and more than 1000.[24a] perhaps even 2500 to 3000[25] of them died in the process. The pathogens and diseases studied by Ishii and his co-workers are listed below till how the Japanese Government has not opened any records on Japanese BW activities except for a three-page document published in 1982[26] together with a report by Kikuo Moriyama, a Social Welfare Ministry official to the lower house of the Diet, that on 'January 1, 1945, there were 3559 men, officers and civilians attached to the Imperial Army's No. 731 unit' [Editorial, 1982a]. State Minister Kumio Tanabe declared that the experiments had been conducted 'during the most extraordinary wartime conditions' and were most regrettable from the view-point of humanity'.

These documents also pronounce that, after the war, US authorities tried not only to describe the results of the Khabarovsk trial (which were confirmed and extended by the disclosed documents) as a fake, but provided immunity from war crimes prosecution to Lt General Shiro Ishii and his co-workers in exchange for exclusive possession of the data yielded by their research. These data were classified as top-secret and therefore the results of the Khabarovsk trial were declared as a 'dead issue'. Owing to the same reasons the public was not informed about the Japanese BW crimes for about three decades, although GIs were also involved and killed during the gruesome experiments. The Japanese BW Unit 731 was offcially described as 'Kwantung Army Boeki Kyusui Bu', which means 'Kwantung Army Anti-Epidemic Water Supply and Purification Department' or 'Anti-Epidemic and Water Supply Unit'. The only official report of the Japanese Government available so far mentions 'its duty (as) study on bacteria, water supply for each unit of Kwantung Army, supply of serum and vaccine, work for preventive medicine, and training of soldiers'. Thus the official purpose of the work done in Unit 731 as well as in the Tokyo laboratory also headed by Ishii could be declared as work for 'prophylactic, protective, or other peaceful purposes', which is permitted by the Biological Weapons Convention. Combined efforts of two governments successfully hid the inhuman work of the Japanese BW research workers under the cloak of 'water purification' and 'vaccine production' to the extent that these activities could be largely concealed for more than forty years.

The Intervening Stage

It was a period of development dependent upon the introduction and development of microbial genetics and of other fields of molecular biology. It lasted for about two to three decades following World War II. 'Since bacteriological (biological) agents exist naturally', it was recognized in the report of the UN Secretary-General that 'their increased potency as weapons has been the result of a process of selection rather than the production of entirely new agents.... Selection has been made possible by advances in our knowledge of the genetics of microbes, and through advances in experimental aerobiology. The identification of DNA as the major genetic material, the elucidation of its structure, as well as the discovery and use of various types of bacterial para-sexual process (e.g., DNA-mediated transformation, transduction, and bacterial conjugation) and the detection and empolyment of physical and chemical mutagens allowed the induction of random genetic changes and the more or less random transfer of genes among related bacterial strains or species. Further, methods were developed which have allowed the selection for microbes with new properties. By these methods, which could also be applied in part to viruses, the virulence of existing pathogens, as well as their resistance against antibiotics and chemotherapeutics, could be raised. Moreover, research could be initiated on bacterial toxins and on their dissemination. During this period there were rather intense BW and TW research programmes including open-air field-testing at least in the USA, the UK and Canada (Cookson and Nottingham, 1969, p. 68-139), and presumably in other countries as well.

No concrete data had been released by Soviet sources, but it has been mentioned that as for biological agents, intensive research can be assumed if only for the same reason as with other advanced countries, i.e. the need to produce vaccines[27]. Both facts and assumptions concerning the research on BW and TW agents during the second stage have been discussed by numerous authors[28]. So that they need not be reviewed here. Some of them, however, will be mentioned in other contexts.

All attempts to make BW and TW agents more efficient and suitable according military requirements depended upon the random genetic change of the organisms studied. BW research workers, therefore, placed their hopes on further genetic advancements.

The Current Stage

The current stage in the development of biological and toxin warfare agents began with the introduction of genetic engineering, a process which coincided with the introduction of the 1972 Biological Weapons Convention. From the very beginning of this turning point in biology, it was suspected that genetic engineering might lead to the development of completely new types of BW and TW agents. The following three statements reveal this :

Further possibilities (to develop new BW agents) are presented by the growing battery of 'genetic engineering' techniques....Such methods might, in the distant future, lead to a strain of pathogen so different from its parent as to be classifiable as a new disease agent (SIPRI, 1973, p. 309).

DNA hybridization must also look an attractive proposition for biological warfare researchers. The new technique offers the prospect of fabricating even nastier BW agents, facilitating the combination of 'desirable characteristics' that cannot be brought together by conventional microbial genetics [29].

With the increase of knowledge in the field of molecular biology, it will in the future be possible to perform genetic engineering in those genetic regions controlling virulence or toxicity of pathogens....Among other potential developments are the exploiting of chemical differences between races and ethnic groups, as well as the further development of already-developed plant diseases,such as rice virus, potato fungi or sugarcane bacteria, into entirely new plant diseases[30].

At the time of a 1977 hearing before the Sub-committee on Health and Scientific Research of the Committee on Human Resources of the US Senate on BW research activities of the Department of Defense, Senator Edward M. Kennedy referred to the potential of recombinant DNA technique (i.e., the core technique of genetic engineering) in the area of BW. The record reads like this:

Senator Kennedy: Just before leaving that subject matter, does the potential in the area of DNA research concern you, how it could be used in-

General Augerson (Brig. Gen. William Augerson, Assistant Surgeon General for Researh and Development): Yes, sir.

Senator Kennedy (continuing): In an adverse way?

General Augerson: Yes sir; potentially very powerful way to altering the way living organisms work (USA, 1977a, p. 8).

Some scientists have expressed concern that such discussions might provide the military and /or groups and nations which are not States Parties to the Biological Weapon Convention with new ideas about how to develop new types of weapon [31]. For some reasons, however, we do not hesitate to specuiate on further developments particularly in this field. First, our ideas will not be much different from those put forth by scientists working on behalf of the military. Second, corresponding ideas discussed in the open literature are already with all parties and will therefore either not be followed up at all because it is not likely that they will provide an advantage in the arms race or, if taken up, they will not lead to an imbalance in armament and weapon development. Third, it is important to foresee possible future developments in order to check whether the Biological Weapons Convention and similar international treaties will cover these new developments or whether additions to the existing treaties or even new treaties are necessary. We will not deal, however, with the possible deveiopment of genetic weapons. Genetic weapons are chemical and biological warfare (CBW) agents which act on the genetic material of attacked organisms. Holmberg (1975) has also pointed out that some CW agents (including TW agents) have carcinogenic and mutagenic effects: 'Mutagenic and carcinogenic weapons may thus be an interesting field of development. Toxicological knowledge may be applied to develop nitrosamines, hydrazines, vinylchloride and other alkylating agents or any volatile and potent mutagenic/carcinogenic or teratogenic substance (into) a future multigeneration drug bomb.

Thus, toxicological warfare may be more dangerous to the human species in comparison to the side effects of the civil industrial use of toxic substances'. Some viruses—that is, potential BW agents-are also mutagenic (Geissler & Theile, 1983). A decade ago it was concluded that 'chemical mutagens..... might one day be made into long-term genetic weapons, although currently it is not possible to control the type of mutation they produce[32]. The subsequent development of site-directed mutagenesis methods has since provided such means. However, these methods are still so sophisticated that although they could conceivably be used to construct BW agents and to study their targets, they are not yet fit for use in war.

Agents that cause random mutations are not likely to be used as CBW agents because they induce recessive mutations. Such recessive mutations are more harmful usually after several generations. It is hard to imagine that an aggressor would make primary use of the mutagenic and/ or carcinogenic activity of a CBW agent for hostile purposes to achieve much, could not be anticipated, and would be of very low efficiency. Conversely, these and other delayed effects of toxic agents might be considered useful by terrorists, to blackmail a society.

Ethnic weapons can be defined as weapons suitable to kill or damage specific ethnic groups. Ethnic weapons would employ diffrences in gene frequencies among specific populations to incapacitate or kill a selected target population. The possible development of such 'genotype-targetable weapons[33], was first suggested by Larson (1970). Even earlier, however, the Japanese World War II BW research programme was said to have included comparisons of the resistance to pathogens of various nationalities and races. These weapons will not be discussed here.

Whether ethnic weapons represent a real threat is still a matter of debate. These weapons would represent no new class of weapon but would belong to BW agents or CW agents (including TW agents). Thus, their use is forbidden by the 1925 Geneva Protocol. The use of ethnic weapons is also forbidden by the 1948 Genocide Convention. And the Biological Weapons Convention forbids the development, production and stockpiling of ethnic weapons that are BW or TW agents.

We will also not go into such unlikely possibilities as cloning or breeding of amoral generals, soldiers, and so on. Concern is sometimes expressed regarding the increasing possibilities of modern genetics to clone human beings or even to breed them taking into consideration their mental and psychic capabilities and/or behaviour. If this were to happen, it could, indeed, be used or misused, as with any other technique. It could be used with a human aim: the cloning or breeding of persons like great writers, highly qualified surgeons, skiled sportsmen, excellent actors, gifted mathematicians, or skilled engineers. It could likewise be used for the cloning or breeding of eficient generals or of amoral, willing and strong soldiers.

However, the cloning or breeding of human beings is not yet possible (Geissler, 1984b). Humans are multifactorially determined both by some 30 000 to 50 000 genes in the germ line cells plus millions of genes (certainly immunoglobin genes and perhaps genes that become active in the central nervous system) in the somatic cells developed by rearrangements of the genetic material during embryonal development, as well as by internal and external (including maternal) environmental (including societal) factors. It is therefore not possible to bring above directed change of human physical or mental capacities and/or behaviour by the changing of one or another of their 30 000 to 50 000 germ-like genes. However, in principle it should be possible to clone human beings with respect to their genetic material, that is, to develop sets of human beings carrying the same genetic material, as do monozygotic twins. Even if it would be technically possible, it would be of no use, however[34]. The cloned early embryos would have to develop in different foster mothers and will thus develop in more or less different manners. Even monozygotic twins, although they develop in one and the same mother, often differ to a greater or lesser extent owing to the random epigenetic interactions between genes, gene products, and cells during embryonal development creating so - called 'developmental noise' (Stent, 1981).

Thus, cloning, although it is described in a well-written science fiction report (Rorvik, 1979), remains impossible in the sense of creating human duplicates (Thomas, 1980), as it is mentioned in a well— written science fiction story.

But affecting the course of normal human development would be possible by genetic manipulation. Physical and psychical damage might result from random injuries of the human genetic material. Such disablement could be induced more efficiently, easily and economically by social means, for instance, by food deprivation, with narcotics, or via educational deprivation. Large-scale misuse of genetic engineering to produce bodily or mental illness is ruled out in near future.

International Law on BW and TW Agents

The Geneva Protocol (1925)

The 'Protocol for the Prohibition of the Use in War of Asphyxiating, Poisonous or Other Gases and of Bacteriological Methods of Warfare' was signed at Geneva on 17 June 1925, came into force on 8 February 1928, and had 108 States Parties as of 31 December 1985, including all five of the permanent members of the UN Security Council. It is among the most important multilateral agreements dealing with CBW agents. As its full name suggests, the States Parties to the Geneva Protocol declared, inter alia, that they 'agree to extend this prohibition to the use of bacteriological methods of warfare'. Concern is occasionally expressed that the language 'bacteriological methods of warfare' might exclude viruses. Such concern is not widespread, however, and may be consideration as not justified. Viruses were not specifically mentioned in the Geneva Protocol because at that time they were not regarded as biological entities different from bacteria. (The definition given for 'virus' in the 1923 edition of an authoritative German dictionary was: 'infectious agent; poison; especially those in living or dead bacteria or poisons excreted by them' Viruses are not mentioned at all in the 24-volume 1929 edition of the Encyclopaedia Britannica [Encyclopaedia, 1929].

In the 1934 edition of an authoritative US dictionary, 'virus' is defined as 'the poison or contagium of a disease, as a pathogenic micro-organism (especially when not identified), which is present in the juices of an organism having an infectious disease and by which, through introduction into another organism, the disease is transmitted; as the virus of vaccinia; now often used as equivalent to filtrable virus'[35]. It became evident only inthe late 1950s that viruses were entirely different from both bacteria and all other organisms because of their possession of only one type of nucleic acid, either DNA or RNA (Lwoff, 1957). Thus 'the prohibition of "bacteriological methods of warfare" as contained in the Geneva Protocol must be understood as a prohibition of biological methods of warfare. Even though in its scientific meaning the term "bacteriological" become narrower than the term "biological", it has always been accepted that in the legal context of the Protocol the two words are exact synonyms[36]. As a matter of fact, the UN Secretary-General has declared that 'various living organisms (e.g. rickettsiae, viruses and fungi), as well as bacteria, can be used as weapons (and that) in the context of warfare all these are generally recognized as "bacteriological weapons".

The Genocide Convention (1948)

The 'Convention on the Prevention and Punishment of the Crime of Genocide' was adopted by the UN General Assembly on 9 December 1948, came into force on 12 January 1951, and had 95 States Parties as of 31 December 1985. In February 1986, the USA ratified the Convention and with this all the five permanent members of the UN Security Council are now States Parties. This Convention holds genocide as a crime under international law which the States Parties undertake to prevent and to punish. In the Convention genocide means 'any of the following acts committed with intent to destroy, in whole or in part, a national, ethnical, racial or religious group, as such; (a) killing members of the group, (b) causing serious bodily or mental harm to members of the group, (c) deliberately inflicting on the group conditions of life calculated to bring about its physical destruction in whole or in part, (d) imposing measures intended to prevent births within the group.

The crimes under it include the use of any possible ethnic weapons. Whereas the use of CBW agents is forbidden by the Geneva Protocol, the use of any possible ethnic weapons—agents which might in course of time be developed by means of genetic engineering-would be forbidden by the Genocide Convention.

The Biological Weapons Convention (1972)

The 'Convention on the Prohibition of the Development, Production, and Stockpiling of Bacteriological (Biological) and Toxin Weapons and on their Destruction' was signed on 10 April 1972, entered into force on 26 March 1975, and has 103 State Parties as of 31 December 1985, which have the UK, the USA and the USSR from among the five permanent members of the UN Security Council. This Convention is also among the most important multilateral agreements dealing with biological weapons and with one important class of CW agents. The States Parties have declared, inter alia, to undertake 'never in any circumstances to develop, produce, stockpile or otherwise acquire or retain: (a) microbial or other biological agents or toxins whatever their origin or method of production, of types and in quantities that have no justification for prophylactic, protective or other peaceful purposes; (b) weapons, equipment or means of delivery designed to use such agents or toxins for hostile purposes or in armed conflict'.

A brief history of the development of the Biological Weapons Convention was made by the Secretariat of the first Review Conference (UN, 1980a) . This report contains a reference to President Nixon's decision of 14 February 1970, that 'the United States renounce offensive preparations for and the use of toxins as a method of warfare' (USA, 1970a). It was this very decision that prompted including TW agents, and hence a certain class of CW agent , in the Biological Weapons Convention. The reason given by the Office of the White House Press Secretary for President Nixon's decision sounded convincing at least in those days: 'The production of toxins in any large quantity would require facilities similar to those needed for the production of biological agents. If the United States continued to operate such facilities, it would not be easy for others to know whether they were being used to produce only toxins but not biological agents. Moreover, though toxins of the type useful for military purposes could conceivably be produced by chemical synthesis in the future, the end products would remain the same and their effects would be indistinguishable from toxins produced by bacteriological or other biological processes' (USA, 1970a). This opinion was first presented by a group of World Health Organisation consultants who in November 1969 noted, commenting on the definition of BW agents given in the report of the UN Secretary General, that 'in some discussions..... toxins are classified as biological agents because the technology of their production is similar to that of biological agents rather than that of chemical agents. The same argument was expressed by M. Meselson in a policy options paper forwarded to the US House of Representatives by John Dellen on 18 February 1970. Toxins, Meselson argued, are usually made using a technology that is indistinguishable from that used to produce bacterial BW agents. Even if toxins could be chemically synthesized (which was not predictable at that time and during the negotiations leading to the Biological Weapons Convention), Meselson further says that their use would give the impression that the USA was using BW agents, since the effects of synthetic toxins would be the same as natural toxins (USA, 1970c). Also, at that time the production of 'artificial toxins' by protein engineering (which now seems to be feasible, was not predictable. Therefore the negotiators seemingly did not worry about definitions of toxins either. Five years after the Biological Weapons Convention's entry into force, the first Review Conference of the Parties to the Biological Weapons Convention was held at Geneva from 3 March to 21 March 1980.

Pursuant to article XII of the Convention, the review was to take into account any new scientific and technological developments relevant to the Convention. (A report describing the Review Conference, its preparation and its results is found in United Nations (1980e, pp. 258-76). The Review Conference was widely cosidered as having been successful. According to this report, the President of the Conference moted in his closing statement, 'that the Review Conference had reaffirmed the importance and validity of the Convention as the first genuine disarmament measure. It had also revealed that the Convention was sufficiently comprehensive to cover recent scientific and technological developments, which was especially significant in that, in other areas, scientific progress had led to newer and more dangerous weapons. As stated in the Final Declaration of the first Review Conference (UN, 1980d), reprinted in appendix 3c, the Conference deeply regretted, howeer, that a comparable chemical weapons agreement was yet to become a reality under article IX of the Biological Weapons Convention.

Another Review Conference of the Parties to the Biological Weapons Convention will be held in 1986. Again, review is to take into account any new scientific and technological developments relevant to the Convention.

References

1. Tigertt *et al.* 1961.

2. Livingstone and Douglas, 1984, Klein, 1985.

3. Geissler, 1985.

4. Damodaran *et al.* 1983, p. 6.

5. Nicholson-Lord, 1981a, b; Stanhope, 1981.

6. Harris and Paxman, 1982, pp. 88-94.

7. Westing, 1982, p. 26.

8. Goldblat, 1982, p. 146.

9. cf. Anherson and King, 1983, p.2.

10. Shank, 1976, p. 90.

11. Ricand, 1984, p. 46.
12. cf. Derbes, 1966, p. 60.
13. Parkman, 1901, p. 44.
14. *Ibid*, p. 45.
15. Sipe, 1929, p. 424.
16. Stearn and Stearn 1945, p. 45.
17. Manchee *et. al*. 1981.
18. Manchee et al. 1983.
19. Harris and Paxman, 1985, p. 109.
20. cf. Perry Robinson, 1981, pp. 83, 91.
21. cf. Lewis, 1982, p. 18.
22. Clarke, 1968, pp. 16, 60, 92, Reid, 1969, p. 307.
23. SIPRI, 1986, p. 568.
24. Tsuneishi, 1985 b.
24a. Tsuneishi, 1986.
25. Uzono, 1985.
26. Truneishi, 1985 a, p. I-I.
27. Vincy, 1968, p. 131.
28. see, e:g., Cookson and Nottingham, 1969, Hersh, 1968, Mccarthy, 1970; Haris and Paxman, 1982; Rose, 1968; SIPRI, 1973.
29. Dixon, 1973, p. 236.
30. Holmberg, 1975.
31. ef., e.g., Milewski 1985.
32. SIPRI, 1973 p. 317.
33. Callahom and Tripis, 1978.
34. Geissler, 1984 b.
35. Webster's, 1934
36. SIPRI, 1973, pp. 42-43

17. Renaud 1984, p. 26
[illegible] Dorbon 1991, p. 30
[illegible] Tassman, 19[illegible], p. 44
18. Ibid., p. 45
19. [illegible] 1992, p. 424
[illegible] and [illegible] 1976, p. 43
[illegible] et al., 1986
[illegible] Manchester et al., 1983
[illegible] Harris and Pickup 19[illegible], p. 190
20. [illegible] 1981, pp. 68[illegible]
21. [illegible] 1987, p. 18
22. [illegible] 1968, pp. 46, 60, 52 and 1[illegible], p. 3[illegible]
23. [illegible] 1988, p. 56
[illegible] 1987
[illegible] 1990
[illegible] 19[illegible]
26. [illegible] 1983, p. 1[illegible]
27. [illegible] 1978, p. 131
28. [illegible] and Harrington, 1969, 41 [illegible]
[illegible] Harris and P[illegible] 1982, [illegible] 1965, 50[illegible]
29. [illegible] 1982, p. [illegible]
30. [illegible]
31. [illegible] 1985
[illegible]
33. [illegible] 19[illegible]
[illegible]
[illegible] 1984
[illegible] 1983, pp. [illegible]

4

Acts of Bioterrorism

Biological weapons have taken us to an era that is marked by violence, killings and spreading diseases; making it easy for the terrorists to attack humanity without the fear of being detected. Following examples would make it further clear.

It was normal for the crowds hurrying to work in the Tokyo rush hour on the morning of 20 March 1995. In the tube system, orderly streams of people negotiated the escalators and underground halls to reach their platforms and be pushed onto the trains. Among the commuters, however, there were five who had a job to do during, rather than after, their journeys. They were members of the apocalyptic religious sect Aum Shinrikyo; and their mission was to kill as many of their fellow passengers as possible. The five terrorists caught trains on the Hibiya, Marunouchi and Chiyoda lines and all of them were due to arrive at Kasumigaseki station between 8.09 and 8.13 a.m. Above this station lies a concentration of government offices: the Ministries of Foreign Affairs, Home Affairs, Health and Welfare, Agriculture, Labour and several others. The terrorists' aim was to cause death and create panic right to the heart of the state. The sect members carried parcels wrapped in brown paper. Once on board, they put them under their seats and punched holes in them with tips of their umbrellas. From the packages, lethal sarin das escaped into the carriages. Only a very faint smell warned of what was to arrive. After about 15 seconds, nearby passengers felt the first effects: tightness in the chest, difficulty in breathing, pain in the eyes and dimmed vision.

One, Akio Masahata, recalls: 'It hurt to breathe. I could feel it in my nostrils. People began collapsing around me'. They fell, giddy, sweating, vomitting, belching, urinating and defecating involuntarily. Some succumbed to convulsions and death.

Panic ensued. At the next station, gasping people searched for the doors. They reeled, tottered on to the platforms. Staggered towards the station exits, many fell on the way. Emergency medical teams arrived. People were stretchered out, vomitting, bubbles coming from their mouths, blood from their noses.

The result of the act was that twelve people died; 5,500 were injured, some permanently. Had the terrorists not used a faulty batch of sarin, and had disseminated it more effectively, their attack could have killed tens of thousands of people. This was an attack with a chemical weapon: a nerve gas. It was not the first the cult had attempted. In June 1994 also they had killed seven people with sarin in a night attack in Matsumoto, a small mountain resort north of Tokyo. But the Aum Shinrikyo were developing biological weapons as well.

The police found they had 160 barrels of media for growing clostridium botulinum bacteria, which produces botulinus toxin. They had already attempted spreading some of this round Tokyo, but without effect. In 1990 and 1993 they had tried to spray the toxin from a vehicle driving around the national parliament and the centre of the city; and they had also triedout with anthrax spores which they sprayed from the roof of an eight-storey building in eastern Tokyo. That killed birds and plants but not people. A US Senate committee alleges that cult members had also made efforts to obtain the Ebola virus—which causes a particularly horrifying infection, in which the body disintegrates in pools of blood—from Zaire.

The aim behind the attack was as bizarre as the cult itself. Documents in Aum files found by the police predicted that the world would undergo a major cataclym by 1997, and that at least 90 per cent of people in major cities would die—some in gas attacks. The cult was evidently working to make these prophecies true. The Tokyo attack was a psychological watershed. The Aum had done what was known to be possible but presumed to be beyond the pale. It was unthinkable that had happened. Given the interest already shown by other groups in biological terrorism, the ease of acquisition of biological materials, the difficulty of detecting them, and their capacity to inflict terror, many feared that it might occur again and at larger scale.

That is Increasing Threat

The increasing terrorist threat is causing concern amongst experts. In the recent past, terrorists have set off massive explosions at a federal building in Oklahoma City and the World Trade Center. Again, these were directed towards civilians. The attackers at the World Trade Center tried to kill everyone trapped in one of the towers by releasing cyanide gas. At the subsequent trial, one of the judges said this was thwarted only because the sodium cyanide burned instead of vaporising. It is only slightly short of a BW dimension. They would increase terror and put extra pressure on public authorities. 'Visualise the World Trade Centre or an Oklahoma-style attack complicated by the inclusion of a kilogram of anthrax spores as a kind of microbiological shrapnel along with the explosives,' says Nobel - Prize winning geneticist Joshua Lederberg. '[Imagine] its implications for salvage and rescue, public health, panic.' The US Central Intelligence Agency is predicting 'a tremendous increase' in terrorism over the next decade: 'rogue nations, terrorists, subnational groups, cells of ethnic or religious zealots, even individuals with a grudge, are expected to create mass urban panic and destruction with easily available chemical and biological agents. The breakdown of state structures in the former Soviet Union, the ever rising economic distress of scientists there who may be tempted to sell their expertise abroad, the rise of ethnic conflicts—all these developments add to the number of non-state entities which may want to attack others, and be able to develop or hire the know-how.

And the fact that biological agents generally take time to have an impact is added advantage for terrorists. By that time, they can slip far away from the scene.

Other Threats : Food and Agriculture

A conference of experts which took place in Georgetown, Washington in September 1998 concluded that 'terrorism against agriculture and the US food supply has largely been neglected as a threat'. Yet the US food and fibre system accounts for 13 per cent of the country's Gross Domestic Product and 17 per cent of its employment. Terrorist attacks on food and agriculture would disrupt domestic food supplies as also the economy of the nation. The last major foreign animal disease outbreak in the US was of avian influenza in 1983-84. It was confined to Pennsylvania and neighbouring states, but over the course of six months, all chickens there had to be killed and all premises decontaminated. It costed US $ 63 million—the most expensive eradication effeort in US history. The US has food exports to the value of $ 140 billion each year. If it were known to be contaminated with a disease, the loss of these markets would eat into whole of country's budget surplus. The conference, which was organised by the National Consortium for Genomic Resources Management and Services (Gen Con), heard that farming is increasingly concentrating animals in specific areas, which reduces the target area for a terrorist, increases the potential for the spread of infectious agents and magnifies the impact of limited use.

Tourists, travellers or terrorists could introduce diseases affecting animals and crops. Yet although the counter-terrorism community is committing resources to tackling bioterrorism against people, it has so far turned a blind eye to the threat to agriculture. The meeting urged the setting up of a national system in order to protect food and agricultural resouces of the country.

Earlier Threats

It is said that Joseph Stalin considered assassinating Joseph Broz Tito by releasing plague bacteria at a reception. The attack never took place. There have been many other incidents in which groups of various hues have been found in possession of biological agents.

(i) In 1972, members of a right-wing group known as 'Order of the Rising Sun' were caught in Chicago carrying between 30 and 40 kg of typhoid bacteria cultures which they were going to use to poison water supplies in Chicago, St. Louis and other cities in the Midwest. Their obsession was to create a new master race.

(ii) In September 1984, members of the Rajneesh cult contaminated salad bars in The Dalles, Oregon, with Salmonella typhi, which causes typhoid fever. They were trying to influence the outcome of a local election. Nobody died but 750 people became sick.

(iii) A US tax protest group called 'The Patriots Council' were convicted in February 1995 of possessing 0.7 grams of the toxin ricin—enough to kill 100 people. They had plans to poison US government agents by smearing ricin on their doorknobs.

(iv) Only six weeks after the Tokyo attack, Larry Harris, who belongs to a white supremacist group called Aryan Nations, telephoned the American Type Culture Collection in Maryland and ordered three vials of freeze-dried bacteria, Y. pestis, that cause pneumonic and bubonic plague. They were duly delivered by Federal Express; but when in transit, Harris became impatient and called again to inquire why they had not arrived. His manner made the supplier suspicious enough to notify federal authorities, and Harris was arrested and charged with mail fraud.

In the light of these and other incidents, it is not surprising that a five-month study by the US Senate concluded, in March 1996 that the threat of a terrorist group using a nuclear, biological or chemical weapon of mass destruction in the United States is real. It is not a question of 'if' but rather 'when' such an event will occur. Discoveries of biological attacks have not been limited to the United states.

A Red Army Faction safe house in Paris was found to contain a bathtub of botulinal toxin in the 1980s. And, in 1994, Prince Mikasa of Japan admitted that Japanese military officials had contaminated fruit with cholera germs in an effort to poison the members of the 1931 League of Nations Lytton Commission, who were investigating the seizure of Manchuria. Seth Carus of the National Defense University in Washington has made an exhaustive study of bioterrorism. He has chronicled 52 confirmed cases this century in which terrorists, criminals or others shown their interest in biological agents, threatened to use them, attempted to acquire them, or possessed or used them.

The cases, which resulted in 982 victims, including nine deaths, were intended to achieve various ends: murder, extortion, incapacitation, mass murder, creating terror, making a political statement, and revenge. They did not include states acting as terrorists (e.g. the Bulgarian Secret Police's assassination of Georgi Markov. His forecast is not comforting. He suggests, 'The available evidence indicates that there is an explosion of interest by criminals in biological agents. There is also reason for concern that future bioterrorism attacks may be more deadly than past incidents. Three factors lead to the change. First, an increasing number of terrorist groups—foreign and domestic— are adopting the tactic of inflicting mass casualties to achieve ideological, revenge or 'religious' goals. Second, the technological sophistication of the terrorist groups is growing. Third, Aum Shinrikyo has shown that terrorist groups now exist with resources akin to some governments. Therefore, it is increasingly likely that some group will become capable of using biological agents to cause massive casualties.'

Easy to Produce

Weapons of terror need not perform efficiently to produce the desired impact. The Aum's sarin was impure and the means of delivery was crude; yet that attack may have changed the face of terrorism. Terrorists want to establish their power to cause panic and death in the face of the authorities; and they can do so with fewer deaths than their equipment is theoretically capable of producing. Their weapons do not have to be very good—just good enough. Even the Iraqi's biological weapons were not sophisticated. Microbiologist Raymond Zilinskas, of the University of Maryland Biotechnology Institute, took part in the United Nations' search for Iraqi weapons after the Gulf War. 'The Iraqis never mastered the art of weaponising their bacterial agents, including anthrax', he says. 'Most of what the UN investigators found were crude preparations mounted on conventional bombs and missiles, which might not have dispersed very well. ' But Zilinskas tells us that crude weapons can be effective. According to him , a slurry of anthrax spores left in the tunnels of an underground railway system, where they would be dried and blown around by the wind caused by the passing trains, could kill thousands of people.

The Iraqis could also have concealed a more sophisticated BW facility from the UN inspectors. They certainly concealed a lot. According to Carus, it has always been easy for terrorists or criminals to gain access to biological agents. They have been able to buy them from legtitimate suppliers, steal them, produce them themselves or use materials taken from nature, which have been contaminated with the agents. Anthrax, plague, brucellosis and tularemia all can be obtained from natural sources in the environment. The spores of anthrax, for example, which persist for decades, could be collected from soil samples in areas where the disease is endemic in cattle; and the same could be done with brucellosis. Ricin can be extracted from castor beans: yields being about one gram of toxin per kilogram of seeds. Tricothecene mycotoxins can be extracted from corn and aflatoxin from peanuts. Once obtained, bacteria can be grown into larger quantities: very easily: they grow very happily in a flask of chicken soup.

Viruses may be less favoured as they generally can not survive long outside a host; but they do proliferate when injected into an ordinary hen's egg. One author rates the process of producing lethal biological agents as only as only as complicated as manufacturing beer and easier than refining heroin.' And Kathleen Bailey, formerly of the US Arms Control and Disarmament Agency, is absolutely sure that 'a major biological arsenal could be built in a room 15-by-15 feet, with $5,000 worth of equipment. The terrorist would, of course, have to have some knowledge of biology and some technical skill. There is a spread of estimates of the level of education required, from college students to post-graduates. According to Lt. Col. Terry N. Mayer of the US Air Force, 'If an attacker has access to the target area, a simple mechanism to aerosolise a substance, and a basic biology laboratory, the prerequisites are complete.

This is not a high-tech arena that needs specialised equipment or core material. This is basic college biology coupled with motivation. Other experts suggest that post-graduate expertise would be necessary. The Aum cult is reported to have included scientists and engineers. It was a sophisticated and wealthy group, reportedly having at least US $ 300 million in assets and recruited 10,000 members. Under optimal conditions, many types of bacteria can divide every 20 minutes. That means that one bacterium can become 1,074,000,000 after ten hours. Even with a crude system like a fish tank, a terrorist could create a slurry containing billions of spores. The slurry could be spread in liquid form using a sprayer, although it may clog the nozzles, and a high quantity of agent spread in this way generally dies as it is sprayed. This might explain why the Aum had so little success in its efforts to spray agent around Tokyo. It is much easier to spread dry agent—perhaps freeze-dried—but this involves a dangerous process. The biotechnology industry uses freeze-dryers, which preserve materials by freezing them and putting them under a vacuum to remove moisture. The most dangerous part of the operation would be grinding the slurry powder into particles of the right size.

The terrorists would have to use some safety techniques to avoid infecting themselves. Either way aerosolisation is complicated; but it would be a folly to rule out the possibility that it could be done. And even if it were done sub-optimally, that could still be enough to serve the purpose of terrorism.

It is settled that laboratory workers can grow and handle biological agents in moderately well-equipped laboratories. There is more disagreement about terrorists' ability to handle some of the most dangerous pathogens known. In light of reports that the Japanese Aum sect had tried to collect samples of the Ebola virus, it is interesting to question whether such a group could feasibly work with such an organism. There is no treatment and no cure for Ebola. It is contagious, although just how contagious is not yet known. While there is no evidence of airborne transmission, epidemiological, studies reveal that it is passed on through blood and infectious body fluids, in the same way as the AIDS virus; so close contact with another person can lead to infection. However, it is quite hard to catch in comparison to influenza. Expert opinions about whether a terrorist group could handle such a virus are disconcerting. Dr Graham Lloyd is Head of Diagnosis at the UK's Centre for Microbiology and Applied Research (CAMR) at Porton Down.

The site used to be part of the UK biological defence effort, but CAMR is part of the public health sector, which reports to the Department of Health. It is associated with the health care research. Graham Lloyd works in the most secure conditions yet devised to handle and diagnose dangerous viruses like Ebola—so-called P4 level containment laboratories. The viruses are handled either in a series of interconnected cabinets or in laboratories in which personnel make use of highly specialised protective suits that look like space suits (and have their own external air supply). The laboratory design, construction and safety practices make sure that the agents do no escape to the community at large. It has its own filtered air supply and is limited to experienced personnel. Before entering, they must decontaminate under showers. They must work in pairs when they handle an agent. The air pressure in the entire laboratory is kept lower than that outside, so that if any agent escapes it will get sucked back into the lab rather than float out. Graham Lloyd has considered whether a terrorist group could manipulate Ebola without such security: 'They could, if they had access to the agent, microbiological skills and wanted to take the risk worksecure environments.

According to him there would be a high risk of disease, and clinical cases would easily be recognised by vigilant health professionals. Dr Graham Pearson, former director of the UK's chemical and biological defence research, warns against being taken in by the western mindset. This, he says, makes supposition that if protective security measures are available, they are necessary. 'In the UK now we'd never dream of handling Ebola in less than P4. We only work with anthrax in P3 [one grade less of laboratory security] or, if it's aerosolised, P4. But during World War Two, the UK made cattle cakes containing anthrax, and the people doing this put anthrax spores into the centre of the cakes without wearing respirators. They worked in a small shed behind a sheet of glass. One person got subcutaneous anthrax, treatable with penicillin. If you took care, it didn't spread.

Also the United Nations teams investigating Iraq's BW potential found that they would work on micro-organisms in straightforward cabinets. This may beg the question of how contagious the micro-organisms are. Anthrax is not contagious but Ebola is. Yet working with it in less than ideal conditions would not horrify Jeffrey Almond, Professor in the School of Animal and Microbial Sciences at the University of Reading. You would, he says, need very good microbiological technique, and ensure the right kind of air-flow. If you were careful, there'd be no reason to get infected. Given these views, and that suicide terrorists have already shown themselves willing and ready to blow themselves up with their victims, it is obviously not far-fetched to imagine sophisticated cults like the Aum being prepared to go to that extent.

Government Initiatives

A 54-year old American citizen Thomas Lewis Lavy hanged himself in his prison cell in December 1995. He was caught by Canadian customs officials to be carrying 130 grams of ricin—enough to kill 32,000 people, according to the FBI. He claimed he had bought the poison in Canada to poison coyotes that were killing chickens on his farm in Arkansas, but he was also found in possession of neo-Nazi literature. He was prosecuted under the US Biological Weapons Anti-Terrorism Act of 1989, which had proved a successful vehicle for prosecuting some people caught with dangerous agents. Since this legislation was passed, the attacks in Tokyo and in the US have concentrated government minds on the problem of terrorism.

Presidential Decision Directive 39, issued in June 1995, declared: 'Terrorist acquisition of weapons of mass destruction is not acceptable and there is no higher priority than preventing the acquisition of such materials/weapons or removing this capability from terrorist groups.' A few months later, a Senate report singled out the particular areas in which the US needed to improve. It asserted that the US was not adequately equipped to respond to terrorists with weapons of mass destruction. 'Much improvement is necessary in support of our country's first responders' - local fire, police, rescue and emergency room personnel. Government efforts require better coordination, and the intelligence and law enforcement communities must make greater strides in information-sharing. These concerns had the Congressional backing in the Nunn-Lugar-Domenici legislation, passed in September 1996 in the light of an attack against an American base in Saudi Arabia, which led to the Domestic Preparedness programme to provide training to 120 cities in how to react to chemical and biological incidents. In April 1996, President Clinton signed the Antiterrorism and Effective Death Penalty Act, which strengthened previous legislation in the field. Part of it is linked to making the transfer of hazardous agents safer.

The Centers for Disease Control and Prevention (CDC) in Atlanta has since drawn up stricter rules for this, which came into being in April 1997. Under the CDC's new regime, mavericks like Larry Harris can no longer order up dangerous pathogens. Most facilities that control these micro-organisms, whether commercial suppliers, government agencies, universities, research institutions or private companies, need to be inspected to make sure that they can handle them properly, and registered. Permission will have to be given and recorded for every transfer of an agent. The scheme is 'designed to ensure that select agents are not supplied to parties who are ill equipped to handle them appropriately or who otherwise lack proper authorisation for their requests. There are some exemptions for clinical laboratories, so that the work of scientists there will not be hampered. All the major bacteria, viruses, rickettsia, fungi and toxins that are generally cited linked to BW are covered by the new rules. The new regime will make it more difficult for terrorists to obtain micro-organisms, but it will not stop them.

According to Michael Moodie, President of the Chemical and Biological Arms Control Institute, 'It will not make much difference concerning classical biological agents. Anthrax is not hard to find. You don't have to go to the CDC to get cultures. Terrorists will still be able to steal them, procure them from abroad, or cultivate them from natural sources. Much less information is available about the UK government's anti-terrorist efforts. The Home Office is responsible for counter-terrorism. All it is ready to say is that it has 'developed over a period of years, a series of contigency plans for responding to a wide range of terrorist threats, including those which might involve the threatened or real use of nuclear, chemical or biological materials. The Government is firmly committed to have firm plans in place in the interests of national security and the protection of the public. These plans are regularly reviewed, tested and updated in view of changing domestic and international circumstances. It is not willing to divulge any details about the plans themselves, except that, as with civil emergencies in general, operational control of any incident would be a matter for the Chief Officer of Police in whose area the offence was committed. The UK has passed the 1974 Biological Weapons Act to prevent any person or group from possessing suspect biological agents or developing biological weapons. The penalty for these offences is life improsonment.

There have not been any prosecutions under the Act. In July 1998, the UK government published a White Paper on strategic export controls, making proposal that regulations on biological weapons should be as stringent as those on chemical weapons. This would mean that it would be an offence for anyone in the UK or any British person abroad to enlist the aid of a foreigner overseas to develop, procure or use a biological weapon. It also involves making publication of technology subject to export control an offence, in an attempt to reach people publishing on the Internet. Many international legal steps are also in place to fight terrorism. The International Convention for the Suppression of Terrorist Bombings opened for signature in January 1999, and specifically applies to biological and toxin agents. In July 1998, 120 states signed an agreement to set up an International Criminal Court which will be able to try people accused of violating laws governing conduct in war, such as the Genocide Convention. Several states have not passed similar legislation to outlaw biological terrorism on their land. The Japanese government, for instance, had no law that would have given it the power to investigate the Aum group's activities to the extent required to stop them before the attack on the Tokyo underground.

In spite of government attempts to deal with the problem, the actual and feared growth in terrorist activities is one of the main dynamos powering the rising threat of biological weapons. If terrorists can develop crude biological weapons, so can many states. Iraq's secret programme brings home the threat of proliferation of biological weapons. And this is what we are going to study now.

Fire Storm

'Fire Storm', an emergency planning exercise in Greater Manchester, started action on Friday, 17 November 1995. Police refused to confirm reports that it was a counter-BW scenario involving terrorists unleashing a canister of anthrax spores. 'The press are not invited', was what one police officer commented. 'It's private.'

Official sources did however made public that it was a large—scale exercise: so large that one officer predicted they were unlikely to have another similar exercise for the next 15 years. About 250 visiting police, security and government officials from round the country were among those taking part. It was reported that the Home Secretary, Michael Howard, followed the exercise from his desk in London. The emerency planning authorities in Manchester conduct various exercises a year involving the police, fire, ambulance and health services. They make use of a geographical information system to exactly pinpoint the putative release, and combine this with weather forecasts to predict the plume of chemical, biological or radiological pollution.

The weather would influence the authorities' response to the release of a biological agent. Evacuation might be considered if there were little wind, in which case the agent would die around and could become a danger. If it was windy, the agent would be dispersed and people would be advised to remain in shelter where they were. The level of toxicity of the agent would also determine the advice given. Given the dangers of mass evacuation and panic, the authorities prefer to advise what they call 'shelter in place' if it is feasible. And operation 'Fire Storm'? Was it practice for a biological release? One officer replied to that : 'There is no publicly-available information on that type of exercise'.

It Can Happen

The United Nations sanctions against Iraq, imposed after the Gulf War, are still in place. For the civilian population of Iraq, these sanctions have resulted in years of poverty, hunger, indignity, inadequate health care and high rate of infant mortality. Saddam Hussein has already discovered many efforts to overthrow him, and has murdered the plotters. He needs to unite the country behind him, to give him breathing space. The UN is about to hold its periodic review of the sanctions. Saddam Hussein consciously decides to attack the two countries keenest to maintain them: the US and the UK.

At I am on a cloudy night with a moderate wind, a small boat casts off from its mooring on the Potomac River just north of Washington DC. Just above the Theodore Roosevelt Memorial it activates its aerosol generator, which throws out 10 kg of anthrax spores as the boat passes down river. The spores spread all over the city. The boat reaches Chesapeake Bay and heads out into the Atlantic. By morning it has been scuttled, the crew having been lifted off by helicopter. Within five days, hundreds of thousands of people met their end in Washington.

The same day in England, the news of the catastrophe in Washington will not break for many more hours. The streets are crowded as people head home from work. A plane takes off from a southern airport and heads north, takes the route to the west of London. There is a westerly crosswind blowing at 10 km per hour. As the plane crosses the Thames it turns on its aerosol sprays. The pilot knows that the bacteria he is releasing are delicate and that barely ten per cent will survive in the spray, and that these will die off at a rate of five per cent per minute. he also knows that a large proportion will be killed by the pollution generated by the city traffic. Nevertheless he is sure that hundreds of the people hurrying along

London's streets will be infected with plague, and that these people wiil later pass the disease on to hundreds more. After two or three days, when the only news is of the American crisis, the first London casualties collapse with high temperatures, chills and headaches. Plague is diagnosed; stocks of antibiotics are rushed to GP's and hospitals. Several of those who receive treatment within 24 hours of the onset of symptoms are saved. Thousands die within a week.

Grapes of Anger

Some disgruntled European winemakers, angry that their profits are being squeezed by the increasing popularity of Californian wines, enter the US as tourists and visit the wine-producing counties in Northern California. Occasionally they stop their car and stroll up to have a look at the vineyards. At these stops they take tins of pate out of their pockets and scrape some of it onto the ground-pate that contains millions of grape aphids (phylloxera vastratrix) which will settle into the soil and then attack the roots of the plants. Long time after the Europeans have disappeared, the aphids will destroy as much as 70 per cent of the vines. They breed prolifically—according to some estimates, one aphid can produce a staggering 48 billion offspring—and they spread by wind, water and in soil sticking to boots or vehicle wheels. The only way to eradicate them is by removing the vines and replanting aphid-resistant plants—costing a great deal of money.

Water Sabotage

It is not as easy as it might appear to sabotage urban water supplies in technologically advanced countries. These countries filter their water and add chlorine in order to kill micro-organisms. The sheer volume of water needed to supply a city would mean, according to a US Department of Defense biological warfare analyst, that somebody wanting to poison New York's supplies would require 'trainloads' of botulinum toxin to overcome the dilution. Where groundwater sources are pure enough to be distributed without additives, they make an easy target to sabotage. And wells have been poisoned in warfare for thousands of years.

Deadly Doughnuts

Early in the morning of 29 October 1996, laboratory workers at St Paul Medical Center, Texas, got invitation to sample pastries in their lunchroom. The invitation came via an email message, and those who responded found two boxes of blueberry muffins and assorted doughnuts. Between 7.15 am and 1.30 pm, eleven employees had enjoyed the treat; one took a muffin home to share that night.

By 9 pm that evening, the first pastry-eater suffered severed gastrointestinal illnesss. All fell sick by 4 am on 1 November. They had been infected with a particular kind of Shigella dysenteriae which causes vomiting, diarrhoea, headache and fever. Of the twelve infected, four had to be hospitalised and five others were treated at emergency clinics. They all survived. Investigations revealed that laboratory kept the same type of Shigella and that some of its stock was missing. On 28 August 1997, laboratory technician Diane Thompson was charged with poisoning the pastries. She was convicted in September 1998, found guilty and sentenced to 20 years in jail.

BW through Mail

In November 1998, anthrax, plague and brucella were offered to reporters posing as middlemen for a medical laboratory in North Africa, who telephoned the Bio Farma research institute in Bandung, Indonesia. For about $ 600 the institute showed inclination to send cultures of these organisms by mail-order, without any check on the identities of the buyers or what would be the end use of organisms.

The reporters identified 450 laboratories world-wide that keep cultures of micro-organisms. Anthrax was found being sold by more than 50, botulinum by 34 and plague by 18. The journalists approached 20 at random. The Veterinary Research Institute in Brno, in the Czech Republic, was ready to sell botulinum for a mere $18 to $50. The reporters were told they could send a representative to pick it up. Only institutes in Mexico, China and Brazil restricted their sales subject to the production of an export licence.

5

Defining Terrorism

Several laws are made and lapsed as the legal instruments to deal with the problem of terrorism. They, however, do not define the term terrorism in a clear-cut way. Let us try to find out what the term terrorism means in these laws.

The National Security Act

First, the National Security Act, 1980[1]. The NSA was a successor to the much-maligned MISA (Maintenance of Internal Security Act) that lost its credibility during the Emergency. The idea behind having the NSA was quite clear and unambiguous; to put people involved "in certain cases for the purpose of maintenance of internal security and matters connected therewith" behind bang. The NSA was applicable across India, and allowed both the central and the state governments to put anyone in preventive detention for a year if there was reason enough to believe that lockup was necessary to stop the person from "acting in any manner prejudicial to the defence of India, the relations of India with foreign powers, or to the security of India.

Any officer of the level of district magistrate could exercise the power of detention under this Act. An Advisory Board (AB) having three members was to hear cases under NSA, and the government was bound to listen to the advise of the Board on whether a person should continue in custody or be allowed to leave. The AB was clearly an effort of the government to make the NSA above board and to lend it an aura of being non-partisan. But the members of the AB were in effect[2] government nominees, so it was all along quite evident whose instructions they were working on.

The NSA is important, because it was the first Act in Indian history to be directed against organised terrorism[3] in its present *avatar*. When the pro-Khalistan movement in Punjab threatened to spin out of control, the government acted quickly to amend the NSA, making it effectively the first anti-terrorism bill. The changes, introduced in 1984, made the NSA 's provisions even harsher in Punjab. The ABs were dispensed, the period of preventive detention was extended up to two years. The power of the courts to release detainees if any of the grounds for their arrest was struck down, was done away with. The post 1984 NSA reflected the government's faith in a legal remedy to terrorism. But its overriding flaw was that the understanding of terrorism was kept so loose and ill-defined—the term 'in certain cases' was as precise as it got—perhaps even deliberately so, that it became an instrument of government abuse. One of the most high profile cases of its abuse- which was made the subject of a huge media campaign by Amnesty International[4]—was the arrest of 324 people who had been flushed out of the Golden Temple premises by security forces after Operation Bluestar. Most of these people were devotees and temple employees who had no link with what led to the siege of the gurdwara. But they were all arrested under the NSA, and held without trial for far more time than even the maximum amount of preventive detention allowed under the Act. The reason for invoking NSA across the board here was, as a commission of enquiry[5] brought out that the authorities, with the full connivance of the government, wanted to bypass the courts and not get entangled in legal procedure. It's a weakness of terrorism laws that human rights activists rightly point out, that government authorities under pressure to produce results in anti-militancy drives use these laws to bypass the Law itself. Its not something unique to India, and as we will see later, has been particularly confounding for the British government in its efforts to combat the low intensity conflict in Northern Ireland.

It's worthwhile mentioning at this stage that the law in India, in dealing with the central question of what terrorism is, has chosen the traditional approach of expanding it to the widest possible spectrum, leaving the possibility therefore of bringing in more categories of offences that may be considered "terroristic" if the situation were to change in near future. This perhaps explains why definitions of terrorism have been what I would call "maximalist" in the sense that they include an exact breakup of the kinds of activities that would be considered acts of terrorism.

Its not a malaise in any case restricted the Law Commission's definition in 2000, which I will come to later. Take another act, arguably the progenitor of the NSA, the Jammu and Kashmir (Public Safety) Act, for instance. This Act, too, allows the detention upto two years of anyone acting against the "security of the state or the maintenance of law and order". To answer the question of what exactly would be before the law such an act, the J & K act lists four categories[6]:

1. Any act which causes or creates, or could create, or is attempted at creating, feelings of enmity, disharmony or hatred, on the grounds of religion caste race or community. In short, anything that is socially divisive.
2. Anything to do with the use of force that distrupts public order.
3. Anything to do with "the commission of mischief" that threatens public order.
4. Committing any act that is punishable with death or over seven years imprisonment—that is, any serious offence—that also threatens public order.

This act was drafted at a time when the aspect of human rights vis-a-vis terrorism laws was hardly in focus, and it reveals. Instead of narrowing the definition of terrorism to reduce the risk of misuse, an effort was being made by keeping such broad categories as "the commission of mischief"— and the very long period of preventive detention allowed — that the only message that the executive was being given was that it was above board in the exercise of its authority.

The first time any Indian law actually tries to define the word "terrorist" appears to be in 1984. That's also the period just after the controversial Operation Bluestar, a time when the government, under criticism for the methods it had employed, found itself under pressure to clear up a massive backlog of cases that had piled up concerning the anti-militant drive. This was frankly not possible under the NSA—most of those arrested under NSA had undergone their maximum terms in prison-because in the period 1982 to 1984, the

NSA had come under increasing judicial scrutiny. The validity of the Act itself had been upheld, but controls were put on the power of detention in a Supreme Court ruling in 1982[7].

The First Definition

With the NSA having outgrown its utility, and with one eye on subverting the judicial system altogether, the government considered for the first time in 1984, of introducing the much criticised "special courts" to deal with terrorist offences. This was not possible without some definition of the word "terrorist" and so we find in the Terrorist Affected Areas (Special Courts) Act 1984 the first, rather cumbersome, definition of who a terrorist is. And this is how it goes:

A terrorist, under this Act is defined as "any person who indulges in wanton killing of persons or in violence or in the disruption of services or means of communications necessary to the community or in damaging property with a view to:

(a) putting the public or any section of the public in fear.

(b) adversely affecting the harmony between various religious, racial, language or regional groups or castes or communities.

(c) coercing or overawing the government established by law.

(d) endangering the sovereignty and integrity of India"[8].

This also, a very maximalist definition of terrorism. It reflects the mood in government at the time of the enactment of this act. Having asserted the will of the state, as it were, to go all out against terrorism, after first having spawned it, Indira Gandhi required a political breather in Punjab. She was in need to keep those who could challenge her methods in Punjab at arm's length from the media and activist organisations.

Those who believe Mrs Gandhi's decision to introduce the TA (Special Courts) ordinance was influenced by a need to buy time, while talking terms with the Congress's biggest political rival, the resurgent Akalis. That also explains why the Gandhi government deliberately kept the definition of terrorism loose in this act, making room its indiscriminate use by security forces who conveniently charged many of the NSA accused under provisions of this new act, keeping them in detention while tempers cooled in Punjab.

As a political strategy, it proved effective over the long term, culminating in the Punjab accord that the then P.M. Rajiv Gandhi signed with the Akalis in 1985. But in terms of India's human rights record and the Indian judiciary's responsibility to protect it, this was perhaps one of the country's darkest chapters. Captain Amarinder Singh, was the first to challenge the constitutional validity of the Act in a writ petition filed before the Supreme Court[9]. The basic argument in the petition was against the special courts, which didn't provide reasonable safeguards to an accused. Rejecting the challenge, all the apex court bench did was to recommend a few rather cosmetic safeguards such as a frequent review of whether areas marked out as 'terrorist affected' really qualified to be put in that category and the disclosure of witnesses against the accused before the trial, giving the accused reasonable opportunity to defend himself. Its this kind of indifference from the judiciary to the clamour of protests against sweeping anti-terrorism laws that provided the government with the confidence to enact the Terrorist and Disruptive Activities Act in 1985. The definition of a terrorist act in TADA was only a slight modification over the Terrorist Affected areas act. Provisions such as trying to overawe the government, alienate a section of the public and causing death, injury or disruption of supplies and services were merely old phrases being rephrased.

The singular difference however, between TADA and the earlier laws was the inclusion of an element of 'motive' behind a terrorist act. Those who drafted TADA believed that any attempt to "strike terror in the people or a section of the people"[10] makes up an act of terrorism. Any larger or more justifiable reason for causing the terror was irrelevant insofar as the enforcement of the act was concerned. In other words, motive was to be read in the immediate impact of the act itself and not the cause behind it.

This is also the basic thrust of the definition of terrorism as laid down in the Prevention of Terrorism Ordinance 2001[11]:

In this controversial law, whoever

(a) with intent to threaten the unity, integrity, security or sovereignty of India or to strike terror in the people or any section of the people does any act or thing.... in such a manner as to cause or likely to cause both death or injury... or detains any person or threatens to kill any person....

(b) or is or continues to be a member of an association declared unlawful under the Unlawful Activities (Prevention) Act.. commits a terrorist act."

So departing from focus on the 'act' itself, here the definition of terrorism is expanded to 'an act of association' with a terrorist group. The idea again is simple, to bring patrons and harbourers of terrorist groups, and fringe supporters within the scope of the anti-terrorist law. This has been drawn directly from the British Law which draws up a list of 'proscribed organisations' to which membership, funding or open support within the territory of the UK is banned. This list is periodically reviewed, with an intention of making the fight against terrorism in line with threats to internal security. The way in which the British Home Office expanded the concept of a Proscribed Organisation to make it applicable across the broadest spectrum is interesting.

On the one hand, it is precise and unambiguous. It even tries to measure and list what acts would constitute 'support' to a banned organisation, something which had so far been left to law enforcers to interpret. In all, while broadening its scope and arbit, it narrows down the definition of terrorism itself.

Therefore, the British Terrorism Act 2000 allows:

- up to ten years of imprisonment for someone who is a member of a proscribed organisation (PO)
- up to ten years jail term for someone who invites support for a PO, or even arranges manages or helps in arranging a meeting in support of a PO
- up to six months jail term for even wearing a uniform, or displaying an article which proves his or her membership of a PO
- up to five years jail term for not disclosing information "as soon as it is reasonably practicable" concerning a PO or an act of terrorism[12].

These provisions have been incorporated into the Law Commission's draft bill also. The period of detention is often less (membership of a terrorist organisation, for instance, is punishable with five years in jail, not ten but for the purposes of defining the act of terrorism per se, that is irrelevant. What stands out isthat the Law Commission, drawing upon the conclusions of the British lawmakers has attempted to make the process of identifying a terrorist more discrete, and in the process more transparent. But that's where its efforts unfortunately end.

Burden of Proof. The BJP-led government has already made it amply clear that the interpretation of these laws is its personal turf, and subject to personal prejudices or opinion. Privately, many NDA stalwarts talk of how its anti-terrorism law will put fear among sections of the population 'more prone' to militancy. Publicly, such honest comments are difficult to elicit. But some idea of how the government opines the anti-terrorism law as anything but sacrosanct and precise came out through a statement issued by the Home Ministry on January 13, 2000, when journalists in New Delhi had started a campaign against one particular provision of the Law Commission's draft which, if applied, could put a journalist in jail for upto a year for not disclosing information about terrorist groups. In an, ill prepared attempt to allay the fears expressed by journalists, the Home Ministry said that:

"The factual position is that the burden of proving that a person has committed an offence under the Act shall rest entirely on the prosecution. However, the court can certainly draw adverse inference against the accused if found in possession of unauthorized arms/ explosives in a notified area, or found in possession of any proceeds of terrorism or if the accused fails to provide samples of his handwriting, fingerprints, footprints, photograph, blood, saliva, semen or hair despite the direction of the court"[13]. Read between the lines, and here is an occasion where the government forcefully telling journalists, 'Don't worry, you'll never be a terrorist until we are convinced you are' or, equally, that 'Only the hardest evidence that you're a terrorist can get you convicted, if you're on our side and don't make too much of a brouhaha about this legislation' or, finally, that 'Don't worry about the courts, they have their limitations and that is where we step in'. Quite frankly, I am surprised the courts had nothing to offer suo moto on this Home Ministry statement.

Having said that, one can say that journalists are an exalted category, and how an anti-terrorist law looks at them and defines their culpability should be peripheral, at most, to the larger debate on whether such laws are at all needed and how far they should go.

For some strange reason, the journalistic fraternity in India has a fear of persecution when it comes to its relationship with the state, which is why it sought to give the impression that the draft anti-terrorism bill was one way of cutting down the freedom of press, Not completely fallacious, but not completely correct either. The bigger concern, which again the Law Commission has failed to address point blank is the question of whether, and if so, to what extent, can activis—religious differentiated political or ideological—be from terrorism, even if it has the same consequences. That's the core issue of any anti-terrorist legislation: Should motive define terrorism? In the words of an ancient Chinese proverb, brief and to the point, the defining characteristic of a terroristic act would be that it would "kill one, frighten ten thousand" implying in other words, that for a terrorist, an act of violence is aimed not to just cause destruction, but in the message of 'terror' being driven home. It is this 'terror' that is the best way to spread word about a certain political/ insurrectionary/insurgent ideology. As Brian Jenkins puts it, "the terrorist wants a lot of people watching rather than a lot of people dead.[14]"

Jenkins here in his pithy remark tells us one of the biggest truths about contemporary terrorism: that it uses violence, or more appropriately the threat of violence, as an instrument to drive home its point of view, its ideology. Should this be treated as form of dissidence which a democracy must not just entertain, but indulge? Jenkins says no, but in the Indian context, the Peoples' Union for Democratic Rights takes a more pedantic, even highbrow line saying: "We should remember that what is called 'terrorism' is not always a matter of mindless violence. Often its roots are socio-political and governed by distinct and conflicting ideologies"

The PUDR's fear of course is that an anti-terrorism law might be used, by unscrupulous or vindictive governments, to decimate its opponents, It's a fear that was expressed in the British Parliament as well, on various occasions when the Home Office then under Jack Straw tried to push the Prevention of Terrorism Bill through[15]. In the House of Lords debate, the feisty Baroness Miller took on straw's deputy, Minister of State for Home Lord Bassam of Brighton on that very point. Arguing that it would diminish the line between terrorism and protest, (in essence the PUDR's argument as well), she said: "From time to time through history the young people see the iniquity of a path the establishment is trying to follow. They may raise their voices, and sometimes their fists, and they may make life very difficult for the establishment, but we should not allow it in perpetuity to decide what causes are really terrorist causes and what are embarrassments to be silenced.[16]"

As all those people who believe arming the state doesn't help, the Baroness too was pushing her point a bit, giving dissidents an innocuous touch, painting them as just a little wayward, petulant youngsters needing direction, not punishment. Its an indulgence the Tony Blair's New Labour government wasn't willing to prosper. Despite a sustained campaign by British minority groups, organisations like Amnesty and Human Rights Watch and even animal rights groups, the British Parliament managed to push through, in 2000, one omnibus bill to tackle terrorism, replacing 19 others[17] and incorporating for the first time, an element of 'motive' in the definition of terrorism. This is how that Bill—which the Law Commission bashfully admits its been inspired by—defines terrorism. "Terrorism means the use or threat, for the purpose of advancing a political, religious or ideological cause, of action which

involves serious violence against any person or property:

endangers the life of any person:

creates a serious risk to the health or safety of the publicor a section of the public:

is designed seriously to interfere with or seriously disrupt an electronic system":

Tony Blair here was trying to remove the possibility of subversive activity cloaking itself as 'conflicting ideology'. Was the method he was adopting in doing so too simplistic to work? Well, it's not easy to say. But this was the first time anything like this was being experimented as part of anti-terrorist legislation. But other European governments had also tried to something similar, and without much success. It's relevant to go back and learn some of these experiences from history. The dangers of trying to sieve sedition or subversive activity from protest first showed up when the West German government tried to act tough with communist party sympathizers in 1950.

It adopted the system of 'Berufsverbot' which banned from public service anyone who adhered to a political philosophy aimed at overturning democracy. There were two instances from contemporary history that West Germany's first post-War Chancellor cited to justify the Berufsverbot. First, the experience of the Nazis in destroying the Weimar Republic of the Thirties. Second, that of the Czech communists who in 1947-48 tried to achieve their aims by "public disorder and disruption of the administration and economy' so that the people, fearing a breakdown of public order and a fear to lose means of livelihood for their families, accepted the totalitarian alternative. Well, in defence of those who laws such as the Berufsverbot oppressive-and by the same logic would oppose the British POT Act as well — it must be admitted that there have been many occasions when the law was used rather stupidly—like the much celebrated example of a train driver dismissed from service because he was a member of the Communist Party. But as Richard Clutterbuck, one of the best known experts of anti-terrorism legislation, writes, the Berufsverbot "has been consistently supported by both the government and the opposition and has contributed to Germany's political system in the past 40 years being the most stable in Europe"[19].

Actually, the necessity to include rather than exclude political motives in coming up with a workable definition of terrorism is recognized by the Washington based RAND foundation, commissioned by the US Cabinet Committee to Combat Terrorism, to look into the 'phenomenon of terrorist activity in the modern world'. According to the RAND foundation, "it is necessary to define terrorism according to the quality of the act, not the identity of the perpetrator or the nature of the cause".

The RAND foundation therefore brings into use a few indices based on which terrorism can be defined:

(1) Political Motive: RAND talks of "an act of terrorism as a crime in the classic sense such as murder or kidnapping, albeit for political motive"

(2) Attention grabbing Motive: RAND argues in its presentation before the US administration that "terrorism contains a psychological component—it is aimed at people watching." The identities of the actual victims or targets of attack, RAND says,

are secondary or irrelevant to the terrorists' objective of spreading fear or alarm or gaining concessions.

There can be no doubt over the usefulness of the second index and the first has all the potiential to set alarm bells ringing among the traditional opponents of special anti-terrorism legislation. RAND says that the logic of separating an act of violence from its political context is simply to criminalise a certain kind of political expression. In the Indian context, this appears largely appropriate, the central idea being to take away from any group—be it the People's War Group which regularly ambushes policemen in Andhra Pradesh and Madhya Pradesh in an effort to challenge power structures[20] or the United Naga Council, which seizes the Highway connecting Imphal and rationalizes this as part of a larger struggle against the Manipuris — the right to legitimize violence as part of a larger social movement.

The inclusion of political, or for that matter religious or ideological motive, behind any definition of terrorism is also quite useful for India because it effectively removes the ambiguous category of 'disruptive activities ' that TADA introduced in 1985. This category carried with it tough punitive measures, varying from five years imprisonment up to life imprisonment.

Disruptive activities were defined as anything which "questions, disrupts or intends to disrupt the sovereignty and integrity of India, or which is intended to bring about or support any claim whether directly or indirectly for the cession of any part of India from the Union" .

Ten Years of TADA

In the ten years that TADA was in force, as many as 22 of the country's 25 states had invoked it, most of them under the 'disruptive activities' clause. The maximum number of detentions under TADA took place in Gujarat where the figure stood at somewhere close to 20,000 arrests.

As an Amnesty report pointed out, the Gujarat government invoked the Act against bootleggers, people campaigning against a power price hike and students who took to the roads in a novel demonstration against the rise in the cost of milk supplied by the government. One particularly hilarious case, but a pointer to how indiscriminately used the Act provision came to light from Assam, where a 12 year old boy was arrested for 'inciting trouble against the state'[21]. In fact, in retrospect, it would not be wrong to say that TADA failed as it clubbed terrorist activity with disruptive activity. It was this that allowed the use of the act for what should ideally have been dealt with under the Criminal Procedure Code. Unfortunately this cannot be put down in black and white before a court, which is why one finds that most of the challenges to TADA—like in the case of the NSA as well—have been on the grounds of violation of Section 21 of the Constitution, the right to life and personal liberty.

It was not a strong argument, borne out by the rather brusque manner in which the Supreme Court dismissed the challenge to TADA in the celebrated Kartar Singh case stating: "It is for parliament ot enact any law without infringing any of the provisions of the Constitution" which of course the Supreme Court had not. In fact, in that very judgment, the court defended the need to frame tougher laws to discriminate between terrorists and ordinary criminals, arguing that "everyday...many innocent, defenceless people particularly the poor, politicians, government officials and army officials have been mercilessly gunned down. No one can deny these stark facts and naked truth by adopting an ostrich-like attitude completely ignoring the impending danger[22]

If the high rhetoric in the Kartar Singh judgment stood out, it was tempered by some other judgments of the Supreme Court itself which drew out the consternation within the judiciary on whether TADA should have been confined to terrorist offences alone. Even before the Kartar Singh judgment in fact, the court had issued warning on police forces using the TADA to misuse criminal law. Consider the judgment in the Hitendra Thakur vs State of Maharashtra case in 1993. Making a call for necessity or a stricter implementation of the law, the court said:

"Every terrorist may be a criminal, but every criminal cannot be given the label of a terrorist only to set in motion the more stringent provisions of TADA. The criminal activity in order to invoke TADA must be committed with the requisite intention as contemplated under section 3 (1) of the Act by use of such weapons as have been enumerated in s. 3.1 and which cause or are likely to result in the offences as mentioned in the section."

This reveals heartburn within the judiciary as well over constituting a category of 'disruptive activity'. Will ascribing more direct motive— religious, political or ideological as the British Law put it-end that? It's not an easy task to answer that one, to be frank. But one way out could be to introduce a third element in the definition of a terrorist act.

So, if the draft Indian law exhaustively details out the act of terrorism, and the British Law at both the act of terrorism and the motive, the law against terrorism in the United States of America has traditionally looked at the act, the motive as also the persons or audience the act is directed at. The Indian and British laws in their defence, also look at who the terror is aimed at, but not as discretely as American law does, that finds a close parallel in th RAND definition we took up earlier. The US Code (Title 22, Section 265. 6.d) defines terrorism—and this definition has been in use since 1983—as "premeditated, politically motivated, violence perpetrated against non-combatant targets by sub-national groups or clandestine agents, usually intended to influence an audience".

The US law is in my view too narrow and cannot be foolproof, potentially leading to a situation where the government is pushed into a corner. In the US this risk has been overcome by total executive supremacy, oftening bordering on disdain. Consider the record of this exchange between Ned Walker, assistant to the under-Secretary for Middle East Affairs and Lee Hamilton, chairman of the sub-committee on Europe and the Middle East. It took place during a hearing of the Foreign Affairs Committee of the US House of Representatives, so it's as close a look as one can have to understanding the US federal government's mind on tackling terrorism legally. The backdrop is provided by talks between the US and the PLO[23]. Hamilton starts the interrogation:

Hamilton : Well, how do you define terrorism, do you define it in terms of non-combatance?

Walker : The State Department definition which is included in the terrorism report annually defines it in terms of politically motivated attacks on non-combatant targets.

Hamilton: So an attack on a military unit in Israel will not be terrorism?

Walker: It does not necessarily mean that it would not have a very major impact on whatever we were proposing to do with the PLO.

Hamilton : I understand that, but it would not be terrorism.

Walker: An attack on a military target. Not according to the definition. Now wait a minute; that is not entirely correct. You know, attacks can be made on military targets which are clearly terrorism. It depends on the individual circumstances.

Hamilton: Now wait a minute. I thought you were giving me the State Department definition.

Walker : Non-combatant is the terminology, not military no civilian.

Hamilton: All right. So any attack on a non-combatant could be terrorism?

Walker : That is right.

Hamilton: And a non-combatant could include military?

Walker: Of course.

Hamilton: It would certainly include civilian, right?

Walker: Right.

Hamilton: But an attack on a military unit would not be terrorism.

Walker: It depends on the circumstances.

Hamilton: And what are those circumstances.

Walker: I don't think it will be productive to get into a description of the various terms and conditions under which we are going to define an act by the PLO as terrorism.

This conversation points to is the inherent subjective element in the implementation of even the most precise, narrow, definition of terrorism. And that is why even a one-line definition of the kind former Israeli Prime Minister Benjamin Netanyahu proposes[24], that "Terrorism is the systematic and deliberate assault on civilians to inspire fear for political ends" is subject to several interpretations.

This is perhaps the reason that at the international level; there is no legislation, no convention, which can be used as a tool for global cooperation against terrorism. Can one be achieved? I believe it can, but again, that will need the elimination—not the inclusion—of all ideology, motive, compulsion, or long-term goal from such a definition, even if it presents itself in such a hallowed form as the integrity of the state, as the Law Commission's definition does. That blurs the definition and makes it a subject of unnecessary debate.

Bridging the ideologial divide between nations could perhaps then be the first logical step towards a universally acceptable definition, and hence campaign against terrorism at least in India if not globally

References

1. Act number 65 of 1980. It replaced the National Security Ordinance 1980.

2. The members of the advisory board were either High Court Judges or persons eligible for appointment as HC judges.

3. One is of course discounting here the insurgencies in the Northeast some of which like the Naga insurgency predate independence.

4. The need to review cases against 324 Sikhs held in a Jodhpur Jail for more than 4 years Amnesty, September 1988.

5. The Commission of enquiry was Headed by a former High Court judge , Justice CS Tikwana.

6. Section 8 (3) J&K (Public Safety) Act 1978.

7. A K Roy *vs* Union of India AIR 1982 SC 710, the SC judgement in this case led to six principal safeguards being made mandatory on the arresting authorities. This included informing relatives about the arrest, special status in relation to convicted prisoners and no "indignity" being meted by the authorites.

8. Section 2(!)h, Terrorist Affected Areas (Special Powers) Act.

9. WP 15432 (1984) Amarinder Singh vs Union of India, SC.

10. Section 2 (f) Terrorist and Disruptive Activities Prevention Bill 1985.

11. Also Part II Section 3 POT Bill 2000, Law Commission.

12. Secions 11 to 20, Part II & III, Terrorism Act 2000, Published by Stationary Office. UK Parliament.

13. Govt for consensus on anti-terrorism law *The Hindu July 14, 2000.*

14. "Internation a Terrorism: A Balance Sheet".

15. Jack Straw, is among the top five Labour leaders, and was know at one time to have strong views against sweeping powers to the executive to crack down on terrorist groups.

16. Hansard 1445, 12/12/1999.

17. Schedule 16 Terrorism Act 2000 "Repeals and revocations".

18. Terrorism Act 200, Part 1 Section 1. 'Interpretation'.

19. Terrorism Drugs and Crime in Europe after 1992.

20. The Terrorist and Disruptive Activities (Prevention) Act lack of scrupulous care" ASA 20.39.94, Nov. 1994.

21. *Indian Express* report 16 July 94.

22. All the quotes are from Kartar Singh *vs* State of Punjab SC 1994.

23. Hearings and Markup before the sub-committe on Europe and the Middle East of the Committe on Foreign Affairs, House of Representatives 101 Congress, First session , p. 66.

24. Benjamin Netanyahu 'Fighting Terrorism', NY, Farrar Strauss and Giroux 1995.

6

International Law Against Terrorism

Terrorism is a global phenomenon. Various governments have made different laws to deal with this malaise. There are international laws too, which help the governments the world over to tackle this problem. But are they really effective? Terrorism today has spread across the globe, and stands at the level of an international industry. In cases like Pakistan where the national economy is weak, governments are dependent—whether they admit it or not—on the proceeds of terrorism or terrorist related activities in order to feed their millions. Terrorism has also become a powerful instrument of international politics, more so in the post-Cold War world where armies patronized by the Superpowers—the best example here is the taliban—have become armed mercenaries having little or no respect for international borders. Which is why its shocking that of date, there is not even single multilateral treaty that can claim to control, if not stem, the rise of international terrorism. In the course of the debate in India over the necessity or not —for an omnibus anti terrorism law, it has been singled out that Indian is signatory to a slew of international conventions. These multilateral agreements, if applied individually, provide enough of a legal remedy to terrorism, doing away with need for a homegrown remedy. In this chapter, we propose to scrape the bottom of the international legal system to highlight why India needs a domestic law, because there is not— effectively— any multilateral one. Let's start by looking at what has led to international terrorism, as we know it today.

The Genesis of Terrorism

Countries all over the world have turned, at one time or the other, to international law to seek a refuge against terrorism. Their interest in the subject however has been sporadic, and inconsistent. It all has died down soon after the shock effect of a terrorist strike has subsided. The first time when international communities, grouped together was, if my archive search is correct, in the League of Nations, after the assassination of King Alexander I and Louis Barthou in Marseilles, France. This gave birth to the first United Nations Convention against terrorism. It was called, "The 1937 Convention for the Prevention and Punishment of Terrorism " and interestingly, India was the only country to ratify it[1] goes to show, just how deep our resolve to tackle terrorisms—without resorting to state terrorism, in turn— has been. The 1937 Convention, following the incident that led to it, criminalized incidents involving heads of state and diplomats. A very narrow focus, or course, but something, which appeared enough at the time. There was a second convention passed as well, which proposed the creation of an International Criminal Court. Till date the ICC has not been formed.

Terrorism raised its head again on an incipient scale in the 1960s. Once again the playing ground of the terrorist movements was Europe, but their morphology was very different. So were the reasons underlying.

(i) The sudden rise in popularity of extreme neo-Marxist and Trotskyist left wing ideologies among the student communities of industrialized societies. As Wilkinson points out, "Their common points were bitter opposition to United States policy in the Vietnam War and to US policy in the Third World generally, which they regarded as neo-imperialism". These kind of movements led to massive "student revolutions" of 1968-69 all over Europe, most notably France, but died down after that. The central core of student leaders refused to acknowledge this, and groups like the Baader-Meinhof in the Federal Republic of Germany, the Japanese Red Army and the Red Brigades in Italy.

(ii) Soviet Spectre: Most of what were grouped as extreme left wing operatives were unlinked in the tactical—not the ideological— sense. But in the Cold War world, it was natural to cast a Soviet spectre over them. The theory of Soviet patronage for these terrorist groups was in place all through the Sixties and the Seventies of last century, but comes across strongest in a book called the "Terror Network" by Claire Sterling[3]. Sterling's theory, which not suprisingly received a standing ovation from the US establishment at the time, is that the Soviets, not wanting to get into full scale conventional War sponsored, financed, trained or armed groups in Libya, Northern Ireland, Cuba and West European countries from causes as diverse as that of the IRA, the Red Brigades and Turkey's PLA. A kind of proxy war, in effect, which led the US to officially acknowledge cross- border terrorism, in the avatar that we know of it in India— for the first time. As Jenkins notes, this was a time when it began to be accepted that "Governments could employ existing terrorist groups to attack their opponents, or they could create their own terrorists. Terrorism only requires a small investment, certainly far less than what it costs to wage conventional war[4]". The US itself began to resort to, and justify as wars of liberation.

Arab Pride: The massive defeat of the Arab States in their June 1967 war against Israel is also perhaps, one of the turning points in the evolution of modern day terrorism. After that, Arab states found themselves too divided to seriously support the Palestinian cause. Israel was just too militarily powerful. If one goes through the chart of terrorist incidents in the period 1968-1972 therefore, one finds a sudden rise in terrorist incidents aimed against the Israelis—hijack attempts, bombings and shootouts. So has the Palestinian caused a multiplier effect on what we've now come to know as "Islamic Terrorism"? Wilkinson opines that it is so . His premise: the "huge international publicity they achieved" which "undoubtedly had the effect of interesting other militant groups in other parts of the world in exploiting the techniques of international terror"

It is common to all the three possile starting points of contemporary terrorism that they transgress international borders with impunity. The 1960s saw the birth of a closely—connected world, and simultaneously the theatre of action for the terrorism was not local or specific, any more , but global. A part from it, this was also the time when terrorists began to use the third party route' to achieve their ends. A third party route essentially means, bringing in outside players to put pressure on interested parties or governments. As Grant Wardlaw writes talking of this trend: "Terrorist theory now enphasizes the ease with which many goals can be achieved by exerting pressure on the target government through third parties. So an airliner carrying passengers of many nationalities may be hijacked in order that the governments representing these individuals will put pressure on the target governments to accede to the demands of the hijackers[5]".

The 'third party route' is brought out well in the Al-Faran kidnapping case in the Indian context. The Al-Faran—which is believed to be a front organisation of the now-renamed Harkat-ul-Ansar—abducted nine foreigners hiking in the Kashmir valley on two separate occasions. Four of them were freed in a rescuse operation by the Indian forces. Of the five others, a Norwegian tourist, Hans Christian Ostro, was killed in August 1995. Ostro's nationality in this case appeared to have been his undoing, because the atempt by the Al- Faran clearly was to pressurize the Indian government, through the influence wielded by the other hostages' countries of origin— the US, UK and Germany—to meet their demands. The 'third party route' has been gaining popularity with terrorists since 1972, when the 'Black September' terrorists killed Israeli athletes in the Munich Olympics to highlight the plight of the palestinian peoples'. This was an amazingly successful operation, given that 11 Israeli athletes were killed even as a German attempt to con the kidnappers failed. So were five of the eight terrorists, but the other three were later released in exchange for the passengers of a Lufthansa aircraft hijacked from Lebanon. Situations when a third, directly unconnected party becomes involved in a terrorist operation have been many since then, among them what almost became a standard modus operandi of embassy sieges' like that at the Hague in 1974, when the Japanese Red Army took over the French embassy. And in Stockholm a year after when just six members of the Baader-Meinhof occupied and blew up the West German embassy in 1975. The point I am trying to make is that somewhere between the early 1960s and the mid-1970, a virtual spate of 'third party attacks' announced the arrival of a new, more dangerous global terrorism.

This was the time when all of Western Euroupe, and later the United States, became involved in a complex web of terrorism having global implications. Unfortunately, at that time, terrorism was yet to hit India. Which is why we find New Delhi's response to efforts at drafting the appropriate international laws against terrorism half-hearted, even nil. We shall go into that later, but before that let us see how the United Nations responded to the new threat, and how it got mired in trying to focus on 'legal and treaty obligations rather than real action'. Just to drive the point home—of how treaties and conventions fail to even remotely address the many complex and unpredictable situations that modern day terrorism can leave governments groping with—let me just quote one particular instance, now famous Canary Islands Case. It's a tragedy that unfortunately even the United Nations has come to stip in its efforts to tackle terrorism.

On the 27th of March 1977, two Boeing 747 planes collided at Tenerife airport in the Canary islands. As many as 580 people died in the accident. The accident occurred as both the 747 jets were diverted from their original destination of Las Palmas, after a terrorist bomb exploded in a flower shop near the Las Palmas airfield. The Canary terrorists were not involved in world's worst disaster in aviation history, but their act resulted in causing this disaster.[7]

We did not need the world's worst air tragedy to bring home the point, but the Canary Islands case raises serious questions over accountability. If the unintended consequences of terrorism can be so damaging, surely nations need to be generous while drafting a law to curb it. Unfortunately, as we will see from what's been happening at the UN, most nations, India included, have not shown that kind of spirit.

The UN Role

A couple of days after the attacks on Israeli athletes at the Munich Olympics, in a note dated the 8th of September 1972, the then United Nations Secretary General Kurt Waldheim made an appeal to the UN General Assembly to include in its 27th Session: "Measures to prevent terrorism and other forms of violence which endanger or take innocent human lives or jeopardize fundamental freedoms.

At that point of time, Israel found itself cornered by the new terrorism of the Palestinians, including a series of letter bombs aimed at its diplomatic corps and the Lod airport massacre in Tel Aviv. So there was encugh justification to let the item[8] Waldheim introduced in the UNGA pass without amendments. Which is why many were surprised when the item—which had the personal backing of the Secretary when the item- which had the personal backing of the Secretary General-was referred to the legal committee of the UN, Two weeks later, the reason why the item had been made to go through the UN bureaucracy became evident when an amended version of the original proposal was returned. It effectively stymied, if not exactly turned around on its head, the original proposal. Now it became: "Measures to prevent international terrorism which endangers or takes innocent human lives or jeopardizes fundamental freedoms, and study the underlying causes of those forms of terrorism and acts of violence which lie in misery, frustration, grievance and despair which causes some people to sacrifice human lives, including their own in an attempt to effect radical chages."

This meant that Kurt Waldheim's proposal, which one may add was the first major effort at tackling the problem of terrorism through international instruments since 1972, never came through. Even if it had, it would have been too double-edged a weapon to be effective. In its place, the Sixth Committee (Legal) of the UN, which had come up with this humungous amended proposal, asked the UN Secretariat to prepare a detailed draft on what contemporary terrorism was all about, including 'its origins'. That took another two months to complete, and it really did not reveal anything on a solution to the global terrorist malaise[9]. One can therefore skip any details of the 'study'.

It is important to mention here what when the US tried to edge out the political dimension to this amended proposal, by introducing a draft resolution and convention on terrorism, aimed primarily at international terrorists. According to Article 1 of the draft:

"Any person who unlawfully kills, causes serious bodily harm or kidnaps another person, attempts to commit any such act or participates as an accomplice of a person who commits or attempts to commit any such act, commits an act on international significance".

The purpose behind it was to ensure acts against civilians (non combatants) to obtain any kinds of concessions, outside the territory at which the act is directed. In that sense, it was a tool against kidnappings, hijackings and embassy sieges, just the scourge of the time. But once again, it faced oppositions over the question of what a definition of terrorism should be, in which India played a major role. This was perhaps the last real opportunity at the level of the UN to draft a law against terrorism, because opposition to it, though intense, was largely uncoordinated. Sensing this, the US redcafted it:

(i) Ask the UN General Assembly to request the International Law Comission to draft an anti-terrorism convention

(ii) Have the UN GA debate the draft in late 1972

(iii) Convene a special conference as soon as possible to adopt a convention.

The US argument was that attempts to follow causes of terrorism should not be made an impediment to the process of combating it. "The study of the political or socio-economic causes" the US representative brought forward "would nessarily take a long time and the completion of the necessary protective measures could not be postponed pending the completion of that study" A group of 16 countries, led by India were opposed to the US. These countries, including some dubious ones, like Algeria and Sudan, twisted the argument to take a philosophically lofty position on issues like " the inalienable right to self determination", "the legitimacy of national liberation struggles" while condemning "repressive and terrorist acts by colonial racist and alien regimes". When the issue came up for vote in the 35 member UN Ad-hoc committee on International Terrorism, the US motion fell, defeated by a vote of 14 to 16. While this was touted around as a victory for the Non- Aligned movement at the time, it effectively blocked attempts to draft, at the international lvel, a law against terrorism. But more than that, the moot point is that the whole episode showed the kind of clout terrorst groups enjoyed even at the UN. It was something , which frustrated large sections of the international community (and India was not in this group).

In fact, the chairman of the Sixth (legal) committee of the UN, which passed this amended version, Eric Soy, was so frustrated that he said that:

"In reality a simultaneous study of causes and measures (to control terrorism) is a condition impossible to sustain the demand to consider the question en bloc was in reality nothing more than a manoeuvre designed to reduce terrorism to a simply political question and to prevent concrete measures from being drafted".

Multilateral Treaties and Their Failure

When there is no umbrella act/ legislation/ convention against terrorism, the only legal defence against terrorism today is a number of specific conventions and protocols, covering a range of terrorist attacks. Included among them are:

1970 Hague Convention: Against Hijacking

1971 Montreal Convention: Against Sabotaging Aircraft

Attacks on internationally protected persons: 1773 New York Convention, this includes heads of state and government, diplomats, etc

1979 New York Convention: Hostage taking

1988 Convention: for the—Suppression of Unlaful Acts against safety of maritive Narigation: Piracy and Masitime Crime.

Apart from these, there is only one—but extremely effective case-of a regional treaty, the 1977 European Convention for the Suppression of terrorism, and of course there remain on the side a number of bilateral treaties, particularly linked to extradition and cooperation between judiciaries of different governments. These are not specifically linked to terrorism, but are supposed to be useful—with very varying degrees of success—in securing the extradition of those who have committed terrorist acts against a particular state's nationals and taken refuge in the territory of the other party to the treaty.

The obvious question which then arises—and which has been asked by human rights groups in India with great enthusiasm—is that when there are already a number of multilateral mechanisms to control acts of violence, is there any need for tougher domestic laws, say in the case of a country like India where the government believes that most terrorism is not homegrown? Quite frankly, there shouldn't have been if not for four fundamental shortcomings of these mutilateral conventions:

I Not many states are party to them. More importantly, quite often, countries that matter are not. The problems with this have been evident in hostage taking situations, like when Algeria declined to hand over the hijackers of a Kuwaiti plane as it wasn't party to the relevant treaties. But my personal favourite, in this regard, is what's popularly come to be known as the Achille Lauro Affair. It was a rare mix of circumstances which ended up exposing the weakness of international law in dealing wiht terrorism related crises.

In October 1985 four Palestinians hijacked a passenger ship called Achille Lauro off Egypt. They wanted the ship to be taken to the Syrian port of Tartus, but were not given permission there . So they went back to Egypt, to negotiate with the local authorities, and PLO men. But before that, frustrated over the intransigence of the Syrian government, the hijackers killed an elderly US tourist called Leon klinghoffer, and dumped his body overboard, Eventually after 48 hours of negotiations, they handed over the ship in exchange for safe passage out of Egypt. The matter however did not end there. The US had reports that the hijackers were still in Egypt, and not out of the country as had been announced by President Hosir Mobarak. The US waited to react, but when and Egyption plane tried to caray the hijackers out of the country, the US Navy was asked to use its F-14 jets to Egyptian plane and force it to land at the US Italian airbase in Sicily. In Sicily, there was a confrontation between the US and Italy over the issue as to who should arrest the hijackers. Italy finally won, it released the prime leader Abu Abbas of the PLO and arrested the other four. Later, Italian officials openly showed their resentment over the US' lack of respect for their jurisdiction, and Egyptian officials said they were angry at the way which their aircraft had been accosted.

It has been pointed out since that the confusion could have been avoidable, had Italy been a party to the 1979 Convention against the Taking of Hostages. There is a specific extradition/prosecution clause in the Convention (Article 8) which makes it obligatory for signatory states to " if not extradite, be obliged, without exception, to submit its case to competent authorities, for the purpose of prosecution."

II. *The Achille Lauro affair* is also interesting because it reveals just how ineffective international conventions are in the absence of any enforcement provisions. Therefore if a country party to an international convention fails to comply with its letter and spirit, other countries can not really do much more than apply sanctions—which again are subject to international scrutiny. In reality that, too, rarely happens. So in the Achille Lauro case, no action was taken against Egypt, which failed to comply with the 1979 Hostages convention, which it had signed. Same way, no action was taken against Italy, which only two years ago, had signed an extradition treaty with the United States.

III. None of the international or regional treaties, excepting the 1977 European Convention and the 1988 Maritime Convention, specifies that terrorist type acts are not to be deemed as 'political offences' and therefore exempt from extradition laws. Even in these two laws, there are many loopholes. The 1988 Maritime Convention for example provides that "these acts shall be regarded to be extraditable offences" in cases where there is an extradition treaty" implying that there is no room for someone to escape the law on the grounds that his / her 's is an act of political violence. Where there is no extradition treaty however, extradition is "subject to conditions provided for by the law of the required state ". And these laws in turn could well include the political offence exception.

The 1977 European Convention is stricter. It spells out that "for the purposes of extradition between contracting states none of the following offences shall b considered as a political offence or as an offence linked to a political offence or inspired by political motives". Article 1 of the Convention then goes on to state the various offences that fall under the ambit of terrorist acts. In addition Article 2 allows contracting states to deem other terrorist type attacks as non-political for purposes of extradition. The problem with the European Convention, which is perhaps a model for SAARC nations to follow, is the provision under Article 13,which provides for a state to reserve " the right to refuse extradition in respect of any offence mentioned in Ariticle I which it regards to be a political offence, or an offence inspired by political motives, provided that it undertakes to take into due consideration, while assesses the character of the offence, any particularly serious aspects of the offence including

(i) That it created a collective danger to the life, physical integrity or liberty of persons

(ii) That it affected persons not knowing the motives behind it

(iii) That cruel or vicious means have been used in the commission of the offence".

The basic problem with the European Convention, therefore, is that it places great faith on the honesty of the states. It is naive in the modern day and age where terrorism involves a large number of interested parties to expect the "extradite or prosecute" route to work. Countries like Italy have already exploited this naivete or international law to the hilt to avoid not only extradition, but also mutual assistance in cases it considers political. In doing so, Italy has taken the shield of its domestic laws, especially Article 10 and 26 of its constitution, which prevent the extradition of Italians for political purposes. Had Italy been willing, it could easily have amended the constitution to bring it more in league with the European Convention. But it didnot do so. The point I am trying to make is that International Conventions are really of no help if they expressly include a "political offence" clause that terrorist sates can take advantage of. The law has to be unforgiving in that sense, which present day international conventions are not.

IV. Finally, the obligations of contracting states to search for, and arrest, suspects are not treated well and in an insufficiently rigorous way. These obligations are crucial because the " extradite or prosecute " rule is meaningless if suspects are allowed to remain go under cover or go underground. The 1988 Maritime Convention for example imposes no specific obligation to search for suspects believed to be in the territory of a 'state' party. As regards arrest, the convention merely needs a state to arrest suspects "upon bing satisfied that the circumstances so warrant" and in accordance with the law". States are therefore allowed to refuse to arrest suspects for reasons more political than they seem.

Indian Position

Nineteen years is an epoch in the world of international affairs, and so one finds, a complete sea-change in the way the so called "NAM lobby" now looks at the menace of global terrorism, and the necessity to have tough instruments to handle it. Torn by the intransigence of this lobby to pass and apply anti-terrorist conventions through the 1970s and 1980s, some countries- most outstandingly the United States and Israel—have resorted to 'coercive responses'. By this I mean cases like in the Achille Lauro affair were aircraft carrying terrorists was intercepted in international airspace, or Israel's bombing of supposed ' nuclear facilities ' in Iraq. Are coercive responses wring , or illegitimate? Do they amount to war? Well, it's difficult to say. It's this confusion that those who believe in taking on terrorists measure for measure exploit.

In the absence of a global anti-terrorist treaty that can be implemented with punitive intent existing UN rules will in the future become irrelevant. But it is worth remembering what these rules are anyway. According to UN rules:

(a) Use of force in international relations is forbidden except in the exercise of the "inherent right of individual or collective self defence if an armed strike occurs.

(b) Armed attack in this regard means a very serious attack on the territory of the injured state or on its citizens while at home or abroad.

(c) To qualify as an armed attack international law needs that terrorist attacks form part of a regular pattern of violent terrorist action, not isolated or sporadic action.

(d) Having established that there has been an armed attack the next step is to have the conditions for self defene met. For individual self-defence the state has to be directly affected. For collective self defence the state has to be directy affected. For collective self defence the state has to be requested or 'previously authorised' to intervene by proportional to the armed attack and necessary in the sense that all efforts at finding a peaceful solution have been previously exhausted .

In practice, these rule are of no use. It is impossible to gauge the degree of seriousness of an armed strike, or to judge the degree of consistency of terrorist strikes, or for that matter to assess how much action is "proportional" to balance the attack. Having understood this—that the rules of war cannot always be applied to terrorism- and also in the aftermath of the World Trade Center bombings and the emergence of Osama Bin Laden as a major threat, the UN finally saw the need for a global mechanism; a network of inter-linked laws to tackle terrorism. The idea[11] was to:

"Establish an adhoc committee to elaborate an international

convention for the suppession of terrorist bombings and, later, a international convention for the suppression of acts of nuclear terrorism, to supplement existing internatioal instruments.. (and) to address means of further developing a comprehensive framework of conventions dealing with international terrorism."

After first obfuscating all efforts to have a workable anti- terrorist convention passed at the UN, India has now been seeking credit for the change of mood by the UN. It is not alone in doing so Countries like Algeria, Tunisia, Sri Lanka and Turkey have also been lobbying for a comprehensive Convention on International Terrorism (the first two after having blocked any such effort in the 1970s). Not to be outdone, India has even circulated a draft for this purpose at the United Nations General Assembly, during its 51st session[12]. A reading of this fraft reveral a dramatic change in the Indian position on legally tackling terrorism over the years.

(a) The Indian draft talks of the need to make it mandatory for countries to have or enact laws domestically that makes all acts of terrorism for political purposes unjustifiable "irrespective of the considerations, political, philosophical, ideological, racial, ethnic religious or any other that may be invoked to justify them".

(b) With one eye on Pakistan, the Indian draft convention on terrorism makes it the duty of all states to keep off from "instigating facilitating, financing, assisting or participating in the commission of terrorist offences " in other states, or even allowing its territory to be used for such purposes .

(c) The Indian draft also connects arms and narcotics trafficking with terrorism, and the use of so called social and cultural organisations by terrorists as a shield for their activities.

It is clear that India— struggling to get a political consensus domestically on anti-terrorism laws— regards a sweeping international law against terrorism an absolute must. By delinking terrorism from political offences, India hopes to make enforcement measures stricter, more narrowly focused. Is that singing an elegy too loud and early for the use of other provisions of international law to combat terrorism government. In our efforts to scrape the bottom of international laws to seek a solution against terrorism, lets examine some other options.

Other Possibilities

Extradition agreements have been recommended as one way of combating international terrorism. It can be, but as the various references to extradition suggest, the success or failure of extradition as an instrument to tackle terrorism remains mired in the political will of the states concerned, Extradition, simply put, is the official surrender of a fugitive without regard to his or her consent, to a requesting state. Some points about extradition:

(a) Each extradition comes under a separate agreement under international law

(b) There is no duty to extradite if a treaty does not exist

(c) Nothing prevents the right to extradite without a treaty

Extradition therefore is a purely subjective matter, and here with lies both its strength and its weakness. First the strength. If countries want, they cn narow down or even stifle the definition of a 'ppolitical ofence' to make extradition of terorists farter. A great eample of this is the US-UK extradition treaty, which frankly that it is impossible to come up with a value neutral definition of terrorism. As a US official put it "Anyone who rebels against a friend and ally of the United States is, for the purposes of extradition, a terrorist.[13]"

If extradition treaties are to be successful, they need to stop confounding themselves with delicate matters of legal interpretation. On the eve of the signing of the US-UK extradition treaty therefore, we find a clear observation by the then legal advisor to the US Department of State[14] that a terrorist is anyone who attacks to destroy "stable democracies in which the political process is available to redress legitimate[15]" grievances and in which the judicial system provides fair treatment."This definition led to great heartburn among human rights groups, which pointed out that stable democracies are often the greatest violators of terrorism, like Israel in the West Band, US backed Contras in Nicaragua and British troops in Northern Ireland. Also, they questioned, how fair is fair under a country's judicial system?

All valid questions, but thing has stopped the US from pushing through a series of extradition treaties defending its national interests. It is here that India should learn from the American experience. Especially in the case of drugs trafficking, a major problem especially along India's North-eastern borders. Given the involvement of secessionist groups in the narcotics business, it is quite natural that efforts will be made by narco- terrorists to find the 'political offence' exception.

It's in India's interests to pre-empt that by entering into a member of extradition treaties with South-east Asian counties and Myanmar removing the 'political offence clause' altogether. That's what the US did with Colombia and Mexico, giving its enforcement officials a big shot in the arem. The difference was that there was virtually no political opposition to such moves, and when another exradition treaty was signed with the Netherlands, without even finding the impact on political fugitives, it ran trough the Senate Committee on Forein relations without as much as a whimper. The point I am trying to make is that somewhere down the line in our advocacy of a global tool to whip terrorism with, India has lost sight of the usefulness of strong bilateral initiatives.

Which is why I honestly believe that as Prime Minister, Inder Kumar Gujral was mouthing a long sidelined slogan, without fathoming the complex nature of extradition when he called upon the United Nations General Assembly to draft an "international extradition law". That's naive, because mutual advantage is the underlying motivation behind extradition treaties.

Just like India and Pakistan to have any reciprocity in the matter, one can't expect Libya— with the experience of the Lockerbie case behind it— to enter into an extradition treaty with any member of the NATO alliance. Then again, if reciprocity implies returning a favour in equal measure, we'd come up with some amazing situations. The United States must therefore be ready to hand over the CIA man who planned the killing of Chile's General Schneider if it wants the Chilean DINA officials who killed Orlando Leladier in Washinton DC, back. Further, if reciprocity means taking a balanced, common opinion of the criminality of the offence, the IRA men who tried, unsuccessfully, to assassinate Margaret Thatcher at a Brighton hotel in 1984 as just as culpable for the purposes of extradition as the US pilots who bombed Libyan leader Mohammad Gadaffi's home in Tripoli.

Finally, even if we look forward to a future situation where most members of the UN do adopt a extradition treaty, its effectiveness will be stymied by the fact that it will remain being based on the 17th century premise of "aut dedere aut judicare" which means 'extradite or prosecute." This leads as to the possibility of sham prosecutions. All nations do not have same interest in suppressig all forms of crime, and so very often, the gravest terrorist crimes—like the Lockerbie bombing - continue to confound courts, the central issue being whether extradition should have priority over prosecution. In the Lockerbie case, the prime accused was ultimately or extradited and punished in Februry 2001, but that was more a victory of Western diplomats than the International Court of Justice.

The Interpol

The Interpol has been regarded as another possibility for countries like India making attempt to track down international terrorists. But for over 30 years, Interpol's effectiveness has been hindered by US interpretation of a partiular clause in the organisation's constitution[16]. The Interpol had been establish as "an association of countries dedicated to promoting the widest possible mutual assistance between all criminal police authorities within the limits of the laws existing in the different countries and the spirit of the 'Universal Declaration of Human Rights'.[17]" The Interpol's chain includes 138 countries, with a National Central Bureau (NCB) in each country.

In the case of India, the CBI performs the role of the NCB. The Interpol network has been used for

(a) Routine and emergency checks concerning identity and criminal history.

(b) Serving International Wanted or 'red corner' notices.

(c) Fugitive and Suspect searches.

(d) Assistance in extradition/ deportation facilities.

(f) Witness location and their interviews.

Also, Interpol has been used as a channel to speed up the process of getting fugitives to justice in the countries where they are wanted, in other words "as a channel of communication alerting police authorities in member countries to the imminence of requests for provisional arrest in order to extradition as such requests proceed formally through diplomatic channels in accordance with bilateral extradition treaties[18].

It seems in the form of Article 3 of the Interpol constitution, which rather innocuously informs member states that they are "barred from undertaking any intervention or activities of a political, military, religious or racial character". This was used in 1950 by the US as an excuse to protect a group of Czech 'refugees' who hijacked an airplane and then took political asyllum. As a member of Interpol, Czechoslovakia wanted an international wanted notice issued to the hijackers. The notices were issued, and the US was so deeply hurt by what was a simple application of the law in a situation Interpol was typically meant to handle that it withdrew from the organisation. At that time the US argued that the hijacking was simply political and any action against the hijackers would be violative of Article 3 of the Interpol Constitution. This dealt a deathblow to the effectiveness of the Interpol against terrorist attacks, It also deepened irretrievably the artificially created divide between activities motivated by political ideology and terrorist acts.

In the three following decades— and this is not to pin the blame on the US alone—instances of hijacking, hostage taking and extortion continued to rise at an alarming rate. The only real vehicle for enforcement agencies worldwide, the Interpol, ended up being severely handicapped due to the US's obduracy in sticking to its version of right and wrong.

The International Criminal Court

For all those in search of a legal remedy to global terrorism, the last recourse remains an International Criminal Court (ICC) its something India again appears to have incredible faith in, despite the fact that the demand for its ccreation has been echoed fruitlessly for over last six decades. France first proposed the creation of an ICC after the dual murder or Yugoslavia's King Alexander and French foreign minister Louis Barthou in Marseilles, along with the assassination of Austrian Chancellor Engelbert Dolfuss.

Records reveal that the League of Nations belatedly responded by calling for an international conference to be held under its auspices for handling the problem of transnational terrorism. So the 1937 Geneva Conference, apart from the resolution on the Prevention and Repression of Terrorism, there was also another passed for "the creation for an International Criminal Court with jurisdiction over terrorist crimes". As usual, we find nearly no movement on this convention for over a decade after that. And when it has, its got mired somehow in the internal bureaucracy of the UN. In 1951, the International Law Commission— a group of legal experts selected by the UN members —presented a daft statute for the creation of an ICC before the UN General Assembly. It took nearly three years after that for the draft to be referred to a committee on International Criminal Jurisdiction—which had 15 members. This resubmitted its second draft statute on the subject in 1954.

The process just carries on after that, and over the years its clear the creation of the ICC, while becoming a much researched subject with every legal luminary throwing wisdom on what it should look like, has also become in fact a bit of an intellectual exercise. As Friedlander rightly points out "to create an international criminal court without first having an international criminal code is putting the cart before the horse". But what worries me is not the way in which the United Nations has failed to deliver on the creation of an ICC, but how its given a completely warped spin to why there is a need to have an ICC in the first place. When the idea had first come up, the ICC was meant to deal with random terrorst attacks, not genocide. Which is why its quite shocking that the US and its allies altered the very purpose of an ICC in 1948 to suit their own post-war urgency to deal with the perpetrators of the Holocaust. It was a coup of shorts therefore when this alliance managed to push through a resolution at the UN seeking to restrict the role and function of an ICC as "an international judicial organ for the trial of persons charged with genocide."[19] It has taken India four decades to wake up to the deviousness with which the purpose of the ICC was change, a deliberate effort to keep terrorists out of its ambit. Speaking at the UN General Assembly Indian delegate Prem Singh Chandumajra lodged a strong protest on this saying that "Terrorism is the most condemnable form of international crime threatening the intergrity and political and social fibre of states and taking toll on lives of innocent civilians". The ICC, he pleaded, must have transnational terrorism as its focus, not the dregs of World War II rivalries. But who was listening? It seems not, because nothing has happened between the otherwise soft- spoken Chandumajra's forceful interventions at the UN and now to give the impression that the ICC will be established with the purpose it first had in mind. Shocking aain, because as even the judgment of the Nuremberg trial put it: "Crimes aainst international law are committed by men, not by abstract entities, and only punishing individuals who commit such crimes can the provisions of international law be enforced". But if India's frustration over the ICC case proves anything, it is that there is a wide divergence today between the letter and the spirit of international law. As[20] earlier pointed out when talking of Gujral's well meaning request for an international convention on terrorism, international diplomacy— especially in the case of anti terrorist measures— has become a product of national interest. In effect, it is just a case of one country's national interest against the other's, and there is no space really for uniformity between nations or highfaluting notions of a global offensive against terrorism.

India has a lesson or two to learn there, begining perhaps with a fine-tuned homegrown response to the terrorist challenge. I will come to that later, but for now, just to drive home the point of how duplicitous countrys are in dealing with international crime, and the pulls and pressures that play on them, let me end this submission by citing Armenian example.

Over one and a half million Armenians were slaughtered in the Armenian Holocaust, where entire convoys of women and children were driven into the Syrian desert and made to die of starvation and rape. In one case the Turks forced thousands of Armenians into caves and them asphyxiated them with smoke from fires: the world's first gas chambers. That was the world's first genocide. In fact, the word genocide was coined for the first time by a jewish writer to describe the Armenian massacre of 1915-16 by Turkey' Ottoman militia. Hitler, planning his genocide of Europe's Jews, is supposed to have asked his generals: "Who remembers the Armenians?" Winston Churchill was the first to describe the Armenian massacre as a Holocaust. Till date however, the United Nations—which has been quick to establish adhoc Committees for Rwanda and Yugoslavia—has not even casually took note of the Armenian genocide. US President Bill Clinton prevailed on the US House of Representatives not to agree to facts of the Armenian holocaust—with an extraordinary warning that US business in Turkey may be at risk if the truth was acknowledged. Britain has also been humming and having over the issue. Outside the British Parliament at the begining of every sitting and along London's Whitehall across the year, Armenian petitioners still stand with banners, assuming the proportions of almost a fixed tourist spectacle. Clearly none of these countries want to follow the French example. The French Parliament passed a bill recognizing the Armenian slaughter as genocide. The Turkish response was quick, Tukey scrapped a $149 million deal with Alcatel for the launch of a remote sensing satellite. It also declared that France's GIAT Industries will be excluded from a $ 10 billion tanks contract.

The Armenian issue and the way the international powers have handled it raises a spectre of 'selective justice' even within an extremely narrow category of international offences. It makes a clear impression that in dealing with crimes against huminity, international law will continue to be shaped by global political interplay and economic interests rather than the principles of unfettered justice.

Helping Own Cause

While discussing India's options, it is impossible not to look at the Israeli example. Tel Aviv has over the years begun its own form of random strike attacks by special forces on the Arab militia, disregarding the finer issues of how far such strikes are legitimate under UN conventions of War. India, too, is known to organize covert operations across the LoC, but not as frequently as a matter of course as Israel does. Officially, Israel never takes the responsibility for such attacks, but over the years a group of very articulate members of the Israeli intelligentsia have been the best defenders of this new form of "hit and run" counter -terrorism. The best instance is of course Professor Benjamin Netanyau, but one of my personal favourites is Professor Rene Beres, who doesn't mince words when describing his contempt for international law as an anti- terrorist measure. So when Yehya Ayyah, a Palestinian terrorist, was assassinated in Gaza- apparently following the orders of the Shin Bet intelligence- Beres in an article titled "Assassination of Terrorists may be Law-enforcing" defended the action by saying thus:" the assassination of this murderer was anything except a crime. Rather it was an essential effort on behalf of the whole community of civilized nations to compensate for the absence of a strong central world authority with needed self- help."

Evidently, those at the forefront of fighting terrorism have given up their search for an elusive global consensus on it. In the twenty first century, the focus will be more on self help. In the case of India, it must start with an honest effort at making the application of the law above board.

References

1. Not even France and Yugoslavia, the affected parties in the Marseilles incident, ratified this corvention.

2. Paul Wilkinson, Foreword, "Contemporary research on terrorism".

3. "The Torror Network" 1981, Claire Sterling.

4. Brian Jenkins; "International Terrorism: a new mode of conflict, 1975".

5. Grant Wardlaw "Politcal Terrorism".

6. *Ibid.*

7. This case has been cited in "Terrorism: Documents of Local and International control RA Friedlander.

8. UN Doc A/8791 Quoted in Friedlander Ibid

9. UN Document A/C 6/418 November 2 1972, Quoted in Friedlander Ibid.

10. UN Charter Article 51.

11. UN Resolution 51/210, 1996.

12. The draft Convention for the Suppression of International Terrorism, November 11, 1996.

13. Asst Attorney General Stephen Trott, Quoted in the *National Law Journal*, July 29, 1985.

14. Justice Abraham D Soafer, Testimony before the Senate Committee on Foreign Relations.

15. De Jure Bath ac Pais, H. Grotus, 1624.

16. This has been examined in detail in Mary Jo Grotenroth's The INTERPOL's role in International Law Enforcement".

17. Article 2, Interpol Constitution.

18. Grotenberg, Ibid.

19. UN General Assembly Resolution 260, December 1948.

20. This was before he became Prime Minister of the UK.

7

Terrorism, Ideology and Law

Terrorism is mostly driven by some ideology. There is a motive, a goal or an objective and to achieve that terrorist practices are employed. This amounts to use of illegal means for achieving what may be a good objective.

Modern day terrorism has much to do with ideology. This is a phenomenon that began, in its present incarnation, with the Left Wing student movements in Europe in the third quarter of twentieth century. One saw then, for the first time, highly motivated groups with radical views against the establishment, using violence as a means to make their point. These groups made targeted attacks to begin with, but in course of time also exploited the vulnerability of the civilian underbelly of the state. Indeed this was a strange phenomenon not easy to understand but possible to justify. The best effort at defining what was happening came in 1964 form H Eclestein, who like a startled observer of ideologically driven acts of terror, wrote that "terrorism is not just the act of a demented few but represents a deeper academic impulse against repression in its most fundamental sense.

Terrorism rises among political activists as well as among psychopaths in direct ratio to control and rationalization of modern technological society and the likely failure of other parts of revolutionary activity[1]. This view of terrorism as a manifestation of "deeper impulse" may look bizarre today, but in the incipient stage of modern day terrorism, it was generally accepted. There was therefore a great degree of indulgence shown to groups like the Baader- Meinhof in Germany, the original terrorists as it were. It's this covert sympathy that led terrorists to cloak their methods in a garb of "revolution" or "jehad", as the case may be. Official pronouncements from the Arab World have often revealed this. After having gleaned through many of these in the archives of Cambridge University, I find one of the resolutions of the Fifth Islamic Summit meeting most blatant. It was passed in early 1987, just the time when roots of trans national terrorism were growing both in India and the United States. It says: "The conference reiterates its absolute faith in the need to distinguish between the brutal and unlawful terrorist activities perpetrated by individuals, by groups, or by states, from the legitimate struggle of oppressed and subjugated nations against foreign occupation of any kind. This struggle is sanctioned by hevavenly law, by human values, and by international conventions".

Driven by Ideology

Those who think terrorism needs a legal remedy to understand what drives a terrorist—or at least what the terrorist claims drives him, there is this explanation.

We can begin by presenting two very divergent opinions by two individuals the United States, for one, would certainly categorise as terrorists. The first is that of a man called Salah Khalef alias Abu Iyad. He was at one time Yaseer Arafat's deputy and one of the leaders of the Fatah. He was involved in many lethal attacks. One among is the killing of a contingent of Olympic athletes from Israel in Murich in 1972. This is how Salah Khalef blurs the line between terrorism and revolution: "By nature", he says "and even on ideological grounds, I am firmly opposed to political murder and, more generally, to terrorism. Nevertheless unlike many others I do not confuse revolutionary violence with terrorism, or operations that constitute political acts with others that do not"[2].

Here Salah Khalef is attempting to confound 'Terrorism' with national liberation' and 'self determination'. So should the law consider all those who try to do so—and almost all Kashmir based Jehadi groups operating out of Pakistan do so. While this a simplistic question, the answer to it could be fundamental to our understanding of terrorism.

It's also significant to look at these basic questions now, seems to be because the government is trying to push through a law on terrorism without regarding whether the fine print of such a law in other countries needs to be modified to suit India.

Let us now look at the second opinion on terrorism, this time by the hero of the Cuban revolution, Che Guevara. Without looking for the kind of excuses Salah presents, "Terrorism", Che says, "is a measure that is generally ineffective and indiscriminate in its impact, since it often makes victims of innocent people and destroys a large number of lives that could be valuable to the revolution." Besides", he goes on, "it hinders all more or less legal or semi- clandestine contact with the masses and makes imposible unification for actions that will be necessary at a critical moment." At the risk of sounding rather simplistic, let me press on the point to prove why definitions of terrorism cannot be value neutral. The main difference between Salah and Che's positions is that while both seek to carry our wars of liberation, Salah avoids committing himself against attacks on civilians, Che does not.

But that does not make Che any less of a terrorist in the perception of the United States? It does not because the United States has consistently defined attacks on 'non-combatants' as the hallmark of terrorist activity. As a matter of fact defending why the United States looks as 'method' over 'idology, a former Secretary of State has been quoted as saying that: "Once we understand terrorism's goals and methods it is not hard to tell, as we look around the world, who are the terrorists and who the freedom fighters. The Contras in Nicaragua, for example, do not blow up school buses or hold mass executions of civilians.[3]"

The US secretary of state, in saying so was implying that his country was value neutral in drawing a line between terorism, on the one hand and wars of national liberation, on the other. This is a controversial claim, in the light of United States' many foreign policy blunders where its teamed up with undemocratic, even fanatic governments and groups:The most obvious example of this is the anti-Sandinista forces supported for many years by Pentagn. "All anti Sandinista counter-revolutionaries and insurgent armed bandits" were, Friedlander states, "in the eyes of the reagn administration, freedom fighters and commando warriors, despite the act that one of them- the 15 September Legion- are according to the US Defence Intelligence aency - terrorist groups involved in assassination and hijacking." We find an obvious ontradiction there. But having said that, it must be conceded that in domestic law enforcement circles in the US, terrorism has to a large extent come to be identified with the "criminal mode of operation, rather than the specific intent or motivation of the actors".

This has been possible even more since Ronald Reagan's presidency, when Washington demarcated clearly between domestic and transnational terrorism. As Benjamin Netanyahu writes, this was a time when the United States, for the first time started to look for a definition of terrorism and came up with one which defined it in terms of their being 'senseless acts'. This is revealed in US domestic laws. Take, for instance, an amendment to the US Internal Security Act 1950 to 'penalise and control terrorists'. It draws up an exhaustive range of acts in order to define crimes of terrorism including espionage kidnapping, sabotage, extortion, robbery, skyjacking holding a person prisoner or hostage or threat of any or these or threat to cause injury to a human being, animal or personal or real property or any conspiracy to do any or the above in order to compel an act or omission by any person, or government entity."[5] At no point is any reference made to the intention behind any of these acts. It it therefore to be understood that the United States government really believes that terrorism has no relationship with ideology? Certainly not. In fact, if anything the ideological underpinnings in Washington's view of terrorism run for deeper than did even USSR at the height of the cold War.

Udeology does not Justify Vidence

No ideology justfies violence- is both contradictory and eminently self-defeating.

On more than one occasion, if one goes through statements made by key US functionaries through the Eighties and Nineties, one comes across evidence of absolute conviction that American values are universal values, and hence attack on American supremacy is an attack on society at large. In fact, the American worldview is reflected clearly in public efforts to define terrorism by its top brass. Like during a speech by former CIA director, John Deutch, recently: "These groups" Deutch says talking of terrorist organizations, " use terror as their only way to combat the popularity of democratic institutions we espouse and our overwhelming military and economic strength. Their goal is to make the price of our leadership so high that we will stop what we are doig abroad and go hoe. They know they will ultimately fail, but we know that they are likely to keep trying."

Deutch's understanding of terrorism would be' anything that stands in the way of American interests outside its own territory. In other words, at the bottom of the US definition of terrorism is a highly driven understanding of what is just and what ujust. The apparent focus on the act is only a way to embellish hat notion with so called objectivity. Therefore, we find that the RAND Corporation, has even maintained an inventory of terrorist incidents for a number of years, the ostensible reason being to arrive at what cn be called the 'identifying characteristics' of a terrorist act. Can this be repcated in India? Let's see what RAND'S indices for a terrorist act really say:

(a) Civilians are main target of violence: In India, the two major militant groups in Kashmir, the Lashkar - e-Tayabba and the Hizb-ul-Mujahideen, are known to target army and para- military bases. In the state of Assam, the Home Ministry confirms that groups like the ULFA and the Bodo Liberation Tigers unleash attacks against the Indian state by bombing installations, like refineries, oil depots, rail lines and bridges. Same is true of Naxalite groups in Andhra and MP also, where ambushes on security personnel are the chosen method. If we go by RAND's definition, these groups would not be terrorist organizations.

Organised groups only resort to terrorism. This is easier to establish, but not always. First, the sheer diversity of terrorist groups and cadre makes it impossible to keep a dossicr on each individual terrorist, which is what the FBI is known to do in the US. Second, the militant groups are generally known to draw from a pool of public support, as in the case of terrorism in its incipient stages in Punjab and Assam. Here, again, it is not easy to discriminate in black and white—like the British law attempts to do—an ordinary criminal from a terrorism a attempt.

The often claim credit for their act of violence: The logic here too is that a terrorist act is aimed at producing effects far beyond the physical damage. In India, there is little record of any of the recent attacks in which civilian lives were lost, being claimed by militant groups, for instance, the killings of Amarnath pilgrims and the shootout at the Jammu railway station, in the immediate aftermath of the failed Indo-Pak Agra summit. Therefore, while the attempt is induce terror, it rarely ever happens that a militant group is ready to compromise its image by claiming an attack on a civilian target.

Still , attacks on 'soft' unsuspecting targets has become more the pattern on passengers of the Tokyo subway by the Aum Shinrikyo cult. This cult never took responsibility for the attack as its own , an attack it had been planning a year in advance. The subway attack renewed focus on the changing tactics of terrorist warfare, their use of high- end scientific information to spread terror, but it wasn't till US installations were made a target that Whasington woke up to the 'sft target' aspect of modern day terrorism. It's difficult to pinpoint why contemporary terrorists choose soft targets. My assumption, apart from the fact that soft targets allow quick response attacks- without much planning or risk—they also have a greater disruptionist element.

Take for example, the hijacking of IC 814 in December 1999. It took place a few months after the Lahore bus ride, engineered by the Pakistani army which has always been skeptical of Nawaz Sharief's attempts at reconciliation, and suddenly put the entire peace initiative between New Delhi and Islamabad into jeopardy, giving a shot in apart from the arm for hawks on both sides. This is just the same method, that on a more frequent scale, the Hamas and the Hizbollah used throughout to both sideline Yaseer Arafat within his own supporters and derail efforts at a bold peace initiative brokered by then US president Bill Clinton.

But if the idea of terrorists is to disrapt processes of reconciliation, there is perhaps no better example than the Moscow bomb blasts which led to the relentless attack by Russian troops in Chechnya worsening the conflict there, and the Nairobi blast at the US diplomatic mission, which fuelled US missile attacks on what it thought were Osama Bin Laden's bases in Afghainstan. Unfortunalety, this aspect to terrorism—that it *disrupts processes of reconciliation and confidence building*—has been entirely overlooked by traditional definitions- and the government of India would be well advised to include it, whenever it does introduce an Anti-Terorist Bill in Parliament. It's a reality that India should have woken up to long back, but which was ironically best made by the Clinton's Director for Counter-Terrorism Michael A Sheehan in the aftermath of the IC 814 hijack when he started that: "Although terrorists still atttack military installations (like the 1996 Khobar Tower attack in Saudi Arabia) and diplomatic missions (as in Nairobi and Dar-Es-Salaam) they have expanded their target list to include attacks on softer targets such as hotels and tourist sites and may be planning to bring these attacks into continental United States - to an extent quite frankly we were not anticipating. Fortunately due—to the outstanding work of intelligence and law enforcement officials here and abroad—we were able to thwart several potentially deadly events."[7]

Therefore, the Indian government should expand section 3.1 of the draft Law Commission draft bill (Chapter 3, 3(1) of the Prevention of Terrorism Ordinance 2001) to include distruption of processes of reconciliation as terrorist acts, not sumply the "disruption of essential services and supplies." In doing so we' d be acknowledging the fact that beyond "seeking a body count."[8] terrorist acts seek to "cause crises, provoke outrage, frag community ties and undermine faith in democratic institutions. Terrorism, in this sense, aims at putting societies under intolerable pressure, even forcing them to react similarly. All this points in one direction: that no act of terrorism is on impulse or accidental, and that very often there is a pronounced political slant to it. For all the claims that it defines terrorism by the act, the fact remains that enen the United States has not been able to detach its own version of national interest from its definition of terrorism. Let us cite two specific examples to explain this The first is linked to US duplicity over extradition policy. Washington has traditionally been the first to heap accuse countries like Libya and even its European friends like France and Italy of adding a long appendix of political motives to terrorist acts, and using this to turn down US demands for extradition. But as a verdict in 1988 brought out, when it comes to US citizens, American courtrooms react in the same, national accused of masterminding an attack on a bus in the West Bengal—an incident which killed four people—a Brooklyn judge flatly declined to send the acused to face trial in Israel. His reasoning: "In the West Bank, today's rebels could become tomorrow's rulers"[10] referring obviously to the Palestine Liberation Organisation, of which the accused American was a member. The bus attack was therefore categorized as an act of 'political' expression, not terrorism. This decision went unchallenged in any higher US court.

In the light of this, the emphasis on a precise, quantifiable definition of terrorism that the United States claims to espouse is a bit of a non-starter. In its implementation , as members of successive US administrations have ben nonest hough to acknowledge, the US definition of trans-national terrorism has been crafted to be in line with US interests abroad. The introduction of the 'attack on civilians, as a defining characteonstic of terrorism was only accdental. But like good advocates, successive secretaries of state of the United States have always stressed on that point. This giveaway has been when the definition of terrorism has been used to justify US intervention abroad, like when George Shultz who served in the Reagan administration said: "Once we understand terrorism's goals and methods it is no hard to tell, as we look around the world, who are the terrorists and who the freedom fight. The Contras in Nicaragua for example do not blow up school buses or hold mass executions of civilians. It is a applied in another context, it risks making the US itself culpable of its own definition of' international terrorism' . This is separate from transnational terrorism' which the US Central intelligence Agency (CIA) describes as "terrorism carried out by autonomous non- state actors, whether or not they have the support to sympathetic states". International terrorism on the other hand, is according to the CIA definition "terrorism carried out by individuals controlled by a sovereign state". The US will of course argue that the Contras in Nicaragua and the Afghan militia were in the 1980s anything but terrorists. But can its definition of terrorism implicate even its oldest adversaries like Mohammad Gadaffi? It can't. That's because in strict legal terms, even after the conviction of one of the prime accused in the Locerbie case, it's not been possible to pinpoint in strict legal terms whether Gadaffi controlled the accused or supported them or, further still, agreed with their motives. That's just a case in point, but the fact is that motive is very difficult to establish in terrorist cases that governments are generally forced to go on 'fishing expeditions' including a slew of offences that can be brought under one legislation. The only exception one finds is the history of anti- terrorist legislation in the UK, where even way back in 1973, terrorism had this definition: "the use of violence for political ends, including any use of violence for the purpose to putting the public in fear."[12]

After deciding to move towards tougher anti- terrorism legislation, India has the choice of following either the US or the British example. Both try to 'drain the swamp' sieving out terrorists in the process. For the US, that ostensibly means disregarding motive, or political persuasion. For the UK,'draining the swamp' is done by the exact opposite identifying the motive, and punishing the ideology, before moving further, anything else.

India's Leanings

Which one should India choose, or at least tilt towards? At well, there seems to be greater honesty in largely following the British example. Only, unlike the British law which links political motive to ideological and religious motive, it may be better to include the clause "secessionist and religious" as the two chief motives behind terrorism that need to be punished. Punishing a person for his ideology is reressive in contemporary times, and in and case, no law can be really effective, as the PUDR points out, if it clubs everything from "secessionist movements to thwarted regional aspirations, from armed revolt to social oppression to outbreaks of communal violence" under a "catch-all category of terrorism".[13] The option, however, is not as PUDR recommened " the complete and unconditional withdrawal" of the anti-terrorist law, but connecting it a more transparent system of implementation. Therefore, the government should, simultaneously with the passage of an anti-terrorist bill, take the following measures.

(i) Bring in a clause for the establishemt of a National Centre for Counter-terrorism. This could be based on the lines of the US Office of Counter-terrorism, headed by a coordinator appointed directly by the President. Apart from coordinating with foreign governments to enhance a joint effort against terrorism, the Counter-terrorism corrdinator in the US also has the intra-agency working group on Counter- terrorism in place. In brief, the coordinator is the nocal point for all American efforts against terrorsim, domestic and international. There is no such organisation in India, where the military intelligence, the Intelligence Bureau and the Research and Analysis Wing can be brought together to create a National Centre for Counter-terrorism and coordinate and implement the Indian government's counter- terrorism efforts.

(ii) To give the Centre maximum autonomy and freedom from government interference, it should be made subject to annual scrutiny by a permanent standing committee of parliament, with equal representation of all political parties.

(iii) The Chief of the Centre would be the government's direct nominee, but it would also include people with experience in low intensity conflict situations, and legal experts who would analyse charges of the misuse of special powers by law enforcing agencies.

(iv) The Centre would be the final arbiter on disputes over the application of the law, and hence on any charge that the anti-terrorist law is being used to subvert the criminal law process. In that sense, the Centre would make decision whether an act of violence is motivated by "religious or secessionist" impulse, bringing it under the unbrella of the anti-terrorist law. This would apply in cases where the attribution of a motive is challenged by the accused, and would have a limited time frame for disposal.

(v) The Centre for Counter-terrorism would also release annual reports on the threat perception arising out of terrorist activity, following the Patterns of Global Terrorism report brought out annually by the US State Department's Office of Counter-terrorism.

The idea behind having a separate National Centre for Counter-terrorism is to detach the government's anti- terrorism agenda from that of any one political party. But more significantly, it doesn't one with the impression that India's politicians are attempting, a silent coup of the judiciary. At least three sections of the proposed anti-terrorism law (CLA Bill 2000) had been opposed on this ground. These sections are :

(i) Section 6 (a): confiscation of property by the police

(ii) Section 6 (g): The transfer of powers of the civil court to the executive

(iii) Section 26: Power to define offences as "terrorist".

So far the government has just kept an obdurate stance when accused taking over from the courts to punish "intentions" opposed to its own political persuasion. The inclusion of the country's entire political spectrum in the anti-terrorist initiative is perhaps the best method to end the air of recrimination and cussedness that has generally marked the executive-judiciary relationship over the issue of special powers, and where the judiciary's writ ends, and the executive's starts . This turf war is encapsulated best in the Supreme

Court order in Joginder Singh vs. Uttar Pradesh where the judge noted that the "existence of power is one thing, the justification for its exercise quite another"[14]. Unfortunately, this turf war has been considered as a police- Judiciary conflict. In away it is. India does, after all, have the dubious distinction of having the highest proportion of arrests not leading in convictions.

So the judiciary has the right to be worried. More so when, even before the full time implementation of anti-terrorist laws the National Police Commission surprised the nation by revealing that as high as 60 per cent of the arrests carried out by the police across India were "either unnecessary or unjustified". But the police are only the instrument, and as numerous example have shown of late, the executive in India is known to be entirely unabashed when it comes to pushing its own agenda. By bridging the ideological divide, therefore, understanding a terrorist's to agenda—as distinct from a dissident's agenda—by arriving at a political consensus on how to deal with the problem.

In the absence of any international conventions that India can invoke to tackle cross border terrorism where it starts budding, there has to be a homegrown response to it. And that is possible only if the government of the day shows much greater generosity (in involving others than it has so far in holding the problem, and opposition parties give up going to extremes—what V.S. Jafa calls 'public whistle blowing'—to confound a malaise that claims lives every single day. Perhaps a truly independent and non partisan National entre for Counter-terrorism could be the right answer.

References

1. H Eclestein "Internal War" 1964.

2. Abu Iyad "Without a Homeland" Mifras; Tel Aviv, 1983.

3. Secy of State George Shultz 1986.

4. RA Friedlander, Volume 1, pp. xii-xiii.

5. HR 1179, US House of Representatives Records, Section 202.

6. Georgetown University; Speach at, Sep. 5 1996.

7. Seech B MA Sheehan at the Brookings Institution February 2000 (Post Millennium Terrorist Review).

8. Reply of Oklahoma City Bomber Timothy Me Veigh when asked why he carried out the bombing.

9. Brian Jenkins.

10. June 1988 Judegement; the judge argues on the basis of a 'political charge' being exempt from the provisions of the US-Israel extradition treaty.

11. George Shultz., 1986 Quote.

12. Northern Ireland (Emergency Provisions) Act 1973.

13. "TADA : Hard Law for Soft State" PUDR, *Economic and Political Weekly,* March 25, 2000.

14. 1994 SSC (GI) 1172.

8

The New Law on Terrorism

Lapse of TADA, a controversial legal instrument to tackle terrorism, coincided with the rise in terrorism in India. It led to the need for a new law on terrorism. Let us go into some depth and find out how the developments about new law took place.

Exactly when the Indian government first thought of creating a special law to deal with terrorism is difficult to pinpoint. But plans to enact an omnibus anti-terrorism law came into public focus only after the hijacking of Indian Airlines flight IC 814 entroute from Kathmandu to New Delhi. The incident had caused the government in power, a major embarrassment. The end game to the entire episode, with External Affairs Minister Jaswant Singh accompanying the wanted militants to Kandahar airport, in exchange for the hostage passengers, had laid bare the soft underbelly of the Indian government, turning the BJP's election slogans against a "soft Centre" on their head. Four months before this incident, the Home Ministry had first toyed with the idea of drafting a new Anti- Terrorism law.

In a letter to the Chairman of the Law Commission of India, Justic BPJeevan Reddy, Home Minister Lal Krishna Advani asked the Commission to look afresh into the issue of a specific legislation for cobating terrorism and anti-national activities.

Lapse of TADA

The brief couldn't have been clearer, or terser. TADA had lapsed in 1995, and the largely recommendatory Law Commission was asked to recommend means to revive "a comprehensive anti-terrorism law", not examine the more contentious issue of whether such a law was needed or not.

At the time this letter was written, Mr Advani did not set the Law Commission any timeframe to complete this job. In fact, no time frame was ever set, but after the hijack of IC 814, the otherwise laid back commission appeared to be working under great pressure. In less than four monts since the incident, the Commission had held two seminars in New Delhi on evolving a legal answer to the terrorist threat. By April 2000, a draft Prevention of Terrorism Bill 2000 had been submitted to the government. The draft Bill seems to have been pegged on the IC 814 incident . In one of the introductory pages, its authors write: "Indeed over the last few months since the working paper was released, the security situation has worsened. The hijacking of the Indian Airlines flight, the release of three notorious terrorists by the Government of India to save the lives of innocent civilians and crew of the flight, the subsequent clarations of the released terrorists and their activities in Pakistan and PoK, have raised the level of terrorism both in quality and extent."[1]

The Law Commission had looked at the country's segcurity environment was in 1972, the last time. Since then, the security situation has changed drastically. Many of these changes had been brought about by socio-political and economic reasons, but the Law Commission started its work on the premise that it was for the reason that the state had gone soft on those who defied its whip.

This 'soft state' argument was the core of the 'working paper' on terrorism that the Law Commission had circulated among a select group.[3] It was well-clothed in the high political rhetoric as well. Take this example:

"A perception has developed among the terrorist groups that the Indian state is inherently incapable of meeting their challenge, that it has become soft and indolent. As a matter of fact, quite a few parties have developed a vested interest in a soft state, a weak government and ineffective implementation of the laws. Foreign funds are flowing substantially to various organisations and groups which serve, willingly or unwillingly, the long term objective of foreign powers.[4]

Rise in Terrorism

In a way, the Government had aleady pinpointed what it thought the principal reason for the rise in terrorism. It has also harped in on the remedy: aiming itself with wider powers. After the IC 814 hijacking, the possibility of quick approval for tough laws—doing away with the chorus that pinpointed the double-edged nature of such laws, and the possibility of their misuse— was high. This was a special situation, the Government argued, and the Law Commission—a body of political appointees—was simply there to echo the opinion that a special law was needed to deal with it. In doing so, however, the Law Commission's tone appears a little too shrill and defensive. Such as in this extract:

"An extraordinary situation needs an extraordinary law, designed to meet and check such extraordinary situations. It is one thing to state that we must develop and provide internal structures and safeguards against possible use and abuse of the act and an entirely different thing to say that because a law is liable to be misused, we should not have an act at all."[5]

The thrust of the government's reasoning, therefore, was three—pronged.

(i) First, that terrorism had gone up in its very nature, leading to need for changes in strategies to counter it.

(ii) Second, that terrorism was not being combated well enough due to weakness of the state.

(iii) Third, that the possible abuse of tough anti- terrorism laws did not create a strong enough case to shelve such laws altogether.

Defending the first point, the Law Commission provided only Home Ministry statistics and Intelligence Bureau reports on terrorist offences. No effort was made to anaylse links between terrorist groups, the conditions in which they had spawned, the politician-militant nexus and other forms of patronage these groups receive, the proliferation of small arms leading to the growth of private armies, all factors that contribute to the 'quality and extent' of internal security threats. The secod point-about how the Government had looked indolent in its anti-terrorist drives—was essentially subjective, but the Law Commission got several people to second a more stringent legal challenge to terrorism. The argument here was at three levels.

(i) First, that the challenge of external terrorism was a new phenomenon.

(ii) Second, that the Indian Penal Code had failed to check organised crime, that it therefore had to be fought at a different level.

(iii) Third, that countries like the USA and UK, too, had effected changes their anti- terrorism laws to deal with new global trends in terrorism.

The third point—that a law can't be shelved only because it can be misused—was supported by previous judgments. Notably, the state of Rajasthan vs. Union of India[6] where the judgment included an observation that merely because power may sometimes be abused, it can not be a ground for denying the existence of power. The wisdom of man has not so far been able to conceive of a government with power enough to answer its legitimate needs and at the same time be incapable of mischief. This was a powerful argument; about the leeway a government can give itself for error in the implementation of laws, a point that's at the basis of the debate over the proposed law.

Essentially, it boils down to a debate over whether the executive-in tracking down terrorists—should be subject to the same bottom line of judicial review or given special status. It's a debate the law Commission, at least, appear to have caught on early, when it quoted from the Kesavananda Bharti vs State of Kerala case of 1973.[7] In that judgment, the court had said," In exercising the power of judicial review the courts cannot be oblivious of the practical needs of the government. Enough has to be left for trial and error. Constitutional law like other mortal contrivances has to take some chances. Opportunity must be allowed for vindicating reasonable belief based on experience.

By agreeing to the possibility of abuse, the Law Conmmission had sidestepped the confounding question of who a terrorist is and what exactly the law should consider an act of terrorism. "Its an obvious thing, isn't it?" the flamboyant P.N. Ghatate, member of the Law Commission, told me. " Those who draw circles around it are merely playing around with words beyond a point!" Mr Ghatate has a valid point. But as he has discovered himself, there are two fundamental questions that require an answer before the law can be amended.

First, while the public perception of a terrorist in the present situation is not exactly that of a Greenpeace activist chaining himself to an oil tanker or a Left leaning JNU academic, there is always a slim chane that a desperate government or a vindictive official could use—and this has happened in the past—the same set of laws for them as he would for a militant.Also, was a rise in incidents of terrorism really a result of weak laws? Or the ineffective implementation of existing laws? If the laws were to be strengthened, made more matter-of-fact, would they go against human righs? As the Peoples Union for Democratic Rights argues forcefully, against bringing in a new legislation:

"The premise of such a demand is that the ordinary law and the normal criminal justice system have failed to cope with these crimes. The failure is not attributed to the law enforing machinery—its inefficiency or corruption—but to a weakness of the law based on Principles of liberal jurisprudence and notions of natural justice. Principles like the right to equal treatment before the law, the right to a fair trial and the right to be deemed innocent until proven guilty beyond reasonable doubt. Ant so if the law is to be effective in dealing with terrorists it can only do so if these principles are overturned and these rights are taken away."[8]

The above argument was certainly not limited to India. The issue of terrorism and human rights, something that has befuddled even the UNHCR, has come up as a subject of debate in India since the late 1980s, when KPS Gill, as Punjab's Director General of Police, cracked down on militancy in the state. since that time, there have often been disagreements between the government and the human rights organisations, notably among them being Amnesty International and Human Rights Watch.

These organisations, while assiduously avoiding the use of the term 'terrorist' at any point—even for mercenaries in Kashmir—have made accusations against Indian security forces of human rights violations in areas of widespread violence, especially Kashmir and the North-east. India has in turn , clarified that there cannot be an across the board guarantee of human rights to all , irrespective of the means they in turn use to achieve their goals, or whether they respect the human rights of local communities at all. It's an argument that has been used by previous governments also. Most combatively, perhaps by then Prime Minister Narasimha Rao before the United

Nations Security Council in 1995, that "I have profound respect for those who are crusading for the protection of human rights. But we cannot countenance a situation where all the human rights. are reserved for the practitioners of terrorism, while Governments dealing with the menace are arraigned day and night on grounds of violation of human rights—real or imaginary. What should really be suggested at this meeting is perhaps to delineate the parameters that harmonise the defence of national integrity with the respect for human rights."

More interesting is the fact that the Indian Prime Minister was making this strong case for diluting the human rights of 'pactitioners of terrorism' in the same year the controversial Terrorists and Distruptive Activities (Prevention) Act—TADA—was allowed to lapse because of the serious human rights violations that accompanied its implementation. Evidently, New Delhi was feeling uncomfortable about lack of a tough instrument to combat terrorism legally, and actually thought that the problem came up as terrorists had votaries in human rights groups. The period 1995-96 is also the time the United Nations, after years of complete confusion on drafting an anti- terrorism draft law at its level, appeared keener to push it through. Perhaps this was happening because acts of terrorism themselves were moving across from European capitals to the United States, but whatever the reason, the UN was suddenly wide awake to the threat of global terrorism.

Take for example, this resolution of the UN High Commissioner for Refugees' Sub- Commission on the Prevention of Discrimination and Protection of Minorities.[9]

Raising demand for terrorism and human rights, it reiterates, "the unequivocal condemnation of all acts, methods and practices of terrorism, regardless of their motivation, in all its forms and manifestations, wherever and by whoever committed, aimed at the annihilation of human rights, fundamental freedoms and democracy. Destabilizing legitimately constituted governments, undermining pluralistic civil society and having adverse consequences on the economic and social development of states." This UNHCR resolution is a landmark in the history of legislating against terrorism, at the international level.

For a change, with some measure of conviction, it removes the aspect of 'motive' from any act of terrorism and public annihilation, snatching away the possibility of describing some acts as political violence, rather than merely terrorism. This is very significant because at the level of the United Nations, the causes of terrorism have always been connected with the acts themselves, in an effort to out-manoeuvre those countries looking for simple definition of terrorism as, say, anything that endangers human lives or jeopardizes individual freedoms.[11] The debate over whether there should at all be a separate category of political violence not to be looked at on par with 'ordinary terrorism' still carries on, and I will look at it in greater detail later.

But the fact that the UN was considering it is noteworthy. More so in the Indian context where at the core of the opposition to an anti- terrorism law is the premise that some perpetrators of violence, are activists since they support sub-regional sentiments (like the Telengana movement in Andhra Pradesh or the kilings by the Peoples' War Group in Madhya Pradesh) or anti-establishment ideologies. Second, it introduces, for the first time at the UN level, the principle that anything that destablises legitimately constituted governments could be termedas terrorism. In other words, all efforts at secessionism using violence, or even challenging governments within their territory, would qualify as terrorism.

This is something that can be grossly abused by governments to inflict their own form of state terrorism on political or ideological opponents like, say, in Pinochet's Chile or Ershad's Bangladesh. But innocent or not, the UN seemed to be looking at terrorism as the subversion of government. Whatever the backdrop, a UN body was practically removing the element of individual 'perception from a definition of terrorism. This was in other words, an attemp to extricate any larger meaning from acts of terror by focusing on the act itself. That's the question that still confounds us in India. What length should we go as a nation in arming ourself against terrorism? Should we provide special leeway for certain groups in order to allow dissent, free speech and even fringe ideologies to flourish? Should we humanise the anti-terrorism laws? And if so, then how? These are some questions that formed the basis of the debate in parliament when the government sought to present a new amended Criminal Law bill in 1995, once TADA lapsed. Defending the argument that opposition to any anti-terrorism bill is institutionalized, one can scan the position taken on the CLA by the Congress when it was in power and now. In contrast to the position taken now by party spokesperson Jaipal Reddy that the "law is full of loopholes and can be used against innocents and political opponents the Congress had adopted a 'hawkish' line every time the question of giving TADA another lease of life emerged when it was in power.

VS Jafa details out particularly acerbic comment—made by the irrepressible Mani Shanker Aiyer—is his essay on 'Terrar and the Law.''[13]. It was made in 1991, during a parliament debate, when MP Syed Shahabuddin opposed the extension to TADA. Summing up his party and government's position, Mr Aiyer says:"Syed Shahabuddin asked a question as to how long it would be necessary for us to have repeated extensions of such on Act. I can only reply that we have to continue extending it so long as terrorism raises its ugly head."[14] It didn't need Mr Aiyer to spell it out, but has done so forcefully and put across his point that most opponents to a new Anti- terrorism Law don't do so, because they feel laws per se are ineffective. Sure, organisations like PUDR and PUCL feel one has to heal the socio-economic reasons that spawned terrorism. But central to their argument is the opinion that there has to be a dividing line brought in between mindless violence, on the one hand, and violence aimed at a larger purpose. In brief, it's over the definition of terrorism.

That's an area the Law Commission has not looked at, at all, in its draft anti- terrorism bill. It's something that requires deeper focus, and more sustained debate. The question to be answered is simply this: Can any motive justify an act of violence?

Lets flip back to Mr Ghatate on that one. "Of course not!" he thundes. "But even if it did, would be so foolish as to actually spell out the sub-sections under which a terrorist can get an alibi?" Well, Mr Ghatate has a point. But when a 21 -line definition of terrorism fails to carry the nation with it, there's no harm in looking deeper to find if it can be made more direct.

References

1. Chapter 2, 173rd Report of the Law Commission, 1.10.1.

2. 43rd Report of the Law Commission on Offences against National Security, 1972.

3. The working paper was circulated to all the concerned authorities, organizations and individuals'' Chapter 1. 173rd Report of the Law

Commission on 'Prevention of Terrorism Bill 2000.

4. Page 13, Chapter 2, 173rd Report (above) 1.16.1

5. Page 10, 173rd Report

6. 1978 I SCR p.1

7. 1973 Supp SCR p.1

8. TADA Hard Law for a Soft State, *Economic and Political Weekly.*

9. Resolution 1996/20, "Human Rights and Terrorism.

10. Working paper submitted by Ms Kalliopi Koufa, Doc E/CN4/ Sy.2/1997/28.

11. Definition mooted by then UN Secy Genl Kurt Waldhet, two days after the Munich massarie.

12. Debate on *STAR* News, Jaipal Reddy vs PN Ghatate October 2000.

13. 10 o'clock to Bed: Insouciance, terror and the law, Volume 5 Faultlines, Bulwark.

14. August 1991, Lok Sabha proceedings.

9

The Botulinum Toxins

Botulinum is a likely candidate for future biological weapons. These toxins are found to be most poisonous.Hence their potency makes them more suitable than other toxins and nerve gas. There are various types of botulinum toxins. Botulinum toxin as a possible BW agent has been the subject of much speculation in recent years, hence it is considered worthwhile to discuss this subject in a little more detail. The materials for the present discussion are derived mainly from some excellent eviews [1-4] which may also be consulted for further details. Botulism was first described in Germany in 1820 by Justinus Kerner. The organism responsible for this was first isolated by Van Ermengem in 1896 as a strict anaerobe now called Clostridium botulinum. It is a spore-forming, rod-shaped bacterial species. This organism derives its name from the Latin word for sausage—botulus, where it was first found, and botulism has been associated with the consumption of sausages, though not exclusively. It has been shown later that botulism is not an infectious disease, but a kind of poisoning caused by eating food having grown botulinum and having produced toxin.

The toxin is intracellular but is released into the growth medium after the major increase in the culture population has been achieved. Hence it is considered to be an exotoxin. Cl. botulinum also produces small amounts of other toxins such as a haemagglutinate, an O-labile haemolysin, and a haemolytic lecithinase.

Cl. Botulinum: Its Kinds

Botulinum organisms are divisible into kinds A, B, C, D, and E, according to the immunologic specificities of the toxins they produce. That is, one strain of organism produces exclusively one of the antigenic types of toxin. Mutation in production from one kind to another, of toxin has never been found, despite the mutability observed with respect to the quantity of a toxin produced under fixed conditions of bacterial growth and mutability of several other characters of Cl. botulinum. They are further distinguishable from one another based on their cultural and biochemical features. For example, deep colonies of Types A and B may be round or leuticular, while those of C and D resemble loose balls of cotton wool. Types A and B are far more proteolytic than the virtually non- proteolytic C, D and E.

All the five kinds are believed to produce their toxicological effects through the same kind of injury to the tissues. Further, it has been established from experiments with mice that the lethal effect of one type is not reinforced or suppressed by the presence of other kinds.

Natural Habitat of Cl. Botulinum

Soil is the natural habitat of this organism and also stagnant water in which vegetation is decaying. It is rather more prevalent in virgin soil than in cultivated, manure, or pasture lands. In comparison with the other important pathogenic clostridia, Cl. botulinum is not a common inhabitant of the intestines of domestic animals or of farmyard manure. It can be found in the excreta of domestic animals in areas where botulism is enzootic, but it has almost never been isolated from human excreta. The various types are found in different region. Type A is more common than Type B in the U.S.A., while the latter is more usual in Europe. Type E bacilli are probably marine organisms. The difference in habitat may be responsible for the greater sensitivity to heat of type E spores than of spores of the other types.

Symptoms in Man

In man the symptoms become visible after periods varying from less than a day (say within 6 hours) to several days after ingestion of the toxin, depending on the amount taken. The symptoms include vomiting, constipation, thirst, double vision, difficulty in swallowing and speaking, and respiratory paralysis. Diarrhoea or vomiting does not, however, necessarily follow ingestion of the toxin. In fact the syndrome is often ushered in with muscular weakness and ocular disturbances, of which diplopia, lack of power of accommodation and loss of the light refled are conspicuons features. Troubles with articulation and swallowing soon follow, brought about in part by weakness and incoordination of the pharyngeal muscles and partly by cessation of salivation. Gradually all the voluntary muscles weaken, and death generally occurs as the result of paralysis of the muscles of respiration. The heart often continues to beat for sometime after breathing has ceased. The mortality rate could be as high as 70 per cent. However, the case-fatality rates widely differ in different epidemics and localities, depending on the kind and quantity, of the contaminated food consumed and the type of toxin prevalent. In survivors convalescence is slow, and partial paralysis may persist for many months. This is an important point to be noted, because there are now well- developed methods for continuous artificial respiration over long periods with mechanical insufflators.

Outbreaks in Human Population

It seems worthwhile to note that in spite of their widespread distribution in soils, botulinum spores in comparison to those of tetanus and gas gangrene fail to germinate readily in the tissues and have only rarely been recorded as a complicating infection of wounds. Only three exceptional clinical cases of botulism because of probably authentic wound infection have been reported in man[3], but for all practical purposes the organism may be regarded as non-invasive. Outbreaks of botulism among humans are sporadic and rare and would be considered as insignificant were it not for the high fatality rate. from 1899 to 1947, there were 462 outbreaks in the United States and Canada with 1,253 cases and 815 deaths. In the United Kingdom only four outbreaks have been recorded. Human cases result from the eating of smoked, salted, spiced or canned foods, which have been allowed to stand for a period and eaten without being cooked.

In Europe, most cases have been because of sausages, ham, spiced meats, game pastes, potted meats and, in Russia, salt fish. In the United States most cases have been because of canned, especially home-canned, vegetables and fruits such as olives, string beans, corn and peas. Affected meats may appear obviously spoiled but the growth of Cl. botulinum in canned vegetables may be slight and apparently not noticeable, although dangerous amounts of toxin may have formed.

Symptoms and Outbreaks in Animals

Botulism occurs far more frequently in animals than in human beings and may be so prevalent in some areas that husbandry becomes virtually impossible unless steps are taken to control the disease. Amongst the more important of these naturally occurring intoxications in animals are 'lamziekte' amongst cattle in South Africa, and horses, cattle and sheep in Western Australia, a form of 'meningoencephalitis' of horses in various parts of France, 'Limber neck' in fowls and ducks in several parts of the world, and a paralytic syndrome amongst wild ducks on reservations in Western United States. In cattle and other herbivora in South Africa and Australia, the intoxication arises from the habit of sarcophagia and osteophagia of carrion which animals grazing on the veldt country develop to satisfy their craving for the phosphorus which is often deficient in their ordinary pasturage.

In France, it appears likely that the horses contract botulism from hay and silage which has been contaminated with the remains of small dead rodents and birds. Farmyard birds may become affected by eating the larvae of the 'green bottle' and other blowflies which are often present in contaminated carcasses. Wild ducks become intoxicated by the consuming marsh weeds that are growing in places and under conditions in which oxygen consuming microorganisms, notably pseudomonas aeruginosa, flourish and create those anaerobic conditions which lead to the profuse proliferation of the clostridium and the formation of large quantities of its toxin. Type D is the cause of lamziekte and type C is the cause of epizootic outbreaks of botulism in wild birds. Differences in susceptibility of specific vertebrates to the types of toxins, differences in geographic distribution of the botulinum types and differences in feeding habits of different animal species, are the factors that determine the frequency of occurrence of particular toxin type as causes of natural food poisoning.

Pathogenicity

Comparative lethal doses for different animal species

The botulinum toxins, taken collectively, are highly pathogenic on parenteral injection for a wide range of both warm and cold blooded animals, in all of which the syndrome of the intoxication follows one common pattern of paralysis. When different kinds of the toxins are analysed individually, it would be interesting to know their relative potencies for a particular species. The problem is, however, a complex one, as has been pointed out recently[3]. For a critical assessment, one must ensure beforehand whether or not the toxin fulfils the criteria of purity. Secondly, it remains to be seen whether these toxins are actually general cellular poison so that there is justification for expressing lethal dose per kilogram of body weight or per unit weight of poison. There is, however, some evidence that indicates otherwise. In the mouse, for example, the potencies of botulinum toxins A, B and C are found to be independent of the weights of the individual animals of different ages whether the potency is measured in terms of the time it takes to kill or in terms of the percentage of animals killed by different concentrations of toxins[5]. Smaller mice have proved to be more resistant to Type B toxin than the heavier ones. Further, the female mouse sometimes proves to be the more hardy member of the species. In the case of other species, the true nature of the relationship between body weights an potency has not yet been determined. Expressions of toxicity in terms of 1-kilogram of body weight are extrapolations from findings with actual animals, although no such thing as mouse, rat or guinea pig of 1-kilogram body weight practically exists in nature. Instead of being so critical, for the present the conventional method of expression may be considered. Earlier data (Table9) utilized for this purpose give some idea of qualitative estimates regarding relative pathogenicities of various botulinum toxins for particular species.

The relative pathogenicities according to this procedure are shown to fluctuate widely. For example, the ratio of the lethal doses for mice and fowls are 1:15 for Type A, 1:2000 for Type C, 1:100,000 for Type D and 1:25 for Type E. Mice, guinea-pigs, rabbits and monkeys are notably susceptible to all types of toxin (except perhaps type D for monkeys), whereas cats, dogs, fowls and pigeons are more refractory. Horses are also highly susceptible to Types A,B, and D.

TABLE 9.1
Comparative Lethal Doses of Different Types of CL. Botulinum Toxin given Parenterally for Some of the Common Laboratory Animals*

Toxin type	Minimum lethal dose per unit weight of animal								
	Mouse	Rat	Guinea-pig	Rabbit	Fowl	Pigeon	Dog	Cat	Monkey
A	1		1/2	1/3	15				
	1	$2^{1}/_{2}$							
	1			1					
B	1	1,000							
	1		1/5						
	1		1/3						
C	1	6	1	1/8	2000	20	1,000	800	1/3
D	1	320	1/4	1/5	100,000	2,000	100,000	15,000	100
E	1	40	1/2	1	25	25	100	400	1

**Based on G. Payling Wright*

Comparative lethal doses as determined by modes of administration.

Since naturally occurring botulism, both in man and animals, is basically a food poisoning, it is important to compare the lethal dosages of toxins preparations when given parenterally and orally. There is again considerable variation in the ratio of oral to parenteral toxicity for the different types and different animals. These differences are almost certainly of major epidemiologic importance. Though several preparations of the botulinum toxins are highly potent when they are taken in food, they are usually less effective orally than when inoculated directly into the tissues (Table 9.2.) Similar comparison of the susceptibility of mouse, ferret and mink has been made in more details in (Table 9.3). To what extent the lessened iethality of the toxin when given orally results from its partial destruction by digestive juices and other agents within the contents of the alimentary canal and to what extent from the incomplete absorption of the toxic protein moleule through the intestinal mucosa is unknown.

The ratio between destruction and unabsorbability almost certainly differs widely from one set of experimental conditions to another. There is yet another important route of entry of the toxin into the circulation, as has been shown recently. The toxin can be absorbed through the respiratory mucous membranes also, constituting an additional hazard to those working with dried toxin particularly. The lower reaches of the respiratory tract possess only a thinlayer of epithelial cells. It is much more toxic—may be many thousand times more toxic—by inhalation than by ingestion. The exact factor is yet to be determined. Its action is also quicker by the respiratory route.

TABLE 9.2

Comparative Lethal Dose Affected by the Mode of Administration of Toxin Preparations*

Toxins type	Species	Ratio of oral to parenteral lethal dose (approx.)	
A	Dog	1,000 : 1	(This gap is narrowed when the animal is starved)
	Rat	1,000,000 :1	
	Horse	100 : 1	
B	Horse	100 :1	
	Rabbits	1,000 :1	(Oral administration by stomach tube)
	Rabbits	1:1	
	Macacus-Monkey	1:1	
	Mice	1:1	
	Guinea-pigs	1:1	
C	Rabbits	100 to 1,000:1	
	Guinea-pigs	100 to 1,000:1	
	Mice	100 to 1,000:1	
D	Rabbits	100 to 1,000:1	
	Guinea-pigs	100 to 1,000:1	
	Mice	100 to 1,000:1	
	Goats	100 to 1,000:1	

**Data taken from G. Payling Wright[2]*

TABLE 9.3

Comparison of the Susceptibility of Mouse, Ferret and Mink to Botulinum Toxin Types A and B Administered by the Intraperitoneal (I.P) and Oral Routes*

Route	Type of toxin	Animal	Average weight (gm.)	Minimum lethal dose (mg.)	Minimum lethal does per gm.	Resistance per gram wt. (based on minimu lethal dose in mouse)	Resistance**
I.P	A	Mouse	20	10^{-6}	$5x10^{-3}$	1	1
I.P	A	Ferret	1620	10^{-2}	$6x10^{-7}$	12	10^{4}
I.P	A	Mink	840	10^{-2}	$1.2x10^{-6}$	24	10^{4}
I.P	B	Mouse	20	10^{-6}	$5x10^{-8}$	1	1
I.P	B	Ferret	1520	1.0	$6x10^{-4}$	1200	10^{6}
I.P	B	Mink	1000	1.0	10^{-4}	2000	10^{6}
Per os	A	Mouse	20	10^{-2}	$5x10^{-4}$	1	1
Per os	A	Ferret	-	Variable	-	-	-
Per os	A	Mink	1000	60-80	$6x10^{-2} = 8x10^{-2}$	120-160	$6x10^{3}$-$8x10^{3}$
Per os	B	Mouse	20	10^{-2}	$5x10^{-4}$	1	1
Per os	B	Ferret	-	Variable	-	-	-
Per os	B	Mink	980	20.0	$2x10^{-2}$	40	$2x10^{4}$

*Based on C. **Lamanna[3]. **Irrespective of weight differences based on minimum lethal dose in mouse.

Fate of Botulinum Toxin in Alimentary Canal

Exposure of toxic filtrates from cultures of Cl. botulinum of Type A to conditions (pH 2.3 to 5.0 at 37°C) simulating those found in the gastric contents seems to have little adverse effect on their potency. Nor does the addition of pepsin or trypsin reduce the toxicity of the solutions. Only when the pH of the broth is brought above 5.0, the potencies are seen to fall. Different results are, however, obtained with a highly purifed preparation of Type A toxin—a crystalline product in a buffered solution. There is a considerable fall in potency, about 90 per cent, both at lower and higher pH values. The addition of pepsin at pH 1.4 and of trypsin and chemotrypsin at pH 6.8 also totally detoxify the toxin solutions by the end of 72 hours..

Apparently purification affects the stability of the toxin by separating it from protective agents such as proteins and other organic materials. Without these agents in the broth, the toxin would have been digested by the enzyme. Another likelihood is that purification separates toxin from factors promoting gut permeability. The toxin is absorbed rapidly through the mucous membrane of the alimentary tract. Based on published evidence the small intestine must be regarded as the major site of systemic absorption in natural cases of poisoning by ingested toxin. The stomach and colon are minor absorption sites [6]. Ingested toxin seems to have every opportunity for contact with proteolytic enzymes. No critical studies delineating the likelihood that the oropharynx and esophagus act as major avenues of systemic absorption have been reported.

Such a demonstration would help to explain reports that botulism has occurred in human beings after just tasting of contaminated foods. The toxin may be absorbed through abrasions and burns of the skin and mucous membranes. Thus, mouth wounds, and perhaps even dental caries may permit absorption of toxin before contact with the proteolytic enzymes of the alimentary tract occurs. What is important is the persistence of residual amounts of toxicity for long periods of time in the face of destruction of toxin by proteolytic enzymes. This means that the toxin need not be resistant to enzymatic proteolysis in an absolute sense in order to act as an oral poison.

It is needful only that the rate of digestion of the toxin before total destruction be such that a lethal dose can pass the barrier of the alimentary tract. Such a situation might be in accordance with the observation that much larger quantities of toxin, say Type A,—larger by as much as 100,000 fold—are needed for a lethal oral than for a lethal parenteral dose. It is also likely that the known difference in potency of oral doses of different types of toxin in a given animal species, or of oral doses of one type of toxin in different species might reflect differences in the resistance of the various types of toxin to the digestive juices of animals of different species. A case in point is the nonsusceptibility of the Rhesus monkey to C and D toxins administered orally. For a clearer picture, it would be required to know whether protein from extraneous sources, such as foods, can slow down or prevent proteolytic destruction of toxin, and whether ingested toxin can seriously interfere with the secretion of enzymes into the alimentary tract—these possibilities are not yet explored in any animal species. It is worth pointing out that botulinum toxin does not characteristically cause the direct irritation of intestinal surfaces that is found in other types of bacterial food poisoning, like salmonellosis and staphylococcus enterotoxin poisoning; diarrhoea or vomiting does not necessarily follow ingestion of botulinum toxin.

Thus there is no self- cleansing mechanism to limit the period of absorption of this toxin. This observation also suggests that in clinical treatment of botulism an allout effort should be made to promptly clear the alimentary tract in toto. It is not known how botulinum toxins having such high molecular weights pass through the membrane of the alimentary tract. The potency of the ingested toxin, as has been suggested, may be attributable to its high level of toxicity alone and not to any unusual ability to excape destructive intestinal processes or to possession of toxophores of small molecular weight released from a larger carrier particle by intestinal mechanism. Very small quantities of a toxin need penetrate the intestine for a fatal result to ensure. The explanation of the permeability of the alimentary tract regarding toxin may rest on some unexpected capacity for proteins in general to escape in small amounts by a lymphatic route, a point which may form basis of a future study.

Susceptibility of Human beings to Different Types

Human—beings are affected mainly by Type A, less frequently by Types B and E. Only two reported outbreaks of poisoning with Type C and one with Type D are documented. Poisoning by Type E results from consumption of improperly preserved food. These differences almost certainly reflect fluctuating human susceptibility to the different types of toxin as much as in the degree of exposure to one or another of them. For example, there is a much lower case mortality (20 per cent or less) in Type B than in Type A (90 per cent) intoxications, and recovery from Type B has been possible even when appreciable amounts of toxin could be illustrated in the blood. In some areas (e.g. South Africa) where there is considerable exposure to C and D toxins, no human cases of in toxication have occurred. Only Types C and D have been found to intoxicate herbivores in nature.

Some Properties of the Pure Toxins

For fundamental studies on the mode of action of botulinum toxin and for exhibiting its different characteristies, it became necessary to obtain the toxin in pure or crystalline form. At Camp Detrick in the United States, two groups of investigators, namely, Lamanna and his colleagues, and Abrams and co-workers, could achieve the signal success in purifying the neurotoxin present in Type A cultures, and further progress has been made there and elsewhere in concentrating the toxins of Types A, B, C, D and E and in finding out their potencies. It is not considered necessary to mention here the methods of cultivation of the different types of Cl. botulinum and of purification of the toxins. Molecular weights and potencies of various preparations of the toxins are shown in Table ?.

Purification of toxins of Types C, D and E has not been achieved to the same extent as those of Types A and B, and thus their molecular weights are not known with sufficient degree of accuracy. Recent data available on potencies of preparations of Types A,B,C and E are those of Duff and co- workers [11, 13, 15, 18] from Camp Detrick, of Types C and D are those of Sterne and Wentzel [14,16] from South Africa, and of Type D of Boroff et al[17] from France. Type A crystalline material is a globulin which contains nineteen amino acid residues, with an unusually high proportion of aspartic acid, tyrosine and threonine. Incidentally, tetanus toxin also contains exceptionally high percentages of aspartic acid and lysine, and the relationships of aspartic acid to glutamic acid and of isoleucine to leucine are very similar to those found with Type A botulinum toxin and are reverse of those typical of many other proteins. In other words, tetanus toxin is also an unusual protein like botulinum toxin. Less than $0.1x10^{-3}$

microgram of botulinum toxin brings death to a mouse. For fifty per cent lethality, the presence of $2.1x10^7$ molecules of Type A toxin or of $1.6x\ 10^7$ mlecules of type B toxin is required. In the case of Type D toxin when dissolved in acid-gelatin phosphate buffer, only some 1,000 molecules are needed to kill a mouse.

The molecular structure of botulinum toxin seems to be unstable. When a solution of Type A toxin is brought to a pH of 7.5 (almost neutral), a major proportion of the large molecules, which were typical of the protein in acid solution, undergo fission into much smaller ones whose molecular weight was estimated to be almost 70,000 [19, 20]. This 'dissociated toxin' still possesses the same level of lethality for mice as the 'complex toxin' from which it is apparently derived, and may prove to be the form in which the toxin is absorbed in naturally occurring botulism.

How a protein with a molecular weight of the order of one million can undergo absorption through the mucosa of the alimentary tract is explained on the basis of such dissociation. Types B and D also appear to occur in forms with different molecular weights. The inference is that botulinum toxin molecules do not seem to be fixed entities but are structures capable of dissociating and repolymerizing in many different ways. Such changes may account for the difference in behaviour of the various types and preparations and possibly also for the ability of the toxin to pass from the gut into the circulation. However, dissociation phenomenon is still in a hypothetical stage.

Potentiation of the Toxins

Another interesting property to which reference may be made is the potentiation of botulinum toxin by serum and other materials. The lethality of Type A toxin has been raised two or three times by an exposure to 2 per cent peptone at 37°C for many hours while similar treatment with serum might raise it more, say ten times. However, such potentiation lasts for a brief period—a few hours at the most. The enhancement of lethality of Type D by the addition of 0.2 per cent gelatin has been of a much greater order. The intraperitoneal toxicity for mice of crude and partially purified Type E toxin was found to improve strikingly when the culture was incubated with trypsin. The protective action of substances like gelatin, peptone, serum, etc., against oxidative or destructive influences acting on dilute solution of the toxins is, however, understandable. Likewise, the presence of other neutral colloids might also reduce the loss of the highly surface active toxin through denaturation or attachment to glass surfaces. But the manner in which potentiating agents operate is still obscure.

Mode of Action

In botulism the immediate cause of death is generally a paralysis of the skeletal musculature, which causes interference with breathing and in terminal asphyxia. The greater the dose of toxin, the more rapidly death ensues, and the less likely it is that histopathological changes will be noticed. It is a neurotoxin which does not harm the central nervous system but acts very widely on all those portions of the peripheral nervous system that are cholinergic in character regardless whether they form pre or post- ganglionic components of the autonomic nervous system or are somatic nerves supplying skeletal muscles.

While producing muscular paralysis the toxin acts, at the myoneural junction, apparently by stopping the release of acetyl choline, the transmitter substance, from the demyelinated ends of the cholinergic motor nerves. This anticholinergic effect of the toxin at the pre-ganglionic level induces secretory paralysis also. The pharmacological actions of the different kinds are found to be identical. but it is not knowhow the release of acetylcholine is inhibited. It is not an inhibitor of cholinesterase activity and varies in this regard from some of the fatal nerve gases which are anticholinesterases. Incidentally, tetanus produces muscular spasticity and convulsions but acts on some site within the central nervous system. Though curare- like poisoning is generally ascribed to botulism, the mechanisms of neuromuscular blockade are different in the two cases . Whereas curare competes for acetylcholine receptors to stop acetylcholine from exerting its depolarizing action, botulinum toxin, as mentioned above, inhibits the release of acetylcholine. Whether or not botulinum toxin is a general cellular poison, is not yet confirmed. Whatever meagre evidence is there in the case of mouse, the toxin seems to act on biochemical substrates which do not keep pace in quantity with increase in body weight. Several species of cold blooded animals, e.g., snails, earthworms, frogs and fish can likewise be intoxicated by botulinum toxin, though the dosage needed to kill them may proportionately be much larger.

In these animals, botulism develops quicker when the temperature of the environment is raised, and an inverse correlation is been between the lethal dose and the temperature. The effect of raised temperature is supposed to accelerate the action of the toxin on susceptible structures once it has become fixed, rather than to hasten the early stages of its absorption and fixation. If the temperature effect holds good in the case of warm blooded animals including man, raised temperature as in febrile condition is expected to render a subject easily susceptible to botulism, and will lessen the survival time as well. It is interesting to mention that all but one of the vertebrates tested have been poisoned; exception is claimed for the American turkey vulture Cathartes aura septentrionalis [21]. Perhaps the vulture contains a neutralizing property in its serum which has originated as an evolutionary adaptation to the natural risk of feeding on the carrion of animals dead of botulism. This reveals the possible existence of unsuspected peculiarities in the avian cholinergic nervous system.

To understand botulism better as well as to gain a more intimate knowledge of the biochemistry of nerve terminals, it is needed to determine the precise site and nature of the reactions leading to the failure of poisoned nerves to release acetylcholine. Since all current medical treatment is merely supportive, a specific therapy which is an urgent need might ultimately evolve from such a study.

Lethal Dose for Man and Some Herbivorous Animals

The current state of knowledge with regard to lethal or semilethal dose of botulinum toxins for man and some herbivorous animals is very meagre. In arriving at such estimates it has been assumed that the dose would be proportional to body weight, and that the mouse data (Table 9.4) would apply to any kind of vertebrate on weight basis. The first estimate of lethal dose of Type A toxin for man was ascribed to Lamanna from Camp Detrick, according oto whom the figure was given as 0.15 microgram roughly for a 165 pound man [22]. For the Abrams crystals which were more potent, the lethal dose would, of course, be smaller. For a man having 65 kilogram body weight, it came to be of the order of 0.1 microgram. In the case of Type D toxin exhibiting ordinary potency, (i.e., without potentiation), the estimated lethal dose for a cattle or horse weighing 366 kilograms would be less than 0.9 microgram. The corresponding lethal dose of Type D toxin with the unprecedented order of potency (after

TABLE 9.4

Comparative Potency of Different Types of Botulinum Toxin and the Estimates of Lethal Dose for Man and Some Domestic Animals

Type	Crystal or concentrate	Molecular weight	Potency per mg. N		Potency per mg. toxin (16% N assumed)		Estimated number of molecules per LD_{50} or m.l.d.	Estimated semi-lethal dose (microgram)*	
		LD_{50}	m.l.d.	LD_{50}	m.l.d		Man (65 kg)		Cattle or horse (366 kg)
1	2	3	4	5	6	7	8	9	10
A	Crystal	900,000(7)	220×10^6 (8)	-	35×10^6	-	2.1×10^7	0.093	0.5
	Crystal	1,130,000(9)	-	220×10^6(10	-	35×10^6	-	0.093	0.5
	Crystal	-	269×10^6 (11)	-	43×10^6	-	-	0.075	0.4
B	Concentrate	60,000(12)	160×10^6 (12)	-	26×10^6		1.6×10^7	0.125	0.7
	Crystal	-	262×10^6 (13)	-	42×10^6	-	-	0.077	0.4

1	2	3	4	5	6	7	8	9	10
C	Concentrate	-	-	$3x10^6$(14)	-	$0.5x10^6$	-	-	36.6
	Concentrate	-	$22x10^6$ (15)	-	$3x10^6$	-	-	-	6.1
D	Concentrate	1,000,000 (14)	-	$130x10^6$(14)	-	-	-		0.9
	Concentrate (in gelatin phosphate buffer at pH 6.2)	-	-	$4x10^{12}$(16)	-	$0.6x10^{12}$	$1x10^3$		$-30.5x10^{-6}$
	Concentrate	-	$14x10^6$ (17)	-	$2x10^6$	-	-	-	9.1
	Concentrate	-	-	10^7(17)	-	$1.6x10^6$	-	-	11.4
E	Concentrate	-	$19x10^6$ (18)	-	$3x10^6$	-	-	1.083	-

*On the basis of twenty grams as more body weight, and the toxins administered parenterally as in mouse.
LD_{50} (semi-lethal0 dose-the amount or dose which kills 50 per cent of a group of mice as test animals (usually 10 or more).
M.l.d. (minimum lethal dose)-the smallest of several does which kills one of a group of mice as test animals.

potentiation) would be $30.5X10^{-6}$ micrograms. For reasons already discussed such estimates can only be provisional [3]. Even the available clinical data do not allow one to make a scientific judgement of the true minimum lethal dose for man. Available evidence points to man as a very susceptible species.

Recently it has been calculated that ingestion of a dose only 3500 times larger than the dose lethal to mice (which is less than $0.1X10^{-3}$ micrograms by parenteral route and 10 micrograms by the oral route) was responsible for the death of a 104 kilogram man [23]. This is considered so far to be the best statement of toxicity for man. Allowing some margin for error, one can then guess that the lethal parenteral dose may be 0.5 microgram and the figures for oral toxicity would be considerably higher. Such type of information gives us a notion of the range within which a fatal dose for man falls, but it gives us no clue as to what lesser quantity of toxin might prove to be fatal. From the standpoint of its use as a BW agent, it is significant to point out again that the size of the oral dose might be several times more than that of the parenteral dose for producing lethal effect. The exact ratio between the doses by these two routes is not known for man or for cattle. For horse, the lethal dose by mouth of Types A and B was reported to be hundredfold that needed when given subcutaneously. [24]

Lethal Dose of Some Infective Germs Estimate

Let us now compare the potency of botulinum toxin with the lethal doses of a few infective BW agents as reported in the literature[22]. A single pair of pneumococci or a single bacillns of tularemia can kill a mouse on injection and the effective weight of such a killing dose may be given as follows. Taking the pneumococcus unit (two bacteria surrounded by a capsule) as a sphere 3 microns in diameter and its density about that of water, the weight of this unit could be estimated at $14X10^{-12}$ gm. As such, the pneumococcal substance at contains $70X10^{-6}$ killing doses per mg. for the mouse or is nearly twice as much potent as botulinum toxin which is shown to contain $35x\ 10^{6}$ killing doses per mg. The bacillus of tularemia is a small one and has a diameter of about 0.2 micron and a length of 0.5 micron. Its total weight could be estimated at about $0.02X10^{-12}$ gm. Accordingly, it has potency of 50000X10 killing doses per mg. That makes it about 1400 times as potent as botulinum toxin. In the case of tobacco mosaic virus, the crystalline material (molecular weight

17 million) is capable of producing disease in a quantity as small as one thousand millionth of a gram or less than 100 molecules. Such estimates are hypothetical because one organism as such does not kill the host. It multiplies inside the host and the combined effect of many such organisms that are formed cause death. Infective doses of some germs for man have also been estimated from laboratory accidents.

In a single human case of streptococcal infection, the dose received by inhalation was reported to be of the order to 1280 germs. Calculation reveals that one gram of these germs can affect about 700 million men. One germ of tularemia or brucellosis is also enough for infecting a man, and this might be the case for plague bacillus as well . In the case of psittacosis infection in another human case, the dose eceived by inhalation was estmated to be not more than 100 mouse units. Each cubic centimetre of the culture fluid handled contained about $1.5x10^9$ mouse units. Hence this volume of the fluid, almost weighing one gram, is adequate to infect at least 15 million men.

Comparative Toxicity of Other Toxins and Nerve Gases

Botulinum toxins are, no doubt, the most potent poisons known as yet, less than $0.1x10^{-3}$ microgram proving lethal to a mouse. Only tetanus and shigella neurotoxins seems to possess potency of this order. Other protein poisons, like diphtheria toxin and animal venoms, are hundreds and tens of thousands of times less poisonous. Aconitine, an alkaloid with the empirical formua- $C_{34} H_{47}O_{11} N$, one of the most poisonous non-protion materials known, is far less toxic than the botulinum toxins. Its toxicity regarding white mouse is given as $3.5X10^3$ LD_{50} per mg. of nitrogen or $3.5X10^3X1000/46$ LD_{50} per gram of solid [3]. The extraordinarily high toxicity recorded for the Type D, needs, however, further confirmation. The toxicity of a nerve gas like disopropyl fluorophosphate (DFP) is comparable with that of hydrogen cyanide, but is no match for that of botulinum toxin.

While it is not possible to give data on lethal dose of any of these nerve gases for man by direct experimentation, the effect of DFP may, however, be mentioned. When men were exposed to DFP at a concentration of $1:10^6$ for five minutes, practically no effects were observed during exposure nor until some five minutes later [25]. Intense myosis, that is, extreme pupil constriction and reduction of the powers of accommodation, for seven days, with little relaxation of symptoms in less than 72 hours. At higher concentrations the toxicity was so high as to cause a quick knock- out action in animals. The LC_{50} (toxicity by inhalation expressed as the concentration in milligrams per litre of air required to kill 50 per cent of the animals after 10 minutes' exposure) was shown to be 0.36 mg.l for rats and 0.44 mg.l for mice. The symptoms included muscular changes,gasping, and finally cessationof respiration.

Biological Sensitivity

Regarding biological sensitivity, botulinum toxin is, however, surpassed by ethyl mercaptan and crocin. In air the odour of mercaptan may be recognized at 0.00001 p.p.m. The number of mercaptan molecules adequate for recognition in this way is estimated to be about $3X10^{10}$, corresponding to $2X10^{12}$ gram in about 100 ml. of air. Approximately one molecule of crocin ($C_{44}H_{64}O_{24}$) is needed to render one germ cell of algae of the genus chlamydomonas motile, corresponding to 10^{-15} microgram. The concentration of the glycoside picrocrocin ($C_{16}H_{26}0_{7}$) needed to fix sex amounts to 1000 molecules per gamete or $0.5X10^{-12}$ microgram, while that of safranal ($C_{10}H_{14}O$) is only 10 molecules per gamete or $0.25X10^{-14}$ microgram.

Botulinum Toxins as BW Agents

As has already been described, man is affected mainly by type A, less frequently by Types B and E, and almost never by Type C or D. When it is known that Type D is a deadly poison for cattle and other herbivorous animals, the focus of attention may be swifted towards a more likely use of this toxin in BW than Type A toxin. It will be easier to contaminate grasssy land and feeds with the expectation that a large number of cattle and other herbivorous domestic animals such as sheep, goats, buffaloes, horses etc., will be affected. For practical use in BW, it is quite possible that the production of Types A and D toxin will receive the greatest attention in comparison to the other types. Being a chemical poison and not an infective agent and owing to factors affecting dissemination, the dose of botulinum toxin to be used in actual BW would have to be very much more than that indicated by any possible estimate of lethal dose.

As has already been mentioned the crude preparation or the

culture filtrate is more stable than the purear material and hence it excludes the need for the complicated steps of purification. If a more potent product is to be used, the problem of purification and stabilization is involved. Its potentiality would be much more if the toxin could be stabilized in the truest sense. The choice of using the crude or the pure product will, however, depend on a number of factors. The use of a crude preparation or culture filtrate will need a heavier weight to be carried for transportation or dissemination. Botulinum toxin can enter the body by ingestion, inhalation and through contact with wounds or infection; through all the possible routes by which an animal can be poisoned. The organism producing it is harmless if injected and its spares fail to germinate easily in the tissues. It can be used only to produce toxin in foodstuffs and water.

Botulinum toxin is distinguished from the tetanus and diphtheria toxins in its ability to be readily absorbed by the mucous membrane of the alimentary tract, whereas the latter are destroyed or rendered inactive by ingestion. So the different types of botulinum toxin might find use in BW either as an aerosol which would lead in unmasked persons or animals to the contamination of the respiratory and alimentary tracts, or as agents for contaminating food, feeds and water supplies.

Protective Measures

Methods of treatment of contaminated foodstuffs and water

For protection against bothlism, which may result from the consumption of polluted foodstuffs and water, some important studies have been made on the resistance of the spores of Cl. botulinum and also of botulinum toxin to heat and other agents.

Generally speaking, spores may survive for many hours at 100°C, and upto 10 minutes at 120°C. The spores of Type E are much less resistant than those of the other types. As is the case with other Clostridia, and with Bacilli, great variation in resistance is found in different strains and in different cultures of the same strain. The interior of a foodstuff generally presents an ideal place for the growth of anaerobes. Cl. botulinum is the only organism that may resist processing temperatures. On the other hand, application of excessive heat is deleterious to the product. In canning industry, sterilization in bulk is required without applying, however, excessive heat. If the whole mass of a food, including the centre of cans , neutral in pH reaches 115°C and is held for 15 minutes, the danger of botulism is apparently nil. It has been observed from the safety record of commercial canned food that the modern method of canning is highly reliable. One may easily protect oneself against botulism by boiling all canned food for 20 minutes after opening them. The toxin is also destroyed by this treatment. In relation to the destructive effects of heat on specimens of all five types of toxin, types A, B, and E have been shown to be relatively thermolabile, in that they are destroyed by exposure to 70°C for a few minutes, while types C and D are much more resistant. Such estimates of thermal destruction can only be very general, for they are dependent upon the pH and other features of the medium in which the toxin is present.

For instance, the same type of toxin often proves more resistant to heat when present in vegetable juices than when in broth: the greater acidity of the former apparently raises its resistance. All the types of toxin, as indicated, are more stable when dissoved in media with an acid reaction. Even at physiological neutrality, they soon lose much of their potency—especially Types A and b—and when made slightly alkaline they rapidly become quite inactive. Nor can this loss of potency be reversed by any later reacidification a of the solution. The toxins remain potent for several days in cold clean water, but are destroyed in a few minutes by exposure to permanganate, chlorine, iodine and other oxidising agents in concentrations ordinarily used for the chemical steriliazation of water supplies (e.g. 1 to 2 p.p.m. of free chlorine at the end of half an hour's contact with). The efficacy of such oxidising agents goes down if there is too much organic matter in the water. If such polluted water is made slightly alkaline, it can be readily detoxicated by warming to 70°C, for a few minutes.

Detoxification may be possible by using the dye crystal violet. Under appropriate conditions, some anionic and cationic surface active agents may also lead to precipitation and inactivation of the toxins. Procedures for detoxifying contaminated forage, pasture, hay stacks, etc. will, however, be different. Prolonged exposure to the sun, inundation, or washing away by rain, will have to be relied on, or the safest way is to discard the suspected materials. where it is possible, some of the principles outlined before for decontaminating human foodstuffs may also be brought into practice.

Prophylaxis and Treatment

For defensive use in human population, large scale production of effective immunizing preparations will be required. It will also be a sound economic policy to immunize domestic animals. Since the toxins of the various kinds of Cl. botulinum are serologically distinct, it is possible to prepare antisera containing active antitoxins in enough quantity for prophylactic purposes by appropriate immunization procedure. Such sera may be specific or polyvalent. While hyperimmune sera to Types A and B are monospecific, hyperimmune sera to Type C usually has a proportion of D- antitoxin and vice-versa. This probably is because Types C and D possessing a moiety of the heterologous toxins. It would be advantageous to have polyvalent antisera to the extent of containinig antibodies to A, B and E, the types to which man is naturally susceptible. Antisera should be administered to all persons suspected of having partaken of contaminated food. Apart from antisera, toxoids may also be used. They are non-toxic, quite stable, specific and are known to produce active immunization against circulating toxins. They are prepared by a simpler and yet safer method which comprise detoxifying the toxins by chemical means without destroying their antigenic properties. The addition of formaldehyde to toxin solution under controlled conditions of reagent concentration, of acidity, and of temperature, is the favoured method. For use in human beings a preparation of highly purified toxoids of great efficacy is now available[26]. It is polyvalent, comprising of a mixture of toxoids of Types A, B, C, D, and E. While the individual toxoids in this preparation vary in degree of purity, a satisfactory response is engendered by each of the five components.

Such toxoids are not necessarily free from haemagglutinins. Human Type C red blood cells can, however, be used as adsorbents for the removal of haemagglutinin. Under ordinary circumstances, naturally occurring botulism in man is so uncommon that active immunization on a large scale is not worthwhile, although it is advisable to protect laboratory workers who are at greater risk. Treatment with antitoxins has marked prophylactic value, but their therapeutic efficacy is slight. It is significant to note here that in botulism, as in tetanus, the symptoms are a result of the injury to the nerve tissue, with which the toxin combines irreversibly, and the administration of antitoxin serves nly to neutralize circulating toxin.

Continued artifical respiration for long periods is recommended since death results from paralysis of the muscles of respiration. As in tetanus, the lesion caused by botulinum toxin may regress, and the paralyses and other clinical manifestations of the disease slowly disappear. This is known from the clinical study of patients who have survived epidemics. In clinicl treatment of botulism, all out effort should be made also to promptly clear the alimentary tract in toto.

The near total lack of therapeutic, effects of botulium antitoxin in human botulism is, without doubt, attributable to the inevitably too late administration or to the administration of too little serum of too poor quality even at earlier stage. For the above reasons, the immunizing procedure may be of only partial utility as a protective measure.

However, such prophylactic steps will be essential under certan circumstances. Into a suspected area of contamination, persons should enter only after active immunization with the appropriate toxioid or most preferably with a combined toxoid which is reported to have been produced of late. No chemotherapeutic agent has so far been found to be an antidote in botulism. To sum up, it is one thing to say that a gram of any given agent contains enough germs to infect, or enough toxin to intoxicate, so many men, but to bring about such an event in practice is altogether a different matter. Various factors such as the kind and size of the disssemination device, the number of such devices and the manner in which they are set in action and , wind, weather and other conditions are obviously involved here even though a BW agent could be potent enough.

Nevertheless, botulinum toxin finds an important place in the list of possible BW agents for several reasons. The toxin is the most potent of all poisons known so far. It can affect man and different modes of entry into the body, inhalation in the form of an aerosol is of considerable importance . Treatment of botulism is only supportive and its timely detection is a great necessity.

References

1. L. Pillemer and K.C. Robbins, Ann. Rev Microbiology, 3:265 (1949).

2. G. Payling Wright, Pharmacol. Rev., 7:413 (1955).

3. C. Lamanna, Science, 130:763 (1959).

4. M. Sterne and W.E. van Heyningen, in Bacterial and Mycotic Infections of Man, edited by R. J. Dubos, 3rd Ed., (Pitman Medical, 1958), p. 359.

5. C Lamanna, W.I. Jensen and I.D. Bross, Am. J. Hyg., 62:21 (1955).

6. A.J. May and B.C. Whaler, Brit. J. Exptl. Pathol., 39:307 (1958).

7. F.W. Putnam, C. Lamanna and D.G. Sharp, J. Biol. Chem. 176: 401 (1948).

8. F. W. Putnam, C. Lamanna and D G. Sharp, J. Biol. Chem., 165: 735 (1946).

9. G. Kegeles, J. Am. Chem. Soc., 68: 1670 (1946).

10. A. Abrams, G. Kegeles and G.A. Hottle, J. Biol. Chem. 164:63 (1946).

11. J.T. Duff, G.G. Wright, J. Klerer, D.E. Moore and R.H. Bibler, J. Bact., 73: 42 (1957).

12. C. Lamanna and H.N. Glassman, J. Bact., 54: 575 (1947).

13. J. T. Duff, J. Klerer, R.H. Bibler, D.E. Moore, C. Gottfried and G.G. Wright, J. Bact., 73: 597 (1957).

14. M. Sterne and L.M. Wentzel., J. Immunol., 65: 175 (1950).

15. M.A. Cardella J.T. Duff, C. Gottfried and J.S. Begel, J. Bact., 75: 360 (1958).

16. L.M. Wentzel, M. Sterne and A. Polson, Nature 166:739(1950).

17. D.A. Boroff, M. Raynaud and A.R. Prevot, J. Immunol., 68: 503 (1952).

18. M. Gordon, M. A. Fiock, A. Yarinsky and J.T. Duff, J. Bact., 74: 533 (1957).

19. J.Wagman, Arch. Biochem.,50: 104 (1954).

20.J.Wagman and J.B. Bateman, Arch. Biochem., 45: 375 (1953).

21. E.R. Kalmbach, J. Am. Vet. Med Assoc., 94: 187 (1939).

22. T. Rosebury, Peace or Pestilence (Mc Graw - Hill, 1949), p.77.

23.K.F. Meyer and B. Eddie, Z. Hyg., 133: 255 (1951).

24. K. Legroux, J.C. Levadite and C Jeramee, Ann. Inst. Pasteur, 72: 409 (1945).

25. B.C. Saunders, Endeavour, 19:36 (1960).

26. M.A. Cardella, M.A. Fiock and G.G. Wright, Bacterial proc., (Soc. Am. Bacteriologist), 58: 78 (1958).

10

New Generation Biological Weapons

Biological weapons are meant to cause suffering to the population attacked. There must be deaths or diseases resultion from the use of biological weapons. These deaths or diseases can be in humans, enimals and plants.

Biological warfare (BW) agents, can be defined as living organisms, having viruses or infectious material derived from them, which are used for attacking purposes to cause disease or death and which usually depend for their basic effects on their ability to multiply in the organism attacked.

To be an effective agent for use in either a strategic or a tactical role, a BW agent should meet specific criteria[1].These criteria can be summarized as follows:

1. The agent should consistently produce a desired effect: death or disease.
2. The agent is supposed to be highly contagious.
3. The concentration of the agent required to cause death or disease— the infective dose— should be low.
4. The agent should have a short and predictable incubation time between exposure to oneset of the disease symtoms.
5. The target population should have little or no natural or acquired immunity or resistance to the agent.
6. The agent should not be easy to identify in the target population,

and little or no treatment for the disease caused by the agent should be available.

7. Prophylaxis against the agent should not be available in areas of the target population.

8. The agent should be amenable to economical mass production.

9. The aggressor should have means to save his own forces and population against the agent clandestinely.

10. The agent should be reasonably robust and stable under production and storage conditions, in munitions and during transportation. Storage methods should be available that stop gross decline in the agent's activity.

11. The agent should have the capability of efficient dissemination. If it cannot be delivered via an aerosol, living vectors (e.g. fleas, mosquitoes or ticks) shoud be available for dispersal or same form of infected substrate.

12. The agent should remain stable during dessemination. If it is to be delivered via an aerosol, it must be able to survive and remain stable in air until it reaches the target population.

13. After delivery, the agent should have a low persistence, surviving only for a short time, thereby allowing a prompt occupation of the attacked area by the aggressor's troops.

Agents which meet at least some of these criteria and which are known to be considered as potential BW agents by the miitary are listed in Table 10.1 and 10.2 . A comparison of the dates from the open literature (see Table 10.1) shows that whereas in 1969 most of the organisms (20 out of 31) regarded to be potential BW agents were bacteria and fungi , by 1983 viruses had become the majority of such agent (19 out of 22). This change appear to have been caused by several factors.

Table 10.1

Putative BW Agents Having the Highest Suitability for Operational Use Against Humans

	1940[a]	*1956*[b]	*1969*[c]	*1983*[d]
VIRUSES				
Poxviruses				
Variola Virus	+	+	+	+
Alphaviruses				
Chikungunya virus (CHIK)		+		+
Eastern encephalitis virus (EEV)		+	+	+
Venezuelan encephalitis virus (VEV)		+	+	+
Western encephalitis virus (WEV)		+	+	+
Flaviviruses				
Dengue virus		+	+	+
Yellow fever virus		+	+	+
Japanese encephalitis virus (JEV)		+	+	+[g]
Russian spring- summer encephalitis virus (RSSEV)[h]	+	+	+	+
St Louis encephalitis virus (SLEV)		+	+	
Arenaviruses				
Junin (Argentine haemorrhagic fever) virus (AHFV)				+
Lassa fever virus				+
Lymphocytic choriomeningitis virus (LCMV)				+
Machupo (Bolivian haemorrhagic fever) virus (BHFV)				+
Bunyaviruses				
Crimean-Congo haemorrhagic fever virus (CCHFV)				+
Hantaan (Korean haemorrhagic fever) virus			+	
Rift valley fever virus				+
Filoviruses				
Marburg virus				+
Ebola virus				+
Picornaviruses				
Hepatitis A virus		+	+	+[g]
Orthomyxoviruses				
Influenza virus	+	+	+	
BACTERIA				
Chlamydia psittaci		+	+	
Coxiella burnetti	+	+	+	
Rickettsia prowazeki		+	+	+

R. rickettsi		+	+	
R. tsutsugamushi		+	+	+
Bacillus anthracis	+	+	+	+
Francisella (Pasteurella) tularensis	+	+	+	+
Pasteurella pestis	+	+	+	
Brucella melitensis, B. suis	+	+	+	
Clostridium tetani	+			
C.perfringens	+			
Meningococcus	+			
Shigella dysenteriae	+			
Salmonella typhi				
S. paratyphi	+	+	+	
S. sp. causing food poisoning	+	+	+	
Vibrio comma	+	+	+	
Corynebacterium diphtheria		+	+	
Actinobacillus mallei	+	+	+	
Pseudomonas pseudomallei		+	+	
Mycobacterium tuberculosis	+	+	+	
FUNGI[i]				
Coccidioides immitis		+	+	
Histoplasma capsulatum		+	+	
Norcardia farcinica		+	+	

a Japanese BW research activities during 1935-45 (USA, 1947b).
b USA. 1956.
c USA.1969,p[1].42.
d Anderson & King. 1983, p.5.
e Additionally, the US Department of Defense performs (in in —home laboratories) or funds via active contract work on Mayaro virus, Ross River virus, O[2] nyong-nyong virus (alpha viruses), and phlebotous fever viurs (bunyavirus) (Anonymous 1985a; USA, 1985b).
f Subtype of Semliki Forest virus.
g Anonymous 1985a.
h Subtype of tick borne encephalitis virus (TBEV).
i Fungi are not currently considered by US Army as anti-personnel BW agents, but might be used as anti— animal and anti—crop BW agents (Anderson & King, 1983, p.19).

First, several of the virses in the list of the potential BW agents have been previously regarded as too dangerous or too difficult to handle for development as potential BW agents. However by 1983, the advancement of genetic engineering techniques had altered this situation. New military interests in biological research have emerged since the first Review Conference on the Biological Weapons Convention at least in the USA. Correspondingly there is a significant rise in the funds obligated by the US Department of Defense for BW research (Table 10.3).

Table 10.2

Some Features of BM Agents Under Recent Consideration[a]

Agent[d]	Disease	latent period	Availability of vaccine	therapy	Infectivity (man-man)	Mortality (%)	Intended effect
Variola V.	Smallpox	7-16	yes	no	high	10-30	death
CHIK	Chikungunya fever	2-6	no[c]	no	-d	low	incap[g]
EEV	Eastern encephalitis	5-15	yes	no	-d	50	death
VEV	Veneznelan encephalities	2-5	yes	no	d	1	incap.
WEV	Western encephalitis	7-21	yes	no	-d	3	incap.
Dengue V.	Dengue fever Dengne hacmorrhagic fever	2-7	no no -d	no	-d	low 20	incap.
YFV	yellow fever	3-6	yes	no	-d	5-19	death
JEV	Japanese encephalitis	5-15	yes	no	-d	2-50	death
RSSEV	Russian spring-summer encephalitis	7-14	yes	no	-d,e	2-20	death
SLEV	St Louis encephalitis	4-21	no	no	-d	2-22	death
Junin V.	Argentian haemorrhagic fever	7-14	no[c]	no	low	5-15	death
LassaV.	Lassa fever	5-21	no[c]	no	low	low	incap.
LCMV	Lymphocytic choriomeningities	6-13	no[c]	no	low	low	inca

MachupoV.	Bolivian haemorrhagic fever	7-14	no-[c]	no	low	5-15	death.
CCHFV	Crimean-corgo hacmorahagic fever	3-16	no-[c]	no	-[d]	13-40	death
HantaanV.	Korean hecmorrhagic fever	12-33	no-[c]	no	moderate	1-30	death
RFV	Gift Valley fever	3-5	yes	no	low	10	aeth
Marburg V.	marburg disease	6-10	no	no	high	35	death
Ebola V.	Ebala hacmorrhagic fever	2-21	no	no	high	65-80	death
HAV	Hepatitis	10-50	no-[f]	no	high		incap
C. burnetti	Q-fever	10-21	yes	yes	low	1	incap
B. anthracis	Anthrax	1-5	yes[h]	yes	low	5-20	death
F. Tularensis	Tularemia	1-10	yes	yes	low	40-60	death

a UN, 1969; Anderson & King, 1983; Fields, 1985.
b For abbreviations of viruses, see table 10.1.
c Under development by US Department of Defense (anderson& King. 1983; Anonymous, 1985a).
d Unless vector present.
e RSSEV and other tick- borne encephalitis viruses are resistant to acidic pH. This allows oral infection and, hence, dissemination by an aerosol.
f Under development.
g incap. =incapacitation.
h Live vaccine under development at USAMRIID(Anderson & King, 1983).

Table10.3
Funds Obligated by the US Department of Defense for Research on Biological Warfare Defence, 1977-84 (Westing, 1985a)

Fiscal year (Oct.-Sep.)	Funds obligated (Current $m.)	Consumer price index(FY)	Funds obligated (1984 $m.)	% Change
1976-7	15.9	0.619	26	-
1977-8	16.5	0.667	25	-4
1978-9	16.5	0.723	23	-8
1979-80	16.0	0.797	20	-13
1980-1	15.1	0.879	17	-15
1981-2	21.6	0.939	23	+35
1982-3	38.8	0.972	40	+74
1983-4	62.5	0.994	63	+58

Sources: Funds obligated are from the annual reports by the US department of Defense to the US Congress on funds obligated in the chemical warfare and biological defence research programmes (done in accordance with Public Laws 91-121, sec. 409, and 93-608, sec.2[4], The value for 1976-7 is from the 1978 Congressional Record 124: 7880.90 Washington, DC; that for 1977-8 from the 1979 Congressional Record 125: 19501-16; that for 1978-9 from the 1980 Cogressional Record 126: 21383-400; that for 1979-80 unpublished (15 dec.1980): that for 1980-1 unpulished (30 Dec. 1981); that for 1981-2 unpublished (30 Sep. 1982); that for 1982-3 unfublished (30 Sep. 1983); and that for 1983-4 unpublished (30 Sep. 1984). the consumer price index is derived from the UN Internationable Monetary Fund yearbook, International Financial Statistics 37: 595 (1984) and 38 (1): 478-9 (Jan. 1985), with an index value of 1 referring to the calendar year 1984 US dollar.

Now for example, the genetic material of highly pathogenic viruses can be replicated, studied and manipulated in the relative protection of the 'biological containment' provided for Escherichia coli K12 or other host bacteria, (Table 10.4). (Because of differences in their gene structure, bacteria are unable to reveal most genes of higher organisms and of their viruses). Moreover, the chains of replicating viral nucleic acids in bacteria now allows them ultiplication of the genomes of those viruses which normally do not replicate outside their natural hosts , such as papilloma viruses and hepatitis B virus. Although until now such viruses have not been considered to be potential BW agents in the open literature, the situation might well alter with the new multiplication methods available. Second, viral diseases can be considered more debilitating than those caused by bacteria because they still cannot be treated by a specific therapy (table 2.2). Most of viral diseases can be treated only symptomaticlly including the prevention of secondary (bacterial) infections. Third, most of the diseases caused by viruses under consideration are not easy to diagnose without virus isolation because the symptoms cannot easily be clinically distinguished from several other infections.

This is true, for example, of viruses causing encephalitis or haemorrhagic fever. Finally, a rising number of vaccines against these viruses are available or under development, allowing the safety of the aggressor's troops.

In any case, genetic engineering might be used to modify potential BW agents more efficiently and in a more specific manner than classical genetic methods . The latter were not highly effective when genes had to be transferred

Table 10.4

Genes of Putative BW Agents Studied by Genetic Engineering Techniques

Agent	Genome structure[a]	Gene(s) cloned	Reference
Poxviruses	DNA, one double strand		
Vaccinia virus		used as gene vector	see p. 166
Alphaviruses	RNA, one single plus-strand		
Flaviviruses	RNA, one single plus-strand		
Yellow fever virus		complete genome cloned and sequenced	*b*
Arenaviruses	RNA, two single minus-strands (segments L & S)		
Lassa fever virus		oligonucleotide mapping, L and S segments cloned,	*i*
		S(=gene N) sequenced	*c*
Lymphocytic chorio-meningitis virus		large parts of L and S cloned and sequenced	*d*
Bunyaviruses	RNA, three single minus strands (segments LMS)		

Rift Valley fever virus		M segment cloned and sequenced	e
Hantaan virus		oligonucleotide mapping and partial sequence analysis	
Filoviruses	RNA, one single minus-strand		
Picornaviruses	RNA, one single plus-stand		
Bacteria	DNA, one double-stranded chromosome +double-stranded plasmids		
Bacillus anthracis		tox genes PA and LF cloned	*fg*

a. Single stranded plus —RNA molecules are infectious, whereas minus -b RNA strands are not infectious because they first have to be transcribed into plus- strands in the infected cell.
b. Rice et al., 1985.
c. Clegg & Oram.1985.
d. Romanowski & Bishop, 1985.
e. Purchio et al. 1984; Collett et al., 1985.
f. Vodkin & Leppla, 1983.
g. Robertson & Leppla. quoted by Leppla et al., 1985.
h. Schmaljohn & Dalrymple, 1984.
i. Gonzalez et al. 1984.

Between bacteria of different species and were not applicable to gene transfer between different taxonomic entities. Furthermore, the method of site—directed mutagenesis now make it very easy to mutate genes at will, including genes which normally do not at once mutate at all or only with very low frequencies, or for which selection cannot be made.

Thus it should be possible to increase the utility of potential BW agents by use of the methods described in this chapter's section II which follows.

Modifying the BW Agents

The symptoms caused by bacteria, viruses and other pathogens are ususally the result of the action of some toxin produced by the agent and/or of certain activities linked to the multiplication of the agent in the infected host organism. Thus pathogenicity and virulence are determined by toxin- coding tox genes and/or by one or more genes included in replication and multication of the agents. Mutation of such genes might raise or reduce the pathogenicity and virulence of the corresponding agents.

Although more knowledge has been obtained during the past few years about the molecular mechanisms of viral replication, there is still little information about genes and mechanisms responsible for the virulence of viruses. One type of 'virulence ' is responsible for the invasiveness of virus for given hosts. For example, viruses disseminated by aerosols do not invade by direct inoculation into the bloodstream but enter their host organisms through the mucosal barriers of the respiratory and gastrointestinal tracts. The surfaces of these tracts are usually protected by proteotytic enzymes, bile salts and large number of other non- specific defence factors. Viruses disseminated by aerosols can initiate a successful infection only if they are resistant to these defence factors. Studies with reoviruses, for instances demonstrate that specific genes may determine such a resistance.

Much in the same way, the ability to spread within an infected host organism to target organs and cells where viral replication and disease induction occur, as also the extension of viral spread throughout the organism, may be determined by specific viral genes.

Additional viral genes code for components of the viral coat and/or envelope needed to interact with specific receptors on the surface of target cells. thus, cell and tissue tropisuns of numerous viruses are coded for by specific genes and therefore may be modified by mutating or rearranging these genes. In the case of bunyaviruses, the glycoproteins of the viral envelope have been identified as the principal determinants of virulence and effective transmission[3].

The M genes of Rift Valley fever virus[4] and of Punta Toro virus, one of the agents that causes phlebotomus fever[5], which code for glycoproteins, have been cloned and sequenced at the US Army Medical Rsearch Institute of Infectious Diseases (USAMRIID). Other 'virulence genes' are responsible for virus-induced cell and tissue damage.

Virus-coded proteins, for example, may interfere with components of the host's protein synthesis apparatus, as do many toxins. Other viral products may interfere with the immune response or with other defence mechanisms of the host. This is well demonstrate by the HTLV-III virus causing the 'acquired immune deficiency syndrome' (AIDS). HTLV-III is a virus exerting a specific tropism for certain cells (T lymphocytes) essential for the immune response. Thus the virulence of this virus evolves as a result of sensitization of the host to other pathogenic agents by paralysing its defence system. In other virus-host systems, adverse effects of the immune response of the host may help in viral pathogenesis. Thus anti-viral antibodies produced by the host in response to viral infection may contribute to the enhanced pathhogenicity of Dengue viruses.

An entirely new possibility to increase the virulence of viruses is provided by genetic engineering, using viruses as molecular vectors for toxin- encoding genes. Vaccinia virus strains have been constructed in vitro, which have the genes coding for many antigens, in order to develop vaccines. Similar experiments have been made with other viruses. Therefore, the same method might possibly be used to develop viral vectors carrying genes coding for highly toxic molecules. As mass vaccination against smallpox is no longer practised, a poxvirus carrying a tox gene would be a highly efficient BW agent. It should also be possible to introduce tox genes into bacteria suitable for BW purposes.

In numerous cases toxins, such as enterotoxins and neurotoxins, are clearly responsible for the main pathological influence. The rule of toxins is also clear in such cases as anthrax, diphtheria and tetanus. Tox genes are of course sensitive to genetic manipulation and thus their expression can be increased both quantitatively and qualitatively. At least some toxin-producing pathogens possess capsule as additional virulence factors. Capsules save these pathogens from host defence mechanisms. Thus, a capsule composed of D- glutamyl polypeptide is a virulence factor of Bacillus anthracis. There exist avirulent mutant strains of Bac. anthracis which produce toxin but not the capsules. Additionally, similar to some viral products, toxins and other bacterial gene products may exert an indirect inflerence by interfering with the host's immune system and/or by inducing immunopathological reactions of the host. The immune system is also damaged by irradiation as also by toxins and poisons including CW and TW agents. Thus additive and even synergistic and / or toxins are infected by BW agents. As a result, BW agents combined with other types of weapon might become tactical warfare agents. Other significant virulence feature of some pathogenic bacteria are colonization - factor antigens which permit specific adhesion of pathogens to target cells and tissues[7]. Several colonization - factors have been dscribed that exhibit distinct spcificities for different cells and for cells of different animals. A large number genes coding for colonization factors as well as for toxins and for antibiotic resistance have been localized on extrachromosomal genetic manipulations. In addition numerous bacterial gene products, including several exoenzymes proteinases, lipases etc) cuncleases, are involved in fixing virulence. Their alteration might also lead to making bacteria to be used as BW agents more virulent *Autigenic structure.*

Natural as well as acquired defence mechanisms shielding host organisms are targeted on the antigenic structure of bacteria, viruses and other agents. By changing the antigenic structure these barriers may be overcome. Such changes can be brought about because antigenic determinants of infectious agents are coded for by specific genes, many of which have already been identified and studied. The possible efficacy of such procedures is demonstrated by the consequences of antigenic changes of influenza virses. Minor (antigenic drift') and major (antigenic shift') Changes of only two genes coding for two components of the viral envelop-haemagglutinin and neuraminidase- are responsible for the continuous natural evolution of new strains of influenza virus. Humans are more sensitive to these new strains than to previous strains against which they have developed antibodies as consequences of infections and/or vaccinations Similarly new strains of BW agents may be developed that carry new antigenic determinants against which no vaccines are available or which are under development in the target countries , whereas specific vaccines can be produced to protect the aggressor's troops and population. Detection of viruses posessing highly variable antigenic structures, such as the AIDS agent HTLV-III, renders the possibility of providing BW agents with such determinants of high plasticity HTLV-III is not considered to be a potential BW agent, although some persons have expressed concern that HTLV-III might bea 'killer virus developed on behalf of the the CIA in order to eliminate male homosexuals. These suggestions however, are useless and ridiculous HTLV-III is not a product of genetic engineering; it is a genuine virus that presumably emerged in Central Africal decades ago as a derivative of a monkey virus[10]. This apart, BW-agent designers might well hesitate to introduce analogous hypervariable antigen- determining genes into the genome of potential BW agents, because it would become very difficult, or even impossible, to develop protection for one's own forces against such agents.

Markers usually used in diagnosis

Various highly sensitive methods have been developed using modern immune techniques to detect and to identify bacteria, viruses and other infectious agents. Monoclonal antibodies, radio- immuno assays (RIA), enzyme- linked immune sorbent assays (ELISA) and other methods are mainly based on the detection of certain specific antigenic sites on the surface of living agents . The techniques just mentioned that are used to change the autigenic structure have the additional advantage that the modified organisms might become more difficult to identify and hence more difficult to be attacked by specific therapeutic means. Also stopping their further dissemination would thus become more difficult. Pathogenic bacteria are identified due to their sensitivity or resistance to bacterial viruses (bacteriophages). The corresponding pattern might also be changed by genetic manipulation. Additionally, the physical map- that is, the primary structure of the genetic material of these agents- might be change . This would come in the way of the identification of the changed agents by means of molecular diagnosis (physical mapping, restriction enzyme analysis, nucleic acid hybridization, oligonucleotide fingerprinting).[12]

Protection of the Aggressor's Forces

Genetic engineering and other modern biotechnological means provide some completely new techniqes or superior methods for the development of vaccines of high specificity. These vaccines might be applied to protect the aggressor's forces against a BW agent they are going to be using. Since the development of more and better vaccines by means of recombinant DNA technology might increase the prospects of some state choosing to use BW agents, the expert panel convened by the US Department of State said that the most significant impact of genetic engineering for BW is that 'an increased protection capability may be an inducement to use biological warfare, since the instigator has a decreased risk of being harmed by his own actions'.

Making them drug resistant

Bacteria carry genes that code for resistance to antibiotics and to other antibacterial agents. (Usually it is not possible to inhibit viruses by such drugs without damaging their host organisms. simultaneously.) These genes are located either on the bacterial chromosome or on extra- chromosomal nucleic acid molecules called plasmids or resistance transfer factors. Plasmid- located resistance genes are especially easily transferred from organism to organism, even under field conditions. Laboratory methods including genetic engineering, greatly increase the probability of resistance-gene transfer, including transfer between unrelated bacterial species. Thus, potential BW agents can be made resistant to antibiotics and to those chemotherapeutics normally used to control them, especially if such resistance is normally not developed by spontaneous mutation, by naturally occurring gene transfer, and/ or by natural selection . Also knowing which drugs are most commonly used in a certain target country, one might change the agent with respect to the drug in question , thus rendering the antibiotic ineffective.

Production and storage

In their background paper submitted to the first Review Conference of the Biological Weapons Convention, the three depositary governments describe[e] the appearance of four previously unknown and severe infectious diseases. ... Marburg disease, ebola, Lassa fever and Legionnaire's disease' After making clear' that micro-organisms responsible for these, and any other new infectious disease are embraced by the Convention' they conclude that 'on the basis of published information no nation has the current ability to use the of these diseases in biological warfare' and that 'knowledge of these agents is far below that required for fundamental assessment of suitability as biological warfare agents. Such knowledge is not likely to increase rapidly through necessary research on public health aspects'. In the meantime, however, all three viruses mentioned, Lassa Fever, Marburg and Ebola virus, have been considered by US Army scientists as among those 'putative BW agents having the highest liability or operational users[13]. This appear to be the consequence of the fact, that the formidable safety requirements for any bacteriological weapon development activity involving pathogenic agents[1]' recognized in the background paper of the depositary governments can now be reduced. First, the experience gained in following the guidelines for research involving recombinant DNA molecules (including the construction of safety laboratories poviding increased degrees of physical containment) has been very helpful in making experiments with highly pathogenic agents safer. Second, the possibility offered by genetic engineering of replicating nucleic acids (including viral genomes in bacterial host cells) greatly reduces the need for safety need to work with these viruses. The genome of Lassa virus has already been studied by physical mapping (oligonucleotide fingerprinting) and its N gene segment has been cloned and expressed in Escherichia coli. Obviously, the new methods make it feasible to develop such viruses into BW agents which can be manufactured on a larger scale.

Since the first Review Conference, AIDS is the only major new infectious disease which has been described [14]. The causative agents, a virus designted HTLV-III,LAV orARV respectively, has been isolatd and studied in detail using the safe laboratory conditions now available. Although HTLV-III is not regarded as a potential BW agents, studies of AIDS and of its caus ative agent may nervertheless be interesting for designers of BW agents. AIDS induces many severe psychoogical reactions, especially among the major risk group, and production of desired psychological effects is oe of the additional characteristics of potential BW agents, as characterized by the US army. Therefore, an agent like HTLV-III might be considered an ideal BW agent by terrorists . This the spread and development of AIDS demostrates the consequences of the introduction of a (new) agent into a population not protected by an immune barrier. In this regard a mathematical model for the global spread of influenza virus (which could be used to model the geographic spread of any pathogen including BW agents) has been created by Soviet scientists.[15] The model received some public attention because fear was expressed that it could used to forecast the geographical consequence of BW attacks.[16] While Rifkin, for instance, understood that Rvachev is concerned that the mathematical model he developed for tracing and tracking viruses could be used for military purposes' , Rvachev (1984) himself clarified in letters to various scientists that he was never expressing alarm about BW and the use to which his work might eventually be put.

Other Changes

It should also be possible to make potential BW agents more resistant to ultraviolet radiation: by changing a large number of genes known to be involved in repair mechanisms, and by making such potential agents more resistant to desiccation so as to make their possible dissemination in aerosol form more efficient. The UN Secretary- General's Committee of experts had discussed whether the high vulnerability of micro-organisms in aerosols might be reduced by encapsulating the aerosol particles in source organic compounds so as to protect them. A lot more progress has since been made in the field of micro-encapsulation. Liposomes (i.e. vesicles formed from phospholipids) and other loaded membranous vesicles have been used as efficient carriers for the introduction of infectious nucleic acids, drugs and toxins into cells and living organism s [17]. Thus, micro organisms destined to be used as BW agents might also be distributed after micro- encapsulation especially since oral applications of liposomes have now been reported. Micro-bomblets' also be developed using these techniques, which may have billions of individual BW agents. It should also be possible to set up more efficient (or even totally new) host- vector systems by developing more arthropod-borne BW systems, in addition to those already existing under natural conditions. Moreover, it should be possible to restrict potential BW agents to defined target organs or tissue by developing specific metabolic demands or new receptor-binding systems. Conversely, one might acquire the reverse by unrestricting these agents.

Recombinant DNA Research Guidelines

Soon after the new techniques of genetic engineering emerged (with their new possibilities for directed change of genetic material), fear arose over whether the new methods or their products would be covered by the Biological Weapons Convention. As early as 1974, a committee headed by Paul Bergh called by the US National Academy of Sciences so as to regared the potential risks of genetic engineering-reterred to the problems of BW agents in an early draft their final conclusions . One member of this committee, David Baltimore, told the participants of the 1975 Asilomar confrence on Recombinant DNA Research at the opening session that the new methods could conceivably lead to more effective instruments for biological warfare. he added, however that this was not an area of investigation for the Asilomar assembly . In a post- Asilomar interview he said that the public health aspect of recombinant DNA research was a more important concern because President Nixon had already dismantled the machinery or biological warfare.[22] A similar position was taken by the British Genetic Manipulation Advisory group in 1977.

Nevertheless, one of the three working panels at the Asilomar Conference on the assessment of risks with the following admonition: 'We believe that perhaps the greatest potential for biohazards involving genetic alteration of microorganisms [is] linked to possible military applications. We believe strongly that construction ofgenetically altered micro-organisms for any military purposes and would be expressly prohibited by international treaty' Following the proposals of the 1974 Berg committee[24] as well as the recommendations of the 1975 Asilomar Conference 1975),[25] the responsible agencies of various governments began to release guidelines regulating recombinant DNA research (see COGENE, 1981).

The evolution and development of these guidelines, concerning problems of BW agents, are summarized elsewhere . Here it should be mentioned only that US scientists repeatedly took action to insert into the guidelines issued by the National Institutes of Health (NIH) paragraphs explicity banning the use of genetic engineering in constrcting BW agents. They did this because the 'use of molecular cloning for the deliberate construction of biological weapons is, per se the most serious biohazard imaginable for this technology.[27] Proposals and comments regarding such an insertion into the guidelines were discussed by the Recombinant DNA Advisory Committee (RAC) (Milewski, 1982). Official representatives of the US department of Defense declared that the USA would follow the Biological Weapons Convention without reservation.

Baltimore stressed that an insertion of this ature would imply the existence of an ambiguity in the Biological Weapons Convention and that this might lead to undermining it specifically, he opined that it could lead to an erosion of the obligations by the USA to follow the Convention. He also felthat this could substantiate the suspicion that genetic engineering for the development of BW agents might be allowed. In the end, the committee resolved that; That Recombinant DNA Advisory Committee advises the Director, NIH , that the existing treaty of 1972 (the Biological Weapons Convention) involves the prohibition on the use of recombinant DNA methodology for development of microbial or other biological agents, or toxins , of kinds or in quantities that have no justifiation for prophylactic, protective or peaceful purposes.[28]

Nevertheless L. Rogers and J. Rifkin in 1985 proposed again-and obviously -that the Recombinant DNA Advisory Group Committee of the NIH establish a working subgroup whose stated purpose would be to examine potential uses of recombinant DNA technology for offensive and defensive biological weapons systems.[29] Their action was (and will be) without success because the RAC members agree that there is no reason to believe the Do d has not complied fully with the Convention and the NIH Guidelines'.[30] Most experts agree that the language of the convention also the use of genetic engineering for development of BW agents for of prohifits ensive purposes.

Latest BW Agents

Fear is sometimes expressed concerning completely new kinds of BW agent which might -at least by intentionally spurious interpretation- not be considered as biological agents' and therefore not be covered by the Biological Weapons Convention. In a discussion on patenting processes and products of genetic engineering Brenner(1982) could for see that by using both new and old methods it should be possible to speed up evolution in the test tube and go through in a few years what might have taken 10 billion years to accomplish in nature, and so produce something that is totally new'. The Soviet scholars Milstein and Semejko (1977) showed their concern that "genetic weapons" can also be qualified as half-synthetic, formed artificially... Those same "genetic weapons can studied in a broader context, could be considered a new independent type of weapon can pable of mass destruction'. However , the editor of the Buletin of the atomic scientists, in which the Mistein- semejko paper was published, noted that 'this contention directly contradicts not only the letter of the Biological Weposn Convention but also the understanding of it by the scientific community, (Editorial, 1977). Nevertheless, it appears obvious that as long as agents are able to multiply, even if they are 'totally new ', they must be defined as BW agents and are thus covered by the Biological Weapons Convention. This also holds true for infectious, self- replicating nucleic acid molecules synthesized in vitro and then assembled into micro-capsulesalso acquired through chemical synthesis. Artificial viruses might thus have been developed that are capable of multiplication and therefore must be regarded as biological agents.

Conclusions

(i) A new generation of potential biological weapons has emerged since the signing of the 1972 Biological Weapons convention. There is an important shift of interest from bacterial to viral BW agents, the latter being more difficult to diagnose and refractory to *specific therapy*. Apart from, genetic engineering and other biotechnological methods allow the development of all kinds of new and far more effective BW agents.

(ii) Nevertheless, BW agents— including viruses and infectious nucleic acids—improved or developed by ganetic engineering and other view biological techniques are covered by the prohibition on the use of CBW agents imposed by the 1925 Geneva Protocol as well as by the prohibition of the development production and stockpiling of BW and TW agents imposed by the 1972 Biological Weapons Convention.

(iii) BW agents are acquiring increasing military importance because new effective means are emerging to protect the aggressor's troops

(iv) BW agents used in combination with CW or TW agents might become transformed from strategic to tactical weapons because organinsms damaged by nuclear and / or chemical weapons are more sensitie to the action of BW agents

(v) The possibiity of a new arms race must be seriously regarded because of mutual accusations with respect to the use of genetic engineering to developnovel BW agents. Further suspicion cannot be avoided that non classified work on the development of vaccines againstBW agents might be used for clandestine construction of new BW agents because there is no barrier between defensive and offensive research in this area.

References

1. USA, 1964, p. 25 Anderson and King, 1983, p. 3.

2. (See Budiansky, 1982; Wright & Sinsheimer, 1983; Westing, 1985a; and others.

3. Shope *et al.*, 1981; Beaty *et al.*, 1981.

4. *Collett et al.*, 1985.

5. Thara *et al.*, 1985.

6. Leppla *et al.*, 1985.

7. Orskov & Orsko, 1977; Smith & Huggins, 1977.

8. Holder, 1985.

9. Cf, Kaplan & Webster, 1977.

10. Kanki *et al.*, 1985.

11. Nowinski *et al.*, 1983; Rytel, 1979.

12. cf. Echeverria *et al.*, 1982.

13. Anderson & King, 1983.

14. Curran *et al.*, 1985.

15. Belowa *et al.*, 1983; Rvachev & Longim, 1985.

16. Editorial, 1985; Anonymous, 1984b; Asinof, 1984.

17. Loyter *et al.*, 1983; Gregoriadis, 1983, 1984.

18. Maierhofer, 1985.

19. Nash *et al.*, 1967.

20. Weiss, 1979, p. 257.

21. Krimsky, 1982b, p. 106.

22. Krimsky, 1982b, p. 106.

23. Yanchinski, 1982.

24. Berg *et al.*, 1974.

25. Berg *et al.*, 1975.

26. Geissler, 1984a.

27. Noviek & Goldstein, 1982.

28. Milewski, 1982.

29. Rogers & Rifkin, 1985.

30. Milewski, 1985, p. 175.

11
Biological Weapons Control

Geneva Protocol, 1925 was the first major effort towards control of biological weapons, though there were earlier attempts to control the calamities of war like St. Petersburg Declaration of 1568 and Hague conferences of 1899 and 1907.

The early part of the portocol provides a link with those earlier developments of international humanitarian law in stating that:

Whereas the use in war of asphyxiating, poisonous or other gases, and of all analogous liquids, materials or devices, has been justly condemned by the general opinion of the civilized world; and

Whereas the prohibition of such use has been declared in Treaties to which the majority of Powers of the World are Parties; and

To the end that this prohibition shall be universally accepted as part of International Law, binding alike the conscience and the practice of nations.

The question of controlling biological (bacteriological) weapons comes up in the following 'Declaration':

That the High Contracting Parties, so far as they are not already Parties to Treaties prohibiting such use, accept this prohibition, agree to extend this prohibition to the use of bacteriological methods of warfare and agree to be bound as between themselves according to the terms of this declaration.

It is important to be clear about exactly what this declaration means. It will be seen first that the prohibition concerns use, not development nor production, of biological weapons. Secondly, it will be noted that the text refers to 'use in war' initially but nowhere does it define war. Thirdly, it will be seen that the text of the declaration ends by making it clear that the prohibitions apply to fellow parties to the agreement.

It must be remembered that the states which negotiated this protocol had recently gone through the experience of the widespread use of chemical weapons in the World War I.

Thus the undertakings in the text were diminished by reservations, made by many states, which restricted the states to which it should apply to fellow parties only. This reservation restricting application to fellow parties only was also supplemented by a further reservation that the prohibition should only apply to an enemy whose armed forces or allies followed the provisions. Thus many commentators have indicated that the protocol is best seen as a 'no-first-use' agreement amongst the parties. Regarding proliferation, the Geneva Protocol is best not regarded as an arms control or disarmament agreement. There are no restrictions, as we have seen, on the development or production of biological (or other) weapons and there are certainly no provisions in the text for any kind of verification, for instance. It was not a legal barrier to the UK developing biological weapons in the 1940s. Also, the United States only became a party to the agreement much later, in 1975. Yet, the control of biological weapons is founded on this fragile base.

International Control Regime

Winfried Lang, the Austrian diplomat who chaired the second Review Conference of the Biological Weapons Convention (BWC) in 1986, has provided a viable framework within which the convention may be discussed. As a lawyer, he pointed to the basic problem of a mismatch between the instrument of control and that which is to be controlled:

...negotiation are required to invent devices that match the static nature of law with dynamics of security perceptions... and scientific/ technological progress.

Bringing into use, his experience in international environmental law negotiations, Lang suggested that this mismatch could be dealt with successfully by the agreement of a series of legal elements over time. These elements, in effect, would ultimately add up to a regime, which he agreed could be seen as a 'network of rules, norms, and procedures that regularise behaviour and control its effects' in a particular sphere of activity. Form his experience in negotiations on environmental issues, which have been rather successful and innovative in recent times Lang drew a number of lessons in regard to the BWC. He argued that first agreements in a new area of environmental concern are frameworks only. They are followed by more detailed protocols at a later stage. He argued further that such later protocols are best made as specific as possible, but with built-in periodic review and revision to keep up with new scientific findings. He believed issues of verification to be just as significant in environmental agreements as in disarmament and arms control negotiations, but argued that the major lesson concerned the need for institutional arrangements. He opined:

.....Treaties become operational only to the extent that they are administered and serviced by intitutions. Institutions have to look into the issue of definition: is the list of substances or activities prohibited or controlled still commensurate with scientific and technical progress?....

Lang further suggests that institutions are needed, for instance, to ask similar questions concerning arrangements for verification and cooperation between rich and poor states.

Opinion of a very experienced diplomat, the crucial problem concerning the regime for controlling biological weapons is that:

..... the biological weapons regime may be qualified as an 'imperfect' regime because it lacks an international organisation for monitoring compliance and adapting legal rules to scientific and technological progress.

He suggests that, if we take this problem seriously, we shall understand the need to establish an international institution in order to help match the static law with the dynamics of security and scientific and technological change.

Currently the regime in place, in addition to the 1925 Geneva Protocol, includes the Convention on the Prohibition of the Development, Production and Stockpiling of Bacteriological (Biological) and Toxin Weapons and on Their destruction of 1972-the BWC.

The convention resulted from intense diplomatic activity in the late 1960s and early 1970s. There are three depository states: the USA, the UK and Russia (succeeding the former Soviet Union). Gradually the number of parties to the convention grew and now there are over 130 states involved and these states meet for three weeks every five years at a review conference. Lang argued that the next element in the biological weapons regime has to be seen to be the results of these reviews, as detailed out in the final documents of 1980, 1986 and 1991. A further element is the set of confidence-building measures established at the second review in 1986 and amended and improved upon at the third in 1991. It is also possible that another element may be developed as a result of the VEREX meetings following the 1991 review. It is possible, that these meetings of experts could end up in the provision of greatly enhanced verification requirements for the BWC through the mechanism of a Special Conference and further meetings leading up to the fourth review in 1996.

With that framework set out we can now discuss the BWC systematically: examining how it came about; what it includes; what are its major drawbacks; how attempts have been made to put these deficiencies right; and finally what is the current state of the treaty.

Concept of Biological Weapons Control Regime

It has been argued that the BWC was a trail-blazing agreement, the first global-level disarmament agreement designed to free the world from a class of weaponry. The convention, rather than being hailed as great success, is roundly criticised for its deficiencies and seen as an almost inevitable result of the suspicions of the Cold War period. As is often the case, the truth may lie between these two extreme positions. The BWC may have been all that could have been achieved at that time of partial detente midway through the Cold War. Whilst the regime-building to date has been largely linked to ettorts to remedy its inadequacies, that does not preclude the development of a really effective agreement on the basis of the BWC. To get to grips properly with these issues we need to understand how the BWC came into being.

The Birth

Biological weapons of mass destruction appeared on the agenda of UN bodies at intervals almost from the moment the organisation was established after the Second World War. Usually, however, chemical and biological weapons were considered together and in the context of discussions of General and Complete Disarmament. The Secretary General's report of 1967-68 indicated the beginning of a period of intense activity. After observing that chemical and biological weapons were usually overshadowed by the question of nuclear weapons, he continued:

....Nevertheless, these too are weapons of mass destruction.... In some respects they may be even more dangerous that nuclear weapons because they do not require the enormous expenditure of financial and scientific resources that are required for nuclear weapons...

As the report went on to observe, even small and poor countries could afford to manufacture such weapons cheaply. By using small facilities, such production could also be done quickly and secretly. The special UN report on chemical and biological weapons referred to earlier was prepared by a group of experts, and forwarded by the Secretary General to member states, the General Assembly, the Security Council and the then-18- nation Committee on Disarmament. Its foreword made a strong call for the conclusion of an agreement to eliminate these weapons. The United Kingdom, which had played a major role in the discussions on biological weapons control, then submitted a draft convention to deal with these systems separately form chemical weapons.

The draft was tough in a number of respects Given the many reservations lodged by parties to the Geneva Protocol, it proposed to provide weightage to the ban on use with a first article which read:

Each of the parties to the Convention undertakes, insofar as it may not already be committed in that respect under Treaties or other instruments in force prohibiting the use of chemical and biological methods of warfare, never in any circumstances.... to engage in biological methods of warfare.

In Article II (b) parties would also have undertaken:

.....not to conduct, assist or permit research aimed at production [of agents, equipment or vectors].....

This is in contrast to the elimination of references to research in the BWC.

Although a process of removing state reservations to the Geneva Protocol has recently started to reduce the saliency of the British point on use, the issue of permitted research is still important. Yet as one prominent commentator has noted, the great difficulty of verifying a ban on research was a likely reason for its eventual removal from the draft. There was initially strong opposition to the idea of keeping biological weapons in a category separate from chemical weapons, particularly from the Soviet Union and its allies. However, this position changed and the two superpowers undertook a period of intense negotiations which led to a draft convention being presented in December 1971. Many interested parties had reservations about the BWC which resulted from these bilateral negotiations. Opinions differ as to whether the superpowers were just wanting to clear the decks for more significant nuclear questions to be discussed, or whether a very cynical exercise had taken place. For what ever reason the resulting convention had many inadequacies.

The Biological Weapon Convention

In comparison to modern treaties such as those covering strategic nuclear or chemical weapons, the BWC is an extraordinarily slight document. It consists of a short preamble and just 15 articles. It was opened for signature in 1972 and became effective in 1975. The full text is set out in Appendix 1 and the provisions are summarised in Table 11.1.

Table 11.1

Summary of the Biological Weapons Convention

1. Not to develop, produce, stockpile or acquire agents, weapons etc.
2. To destroy stocks.
3. Not to transfer to or assist others.
4. To take national measures.
5. To consult and co-operate in solving problems.
6. May lodge complaint with the Security Council.
7. To provide assistance in the event of a violation.
8. No detraction from Geneva Protocol.

9. Obliged to continue negotiations on chemical weapons.
10. Co-operation for peaceful purposes.
11. Amendment.
12. Review.
13. Duration.
14. Signature, ratification, deposition.
15. Languages.

To compare, we may consider the recently agreed Chemical Weapons Convention (CWC) which has the primary objectives of destroying all chemical weapons and of stopping the proliferation and production of new ones. The long and detailed text was negotiated over a period of nine years. The organisation to take charge of the treaty will include a Conference of the States Parties, an Executive Council and a Technical Secretariat and it will have its headquarters at The Hague. A charactristic of the convention is the very careful delineation of the lists of chemicals that are to be controlled and the different means of verification that will be used. Such means involve on-site challenge inspections.

The essence of the BWC lies in Article 1 in which each party:

...undertakes never in any circumstances to develop, produce, stockpile or otherwise acquire or retain:

1. Microbial or other biological agents, or toxins whatever their origin or method of production, of types and in quantities that have no justification for prophylactic, protective or other peaceful purposes;
2. Weapons, equipment or means of delivery designed to use such agents or toxins for hostile purposes or in armed conflict.

This all sounds splendid, but, as many people have singled out, it gives no idea about what is legal or illegal. How can a judgement be made about whether some activity has no justification for peaceful purposes if no list of agents or substances which might cause worry is given and there is also no indication of what quantity of an agent or substance might be acceptable? Considerable attention has been paid to this article at the review conferences, but the basic difficulty remains today. In Article 2 the parties undertake, within nine months of the convention entering into force, to safely destroy or divert for peaceful purposes the elements banned in Article 1.

In order to stress on the lack of effective verification for the BWC, it only requires to be remarked that the Soviet Union apparently decided to raise its offensive biological weapons programme just at the time the convention came into force and continued this programme for more than a decade and a half. Under Article 3 parties undertake not to transfer to other states, nor help them in any other way to manufacture or procure , agents, toxins or weapons. As we shall see in Chapter 9, the Australia Group of countries has extended the informal co-operation that it developed concerning export controls linked to chemical weapons to the field of biological weapons. This arrangement, however, is not formally related to the BWC.

Article 4 needs parties to enact national legislation to check the banned activities from taking place in their territories. Like much else linked to the BWC, the implementation of this article by states has taken place only slowly. In Article 5 parties undertake to 'consult one another and co-operate in solving any problems which may arise with regard to the objective of, or in the application of the Conventio'. Consultation and co-operation, it is observed, 'may also be undertaken through appropriate international procedures within the framework of the United Nations.' Furthermore, in Article 6, parties which believe another party 'is acting in breach of obligations' given the right to file a complaint with the Security Council.' Other states party to the convention undertake to co-operate with any later investigation. Not surprisingly, these two articles, embodying what passes for verification provisions in the BWC, though never used have been the subject of intense discussion, and some development, at review conferences. In Article 7 parties agree to provide help to other parties which are believed by the Security Council to have 'been exposed to danger as a result of violation of the Convention'. Aritcle 8 makes clear that the BWC in no way restricts or detracts from obligations undertaken under the Geneva Protocol.

In Article 9 parties then undertake to continue negotiations towards a Chemical Weapons Convention. Those negotiations eventually led to a major treaty being agreed and implemented in the 1990s, about two decades later. Article 10 has caused considerable strain between developed and developing countries. In potential contradiction to the objective of Article 3, parties undertake:

.... to facilitate, and have the right to participate in, the fullest possible exchange of equipment, materials and scientific and technological information...

on the use of agents and toxins for peaceful purposes. It is also agreed that the convention should be implemented:

....in a manner designed to avoid hampering the economic or technological development of State Parties....

or international co-operation in peaceful purposes related to the convention. This seeming clash between Article 3 and 10 brings up the question of how to check dual-use technology from being misused, as it implies some restriction of the developing countries by the developed countries while at the same time helping them in their industrial development.

It is perhaps not as well absorbed as it should be in the West that the possibility of restriction works both ways in such issues. As Lang emphasised:

... the North-south dimension cannot be easily dismissed... Developing countries know very well that such international regimes are unlikely to work without their full participation....they demand special treatment concerning access to research and development...

As the concerns of the poorer countries have not, in their opinion, been reasonably addressed, it is not surprising that they have sometimes been less than enthusiastic supporters of some Western ideas. This significant theme runs through the remaining chapters of this book.

The subject of Article 11 is amendment of the convention. Any state party to the convention may propose amendments, but the text states:

....Amendments shall enter into force for each State Party accepting the amendments upon their acceptance by a majority of the State Parties...

A reluctance to amend arms control agreements is always there for fear of unpicking the whole of what is usually a complex set of balances but, for the BWC, an amendment risks producing a situation in which two different treaties are in operation: one for states that accept and another for those that do not accept the amendment! Under standabley, there has been a reluctance to go down this road.

The first review of the convention was mandated in Article 12. The conference was to:

....review the operation of the Convention, with a view to assuring that the purposes of the preamble and the provisions....are being realised....

It was also needed that:

....Such review shall take into account any new scientific and technological developments relevant to the Convention.

The second Review Conference was agreed by parties to the first, and so on to date. Noting only that the convention is of unlimited duration but allows for withdrawal (Article 13), that the mechanisms of signature, ratification, etc. are covered in Article 14 and treaty languages in Article 15, we look at the results of the reviews.

The Review Conferences)

The Review Conferences order the first declaration in terms of the articles of the convention. It is convenient therefore to discuss the evolution of the convention in terms of the crucial individual articles.

Article 1 : At the first Review Conference the parties reaffirmed their support for the provisions of this article and expressed the faith that it:

....has proved sufficiently comprehensive to have covered recent scientific and technological developments relevant to the convention.

This reflected the reviews of these developments presented by the three depository states and the discussions at the conference.

At the second review more concern was seen regarding new scientific and technological developments and it was though necessary to state that the conference:

...reaffirms that the undertakings given by the State Parties in Article 1 apply to all such developments.

In a second point the conference tried to deal with the possible production of toxins by new methods, holding that the convention applied to all natural or artificial agents or toxins and:

...Consequently, toxins (both proteinaceous and non-proteinaceeous) of a microbial, animal or vegetable nature and their synthetically produced analogues are covered.

These points were reaffirmed at the third Review Conference. Also, at the third review the parties tried to the requirements by stating that:

....experimentation involving open-air release of pathogens or toxins harmful to man, animals or plants that has no justification for prophylactic, protective or other peaceful purposes is inconsistent with the undertakings contained in Article 1.

Open-air testing of pathogens is, of course, major element in an offensive research programme. It should be understood also that in reference to this article the final declarations of the second and the third reviews involved expressions of grave concern over possible non-compliance with the convention by some state and over the inability of the parties to resolve these doubts.

Article 4 : The first and the second Review Conference called upon parties which had not already done so to take the necessary steps to ban and check acts in contravention of the convention in their national legislation. Parties were also exhorted to supply the necessary informantion on what had been done to the UN Department of Disarmament Affairs. The second review gave more explicit instructions on what was needed and this all was incorporated into the enhanced confidence-building measures (Declaration of legislation and regulations, and other measures) agreed at the third Review Conference.

Article 5 : The doubts about the sufficiency of the verification provisions of the BWC resurfaced at the first Review Conference, particularly from Sweden. In the end, however, only a modest advance could be agreed. This allowed that the consultation procedures:

....include, inter alia, the right of any State Party subsequently to request that a consultative meeting open to all State Parties be convened at expert level.

By the time of the second review, concerns over scientific and technological developments and over possible illegal activities had considerably gone up. Sweden had also, in 1982, unsuccessfully attempted to have a special conference called with a view to establishing 'a flexible, objective and non-discriminatory procedure' to deal with compliance issues related to the BWC. Considerable progress therefore became possible at the second review because of these pressures.

It was agreed, for instance, that the consultative meeting should be promptly convened, that it could consider any problem, suggest means in which clarification might be achieved, use technical experts and initiate international procedures through the United Nations. Lang remarked that the consultative meeting was thus more clearly defined and the former bilateral procedures more firmly transformed into a multilateral system. However, he was also critical of the fact that:

....All efforts...failed to make the Secretary-General of the United Nations the key to this machinery, the depositories (Soviet Union, UK, US) refused to relinquish their dominating position.

Still, at the third Review Conference in 1991 the procedures were again substantially elaborated. A request for a formal consultative meeting could be preceded by bilateral or other consultations, it had to be addressed to the depositories, and they were needed to convene the meeting within 60 days. The rules and costs of the meeting were defined and it was agreed that 'the Secretary-general may be kept informed' under certain conditions.

Under Article 5 the second and the third Review Conferences also elaborated a number of confidence—building measures which we shall discuss in the next section, and the third review put in place the VEREX experts' meetings that shall be taken up separately.

Article 8: The first and the second reviews strongly reaffirmed the significance of the 1925 Geneva Protocol and that the BWC in no way limited or detracted from it. Both final documents urged states not yet party to the protocol to adhere to it at the earliest possible date. The final document of the third review went beyond it and stressed:

....the importance of the withdrawal of all reservations to the 1925 Geneva Protocol related to the biological and toxin weapons Convention.

This reflected the process whereby rising number of states had removed such reservations over the period since the BWC was agreed.

Article 9: The final documents of the BWC Review Conferences undoubtedly revealed that a link was still felt to be in place between the issues of chemical and biological weapons. The first review document stated that:

....The Conference deeply regrets that such agreement-[on chemical weapons] has not yet become a reality despite the fact that eight years have already elapsed since the [BW] Convention was opened for signature.

The second and the third reviews, on the other hand, observed with satisfaction the progress being made in negotiations on the CWC. The general easing of East-West relations was clearly behind the progress made in the CWC and the BWC during this period. However, the divide between the North and the South—developed and developing—states surfaced very strongly concerning Article 10.

Article 10 : Noting the significance increasingly attached to the opinion that disarmament should assist economic and social development, the first Review Conference concluded that developed countries should raise their co-operation with developing countries in the peaceful uses of biological agents and toxins. The final document specified that:

....Such co-operation should include, inter alia, the transfer and exchange of information, training of personnel and transfer of materials and equipment on a more systematic and long-term basis.

This subject was given much more exhaustive treatment in the second review final document. Pointing to the 'increasing gap' between the developed and the developing countries in the fields of biotechnology and genetic engineering the conference called for the greater sharing of knowledge. Parties to the convention were urged to take a wide range of specific steps in order to bring this about. The link between disarmament and economic development was again stressed and it was noted in conclusion that the fulfilment of the measures recommended would 'positively strengthen' the convention. Unfortunately, even as sympathetic a commentator as Winfried Lang was forced to conclude that:

....In interpreting such understandings one should take into account that, under real life conditions, the transfer of technology takes place on the basis of commercial contracts; it cannot be organised by decrees issued by national governments....

He opined that they do not carry much weight, but they do serve to remind parties that developing countries cannot be taken for granted. At the third review this point was stressed once again. The final document referred to the increasing importance of Article 10 and the gulf between developed and developing countries. It again pointed out a wide range of measures that could help the developing countries, including new elements such as co-operation in epidemiological surveillance to improve identification of major outbreaks of disease. The document also welcomed attempts to elaborate an international programme of vaccine development. Yet even as committed a supporter of the convention as Nicholas Sims was forced to comment that all of these proposals presented:

....problems for the North, where the benefits expected from the Convention are primarily security benefits: the reduced risk of being attacked with BTW (biological and toxin weapons). From the point of view of the North. Article X is being misread....there is not true consensus.

Some recommended that the way forward was to concentrate on the prevention of disease as a co-operative activity, as it is clearly in the treaty itself (Article 10), whereas economic development is not. To a Western reader that may appear reasonable and realistic approach. However, it sits uneasily with Lang's idea of a developing treaty regime in which the final documents of the five-yearly Review Conferences are central themes, for there is no doubt that Third World states have shown their concerns over Article 10 very clearly into these documents.

While there may have been some reasons for their actions, the

Third World states revealed clearly at the third review that their co-operation is needed for progress to be made. As Sims has emphasised, the third review failed to set up any supportive institutions because some parties refused to allow a fund, which would have cost very little, to be set up. The fund would have financed a small unit in the UN Secretariat to deal with the convention's confidence-building measures. He continued:

> ...These State Parties, overwhelmingly from the Third World, had already blocked all proposals for even the most minimal form of intersessional committee; now they sought, and again with regrettable success, to prevent the creation of just two Secretariat posts, within the Geneva Branch of the Department of Disarmament Affairs.

It was no small matter for supporters of the convention because the implementation of the confidence-building measures agreed in the second and the third reviews could undoubtedly have been helped by such a small organisational initiative.

Confidence-Building Measures

The second Review Conference of the BWC was held even as the first signs of the thaw in the Cold War were seen. The successful conclusion of the Stockholm Conference, with its recognition of the role of confidence-building measures (CBMs), occurred in the same month as the review. Thus a positive atmosphere developed for the introduction of such new steps into the convention. The final document, in its section on Article 5, stated that 'mindful of the provisions of Article V and Article X' and in order to strengthen confidence in the convention and its implementation, parties had agreed to implement measures.

> ....in order to prevent or reduce the occurrence of ambiguties, doubts and suspicions, and in order to improve international co-operation in the field of peaceful bacteriological (biological) activities.

The agreed measures are summarised in Table 11.7. It is clear that, while the security implications are usually emphasised in the West, the measures clearly also refer to issues of international co-operation covered by Article 10. The Review Conference took decision that a special group of scientific and technical experts should meet in the following year (1987) to work out the details of how data would be exchanged and the system was then put in to operation.

Table 11.2
Summary of the Confidence-building Measures agreed in 1986

Measure	*Description*
1	Exchange of data on research centres and laboratories that have very high safety standards in handling biological materials that pose a high risk.
2	Exchange of information on outbreaks of disease and similar occurrences caused by toxins that appear to be different from normal.
3	Encouragement of publication of results of research directly related to the convention and promotion of the use of such knowledge for permitted purposes.
4	Active promotion of contacts between scientists engaged in research directly related to the convention, including exchanges for joint research.

But sadly, the results of this data exchange CBM exercise were extremely disappointing. Reporting on the results of the first three rounds of data exchange in 1987, 1988 and 1989, Geissler observed that 18 parties participated in the first, 23 in the second and 14 in the third. The total number of different states participating in the first three rounds was only 27, with the majority of parties to the convention refusing to do so. Geissler reported a slight improvement in the fourth round of 1990. By that time 36 states had taken part , but the majority of parties to the convention had still not participated. In both reports Geissler pointed to the disturbingly low level of participation by developing countries from the Third World. Regarding the information provided, there were also wories because it was less than complete in some cases and there were ambiguities, for example, about what was meant by the words 'directly related to the Convention' in the questions provided the foundation for the exchange. As an example, Geissler noted that although something like 70 unusual outbreaks of disease or similar outbreaks caused by toxins had occurred and should therefore have been reported by parties during the period of the information exchange but only one such outbreak was reported under the confidence-building measures. This was an occurrence of Q-fever in the West Midlands in 1989 affecting more than 100 people and was reported by the UK in 1990. Although Geissler's second report was somewhat more enthusiastic about the promotion of contacts through symposia, its general conclusion was not positive about the level and the quality of the responses.

Nevertheless, the value of CBMs in increasing confidence is well understood by various government specialists. The greater the transparency about activities in this area of biological research, at least in the short term, the fewer suspicions there are likely to be. The third Review Conference tried both to improve the previously agreed confidence-building measures and to add more. The CBMs agreed in 1991 are summarised in Table 11.3. A detailed set of forms relevant to all the measures was attached as an annex to the final document of the Review Conference. As the poor response to the first effort at CBMs in the period 1987-91 may have been partly because of states with nothing to declare failing to return the documents, a new additional initial declaration form listed each of the new measures in turn and asked, for each of them, whether there was nothing to declare or nothing new to declare.

Table 11.3
Summary of the Confidence-building Measures Agreed in 1991

Measure		*Description*
Declaration Form		Nothing to declare or Nothing new to declare
A	(1)	Exchange of data on research centres and laboratories.
	(2)	Exchange of information on national biological defence research and development programmes.
B		Exchange of information on outbreaks of infectious diseases and similar occurrence caused by toxins.
C		Encouragement of publication of results and

	promotion of use of knowledge.
D	Active promotion of contacts.
E	Declaration of legislation, regulations and other measures.
F	Declaration of past activities in offensive and/or defensive biological research and development programmes
G	Declaration of vaccine production facilities.

One aspect, an important one, of building confidence and eventually having an effective verification system for the BWC is to develop understanding of the different national patterns of activity in relevant areas of biological research. A brief review of the submission by the UK in 1992 reveals how such a picture could be built up from these enhanced CBMs.

The initial declaration form (nothing to declare or nothing new to declare for each of the measures) was left blank, indicating that a full response would be needed for each of the CBM measures.

Nine facilities were listed in form A(1). These included the Coppetts Wood Unit of the Royal Free Hospital and Medical school in Muswell Hill, London. This was said to be financed by the Department of Health, to have a laboratory isolator of 1.5 m^2 and to be 'the only comprehensive, high-containment patient management laboratory in the UK' dealing with patients having, or suspected of having, diseases such as Lassa, Ebola and Marburg fevers.

Also listed was the Chemical and Biological Defence Establishment at Porton Down in Wiltshire, recorded as wholly financed by the Ministry of Defence and having a BL3 (lesser) containment unit of 300 m^2. It was clearly stated that there was no BL4 facility. The work of the establishment was summarised as:

> Research and development into protective measures as defence against the hostile use of toxins and micro-organisms such as anthrax, tularemia, flaviviruses and arenaviruses.

This piece of information on the current National Biological Defence Research and Development Programme in the UK was highly amplified over the next 14 pages of the report. An organisational structure was described for CBDE at Porton Down. The annual budget was reportedly in the region £ 30 m, of which the biological defence element accounted for about £10 m. Extra-mural contracts to universities and industry totalled about £ 4 m, approximately one-third of which was linked to biological defence. The total numbers of personnel involved in biological defence work at Porton Down are detailed out in Table 11.4.

Table 11.4
Number of People Involved in the Biological Defence Research and Development Programme at CBDE Porton Down

Description		*Numbers*
I.	Total number	215
II.	Division of personnel	
	Civilian	210
	Military	5
III.	Division of civilians	
	Scientists	105
	Engineers	5
	Technicians	70
	Administration/support	30

The programme was put under four headings : hazard assessment; detection; protection; and medical counter measures. Here, we do not have space here to detail the whole programme but some examples may help to illustrate its nature. Under hazard assessment, recent publications had included:

...a comprehensive and authoritative review of the survival of micro-organisms, particularly bacteria, in the atmosphere and methods for their assaying and monitoring....

and:

.....a paper on the molecular biology of a model toxin, the alpha toxin of Clostridium perfringens, to facilitate the understanding of the potential hazard together with underpinning gene probe technology for detection.

Under detection, an example of a recent publication was

provided which:

....outlines the ability specifically to identify a strain of a model DNA virus (Herpes B virus) using genetic fingerprinting.

Under medical counter measures, a recent paper described:

....The use of an anti-viral drug to counter a model DNA virus (Herpes B virus).

Under current projects there, work on vaccines included:

....the development of improved vaccines for anthrax and tularemia, including the use of recombinant vaccines and the use of vaccinia virus as a multi-agent vaccine carrier.

Concerning to confidence-building measure B, specified at the third Review Conference, the recording of outbreaks of reportable infectious diseases was dominated numerically by BSE in animals, 22,607 cases of which were registered for 1991. Particular attention was paid to an outbreak of blue-eared pig disease which started Humberside and spread across the country, deviating from the normal expected pattern of disease. The disease was first recognised in North America in 1987 and arrived in continental Europe late in 1990. The agent of the disease can be spread by the airborne route and cause economic losses, through reproductive disorders in particular. Suggestions of economic sabotage were dismissed as very unlikely in causing the outbreak. Under measure C it was stressed that it was UK policy for basic research, particularly that related to the convention, to be generally unclassified.

To the extent possible without infringing national or commercial interests, applied research was also to be unclassified.

The UK had a stated nil return for measure D on promotion of contacts. Under measure E legislation was reported in concerning matters specified in Article 1 of the convention and regulations concerning the export and import of micro-organisms and toxins relevant to the convention. Finally under measure G, eight vaccine production facilities were detailed out. One of these was the Public Health Laboratory Service Vaccine Production Unit, at the Centre for Applied Microbiology and Research (CAMR), Porton Down. It was reported to be linked to anthrax and Kveim skin test antigen. Whilst all such information might previously have been obtainable by a foreign intelligence service, such a level of disclosure by parties could not help but clarify national patterns of activity for all concerned. It remains to be seen whether the data exchange lives up to expectations when it is evaluated at the fourth Review Conference in 1996. The lack of organisational back-up for the BWC leaves many observers to doubt that it will meet any success.

The BWC : Current Scenario

In the period before the third Review Conference the United Nations Institute for Disarmament Research in Geneva brought out a research report on the issues that needed to be addressed and proposals for solutions. Its two experienced authors also issued a summary of the paper and reflected on the outcome of the review shortly afterwards. Together with the latest annual review by SIPRI, these publications provide a good foundation for a current general assessment of the health of the BWC and the biological weapons control regime. In their post-conference review, Goldblat and Bernauer pointed first to the continuing need to add new parties to the convention. Despite the welcome rise in the number of states joining, they stressed the large number of states still remaining outside this agreement. Particularly worrying are the states in conflict-prone regions of the world, like the Middle East and North Africa, which have not joined the convention (they cite Algeria, Egypt, Israel, Morocco and Syria as examples).

Goldblat and Bernauer opined that the scope of the convention would remain imprecise until what was actually prohibited was spelt out clearly and it is to be hoped that the VEREX process will encourage this clarification. They remained dissatisfied with the relationship between the BWC and the 1925 Geneva Protocol, noting that in 1992 over 20 states retained reservations to the protocol. In their opinion, the Review Conference should have stated forcefully that such reservations contradict the undertakings given in the BWC never in any circumstance to procure biological or toxin weapons. They also pointed out that few states have enacted the legislative or administrative procedures required by Article 4. Following a careful review of the development of the new consultative mechanisms in Article 5, Goldblat and Bernauer recommonded that 'the competence of the consultative meeting is still not quite clear', and they were fairly pessimistic about the possibility of international economic and technological co-operation under Article 10 of the convention, viewing it 'primarily as a disarmament measure'.

The basic weakness of the BWC is its lack of any organisational underpinning between the brief five-yearly reviews. The real scale of the deficiency may be assessed from sims' analysis of what might best serve the purposes of the convention. He suggested a Committee of Oversight composed of some 20 representatives of parties to the convention, chosen with due consideration to geographical and political factors and charged with promoting the effectiveness of the convention in all its aspects, including its constructive evolution. This committee would be supported by a scientific advisory panel and a legal advisory panel. The state which held the presidency of the Review Conference would also make available a small secretariat for the Committee of Oversight and its advisory panels until the next review, when it would hand over to the next president. Unfortunately no such organisational system is in place, and, given the expenditure necessary to implement the Chemical Weapons Convention, it must be doubtful whether extra expenditure for the BWC will be easily obtained. Perhaps the best that can be hoped for is that a small sub-section of the CWC organisation will ultimately be mandated to handle verification issues associated with the BWC.

Meanwhile the 1993 yearbook of the Stockholm International Peace Research Institute thought fit to add a appendix on 'Benefits and threats of developments in biotechnology and genetic engineering' to its chapter on chemical and biological weapons. Written jointly by a former Senior Director of Research at Sweden's National Defence Research Establishment (FOA), the current head of Stockholm University's Department of Neurochemistry and Neurotoxicology, and the Director-General of FOA, this appendix is a sobering reminder of the pace of technical change in biotechnology related to the development and production of biological weapons.

References

1. Data from Appendix-1.

2. Data from Reference 10.

12

The British Experience

The British have come across terrorism many a time. To deal effectively with this, they have made some legal provisions. These provisions are far more effective than the laws prevailing in India. India can do well to learn lessons from the British experience.

In its report to the Government, the Law Commission virtually lifts entire parts of the anti-terrorism bill as they were introduced in the British House of Commons in December 1999. But that's where it ends. There's no foreground, no background, no history of why the United Kingdom has to enforce such a tough measure, or of where previous laws have failed. Perhaps that reflects on the haste with which the Law Commission made its draft bill, because Britain's anti-terrorist measures don't begin and end with the Terrorism Act of 2000.

The British experience is all the more important from the Indian context because at the core of the problems there is the Irish insurgency, akin to the Kashmir tangle which has spilled over from being a localized problem to one with international ramifications. The Irish resistance has been on for over two hundred years. The problem is essentially demographic and sectarian, with the minority Catholic community in Northern Ireland opposing direct rule from London. Like in the case of Kashmir, there is ample evidence of support from across the border. And like in the case of Kashmir, the government has made efforts to crush the terrorism rather than find a permanent political solution. In this chapter, let us try to understand British experience in tackling terrorism, homegrown and extrapolated, over the last thirty years. There have been four major terrorist campaigns since the establishment of Northern Ireland: in the 1920s, during the 1939-45 World War, between 1956 and 1962 and the present campaign which started in 1969. In 1972, following the prorogation of the Northern Ireland parliament and the imposition of direct rule from Westminster, the UK government appointed a committee under the chairmanship of eminent jurist I ord Diplock to find out what arrangements for the administration of justice in Northern Ireland could be made to effectively deal with terrorist organizations.

Diplock found that the main obstacle to dealing with terrorists in ordinary courts was the intimidation of jurors and witnesses by terrorist organisations. His main recommendations were embodied in the first real law passed by the UK specifically means terrorism, outside the purview of ordinary criminal law. It was called the Northern Ireland (Emergency Provisions) Act 1973, and under it

(a) All terrorism related offences were categorized as "scheduled offences".

(b) Trial of scheduled offences were to be conducted by a senior judge, sitting alone.

Bail in scheduled cases was to be given by the High Court and that , too, only after taking stringent precautions.

(c) Arrest without warrant was allowed and the period of detention by the police of a person suspected of being a terrorist was increased to 72 hours, from the usual 48 hours.

(d) The army was given the power to arrest and detain a suspect up to four hours.

(e) The normal onus of proof—which lies on the detaining authority -is reversed in cases involving the possession of arms and explosives

(f) Supremacy to the executive over criminal law: Detention orders can be made by the secretary of state based on information which security forces believed to be valid, whereas conviction for offences under normal criminal law is on the basis of evidence tested in court.

The NI (EP) Act is the first time that in UK statute law, terrorism has been defined as the use of violence for political motives, including the use of violence for the purpose of creating fear in the public. It's a characteristic British opinion of terrorism, which, as we've seen earlier, is embossed in the new Terrorism Act 2000 also. But in any case, going back to the chronology of events leading to that act, the NI (EP) Act was reassessed by a government committee headed by Lord Gardiner in 1974. The idea of the Gardiner Committee was not to limit the powers in the Northern Ireland Act, but expand it.

The transgression of individual rights, Gardiner argued, was but a necessary compromise citizens would have to be willing to accept, if they sought lasting peace. So he says:

"Any legislation of this kind necessitates some loss of liberty and human freedom. The powers which have evolved nevertheless represent a determination by successive British governments that such legislation will depart as little as possible from internationally agreed principles and from the traditions of British justice. The aim is to ensure both that the security forces have every assistance in their task of bringing terrorists before the courts and that the integrity of the legal system is maintained".

Was it an expression of the frustration of the British government at the time to prevent random terrorist attacks? Possibly, yes. Lord Gardiner's recommendations, are much like the Law Commission's in the sense that they are high on rhetoric and came at a time when the government was under pressure for being unable to handle the new threat. They came just after the attack on two public houses in 1974 that killed 24 people and led to the creation of an even tougher law, the Prevention of Terrorism (Temporary Provisions) Act. Under the garb of "prosecuting terrorists for criminal offences and not the political beliefs they hold" the PTA 1974 armed the executive with three major powers:

(i) The Home Secretary was given the right to "exclude" a person from the UK if convinced that the person is involved in "the commission, preparation or instigation of acts of terrorism". This power was also given to the Northern Ireland Secretary.

(ii) The Home Secretary was allowed to detain without producing in court, for up to a week if necessary, any person suspected of terrorist offences.

(iii) Organisations suspected of terrorism in Northern Ireland were to be put in a "proscribed list" in Great Britain.

These two acts —the NI (EP) Act and the PTA—for several years remained the basis of British anti-terrorist legislation. At the time of their enactment there was heartburn over how long these provisions, which were largely drawn from British Emergency legislation—should be allowed to stay on. Which is why. Justice Gardiner warned , that the country needed to remain the addictive effect of anti-terrorist measures - once introduced into the body politic it is difficult to contemplate giving them up.

Both acts were therefore to be extended time and again, the EPA every six months by both houses of parliament, and the PTA every year. Over the years, that became a ritual, review was almost non-existent. In the words of the then home secretary, Lord Jenkins, "I do not think that anyone would wish these exceptional powers to remain in force a moment longer than necessary" became irrelevant. Data reveals that between 1974 and 1999, more than 2,500 people were killed in Irish and international terrorism in the UK[1]. Statistically therefore one can make an argument that the PTA-EPA combination failed in UK because terrorism needs a political remedy, not a legal antidote.

So why did the Tony Blair government think of revising the laws that combat terrorism? Well, the centrepoint of Blair's defence of a new omnibus anti-terrorism law is that the laws have not failed; they've just been unable to adopt to the changing nature of terrorism in the UK. To justify a change in the laws, the Tony Blair government in 1996 appointed a committee under the supervision of Lord Lloyd of Berwick, to examine in detail the issue of "legislation against terrorism". The Lord Lloyd report is the bulwark of the govvernment's defence of the Terrorism Act 2000. Drawing from the report, the government says that "Experience in the last 25 years in this country and abroad has shown that terrorism methods have been, and are being , adopted by people who purse a growing range of political or more broadly ideological or religious ends".

The Blair government went to a length to explain that the new anti-terrorism act is not aimed at Northern Ireland. In fact Home Secretary Jack Straw told the House of Commons that the assumption in the existing legislation that terrorism must be either Northern

Ireland related or in certain circumstances, international, is no longer valid. But not everyone was willing to accept that argument. The opposition came not just from the opposition, but from Balir's own party. On a cold February morning in London, I asked the left leaning Rt Hon'ble Jeremy Corbyn, Labour MP from a London borough, why he so stuck his neck out against the Terrorism Act in the House of Commons. "Well I represent Islington North" Corbyn elaborated, "and I have to make sure that the large population of people of Bangladeshi and Pakistani origin in my constituency do not become innocent victims of the draconian provisions of the law. It is a question of retaining the trust of these minorities in our increasingly multi-cultural society. Somebody has to stand up for these people," he said.

And, Corbyn did stand up for his constituents. Despite his valiant efforts, his own Labour colleague, Jack Straw, pushed through the Terrorism Bill. It was expected Corbyn to be rejected by a cynical constituency, out to punish Labour for pushing through the "invasive' legislation. So when Corbyn came back to Westminster with trice as many votes as his closest rival, it could mean either of two things. First, that his voters considered that Corbyn couldn't, frankly, have done any better. Or second, that the human rights lobbies had overstated their case, that the Terrorism Act was not as bad as it had been made out to be. Lets read through the Act, therefore, in the context of previously existing acts, in India and the UK is particular, and also in other countries.

Proscription

Proscription is central to the British efforts at fighting militancy[2]. Membership of a proscribed organisation, support to a proscribed organisation (direct or indirect), even displaying an article that could "arouse reasonable suspicion[3]" in a policeman that the bearer is a terrorist, is punishable from anywhere betwen six months to ten years. So large is the scope of this particular clause of the Terrorism Act that in the UK today, even a person who attends a meeting which a member of a proscribed organisation has addressed, can be arrested[4]. Quite naturally therefore, the power to proscribe has been linked to fears that it "infringes on the rights of freedom of association and expression". This fear is reflected in the Prevention of Terrorism Ordinance 2001 as well. In its report on the bill, PUDR says Section 3.5 punishing "anyone who is a member of a terrorist gang or a terrorist organisation, which is involved in terrorist acts" is vulnerable to misuse in the absence of a definition of what a 'terrorist gang' is.

The draft bill gives one the impression that Section 3.5 is to be read separately from Section 3.1.b which has provision for anywhere between five years imprisonment to life for "being or continuing to be a member of an association declared unlawful under the Unlawful Activities (Prevention) Act 1967", or even aiding or abetting such an outfit. So what actually we have is a rather hazy and imprecise attempt at proscription, giving the impression that unlike the British law, the concept of 'targeting the group' is not the theme the Law Commission's recommendation of proscriptive powers. Instead, it's only one more way of empowering the executive. So is the power to proscribe terrorist organisations largely symbolic? Well, experts like Paul Wilkinson and Walker opine thus.

As Lord Lloyd admits in his seminal report, there have been very few convictions under Section 2 of the 1989 Act on Proscription in the UK. But however successful, proscription is one of the key features of the Act" Lloyd insists. So are there other parallels to look at? In Germany, it is an offence to take part in activities of a terrorist organisation. Under Article 129A of the German Penal Code it is illegal to form or be a member of an organisation which engages in murder or other specified criminal activities. Unlike the UK, Article 129A is the basis of almost all terrorism linked prosecutions in Germany. In Italy, too, there is a similar crime of association with "the aim of terrorism and subversion of the democratic order". But the United States probably attaches the highest importance to proscription. The new Terrorism Prevention Act in the US gives powers to the Secretary of State to designate foreign terrorist organisations. The purpose of the power is to sap a terrorist organisation of its material base, stopping routes of material replenishment and seizing its existing assets. Membership therefore of a "Designated Organisation" (DO) can lead to deportation from and denial of entry to the US.

But what of individual acts of terrorism? Well that's where the efficacy of a law that makes one dependent on proscription alone is in doubt. After all, as Lord Lloyd points out, if membership of a group whose objects include the promotion or commission of terrorist acts is acceptable as an offence, why should the same not apply to an individual terrorist working on its own? This argument is largely valid in the Indian context, where the militant groups are known to be tremendously fissile, known to frequently change their names to confuse security forces. It is to trap individual terrorists that Lord Lloyd suggested creating an offence on the "preparation of terrorisms". If the preparation is at an advanced stage, then material evidence can be used to arrest the person under existing offences, such as the terrorist act, but the idea is to pre-empt such an act. Against this backdrop, the government has taken the right decision by drawing up a list of 23 proscribed organisations. But a lot more needs to be done.

(a) A body need to be created on the lines of the British POAC (Proscribed Organisations Appeal Commission) which will have the power on the inclusion or otherwise of organisations on the PO list.

(b) Section 3.5 and 3.1.b should be merged and the Unlawful Activities (Prevention Act) of 1967 must be thoroughly revised and reviewed by a group of experts appointed by the government.

Interception of Communications.

Intercepting communications is the essential need to gather intelligence about terrorist organisations. In India, this is one area where the law needs to be amended, perhaps by introducing a provision in the Criminal Law Amendment Bill itself. The main theme behind strengthening the laws on interception to allow the government intrusive rights is to collect evidence to charge those terrorists who plan and direct terrorist activities, but are not involved in execution of the same. In the British case, the lawful interception of communication has been allowed for the last seventeen years. But like in India, the use of material gathered through interception is inadmissible as evidence in court under Section 9 of the Interception of Communications act 1985 (IOCA).

Then, what is the importance of interception ? Well, it does provide telling evidence on some occasions. In Britain alone, figures from a consultation paper prepared for parliament suggest that between 1986 and 1997, interception as a tool of investigation played a crucial part and led to :

- (a) 1,200 arrests.
- (b) seizure of nearly three tonnes of class A drugs, and 112 tonnes of other drugs, worth over $ 800 million.
- (c) seizure of 450 firearms[6].

But interception also carries with it the risk of creating a 'surveillance society'. And there are political overtones to it as well, India perhaps being the only country where a political row over 'interception' has actually led to fall of a government. Perhaps it is appropriate therefore to allow the use of intercepted material as evidence, but only in terrorism or narcotics related cases. In the case of the UK, Lord Lloyd recommends that the problematic Section 9 of the IOCA be amended so as to allow the prosecution to adduce, interpret material in cases related to national security, that is to say, cases where the warrant authorizing the interception has been issued under Section 2.2 a of the IOCA.

In fact, India is one of the few countries today where interception to gather terrorism-related information still has covert, undercover overtones. We need to change that mindset because in most countries facing similar or much lower threat perceptions, interception has become a handy tool in criminal investigation. The ethical dimension to the use of interception in investigation was addressed by the European Commission in Preston vs United Kingdom[7]. Arguing around the principle of 'equality of arms', the applicants claimed that the use in evidence of data related to communications—while intercepted data was excluded-was unfair. They said it gave the prosecution an unfair advantage in preparing their case.

The Commission did not agree, noting that Section 9 of the IOCA prevented either party from adducing evidence that could tend to indicate that interception had taken placee. The case was rejected; proving therefore that an intelligent use of the information culled through intercepts is necessary to building a case against terrorism. I don't want to go into too many other precedents at this stage, but this is not the only case where intercepted evidence has been used in criminal cases in other European countries[8]. At what level should interception be allowed? It is suggested that this should be toned down to the level of superintendents of police, commandants of military and para-military units posted in counter-insurgency roles (especially the Rashtriya Rifles in J&K) and senior officials of the Home Ministry.

A more appropriate approach is to order the interception by an investigating judge to make the entire process above board, as is the case in both France and Spain. In the US, the use of intercept material as evidence is considered as essential. In many cases, including the high profile cases involving the New York mafia, convictions otherwise unobtainable have been secured by the use of intercept material. "I put to officers of the FBI the suggestion that they were having second thoughts on the use of intercept material" Lord Lloyd writes in his report, "I could find no support for this suggestion."

Perhaps the most striking use of intercepts has been in Australia. Here, terrorism is yet to make inroads, but criminal prosecutors routinely use intercepted material to support their courtroom arguments. According to the Australian Attorney General's office, between 1993-1994 there were 664 prosecutions for offences ranging from murder to serious fraud based on intercepts, nearly 500 of these were in cases of drugs related offences. But most striking of all, as many as 87 per cent of the cases resulted in convictions. Clearly when presented with the evidence of an intercept, even tough defendants pleaded guilty. All in all, there's a strong case in India for not just amending the law for the use of intercepts routinely to intercept communication between terrorism related suspects, but also to make the use of the material gathered qualify as admissible evidence in court. It might help in nailing suspects.

Powers of Police

The central idea behind expanding the powers of arrest for the police is to increase the pre-emptive element in combating terrorism. In other words, the police are given a chance to act against suspects under surveillance instead of waiting for the surveillance to reach fruition before actually enforcing the arrest. Under ordinary criminal law in the UK (PACE) the police may arrest a person only when it has "reasonable grounds for suspecting that he has committed, or is about to commit, an offence". This is raised in the Prevention of Terrorism Act. Under the PTA, an officer can arrest a person whom he suspects guilty of certain scheduled offences, or involved in the commission preparation or instigation of Irish or international terrorism. The justification of the special power of arrest is the one universally used across the world, "including India. Namely, that or if the police had to rely on the PACE powers of arrest they would be obliged to hold back till they acquire sufficient information to link the individual with a particular offence. In some cases it becomes too late to prevent the prospective crime. Provided that public safety is an issue that is a risk neither the police nor the public can afford to take[10]. Simply put, under pre-emptive arrest.

(i) The police is given an opportunity to interview the person concerned

(ii) The police can in the meantime conduct enquiries to confirm his identity searching records and making international enquiries, if necessary

(iii) The police gets time to carry out forensic arrests and search premises if necessary

The argument against a pre-emptive power of arrest in India, on the other hand is at two levels. First, that it goes against the basic principle that a person should be liable for arrest only when he is suspected of having committed a certain crime. Second, and more importantly, that even in the UK—where the police force is much more sensitized than India's — the number of actual convictions, as a fraction of detentions continues to be very low. The figures given below are for the period 1985-1995.

Between 1985-95 action was eventually taken against just 22 per cent of the 1,547 people held by the police for Irish/International terrorism. Of this, just 66 persons or four per cent of the total arrests were actually charged under provisions of the PTA, as against thrice as many or 11 per cent under non-PTA offences. Of the 233 arrests under the category of international terrorism not even a single person was actually charged under the PTA, though 12 per cent of the arrests resulted in convictions for non-PTA offences. The power of pre-emptive arrest seems therefore to have been used quite indiscriminately by security forces in the UK. But even so, the process of scrutiny and interrogation seems to have been done more exhaustively, because only one in every four people arrested were, at most, charged under the relevant acts.

The figures for India reveal the exactly opposite. Under TADA, only one in every four cases of people arrested was dropped without framing any charges. And as many as 95 per cent of all cases ended in acquittals. Whether as a result of sheer misuse or lack of knowledge, extending a pre-emptive power of arrest in India will be counter-productive.

A way to make the police more efficient in the application of anti-terrorism laws is by introducing the threat of punishment if the letter of the law is not followed. That's what the Supreme Court stopped just short of suggesting in DK Basu vs Govt. of West Bengal[11]. The Supreme Court judgment in that case laid down an extensive drill that police personnel were asked to follow while making arrest. Among others:

(a) Police personnel making the arrest and handling the interrogation were to wear accurate visible identity tags with their designations. The details of people who conduct such investigation must be recorded in a register.

(b) The police officer shall make a memo of arrest (with details like time, grounds of arrest etc.) which will then be signed by a witness, preferably a family member of the person arrested.

(c) The arrestee shall be subjected to a medical examination by a trained doctor every 48 hours during the period of detention by an empanelled doctors

(d) The person under arrest must be given chancc to meet his lawyer during interrogation.

The idea behind it seems to be to lay down so complex a set of rules that the law enforcers are careful not to transgress it. Failure to comply with these rules, the apex court warned, would be regarded as contempt of court. The problem with judgments like the one above is the almost naive way in which they place absolute faith with the executive. At the risk of being judged for contempt, it appears the courts often pass the buck on, as it were, to the executive, so that in the event of the misuse of the law, the accountability lies elsewhere. The naivete's draft bill, which imforme police offices that the confession is also seen in the Law Commission's decision to allow confessions to policemen as admissible evidence in special courts handling terrorism related offences. How, for instance, can one explain Section 27.3 of the Law Commission's draft bill, which inform a police officer that the confession shall be recorded in an atmosphere free form threat or inducement. As any officer knows, these provisions amount to nothing. Under pressure to show results, these sections of the proposed law can be used to distort figures.

These special leeways for 'executive excess' are not unique to India. They simply assume different shapes in different countries and sometimes give the impression of having emerged almost overnight. In the United Kingdom, for example, they appear in the shape of the powers of executive internment, i.e., imprisonment without trial. In 1998, Prime Minister Tony Blair called internment a 'retrograde step'. In a lofty speech after the Omagh terrorist attack, Balir took pains to explain why he was against keeping anyone, even the most hardened terrorists, in jail without trial. "All the way through," he said,"we are trying to tackle carefully targeted measures that allow us to deal with these terrorist groups but do not provoke a backlash in other parts of the community that they undermine the right that we are trying to secure". What Blair failed to add was that the powers of internment would continue to operate in Northern Ireland, where the power of internment has been frequently misused.

The outcome is what the Americans like to call 'fishing expeditions' or "trawler operations" implying arrests conducted in order to obtaining evidence, not following evidence. This has been in practice in Northern Ireland since 1970s. In fact, the Benet Committee, which examined the use of special powers in the early Eighties found that in almost all cases, security forces use their general power of arrest for questioning under the NI (EP) Act 1978 and the PTA 1976 in preference to their power to arrest suspects for specific criminal offences.

Talking of how the government forces have used these acts, the Benet Committee report confesses thus : "We have been told by the royal Ulster Constabular that it is their policy to arrest every terrorist suspect, even if caught in the act of committing a specific offence, under the provisions of either Section 11 of the 1978 Act or Section 12 of the 1976 Act. One clear advantage to the police of doing so is to give them more time in which to carry out their investigations".

The legal requirements for a valid arrest under NI (EP) Act 1978 are far less demanding than those under ordinary criminal law. Under this act, the police officer need not specify to the defendant what the arrest is for or even have in mind any particular offence other than a suspicion — even the provision of a 'reasonable suspicion' is not required here - that the person arrested is a terrorist. Based on it, a person can be held in detention up to three days. The effect of having such flexible powers is again that a large number of arrests are found to have been unnecessary and perhaps even avoidable. Between September 1977 and August 1978 therefore, one notes that only one-third of the 2,814 people arrested under the EPA were actually charged. True, that was also accompanied by a particularly bad spell of Irish militancy. But even if we take a look at a longer time frame, the figures aren't too rosy. Between November 1974 and September 1979 therefore only 46 per cent all the of arrestees were actually charged[12]. But there's a larger story behind these figures, one that the Indian government should not overlook while attempting to spin a more stringent law. Simply put, it is that in the absence of effective judicial scrutiny, the law-enforcers generally become law-breakers. I cannot think of a more appropriate way to hammer the point across than by reeling yet another statistic.

In the make or break year of international terrorism, 1989-90, when acts of Irish militancy also reached peack its, the simple cardinal point following all arrests, allowing access to a lawyer, was denied in as many as 26 per cent of all cases. As the levels of violence got reduced so did the figures of people who had been delayed the rithe legal advice. By 1994 it was down to 7 per cent. That's the kind of situation the British experience should forewarn Indian lawmakers of.

True, anti-terrorism laws are in a sense emergency provisions, but that doesn't require an obfuscation of the legal process. In the UK, that happens under the guise of national interest. Explaining therefore why the extension of detention in terrorist cases has to be made by the executive, the British government says "decisions to authorize the detention of suspects beyond 48 hours may be, and often are, taken based on information the nature and source of which could not be leaked to a suspect or his legal advisor without serious risk to individuals helping the police or the prospect of further valuable intelligence being lost". In effect, what the British government is saying is that it cannot trust even the judicial system with 'sensitive' information. The results have already been disastrous.

But fortunately, the Indian judiciary has been spared the charge of not being trustworthy enough to vest national secrets with. But then there has never been any real need to do so, because the special courts in India under TADA have so far been laws unto themselves, leaving very little scope of review by the superior judiciary. That's where the decision to allow appeals in the High Court—not just the apex court like under TADA—is welcome. But its perhaps okay to go a step further, and scrap the special courts altogether. True, the criminal justice system in our country is notorious for inordinate delays. But is it possible, as the National Human Rights Commission has suggested, to create additional courts with fixed time frames to dispose cases linked to terrorism to handle trial?[14] Perhaps the government ought to study the NHRC's recommendation in this regard a little more in detail. After all, an anti-terrorism law is an article of public faith, and the courts have in the post—Emergency years shown a willingness to adopt a more activist human rights jurisprudence, particularly in relation to ordinary criminal law regime.[15]

Whether it is in ordering the release of prisoners detained for long periods without trial[16] or calling for a more humane sentencing policy[17] the much maligned criminal justice system has revealed itself to be eminently responsive to public concerns. If an outside limit can be put on how long a case should be allowed to drag on for, special courts can be done away with altogether. This will also have the dual effect of making peace with the human rights lobbyists who claim excessive powers have been self-conferred by the executive, but then that's neither the intention nor the primary incentive. To sum up then, let us revisit the areas of possible review parliament can consider as and when the Draft Prevention of Terrorism Bill Comes before it. So in no particular order of following priority, are a few steps the government can take:

(i) Focus in greater detail on expanding the category of proscribed organisations. Revise the list of banned organisations in the Unlawful Activities (Prevention) Act, and develop a separate appellate commission for proscribed organisations.

(ii) Allow the lawful use of interception as an investigative tool. Further, make the use of evidence collected through such interception admissible as evidence in courtrooms all over the country.

(iii) Skim powers of arrest, and shorten the period of detention without trial.

(iv) Increase and where applicable, restore the power of judicial scrutiny, scrap special courts and create more sessions courts to dispose offences related to terrorism within a fixed time frame.

There must of course be several other areas where legal experts might want the Law Commission's draft bill revised, but these are just some areas where we'll be drawing from the British experience in search for a legal remedy to tackle terrorism.

References

1. This figure was provided by the Under-secretary for state in the Home Office Lord Bassam in a House of Lords debate in December 1999.

2. Part II Clause 11 'Membership'.

3. Part II Section 13 (1) a & b.

4. Amnesty International, UK: Briefing on the Terrorism Bill www.amnesty.org/ai.nsf.index/EUR45043200.

5. Section 40.1b A Terrorist is "or has been concerned in the commission preparation or insumption of acts of terrorism."

6. Consuitation paper on the Interception of Communications in the UK, Parham Stationary Office.

7. July 2 1997.

8. Valenzuala Cotraras *vs* Spain 1998 and Lambert *vs* France 1998 are two recent examples.

9. These figures were made available to Lord Iloyd by the Security Division of the Australian AG'S office.

10. References are made from Lord Ilioyd's report.

11. 1997 CD SCC 416.

12. Lord Shackleton "Review of the operation of the PTA 1974 and 1976".

13. In Murray *vs* UK, the ECHR found that denial of access to a lawyer combined with the right to draw adverse inferences from silence under questioning, violated the detainees right under Section 6 of the ECHR.

14. NHRC Newsletter August 2000 page 3.

15. Venkat Iyer, States of Emergency: The Indian experience 1978-97.

16. Hussainara Khatoon *vs* Home Secretary of Bihar 1980 ISCC 81.

17. In Santa Singh *vs* Punjab the court noted that penal law should be used as a tool to reform and rehabilitate criminals.

13

Preventive Acts

Given below are some Acts that remained in force from time to time, in order to contain terrorism.

I

DISTURBED AREAS (SPECIAL COURTS ACT), 1976

An Act to provide for the speedy trial of certain offences in certain areas

1. **Short title, extent and commencement-** (i) This Act may be called the Disturbed Areas (Special Courts) Act, 1976.

(ii) It extends to the whole of India except the State of Jammu and Kashmir.

(iii) It shall come into force on such date as the Central Government may, by notification in the Official Gazette, appoint and different dates may be appointed for different States or for different Parts thereof.

2. **Definitions-** In this Act, unless the context otherwise requires,-

(a) "Code" means the Code of Criminal Procedure, 1973; (2 of 1974)

(b) "disturbed area" means an area declared as a disturbed area under section 3;

(c) period of disturbance. in relation to a disturbed area, means the period during which it is to be a disturbed area for the purposes of section3;

(d) "Scheduled offence" means an offence specified in the Schedule being an offence forming part or arising out of, or connected with, any such disturbance as is referred to in section 3;

(e) "Special Court" means a Special Court constituted under section 4;

(f) Words and expressions used but not defined in this Act, and defined in the Code shall have the meanings respectively assigned to them in the Code.

3. Declaration of an Area as Disturbed Area-(1) Where a State Government is satisfied that-(i) there was, or (ii) there is, in any area within a State extensive disturbance of the public peace and tranquillity, by reason of differences or disputes between members of different religious, racial, language or regional groups or castes or
4. 15-8-1976: Vide Notification S.O. 549(E), dt. 13-8-1976.
communities, it may, by notification in the Official Gazette, declare such area to be a disturbed area.

(2) A notification issued under sub-section (1) in respect of any area shall specify the period during which the area shall, for the purposes of this section, be a disturbed area and where the State Government is satisfied that there was such disturbance of public peace and tranquillity as is referred to in sub-section (1) in that area from any date prior to the issue of such notification, the period specified in the notification may commence from that date: Provided that - (a) no period commencing from a date earlier than three months before the date of publication of the notification shall be specified therein; and (b) so much of the period specified in such notification as is subsequent to the date of publication of the notification shall not, in the first instance, exceed three months but the State Government may amend such notification to extend such period from time to time by any period not exceeding three months at any one time if in the opinion of the State Government there continues to be in such area such disturbance of public peace and tranquillity as is referred to in sub-section (1): Provided further that where the State Government is satisfied that there is no longer such disturbance of public peace and tranquillity as is referred to in sub-section (1) in such area, it shall amend the notification issued under that sub-section in respect of that area to limit the period specified therein

(whether originally or by amendment under the preceding proviso) accordingly.

4. **Constitution of Special Courts-**(1) The State Government may, for the purpose of providing speedy trial of scheduled offences committed in disturbed areas, by notification in the Official Gazette, constitute as many Special Courts as may be necessary in or in relation to such disturbed area or area as may be specified in the notification.

(2) A Special Court shall consist of a single judge who shall be appointed by the High Court upon a request made by the State Government.

Explanation- In this sub-section, the worked "appoint" shall have the meaning given to it in the Explanation to section 9 of the Code.

(3) A person shall not be qualified for appointment as a judge of a Special Court unless-(a) he is qualified for appointment as a judge of a High Court, or (b) he has, for period of not less than one year, been a Sessions Judge or an Additional Sessions Judge.

(4) Notwithstanding anything contained in sub-section (3), a person shall not be eligible for being appointed as, and for being, a Judge of a Special Court in any State after he has attained the age at which Sessions Judges in that State have to retire from service.

5. **Jurisdiction of Special Courts-** (1) Notwithstanding anything contained in the Code or any other law, a scheduled offence committed in any disturbed area at any time during the period during which it is a disturbed area shall be triable, whether during or after such period, only by the Special Court constituted in or in relation to the disturbed area in which the offence has been committed.

(2) When trying any scheduled offence, a Special court may also try any offence other than the scheduled offence with which the accused may, under the Code, be charged at the same trial if the offence is connected with the scheduled offence.

6. **Procedure and Powers of Special Courts -** (1) Every scheduled offence shall be cognizable.

(2) A Special Court may take cognizance of any scheduled

offence - (a) where under the Code such offence is an offence triable exclusively by a Court of Session, upon its being committed to it under section 209 of the Code as if the Special Court were a Court of Session; (b) in any other case, upon a police report of the facts together with a certificate from the public prosecutor to the effect that the offence is triable exclusively by the Special Court.

(3) Where a scheduled offence is an offence triable exclusively by a Court of Session under the Code, a Special Court shall have all the powers of a Court of Session and shall try such offence as if it were a Court of Session, so far as may be in accordance with the procedure prescribed in the Code for trial before a Court of Session.

(4) Where a scheduled offence is an offence which is punishable with imprisonment for a term exceeding three years but which, according to the provisions of the Code, is not an offence triable exclusively by a Court of Session, a Special Court may on taking cognizance of the offences perform the functions of a Magistrate under section 207 of the Code and thereafter try such offence so far as may be in accordance with the procedure prescribed in the Code for trial before a Court of Session as if the Special Court were a Court of Session and the case had been committed to it for trial under the provisions of the Code.

(5) Where a scheduled offence is punishable with imprisonment for a term not exceeding three years or with fine or with both, a Special. Court may, notwithstanding anything contained in sub-section (1) of section 260 or section 262 of the Code, try the offence in a summary way in accordance with the procedure prescribed in the Code and the provisions of sections 263 to 265 of the Code, shall so far as may be, apply to such trial: Provided that when, in the course of a summary trial under this sub-section, it appears to the Special Court that the nature of the case is such that it is-undesirable to try it summarily, the Special Court shall recall any witnesses who may have been examined and proceed to rehear the case in the manner provided by the provisions of the Code for the trial of such offence and the said provisions shall apply to and in relation to a Special Court as they apply to and in relation to a Magistrate: Provided further that in the case of any conviction in a summary trial under this section, it shall be lawful for a Special Court to pass a sentence of imprisonment for a term not exceeding two years.

(6) A Special Court may, with a view to obtaining the evidence of any person suspected to have been directly or indirectly concerned in, or privy to, an offence, tender a pardon to such person on condition of his making a full and true disclosure of the whole circumstances within his knowledge relating to the offence and to every other person concerned whether as principal or abettor in the commission thereof and any pardon so tendered shall, for the purposes of section 308 of the Code, be deemed to have been tendered under section 307 thereof.

7. **Power to Transfer Cases to Regular Court-**Where, after taking cognizance of any offence, a Special Court is of opinion that the offence is not a scheduled offence, it shall, notwithstanding that it has no jurisdiction to try the case, transfer the case for trial, to any court having jurisdiction under the Code and the court to which the case is transferred may proceed with the case as if it had taken cognizance of the offence.

8. **Appeal and Revision-** The High Court may exercise, so far as they may be applicable, all the powers conferred by chapters XXIX and XXX of the Code on a High Court, as if a Special Court is a Court of Session trying cases within the local limits of the jurisdiction of the High Court.

9. **Overriding Effect of Act-**(1) The provisions of this Act shall have effect notwithstanding anything contained in the Code or any other law, but save as expressly provided in this Act, the provisions of the Code shall, insofar as they are not inconsistent with the provisions of this Act apply to the proceedings before a Special Court; and for the purposes of the said provisions of the Code, the Special Court shall be deemed to be a Court of Session and the person a prosecution before Special Court shall be deemed to be a public prosecutor.

(2) In particular and without prejudice to the generality of the provisions contained in sub-section (1), the provisions of sections 326 and 475 of the Code shall, so far as may be, apply to the proceedings before a Special Court, and for this purpose references in those provisions to a Magistrate shall be construed as references to the Special Court.

10. **Savings-**(1) Nothing in this Act shall affect the jurisdiction

exercisable by, or the procedure applicable to, any court or other authority under any law relating to the naval, military or air forces or any other armed forces of the Union.

(2) For the removal of doubts, it is hereby declared that for the purposes of any such law as is referred to in sub-section (1), a Special Court shall be deemed to be a court of ordinary criminal Justice.

THE SCHEDULE

[See section 2 (d)]

1. Offences under the following provisions of the Indian Penal Code:

945 of 1860)

Section 120B;

Sections 143 to 145, 147, 148, 151 to 155, 157, 158 and 160;

Sections 182, 183, 186 to 190;

Sections 193 to 195, 199, 201 to 203, 211 to 214, 216, 216A and 225

Sections 295 to 298;

sections 302, 303, 304, 307, 308, 323 to 335, 341 to 348, 352 to 358, 363 to 369 and 376;

Sections 379, 380, 382, 384 to 387, 392 to 399, 402, 411, 412, 426, 427, 431, 435, 436, 440, 447 to 462;

Sections 504 to 506 and 509.

2. Offences under the following provisions of the Arms Act, 1959: (54 of 1959) Sections 25 to 30.

3. Offences under the following provisions of the Indian Explosives Atc, 1884:- (of 1884) Sections 6 (3) and 8 (2).

II

THE NATIONAL SECURITY ACT, 1980

Enactment Date: [27th December, 1980]

1. **Act Objective-** An Act to provide for preventive detention in certain cases and for matters connected therewith. BE it enacted by Parliament in the Thirty-first Year of the Republic of India as follows:

2. **Definitions-** In this Act, unless the context otherwise requires,-

(a) "appropriate Government" means, as respects a detention order made by the Central Government or a person detained under such order, the Central Government, and as respects a detention order made by a State Goveronment or by an officer subordinate to a State Govenment or as respects a person detained under such order, the State Government;

(b) "detention order" means an order made under section 3;

(c) "foreigner" has the same meaning as in the Foreigners Act, 1946 (31 of 1946);

(d) "person" includes a foreigner;

(e) "State Government ", in relation to a Union territory, means the administrator thereof.

3. **Power to Make Orders Detaining Certain Persons-** (1) The Central Government or the State Government may,- (a) if satisfied with respect to any person that with a view to preventing him from acting in any manner prejudicial to the defence of India, the relations of India with foreign powers, or the security of India, or (b) if satisfied with respect to any foreigner that with a view to regulating his continued presence in India or with a view to making arrangements for his expulsion from India, it is necessary so to do, make an order directing that such person be detained.

(2) The Central Government or the State Government may, if satisfied with respect to any person that with a view to preventing him from acting in any manner prejudicial to the security of the State or from acting in any manner prejudicial to the maintenance of Public

order or from acting in any manner prejudicial to the maintenance of supplies and services essential to the community it is necessary so to do, make an order directing that such person be detained.

Explanation- For the purposes of this sub-section, "acting in any manner prejudicial to the maintenance of supplies and services essential to the community" does not include "acting in any manner prejudicial to the maintenance of supplies of commodities essential to the community" as defined in the Explanation to sub-section (1) of section 3 of the Prevention of Black-marketing and Maintenance of Supplies of Essential Commodities Act, 1980 (7 of 1980), and accordingly, no order of detention may be made under that Act on any ground on which an order of detention may be made under that Act.

(3) If, having regard to the circumstances prevailing or likely to prevail in any area within the local limits of the jurisdiction of a District Magistrate or a Commissioner of Police, the State Government is satisfied that it is necessary so to do, it may, by order in writing, direct, that during such period as may be specified in the order, such District Magistrate or Commissioner of Police may also, if satisfied as provided in sub-section (2), exercise the powers conferred by the said sub-section: Provided that the period specified in an order made by the State Government under this sub-section shall not, in the first instance, exceed three months, but the State Government may, if satisfied as aforesaid that it is necessary so to do, amend such order to extend such period from time to time by any period not exceeding three months at any one time.

(4) When any order is made under this section by an officer mentioned in sub-section (3), he shall forthwith report the fact to the State Government to which he is subordinate together with the grounds on which the order has been made and such other particulars as, in his opinion, have a bearing on the matter, and no such order shall remain in force for more than twelve days after the making thereof unless, in the meantime, it has been approved by the State Government: Provided that where under setion 8 the grounds of detention are communicated by the officer making the order after

five days but not later than ten days from the date of detention, this sub-section shall apply subject to the modification that, for the words "twelve days", the words "fifteen days" shall be substituted.

(5) When any order is made or approved by the State Government under this section, the state Government shall, within seven days, report the fact to the Central Government together with the grounds on which the order has been made and susch other particulars as, in the opinion of the State Government, have a bearing on the necessity for the order.

4. **Execution of Detention Orders-**A detention order may be executed at any place in India in the manner provided for the execution of warrants of arrest under the Code of Criminal Procedure, 1973 (2 of 1974).

5. **Power to Regulate Place and Conditions of Detention**- Every person in respect of whom a detention order has been made shall be liable—(a) to be detained in such place and under such conditions, (b) including conditions as to maintenance, discipline and punishment for breaches of discipline, as the appropriate Government may, by general or special order, specify; and (c) to be removed from one place of detention to another place of detention, whether within the same State or in another State, by order of the appropriate Government: Provided that no order shall be made by a State Government under clause (d) for the removal of a person from one State to another State except with the consent of the Government of that other State.

6. **Detention Orders not to be Invalid or Inoperative on Certain Grounds—** No detention order shall be invalid or inoperative merely by reason—(a) that the person to be detained thereunder is outside the limits of the territorial jurisdiction of the Government or officer making the order, or (b) that the place of detention of such person is outside the said limits.

7. **Powers in Relation to Absconding Persons-** (1) If the Central Government or the State Government or an officer mentioned in sub-section (3) of section 3, as the case may be, has reason to believe that

a person in respect of whom a detention order has been made has absconded or is concealing himself so that the order cannot be executed, that Government or officer may—(a) make a report in writing of the fact to a Metropolitan Magistrate or a Judicial Magistrate of the first class having jurisdiction in the place where the said person ordinarily resides; (b) by order notified in the Official Gazette direct the said person to appear before such officer, at such place and within such period as may be specified in the order.

(2) Upon the making of a report against any person under clause (a) of sub-section (1), the provisions of sections 82, 83, 84 and 85 of the Code of Criminal Procedure, 1973 (2 of 1974), shall apply in respect of such person and his property as if the detention order made against him were a warrant issued by the Magistrate.

(3) If any person fails to comply with an order issued under clause (b) of sub-section (1), he shall, unless he proves that it was not possible for him to comply therewith and that he had, within the period specified in the order, informed the officer mentioned in the order of the reason which rendered compliance therewith impossible and of his whereabouts, be punishable with imprisonment for a term which may extend to one year, or with fine, or with both.

(4) Notwithstanding anythin contained in the Code of Criminal Procedure, 1973 (2 of 1974), every offence under sub-section (3) shall be cognizable.

8. **Grounds of Order of Detention to be Disclosed to Persons Affected by the Order**-(1) When a person is detained in pursuance of a detention order, the authority making the order shall, as soon as may be, but ordinarily not later than five days and in exceptional circumstances and for reasons to be recorded in writing, not later than ten days from the date of detention, communicate to him the grounds on which the order has been made and shall afford him the earliest opportunity of making a representation against the order to the appropriate Government.

(2) Nothing in sub-section (1) shall require the authority to disclose facts which it considers to be against the public interest to

disclose.

9. **Constitution of Advisory Boards** - (1) The Central Government and each State Government shall, whenever necessary, constitute one or more Advisory Boards for the purposes of this Act.

(2) Every such Board shall consist of three persons who are, or have been, or are qualified to be appointed as, Judges of a High Court, and such persons shall be appointed by the appropriate Government.

(3) The appropriate Government shall appoint one of the members of the Advisory Board who is, or has been, a Judge of a High Court to be its Chairman, and in the case of a Union territory, the appointment to the Advisory Board of any person who is a Judge of the High Court of a State shall be with the previous approval of the State Government concerned.

10. **Reference to Advisory Boards**- Save as otherwise expressly provided in this Act, in every case where a detention order has been made under this Act, the appropriate Government shall, within three weeks from the date of detention of a person under the order, place before the Advisory Board constituted by it under section 9, the grounds on which the order has been made and the representation, if any, made by the person affected by the order, and in case where the order has been made by an officer mentioned in sub-section (3) of section 3, also the report by such officer under sub-section(4) of that section.

11. **Procedure of Advisory Boards** - (1) The Advisory Board shall, after considering the materials placed before it and, after calling for such further information as it may deem necessary from the appropriate Government or from any person called for the purpose through the appropriate Government or from the person concerned, and if, in any particular case, it considers it essential so to do or if the person concerned desires to be heard, after hearing him in person, submit its report to the appropriate Government within seven weeks from the date of detention of the person concerned.

(2) The report of the Advisory Board shall specify in a separate

part thereof the opinion of the Advisory Board as to whether or no there is sufficient cause for the detention of the person concerned.

(3) When there is a difference of opinion among the members forming the Advisory Board, the opinion of the majority of such members shall be deemed to be the opinion of the Board.

(4) Nothing in this section shall entitle any person against whom a detention order has been made to appear by any legal practitioner in any matter connected with the reference to the Advisory Board; and the proceedings of the Advisory Board and its report, excepting that part of the report in which the opinion of the Advisory Board is specified, shall be confidential.

12. **Action upon the Report of the Advisory Board-** (1) In any case where the Advisory Board has reported that there is, in its opinion, sufficient cause for the detention of a person, the appropriate Government may confirm the detention order and continue the detention of the person concerned for such period as it thinks fit.

(2) In any case where the Advisory Board has reported that there is, in its opinion , no sufficient cause for the detention of a person, the appropriate Government shall revoke the detention order and cause the person concerned to be released forthwith.

13. **Maximum Period of Detention-** The maximum period for which any person may be detained in pursuance of any detention order which has been confirmed under section 12 shall be twelve months from the date of detention: Provided that nothing contained in this section shall affect the power of the appropriate Government to revoke or modify the detention order at any earlier time.

14. **Revocation of Detention Orders** - (1) Without prejudice to the provisions of section 21 of the General Clauses Act, 1897 (10 of 1897), a detention order may, at any time, be revoked or modified,— (a) notwithstanding that the order has been made by an officer mentioned in sub-section (3) of section 3, by the State Government to which that officer is subordinate or by the Central Government; (b) notwithstanding that the order has been made by a State Government, by the Central Government.

15. **Temporary Release of Persons Detainea** - (1) the appropriate Government may, at any time, direct that any person detained in pursuance of a detention order may be released for any specified period either without conditions or upon such conditions specified in the direction as that person accepts, and may, at any time, cancel his release.

(2) In directing te release of any person under sub-section (1), the appropriate Government may require him to enter into a bond with or without sureties for the due observance of the conditions specified in the direction.

(3) Any person released under sub-section (1) shall surrender himself at the time and place, and to the authority, specified in the order directing his release or cancelling his release, as the case may be.

(4) If any person fails without sufficient cause to surrender himself in the manner specified in sub-section (3), he shall be punishable with imprisonment for a term which may extend to two years, or with fine, or with both.

(5) If any person released under sub-section (1) fails to fulfil any of the conditions imposed upon him under the said sub-section or in the bond entered into by him, the bond shall be declared to be forfeited and any person bound thereby shall be liable to pay the penalty thereof.

16. **Protection of Action Taken in Good Faith**- No suit or other legal proceeding shall lie against the Central Government or a State Government, and no suit, prosecution or other legal proceeding shall lie against any person, for anything in good faith done or intended to be done in pursuance of this Act.

17. **Act not to have Effect with Respect to Detentions under State Laws**-(1) Nothing in this Act shall apply or have any effect with respect to orders of detention, made under any State law, which are in force immediately before the commencement of the National Security Ordinance, 1980 (11 of 1980), and accordingly every person in respect of whom an order of detention made under any State law

is in force immediately before such commencement, shall be governed with respect to such detention by the provisions of such State law or where the State law under which such order of detention is made is an Ordinance (hereinafter referred to as the State Ordinance) promulgated by the Governor of that State and the State Ordinance has been replaced —(i) before such commencement, by an enactment passed by the Legislature of that State, by such enactment; or (ii) after such commencement, by an enactment which is passed by the Legislature of that State and the application of which is confined to orders of detention made before such commencement under the State Ordinance, by such enactment, as if this Act had not been enacted.

(2) Nothing in this section shall be deemed to bar the making under section 3, of a detention order against any person referred to in sub-section (1) after the detention order in force in respect of him as aforesaid immediately before the commencement of the National Security Ordinance, 1980 (11 of 1980), ceases to have effect for any reason whatsoever.

Explanation- For the purposes of this section, "State law" means any law providing for preventive detention on all or any of the grounds on which an order of detention may be made under sub-section (2) of section 3 and in force in any State immediately before the commencement of the said Ordinance.

18. **Repeal and Saving** - (1) The National Security Ordinance, 1980 (11 of 1980), is hereby repealed.

(2) Notwithstanding such repeal, anything done or any action taken under the said Ordinance shall be deemed to have been done or taken under the corresponding provisions of this Act, as if this Act had come into force on the 23rd day of September, 1980, and, in particular, any reference made under section 10 of the said Ordinance and pending before any Advisory Board immediately before the date on which this Act receives the assent of the President may continue to be dealt with by that Board after that date as if such Board had been constituted under section 9 of this Act.

III

TERRORIST AFFECTED AREAS (SPECIAL COURTS) ACT, 1984

1 **Objective-** An Act to provide for the speedy trial of certain offences in terrorist affected areas and for matters connected threwith. BE it enacted by Parliament in the Thirty-fifth Year of the Republic of India as follows:-

2. **Definitions-** (1) In this Act, unless the context otherwise requires,-

(a) "Code" means the Code of Criminal Procedure, 1973 (2 of 1974);

(b) "High Court", in relation to a Special Court, means the High Court within the territoral limits of whose jurisdiction such Special Court is proposed to be, or is, established;

(c) "judicial zone" means a judicial zone constituted under sub-section (1) of section 3;

(d) " Notification" means a notification published in the Official Gazette;

(e) "Public Prosecutor" means a Public Prosecutor or an Additional Public Prosecutor or a Special Public Prosecutor appointed under section 9 and includes any person acting under the directions of the Public Prosecutor;

(f) "Scheduled offence" means an offence specified in the Schedule being an offence committed in a terrorist affected area;

(g) "Special Court" means a Special Court or an Additional Special Court established under section 4;

(h) "Terrorist" means a person who indulges in wanton killing of persons or in violence or in the disruption of services or means of communications essential to the community or in damaging property with a view to- (i) putting the public or any section of the public in fear; or (ii) affecting adversely the harmony between different religious, racial, language or regional groups or castes or communities; or (iii) coercing or overawing the Government established by law; or (iv) endangering the sovereignty and integrity of India;

(i) "terrorist affected area" means an area declared as a terrorist affected area under section 3;

(j) words and expressions used but not defined in this Act and defined in the Code shall have the meanings respectively assigned to them in the Code.

(2) Any reference in this Act to the Code or any provision thereof shall, in relation to an area in which the Code or such provision is not in force, be construed as a reference to the corresponding law or the relevant provision of the corresponding law, if any, in force in that area.

3. **Declaration of Terrorist Affected Area** - (1) If the Central Government is of the opinion that offences of the nature specified in the Schedule are being committed in any area by terrorists on such a scale and in such a manner that it is expedient for the purpose of coping with the activities of such terrorists to have recourse to the provisions of this Act, it may, by notification, - (a) declare such area to be a terrorist affected area; and (b) constitute such area into a single judicial zone or into as many judicial zones as it may deem fit.

(2) A notification issued under sub-section (1) in respect of an area shall specify the period during which the area shall, for the purposes of this Act, be a terrorist affected area, and where the Central Government is of the opinion that terrorists had been committing in that area, from a date earlier than the date of issue of the notification, offences of the nature specified in the Schedule on such a scale and in such a manner that it is expendient to commence the period specified in the notification from such earlier date, the period specified in the notification may commence from that date: Provided that - (a) no period commencing from a date earlier than six months from the date of publication of the notification shall be specified therein; and (b) so much of the period specified in such notification as is subsequent to the date of publication of the notification shall not, in the first instance, exceed six months, but the Central Government may, by notification, extend such period from time to time by any period not exceeding six months at any one time, if the Central Government, having regard to the activities of terrorists in

such area, is of the opinion that it is expedient so to do.

Explanation- For the avoidance of doubts, it is hereby declared that the period specified in a notification issued under this section may fommence from a date earlier than the date of commencement of this Act.

4. **Establishment of Special Courts**- (1) For the purpose of providing for speedy trial of scheduled offences committed in a judicial zone, the Central Government may establish, by notification, a Special Court in relation to such judicial zone - (a) within such judicial zone; or (b) if the Central Government having regard to the exigencies of the situation in such judicial zone considers it expedient so to do, at any place outside such judiscial zone considers it expedient so to do, at any place outside such judicial zone but within the State in which such judicial zone is situated.

(2) Notwithstanding anything contained in sub-section (1), if, having regard to the exigencies of the situation prevailing in a State, the State Government is of the opinion that it is expedient to establish in relation to a judicial zone, or in relation to two or more judicial zones, in the State, an Additional Special Court outside the State, for the trial of such scheduled offences committed in the judicial zone or judicial zones, the trial whereof within the State - (a) is not likely to be fair or impartial or completed with utmost dispatch; or (b) is not likely to be feasible without occasioning a breach of peace or grave risk to the safety of the accused, the witnesses, the Public Prosecutor and the Judge or any of them; or (c) is not otherwise in the interests of justice, the State Government may request the Gentral Government to establish in relation to such judicial zone or judicial zones an Additional Special Court outside the State and thereupon the Central Government may, after taking into account the information furnished by the State Government and making such inquiry, if any, as it may deem fit, establish, by notification, such Additional Special Court at such place outside the State as may be specified in the notification.

5. **Composition and Appointment of Judges of Special Courts**- (a) A Special Court shall be presided over by a judge to be appointed by the Central Government with the concurrence of the Chief Justice of the High Court.

(2) The Central Government may also appoint, with the concurrence of the Chief Justice of the High Court, Additional Judges to exercise jurisdiction in a Special Court.

(3) A person shall not be qualified for appointment as a Judge or an Additional Judge of a Special Court unless he is immediately before such appointment a Sessions Judge or an Additional Judge in any State.

(4) For the removal of doubts, it is hereby provided that the attainment by a person, appointed as a Judge or an Additional Judge of a Special Court, of age of superannuation under the rules applicable to him in the Service to which he belongs, shall not affect his continuance as such Judge or Additional Judge.

(5) Where any Additional Judge or Additional Judges is, or are, appointed in a Special Court, the Judge of the Special Court may, from time to time, by general or special order, in writing, provide for the distribution of business of the Special Court among himself and the Additional Judge or Additional Judges and also for the disposal of urgent business in the event of his absence or the absence of any Additional Judge.

6. **Place of Sitting** - A Special Court may, if it considers it expedient or desirable so to do, sit for any of its proceedings at any place, other than the ordinary place of its sitting, in the State in which it is established: Provided that if the Public Prosecutor certifies to the Special Court that it is in his opinion necessary for the protection of the accused or any witness or otherwise expedient in the interests of justice that the whole or any part of the trial should be held at some place other than the ordinary place of its sitting, the Special Court may, after hearing the accused, make an order to that effect unless, for reasons to be recorded in writing, the Special Court thinks fit to make any other order.

7. **Jurisdiction of Special Court**-(1)Notwithstanding anything contained in the Code or in any other law, a scheduled offence committed in a judicial zone in a State at any time during the period during which such judicial zone is, or is part of, a terrorist affected area shall be triable, whether during or after the expiry of such period, only by the Special Court established for such judicial zone in the State: Provided that where the period specified under sub-secton (2)

of section 3 as the period during which an area declared by notification under sub-section (1) of that section to be a terrorist affected area commences from a date earlier than the date on which such notification is issued, then-(a) nothing in the foregoing provisions of this sub-section shall apply to a scheduled offence committed in such area in which the whole of the evidence for the prosecution has been taken before the date of issue of such notification; and (b) all other cases involving scheduled offences committed in such area and pending before any court immediately before the date of issue of such notification shall stand transferred to the Special Court having jurisdiction under this section and the Special Court to which such proceedings stand transferred shall proceed with such cases from the stage at which they were pending at that time.

(2) Notwithstandin anything contained in sub-section (1), if in respect of a case involving a scheduled offence committed in any judicial zone in a State, the Central Government, having regard to the provisions of sub-section (2) of section 4 and the facts and circumstances of the case and all other relevant factors, is of the opinion that it is expedient that such offence should be tried by the Additional Special Court established in relation to such judicial zone outside the State, the Central Government may make a declaration to that effect: Provided that no such declaration shall bc made unless the State Government has forwarded to the Central Government a report in writing containing a request for making of such declaration.

Explanation- Where an Additional Special Court is established in relation to two or more judicial zones, such Additional Special Court shall be deemed, for the purposes of this sub-section, to have been established in relation to each of such judicial zones.

(3) A declaration made under sub-section (2) shall not be called in question in any court.

(4) Where any declaration is made in respect of any offence committed in a judicial zone in a State, any prosecution in respect of such offence shall be instituted only in the Additional Special Court established in relation to such judicial zone outside the State, and if any prosecution in respect of such offence is pending immediately before such declaration in any other court, the same shall stand

transferred to such Additional Special Court and such Additional Special Court shall proceed with such case from the stage at which it was pending at that time.

8. **Powers of Special Courts with Respect to other Offences-** (1) When trying any scheduled offence, a Special Court may also try any offence other than the scheduled offence with whch the accused may, under the Code, be charged at the same trial if the offence is connected with the scheduled offence.

(2) If, in the course of any trial under this Act, it is found that the accused person has committed any offence, the Special Court may, whether such offence is or is not a scheduled offence, convict such person of such offence and pass any sentence authorised by law for the punishment thereof.

9. **Public Prosecutors** - (1) For every Special Court, the Central Government shall appoint a person to be the Public Prosecutor and may appoint one or more persons to be the Additional Public Prosecutor or Additional Public Prosecutors: Provided that the Central Government may also appoint for any case or class of cases a Special Public Prosecutor.

(2) A person shall be eligible to be appointed as a Public Prosecutor or an Additional Public Prosecutor or a Special Public Prosecutor under this section only if he has been in practice as an Advocate for not less than seven years or has held any post, for a period of not less than seven years, under the Union or a State, requiring special knowledge of law.

(3) Every person appointed as a Public Prosecutor or an Additional Public Prosecutor or a Special Public Prosecutor under this section shall be deemed to be a Public Prosecutor within the meaning of clause (u) of section 2 of the Code, and the provisions of the Code shall have effect accordingly.

10. **Procedure and Powers of Special Courts-** (1) A Special Court may take cognizance of any scheduled offence, without the accused being committed to it for trial, upon receiving a complaint of facts which constitute such offence or upon a police report of such facts.

(2) Where a scheduled offence is punishable with imprisonment for a term not exceeding three years or with fine or with both, a

Special Court may, notwithstanding anything contained in sub-section (1) of section 260 or section 262 of the Code, try the offence in a summary way in accordance with the procedure prescribed in the Code and the provisions of sections 263 to 265 of the Code, shall, so far as may be, apply to such trial: Provided that when, in the course of a summary trial under this sub-section, it appears to the Special Court that the nature of the case is such that it is undersirable to try it in a summary way, the Special Court shall recall any witnesses who may have been examined and proceed to re-hear the case in the manner provided by the provisions of the Code for the trial of such offence and the said provisions shall apply to and in relation to a Special Court as they apply to and in relation to a Magistrate: Provided further that in the case of any conviction in a summary trial under this section, it shall be lawful for a Special Court to pass a sentence of imprisonment for a term not exceeding two years.

(3) A Special Court may, with a view to obtaining the evidence of any person supposed to have been directly or indirectly concerned in, or privy to, an offence, tender a pardon to such person on condition of his making a full and true disclosure of the whole circumstances within his knowledge relative to the offence and to every other person concerned whether as principal or abettor in the commission thereof, and any pardon so tendered shall, for the purposes of section 308 of the Code, be deemed to have been tendered under section 307 thereof.

(4) Subject to the other provisions of this Act, a Special Court shall, for the purpose of trial of any offence, have all the powers of a Court of Session and shall try such offence as if it were a Court of Session so far as may be in accordance with the procedure prescribed in the Code for the trial before a Court of Session.

(5) Subject to the other provisions of this Act, every case before an Additional Special Court shall be dealt with as if such case had been transferred under section 406 of the Code to such Additional Special Court.

11. **Power of Supreme Court to Transfer Case**-Whenever it is made to appear to the Supreme Court that an order under this section is expedient for the ends of justice, it may direct that any particular case be transferred from one Special Court to another Special Court.

12. **Protection of Witnesses**-(1) Notwithstanding anything contained in the Code, all proceedings before a Special court shall be conducted in camera: Provided that where the Public Prosecutor so applies, any proceedings or part thereof may be held in open court.

(2) A Special Court may, on an application made by a witness in any proceedings before it or by the Public Prosecutor in relation to such witness or on its own motion, take such measures as it deems fit for keeping the identity and address of the witness secret.

(3) In particular and without prejudice to the generality of the provisions of sub-section (2), the measures which a Special Court may take under that sub-section may include - (a) the holding of the proceeding at a protected place; (b) the avoiding of the mention of the names and addresses of the witnesses in its orders or judgments or in any records of the case accessible to public; (c) the issuing of any directions for securing that the identity and addresses of the witnesses are not disclosed.

(4) Any person who contravenes any direction issued under sub-section (2) shall be punishable with imprisonment for a term, which may extend to one year and with fine, which may extend to one thousand rupees.

13. **Power to Transfer Cases to Regular Courts**- Where after taking cognizance of any offence, a Special Court is of opinion that the offence is not a scheduled offence, it shall, notwithstanding that it has no jurisdiction to try such offence, transfer the case for trial of such offence to any court having jurisdiction under the Code and the court to which the case is transferred may proceed with the trial of the offence as if it has taken cognizance of the offence.

14. **Appeal** -(1) Notwithstanding anything contained in the Code, an appeal shall lie as a matter of right from any judgement, sentence or order, not being interlocutory order, of a Special Court to the Supreme Court both on facts and on law.

(2) Except as aforesaid, no appeal or revision shall lie to any court from any judgement, sentence or order of a Special Court.

(3) Every appeal under this section shall be preferred within a period of thirty days from the date of the judgement, sentence or

order appealed from: Provided that the Supreme Court may entertain an appeal after the expiry of the said period of thirty days if it is satisfied that the appellant had sufficient cause for not preferring the appeal within the period of thirty days.

15. **Modified Application of Certain Provisions of the Code**-(1) Notwithstanding anything contained in the Code or any other law, every scheduled offence shall be deemed to be a cognizable offence within the meaning of clause (c) of section 2 of the Code and "cognizable case" as defined in that clause shall be construed accordingly.

(2) Section 167 of the Code shall apply in relation to a case involving a scheduled offence subject to the modifications that - (a) the reference in sub-section (1) thereof to "Judicial Magistrate" shall be construed as a reference to "Judicial Magistrate or Executive Magistrate"; (b) the references in sub-section (2) thereof to "fifteen days", "ninety days" and sixty days", wherever they occur, shall be construed as references to "thirty days", "one year" and "one year", respectively; and (c) sub-section (2A) thereof shall be deemed to have been omitted.

(3) Sections 366 to 371 and section 392 of the Code shall apply in relation to a case involving a scheduled offence subject to the modifications that the references to "Court of Session" and "High Court", wherever occurring therein, shall be construed as references to "Special Court" and "Supreme Court", respectively.

(4) Nothing in section 438 of the Code shall apply in relation to any case involving the arrest of any person on an accusation of having committed a scheduled offence in a terrorist affected area.

(5) Notwithstanding anything contained in the Code, no person accused of a scheduled offence shall, if in custody, be released on bail or on his own bond unless—(a) the Public Prosecutor has been given an opportunity to oppose the application, for such release, and (b) where the Public Prosecutor opposes the application, the court is satisfied that there are reasonable grouds for believing that he is not guilty of such offence and that he is not likely to commit any offence while on bail.

(6) The limitations on granting of bail specified in sub-section

(5) are in addition to the limitations under the Code or any other law for the time being in force on granting of bail. [Ins. by Act 45 of 1985, S.2.]

[15A. **Abolition of Certain Special Courts**- Where the area comprising a judicial zone has ceased to be a terrorist affected area and no cases are pending berore a Special Court or an Additional Special Court established in relation to such judicial zone, the Central Government may, by notification in the Official Gazettte, abolish such Special Court or Additional Special Court.]

16. **Overriding Effect of Act**- (1) The provisions of this Act shall have effect notwithstanding anything contained in the Code or any other law, but save as expressly provided in this Act, the provisions of the Code shall, in so far as they are not inconsistent with the provisions of this Act, apply to the proceedings before a Special Court; and for the purpose of the said provisions of the Code, the Special Court shall be deemed to be a Court of Session.

(2) In particular and without prejudice to the generality of the provisions contained in sub-section (1), the provisions of sections 326 and 475 of the Code shall, as far as may be, apply to the Proceedings before a Special Court, and for this purpose any reference in those provisions to a Magistrate shall be construed as a reference to the Special Court.

17. **Delegation**- The Central Government may, by notification, delegate, subject to such conditions as may be specified, all or any of the powers exercisable by it under this Act [except the power under sub-section (2) of section 4 and the power under sub-section (2) of section 7] to the State Government.

18. **Power to Make Rules**- The Supreme Court may, by notification, make such rules, if any, as it may deem necessary for carrying out the purposes of this Act.

19. **Saving**- (1) Nothing in this Act shall affect the jurisdiction exercisable by, or the procedure applicable to, any court or other authority under any law relating to the naval, military or air forces or any other armed forces of the Union.

(2) For the removal of doubts, it is hereby declared that for the purposes of any such law as is referred to in sub-section (1), a Special Court shall be deemed to be a Court of ordinary criminal justice.

IV
(THE) TERRORIST AND DISRUPTIVE ACTIVITIES (PREVENTION) ACT, 1987

The full text of the Act follows.

(Act No. 28 of 1987) (Amended by Act 43 of 1993) [3rd September, 1987]

CONTENTS

PART I

PRELIMINARY

Part II

Punishments for, and Measures for Coping with, Terrorist and Dissruptive Activities

Part III

Designated Courts

An Act to make special provisions for the prevention of, and for coping with, terrorist and disruptive activities and for matters connected therewith or incidental thereto.

Be it enacted by Parliament in the Thirty- eighth year of the Republic of India as follows:

Part I

Preliminary

1. **Short title, extent, application, commencement, duration and savings-** (1) This Act may be called the Terrorist and Disruptive Activities (Prevention)Act, 1987.

(2) It extends to the whole of India, and it applies also,-

(a) to citizens of India outside India;

(b) to persons in the service of the Government, wherever they may be; and

(c) to persons on ships and aircraft registered in India, wherever they may be.

(3) Sections 5, 15, 21 and 22 shall come into force at once and the remaining provisions of this Act shall be deemed to have come into force on the 24th day of May, 1987.

(4) It shall remain in force for a period of [eight years] from the 24th day of May, 1987, but its expiry under the operation of this sub-section shall not affect,-

(a) the previous operation of, or anything duly done or suffered under this Act or any rule made thereunder or any order made under any such rule, or

(b) any right, privilege, obligation or liability acquired accrued or incurred under this Act or any rule made thereunder or any order made under any such rule, or

(c) any penalty, forfeiture or punishment incurred in respect of any offence under this Act or any contravention of any rule made under this act or of any order made under any such rule, or

(d) any investigation, legal proceeding or remedy in respect of any such right, privilege, obligation, liability, penalty, forfeiture or punishment as aforesaid.

and any such investigation, legal proceeding or remedy may be instituted , continued or enforced and any such penalty, forfeiture or punishment may be imposed as if this Act had not expired.

2. **Definitions**- (1) In this Act, unless the context otherwise requires,-

(a) "*abet*", with its grammatical variations and cognate expessions, includes,-

(i) the communication or association with any person or class of persons who is engaged in assisting in any manner terrorists or disruptionists

(ii) the passing on, or publication of, without any lawful authority and information likely to assist the terrorists or disruptionists and the passing on, or publication of or distribution of, any document or matter obtained from terrorists or distuptionists;

(iii) the rendering of any assistance,whether financial or otherwise, the terrorists or disruptionists;

(b) "*Code*" means the Code of Criminal Procedure 1973 (2 of1974);

(c) "*Designated Court*" means a Designated Court constituted under Section 9;

(d) "*Disruptive activity*" has the meaning assigned to it in Section 4, and the expression "disruptionist" shall be construed accordingly;

(e) "*High Court*" means the High Court of the State in which a judge or an additional judge of a Designated Court was working immediately before his appointment as such judge or additional judge;

(f) "*notified area*" means such area as the State Government may, by notification in the official Gazette, specify;

(g) "*public prosecutor*" means a Public Prosecutor or an Additional Public Prosecutor or a Special Public Prosecutor appointed under Section 13, and includes any person acting under the directions of the Public Prosecutor;

"*Property*" means property and assets of any description, whether corporeal or incorporeal, movable or immovable, tangible or intangible and deeds and instruments evidencing title to, or interest in, such property or assets, derived or obtained from the terrorist Act and includes proceeds of terrorism;

(h) "*terrorist act*" has the meaning assigned to it in sub- section(1) of Section 3, and the expression "terrorist" shall be construed accordingly;

(i) words and expressions used but not defined in this Act and defined in the code shall have the meaning respectively assigned to them in the Code.

(2) Any reference in this Act to any enactment or any provision thereof shall, in relation to an area in which such enactment or such provision is not in force, be construed as a reference to the corresponding law or the relevant provision of the corresponding law, if any, in force in that area.

Part II

Punishments For, and Measures for Coping with, Terrorist and Disruptive Activities

3. **Punishment for Terrorist Acts**- (1) Whoever with intent to overawe the Government as by law established or to strike terror in the people or any section of the people or to alienate any section of the people or to adversely affect the harmony amongst different sections of the people does any act or thing by using bombs, dynamite or other explosive substances or inflammable substances or lethal weapons or poisons or noxious gases or other chemicals or by any other substances (whether biological or otherwise) of a hazardous nature in such a manner as to cause, or as is likely to cause , death of, or injuries to, any person or persons or loss of, or damage to, or destruction of, property or disruption of any supplies or services essential to the life of the community, or detains any person and threatens to kill or injure such person in order to compel the Government or any other person to do or abstain from doing any act, commits a terrorist act.

(2) Whoever commits a terrorist act, shall,-

(i) if such act has resulted in the death of any person, be punishable with death or imprisonment for life and shall also be liable to fine;

(ii) in any other case, be punishable with imprisonment for a term which shall not be less than five years but which may extend to imprisonment for life and shall also be liable to fine.

(3) Whoever conspires or attempts to commit, or advocates, abets, advises or incites or knowingly facilitates the commission of, a terrorist act or any act preparatory to a terrorist act, shall be punishable with imprisonment for a term which shall not be than five years but which may extend to imprisonment for life and shall also be liable to fine.

(4) Whoever harbours or conceals, or attempts to harbour or conceal, any terrorist shall be punishable with imprisonment for a term which shall not be less than five years but which may extend to imprisonment for life and shall also be liable to fine.

(5) Any person who is a member of a terrorist's gang or a terrorist organisation, which is involved in terrorist acts, shall be punishable with imprisonment for a term which shall not be less tan five years but which may extend to imprisonment for life and shall also be liable to fine.

(6) Whoever holds any property derived or obtained from commission of any terrorist act or has been acquired through the terrorist funds shall be punishable with imprisonment for a term which shall not be less than five years but which may extend to imprisonment for life and shall also be liable to fine.]

4. **Punishment for Distrptive Activities-** (1) Whoever commits or conspires or attempts to commit or abets, advocates, advises, or knowingly facilitates the commission of, any disruptive activity or any act preparatory to a diisruptive activity sshall be punishable with imprisonment for a term which shall not be less than five years but which may extend to imprisonment for life and shall also be liable to fine.

(2) For the purposes of sub-section (1), "disruptive activity" means any action taken, whether by act or by speech or through any other media or in any other manner whatsoever-,

(i) which questions, disrupts or is intended to disrupt, whether directly or indirectly, the sovereignty and territorial integrity of India; or

(ii) which is intended to bring about or supports any claim, whether directly or indirectly, for the secession of any part of India or the secession of any part of India from the Union.

Explanation- For the purposes of this sub-section-,

(a) "cession" includes the admission of any claim of any foreign country to any part of India, and

(b) "secession" includes the assertion of any claim to determine whether a part of India will remain within the Union.

(3) Without prejudce to the generality of the provisions of sub-section (2), it is hereby declared that any action taken, whether by act or by speech or through any other media or in any other manner whatsoever, which—

(a) advocates, advises, suggests or incites; or

(b) predicts, prophesies or pronounces or otherwise expresses, in such manner as to incite, advice, suggest or prompt, the killing or the destruction of any person bound by oath under the constitution to uphold the sovereignty and integrity of India or any public servant shall be deemed to be a disruptive activity within the meaning of this section.

(4) Whoever harbours or conceals, or attempts to harbour or conceal, any disruptionist shall be punishable with imprisonment for a term which shall not be less than five years but which may be extended to imprisonment for life and shll also be liable to fine.

2. **Habeas Corpus**- In habeas corpus proceedings if the detention is legal at the time of the disposal of the petition the Court cannot order release of the person detained by issuing a writ of habeas corpus. Therefore, the legality or otherwise of the detention shall also be considered on the date of final disposal of the petition. Bacha Bora v. State of Assam, 1991 Cr LJ 2782 (Gau).

5. **Possession of Certain Unauthorised Arms, etc. in Specified Areas**- Where any person is in possession of any arms and ammunition specified in Column 2 and 3 of Category I or category III (a) of Schedule I to the Arms Rules, 1962, or bombs, dynamite or other explosive substances unauthorisedly in a notified area, he shall, notwithstanding anything contained in any other law for the time being in force, be punishable with imprisonment for a term

which shall not be less than five years but which may extend to iimprisonment for life and shall also be liable to fine.

6. **Enhanced Penalties-** (1) If any person with intend to aid any terrorist or disruptionist, contravenes any provision of, or any rule made under the Arms Act, 1959, the Explosives Act, 1884, the Explosives substances act, 1908 or the Inflammable Substances act, 1952, he shall, notwithstanding anything contained in any of the aforesaid Acts or the rules made thereunder, be punishable with imprisonment for a term which shall not be less than five years but which may extend to imprisonment for life and shall also be liable to fine.

(2) For the purposes of this section, any person who attempts to contravene or abets, or attempts to abet, or does any act preparatory to the contravention of any provision of any law, rule or order, shall be deemed to have contravened that provision, and the provision of subsection(1) shall, in relation to such person, have effect subject to the modification that the reference to "imprisonment for life" shall be construed as a reference to "imprisonment for ten years".

7. **Conferment of Powers-** (1) Notwithstanding anything contained in the Code or in any other provision of this Act, the Central Government may, if it considers it necessary or expedient so to do,-

(a) for the prevention of, and for coping with, any offence under Section 3 or Section 4; or

(b) for any case or class or group of cases under Section 3 or Section 4;

in any State or part thereof, confer, by notification in the official Gazette, on any officer of the Central Government, powers exercisable by a police officer under the Code in such State or part thereof or, as the case may be, for such case or class or group of cases and in particular, the powers of arrest, investigation and prosecution of persons before any Court.

(2) All officers of police and all officers of Government are hereby required and empowered to assist the officer of the Central Government referred to in sub-section (1), in the execution of the provisions of this act or any rule or order made thereunder.

(3) The provisions of the Code shall, so far as may be and subject to such modifications mde in this Act, apply to the exercise of the powers by an officer under sub- section (1).

[7-A. **Powers of Investigating Officers**- If an officer investigating an offence committed under the Act has reason to believe that any property in relation to which an investigation is being conducted is a property derived or obtained from the commission of any terrorist Act, and includes proceeds of terrorism he shall, with the approval of the Superintendent of Police, make an order seizing such property and where it is not practicable to seize such property, he may take an order of attachment directing that such property shall not be transferred or otherwise dealt with except with the prior permission of the officer making such order, or of the Designated Court and a copy of such order shall be served on the persons concerned:

Provided that the investigating officer shall duly infom the Designated Court within forty- eight hours of the attachment of such propety and the said Court shall either confirm or revoke the order of attachment so issued.]

8. **Forfeiture of Property of Certain Persons**- (1) Where a person has been convicted to any offence punishable under this Act or any rule made thereunder, the Designated Court may, in addition to awarding any punishment, by order in writing, declare that any property, movable or immovable or both, belonging to the accused and specified in the order, shall stand forfeited to the Government free from all encumbrances.

(2) Where any person is accused of any offence under this Act or any rule made thereunder, it shall be open to the Designated Court trying him to pass an order that all or any properties, movable or immovable or both belonging to him, shall, during the period of such trial, be attached, and where such trial ends in conviction, the properties so attached shall stand forfeited to Government free from all encumbrances.

(3) (a) If upon a report in writing made by a police officer or an officer referred to in sub-section (1) of Section 7, any Designated Court has reason to believe that any person, who has committed an offence punishable under this act or any rule made thereunder, has absconded or is concealing himself so that he may not be

apprehended, such court may, notwithstanding anything contained in Section 82 of the Code, publish a written proclamation requiring him to appear at a specified place and at a specified time not less than fifteen days but not more than thirty days from the date of publication of such proclamation.

(b) The Designated Court issuing a proclamation under Clause (a) may, at any time, order the attachment of any property, movable or immovable or both belonging to the proclaimed person, and thereupon the provisions of Sections 83 to 85 of the Code shall apply to such attachment as if such attachment were made under the Code.

(c) If, within six months from the date of the attachment, any person, whose property is, or has been, at the disposal of the Government under sub- section (2) of section 85 of the code, appears voluntarily or is apprehended and brought before the Designated Court by whose order the property was attached, or the Court to which such Court is subordinate, and proves to the satisfaction of such Court that he did not abscond or conceal himself for the purpose of avoiding apprehension and that he had not received such notice of the proclamation as to enable him to attend within the time specified therein, such property or, if the same has been sold, the net proceeds of the sale and the residue of the property, shall, after satisfying therefrom all costs incurred in consequence of the attachment, be delivered to him.

(4) Where any share in a company stand forfeited to the Government under this sub-section, then, the company shall, notwithstanding anything contained in the Companies Act, 1956, or the articles of association the company, forthwith register the Government as the transferee of such shares.

Part III

Designated Courts

9. **Designated Courts**- (1) The Central Government or a State Government may, by notification in the official Gazette, constitute one or more Designated Courts for such area or areas, or for such case or class or group of cases as may be specified in the notification.

(2) Where a notification constituting a Designated Court for any area or areas or for any case or class or group of cases is issued

by the Central Government under sub-section (1), and a notification constituting a Designated Court for the same area or areas or for the same case or class or group of cases has also been issued by State Government under that sub- section, the Designated Court constituted by the Central Government, whether the notification constituting such Court is issued before or after the issue of the notification constituting the Designated Court by the State Government, shall have, and the Designated Court constituted by the State Government shall not hve, jurisdiction to try any offence committed in that area or areas or, as the case may be, the case or class or group of cases, and all cases pending before any Designated Court constituted by the State Government shall transferred to the Designated Court constituted by the Central Government.

(3) Where any question arises as to the jurisdiction any Designated Court, it shall be referred to the Central Government whose decision thereon shall be final.

(4) A Designated Court shall be presided over by a Judge to be appointed by the Central Government or, as the case may be, the State Government, with the concurrence of the Chief Justice of the High Court.

(5) The Central Government or, as the case may be, the State Government may also appoint, with the concurrence of the Chief Justice of the High Court additional Judges to exercise jurisdiction in a Designated Court.

(6) A person shall not be qualified for appointment as a judge or an additional Judge of a Designated Court unless he is immediately before such appointment a Sessions Judge or an additional Sessions Judge in any State.

(7) for the removal of doubts , it is hereby provided that the attainment by a person appointed a Judge or an Additional Judge of a Designated Court of the age of superannuation under the rules applicable to him in the service to which he belongs, shall not affect his continuance as such Judge or additional Judge.

(8) Where any Additional Judge or Aditional Judges is or are appointed in a designated Court, the Judge of the Designated Court may, from time to time, by general or special order, in writing, provide for the distribution of business of the Deisgnated Court among

himself and the additional Judge or Additional Judges and also for the disposal urgent business in the event of his absence or the absence of any Additional Judge.

10. **Place of Sitting**- A Designated Court may, on its own motion or on an application made by the Public Prosecutor, and if it considers it expedient or desirable so to do, sit for any of its proceedings at any place, other than its ordinary place of sitting:

Provided that nothing in this section shall be construed to change the place of sitting of a Designated Court constituted by a State Government to any place outside that State.

11. **Jurisdiction of Designated Courts**- (I) Notwithstanding anything contained in the Code, every offence punishable under any provision of his Act or any rule made thereunder shall be triable only by the Designated Court within whose local jurisdiction it was committed or as the case may be, by the Designated Court constituted for trying such offence under sub-section (1) of Setion 9.

(2) If, having regard to the exigencies of the situation prevailing in a State, the Central Government is of the opinion that,-

(a) the situation prevailing in such State is not conducive to a fair, impartial or speedy trial, or

(b) it is not likely to be feasible without occasioning the breach of peace or grave risk to the safety of the accused, the witnesses, the Public Prosecutor and the Judge of the Designated Court or any of them, or

(c) it is not otherwise in the interests of justice,

It may, with the concurrence of the Chief Justice of India (such occurrence to be obtained on a motion moved in that behalf by the Attorney- General), transfer any case pending before a Designated Court in that State to any other Designated Court within that State or in any other State.

(3) Where the whole or any part of the area within the local limits of the jurisdiction of a Designated Court has been declared to be, or forms part of, any area which has been declared to be a disturbed area under any enactment for the time being in force making provision for the suppression of disorder and restoration and maintenance of

public order, and the Central Government is of opinion that the situation prevailing in the State is not conducive to fair, impartial or speedy trial within the State, of offences under this Act or the rules made thereunder which such Designated Court is competent to try, the Central Government may, with the concurrence of the Chief Justice of India, specify, by notification in the official Gazette, in elation to such Court (hereafter in this sub-section referred to as the local Court) a Designated Court outside the State (hereinafter in this section referred to as the specified court), and thereupon,-

(a) it shall not be competent at any time during the period of operation of such notification, for such local court to exercise any jurisdiction in respect of, or try, any offence under this Act or the rules made thereunder;

(b) the jurisdiction which would have been, but for the issue of such notification, exercisable by such local court in respect of such offences committed during the period of operation of such notification shall be exercisable by the specified court;

(c) all cases relating to such offences pending immediately before the date of issue of such notification before such local court shall stand transferred on that date to the specified court:

(d) all cases taken cognizance of by, or transferred to, the specified court under Clause (b) or Clause (c) shall be dealt with and tried in accordance with this Act (whether during the period of operation of such notification or thereafter) as if such offences had been committed within the local limits of the jurisdiction of the jurisdiction of the specified court or, as the case may be, transferred for trial to it under sub-section (2).

Explanation 1- A notification under this sub- section in relation to any locl court shall cease to operate on the date on which the whole or, as the case may be, the aforementioned part of the area within the local limits of its jurisdiction, ceases to be a disturbed area.

Explanation 2- For the purposes of this section, "Attorney-General" means the Attorney General of India or, in his absence, the Solicitor-General of India or, in the absence of both, one of the additional Solicitors-General of India.

12. **Power of Designated Courts with respect to Other Offences-** (1) When trying any offence, a Designated Court may also try any other offence with which the accused may, under the code, be charged at the same trial if the offence is connected with such other offence.

(2) If, in the course of any trial under this Act of any offence, it is found that the accused person has committed any other offence under this Act or any rule made thereunder or under any other law, the Designated Court may convict such person of such other offence and pass any sentence authorised by this Act or such rule or, as the case may be, such other law, for the punishment thereof.

13. **Public Prosecutors-**(1) For every Designated Court, the Central Government or, as the case may be, the State Government, shall appoint a person to be the Public Prosecutor and may appoint one or more persons to be the Additional Public Prosecutor or Additional Public Prosecutors;

Provided that the Central Government or, as the case may be, the State Government, may also appoint for any case or class or group of cases a Special Public Prosecutor.

(2) A person shall not be qualified to be appointed as a Public Prosecutor or an Additional Public Prosecutor or a Special Public Prosecutor under this section unless he has been in practice as an Advocate for not less than seven years or has held any post, for a period of not less than seven years, under the Union or a State, requiring special knowledge of law.

(3) Every person appointed as a Public Prosecutor or an Additional Public Prosecutor or a Special Public Prosecutor under this Sction shall be deemed to be a Public Prosecutor within the meaning of clause (u) of Section 2 of the Code and the provisions of the Code shall have effect accordingly.

14. **Procedure and Power of Designated Courts-** A Designated Court may take congnizance of any offence, without the accused being committed to it for trial, upon receiving a complaint of facts which constitute such offence or upon a police report of such facts.

(2) Where an offence triable by a Designated Court is punishable with imprisonment for a term not exceeding three years or with fine

or with both, the Designated Court may, notwithstanding anything contained in sub-section (1) of Section 260 or Section 262 of the Code, try the offence in a summary way in accordance with the procedure prescribed in the Code and the provisions of Section 263 to 265 of the Code, shall, so far as may be, apply to such trial:

Provided that when, in the course of a summary trial under this sub-section, it appears to the Designated Court that the nature of the case is such that it is undesirable to try it in a summary way, the Designated Court shall recall any witnesses who may have been examined and proceed to re-hear the case in the manner provided by the provisions of the code for the trialof such offence and the said provisions shall apply to and in relation to a Designated Court as they apply to and in relation to a Magistrate:

Provided further that in the case of any conviction in a summary trial under this section, it shall be lawful for a Designated Court to pass a sentence of imprisonment for a term not exceeding two years.

(3) Subject to the other provisions of this Act, a Designated Court shall, for the purpose of trial of any offence, have all the powers of a Courts of Session and shall try such offence as if it were a Court of Session so far as may be in accordance with the procedure prescribed in the Code for the trial before a Court of Session.

(4) Subject to the other provisions of this Act, every case transferred to a Designated Court under sub- section (2) of Section 11 shall be dealt with as if such case had been transferred under Section 406 of the code to such Designated Court.

(5) Notwithstanding anything contained in the Code, a Designated Court may, if it thinks fit and for reasons to be recorded by it, proceed with the trial in the absence of the accused or his pleader and record the evidence of any witness, subject to the right of the accused to recall the witness for cross- examination.

15. **Certain Confessions made to Police Officers to be Taken into Consideration**- (1) Notwithstanding anything in the Code or in the Indian Evidence Act, 1872, but subject to the proisions of this section, a confession made by a person before a policlo officer not lower in rank than Superintendent of Police and recorded by such police officer either in writing or on any mechanical device like cassettes, tapes or sound tracks from out of which sounds or images

can be reproduced, shall be admissible in the trial of such person [or co- accused, abettor or conspirator] for an offence under this Act or rules made thereunder:

[Provided that co-accused, abettor or conspirator is charged and tried in the same case together with the accused].

(2) The police officer shall, before recording any confession under sub-section (1), explain to the person making it that he is not bound to make a confession and that, if he does so, it may be used as evidence against him and such police officer shall not record any such confession unless upon questioning the person making it, he has reason to believe that it is being made voluntarily.

16. **Protection of Witnesses**-[(1) Notwithstanding anything contained in the Code, the proceedings under this Act may be held in camera if the Designated Court so desires.]

(2) A Designated Court may, on an application made by a witness in any proceedings before it or by the Public Prosecutor in relation to such witness or on its own motion, take such measures as it deems fit for keeping the identity and address of any witness secret.

(3) In particular, and without prejudice to the generality of the provisions of sub-section (2), the measures which a Designated Court may take under that sub-section may include,-

a. the holding of the proceedings at a place to be decided by the Designated Court;

b. the avoiding of the mention of the names and addresses of the witnesses in it orders or judgments or in any records of the case accessible to public;

c. the issuing of any directions for securing that the identity and addresses of the witnesses are not disclosed.

d. that it is in the public interest to order that all or any of the proceedings pending before such a court shall not be published in any manner.

(4) Any person who contravenes any direction issued under sub-section (3) shall be punishable with imprisonment for a term which may extend to one year and with fine which may extend to

one thousand rupees.

17. **Trial by Designated Courts to have Precedence**- The trial under this Act of any offence by a Designated Court shall have precedence over the trial of any other case against the accused in any other court (not being a Designated Court) and shall be concluded in preference to the trial of such other case and accordingly the trial of such other case shall remain in abeyance.

18. **Power to Transfer Cases to Regular Courts**- Where, after taking cognizance of any offence, a Designated Court is of opinion that the offence is not triable by it, it shall, notwithstanding that it has no jurisdiction to try such offence, transfer the case for the trial of such offence to any court having jurisdiction under the Code and the court to which the case is transferred may proceed with the trial of the offence as if it had taken cognizance of the offence.

19. **Appeal**- (1) Notwithstanding anything contained in the Code, an appeal shall lie as a matter of right from any judgment, sentence or order, not being an interlocutory order, of a Designated Court to the Supreme Court both on facts and on law.

(2) Except as aforesaid, no appeal or revision shall lie to any court from any judgment, sentence or order including an interlocutory order of a Designated Court.

(3) Every appeal under this section shall be preferred within a period of thirty days from the date of the judgment; sentence or order appealed from:

Provided that the Supreme Court may entertain an appeal after the expiry of the said period of thirty days if it is satisfied that the appellant had sufficient cause for not preferring the appeal within the period of thirty days.

Part IV Miscellaneass

20. **Modified Application of Certain Provisions of the Code**-(1) Notwithstanding anything contained in the Code or any other law, every offence punishable under this Act or any rule made thereunder shall be deemed to be a cognizable offence within the meaning of clause (c) of section 2 of the Code, and "congnizable case" as defined in that clause shall be construed accordingly.

(2) Section 21 of the Code shall apply in relation to a case involving an offence punishable under this Act or any rule made therunder subject to the modification that the referrence to "the State Government" therein shall be construed as a reference to "the Central Government or the State Government".

(3) Section 164 of the Code shall apply in relation to a case involving an offence punishable under this Act or any rule made thereunder, subject to the modification that the reference in subsection (1) thereof to "Metropolitan Magistrate, Judicial Magistrate" shall be construed as a reference to "Metropolitan Magistrate, Judicial Magistrate, Executive Magistrate or Special Executive Magistrate.

(4) Section 167 of the Code shall apply in rilation to a case involving an offence punishable under this act or any rule made thereunder subject to the modifications that-

a. the reference insub- section (1) thereof to "Judicial Magistrate" shall be construed as a reference to Judicial Magistrate or Executive Magistrate or Special Executive Magistrate;

b. the reference in sub-section (2) thereof to "fifteen days," ninety days" and "sixty days", wherever they occur shall be construed as references to sixty days." [one jundred and eighty days] and [one hundred and eighty days] , respectively; and

(bb) sub-section (2-A) thereof shall be deemed to have been ommitted.

[(bbb) in sub-section (2),[1] after the proviso, the following proviso shall be inserted namely:-

"Provided further that, if it is not possible to complete the investigation within the said period of one hundred and eighty days, the Designated Court shall extend the said period up to one year, on the report of the Public Prosecutor indicating the progress of the investigation and the specific reasons for the detention of the accused beyond the said period of one hundred and eighty days.]

(5) Section 268 o the Code shall apply in relation to a case involving an offence punishable under this Act or any rule made thereunder subject to the modifications that-

(a) the reference in sub-section (1) thereof-

(i) to "the State Government" shall be construed as a reference to "the Central Government" or the State Government;"

(ii) to "order the State Government "shall be construed as a reference to "order of the Central Government or the State Government, as the case may be;" or

(b) the reference in sub- section (2) there of , to "State Government" shall be construed as a reference to "Central Government or the State Government, as the case may be".

(6) Sections 366 to 371 and section 392 of the Code shall apply in relation to a case involving an offence triable by a Designated Court subject to the modifications that the references to "Court of Session" and "High Court" , wherever occurring therein, shall be construed as references to "Designated Court" and "Supreme Court", respectively.

(7) Nothing in Section 438 of the Code shall apply in relation to any case involving the arrest of any person on an accusation of having committed an offence punishable under this act or any rule made thereunder.

(8) Notwithstanding anything contained in the Code, no person accused of an offence punishable under this Act or any rule made thereunder shall, if in custody, be released on bail or on his own bond unless,-

a. the Public Prosecutor has been given an opportunity to oppose the application for such release, and

b. where the Public Prosecutor opposes the application, the Court is satisfied that there are reasonable grounds for believing that he is not guilty of such offence and that he is not likely to commit any offence while on bail.

(9) The limitations on granting of bail specified in sub- section (8) are in addition to the limitations under the Code or any other law for the time being in force on granting of bail.

[20-**A. Cognizance of Offence**- (1) Notwithstanding, anything contained in the code, no information about the commission of an offence under this Act shall be recorded by the police without the prior approval of the District Superintendent of Police.

(2) No court shall take cognizance of any offence under this Act without the previous sanction of the Inspector- General of Police, or as the case may be, the Commissioner of Police.]

21. **Presunption as to Offences Under Section** 3- (1) In a prosecution for an offence under sub- section (1) of Section 3, if it is proved-

(a) that the arms or explosives or any other substances specified in Section 3 were recovered from the possession of the accused and there is reason to believe that such arms or explosives or other substances of similar nature, were used in the commission of such offence; or

(b) that by the evidence of an expert the fingerprints of the accused were found at the site of the offence or on anything including arms and vehicles used in connection with the commission of such offence.

(2) In a prosecution for an offence under sub-section 3 of Section 3, if it is proved that the accused rendered any financial assistance to a person accused of, or reasonably suspected of, an offence under that section, the Designated Court shall presume, less the contrary is proved , that such person has committed the offence under that subsection.

22. **Identification of Accused**- Where a person has been declared a proclaimed offender in terrorist case, the evidence regarding his identification by witnesses on the basis of his photograph shall have the same value as the evidence of a test identification parade.

23. **Saving**- (1) Nothing in this Act shall affect the jurisdiction exercisable by, or the procedure applicable to, any Court or other authority under any law relating to the naval, military or air forces or other armed forces of the Union.

(2) For the removal of doubts, it is hereby declared that for the purposes of any such aw as is referred to in sub-section (1), a Designated Court shall be deemed to be a Court of ordinary criminal justice.

24. **Saving as to Orders-** Where an order purports to have been made and signed by any authority in exercise of any power conferred by or under this Court shall, within the meaning of the Indian

Evidence Act, 1872, presume that such order was so made by that authority.

25. **Overriding Effect-** The provisions of this Act or any rule made thereunder or any order made under any such rule shall have effect notwithstanding anything inconsistent therewith contained in any enactment other than this Act or in any instrument having effect by virtue of any enactment other than this Act.

26. **Protection of Action taken under this Act**- No suit, prosecution or other legal proceeding shall lie against the Central Government or State Government or any other authority on whom powers have been conferred under this Act or any rules made thereunder, for anything which is in good faith done or purported to be done in pursuance of this Act or any rules made thereunder or any order issued under any such rule.

27. **Power of the Supreme Court to Make Rules-** The Supreme Court may, by notification in the official Gazette, make such rules, if any, as it may deem necessary for carrying out the provisions of this Act relating to Designated Court.

28. **Power to Make Rules-** (1) Without prejudice to the powers of the Supreme Court to make rule under Section 27, the Central Government may, by notification in the Official Gazette, make rules for carrying out the provisions of this Act.

(2) In particular , and without prejudice to the generality of the foregoing power, such rules may provide for all or any of the following matters namely:

(a) regulating the conduct of persons in respect of areas the control of which is considered necessary or expedient and the removal of such persons from areas.

(b) The entry into, and search of-

(i) any vehicle, vessel or aircraft; or

(ii) any pace, whatsoever,

reasonably suspected of being used for committing the offence referred to in Section 3 or Section 4 or for manufacturing or storing anything for the commission of any such offence.

(c) Conferring powers upon,-

(i) the Central Government;

(ii) a State Government;

(iii) an Administrator of a Union Territory under Article 239 of the Constitution;

(iv) an officer of the Central Government not lower in rank than of a Joint Secretary, or

(v) an officer of a State Government not lower in rank than that of a District Magistrate;

to make general or special orders to prevent or cope with terrorist acts or disruptive activities:

(d) the arrest and trial of persons contravening any of the rules or any order made thereunder;

(e) the punishment of any person who contravenes or attempts to contravene or abets or attempts to abet the contravention of any rule or order made thereunder with imprisonmennt for a term which may extend to seven years or for a term which may not be less than six months but which may extend to seven years or with fine or with imprisonment as aforesaid and fine;

(f) Providing for the seizure and detention of any property in respect of which such contravention, attempt or abetment as is referred to in Clause (e) has been committed and for the adjudication of such seizure and detention, whether by any court or by any other authority.

29. **Rules to be laid before Houses of Parliament**- Every rule made by the Central Government under this Act shall be laid, as soon as may be after it is made, before each House of Parliament, while it is in session, for a total period of thirty days which may be comprised in one session or in two or more succcessive sessios, and if, before the expiry of the session immediately following the session or the successive sessions aforesaid, both Houses agree in making any modification in the rule or both Houses agree that the rule should not be made, the rule shall thereafter have affect only in such modified form or be of no effect, as the case may be; so, however that any such modification or annulment shall be without prejudice to

the validity of anything previously done under that rule.

30. **Repeal and Saving-** (1) The Terrorist and Disruptive Activities (Prevention) Ordinance, 1987 (2 of 1987) is hereby repealed.

(2) Notwithstanding such repeal, anything done or any action taken under the said Ordinance shall be deemed to have been done or taken under the corresponding provisions of this Act.

V

THE SAARC CONVENTION (SUPPRESSION OF TERRORISM) ACT, 1993 ENACTMENT DATE: [26TH APRIL 1993]

1. **Act Objective-** An Act to give effect to the South Asian Association for Regional Cooperation Convention on Suppression of Terrorism and for matters connected therewith or incidental thereto. WHEREAS a Convention on the Suppression of Terrorism was signed on behalf of the Government of India at Kathmandu on the 4th day of November, 1987; AND WHEREAS India, having ratified the said Convention, should make provisions for giving effect thereto and for matters connected therewith or incidental thereto; BE it enacted by Parliament in the Forty- fourth Year of the Republic of India as follows:

2. **Definitions-** In this Act, unless the context otherwise requires: (a) "Convention" means the South Asian Association for Regional Cooperation Convention on Suppression of Terrorism signed at Kathmandu on the 4th day of November, 1987 as set out in the Schedule;

(b) "Convention country" means a country in which the Convention is for the time being in force.

3. **Application of the Convention-** Notwithstanding anything to the contrary contained in any other law, the provisions of Articles I to VIII of the Convention shall have the force of law in India.

4. **Hostage-taking-**(1) Whoever, by force or threat of force or by any other form of intimation, seizes or detains any person and threatens to kill or injure that person with intent to cause a Convention country to do or abstain from doing any act as the means

of avoiding the execution of such threat, commits the offence of hostage-taking.

(2) Whoever commits the offence of hostage-taking shall be punished with imprisonment for a term which may extend to ten years, and shall also be liable to fine.

5. **Provisions as to Extradition Act**- For the purposes of the Extradition Act, 1962 (34 of 1962), in relation to a convention country, an offence under sub-section (1) of section 4 or any other offence specified in Article I of the convention , shall not be considered to be an offence of a political character.

6. **Offences Committed Outside India**- (1) When an offence under sub-section (1) of section 4 or any other offence specified in Article I of the convention is committed outside India,- (a) by a citizens of India, whether on the high seas or elsewhere; (b) by person, not being such citizen, on any ship or aircraft, registered in India; or (c) by a person, not being such citizen, in a Convention country, he may be deat with in respect of such offence as if it had been committed at any place within India at which he may be found.

(2) Notwithstanding anything contained in sub-section (1), the Central Government may, by general or special order published in the Official Gazette, direct that the offence under sub- section (1) of section 4 or any other offence specified in Article I of the Convention may be inquired into or tried at any place within India.

7. **Previous Sanction Necessary for Prosecution**- No prosecution for an offence under this Act shall be instituted except with the previus sanction of the central Government and the sanctin granted under this section shall be deemed to be a sanction granted under section 188 of the Code of Criminal Procedure, 1973 (2 f 1974).

8. **Protection of Action Taken in Good Faith**- (1) No suit, prosecution or other legal proceeding shall lie against any person for anything which is in good faith done or intended to be done in pursuance of the provisions of this act.

(2) No suit or other legal proceeding shall lie against the Central Government for any damage caused or likely to be caused for anything which is in good faith done or intended to be done in pursuance of the provisions of this Act.

VI

THE PREVENTION OF TERRORISM ORDINANCE, 2001

No. 9 Of 2001

Promulgated by the President in the Fifty-second Year of the Republic of India.

An ordinance to make provisions for the prevention of, and for dealing with, terrorist activities and for matters connected therewith.

WHEREAS Parliament is not in session and the President is stisfied that circumstances exist which render it necessary for him to take immediate action;

Now THEREFORE, in exercise of the powers conferred by clause

(1) of article 123 of the Constitution, the President is pleased to promulgate the following Ordinance:-

Chapter-1

Preliminary

1. **Short Title, Extent, Application, Commencement, Duration and Saving**- (1) This Ordinance may be called the Prevention of Terrorism Ordinance, 2001.

(2) It extends to the whole of India.

(3) Every person shall be liable to punishment under this Ordinance for every act or omission contrary to the provisions thereof, of which he is held guilty in India.

(4) Any person who commits an offence beyond India which is punishable under this Ordinance shall be dealt with according to the provisions of this Ordinance in the same manner as if such act had been committed in India.

(5) The provisions of this Ordinance apply also to-

(a) Citizens of India outside India,

(b) persons in the service of the Government, wherever they may be; and

(c) persons on ships and aircraft, registered in India, wherever

they may be.

(6) It shall come into force at once and shall remain in force for a period of five years from the date of its commencement, but its expiry under the operation of this sub-section shall not affect-

(a) the previous operation of, or anything duly done or suffered under this Ordinance, or

(b) any right, privilege, obligation or liability acquired accrued or incurred under this Ordinance or

(c) any penalty, forfeiture or punishment incurred in respect of any offence under this Ordinance, or

(d) any investigation, legal proceeding or remedy in respect of any such right, privilege, obligation, liability, penalty, forfeiture or punishment as aforesaid.

and, any such investigation, legal proceeding or remedy may be instituted, continued or enforced and any such penalty, forfeiture or punishment may be imposed as if this Ordinance had not expired.

2. **Definitions**- (1) In this Ordinance, unless the context otherwise requires,

(a) "Code ' means the Code of Criminal Procedure, 1973;

(b) "Designated Authority" shall mean such officer of the Central Government not below the rank of Joint Secretary to the Government, or such officer of the State Government not below the rank of Secretary to the Government, as the case may be, as may be specified by the Central Government or as the case may be, the State Government, by a notification published in the official Gazette;

(c) "proceeds of terrorism" shall mean all kinds of properties which have been derived or obtained from commission of any terrorist act or have been acquired through funds traceable to a terrorist act, and shall include cash, irrespective of person in whose name such proceeds are standing or in whose possession they are found;

(d) "property" means property an assets of every description, whether corporeal or incorporeal, movable or immovable, tangible or intangible and deeds and instruments evidencing title to, or interest in, such property or assets;

(e) "Public Prosecutor" means a Public Prosecutor or an Additional Public Prosecutor or a Special Public Prosecutor appointed under section 28 and includes any person acting under the directions of the Public Prosecutor;

(f) "Special Court" means a Special Court constituted under section 23;

(g) "terrorist act" has the meaning assigned to it in sub-section (1) of section 3, and the expression "terrorist" shall be construed accordingly;

(h) "State Government", in relation to a Union territory, means the Administrator thereof;

(i) words and expressions used but not defined in this Ordinance and defined in the Code shall have the meanings respectively assigned to them in the Code.

(2) Any reference in this Ordinance to any enactment or any provision therof shall, in relation to an area in which such enactment or such provision is not in force, be construed as a reference to the corresponding law or the relevant provision of the corresponding law, if any, in force in that area.

Chapter II

Punishment for, and Measures for Dealing with, Terrorist Activities

3.(1) Whoever,- (a) with intent to threaten the unity, integrity, security or sovereignty of India or to strike terror in the people or any section of the people does any act or thing by using bombs, dynamite or other explosive substances or inflammable substances or fire arms or other lethal weapons or poisons or noxious gases or other chemicals or by any other substances (whether biological or otherwise) of a hazardous nature or by any other means whatsoever, in such a manner as to cause, or likely to cause, death of, or injuries to any person or persons or loss of, or damage to, or destruction of property of disruption of any supplies or services essential to the life of the community or causes damage or destruction of any property or equipment used or intended to be used for the defence of India or in connection with any other purposes of the Government of India any State Government or any of their agencies, or detains any person and threatens to kill or injure such person in order to compel the Government or any other person to do or abstain from doing any act;

(b) is or continues to be a member of an association declared unlawful under the Unlawful Activities (Prevention) Act, 1967, or voluntarily does an act aiding or promoting in any manner the objects of such association and in either case is in possession of any unlicensed firearms, ammunition, explosive or other instrument or substance capable of causing mass destruction and commits any act resulting in loss of human life or grievous injury to any person or causes significant damage to any property, commits a terrorist act.

Explanation- For the purposes of this sub-section, "a terrorist act" shall include the act of raising funds intended for the purpose of terrorism.

(2) Whoever commits a terrorist act, shall,-

(i) if such act has resulted in the death of any person, be punishable with death or imprisonment for life and shall also be liable to fine;

(ii) in any other case, be punishable with imprisonment for a term which shall not be less than five years but which may extend to imprisonment for life and shall also be liable to fine.

(3) Whoever conspires of attempts to commit, or advocates, abets, advises or incites or knowingly facilitates the commission of, a terrorist act or any act preparatory to a terrorist act, shall be punishable with imprisonment for a term which shall not be less than five years but which may extend to imprisonment for life and shall also be liable to fine:

(4) Whoever voluntarily harbours or conceals, or attempts to harbour or conceal any person knowing that such person is a terrorist shall be punishable with imprisonment for a term which shall not be less than three years but which may extend to imprisonment for life and shall also be liable to fine:

Provided that this sub-section shall not apply to any case in which the harbour or concealment is by the husband or wife of the offender.

(5) Any person who is a member of a terrorist gang or a terrorist organisation, which is involved in terrorist acts, shall be punishable with imprisonment for a term which may extend to imprisonment for life or with fine which may extend to rupees ten lakh or with both.

Explanation- For the purposes of ths sub-section, "terrorist organisation" means an organisation which is concerned with or involved in terrorism.

(6) Whoever knowingly holds any property derived or obtained from commission of any terrorist act or has been acquired through the terrorist funds shall be punishable with imprisonment for a term which may extend to imprisonment for life or with fine which may extend to rupees ten lakh or with both.

(7) Whoever threatens any person who is a witness or any other person in whom such witness may be interested, with violence, or wrongfully restrains or confines the witness, or any other person in whom the witness may be interested , or does any other unlawful act with the said intent, shall be punishable with imprisonment which may extend to three years and fine.

(8) A person receiving or in possession of information which he knows or believes to be of material assistance-

(i) in preventing the commission by any other person of a terrorist act, or

(ii) in securing the apprehension, prosecution or conviction of any other person for an offence involving the commission, preparation or instigation of such an act, and fails, without reasonable cause, to disclose that information as soon as reasonably practicable to the police, shall be punishable with imprisonment for a term which may extend to one year or with fine or with both:

Provided that a legal practitioner of the accused shall not be bound to disclose such information which he might have received while defending the accused.

4. **Possession of Certain Unauthorized Arms, etc.**- Where any person is in unauthorized possession of any,-

(a) arms or ammunition specified in columns (2) and (3) of

Category I or Category III (a) of Schedule I to the Arms Rules, 1962, in a notified area,

(b) bombs, dynamite or hazardous explosive substances or other lethal weapons capable of mass destruction or biological or chemical substances of warfare in any area, whether notified or not, he shall be guilty of terrorist act notwithstanding anything contained in any other law for the time being in force, and be punishable with imprisonment for a term which may extend to imprisonment for life or with fine which may extend to rupees ten lakh or with both.

Explanation- In this section "notified area" means such area as the State Government may, by notification in the Official Gazette, specify.

5. **Enhanced Penalties**- (1) If any person with intent to aid any terrorist contravenes any provision of, or any rule made under, the Arms Act, 1959, the Explosives Act, 1884, the Explosive Substances Act, 1908 or the Inflammable Substances Act, 1952, he shall, notwithstanding anything contained in any of the aforesaid Acts or the rules made thereunder, be punishable with imprisonment for a term which may extend to imprisonment for life and shall also be liable to fine.

(2) For the purposes of this section, any person who attempts to contravene or abets, or does any act preparatory to the contravention of any provision of any law, role or order, shall be deemed to have contravened that provision, of law, rule or order, shall be deemed to have conravened and the provisions of sub- section (1) shall, in relation to such person, have effect subject to the modifiction that the reference to "imprisonment for life" shall be construed as a reference to "imprisonment for ten years".

6. **Holding of Proceeds of Terrorism Illegal**- (1) No person shall hold or be in possession of any proceeds of terrorism.

(2) Proceeds of terrorism, whether held by a terrorist or by any other person and whether or not such person is prosecuted or convicted under this Ordinance, shall be liable to be forfeited to the Central Government or the State Government, as the case may be, in the manner provided under this Chapter.

7. **Powers of Investigating Officers**- (1) If an officer (not below

the rank of Superintendent of Police) investigating an offence committed under this Ordinance, has reason to believe that any property in relation to which an investigation is being conducted, represents proceeds of terrorism, he shall, with the prior approval in writing of the Director General of the Police of the State in which such property is situated, make an order seizing such property an where it is not practicable to seize such property, make an order of attachment directing that such property shall not be transferred or otherwise dealt with except with the prior permission of the officer making such order, or of the Designated Authority, or the Special Court, as the case may be, before whom the properties seized or attached are produced and a copy of such order shall be served on the person concerned.

(2) The investigating officer shall duly inform the Designated Authority or, as the case may be, the Special Court, within forty-eight hours of the seizure or attachment of such property.

(3) It shall be open to the Designated Authority or the Special Court before whom the seized or attached properties are produced either to confirm or revoke the order of attachment so issued:

Provided that an opportunity of making a representation by the person whose property is being attached shall be given.

(4) In the case of immovable property attached by the investigating officer, it shall be deemed to have been produced before the Designated Authority or the Special Court , as the case may be, when the investigating officer notifies his report and places it at the disposal of the Designated Authority or the Special Court, as the case may be.

(5) The investigating officer may seize and detain any cash to which this Chapter applies if he has reasonable grouds for suspecting that-

(a) it is intended to be used for the purposes of terrorism;

(b) it forms the whole or part of the resources of an organisation declared as terrorist organisation under this Ordinance:

Provided that the cash seized under this sub-section by the investigating officer shall be released not later than the period of forty- eight hours beginning with the time when it is seized unless the matter involving the cash is before the Designated Authority, or as the case may be, the Special Court and such authority or, as the case may be, the Court passes an order allowing its retention beyond forty- eight hours.

Explanation-For the purposes of this sub-section "cash" means—

(a) Coins and notes in any currency;

(b) postal orders;

(c) traveller's cheques;

(d) banker's drafts; and

(e) such other monetary instruments as the Central Government, or as the case may be, he State Government may specify by an order made in writing.

8. **Forfeiture of Proceeds of Terrorism**- Where any property is seized or attached in the belief that it constitutes proceeds of terrorism and is produced before the Designated Authority, it shall, on being satisfied that the said property consists of proceeds of terrorism, order forfeiture of such property, whether or not the person from whose possession it is seized or attached, is prosecuted in a Special Court for an offence under this Ordinance.

9. **Issue of Show Cause Notice Before Forfeiture of Proceeds of Terrorism**-(1) No order forfeiting and proceeds of terrorism shall be made under section 8 unless the person holding or in possession of such proceeds is given a notice in writing informing him of the grounds on which it is proposed to forfeit the proceeds of terrorism and such person is given an opportunity reasonable time as may be specified in the notice against the grounds of making a representation in writing within such reasonable time as may be specified in the notice against the grounds of forfeiture and is also given a reasonable opportunity of being heard in the matter.

(2) No order of forfeiture shall be made under sub- section (1), if such person established that he is a bona fide transferee of such proceeds for value without knowing that they represent proceeds of terrorism.

(3) It shall be competent for the Designated Authority to make an order in respect of property seized or attached,—

(a) directing it to be sold if it is perishable property and the provisions of section 459 of the Code shall, as nearly as may be practicable, apply to the net proceeds of such sale;

(b) nominating any officer of the Central or State Government, in the case of any other property, to perform the function of the Administrator of such property subject to such conditions as may be specified by the Designated Authority.

10. **Appeal**- (1) Any person aggrieved by an order of forfeiture under section 8 may, within one month from the date of the receipt of such order, appeal to the High Court within whose jurisdiction, the Designated Authority, who passed the order appealed against, is situated.

(2) Where an order under section 8 is modified or annulled by the High Court or where in a prosecution instituted for the contravention of the provisions of this Ordinance, the person against whom an order of forfeiture has been made under section 8 is acquitted, such property shall be returned to him and in either case if it is not possible for any reason to return the forfeited property, such person shall be paid the price therefore as if the property had been sold to the Central Government with reasonable interest calculated from the day of seizure of the property and such price shall be determined in the manner prescribed.

11. **Order of Forfeiture not to Interfere with Other Punishments**-The order of forfeiture made under this Ordinance by the Designated Authority, shall not prevent the infliction of any other punishment to which the person affected thereby is liable under this Ordinance.

12. **Claims by Third Party**- (1) Where any claim is preferred, or any objection is made to the seizure of any property under section 7 on the ground that such property is not liable to seizure, the Designated Authority, or as the case may be, the Special Court, before whom such property is produced, shall proceed to investigate the claim or objection:

Provided that no such investigation shall be made where the Designated Authority or the Special Court considers that the claim or objection was designed to cause unnecessary delay.

(2) In case claimant or objector establishes that the property specified in the notice issued under section 9 is not liable to be attached or forfeited under the Ordinance, the said notice shall be withdrawn or modified accordingly.

13. **Powers of Designated Authority**- The Designated Authority, acting under the provisions of this Ordinance, shall have all the powers of a Civil Court required for making a full and fair enquiry into the matter before it.

14. **Obligation to Furnish Information**- (1) Notwithstanding anything contained in any other law, the officer investigating any offence under this Ordinance, with prior approval in writing of an officer not below the rank of a Superintendent of Police, may require any officer or authority of the Central Government or a State Government or a local authority or a Bank, company, or a firm or any other institution, establishment, organisation or any individual to furnish information in their possession in relation to such of fence, on points or matters, where the investigating officer has reason to believe that such information will be useful for, or relevant to, the purposes of this Ordinance.

(2) Failure to furnish the information called for under sub- ection (1), or deliberately furnishing false information shall be punishable with imprisonment for a term which may extend to three years or with fine or with both.

(3) Notwithstanding anything contained in the Code, the offence under sub-section (1) shall be tried as a summary case and the procedure prescribed in Chapter XXI of the said Code [except sub-section (2) of section 262] shall be applicable thereto.

15. **Certain Trasfers to be Null and Void**- Where, after the issue of an order under section 7 or issue of a notice under section 9, any property referred to in the said order or notice is transferred by any mode whatsoever, such transfer shall, for the purpose of the proceedings under this Ordinance, be ignored and if such property is subsequently forfeited, the transfer of such property shall be deemed to be null and void.

16. **Forfeiture of Property of Certain Persons**- (1) Where any person is accused of any offence under this Ordinance, it shall be open to the Special Court trying him to pass an order that all or any

of the properties, movable or immovable or both belonging to him, shall, during the period of such trial, be attached, if not already attached under this Ordinance.

(2) Where a person has been convicted of any offence punishable under this Ordinance, the Special Court may, in addition to awarding any punishment, in by order writing, declare that any property movable or immovable or both belonging to the accused and specified in the order, shall stand forfeited to the Central Government or the State Government, as the case may be, free from all encumbrances.

17. **Company to Transfer Shares to Government**- Where any shares in a company stand forfeited to the Central Government of the State Government, as the case may be, under this ordinance, then, the company shall on receipt of the order of the Special Court, notwithstanding anything contained in the Companies act, 1956, or the articles of association of the company, forthwith register the Central Government or the State Government, as the case may be, as the transferee of such shares.

Chapter III

Terrorist Organisations

18. **Declaration of An Organisation as a Terrorist Organisation-**

(1) For the purposes of this Ordinance an organisation is a terrorist organisation if-,

(a) it is listed in the Schedule, or

(b) it operates under the same name as an organisation listed in that Schedule.

(2) The Central Government may be order , in the Official Gazette,-

(a) add an organisation to the schedule;

(b) remove an organisation from that Schedule;

(c) amend that Schedule in some other way.

(3) The Central Government may exercise its power under clause (a) of sub-section (2) in respect of an organisation only if it believes that it is involved in terrorism.

(4) For the purposes of sub- section (3) an organisation shall be

deemed to be involved in terrorism if it-

(a) commits or participates in acts of terrorism,

(b) prepares for terrorism,

(c) promotes or encourages terrorism, or

(d) is otherwise involved in terrorism.

19. **Denotification of a Terrorist Organisation-** (1) An application may be made to the Central Government for the exercise of its power under clause (b) of sub-section (2) of section 18 to remove an organisation from the Schedule.

(2) An application may be made by-

(a) the organisation, or

(b) any person affected by inclusion of the organisation in the Schedule as a terrorist organisation.

(3) The Central Government may make rules to prescribe the procedure for admission and disposal of an application made under this section.

(4) Where an application under sub-section (1) has been refused, the applicant may apply for a review to the Review committee constituted by the Central Government under sub-section (1) of section 59 within one month from the date of receipt of the order by the applicant.

(5) The Review Committee may allow an application for review against refusal to remove an organisation from the Schedule, if it cosiders that the decision to refuse was flawed when considered in the light of the principles applicable on an application for judicial review.

(6) Where the Review committee allows review under sub- section (5) by or in respect of an organisation, it may make an order under this sub-section.

(7) Where an order is made under sub-section (6), the Central Government shall as soon as the certified copy of the order is received by it, make an order removing the organisation from the list in the Schedule.

20. **Offence Relating to Membership of a Terrorist Organisation** (1) A person commits an offence if he belongs or professes to belong to a terrorist organisation:

Provided that this sub-section shall not apply where the person charged is able to prove-

(a) that the organisation was not declared as a terrorist organisation at the time when he became a member or began to profess to be a member, and

(b) that he has not taken part in the activities of the organisation at any time during its inclusion in the Schedule as a terrorist organisation.

(2) A person guilty of an offence under this section shall be liable, on conviction, to imprisonment for a term not exceeding ten years or with fine or with both.

21. **Offence Relating to Support Given to a Terrorist Organisation-**

(1) A person commits an offence if-

(a) he invites support for a terrorist organisation, and

(b) the support is not, or is not restricted to, the provision of money or other property within the meaning of section 22.

(2) A person commits an offence if he arranges, manages or assists in arranging or managing a meeting which he knows is-

(a) to support a terrorist organisation,

(b) to further the activities of a terrorist organisation, or

(c) to be addressed by a person who belongs or professes to belong to a terrorist organisation.

(3) A person commits an offence if he addresses a meeting for the purpose of encouraging support for a terrorist organisation or to further its activities.

(4) A person guilty of an offence under this section shall be liable on conviction, to imprisonment for a term not exceeding ten years or with fine or with both.

Explanation.- For the purposes for this section, the expression "meeting' means a meeting of three or more persons whether or not the public are admitted.

22. **Fund Raising for a Terrorist Organisation to be An Offence—**

(1) A person commits an offence if he-

(a) invites another to provide money or other property, and

(b) intends that it should be used, or has reasonable cause to suspect that it may be used, for the purposes of terrorism.

(2) A person commits an offence if he-

(a) receives money or other property, and

(b) intends that it should be used, or has reasonable cause to suspect that it may be used, for the purposes of terrorism.

(3) A person commits an offence if he-

(a) provides money or other property, and

(b) knows or has reasonable causetosuspect that it will or may be used for the purposes of terrorism.

(4) In this section , a reference to the provision of money or other property is a reference to its being given, lent or otherwise made available, whether or not for consideration.

(5) A person guilty of ans offence under this section shall be liable on conviction, to imprisonment for a term not exceeding fourteen years, or with fine or with both.

Chapter IV
Special Courts

23. **Special Courts**- (1) The Central Government or a State Government may, by notification in the Official Gazette, constitute one or more Special Courts for such area or areas , or for such case or class or group of cases, as may be specified in the notification.

(2) Where a notification constituting a Special Court for any area or areas or for any case or class or group of cases is issued by the Central Government under sub-section (1), and a notification

constituting a Special Court for the same area or areas or for the same case or class or group of cases has also been issued by the State Government under that sub- section, the Special court constituted by Central Government. Whether the notification constituting such Court is issued before r after the issue o the notification constituting the Special Court by the State Government, shall have, and the Special Court constituted by the State Government shall not have, jurisdiction to try any offence committed in that area or areas or, as the case may be, the case or class or group of cases and all cases pending before any Special Court constituted by the State Government shall stand transferred to the Special Court constituted by the Central Government.

(3) Where any question arises as to the jurisdiction of any Special Court, it shall be referred to the Central Government whose decisionin the matter shall be final.

(4) A Special Court shall be presided over by a judge to be appointed by the Central Government or, as the case may be, the State Governments, with the concurrence of the chief Justice of the High Court.

(5) The Central Government or, as the case may be, the State Government may also appoint with the concurrence of the Chief Justice the High Court, additional judges to exercise jurisdiction of a Special Court.

(6) A person shall not be qualified for appointment as a judge or an additional judge of a Special Court unlesss he is, immediately before such appointment, a sessions judge or an additional sessions judge in any State.

(7) For the removal of doubts, it is hereby provided that the attainment, by a person appointed as a judge or an additional judge of a Special Court, of the age of superannuation under the rules applicable to him in the service to which he belongs, shall not affect his continuance as such judge or additional judge.

(8) Where any additional judge or additional judges is or are appointed in a Special Court, the Judge of the Special Court may, from time to time, by general or special order, in writing , provide for the distribution of business of the Special Court among all judges including himself and the additional judge or additional judges

and also for the disposal of urgent business in the event of his absence or the absence of any additional judge.

24. **Place of Sitting-** A special Court may, on its own motion, or on an aplication made by the Public Prosecutor and if it considers it expedient or desirable so to do, sit for any of its proceedings at any place, other than its ordinary place of sitting:

Provided that nothing in this sectin shall be construred to chage the place of sitting of a Special Court ostituted by a State Government to any place outside that State.

25. **Jurisdiction of Special Courts-** (1) Notwithstanding anything contained in the Code, every offence punishable under any provision of this Ordinance shall be triable only by the Special Court within whose local jurisdiction it was committed or,as the case may be,by the Special Court constituted for trying such offence under section 23.

(2) If, having regard to the exigencies of the situation prevailing in a State;

(i) it is not possible to have a fair, impartial or speedy trial; or

(ii) it is not feasible to have the trial without occasioning the breach of peace to or grave risk ot the safety of the accused, the witnesses, the Public Prosecutor and a Judge of the Special Court or any of them; or

(iii) it is not otherwise in the interests of justice, the Supreme Court may transfer any case pending before a Special Court to any other Special Court within that State or in any other State and the High Court may transfer any case pending before a Special Court situated in that State to any other Special Court within the State.

(3) The Supreme Court or the High Court, as the case may be, may act under this section either on the applicationot of the CentralGovernment or a party interested and any such application shall be made by motion, which shall, except when the applicant is the Attorney-General of India, be supported by an affidavit or affirmation.

26. **Power of Special Courts with respect to Other Offences-**(1) When trying any offence, a Special Court may also try any other

offence with which the accused may, under the Code, be charged at the same trial if the offence is connected with such other offence.

(2) If, in the course of any trial under this Ordinance of any offence, it is found that the accused person has committed any other offence under this Ordinance or under any other law, the Special Court may convict such person of such other offence and pass any sentence or award punishment authorized by this ordinanae or such rule or, as the case may be, under such other laws.

27. **Power to Direct for Samples etc.**- (1) When a police officer investigating a case requests the Court of a Chief Judicial Magistrate or the Court of a Chief Metropolitan Magistrate in writing for obtaining samples of hand writing, finger prints, foot prints, photographs, blood, saliva, semen, hair, voice of any accused person reasonably suspected to be involved in the commission of an offence under this Ordinance, it shall be lawful for the Court of a Chief Judicial Magistrate or the Court of a Chief Metropolitan Magistrate to direct that such sampales be given by the accused person to the police officer either through a medical practitioner or otherwise, as the case may be.

(2) If any accused person refuses to give samples as provided in sub-section (1), the court shall draw adverse inference against the accused.

28. **Public Prosecutors**- (1) For every Special Court, the Central Government or, as the case may be, the State Government, shall appoint a person to be the Public Prosecutor and may appoint one or more persons to be the Additional Public Prosecutor or Additional Public Prosecutors:

Provided that the Central Government or, as the case may be, the State Government, may also appoint for any case or class or group of cases, a Special Public Prosecutor.

(2) A person shall not be qualified to be appointed as a Public Proseutor or an Additional Public Prosecutor or a Special Public Prosecutor under this section unless he has been in practice as an Advocate for not less than seven years or has held any post, for a period of not less than seven years, under the Union or a State, requiring special knowledge of law.

(3) Every person appointed as a Public Prosecutor or an Additional Pubic Prosecutor or a Special Public Prosecutor under this section shall be deemed to be Public Prosecutor within the meaning of clause (u) of section 2 of the Code, and the provisions of the code shall have effect accordingly.

29. **Procedure and Powers of Special Courts-** (1) Subject to the provisions of section 49, Special Court may take cognizance of any offence, without the accused being committed to it for trial, upon receiving a complaint of facts that constitute such offence or upon a police report of such facts.

(2) Where an offence triable by a special Court is punishable with imprisonment for a term not exceeding three years or with fine or with both, the Special Court may, not withstanding anything contained in sub-section (1) of section 260 or section 262 of the Code, try the offence in a summary way in accordance with the procedure prescribed in the Code and the provisions of sections 263 to 265 of the Code, shall so far as may be, apply to such trial:

Provided that when, in the course of a summary trial under this sub-section, it appears to the Special Court that the nature of the case is such that it is undesirable to try it in a summary way, the Special Court shall recall any witnesses who may have been examined and proceed to re-rehear the case in the manner provided by the provisions of the code for the trial of such offence and the said provisions shall apply to and in relation to a Special Court as they apply to and in relation to a Magistrate:

Provided further that in the case of any conviction in a summary trial under this section, it shall be lawful for a Special Court to pass a sentence of imprisonment for a term not exceeding one year and with fine which may extend to rupees five lakh.

(3) Subject to the other provisions of this Ordinance, a Special Court shall, for the purpose of trial of any offence, have all the powers of a Court of Session and shall try such offence as if it were a Court of Session so far as may be in accordance with the procedure prescribed in the Code for the trial before a Court of Session.

(4) Subject to the other provisions of this Ordinance, every case transferred to a Special Court under section 25 shall be dealt with as if such case had been transferred under section 406 of the Code to

such Special Court.

(5) Notwithstanding anything contained in the Code, but subject to the provisions of section 299 of the Code, a Special Court may, if it thinks fit and for reasons to be recorded by it, proceed with the trial in the absence of the accused or his pleader and record the evidence of any witness, subject to the right of the accused to recall the witness for cross-examination.

30. **Protection of Witnesses**- (1) Notwithstanding anything contained in the Code, the proceedings under this Ordinance may, for reasons to be recorded in writing, be held in camera if the Special Court so desires.

(2) A Special Court, if on an application made by a witness in any proceeding before it or by the Public Prosecutor in relation to such witness or on its own motion, is satisfied that the life of such witness is in danger, it may, for reasons to be recorded in writing, take such measures as it deems fit for keeping the identity and address of such witness secret.

(3) In particular, and without prejudice to the generality of the provisions of sub-section (2), the measure which a Special Court may take under that sub-section may include-

(a) the holdig of the proceedings at a place to be decided by the Special Court;

(b) the avoiding of the mention of the names and addresses of the witnesses in its orders or judgements or in any records of the case accessible to public;

(c) the issuing of any directions for securing that the identity and address of the witnesses are not disclosed;

(d) a decision that it is in the public interest to order that all or any of the proceedings pending before such a court shall not be published in any manner.

(4) Any person who contravenes any decision or direction issued under sub-section (3) shall be punishable with imprisonment for a term which may extend to one year and with fine may extend to one thousand rupees.

31. **Trial by Special Courts to Have Precedence**- The trial under

this Ordinance of any offence by a Special Court shall have precedence over the trial of any other case against the accused in ay other court (not being a Special Court) and shall be concluded in preference to the trial of such other case and accordingly the trial of such other case shall remain in abeyance.

32. **Certain Confessions made to Police Officers to be Taken into Consideration**- (1) Notwithstanding anything in the Code or in the Indian Evidence Act, 1872, but subject to the provisions of this section, a confession made by a person before a police officer not lower in rank than a Superintendent of police and recorded by such police officer either in writing or on any mechanical or electronic device like cassettes, tapes or sound tracks from out of which sound or images can be reproduced, shall be admissible in the trial of such person for an offence under this Ordinance or rules made thereunder.

(2) A police officer shall, before recording any confession made by a person under sub-section (1) explain to such person in writing that he is not bound to make a confession and that if he does so, it may be used against him:

Provided that where such person prefers to remain silent, the police officer shall not compel or induce him to make any confession.

(3)The confession shall be recorded in an atmosphere free from threat or inducement and shall be in the same language in which the person makes it.

(4) The person from whom a confession has been recorded under sub-section (1), shall be produced before the Court of a chief metropolitan Magistrate or the Court of a Chief Judicial Magistrate along with the original statement of confession, written or recorded on mechanical or electronic device within forty-eight hours.

(5) The Chief Metropolitan Magistrate or the chief Judicial Magistrate, shall, record the Cstatement, if any, made by the person so produced and get his signature or thumb impression and if there is any complaint of touture, such person shall be directed to be produced for medical examination before a Medical Officer not lower in rank than an Assistant Civil Surgeon and thereafter, he shall be sent to judicial custody.

33. **Power to Transfer Cases to Regular Courts**- Where, after

taking cognizance of any offence, a Special Court is of the opinion that the offence is not triable by it, is shall, notwithstanding that it has no jurisdiction to try such offenece, transfer the case for the trial of such offence to any court having jurisdiction under the Code and the the court to which the case is transferred may proceed with the trial of the offence as if it had taken cognizance of the offence.

34. **Appeal-** (1) Notwithstanding anything contained in the Code, an appeal shall lie from any judgment, sentence or order, not being an interlocutory order, of a Special Court to the High Court both facts and on law.

Explanation- For the purposes of this section, "High Court" means a High Court within whose jurisdiction, a Special Court which passed the judgment, sentence or order, is situated.

(2) Every appeal under sub-section (1) shall be heard by a bench of two judges of the High Court.

(3) Except as aforesaid, no appeal or revision shall lie to any court from any judgment, sentence or order including an interlocutory order of a Special Court.

(4) Notwithstanding anything contained in sub-section (3) of section 378 of the Code, an appeal shall lie to High Court against, an order of the Special Court granting or refusing bail.

(5) Every appeal under this section shall be preferred within a period of thirty days from the date of the judgment, sentence or order appealed from:

Provided that the High Court may entertain an appeal after the expiry of the said period of thirty days if it is satisfied that the appellant had sufficient cause for not preferring the appeal within the period of thirty days.

Chapter V

Interception of Communication In Certain Cases

35. **Definitions-** In this Chapter, unless the context otherwise requires,-

(a) "an electronic communication" means any transmission of signs, singnals, writings, images, sounds, data or intelligence of any nature transmitted in whole or in part by a wire, radio, electromagnetic, photo electronic or photo optical system that affects inland or foreign commerce but does not include,-

(i) the radio portion of a cordless telephone communication that is transmitted between the wireless telephone hand-set and the base unit;

(ii) any wire or oral communication;

(iii) any communication made through a tone only paging device, or

(iv) any communication from a tracking device;

(b) "intercept' means the aural or other acquistion of the contents by wire, electronic or oral communication through the use of any electronic, mechanical or other device;

(c) [1]oral communication' means any oral communication uttered by a person exhibiting an expectation that such communication is not subject to interception under circumstances justifying such expectation but such term does not include any electronic communication;

(d) 'wire communication ' means any aural transmission made in whole or part through the use of facilities for the transmission of communications by the aid of wire, cable or other like connection between the point of origin and the point of connection, between the point of origin and the point of reception (including the use of such connection in switching station) and such term includes any electronic storage of such communication.

36. **Appointment of Competent Authority**- The Central Government or the State Government, as the case may be, may appoint an officer not below the rank of Secretary to the Government in case of State Government and not below the rank of Joint Secretary to the Government in the case of Central Government, to be the Competent Authority for the purposes of this Chapter.

37. **Application for Authorization of Interception of Wire, Electronic or Oral Communication**- (1) A police officer not below the rank of Superintendent of Police supervising the investigation of any terrorist act under this Ordinance may submit an application in

writing to the Competent Authority for an order authorizing or approving the interception of wire, electronic or oral communication by the investigating officer when he believes that such interception may provide, or has provided evidence of any offence invloving a terrorist act.

(2) Each application shall include the following information:-

(a) the identity of the investigating officer making the application, and the head of the department authorizing the application;

(b) a statement of the facts and circumstances relied upon by the applicant to justify his belief that an order should be issued, including-

(i) details as to the offence of terrorist act that has been is being, or is about to be committed;

(ii) a particular description of the nature and location of the facilities from which or the place where the communication is to be intercepted;

(iii) a particular description of the type of communications sought to be intercepted ; and

(iv) the identity of the person, if known, committing the terrorist act whose communications are to be intercepted;

(c) a statement of the period of time for which the interception is required to be maintained, if the nature of the enquiry is such that the authorization of interception should not automatically terminate after the described type of communication has been first obtained;

(d) a particular description of facts establishing probable cause to believe that additional communications of the same type will occur thereafter; and

(e) where the application is for the extension of an order, a statement setting forth the results thus far obtained from the interception, or a reasonable explanation of the failure to obtain such results.

(3) The Competent Authority may require the applicant to furnish additional oral or documentary evidence support of the application.

38. **Decision by Competent Authority on Application for Interception-** (1) Upon such application, the Competent Authority may reject the application or issue an order, as requested or as modified, authorizing or approving interception of wire, electronic or oral communications, if the Competent Authority determines on the basis of the facts submitted by the applicant that-

(a) there is probable cause for belief that an individual is committing, has committed, or is about to comm it a particular offence described and made punishable under sections 3 and 6 of this Ordinance;

(b) there is a probable cause of belief that particular comunications concerning that offence may be obtained throught such interception;

(c) there is probable cause of belief, that the facilities from which, or the place where , the wire, electronic or oral communications are to be intercepted are being used or are about to be used, in connection with the commission of such offence, leased to , or are listed in the name of or commonly used by such person.

(2) Each order by the Competent Authority authorizing or approving the interception of any wire, electronic or oral communication under this section shall specify-

(a) the identity of the person, if known, whose communications are to be intercepted;

(b) the nature and location of the communication facilities as to which, or the place where, authority to intercept is granted;

(c) a particular description of the type of communication sought to be intercepted, and a statement of the particular offence to which it relates;

(d) the identity of the agency authorized to intercept the communications, and the person authorizing the application; and

(e) the period of time during which such interception is authorized, including a statement as to whether or not the interception shall automatically terminate after the described communication has been first obtained.

39. **Submission of Order of Interception to Review**

Committee— (1) The Competent authority shall immediately after passing the order under sub-section (1) of section 38, but in any case not later than seven days form the passing of the order, submit a copy of the same to the Review Committee constituted under section 59 along with all the relevant underlying papers, record and his own findings, in respect of the said order, for consideration and approval of the order by the Review Committee.

(2) An order authorizing the interception of a wire, electronic or oral communication under this section shall, upon request of the applicant direct that a provider of wire or electronic communication service, landlord, custodian or other person shall furnish to the applicant forthwith all information, facilities, and technical assistance necessary to accomplish the interception unobtrusively and with a minimum of interference with the services that such service provider, landlord, custodian, or person is providing to the person whose communications are to be interecepted.

40. **Duration of An Order of Interception etc.**- (1) No order issued under this section may authorize or approve the interception of any wire, electronic or oral communication for any period longer than is necessary to achieve the objective of the authorization, nor in any event longer than sixty days and such sixty days period shall begin on the day immediately preceding the day on which the investigation officer first begins to conduct an interception under the order or ten days after order is issued whichever is earlier.

(2) The extension of an order may be granted , but only upon an application for an extension made in accordance with sub-section (1) of section 37 and the Competent Authority making the findings required by sub-section (I) of section 38, and the period of such extension shall be no longer than the Competent Authority deems necessary to achieve the purposes for which it was granted and in no event for longer than sixty days at a time.

(3) Every order and extension thereof shall contain a provision that the authorization to intercept shall be executed as soon as practicable and shall be conducted in such manner as to minimize the interception of communications not otherwise subject to inerception under this section and shall terminate upon attainment of the authorized objective, or in any event on the expiry of the period of said order of extension there of.

41. **Authority Competent to Carry Out Interception**- (1) An interception under this Chapter may be conducted in whole or in part by a public servant, acting under the supervision of the investigating officer authorized to conduct the interception.

(2) Whenever an order authorizing an interception is issued pursuant to this section , the order may require reports to be made to the Competent Authority ho issued the order showing that progress has been made towards achievement of the authorized objective and the need for continued interception and such report shall be made at such intervals as the competent Authority may require.

42. **Interception of Communication in Emergency**-(1) Notwithstanding anything contained in any other provision of this section, an officer not below the rank of Additional Director General of Police or a police officer of equivalent rank who reasonably determines that-

(a) an emergency situation exists that involves-

(i) immediate danger of death or serious physical injury to any person;

(ii)conspiratorial activities threatening the security of interest of the State; or

(iii) Conspiratorial activities, characteristic of a terrorist act, that requires a wire, electronic or oral communication to be intercepted before an order from the Competent Authority authorizing such interception can, with due diligence, be obtained, and

(b) there are grounds on which an order should be issued under this section to authorize such interception, may authorize, in writing, the investigating officer to intercept such wire, electronic or oral communication, if an application for an order approving the interception is made in accordance with the provisions of sub-sections (1) and (2) of section 37 within forty-eight hours after the interception has occurred, or begins to occur.

(2) In the absence of an order approving the interception made under sub-section (1), such interception shall immediately terminate when the communication sought is obtained or when the application for the order is rejecteder, whichever is earlier; and in the event of an application, for permitting interception being rejected under sub-

section (1) of section 38 or an application under sub-section (1) of section 42 for approval being rejected or in any other case where the interception is terminated without an order having been issued, the contents of any wire, electronic or oral communication intercepted shall be treated as having been obtained in violation of this section.

43. **Protection of Information Collected**-(a) The contents of any wire, electronic or oral communication intercepted by any means authorized by this section shall as far as possible, be recorded on tape or wire or other comparable device and shall be done in such manner as to protect the recording from editing or other alterations.

(b) Immediately upon the expiration of the period of order, or extension there of, such recording shall be made available to the Competent Authority issuing such order and shall be sealed under his directions and kept in the custody of such person or authority as the Competent Authority orders, and such recordings shall not be destroyed except upon an order of the Competent Authority and in any event shall be kept for ten years.

(c) Applications made and orders issued under this section shall be sealed by the Competent Authority and custody of the applications and orders shall be kept in such manner as the Competent Authority directs, and shall not be destroyed except on an order of the Competent Authority, and in any event shall be kept for ten years.

44. **Admissibility of Evidence Collected through the Interception of Communications**- Notwithstanding anything in the Code or in any other law for the time being in force, the evidence collected through the interception of wire, electronic or oral communication under this Chapter shall be admissible as evidence against the accused in the Court during the trial of a case:

Provided that, the contents of any wire, electronic or oral communication intercepted pursuant to this Chapter or evidence derived therefrom shall not be received in evidence or otherwise disclosed in any trial, hearing or other proceeding in any court unless each accused has been furnished with a copy of the order of the Competent Authority, and accompanying application, under which the interception was authorized or approved not less than ten days before trial, hearing or proceeding:

Provided further that, the period of ten days may be waived by the judge trying the matter if he comes to the conclusion that it was not possible to furnish the accused with the above information ten days before the trial, hearing or proceeding and that the accused will not be prejudiced by the delay in receiving such information.

45. **Review of Authorisation Order**- (1) The Review Committee constituted by the Central Government or the State Government, as the case may be, shall review every order passed by the Competent Authority under section 38.

(2) Every order passed by the Competent Authority under section 38, or disapproved by the officer under section 42, shall be placed before the Review Committee, which shall be considered by the Review Committee within ten days after its receipt, to decide whether the order, was necessary, reasonable and justified.

(3) The Review Committee, after examining the entire record and holding such enquiry, if any, deemed necessary may, by order in writing, either approve the order passed by the Competent Authority or may issue order disapproving the same.

(4) On issue of an order of disapproval by Review Committee, the interception, if any, already commenced shall by forthwith discontinued and the intercepted communication, if any, in the form of tape, wire or other device shall, thereupon, not be admissible as evidence in any case and shall be directed to be destroyed.

46. **Interception and Disclosure of Wire, Electronic or Oral Communications Prohibited**- Except as otherwise specifically provided in section 38, any police officer who-

(a) intentionally intercepts, endeavours to intercept, or procures any other person to intercept or endeavour to intercept any wire, electronic or oral communication.

(b) intentionally used, endeavours to use , or procures any other person to use or endeavours to use any electronic, mechanical or other device to intercept any oral communication when-

(i) such device is affixed to, or otherwise transmits a signal through a wire cable, or other like connection used in wire communications; or

(ii) such device transmits communications by radio, or interferes with the transmission of such communication;

(c) intentionally discloses, or endeavours to disclose, to any other person the contents of any wire, electronic or oral communication, knowing or having reason to know that the information was obtained through the interception of a wire, electronic or oral communication in violation of this Chapter;

(d) intentionally uses, or endeavours to use, the contents of any wire, electronic or oral communication, knowing or having reason to know that the information was obtained through the interception of a wire, electronic or oral communication in violation of this Chapter; or

(e) intentionally discloses, or endeavours to disclose, to any other unauthorized person the contents of any wire, electronic or oral communication, intercepted by means authorized by section 38; the interception of wire, electronic or oral communication after the issue of an order of rejection by the Competent Authority under this Chapter.

(f) intentionally continnes

(g) intentionally continues the interception of wire, electronic or oral communication after the issue of an order of disapproval by the Review Committee under sub-section (3) of section 45, shall for such violation be punishable with imprisonment for a term which may extend to one year and with fine upto rupees fifty thousand.

47. Annual Report of Interceptions- (1) The Central Government and the State Government, as the case may be, shall cause an annual report to be prepared giving a full account of-

(i) the number of applications for authorization of interceptions received by the competent Authority from the Police Department in which prosecutions have been launched;

(ii) the number of such applications permitted or rejected;

(iii) the number of interceptions carried out in emergency situations and the number of approvals granted or rejected in such matters;

(iv) the number of prosecutions launched based on such interceptions and convictions resulting from such interceptions, along with an explanatory memorandum giving general assessment of the utility and importance of the interceptions authorized.

(2) An annual report shall be laid by the State Government before the State Legislature within three months of the completion of every calendar year:

Provided that, if the State Government is of the opinion that the inclusion of any matter in the annual report would be prejudicial to the security of the State or to the prevention of detection of any terrorist act, the State Government may exclude such matter from being included in such annual report.

(3) An annual report shall be laid by the Central Government before each House of Parliament within three months of the completion of every calendar year:

Provided that, if the Central Government is of the opinion that the inclusion of any matter in the annual report would be prejudicial to the security of the country or to the prevention or detection of any terrorist act, the Central Government may exclude such matter from being included in such annual report.

Chapter VI

Miscellaneous

48. **Modified Application of Certain Provisions of the Code**- (1) Notwithstanding anything contained in the Code or any other law, every offence punishable under this Ordinance shall be deemed to be a congnizable offence within the meaning of clause (c) of section 2 of the Code, and "congizable case" as defined in that clause shall be construed accordingly.

(2) Section 167 of the Code shall apply in relation to a case involving an offence punishable under this Ordinance subject to the modification that in sub-section (2)-

(a) the references to "fifteen days", "ninety days" and "sixty days", wherever thay occur, shall be construed as references to "thirty days" "ninety days" and 'ninety days", respectively; and

(b) after the proviso, the following provisos shall be inserted, namely:-

"Provided further that if it is not possible to complete the investigation within the said period of ninety days, the Special Court shall extend the said period up to one hundred and eighty days, on the report of the Public Prosecutor indicating the progress of the investigation and the specific reasons for the detenti on of the accused beyond the said period of ninety days:

Provided also that if the police officer making the investigation under this Ordinance, requests, for the purposes of investigation, for police custody from judicial custody of any person from judicial custody, he shall file in assidavit stating the reasons for doing so and shall also explain the delay, if any, for requesting such police custody."

(3) Section 268 of the Code shall apply in relation to a case involving an offence punishable under this Ordinance subject of the modification that-

(a) the preference in sub- section (1) thereof-

(i) to "the State Government" shall be construed as a reference to the Central Government or the State Government",

(ii) to " order of the State Government" shall be construed as a reference to "order of the Central Government or the State Government, as the case may be" , and

(b) the reference in sub-section (2) thereof, to "State Government" shall be construed as a reference to "Central Government or the State Government, as the case may be"

(4) Sections 366, 367 and 371 of the Code shall apply in relation to a case involving an offence triable by a Special Court subject to the modification that the reference to "Court of Session" , wherever occurring therein, shall be construed as the reference to " Special Court".

(5) Nothing in section 438 of the code shall apply in relation to any case involving the arrest of any person accused of having ommitted and offence punishable under this Ordinance.

(6) Notwithstanding anything contained in the Code, no person

accused of an offence punishable under this Ordinance shall, if in custody, be released on bail or on his own bond unless the Court gives the Public Prosecutor an opportunity of being heard.

(7) Where the Public Prosecuctor opposes the application of the accused to release on bail, no person accused of an offence punishable under this Ordinance or any rule made thereunder shall be released on bail until the court is satisfied that there are grounds for believing that he is not guilty of committing such offence:

Provided that after the expiry of a period of one year from the date of detention of the accused for an offence under this Ordinance, the provisions of sub- section (6) of this section shall apply.

(8) The restrictions on granting of bail specified in sub-sections (6) and (7) are in addition to the restriction under the code or any other law for the time being in force on granting of bail.

(9) Notwithstanding anything contained in sub-sections (6), (7) and (8), no bail shall be granted to a person accused of an offence punishable under this Ordinance , if he is not an Indian citizen and has entered the country unauthorisedly of illegally except in very exceptional circumstances and for reasons to be recorded in writing.

49. **Cognizance of offences-** No Court shall take cognizance of any offence under this Ordinance without the previous sanction of the Central Government or as the case may be, the State Government.

50. **Officers Competent to Investigate Offences Under This Ordinance-** Notwithstanding anything contained in the Code, no police officers

(a) in the case of the Delhi Special Police Establishment, not below the rank of a Deputy Superintendent of Police or a police officer of equivalent rank;

(b) in the metropolitan areas of Mumbai, Kolkata, Chennai and Ahmedabad and any other metropolitan area notified as such under sub section (1) of section 8 of the Code, not below the rank of and Assistant Commissioner of Police;

(c) in any other case not relatable to clause (a) or caluse (b) or , not below the rank of a Deputy Superintendent of Police or a police officer of an equivalent rank, shall investigate any offence punishable under this Ordinance.

51. **Arrest**- (1) Where a police officer arrests a person, he shall prepare a custody memo of the person arrested.

(2) The person arrested shall be informed of his right to consult a legal practitioner as soon as he is brought to the police station.

(3) Whenever any person is arrested, information of his arrest shall be immediately communicated by the police officer to a family member or in his absence to a relative of such person by telegram, telephone or by any other means and this fact shall be recorded by the police officer under the signature of the person arrested.

(4) The person arrested shall be permitted to meet the legal practitioner representing him during the course of interrogation of the accused person:

Provided that nothing in this sub-section shall entitle the legal practitioner to remain present throughout the period of interrogation.

52. **Presumption as to Offences Under Section 3**- (1) In a prosecution for an offence under sub-section (1) of section 3, if it is proved-

(a) that the arms or explosives or any other substances specified in section 4 were recovered from the possession of the accused and there is reason to believe that such arms or explosives or other substances of a similar nature, were used in the commission of such offence; or

(b) that the finger-prints of the accused were found at the site of the offence or on anything including arms and vehicles used in connection with the commission of such offence.

the Special Court shall draw adverse inference against the accused.

(2) In a prosecution for an offence under sub-section (3) of section 3, if it is proved that the accused rendered any financial assistance to a person, having knowledge that such person is accused of, or reasonably suspected of, an offence under that section, the Special Court shall draw adverse inference against the accused.

53. **Bar of Jurisdiction of Courts, etc.**- No civil court or other authority shall have, or be entitled to exercise any jurisdiction,

powers or authority in relation to the matters referred to in section 19 and section 39 of the Ordinance.

54. **Saving**-(I) Nothing in this Ordinance shall affect the jurisdiction exercisable by, or the procedure applicable to , any court or other authority under any law relating to the naval, military or air forces or other armed forces of the Union.

(2) For the removal of doubts, it is hereby declared that for the purposes of any such law as is referred to in sub- section (l), a Special Court shall be deemed to be a court of ordinary criminal justice.

55. **Overriding effect**- The provisions of this Ordinance shall have effect notwithstanding anything inconsistent therewith contained in any enactment other than Ordinance or in any instrument having effect by virtue of any enactment other than this Ordinance.

56. **Protection of Action Taken in Good Faith**- No suit, prosecution or other legal proceeding shall lie against the Central Government or State Government or any authority of the Central Government or State Government or any other authority on whom powers have been conferred under this Ordinance, for anything which is in good faith done or purported to be done in pursuance of this ordinance:

Provided further that no suit, prosecution or other legal proceedings shall lie against any serving member of the armed forces or other paramilitary forces in respect of any action taken or purported to be taken by him in good faith, in the course of any operation directed towards combating terrorism.

57. **Punishment and Compensation for Malicious Action**- (1) Any police officer who exercises powers corruptly or maliciously, knowing that there are no reasonable ground for procuding under this Ordinance, shall be punishable with imprisonment which may extend to two years, or with fine, or with both.

(2) If the Special Court is of opinion that any person has been corruptly or maliciously proceeded against under this Ordinance, the court may award such compensation as it deems fit to the person, so proceeded against and it shall be paid by the officer, person, authority or Government, as may be specified in the order.

58. **Impounding of Passport and Arms Licence of Person charge sheeted under the Ordinance**- Notwithstanding anything contained in any other law for the time being in force, the passport and the arms licence of a person, who is chargesheeted for having committed any offence under this Ordinance, shall be deemed to have been impounded for such period as the Special Court may deem fit.

59. **Review Committees**- (1) The Central Government and each State Government shall, whenever necessary, constitute, one or more Review Committees for the purposes of this ardinance.

(2) Every such committee shall consist of a Chairperson and such other members not exceeding there and possessing such qualifications as may be prescribed.

(3) A Chairperson of the Committee shall be a person who is , or who has been, a Judge of a High Court, who shall be appointed by the Central Government, or as the case may be, the State Government, so however, that the oconcurrence of the Chief Justice of the High Court shall be obtained in the case of a sitting Judge:

Provided that in the case of a Union territory, the appointment of a person who is a Judge of the High Court of a state shall be made as a Chairperson with the concurrence of the Chief Justice to the concerned High Court.

60. **Power of High Courts to make Rules**- The High Courts may, by notifications in the Official Gazette make such rules, if any, as they may deem necessary for carrying out the provisions of this Ordinance relating to special Courts within their territories.

61. **Power to Make Rules**- (1) Without prejudice to the powers of the High Courts to make rules under section 60, the Central Government may, by notification in the Official Gazette, make rules for carrying out the provisions of this Ordinance.

(2) In particular, and without prejudice to the generality of the foregoing power, such rules may provide for all or any of the following matters, namely:-

(a) regulating the conduct of persons in respect of areas the control of which is considered necessary or expedient and the removal of such persons from such areas;

(b) the entry into, and search of,-

(i) any vehicle, vessel or aircraft; or

(ii) any place, whatsoever,

reasonably suspected of being used for committing the offences refferred to in section 3 or section 4 for manufacturing or storing anything for the commission of any such offence;

(c) Conferring powers upon,-

(i) the Central Government;

(ii) a State Government:

(iii) an Administrator of a Union territory under article 239 of the Constitution;

(iv) an officer of the Central Government not lower in rank than that of a Joint Secretary ; or

(v) an officer of a State Government not lower in rank than that of a District Magistrate,

to make general or special orders to prevent or deal with terrorist acts;

(d) the arrest and trial of.persons contravening any of the rules or any order made there under;

(e) the punishment of any person who contravenes or attempts to contravene or abets or attempts to abet the contravention of any rule or order made thereunder with imprisonment for a term which may extend to one year or fine or both.

(f) providing for the seidiure and detention of any property in respect of which such contravention attempt or abetment as is referred to in clause (e) has been committed and for the adjudication of such seizure and detention, whether by any court or by any other authority.

(g) determination of the price of the forfeited property under sub- section (2) section 10;

(h) the procedure of making application under sub-section (3) of section 19.

(i) the qualifications of the members of the Review committee under sub-section (2) of section 59.

SCHEDULE

(see section 18)

TERRORIST ORGANISATIONS

1. BABBAR KHALSA INTERNATIONAL.
2. KHALISTAN COMMANDO FORCE
3. KHALISTAN ZINDABAD FORCE
4. INTERNATIONAL SIKH YOUTH FEDERATION.
5. LASHKAR-E TAYABBA / PASBAN- E- AHLE HADIS.
6. JAISH-E- MOHAMMED / TAHRIK-E-FURQAN.
7. HARKAT-UL- MUJAHIDEEN / HARKAT-UL- ANSAR / KARKAT-UL-JEHAD-E-ISLAMI.
8. HIZB-UL-MUJAHIDEEN / HIZB-UL-MUJAHIDEEN PIR PANJAL REGIMENT.
9. AL- UMAR-MUJAHIDEEN.
10. JAMMU AND KASHMIR ISLAMIC FRONT.
11. UNITED LIBERATION FRONT OF ASSAM (ULFA).
12. NATIONAL DEMOCRATIC FRONT OF BODOLAND (NDFB).
13. PEOPLE'S LIBERATION ARMY (PLA).
14. UNITED NATIONAL LIBERATION FRONT (UNLF).
15. PEOPLE'S REVOLUTIONARY PARTY OF KANGLEIPALK (PREPAK).
16. KANLEIPAK COMMUNIST PARTY (KCP).
17. KANGLEI YAOL KANBA LUP (KYKL)
18. MANIPUR PEOPLE'S LIBERATION FRONT (MPLF).
19. ALL TRIPURA TIGER FORCE.

20. NATIONAL LIBERATION FRONT OF TRIPURA.
21 LIBERATION TIGERS OF TAMIL EELAM (LTTE).
22. STUDENTS ISLAMIC MOVEMENT OF INDIA (SIMI).

Bibliography

Aldrich, F.D. & Gooding, J.F., 1976. Pesticides. In: Newberne, P.M. (ed.), 1976. *Trace Substances and Health. A Handbook.* Part I. New York and Basel : Marcel Dekker.

Allured, V.S., Case, L.M., Leppla, S.H. & McKay, D.B., 1985. Crystallization of the protective antigen protein of *Bacillus anthracis. Journal of Biological Chemistry,* **260**(8): 5012-13.

Alouf, J.E., Fehrenback, F.J., Freer, J.H. & Jeljaszewicz, J., 1984. *Bacterial Protein Toxins.* London: Academic Press.

Anderson III, W.C. & King, J.M., 1983. Vaccine and antitoxin availability for defense against biological warfare threat agents. *U.S. Army Health Care Studies Division Report No. 83-002.* Fort Sam Houston, TX: US Army Health Services Command.

Anonymous, 1976. Between 1950 and 1966, eight germ-war tests in U.S. are acknowledged by Army. *International Herald Tribune,* (23 Dec.): 1.

Anonymous, 1981 a, Biological protection against chemical warfare. Military record of CBR/atomic happenings. *Aviation Studies Atlantic, Report WS 112/81:4.*

Anonymous, 1981b. US accused by Cuba of germ warfare. *The Times,* (26 Sep.).

Anonymous, 1984a. Chemical and bacteriological weapons in the 1980s. *Lancet,* London (2), (21 July): 141-3.

Anonymous, 1984b. Russian tells West's scientists of dangers of biological war. *International Herald Tribune* (31 May): 5.

Anonymous, 1984c, Documents show U.S. tested germs in public. *New York Times,* (4 Dec.): 8.

Anonymous, 1985a. Recombinant DNA research projects. *gene WATCH,* Boston, MA, 2: 14-15.

Anonymous, 1985b. Exposed-ghastly truth of Japanese death camps. *Liverpool Daily Post,* (10 Aug.).

Anonymous, 1985c. Japanese biological research atrocities claimed. British POWs tell how they were germ lab 'guinea-pigs'. *The Times,* (12 Aug.).

Anonymous, 1985d. AIDS germ warfare fear. Morning Star, London, (20 Dec.): 5.

Anonymous, 1985e. *New York Times,* (1 June).

Anonymous, 1986a. 1948 genocide pact approved in U.S. *International Herald Tribune,* (21 Feb.): 2.

Anonymous, 1986b. The anti-genocide treaty. *International Herald Tribune*, (22-23 Feb.): 6.

Asinof, R., 1984. Averting genetic warfare. *Environmental Action*, Washington, **16** (1): 1, 16-22.

Audibert, F., Jolivet, M., Chedid, L., Alouf, J., Boquit, P., Rivaille, P. & Siffert, O., 1981. Active antitoxic immunization by a diphtheria toxin synthetic oligopeptide. *Nature*, **284**: 593-5.

Audibert, F., Jolivet, M., Chedid, L., Gras-Masse, H. & Tartar, A., 1985. Construction of antimicrobial polyvalent synthetic vaccines active in saline. In: Lerner, R.A. et al., 1985: 139-42.

Beaty, B.J., Holterman, M., Tarachnick, W., Shope, R.E., Rozhon, J. & Bishop, D.H.L., 1981. Molecular basis of bunyavirus transmission by mosquitoes: The role of the M RNA segment. *Science*, **211**: 1433-5.

Besiel, W.R., 1976. Enterotoxin-mediated diseases. In: Newberne, P.M. (ed.). *Trace Substances and Health, A Handbook Part 1.* New York and Basel: Marcel Dekker.

Berg, P., Baltimore, D., Boyer, H.W., Cohen, S.N., Davies, R.W., Hogness, D.S., Nathans, D., Roblin, R., Watson, J.D., Weissman, S. & Zinder, N.D., 1974. Potential biohazards of recombinant DNA molecules. *Proceedings of the National Academy of Sciences (USA)*, **71** (7): 2593-4.

Berg, P., Baltimore, D., Brenner, S., Roblin III, R.O. & Singer, M. F., 1975. Summary statement of the Asilomar conference on recombinant DNA molecules. *Proceedings of the National Academy of Sciences (USA)*, **72**: 1981-4.

Betley, M. J. & Lofdahl, S., Kreiswirth, B. N., Bergdoll, M. S. & Novick, R. P., 1984. Staphylococcal enterotoxin A gene is associated with a variable genetic element. *Proceedings of the National Academy of Sciences* (USA), 81: 5179-83.

Betley, M. J. & Mekalanos, J. J., 1985. Staphylococcal enterotoxin A is encoded by phage. *Science*, **229** (4709): 185-7.

Bezdenezhnzkh, I. S. & Nikoforov, V. N., 1980. Epidemiologic analysis of cases of Siberian ulcer (anthrax) in Sverdlovsk. *Zhurnal Mikrobiologii, Epidemiologii i Immunbiologii*, 51: 111-13. (In Russian).

Bittle, J. L., Houghten, R.A., Alexander, H., Shinnick, T. M., Sutcliffe, J. G., Lerner, R.A., Rowlands, D. J. & Brown, F., 1982. Protection against foot and mouth disesase by immunization with a chemically synthesized peptide predicted from the viral nucleotide sequence. *Nature*, **298** (5869): 30-3.

Blöcker, H. & Frank, R., 1986. Synthetic genes. In: Silver, S. (ed)., 1986. *Biotechnology: Potentials and Limitations*. Dahlem Konferenzen. Berlin: Springer-Verlag.

Blount, R. E.. & Crozier, D., 1963. Antibiotic prophylaxis and treatment. *Military Medicine* **128**(2): 129-31.

Blundell, T. & Sternberg, M. J. E., 1985. Computer-aided design in protein engineering. *Trends in Biotechnology,* **3**(9): 228-34.

Borisov, K., 1983. For strict observance of the Bacteriological Weapons Ban. *International Affairs,* Moscow (Aug.) **(8)**: 98.

Bornheimer, A. W. & Schwartz, L. L., 1963. Isolation and composition of staphylococcal alpha toxin. *Journal of General Microbiology,* **38**: 455-9.

Botstein, D. & Shortle, D., 1985. Strategies and applications of *in vitro* mutagenesis. *Science,* **229**(4719): 1193-201.

Boulter, J., Evans, K., Goldman, D., Martin, G., Treco, D., Heinemann, S. & Patrick, J., 1986. Isolation of a DNA clone coding for a possible neural nicotinic acetylcholine receptor subunit. *Nature,* **319**(6052): 368-74.

Boyle, F. A., 1986. Memorandum of Francis A. Boyle to Committee for Responsible Genetics containing text of Draft Biological Weapons Act of 1986 (7pp).

Brenner, S., 1982. Recombinants that are the same but different. In: Plant, D. W., Reimers, J. J. & Zinder, N. D. (eds), 1982. *Patenting of Life Forms.* Banbury Report 10. Cold Spring Harbor, NY: Cold Spring Harbor Laboratory.

Brinster, R. L. & Palmiter, R. D., 1982. Induction of foreign genes in animals. *Trends in Biochemical Science,* **7**: 438-40.

Brockhaus, 1923. *Brockhaus' Handbuch des Wissens in vier Banden.* Leipzig: Brockhaus-Verlag.

Brown, F., Schild, G.C. & Ada, G. L., 1986. Recombinant vaccinia viruses as vaccines. *Nature,* **319**(6054): 549-50.

Budiansky, S., 1982. US looks to biological weapons. Military takes new interest in DNA devices. *Nature,* **297** (5868): 615-16.

Buller, R. M. L., Smith, G. L., Cremer, K., Notkins, A. L. & Moss, B., 1985. Decreased virulence of recombinant vaccinia virus expression vectors is associated with a thymidine kinase-negative phenotype. *Nature,* **317** (6040):813-15.

Busby, Jr, W. F. & Wogan, G. N., 1981a. Aflatoxins. In: Shank, R. C. (ed), 1981. *Mycotoxins and N-nitroso Compounds: Envirionmental Risks.* Boca Raton, FL: CRC Press.

Busby, Jr, W. F. & Wogan, G.N., 1981b. Trichothecenes. In: Shank, R. C. (ed), 1981. *Mycotoxins and N-nitroso Compounds: Environmental Risks.* Boca Raton, FL: CRC Press.

Callaham, M.B. & Tsipis, K. M., 1978. Biological warfare and recombinant DNA. *Bulletin of the Atomic Scientists,* **34** (9 Nov.): 11-50.

Cambray, G., 1985. High containment laboratory systems and safety cabinets. *International Labmate*, Herts, UK: St. Albans, **10**(5): 33-5.

Chahl, L. A. & Kirk, E. J., 1975. Toxins which produce pain. *Pain*, 1(1):3-49.

Chan, S.J., Noyes, B., Agarwal, K. & Steiner, D., 1979. Construction and selection of recombinant plasmids containing full-length complementary DNAs corresponding to rat insulin I and II. *Proceedings of the National Academy of Sciences (USA)*, **76**: 5036-40.

Changeux, J. P., Devillers - Thiery, A. & Chemouilli, P., 1984. Acetylcholine receptor: An allosteric protein. *Science*, **225**: 1335-45.

Chanock, R. M. & Lerner R. A. (eds), 1984. *Modern Approaches to Vaccines. Molecular and Chemical Basis of Virus Virulence and Immunogenicity*. Cold Spring Harbor, NY: Cold Spring Harbor Laboratory.

Clarke, R., 1968. *We All Fall Down. The Prospect of Biological and Chemical Warfare*. London: Penguin Press.

Clark-Lewis, I., Aebersold, R., Ziltener, H., Schrader, J. W., Hood, L. E. & Kent, S. B. H., 1986. Automated chemical synthesis of a protein growth factor for hemopoietic cells, interleukin-3. *Science*, **231** (4734): 134-9.

Clegg, J. C. S. & Oram, J. D., 1985. Molecular cloning of Lassa virus RNA: Nucleotide sequence and expression of the nucleocapsid protein gene. *Virology*, **144**: 363-72.

COGENE (Committee on Genetic Experimentation), 1980. *Report to COGENE from the Working Group on Recombinant DNA Guidelines*, Miami, FL.

Cohen, P. & van Heyningen, S. (eds), 1982. *Molecular Action of Toxins and Viruses*. Vol. 2 of *Molecular Aspects of Cellular Regulation*. Amsterdam: Elsevier Biomedical Press.

Cold Spring Harbor Laboratory, 1984. *Molecular Neurobiology*. Cold Spring Harbor Symposia on Quantitative Biology, Vol. 48. Cold Spring Harbor, NY.

Cole, L. A., 1982. Americans as guinea pigs: The Army's secret germ-war testing. *The Nation* **235** (23 Oct.): 397-9.

Cole, L. A., 1984. Yellow rain or yellow journalism? *Bulletin of the Atomic Scientists*, **40**(7): 36-8.

Cole, L. A., 1985. Operation Bacterium. Testing germs on the A Train. *Washington Monthly*, **17**(6, 7): 38-45.

Collett, M. S., Purchio, A. F., Keegan, K., Frazier, S., Hays, W., Anderson, D. K., Parker, M. D., Schmaljohn, C., Schmidt, J. & Dalrymple, J. M., 1985. Complete nucleotide sequence of the M RNA segment of Rift Valley fever virus. *Virology*, **144**: 228-45.

Collier, R. J. & Kaplan, D. A., 1984. Immunotoxins. *Scientific American*, **251** (1): 44-52.

Collins, J., 1986. Animals and medicines. In: Silver, S. (ed), 1986. *Biotechnology: Potentials and Limitations*. Dahlem Konferenzen. Berlin: Springer-Verlag.

Collins, J. M. & Cronin, P. M., 1985. *U. S. -Soviet Military Balance 1980-1985*. Washington, New York, Oxford, London, Toronto, Sydney, Frankfurt: Pergamon-Brassey's.

Cookson, J. & Nottingham, J., 1969. *A Survey of Chemical and Biological Warfare*. London and Sydney: Sheed and Ward.

Curran, J. W., Morgan, W. M., Hardy, A. M., Jaffe, H. W., Darrow, W. W. & Dowdle, W. R., 1985. The epidemiology of AIDS: current status and future prospects. *Science*, **229**: 1352-7.

Cushman, J., 1985. Experts raise specter of biological warfare. *Defense Week*, **6**(26): 1, 5.

Dallas, W. S. & Falkow, S., 1979. The molecular nature of heat-labile enterotoxin (LT) of *Escherichia coli*. *Nature*, **277**: 406-7.

Damodaran, A. K., Kothari, R.& Subrahmanyam, K., 1983. *Common Security and the Developing World*. New Delhi: Institute for Defence Studies and Analysis.

Dasey, C., 1984. Biotechnology and its applications to military medical R & D. *Army R, D & A Magazine*, **25**(4):12-13.

Davies, J. C., 1982. A major epidemic of anthrax in Zimbabwe. *Central African Journal of Medicine*, **12**: 291-8.

Derbes, V. J., 1966. De Mussis and the Great Plague of 1348. A forgotten episode of bacteriological warfare. *Journal of the American Medical Association*, **196**:59-62.

Dick, G., 1966. Smallpox: a reconsideration of public health policies. *Progress in Medical Virology*, **8**: 1-29.

Dixon, B., 1973. Biological research. *New Scientist*, **60**(869): 236.

Douglass, Jr, J. D., 1982. Chemical weapons. An imbalance of terror. *Strategic Review*, **10**(3): 36-47.

Douglass, Jr, J.D. & Lukens, H. R., 1984. The expanding arena of chemical-biological warfare. *Strategic Review*, **12**(4): 71-9.

Doyle, J., 1985. *Altered Harvest*. New York: Viking Press.

Dubois, J. M. & Cohen, J. B., 1977. Effect of palytoxin on membrane potential and current of frog myelinated fibers. *Journal of Pharmacology and Experimental Therapy*, **201**: 148-55.

Echeverria, P., Seriwatana, H., Chityothin, O., Chaicumpa, W. & Tirapat, C., 1982. Detection of enterotoxigenic *Escherichia coli* in water by filter hybridization with three enterotoxin gene probes. *Journal of Clinical Microbiology*, **16**: 1086-90.

ECN Process Supplement, 1985. European firms set for biotech equipment boom. (Nov.): 20.

Edelmann, F., 1985. Zu wissenschaftlichen Grundlagen des potentiellen Missbrauches ausgewählter genetisch determinierter. ethnisch relevanter Proteinpolymorphismen-Beitrag zur Kenntnis der Problematik. Dissertation. Leipzig: Karl-Marx Universität.

Editorial, 1971. Isolation of the cholinergic receptor protein. *Nature*, **229**(5286): 523-4.

Editorial, 1977. *Bulletin of the Atomic Scientists*, **33**(2): 36.

Editorial, 1979. How the U. S. used its citizens as guinea pigs. *Saturday Review*, **6**(22): 10.

Editorial, 1982a. Japan's biological weapons: 1930-1945—an update. *Bulletin of the Atomic Scientists*, **38**(8): 62.

Editorial, 1982b. Chemical inspections. *Nature*, **296**(5852): 2.

Editorial, 1983. More tests in anthrax bland. *Daily Telegraph*, (25 Apr.): 10.

Editorial, 1985. 'A mathematical model for the global spread of influenza' by Leonid A. Rvachev and Ira M. Longini, Jr. *Mathematical Biosciences*, **75**: 1.

Elwell, L. P. & Shipley, P. L., 1980. Plasmid-mediated factors associated with virulence of bacteria to animals. *Annual Review of Microbiology*, **34**: 465-96.

Eto, M. 1974. *Organophosphorus Pesticides: Organic and Biological Chemistry*. Cleveland, OH: Chemical Rubber Company.

Faras, A., Sadowski, P., Pilacinski, W., Hu, S-L., Halling, S., Collett, M., Salström, J., Watson, R., Robbins, A., Muscoplat, C., Enqvist, L., Sherman, D. & Acres, S., 1983. The efficiency of bioengineered anti-toxins and vaccines for animal health care. In: Downey, K. (ed.), 1983. *Advances in Gene Technology*. New York: Academic Press.

Fenner, F., 1985. Lessons from the smallpox eradication campaign. In: Lerner, R.A. *et al.*, 1985

Fields, B.N. (ed.), 1985. *Virology*. New York: Raven Press.

Fiers, W., 1986. The future role in medicine of proteins made by genetic engineering. In: Silver, S. (ed)., 1986. *Biotechnology: Potential and Limitations*. Dahlem Konferenzen. Berlin: Springer-Verlag.

Finn, Jr, C. W., Silver, R. P., Habig, W. H., Hardegree, M.C., Zon, G. & Garon, C. F., 1984. The structural gene tetanus neurotoxin is on a plasmid. *Science*, **224**: 881-4.

Fischer, D. A. V., 1982. Safeguards—a model for general arms control? *IAEA Bulletin*, (June), **24**(2): 45-9.

Fischer-Fabian, S., 1985. *Der jüngste Tag*. Munich: Droemer-Knaur Verlag.

Franck, B., 1984. Mycotoxins from mold fungi-weapons of uninvited fellow-boarders of man and animal: structures, biological activity, biosynthesis, and precautions. *Angewandte Chemic* (International Edition in English), **23**: 493-505.

Franke, S., 1977. *Lehrbuch der Militärchemie*. 2 Vols, 2nd ed. Berlin: Militärverlag der DDR.

FRG (Federal Republic of Germany), 1955. Gesetz betreffend den Beitritt der Bundesrepublik Deutschland zum Brüsseler Vertrag und zum Nordatlantik vertrag. (May) No. 24. *Bundesgesetzblatt*, Part II (25 Mar.), 7: 256-94 (Protokoll III über die Rustüngskontrolle: 266-73).

FRG, 1978, H. Schmidt's Address presented before the tenth Special Session of the UN General Assembly Devoted to Disarmament, New York, 26 May. Reprinted in *Chemical and Biological Warfare: Selected Issues and Developments during 1978 and January 1-June 30, 1979* by J. M. McCullough. US Congress, Congressional Research Service, Document UG447 of 1 July 1979; 32-3.

FRG, 1984. Deutscher Bundestag, Antwort der Bundesregierung, Wehrmedizinsche Entwicklungsamfträge und Forschungen im Bereich von "B-Waffen". Drucksache 10/3718 , (12 Aug.) (quotation: *Drucksache* 10/3718).

FRG, 1986. Anfrage des Mitglieds des Deutschen Bundestages Torsten Lange an die Bundesregierung (1 June).

Funatsu, A., Yoshitake, S. & Funatsu, M. 1978. Primary structure of Ile chain of ricin D. *Agricultural and Biological Chemistry*, **42**: 501-3.

Gaastra, W. & de Graaf, F. K., 1982. Host-specific fimbrial adhesions of noninvasive enterotoxic *Escherichia coli* strains. *Microbiological Reviews*, **46**: 129-61.

Geffard, M., McRae-Degueurce, A. & Sovan, M. L., 1985. Immunocytochemical detection of acetylcholine in the rat central nervous system. *Science*, **229**(4708): 77-9.

Geissler, E., 1984a. Implications of genetic engineering for chemical and biological warfare. In: SIPRI, 1984. *World Armaments and Disarmament: SIPRI Yearbook 1984*. London and Philadelphia: Taylor & Francis, 421-54.

Geissler, E., 1984b. *Bruder Frankenstein oder-AF Pflegefälle aus der Retorte, Sinn und Form*, Berlin, **36**(6): 1289-319.

Geissler, E., 1995. B-Waffen und Geningenieure. In: Dosch, W. & Herrlich, P. (eds), 1985. *Achtung der Giftwaffen. Naturwissenschaftler warnen vor Chemischen und Biologischen Waffen*. Frankfurt am Main: Fischer Taschenbuch Verlag.

Geissler, E. & Theile, M., 1983. Virus-induced gene mutations of eukaryotic cells. *Human Genetics*, **63**: 1-12.

Gilbert, W., 1981. DNA sequencing and gene structure. *Science*, **214**: 1305-12.

Gill, D. M., 1982. Bacterial toxins: a table of lethal amounts. *Microbial Reviews*. **46**: 86-94.

Glover, D.M., 1985. See Appendix 5, Recommendations for Further Reading, page 158.

Gluzman, Y. (ed), 1982. *Eukaryotic viral vectors*. Cold Spring Harbor, NY: Cold Spring Harbor Laboratory.

Goldblat, J., 1982. *Agreements for Arms Control. A Critical Survey*. (A SIPRI book).London and Philadelphia: Taylor & Francis.

Gonzalez, J. P., Buchmeier, M. J., McCormick, J. B., Mitchell, S. W., Elliott, L. H. & Kiley, M. P., 1984. Comparative analysis of Lassa and Lassa-like arenavirus isolates from Africa. In: Compans, R. W. & Bishop, D. H. L., (eds), 1984. *Segmented Negative Strand Viruses*. Orlando, San Diego: Academic Press.

Gray, G. S. & Kehoe, M., 1984. Primary sequence of the λ-toxin gene from *Staphylo-coccus aureus* Wood **46**. *Infection and Immunology*, **46**(2): 615-18.

Greenfield, L., Bjorn, M. J., Horn, G., Fong, D., Buck, G. A., Collier, R. J. & Kaplan. D. A., 1983. Nucleotide sequence of the structural gene for diphtheria toxin carried by corynebacteriophage β. Proceedings of the *National Academy of Sciences (USA)*, **80**(22) 6853-57.

Gegoriadis, G., 1983. Liposomes as drug carriers. *Pharmacology International*, **4**: 33-7.

Gregoriadis, G., 1984. *Liposome Technology*. **3** Vols. Boca Raton, FL: CRC Press. Hackett, D., 1985. Television. Japan's dreadful secret. *The Times* (14 Aug.).

Hammerschlag, R., 1974. Ethnic weapons. In: *Chemical Weapons and U.S. Public Policy*, Washington, DC: American Chemical Society.

Harris, R. & Paxman, J., 1982. *A higher form of killing. The Secret Story of Gas and Germ Warfare*. London: Chatto and Windus.

Harris, R. & Paxman, J., 1985. *Eine hohere Form des Totens. Die undekannte Geschichte der B-und C-Waffen*. Von den Autoren aktualisierte Ausgabe. Munich: Deutscher Taschenbuch Verlag.

Harrison, K. & Hattis, D., 1985. *Containment of Genetically Engineered Microorganisms*: A Comparison *of Expected Releases during Greenhouse Trials with Releases in Ordinary Research and Development*. Report No. CTPID 85-2. Cambridge, MA: Center for Technology, Policy, and Industrial Development, MIT.

Hayakawa, S., Uchida, T., Mekada, E., Moynihan, M. R. & Okada, Y., 1983. Monoclonal antibody against diphtheria toxin. Effenct on toxin binding and entry into cell. *Journal of Biological Chemistry*, **258**: 4311-17.

Hayes, A. W., 1981. *Mycotoxin Teratogenicity and Mutagenicity*. Boca Raton, FL: CRC Press.

Hersh, S. M., 1968. *Chemical and Biologial Warfare. America's Hidden Arsenal*. London: MacGibbon & Kee.

Hilleman, M. R., 1985. Newer directions in vaccine development and utilization. *Journal of Infectious Diseases*, **151**(3): 407-19.

Ho, C., Jasin, M. & Schimmel, P., 1985. Amino acid replacements that compensate for a large polypeptide deletion in an enzyme. Science, **229**(4711): 389-93.

Hoeber, A. & Douglass, Jr, J. D., 1978. Das Problem chemischer Kriegfuhrung. *Europäische Wehrkunde*, **10**: 489-95.

Hofschneider, P. H. & Goebel, W., 1982. Gene cloning in organisms other than *Escherichia coli*. *Current Topics in Microbiology and Immunology*. Vol. 96. Berlin, Heidelberg, New York: Springer-Verlag.

Holder, I. A., 1985. *Bacterial enzymes and virulence*. Boca Raton, FL: CRC Press.

Holmberg, B., 1975. Biological aspects of chemical and biological weapons. *Ambio*, **4**(5-6): 211-15.

Holmgren, J., 1985. Toxins affecting intestinal transport processes. In: Sussman, M. (ed.), 1985. *The Virulence of Escherichia coli*. London: Academic Press.

Hotz, R. L., 1985. Biowarfare: Specter of the ultimate nightmare. *Atlanta Constitution*, (17 Apr.): 1.

Hunkapiller, M. W. & Hood, L. E., 1983. Protein sequence analysis: Automated microsequencing. *Science*, **219**(4585): 650-59.

Hutwitz, E., 1982. Terrorists and chemical/biological weapons. *Naval War College Review*, Newport, RI, **35**(3): 36-40.

Ihara, T., Smith, J., Dalrymple, J.M. & Bishop, D. H.L., 1985. Complete sequences of the glycoproteins and M RNA of Punta Toro phlebovirus compared to those of Rift Valley fever virus. *Virology*, 144: 246-59.

Inoue, K. & Iida, H., 1971. Phage-conversion of toxigenicity in *Clostridium botulinum* types C and D. *Japanese Journal of Medical Science and Biology*, **24**: 53-6.

Japan, 1982. *Brief History of the Kwantong Army Anti-Epidemic Water Supply Unit*. Submitted to one of the committees of the Diet from the Japanese Ministry of Health and Welfare. Reprinted and translated by Tsuneishi, K., 1985:1-2-1-5.

Jones, L., Ristow, S., Yilma, T. & Moss, B., 1986. Accidental human vaccination with vaccinia virus expressing nucleoprotein gene. *Nature*, **319**(6054):543.

Kaczorek, M., Delpeyroux, F., Chenciner, N. & Streeck, R. E., 1983. Nucleotide sequence and expression of the diphtheria tox 228 gene in *Escherichia coli*. *Science*, **221**: 855-8.

Kanki, P. J., Alroy, J. & Essex, M., 1985. Isolation of T-lymphotropic retrovirus related to HTLV-III/LAV from wild-caught African Green Monkeys. *Science*, **230**(4728): 951-4.

Kaplan, M. M. & Webster, R. G., 1977. The epidemiology of influenza. *Scientific American*. **237**(6): 88-106.

Kasahara, S., 1985. Interview published in a TVS documentary 'Unit 731- Did the emperor know?'. First shown on ITV, London, 13 Aug.

Kauffman, R. S. & Fields, B. N., 1985. Pathogenesis of viral infections. In: Fields, B. N. (ed.), 1985: 153-167.

Kazazian, Jr, H. H., Antonarakis, S. E., Cheng, T., Boehm, C. D. & Waber, P. G., 1983. DNA polymorphisms in the β-globin gene cluster: Use in discovery of mutations and prenatal diagnosis. In: Caskey, C. T. & White, R. L. (eds), 1983. *Recombinant DNA Applications to Human Disease*, Banbury Report 14. Cold Spring Harbor, NY: Cold Spring Harbor Laboratory.

Kehoe, M., Dougan, G., Foster, T., Kennedy, S., Duncan J., Timmis, K., Grey, G. & Fairweather, N., 1984. Genetic analysis of toxins from gram positive cocci. In: Alouf, J. E. et al., 1984.

Kehoe, M., Duncan, J., Foster, T., Fairweather, N. & Dougan, G., 1983. Cloning, expression and mapping of the *Staphylococcus aureus* α-hemolysin determinant in *Escherichia coli* K-12. *Infection and Immunology*, **41**: 1105-11.

Kelly, R. B., Oberg, S. G., Strong, P. N. & Wanger, G. M., 1976. β-Bungarotoxin, a phospholipase that stimulates transmitter release. Cold Spring Harbor Symposia on Quantitative Biology (*The Synapse*), Vol. 40. Cold Spring Harbor, NY: Cold Spring Harbor Laboratory.

Kenny, M., 1985. The butchers who killed in the name of science. *Daily Mail*, (14 Aug.).

Khorana, H. G., 1979. Total synthesis of a gene. *Science*, 203 (4381): 614-25.

Kieny, M. P., Lathe, R., Drillien, D., Spehner, D., Skory, S., Schmitt, D., Wiktor, T., Koprowski, H. & Lecocq, J. P., 1984. Expression of rabies virus glycoprotein from a recombinant vaccinia virus. *Nature*, **312**: 163-66.

Kibourne, E.D., 1975. Introduction to viral diseases. In: Beeson, P.B. & McDermott, W. (eds), 1975. *Textbook of Medicine*, 14th ed. Philadelphia: W. B. Saunders.

King, J., 1982. The threat of biological weapons. *Technology Review*, **85**: 10-11.

King, J., 1985. The threat and falacy of a biological arms race. *Gene WATCH*, **2**(2): 13-20.

Klein, G., 1985. Book warns of chemical, biological terrorism. *Richmond Times-Dispatch*, (23 June): 2.

Klein, L. D., 1983. Chemical and biological warfare: Focus on Asia. *Vanderbilt Journal of Transnational Law*, **16**: 387-471.

Kohler, G. & Milstein, C., 1975. Continuous cultures of fused cells secreting antibodies of predefined specificity. *Nature*, **256**: 495-7.

Krass, A. S., 1985. *Verification: How Much is Enough?* (A SIPRI book). London and Philadelphia: Taylor & Francis.

Krimsky, S., 1982a. Social responsibility in an age of synthetic biology. *Environment*, 24(6): 2-11.

Krimsky, S., 1982b. *Genetic Alchemy. The Social History of the Recombinant DNA Controversy*. Cambridge, MA, and London: MIT Press.

Kucewicz, W., 1984a. Soviets search for eerie new weapons. Beyond Yellow Rain: The threat of Soviet genetic engineering. First of a series in *Wall Street Journal*, (23 Apr.): 30.

Kucewicz, W., 1984b. The science of snake venom. Beyond Yellow Rain: The threat of Soviet genetic engineering. Second of a series in *Wall Street Journal*, (25 Apr.): 30.

Kucewicz, W., 1984c. Surveying the lethal literature. Beyond Yellow Rain: The threat of Soviet genetic engineering. Third of a series in *Wall Street Journal*, (25 Apr.): 28.

Kucewicz, W., 1984d. Lead scientist in a scourge search. Beyond Yellow Rain: The threat of Soviet genetic engineering. Fourth of a series in *Wall Street Journal*, (1 May): 34.

Kucewicz, W., 1984e. Accident prone and asking for calamity. Beyond Yellow Rain: The threat of Soviet genetic engineering. Fifth of a series in *Wall Street Journal*, (3 May): 28.

Kucewicz, W., 1984f. When arms control falls short. Beyond Yellow Rain: The threat of Soviet genetic engineering. Last of a series in *Wall Street Journal*, (18 May): 26.

Kupperman, R. H., 1982. *The Challenge of Terrorism to the Military*. Washington, DC: Army Science Board.

Lamanna, C., 1959. The most poisonus poison, *Science*, **130** (3378): 763-72.

Lamanna, C., 1961. Immunological aspects of airborne infection: Some general considerations of response to inhalation of toxins. *Bacterial Reviews*, **25**: 323-30.

Lamanna, C. & Carr, C. J., 1967. The botulinal, tetanal and enterostaphylococcal toxins: A review. *Clinical Pharmacology and Therapecutics*, **8**: 286-332.

Lazdunski, M., Fosset, M., Renaud, J. F., Schweitz, H., Vigne, P. & Vincent, J. P., 1984. Toxins to analyse the properties of ionic channels in nerve, muscle and cardiac cells. In: Alouf, J. E. et al., 1984.

Leeper, P., 1984/1985. Which diseases? What vaccines? How to set priorities. *News Report*, National Research Council, **35** (1): 4-11.

Leong, D., Coleman, K. D. & Murphy, J. R., 1983. Cloned fragment A of diphtheria toxin is expressed and secreted into the periplasmic space of *Escherichia coli* K 12. *Science*, **220**(4596): 515-17.

Leppla, S. H., Ivins, B. E. & Ezzel, Jr, J. W., 1985. Anthrax toxin. In: Leive, L. (ed.), 1985. *Microbiology-1985*. Washington, DC: American Society for Microbiology.

Lerner, R. A., Chanock, R. M. & Brown, F. (eds), 1985. *Vaccines 85. Molecular and Chemical Basis of Resistance to Parasite, Bacterial, and Viral Diseases*. Cold Spring Harbor, NY: Cold Spring Harbor Laboratory.

Lewin, I., 1976. *The Boys from Brazil*. London: Pan Books.

Lewis, J., 1982. Churchill and the 'Anthrax Bomb', the plan that never was. *Encounter*, **43** (2):18-28.

Lindenfelser, L. A., Lillehoj, E. B. & Burmeister, J. R., 1974. Skin tumor induction and synergistic acute toxicity in white mice. *Journal of the National Cancer Institute*, **52**: 113-16.

Lindholm, L., Holmgren, J., Wikström, M., Karlsson, V., Andersson, K. & Lycke, N., 1983. Monoclonal antibodies to cholera toxin with special reference to cross-reactions with *Escherichia coli* heat-labile enterotoxin. *Infection and Immunology*, **40**: 570-76.

Livingstone, N. C. & Douglass, Jr. J. D., 1984. *CBW: The Poor Man's Atomic Bomb*. Cambridge, MA: Institute for Foreign Policy Analysis.

Lockman, H. & Kaper, J. B., 1983. Nucleotide sequence analysis of the A2 and B subunits of *Vibrio cholerae enterotoxin*. *Journal of Biological Chemistry*, **258**: 13722-26.

Löfdahl, S., Guss, B., Uhlen, M., Philipson, L. & Lindberg, M., 1983. Gene for staphylococcal protein A. *Proceedings of the National Academy of Sciences (USA)*, **80**: 697-701.

Lohs, K., 1968. Uber schmerzerzeugende Substanzen (Algogene). *Zeitschrift für Militärmedizin*, **9**(5): 281-85.

Lohs, K., Trapp, R. & Kläss, V., 1984. Gelber Regen-Hintergründe einer Verleumdungskampagne. *Wissenschaftliche Welt*, **28** (1): 18-20.

Longini, Jr, I. M., Fine, P. E. M. & Thacker, S.B., 1986. Predicting the global spread of new infectious agents. *American Journal of Epidemiology*, **123** (3): 389-91.

Loyter, A., Vainstein, A., Graessmann, M. & Graessmann, A., 1983. Fusion-mediated injection of SV40-DNA. Experimental Cell Research, **143**: 415-25.

Luria, S. E., 1965. Discussion remark. In: Sonneborn, T. M. (ed.), 1965. *The Control of Human Heredity and Evolution*. New York: Macmillan; and London: Collier-Macmillan.

Lwoff, A., 1957. The concept of virus. *Journal of General Microbiology*, **17**: 239-53.

Mackett, M., Yilma, T., Rose, J. K. & Moss, B., 1985. Vaccinia virus recombinants: Expression of VSV genes and protective immunization of mice and cattle. *Science*, **227**: 433-35.

Maierhofer, G., 1985. Liposomes, preparation and application. *International Laboratory*, **15** (5): 92-104.

Manchee, R. J., Broster, M. G., Anderson, I. S. & Henstridge, R. M., 1983. Decontamination of *Bacillus anthracis* on Gruinard Island? *Nature*, **303**: 239-49.

Manchee, R. J., Broster, M. G., Melling, J., Henstridge, R. M. & Stagg, A. J., 1981 *Bacillus anthracis* on Gruinard Island. *Nature*, **294**: 254-55.

Maniatis, T., Fritsch, E. F. & Sambrook, J., 1982. *Molecular Cloning, A Laboratory Manual*. Cold Spring Harbor, NY: Cold Spring Harbor Laboratory.

Maxam, A. M. & Gilbert, W., 1977. A new method of sequencing DNA. *Proceedings of the National Academy of Sciences (USA)*, **74**: 560-64.

McCarthy, R. D., 1970. *The Ultimate Folly. War by Pestilence, Asphyxiation and Defoliation*. New York: Alfred A . Knopf.

McGill, P., 1985. Deadly germ war secrets of unit 731. *Sunday Observer*, (11 Aug.).

McNinch, J., 1953. Far East Command conference on epidemic hemorrhagic fever: Introduction. *Annals of Internal Medicine*, **38**: 53-60.

Mekalanos, J. J., Swartz, D. J., Pearson, G. D. N., Harford, N., Groyne, F. & De Wilde, M., 1983. Cholera toxin genes: nucleotide sequence, deletion analysis and vaccine development. *Nature*, **306** (5943):551-57.

Mellanby, J., 1984. Neurophysiology of tetanus (and botulinum) toxin. In Alouf, J. E. et al., 1984: 403-12.

Meselson, M. S., 1984. Interview in *Omni*, (Dec. 1984): 104-10, 174-80.

Mikulak, R., 1983. International efforts at control. Paper presented to the symposium Chemical and Biological Weapons: Detection Control and Disarmament held at the annual meeting of the American Association for the Advancement of Science, 31 May.

Mikulak, R., 1984. Possible improvements in the Biological Weapons Convention. Speech presented to the annual meeting of the American Association for the Advancement of Science, 26 May.

Milewski, E., 1982. RAC discussion on the construction of biological weapons. *Recombinant DNA Technical Bulletin*, **5**:188-91.

Milewski, E., 1985. Discussion on a proposal to form a RAC Working Group on biological weapons. *Recombinant DNA Technical Bulletin*, (Dec.), **8**: 173-35.

Miller, J. A., 1985a. Toward a "Magic Bullet" for melanoma. *Science News*, (13): 199.

Miller, J. D., 1985b. The attitude of religious, environmental and science policy leaders towards biotechnology. *Recombinant DNA Technical Bulletin*, **8**(4): 141-64.

Milstein, C., 1980. Monoclonal antibodies. *Scientific American*, **243**(4): 56-64

Milstein, M. A. & Semeyko, L. S., 1977. U. S. military 'R & D' through Soviet eyes. *Bulletin of the Atomic Scientists*, **33**(2): 33-8.

Mintz, B., 1983. Putting genes into mice. In: Robberson, D. L. & Saunders, G. F. (eds), 1983. *Perspectives on Genes and the Molecular Biology of Cancer*. New York: Raven Press, 203-20.

Mishina, M., Tobimatsu. T., Imoto, K., Tanaka, K., Fujita, Y., Fukuda, K., Kurasaki, M., Takahashi, H. Morimoto, Y., Hirore, T., Inayama, S., Takahashi, T., Kuno, M.& Numa, S., 1985. Location of functional regions of acetylcholine receptor α-subunit by site-directed mutagenesis. *Nature*, **313**: 364-69.

Mitscherlich, A. & Mielke, F. (eds), 1983. *Medizin ohne Menschlicheit. Dokumenie des Nürnberger Ärzteprozesses*. Frankfurt am Main: Fischer Taschenbuchverlag.

Modrich, P. & Roberts, R. J., 1982. Type-II restriction and modification enzymes. In: Linn, S. M. & Roberts, R. J. (eds), 1982. *Nucleases*. Cold Spring Harbor, NY: Cold Spring Harbor Laboratory.

Murphy, B. R. & Chanock, R. M., 1985. Immunization against viruses. In: Fields, B. N., 1985.

Murphy, J., Pappenheimer, Jr., A. M. & De Broms, S. T., 1974. Synthesis of diphtheria tox-gene products in *Escherichia coli extracts. Proceedings of the National Academy of Sciences (USA)*, **71**: 11-15.

Murray, E. S., 1975. Rickettsial diseases. In: Beeson, P. & McDermott, W. (eds), 1975. *Textbook of Medicine*. Philadelphia: W. B. Saunders.

Myers, R. M., Lerman, L. S. & Maniatis, T., 1985. A general method for saturation mutagenesis of cloned DNA fragments. *Science*, **229**(4710): 242-47.

Nakano, E., Panicali, D. & Paoletti, E., 1982. Molecular genetics of vaccinia virus: demonstration of marker rescue. *Proceedings of the National Academy of Sciences (USA)*, **79**: 1593-6.

Nash, J. H., Elomqvist, A. W., Cooney, W. J., Peperson, P. D. & Leiter, G. G., 1967. *Dissemination Properties of Encapsulate Particles. Applied Science Doc., Report No. ASD-3105*. Minneapolis, MI: Litton Systems.

Newland, J. W., Strockbine, N. A., Miller, S. F., O'Brine, A. D. & Holmes, R. K., 1985. Cloning of Shiga-like toxin structural genes from a toxin converting phage of *Escherichia coli*. *Science*, **230**: 179-81.

Newmark, P. 1983. Will peptides make vaccines? *Nature*, **305**(5929): 9.

Nicholson-Lord, D., 1981a. Anthrax protest, puts whole country at risk. *The Times*, (12 Oct.): 26.

Nicholson-Lord, D., 1981b. Anthrax soil alert near Tory conference. *The Times*, (15 Oct.): 2.

Noack, H. J., 1985. Plotzlich stirbst dueiň Stuck weit. *Der Spiegel*, (28 Jan.), **5**: 178-83.

Notermans, S. & Dufrenne, J. B., 1982. A simple purification method for enterotoxin F produced by *Staphylococcus aureus* and some properties of the toxin. *Antoine van Leeuwenhoek Journal of Hygiene, Microbiology and Serology*, **48**: 447-55.

Novick, R. & Goldstein, R., 1982. Letter to NIH Recombinant Advisory Committee on May 7, 1982. Quoted by: Milewski, E., 1982.

Nowinski, R. C., Tam, M. R., Goldstein, L. C., Stong, L., Kuo, C.-C., Corey, L., Stamm, W. E., Handsfield, H. H., Knapp, J. S. & Holmes, K. K., 1983. Monoclonal antibodies for diagnosis of infectious diseases in humans. *Science*, (11 Feb.), **219** (4585): 637-44.

Nunberg, J. H., Gilbert, J. H., Rodgers, G., Snead, R.M., Nitecki, D. E. & Winston, S., 1985. Localization of a determinant of virus neutralization on feline leukemia virus envelope protein gp 70. In: Lerner, R. A. et al, (eds), 1985.

Olivera, B., Gray, W. R., Zeikus, R., McIntosh, J. M., Varga, J., Rivier, J., De Santos, V. & Cruz, L. J., 1985. Peptide neurotoxins from fish-hunting conesnails. *Science*, **230**(4732):1338-43.

Olsnes, S., 1986. Personal communication. Oslo: Norwegian Radiology Hospital, Department of Biochemistry.

Odsnes, S. & Eiklid, K., 1984. Structure and mechanism of action of *Shigella dysenteriae toxin*. In : Alouf, J. E. et al., 1984.

Olsnes, S. & Pihl, A., 1982a. Cytotoxic proteins with intracellular site of action: Mechanism of action and anti-cancer properties. *Cancer Surveys*, 1(3): 479-87.

Olsnes, S. & Pihl, A., 1982b. Chimeric toxins. *Pharmacological Therapy*, **15**: 355-81.

Olsnes, S. & Pihl, A., 1982c. Toxic lectins and related proteins. In: Cohen & van Heyningen, (1982): 51-105.

Olsnes, S., Refsnes, K. & Pihl, A., 1974. Mechanism of action of the toxic lectins abrin and ricin. *Nature*, 249(5458): 627-31.

Olsnes, S. & Sandvig, K., 1985. Entry of polypeptide toxins into animal cells. In: Pastan, I. & Willingham, M. C. (eds), 1985. *Endocytosis*. New York: Plenum.

Olsnes, S., Sandvig, K., Sundan, A., Eiklid, K. & Pihl, A., 1985. How do protein toxins kill cells? In: Gregoriadis, G., Poste, G., Senior, J. & Tovet, A. (eds), 1985. *Receptor-Mediated Targeting of Drugs*. New York: Plenum.

Orskov, I. & Orskov, F., 1977. Special O: K: H serotypes among enterotoxigenic *E. coli* strains from diarrhea in adults and children. Occurrence of the CF (colonization factor) antigen and of hemagtlutinating abilities. *Medical Microbiology and Immunology*, **163**: 99-110.

Oshiro, S. S., 1984. Secret germ tests were held on isles. *Sunday Star-Bulletin & Advertiser*, Honolulu, (8 July): 1,4.

Palmiter, R. D., Brinster, R. L., Hammer, R. E., Trumbauer, M. E., Rosenfeld, M. G., Birnberg, N. C. & Evans, R. M., 1982. Dramatic growth of mice that develop from eggs microinjected with metallothionein-growth hormone fusion genes. *Nature*, **300**: 611-15.

Panicali, D., Davis, S., Weinberg, R. L. & Paoletti, E., 1983. Construction of live vaccines by using genetically engineered poxviruses: Biological activity of recombinant vaccinia virus expressing influenza virus hemagglutinin. *Proceedings of the National Academy of Sciences (USA)*, **80**: 5364-68.

Paoletti, E., Lipinskas, B. R., Samsonoff, C., Mercer, S. & Panicali, D., 1984. Construction of live vaccines using genetically engineered poxviruses: Biological activity of vaccinia virus recombinants expressing the hepatitis B virus surface antigen and the herpes simplex virus glycoprotein D. *Proceedings of the National Academy of Sciences (USA)*, **81**:193-7.

Paoletti, E., Perkus, M. E., Piccini, A., Lipinskas, B. R. & Mercer, S. R., 1986. A modern approach to live vaccines: Recombinant poxviruses. In: Silver, S. (ed.), 1985. *Biotechnology; Potentials and Limitations*. Dahlem Konferenzen. Berlin: Springer-Verlag.

Parkman, F., 1901. *The Conspiracy of Pontiac and the Indian War after the Conquest of Canada*. In two volumes, Vol. II. 10th ed. Boston: Little, Brown and Co.

Peattie, D. A., 1979. Direct chemical method for sequencing DNA. *Proceedings of the National Academy of Sciences (USA)*, **76**: 1760-64.

Perera, J., 1985. Australia's chemical war tests. *New Scientist*, **105**(1438): 5.

Perkus, M. E., Piccini, A., Lipinskas, B. R. & Paoletti, E., 1985. Recombinant vaccinia virus: Immunization against multiple pathogens. *Science*, **229**(4717): 981-84.

Perpich, J. G., 1983. Biotechnology- International policy considerations. *Politics and the Life Sciences*, **2**: 63-67.

Perry Robinson, J. P., 1981. Environmental effects of chemical and biological warfare. In: *War and Environment. Stockholm*: Liber. Ministry of Agriculture, Environmental Advisory Council.

Perry Robinson, J. P., 1985a. Chemical and biological warfare: developments in 1984. In: SIPRI, 1985. *World Armaments and Disarmament: SIPRI Yearbook 1985* (London and Philadelphia: Taylor & Francis).

Perry Robinson, J. P., 1986. Chemical and biological warfare: developments in 1985. In: SIPRI, *World Armaments and Disarmament: SIPRI Yearbook 1986*. Oxford: Oxford University Press.

Perutz, M., 1985. The birth of protein engineering. New Scientist, **106**(1460): 12-15.

Pestka, S., 1983. The human interferons-form protein purification and sequence to cloning and expression in bacteria: before, between, and beyond. *Archives of Biochemistry and Biophysics*, **221**:1-37.

Pfaff, E., Kuhn, C., Schaller, H., Leban, J., Thiel, H.-J., & Böhm, H.-O., 1985. Structural analysis of the foot-and-mouth disease virus antigenic determinant. In: Lerner, R. A. *et al.*, 1985.

Pfaff, E., Mussgay, M., Böhm, H. O., Schulz, G. E. & Schaller, H., 1982. Antibodies against a preselected peptide recognize and neutralize foot-and-mouth disease virus. *EMBO Journal*, **1**: 869-74.

Piller, C., 1983. Ultimate vaccines: DNA-Key to biological warfare? *The Nation*, **237**(19): 585, 597-601.

INDEX

BIOLOGICAL WEAPONS AND TERRORISM

BIOLOGICAL WEAPONS AND TERRORISM

(In Two Volumes)

Volume-2

Dr. G.C. Satpathy

Publications

KALPAZ PUBLICATIONS

DELHI-110052

Biological Weapons and Terrorism

(*Terrorism*)

Rs. 1800 (Set)

ISBN: 81-7835-168-4 (Set)
81-7835-170-6 (Vol. 2)

Published in 2004 in India by
Kalpaz Publications
C-30, Satyawati Nagar
Delhi-110052
E-mail : kalpaz@hotmail.com

Laser Typesetting at: Sharma Graphic, Delhi
Printed at: Mehra Offset Press, Delhi

Contents

Introduction

This two volume work on Anthrax and Biological Weapons broadly looks into two aspects. These are (i) Use of these weapons by terrorists and (ii) Use of these weapons in a warfare between two or more countries. The first volume is devoted to study of these weapons with a view to their use in terrorism. This volume namely the second volume 100 kg at the possibility and impact of use of such weapons in a full scale war between countries. Also covered in this work are the various potential BW agents, their destruction capabilities, qualities of effective agents, vaccines against these agents, counter measures to WMD etc. This all and more, make this a worthy book giving out vast amount of information, knowledge and exposure about the destructive capabilities of anthrax and other biological weapons. The work is systematically divided into thirteen chapters.

Chapter one discusses how the spectre of biological warfare after lying dormant for a few decades again captured the imagination of military and the general public alike. Expectations that end of cold war would bring about a more bening world order received a setback with the warfare that was undertaken by coalition forces to remove Iraqi from Kuwait in 1991. This warfare also brought back into attention the biological weapons which had become a non-issue for about two decades then. Iraq had a large-scale military programme based on anthrax and botulinun toxin as agents. This chapter discusses biological weapons of mass destruction, reports of SIPRI and the UN, issue of international security, rationale behind the US renunciation of biological weapons etc.

The next chapter discusses the advancement of knowledge about biological organism and its use to develop biological weapons. The new understanding of genetics at molecular level has been quite significant in this regard. This chapter intend to convey the reality of a new mechanistic biology. If the revolution at the end of 19th century allowed the development and use of chemical weapons in the first world war; the resolution in nuclear physics allowed the development and use of nuclear weapons in the second world war, can the development and use new biological weapons be much far off?

Third Chapter of the book look at the state of development of offensive biological weapons before 1969. Fourth chapter is of great interest as it brings out the criteria for selection of an ideal biological agent.

The potential value of an infective organism can be understood to a reasonable extent by such features like-*potency*, *transmitability*, epidemicity, infectivity, resistivity, availability, means of protection, *detectivity*, retroactivity and rapidity of action.

Next we come to selection of potential biological weapons agents. Herein various agents of human diseases are discussed. *Bubonic plague*, *cholera influenza*, *leprosy*, *measles*, *smallpox*, *tuberculosis*, *typhoid* etc. are some major diseases that mankind has come across. These diseases and their agents are studied to find their potential for developing a biological weapon which can be used militarily. Such weapons employ living organisms which multiply within the target organisms or extremely toxic chemicals which can be produced by these living organism. Biological agents for possible use against mankind can be *viral*, *rickettsial* or bacterial or *fungal*. A number of consideration go into selection of a potential *agent for use* from the military point of view.

Sixth Chapter is an extension of chapter five and studies the agents suitable for weapons of mass destruction.

Chapter number seven undertakes the study of toxin weapon. Toxins are considered poisonous substances produced by living organisms. Toxins which kill bacteria are generally developed into antibiotics.

Owing to features such as their toxicity, availability and stability, toxins are known to be of military interest as toxin warfare agents.

The degree of toxicity is not always the deciding factor for the military use of toxins. Some agents though low on toxicity but capable as in capacitating agents are of great military interest. An example is staphylococcal enterotoxin B.

Chapter eight is focused on the vaccines against toxin and

biological agents, their development and production. From military point of view toxins are important for three different reasons. First, vaccing can be used to protect the armed forces and civilians against BW and TW agents used by an aggressor. Secondly, vaccing can be used to protect aggressors own armed forces. Thirdly they can be used to protect troops against the natural outbreak of diseases.

Eminent scholars across the political spectrum have warned about the lurking dangers of new biological weapons. Chapter number nine takes a look at the works of these scholars as also the papers of various governments on the same topic. These papers represent the view how the governments have seen the problems.

The involvement of Iraq in carrying out a large scale biological weapons programme is all too well known. After the 1991 gulf war, the United Nations kept trying to find out the extent of Saddam Hussain's biological weapons. Iraq continued to outwital these efforts for obvious reasons. It took several years and another bombardment of Iraq by the US and British forces before any major breakthrough could be made in this direction. Iraq could play hide and seek as it is vary difficult to detect a biological weapons programme in comparison to a nuclear weapons programme detecting which is quite easy.

Inspectors, inspecting in Iraq had formidable powers on paper. They could inspect anything site, activity, material as after as they often like; they could fly in whatever region they wanted for surveillance; they could take pictures, install sensors in sensitive locations but still they could not make much headway until January, 1994 when Iraq provided them enough information to conduct meaningful inspections.

Iraq, later claimed that it destroyed most of its BW facilities after the war, but these reports were not backed by any concrete proof. However, Iraq's clandestine efforts to develop biological weapons are by no means the first. Since 1920, the western allies, Japan and erstwhile Soviet Union have all done extensive research on agents and weapons.

Eleventh Chapter is focused on the defensive biological weapons programme. Within both national and international spheres, the legitimacy of development of a defensive biological weapon programme lies on two major assumption - (i) That the content of defensive programme differs fundamentally from the content of an offensive programme; and (ii) that it would in facts be possible to defend populations of humans, plants and animals from an adversary bent on utilizing biological agents.

A defensive vaccine programme is useful only against viral agents that an adversary is likely to choose or develop. The development of the vaccine generally involve islation, identification, modification and growth of the potential BW agent. Studies of vaccin's efficacy involve exposure of test animals and even human beings to the agent. All these components would also be associated with an offensive BW programme. So, both the programmes share similar components. Thus it becomes possible to guise the offensive programme under the garb of a defensive programme.

Technology has a great influence on the warfare in today's world. And biotechnology is considered important in the US assessments of critical technologists. This is also reflected in Europe where life science find a prominent place in the fourth framework programme. The fact is that biotechnology is cheaper and simpler to master than the advanced information technologies. Not surprisingly, therefore the American literáture contains frequent references to the likely development of biological weapons as a relatively inexpensive means of countering sophisticated western conventional military technology. The nature of this biotechnology needs a careful study. This topic finds detailed discussion in the chapter now the future.

WMD counter measures are discussed in the second last chapter of this work. Chemical and biological weapons are rising in numbers and experience tells on that when a country makes a decisión to acquire a WMD capability, the acquisition of BWs and CWs takes place simultaneously.

Dissension, *Denial*, *Arms control* and *International Pressure* are the means used as effective counter measures to check the rise in the number of weapons of mass destruction. While the prevention efforts are largely diplomatic in nature, defence-related agencies play a great supporting role.

Nuclear deterrence was the chief instrument of response in cold war period. However, last years of cold war saw a large scale drawdown in the size and variety of nuclear arsenal. It was partly negotiated and partially by unilateral choice.

Today, even the US forces need to be prepared to operate in the ever widening presence of chemical and biological weapons. The case with which biological weapons can be produced and delivered means that threats may be there even in peace keeping operations.

All this information and knowledge makes as up to the reality of the spectre of biological warfare. This volume is written to create awareness and awakening among the masses about the threat looming large on the mankind. Irony is that diseases that God bestowed on mankind with a purpose are being used by the man to upset the calculating of even the almightly. One does not know where all this development or negative development will lead us to. Efforts are made by authors to make the subject interesting by use of good language and interesting example from past history.

1

Biological Warfare : Back in Focus

Biological Warfare is not a new term known to mankind. In fact, agreement of 1925 Geneva Protocol focused on the efforts to control the production and use of the Biological weapons. During past few decades, the spectre of biological warfare lay dormant but only to come back with a renewed vigour in the 1990s.

Expectations that the ending of the Cold War would usher in a more benign new world order took a severe beating when large-scale warfare was undertaken by coalition forces to remove Iraq from Kuwait in 1991. One unwelcome surprise for the general public was the realisation that the coalition forces were very concerned that they might have been attacked with biological weapons. Even for most people involved with security and international affairs, biological weapons had been virtually a non-issue for about two decades. And the general public simply had not thought about the potential use of such weapons.

Writing in the popular science journal *New Scientist* in early 1992, Graham Pearson, the Director General of the UK Chemical and Biological Defence Establishment (CBDE) at Porton Down, tried to focus readers' attention to the importance of preventing biological warfare : As to the suggestion..... that the use of biological weapons is widely recognised by many military commanders as the least effective option, it is interesting to ask why some 10 nations have biological weapons programmes.

Turning in particular to the events of the previous year he added. Why did the Iraqis have a military programme, uncovered by the

UN Special Commission, focused on anthrax and botulinum toxin as agents? Why was there so much concern that such agents might be used by Saddam Hussein? Why is the UN instituting such a stringent future compliance regime?....

In brief, Pearson argued that the potential for proliferation and use of biological weapons is something that we should take seriously and act to prevent now if we possibly can. A similar stand was taken in late 1992 by General Friel, Commander of the US Chemical and Biological Defense Agency. He was reported as saying that concerns over nuclear and chemical weapons during the Cold War had masked similar worries over biological weapons. Looking to the world after the Cold War he stated .... the biological threat has been recently singled out as the one major threat that still poses the ability for catastrophic effects on a theater-deployed force.....

More generally former President Clinton, in his autumn 1993 address to the United Nations, looked forward to a peaceful, prosperous world of market-based democracies. He pointed out the problems that could come in the way of its achievement. In particular, he noted that if proliferation was not prevented no democracy could feel secure. In his view : One of our most urgent priorities must be attacking the proliferation of weapons of mass destruction, whether they are nuclear, chemical or biological; and the ballistic missiles that can rain them down on populations hundreds of miles away.

When the realisation dawned amongst the general public that the erstwhile Soviet Union had an offensive biological weapons programme for the last two decades of the Cold War, it served strongly to reinforce that point regarding biological weapons. It is true, of course, that concerns over the Soviet programme were voiced during the latter stages of the Cold War. The accusations of the alleged use of 'yellow rain' in the Far East appear not to have stood up well to detailed studies. But the latest information strongly reinforces the view that the anthrax outbreak at Sverdlovsk in 1979 did result from an accident at a military research facility.

Moreover, the development in various countries of novel kinds of agents capable of affecting behaviour clearly requires careful analysis. Western governments have made their concerns over the proliferation of biological weapons very clear in recent years.

There has also been a number of estimates of the extent of proliferation presented in the open literature. The widely respected Office of Technology Assessment (OTA) in the United States tried to summarise these sources in mid-1993. In its view 'countries generally reported as having undeclared offensive biological warfare programmes' were as follows:

Middle East	(i) Iran
	(ii) Iraq
	(iii) Israel
	(iv) Libya
	(v) Syria
East Asia	(i) China
	(ii) North Korea
	(iii) Taiwan

There is a considerable overlap between the nations in these two conflict-prone regions which are regarded to have biological weapons programmes and those which are seeking other weapons of mass destruction and ballistic missiles, noted by OTA. The objective of this book is to provide the reader with the necessary information to make judgements about the dangers of the proliferation of biological weapons and how that process might be checked . The conclusion is that we do have a chance to restrict the spread and use of these weapons, but success in that endeavour is not assured. In particular, it will be argued that the rapid advances in commercial biotechnology will considerably complicate any attempt to achieve effective control. If we do not act effectively, it appears possible that we will see biological weapons used on a large scale sooner rather than later in the next century . In the following part an effort is made to bring together some of the openly-available quantitative information on the effects of the use of biological weapons.

It will be argued that the only possible conclusion from this evidence is that biological weapons are weapons of mass destruction, in many ways more equivalent to nuclear weapons than chemical weapons. A brief review will then be given of how biological weapons might be used.

Biological Weapons of Mass Destruction (BWMDs)

To understand a proper factual basis for the analysis presented in the rest of this book we now consider some open quantitative estimates of the potential effects of the use of biological weapons. These estimates are summarised in Table 1.1. The first column of the table gives the four major studies that we shall analyse. Within each study the cases investigated are then numbered and, where possible, described in short. The second column details out the weapon system or agent; the third and the fourth column give, respectively, the data available on the area affected and the casualities in the target area. It will, of course, comes as no surprise that the publicly-available information on this topic is fragmentary, but enough is to be found to get a reasonable picture of the deadly effects of biological weapons.

Table 1.1

Some publicly-available information concerning large-scale attacks using biological weapons

Study (Case)	*Weapon System*	*Affected Area (km^2)*	*Casualities**
Sipri			
(i) bomber	10-kt nuclear	30	-
	biological agent	0-50	-
	VX nerve gas	0.75	-
	5—6-t high explosive	0.22	-
(ii) WEU	1.75-17.5 kg anthrax spores	1	-
(iii)	500-125,000 kg biological agent	500	50%
United Nations			
(i) line attack	10^{10} agent per gm along 100 km	5,000	50%
(ii)	1Mt nuclear	300	90%
	15t Sarin	60	50%
	10t biological	100,000	50% ill; 25% dead

Study (Case)	*Weapon System*	*Affected Area (km²)*	*Casualities**
International Security			
(i) missile on sparsely populated city	20-kt nuclear	-	40,000 dead; 40,000 injured
	300 kg Sarin	-	200-3,000
	30 kg anthrax spores	-	20,000-80,000
(ii)	1 kg anthrax	0.2-2.6	50%
OTA			
(i) missile on sparse to moderately populated city	12.5-kt nuclear	7.8	23,000-80,000
	300 kg Sarin	0.22	60-200
	30 kg anthrax spores	10	30,000-100,000
(ii) line attack	100 kg anthrax spores	46 (clear day)	130-460,000
		140 (overcast)	420,000-1.4m
		300 (clear night)	1-3m

* Numbers Killed, unless otherwise indicated.

SIPRI

In the early 1970s the Stockholm International Peace Research Institute brought out series of volumes under the general title *The Problem of Chemical and Biological Warfare.* In the second volume of the series, *CB Weapons Today*, an effort was made to compare the relative potencies of chemical, biological and other types of weapon both nuclear and conventional. It was estimated that a 10-15-kt nuclear weapon airburst over an urban target might cause 50 per cent casualties, half of which would be fatal, over an area of 3,000 hectare (30 km²). The area over which a biological weapon would cause 50 per cent primary casualties was estimated at 0-5,000 hectares (0-50 km²), a footnote pointing out that the end result would be highly weather-dependent. The attack scenario was for a single aircraft with a bombload of 5-6 tons and, for comparison, the area for 50 per cent casualties from the use of VX nerve gas was given as 75 hectares and for high-explosive bombs as 22 hectares.

Of course, the effect of the chemical weapon would be weather-dependent and that of the high-explosive bombs on the amount of shelter available. The general import of the figures, however, puts biological and nuclear weapons in a class that is different from other weapon systems. Another indication of the potency of biological weapons was given in Volume V of the SIPRI study, *The Prevention of CBW*. In this volume the authors were trying to estimate the scale of a militarily-significant offensive biological weapons programme. What is of interest here is that the authors referred back to the work on the usage of these weapons in volume II and suggested that, to inflict 50 per cent casualties with a non-communicable agent in a city of half a million inhabitants, some 10^{17}-10^{19} pathogens would be needed. They then tried to calculate the weight of agent necessary to provide that number of pathogens and suggested that a figure of 'something between hundreds of kilos and hundreds of tons of BW agent' would be needed . The SIPRI authors then went on to argue that their estimates were of a similar order of magnitude to those made by the Armaments Control Agency of the Western European Union.(WEU).

This agency was concerned with verifying that WEU members were observing the armament limitations agreed in 1955. As the SIPRI authors observed, the official WEU figures available were somewhat deficient in that precise concentrations were not given, but biological and military experts had calculated what amounts of various agents would be required to obtain 'direct military effect' over an area of 1 km^2. In the accompanying table this weight of agent was, for instance, given as 0.007 kg for botulinal toxins and 1.75-17.5 kg for anthrax spores. Scaling up from the least and the most effective agents given, the SIPRI authors stated that : .... for an attack of a 500 km^2 town, the WEU would reckon that something between 500 kg and 125 tons of BW agent would be required.

An imperial ton is equivalent to 1,016 kg so the range of potency is wide, but the message comes loud and clear : biological weapons could have devastating effects if used in right amounts which are capable of being delivered on to a target.

The United Nations

This point finds ample support from the figures of a major United Nations study carried out at about the same time in the late 1960s. It was suggested that pathogens can be produced at a concentration of 10^{10} per gm. The authors then pictured a scenario in which an aircraft sprayed such a mixture along a 100 km line when a 10 km per hour cross-wind was blowing. Assuming that a comparatively fragile agent was used and therefore that only 10 per cent of the organisms survived aerosclisation in the spray, and that they then died off in the environment at a rate of five per cent per minute, it was found that 50 per cent of unprotected people over an area of about 5,000 km^2 would inhale a dose sufficient to cause infection (about 100 of the individual organisms).

The report continued thus : .... This particular calculation is valid for agents such as those which cause tularaemia or plague, as well as for some viruses. The decay rate of the causative agents of Q-fever, anthrax and some other infections is much lower....

These organisms would therefore exert their effects over a much larger area. Again a comparative table was presented in which it was suggested that a one-megaton nuclear weapon could kill 90 per cent of people not protected people in an area of 300 km^2 that 15 tons of nerve agent could cause 50 percent deaths over 60 km^2, and that 10 tons of biological agent could make 50 percent people sick, and death in 25 percent of people over an area of 100,000 km^2. The real equivalence of biological and nuclear weapons of mass destruction is again strongly illustrated here.

International Security

An even more precise comparison was provided by Steve Fetter in the journal *International Security* in 1991. He estimated the number of people that could get killed if a missile with a throw-weight of one tonne were aimed at a large, sparsely-populated (30 people per hectare) city using different kinds of warheads. He calculated that a 20-kt nuclear warhead could kill 40,000 people and injure another 40,000 in the absence of civil defence measures. A chemical warhead of 300 kg of Sarin (nerve agent) could, under the same conditions, kill 200 to 3,000 people, but in comparison 30 kg of anthrax spores could kill between 20,000 and 80,000 people. As Fetter explained, anthrax readily forms spores which are resistant to environmental stress and therefore suitable for dispersal in weapon systems.

As it is not infectious in the sense that a person who caught the disease as a direct consequence an attack would pass it on to another person, Fetter argued that the organism could be used with some discrimination in an attack. Moreover, it is deadly at much lower concentrations than nerve gases. The likely dose rate at wnich 50 percent of an unprotected target population would catch the disease, assuming ideal infective-agent particle sizes of one to five micrometers m^{-6}, is incredibly small. On Fetter's figures, just 1 kg of anthrax spores could produce such conditions, over 0.2 to 2.6 km^2, depending on the prevalent weather. If untreated, anthrax contracted from the air in such an attack, by inhalation through the lungs, would kill almost everyone affected within a few days. Though vaccines are available they would have to be given *before* exposure and their effects following high infective doses of the organism are uncertain. Ultimately, whilst antibiotics can be used successfully, they have to be administered early; before signs of the disease show themselves. Given the numbers of people who could be affected in the scenarios discussed here, it is doubtful whether any effective assistance could be organised in the time available. Theoretically, civil defence measures could be more effective against attack with biological weapons rather than against nuclear weapons but, as Fetter himself concluded :.....even when used against a prepared population, anthrax warheads could rival small nuclear weapons in their ability to kill people....

This point was brought out very clearly in the detailed OTA study released in 1993[10], which also clarified the reasons why different attack scenarios with biological weapons cause such diverse effects.

Office of Technology Assessment (OTA)

The OTA outlined two hypothetical cases : first, an attack with a missile delivered on an overcast day or night, with a moderate wind, on to a city with 3,000 to 10,000 unprotected people per km^2. The authors stated that 300 kg of Sarin nerve gas has potential to kill between 60 and 200 people in an area of 0.22 km^2. 30 kg of anthrax spores spread out in a cigar-shape over the city from the missile warhead could kill 30,000 to 100,000 in an area of 10 km^2. For a 12.5-kt nuclear weapon there would be a circular area of destruction of 7.8 km^2 and possibly kill 23,000 to 80,000 people. In the second case, 100 kg of anthrax spores were released by an aircraft along a line to the windward side of the city (as in the case given in the 1969 United Nations report). The city chosen for demonstration purposes was Washington, DC. On a clear sunny day with a light breeze, 46 km^2 would be affected and 130-460,000 people could die. On an overcast day or night with a moderate wind, 140 km^2 would be affected and 420,000 to 1,400,000 people could get killed.

On a clear, calm night an area of 300 km^2 would be affected and between 1 and 3 million people could die. Using the line source is far more effective means of delivering a biological agent. Whilst the central message of the potentially devastating consequences of the use of biological weapons is clear from these examples, an understanding of the situation is sometimes complicated by the fact that the efficiency with which biological weapons could be produced and used undoubtedly improved from 1940 to 1969. It might also seem from the different scenarios and measures used (Table 1.1) that the results given in the examples were created by *ad hoc* 'back-of-the-envelope' calculations. Nothing, of course, could be further from the truth. Much work has gone into the study of how micro-organisms react to environmental factors and how they infect individuals. The information gained has been used to develop complex mathematical models for predicting the results of employing biological weapons and assuming various conditions for attack.

US Army

It would not be sensible to put all official information and calculations on the public domain, but some of the relevant general data have been released. As an example, we may consider the study, *Biological Vulnerability Assessment* : The *US East Coast*, produced by the US Army at Dugway Proving Ground in 1983. The document studied potential clandestine biological attacks on the whole of the east coast, on Washington DC and on two large military facilities in the area. The report has two major sections, one is concerned with the topography and meteorology of the area and the other with modes of attack, potential agents and examples of hypothetical attacks. Appendices cover the computerised methods used to study weather conditions and the attack scenarios . For a region like the east coast of the USA the meteorological conditions are very well known. The types of weather condition that occur at different times of year and how these can be predicted-at least over the short term-are well understood.

Also, as previously pointed out, much is now known about how aerosols behave in different weather conditions, how various disease agents are affected by environmental stresses, and the mechanisms by which infection takes place through the lungs. As examples, the conferences conducted in part by the US Army on aerobiology in the 1960s may be cited. Thus it is possible to know what specific set of weather conditions would be best to ensure dispersal of the aerosolised agent and its ideal spread over the envisaged target area on the wind. In this specific study one aim was to ascertain the amount of anthrax necessary to attack various targets in the area.

The types of favourable meteorological condition likely to occur in the area were analysed and a mathematical cloud-diffusion model was used to determine the concentrations of the agent which would arrive downwind from the source in such conditions. The best kind of conditions would occur in what is called neutral air stability under cloudy or overcast skies. Since the micro-organism are damaged by UV light, night would be the best time for making say that high levels of most agents arrived at the target. Calculations can be made of the probable dose rate needed to infect 50 per cent of people in a particular target area if the following are known: the concentration of the organism in the source material spread along a line of attack; the efficiency of the munition in aerosolising the agent; the speed of wind the rate of decay of the agent in the air; and the number of organisms necessary to be inhaled, assuming normal rates of respiration in the target population. One such calculation suggested that a 900-km^2 area of Washington could be successfully attacked to cause 50 per cent deaths with 40 kg of anthrax, assuming ideal conditions of neutral stability and a 4m/sec wind speed.

This is similar to the OTA figures as the authors suggested that because of uncertainties in the actual attack conditions, several times the calculated amount might be used. The study includes a number of other relevant calculations for different scenarios, but the general point to be made is that there would be nothing necessarily *ad hoc* about biological warfare. Sophisticated calculations could be made in order to achieve different effects with different kinds of agent. For instance, the required application rate for the fungal agent which causes black stem rust of cereals is 0.01 kg/km^2 to achieve an 85 percent reduction in crop yield.

In the light of the information that is publicly known , it is very necessary to carefully investigate why the United States renounced these weapons unilaterally.

The US Renunciation

Professor Matthew Meselson of Harvard University, who has long been associated with to prevent the use or spread of biological weapons, gave testimony to the US Congress on this subject in 1989. He set out the reasons for the US renunciation as follows: First, it was understood that biological weapons could be as great a threat to large populations as nuclear weapons and that no reliable defence is likely....

The USA already had acquired nuclear weapons which could be seen as more versatile, for example being also suitable for use against small hardened military installations like missile silos. Meselson continued: Second, it was evident that biological weapons could be much simpler and less expensive than nuclear weapons to develop and produce... and: Third, it was realised that our biological weapons program was pioneering an easily duplicated technology and that our program was likely to inspire others to follow suit.

Thus, according to Meselson, the biological weapons programme was a major threat to the United States' own security. Better than to put up a convincing show of giving up the weapons and try to erect some barriers to proliferation.

It will be noticed that this explanation does not involve the widely-accepted and propagated argument that 'biological weapons are not effective military weapons'. This argument was also strongly rejected in 1992 by a senior official from the British Chemical and Biological Defence Establishment at Porton Down. Writing in the *Journal of the Royal United Services Institute*, Gordon Carter stated that President Nixon's decision was a result of political considerations. He specifically rejected the idea that it was due to the stated rationale of the uncontrollability and unpredictability of these weapons. In his opinion: ... The utility of BW had been demonstrated by all means, short of use in war, and the established feasibility could clearly not become disestablished with time....

He reinforced the point like this: ... The US had sustained its offensive BW capability for nearly a quarter of a century. During this period, the concept of uncontrollability and unpredictability (which would only be possible if certain agents of great epidemic potential were used) had nor arisen...

Thus in Carter's view, there was no 'scientific, military or technical reason' as to why an argument of this kind should have been put forward in 1969. By implication, the same holds true today and underlies the statement from the Director General of Porton Down. We should therefore proceed on the assumption that biological weapons could be considered militarily useful in some circumstances.

The proliferation of these weapons is therefore a real problem, not just an empty threat used in a propaganda war over the shape of the new world order. We need to turn finally in this introduction to the question of various ways in which biological weapons might be used, because it is not simply in relation to massive attacks on unprotected civilians that they have been considered.

Other Uses for Military

We have been chiefly discussing about the use of biological weapons on a large scale against civilian populations. As the OTA report noted, it is perfectly possible that a major state might decide to have biological weapons in order to deter any such attack or even for symbolic purposes just to demonstrate its capability. Furthermore, an attack with biological weapons need not necessarily be an over act or be directed against only the human population. As Commander Rose pointed out in his prizewinning essay in the *US Naval War College Review*, Cuba charged the USA with a multifaceted, covert attack in the 1970s:...Allegedly, this campaign targeted vital crops such as tobacco (blue mold) and sugar cane (cane smut), livestock (African swine fever), and also the populace itself (hemorrhagic strain of dengue fever)...

As Rose commented, whatever the source(s) of these diseases (natural or otherwise), they were certainly costly for Cuba. Covert use of biological weapons against people, plants and animals could form a means of economic warfare which serves to weaken an enemy indirectly before military action.

Similarly, as the original SIPRI study noted biological weapons could be used in a covert strategic attack against troops, either massively or against key facilities, for instance, before a major invasion. Covert use would be suggested by the continuing difficulties of developing an effective detector system for biological weapons, and the possibility of protecting troops with masks, etc. if a biological attack were known to be under way. Once hostilities had commenced between parties equipped with biological weapons, a number of both covert and overt uses would clearly be possible. Raymond Zilinskas has suggested that if two Third World states became bogged down in attrition warfare there might well be a temptation to use biological weapons against the enemy's front-line forces, if only to cause logistic and morale problems.

Moreover, as efforts were made to circumvent the front-line stalemate, biological weapons could obviously offer means of attack at other points. As he suggested, terrorists might be made use of to contaminate key transport nodes, like airports and railway stations with persistent and deadly agents. Lest anyone should find such ideas far-fetched we can again refer to official US studies. A 1975 paper entitled *Covert Biological Weapons Literature Review* set out to give an overview of likely operations and the studies that had been made of them. After noting examples involving agents carried in aerosols, by insects or by other methods the paper stated that: In the past several years, all of these methods have been studied, prototype models have been produced, scenarios in their application have been written and tested, and hardware has been evaluated for covert use by unconventional forces...

Such work stopped in the USA, the study stated, after the renunciation of biological weapons. Nevertheless, similar work could certainly have gone on elsewhere, and the USA has continued to study vulnerabilities and the difficulties of taking effective defensive steps against terrorists. A final reason we might note for a major Third World state attempting to possess biological weapons could be to deter intervention in its region by forces from the rich industrial world, or even to use such weaponry if it was fighting forces from the West.

That surely was the reason for concern about Iraq's biological weapons in 1991 and the thinking behind General Friel's worries over the 'biological threat' and ' catastrophic effects on a theater-deployed force. Given that framework, which is intended to stress again the reality of the problem of the proliferation of biological weapons. Let us go into a more detailed study of biological agents.

2

The New Biotechnology

Biological organisms have always fascinated the mankind. Their uses and abuses are known to us since ancient times but the latest research involving manipulation of genetic structure has opened new frontiers for the human being.. With this, new biotechnologies came into being.

To fulfil our present purposes it is necessary to get a sense of the huge scale of investment in modern biotechnology brought about by clear commercial possibilities, and then to review briefly the basic biology and techniques on which current advances are based . With that information it will be possible to focus on what new knowledge has become available which might be have relevance to the manufacture of biological weapons.

Biological organisms have been used by human societies since long, long ago, for example in the brewing of beer, the baking of bread and in cheese-making. Bread is made from wheat flour, salt, sugar and yeast. Water is mixed and the thick sticky dough is repeatedly folded. The mixture is then left to rest for some time. Enzymes from the yeast cells then act on sugars in the mixture to produce carbondioxide through fermentation. As this gas does not find escape from the mixture, it causes the dough to rise. At the same time, other enzymes from the yeast act on proteins in the flour to make them less tough.

Baking then inactivates the yeast, stops the enzymatic reactions and drives off by-products such as alcohol produced by the fermentation of sugars. This system of making bread is quite old,. Genetic engineers are currently making efforts to improve yeasts, for example by making them more active and able to operate more quickly at lower temperatures. Beer is produced from the starch and proteins of barley through a series of stages. In the first, called melting, the seeds are allowed to germinate. Enzymes in the seeds break down the stored material there into simpler compounds that yeast is able to ferment. The germination is stopped by slowly heating the barley. The malted barley is then milled and mashed. Hot water is percolated through the mash to get a rich solution of nutrients called wort. The wort is then mixed with hops to provide the required flavour and heated to obtain a sterile solution. Fermentation of this sterile liquid is done by adding yeast. This stage takes between a week and ten days. As a thick crust builds up on the surface, carbon dioxide produced during fermentation dissolves in the liquid and makes it effervesce. Final processing involves filtering off the solid material from the beer and finishing its presentation in bottles, cans and barrels. Beer usually consists of four to six percent alcohol.

Low-alcohol beers can be made by removing alcohol from ordinary beers or directly, by use of an engineered yeast strain that produces beer of only low-alcohol concentration. Vinegar is produced by a second fermentation of beer, cider or wine. A mixture of *Acetobacter* species is used to convert alcohol to acetic acid. Traditionally, this was carried out in large pine vats and the bacteria were obtained by passing the liquid repeatedly over bundles of birch twigs coated with the bacteria. Nowadays the process is done in aerated fermenters. In cheese-making process, the milk is first pretreated by pasteurisation in order to kill off any contaminating micro-organisms. The milk is then coagulated involving lactose-fermenting bacteria and rennet. The liquid which is separated from the solid curd which is processed further to produce cheese.

Gas-producing bacteria are used to create in the cheese its particular texture and acid-producing bacteria give it flavour. The ripening of cheeses needs storage under conditions that allow micro-organisms to improve the flavour. Fungi are used at this stage to give some cheeses their individual characteristics of flavour, colour, texture and appearance. Official reports in various countries have emphasised the increasing importance of biotechnology. For instance, the UK Advisory Council on Science and Technology (ACOST), in a 1990 report, *Developments in Biotechnology*, suggested that:

> Biotechnology is a broad term used to describe the production of innovative products, devices and organisms by exploitation of biological processes....

The report explained the crucial characteristic of the new developments as follows:

.....Traditional biotechnology was based on enrichment and purification, modern biotechnology on the *manipulation of genes and on the alterations of the genetic structure of cells*. Much of its importance stems from recent advances in genetics and biochemistry and from the emergence of molecular biology.

The central importance of the new understanding of genetics at a molecular level was clearly stressed. In the view of the report's authors:

Underpinning the future progress on genetic manipulation will be advances in molecular genetics and the knowledge of genomes of organisms.....

New commercial opportunities are confidently supposed to arise from the acquisition of this deeper understanding.

Five distinct new technologies were identified in the report Table 2.1 and it was suggested that these have led to advances in the production of : high-value chemicals chiefly for medical use; intermediate-value chemicals or enzymes; monoclonal antibodies for diagnostic purposes; novel plant species or improved yields; transgenic animals; and detection of particular genetic factors in human beings. A paper produced for the European Community 's Forecasting and Assessment in Science and Technology (FAST) Programme in 1992 has summarised some of the progress and prospects in these different areas of application.

Table 2.1
Novel Technologies

1. *Sequencing of genes and proteins*: elucidating the order of the constituent chemicals.
2. *Genetic engineering*: cutting and splicing of DNA, moving genes between organisms and getting these genes to work.
3. *Fused cell techniques*: fusing two cells to produce a new cell with all or parts of the genetic material of the two parent cells, for example to produce monoclonal antibodies or new plants.
4. *Protein engineering*: altering the structure and thus the properties of proteins by manipulation of the DNA which controls their production.
5. *Fermentation and cell culture*: growing large amounts of microbial or animal or plant cells.

Fifteen first-generation protein drugs and vaccines were reported in the FAST, paper to have been approved for use in the USA and a hundred others created by recombinant DNA techniques were said to be awaiting approval. Great advances in understanding are expected to lead to better or more sophisticated and specific products being available in the future. Several genetically-engineered Hepatitis B vaccines are already on the market and human growth hormone has been used to treat dwarfism in children.

Concerning intermediate-value chemicals , it is hoped that over 50 percent of the industrial enzyme market will be taken over by biotechnology products in about a decade. Numerous medical diagnostic kits depending on monoclonal antibodies are already in clinical use. Examples include an AIDS diagnosis kit and a *Legionella* rapid assay include.Plant biopesticides based on toxins produced by the bacterium *Bacillus thuringiensis* (Bt) have been commercially produced for last three decades.

Two rDNA Bt products have now been approved in the USA. Toxic genes have been cloned, sequenced and introduced into different organisms and further applications are likely despite concerns such as those over the development of resistant strains of insects. Plants, of course, have been subjected to mutagens and selected for altered genes for several years. Now various new plant transgenic techniques are available and more than 50 species of crop plant have been transformed using these methods. Progress has been rapid in the development of plants with resistance to herbicides, insects and viruses. Genes which encode for an enzyme that inactivates a herbicide have, for instance , been transferred into cotton and oilseed rape. Regarding animal husbandry, bovine growth hormone (bovine somatotrophin, BST) can now be produced by microbial organisms and fed to cattle. Some 15-30 percent increases in milk production have been reported.

Monoclonal antibody technology is also being used in the diagnosis of animal diseases. There is, for instance, a system that screens for a wide range of poultry diseases. The general impression is that during the next few decades we may expect major benefits from applications of the new biotechnology to the food and drinks industry, health pharmaceuticals, chemicals, agriculture, and the environment . What then is this new technology, and on what scientific knowledge is it based?

Table 2.2
Commercial areas affected by biotechnology

1. Foods and drinks.
2. Pharmaceuticals and health care:
   - -Human medicine;
   - -Veterinary medicine.
3. Chemicals and fuels.
4. Agriculture and horticulture.
5. Environment clean-up.

Basic Facts

The basic facts we need to follow are simple , even though the detail of how living cells operate may be very complex. There are differences in the details of how simple bacterial (prokaryotic) and more advanced (eukaryotic) cells function. Bacterial cells do not have their genetic material or DNA (deoxyribonucleic acid) enclosed in a distinct nucleus as, for example, do the cells in our bodies and this has profound implications.

Nevertheless, for both prokaryotic and eukaryotic cells, we know that the enzymes that and affect their operations, and many other biological compounds of significance, are proteins. These are made up of one or more chains of amino acids called peptides. The sequence of amino acids decides the three- dimensional structure of the chains and this is crucial to the function of the protein. The sequence of amino acids in the peptide chain is determined by the information coded in the DNA gene for that particular chain. In a eukaryotic cell the information in the DNA is transferred out from the nucleus to the cytoplasm surrounding it by a particular type of RNA or ribonucleic acid called messenger (mRNA).

The mRNA has a structure which is complementary to the DNA from which it has been transcribed. The peptide chain is then synthesised on the mRNA by a process known as translation. In bracteria which do not have their DNA separated off in a nucleus, mRNA operates in a similar fashion but tends to be much shorter-lived. The sequence of events is summarised thus: transcription of the coded information from DNA to mRNA and then translation from mRNA to form the peptide chain of amino acids.

The particular sequence of amino acids of the peptide chain then the three-dimensional structure and therefore the properties of the protein coded for by the original DNA gene. Although the existence of nucleic acids has been known for more than a century, the hereditary function of the material was only clearly shown in the early 1950s. The detailed investigation of the structure and function of DNA and RNA effectively dates from that time. Hence our this understanding is very recent and has developed very rapidly. The structure of DNA was suggested by Watson and Crick in 1953. The structure of the DNA double helix is now well known. The DNA molecule is composed of two linked stands of nucleotides.

Each nucleotide has a base, a sugar called deoxyribose, and a phosphate. The backbone of each DNA strand consists of linked and linearly alternating deoxyriboses and phosphates. The base can be one of adenine (A), guanine (G), cytosine (C) or thymine (T). Owing to their particular characteristics A on one strand always connects to T on the other, and similarly G always links with C. The significant point is that the genetic information is encoded in the order of the bases. In the code a particular non-overlapping triplet of bases determines a particular amino acid of a peptide chain. Some other characteristics of DNA should be noted. First, the two strands are coiled around each other in a helical manner. The sugar and phosphate backbones of the strands are on the outside while the linked base pairs are on the inner side (forming the 'rungs' of the helical 'ladder').

It is also known that the phosphate may be attached at either of two positions of the deoxyribose conventionally numbered 5′ and 3′. The two DNA strands have opposite polarity in the sense that in one the attachments run from 5' to 3' and in the other from 3' to 5'. When DNA replicates itself the two strands split apart and a new strand comes up on each in what is a semi-conservative process—each new length of DNA being made up of one old or conserved strand and one new 'daughter' strand. The structure of genes is, of course, by not as simple as this description might indicate. There are, for example, specific sets of triplets which determine where protein synthesis will start and finish on mRNAs, and segments which regulate the transcription of mRNA from the DNA. RNA or ribonucleic acid differs from DNA in that the sugar present is ribose and the base uracil occurs instead of thymine; RNA is also single-stranded but the same principle of a non-overlapping triplet code determining amino acids is applicable here. Messenger RNA is produced on the DNA template, in the 5' to 3' direction, by the action of enzymes known as RNA polymerases. The DNA strands separate locally, but only one is used for copying into mRNA. The mRNA then undergoes a variety of further processing stages before it is ready to act as a template for protein synthesis.

In the simpler bacteria groups of genes are often transcribed together as they are located close together along the bacterial DNA. Such a group of genes is called an operon; the individual genes of the group are called cistrons. The mRNA remains in one piece as the different cistrons are translated into proteins. In more advanced eukaryotic cells each mRNA codes for only one amino acid chain or peptide. Moreover, when the mRNA is first transcribed there are several apparently non-functional pieces (introns) between the pieces (exons) which code for peptide. The introns are sliced away within the nucleus before the passage of the mRNA into the cytoplasm and the later production of the peptide. Protein synthesis takes place in the cytoplasm on ribosomes. These are proteins where mRNA can be brought together with the appropriate amino acids.

The genetic code includes the signals of initiation (AUG) and termination (UAA, UAG and UGA) of protein synthesis and 61 other possible base combinations which code for the 20 different, naturally-occurring amino acids. The code is therefore degenerate since some amino acids are specified by more than one type of triplet. This simplified description of the basics of molecular biology will raise as many questions as it answers. For instance, if the same DNA is present in each of the cells of our bodies why are liver cells different from skin cells? Therefore, there have to be very complex means by which the operation of genes is controlled and means by which these central processes within cells can be integrated with regulatory elements outside the cell. In brief, while it is not necessary for us to follow all the details here, it is clear that an enormous amount of work has gone into elucidating how the basic mechanisms of heredity actually function within the intact cell and the whole organism.

It can be logically argued that, amongst other things, a gene would need.

(i) the code for the protein

(ii) a switch to turn it on and off;

(iii) a regulator to ensure that it produced the correct amount of protein.

Some of these elements have certainly been identified, and the fact that they appear to operate in the same way in a wide variety of organisms indicates that certain very important aspects of the operation of the genetic machinery have been conserved essentially intact through long periods of evolution. This allows the elements to be manipulated between different organisms by man.

The Latest Technology

Here we shall not try to give a comprehensive listing of the major technologies now available in this rapidly- advancing field, nor to detail the technical aspects of those we do describe. The aim rather is to give adequate information on some of the crucial technologies for the reader to be easily able to follow what is being done regarding the organisms of interest. It is significant to stress that the techniques to be described did not arise *de* novo but from an extended background of scientific research. For instance, much of the work which will be of interest to us later has concerned micro-organisms: bacteria and viruses in particular. There has been a long period of intensive study of such organisms including the initial 'Golden Age' of work from the last quarter of the last century through to the beginning of the First World War. Nevertheless, advances are now being made very rapidly and the pace of developments over the last two decades has accelerated.

Sequencing of DNA

One standard way of examining the sequence of bases in DNA is named the Maxam-Gilbert method after its originators. Identical pieces of DNA are cut into fragments (by methods detailed later) and the fragments are then sorted depending on the size by subjecting the whole set to gel electrophoresis. In this technique the DNA fragments are acted upon by an electric current and migrate along the gel to a distance depending on their size, the smallest migrating furthest. Batches of similar-sized fragments can then be received directly by washing them off different sections or bands of the gel. Batches of DNA pieces of identical length are then radioactively labelled at one end and split into four distinct lots Figure 2.1. Each lot of DNA fragments is then treated with a different reagent. The reagent attacks the DNA at one (or two) specific bases.

Conditions are set so that only a small number of sites will be attacked by each reagent, but every potential site should be cut in each lot of DNA. The result is a series of differently-sized fragments in each of the four lots, having different sizes depending on how far away from the radioactive end they were attacked. The four lots of fragments can therefore be subjected to gel electrophoresis again to separate out the different lengths of fragments. The bands thus obtained can then be detected in each case by autoradiographs exhibiting the labelled fragments, and the sequence of the DNA can be deduced by comparing across the four sets: For instance, in the third lot of DNA shown in figure 2.1, the strand can be cut at T immediately after the radioactive label. Thus a band will be obtained at the far end of the electrophoresis gel. This is so because small fragments migrate furthest. Alternatively, the strand can also be cut at the T at the far end of the strand away from the radioactive label. This is the largest and therefore slowest-running band. The more complex problems of sequencing much larger strands of DNA can be sorted out cutting the long sequence of bases at different places to get different initial sets of indentical fragments.

1. Label one end of single DNA strands
2. Divide into four lots
3. Cut DNA strands with specific reagents at:
4. Therefore obtaining fragments in each case of:
5. Run Electroproresis and Autoradiograph

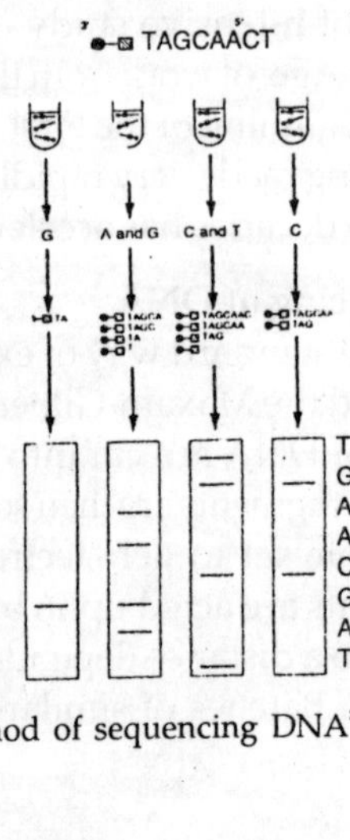

Fig. 2.1. The Maxam-Gilben method of sequencing DNA*.

The results obtained for the different sets of DNA fragments can then be pooled and the total sequence built up. Another method of sequencing, according to Sanger, relies not on breaking the DNA, but on stopping its replication in a controlled way. There is also steady automation of sequencing techniques.

The Polymerase Chain Reaction (PCR)

This is a more recent technique which finds wide application. It allows the generation of large amounts of DNA from small initial quantities. The DNA region of interest is heated in order to separate the two strands. Then two synthetic primers with nucleotide sequences complementary to the parts of the gene of interest are attached to opposite ends to the separated gene. The primer then directs DNA polymerase enzyme to copy each of the strands in opposite directions. This results in the doubling of the amount of DNA. The new quantity of DNA can then be reheated and subjected to the same cycle of treatment to double the quantity again. The cycle can be repeated ten times which gives a 1,000-fold increase in the specific DNA of interest.

Recombining DNA (rDNA)

DNA is recombined in animal reproduction when the paternal DNA in a sperm joins with the maternal DNA in the egg. Human beings have manipulated such processes for several years in order to breed animals for particular purposes, and have done the same with plants. There were severe limits though to what was achievable. As Gerald J. Stine commented:

Entry of such DNA into the cell stimulates production of these enzymes which specifically attack and therefore degrade the function of the foreign DNA. Type II restriction enzymes have been chiefly used in rDNA techniques because they cut DNA at absolutely specific sites without regard to where that DNA originates. Thus it is possible

> ....for millions of years of biological evolution recombination of DNA as it generally occurs in nature, stays within species lines and within their mechanism of reproduction..... the investigator only brought together packages of evolutionarily-prepared DNA and asked whether or not the DNA within these packages (gametes) would recombine. The discovery of site-specific restriction enzymes in 1970 dramatically altered that situation and caused the rapid developments in genetic engineering that we see today. Restriction enzymes occur in bacteria where they function to protect the bacteria against invading foreign DNA.

to cut two different types of DNA at the same site and then to join the two different types together.

As revealed in Fig. 2.2 two species of DNA can be cut by the EcoR1 restriction enzyme which makes a staggered symmetrical cut leaving bases exposed on both. These bases can then join up and be sealed together to create a new mixture of DNAs. By the late 1980s over a thousand such enzymes had been isolated, mostly of type II. Several of these enzymes were isolated from various bacterial species cut at the same site, but, even so, one hundred specific cleavage sites were known and about 150 restriction enzymes were commercially available. In order to use such a restriction enzyme, for instance to produce large amounts of the product of an animal gene, it is necessary not only to develop a way of inserting the gene into another piece of DNA but to get it to function in another cell such as a bacterium which can be easily cultured.

This may be done, for example by inserting the DNA from the higher organism into a plasmid vector. Plasmids are autonomously replicating DNA molecules able to function in bacterial cells. The example shown in Fig. 2.3 outlines the steps that are taken. The plasmid DNA is in the form of a circle which is cut or opened up by a specific restriction enzyme.

The DNA to be inserted is cut by the same enzyme and the fragments of the two types of DNA (gene and plasmid) are mixed . The 'sticky ends' join up and are sealed with DNA ligase. As the joining-up is not a controlled process, some plasmids simply close up again, but some will incorporate the foreign DNA. These are called recombinants. In the next stage the plasmids are mixed with bacteria and some enter the bacterial cells. This process is called transformation, and some of the bacterial cells so transformed will have incorporated the recombinant DNA plasmids. The bacteria having recombinant DNA may be chose in various ways, for instanlet by having recombinant plasmids confer antibiotic resistance on the bacteria which then allows the ones containing such plasmids to be selected out by exposing the whole batch to the action of an antibiotic. Once the selected bacteria having the foreign DNA are identified, they can be grown on (cloned) to yield large quantities of this DNA and its products. Just how large are the quantities that can be produced is demonstrated by the fact that a concentration of *Escherichia coli* bacterial cells of one per millilitre may be transformed into a concentration of one billion cells per millilitre in 24 hours. If each cell has a copy of the plasmid, there will be billions of copies available. Also, a plasmid of *E* coli can be enabled to multiply in the bacterial cell without the bacterium reproducing and thereby splitting itself. In this fashion, 1,000-3,000 plasmids can be obtained within each bacterial cell and each of these plasmids will also reproduce when the bacterium itself does. Although the use of plasmids is a very successful means of producing functioning rDNA in bacteria it has the drawback only relatively short pieces of DNA can be carried.

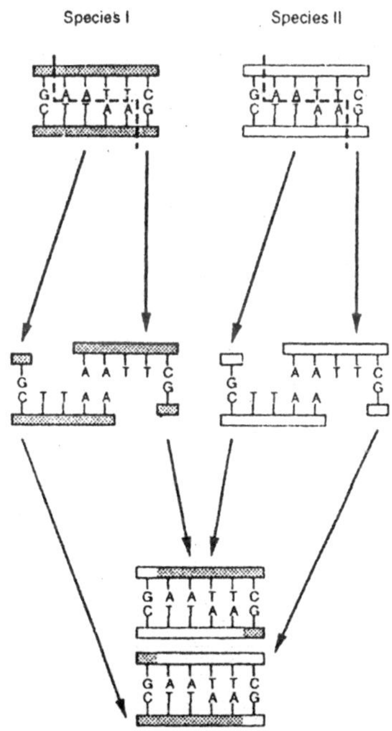

Fig. 2.2. Joining up DNA from different species using a restriction enzyme.*

One way of carrying larger sections of DNA is to use bacteriophages (or phages). These are viruses which attack bacteria. They naturally insert their own DNA into bacteria where it can replicate and produce many new phage particles (lytic phase) or become integrated within the bacterial chromosome and replicate at the same time as the bacterial cell (lysogenic phase). The phage lambda (λ) has been thoroughly studied. It has 60 genes which have all been mapped and the complete sequence of its 48,000 base pairs is now known.

The genes which govern the integration of the phage into the bacterial chromosome and replication alongside the bacterium can be removed from the phage DNA. Then foreign DNA inserted into the phage DNA will be injected into other bacteria when new phages are produced in the lytic phase. Over 100 vectors have been derived from the l phage, as there are several sites where restriction enzymes may be used and which do not interfere with the independent phage replication. There are further ways of cloning still larger pieces of DNA. Advances in the understanding of yeast genetics, for instance, have made it possible to develop cloning vectors called yeast artificial chromosomes (YACs) which can be transferred into yeast cells.

Gene Probes

With the techniques discussed above, it is possible to take the fragments of DNA produced by a number of different restriction enzymes and to prepare a 'library' of clones of these fragments for the whole DNA of a particular organism of interest.

1 Restriction Enzyme Used to Cut Plasmid and Foreign DNA

2. Mixed and Sealed to Produce Recombinant DNA

3. Transformed into Bacterial Cell

4. Selected and Millions of copies Produced in the Bacterium

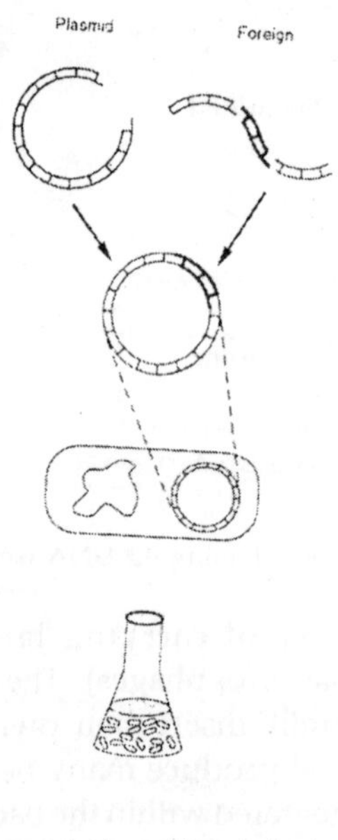

Fig. 2.3 Genetic engineering of a bacterial plasmid and cloning of foreign DNA.*

The question that ultimately arises is as to how the investigator can recognise what gene has been cloned. What does a particular piece of DNA that is now functioning within the bacterial cell do within the whole living organism? The enzyme reverse transcriptase became known in 1970 in certain viruses which cause cancer and which have RNA as their genetic material. In a viral infection the enzyme produces a DNA strand complementary to the virus RNA . In the laboratory, therefore, the same enzyme may be used to produce a DNA copy (complementary DNA or cDNA) from any piece of messenger RNA. Take the simple case of human reticulocytes (red blood cells). The mRNA in these cells is almost totally made up of material used to produce the globin chains that compose the oxygen-carrying haemoglobin molecule.

So it is not too difficult to purify the mRNAs for single globin chains and to make radioactively labelled cDNA from this mRNA. Given that DNA bases always pair A to T and C to G, such DNA molecules can be used to 'recognise ' chemically exactly the same sequences to their own. Thus it would be possible to use a cDNA made from the globin mRNA to find the 'gene' amongst a set of fragments of DNA that have earlier been cloned. A standard procedure for screening cloned DNA shown sequences was developed by Grunstein and Hogness. This is shown Fig. 2.4 . The transformed bacterial cells are grown to visible size in a solid medium. The colonies are then transferred on to a replica plate (basically by stamping the replica plate into the original and this picking up some of the material from each colony. Chemical treatment of the replica colonies then destroys the cells and denatures the DNA. The denatured DNA sticks to the replica plate and protein material etc. may be washed away. Radioactive cDNA can then be flooded on to the replica plate where it will hybridise or join up with any DNA which it specifically complements.

Unhybridised DNA is then washed away and the replica plate subjected to autoradiography. If there is a match with the cDNA it will reflect on the radiograph of the replica plate and this will indicate the colony on the original plate which has the DNA of interest in its plasmids.

Monoclonal Antibodies

When foreign proteins (antigens) enter an animal, its immune system reacts by producing clones of different individual plasma cells, each clone of which produces a different single antibody. A disease known as multiple myeloma develops when an individual clone of plasma cells becomes malignant and proliferates uncontrollably. The antibody it produces, however, is against an unknown antigen. A revolutionary technique was developed in 1975 by Kohler and Milstein in order to take advantage of such cells. The technique involves fusing the malignant cells with antibody-producing cells (from an animal spleen) which are functioning in their normal manner and producing a specific antibody to a known specific antigen Fig. 2.5. In practice, mouse myeloma cells are used and the programmed spleen cells also come from the mouse.

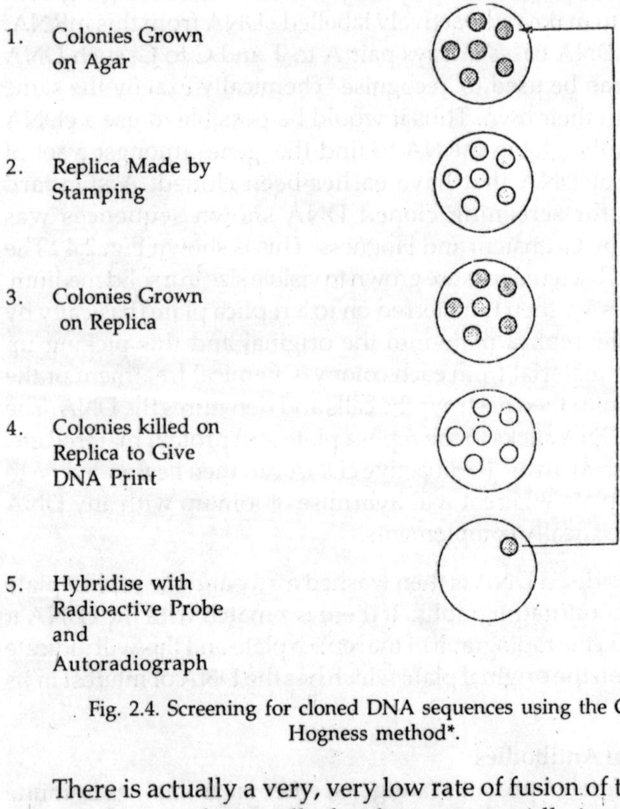

Fig. 2.4. Screening for cloned DNA sequences using the Grunstein Hogness method*.

There is actually a very, very low rate of fusion of the two cell types and as myeloma cells develops very rapidly in culture they would soon swamp any hybrids if special measures are not taken. Since the myeloma cells lack an enzyme that spleen cells possess it is possible, by choosing the correct growing medium, to block the growth of myeloma cells but allow the growth of the hybrids (spleen cells themselves do not develop and divide in this situation). The result is a hybrid cell which proliferates as the myeloma cell did but also produces a specific antibody as the spleen cell did. Clearly the capability for producing large amounts of specific antibodies has given rise to a wide range of new applications, for instance diagnosis, because the antibodies produced have affinity of a precise character for specific antigens.

Bioprocessing Technique

Though it is perhaps less fascinating than the key recombinant DNA (rDNA) and monoclonal antibody techniques, equally critical for the advance of biotechnology has been the steady progress in understanding of how to use cells and molecules in industrial processes. Progress may be categorised in four areas. Firstly, means have been found of conducting large-scale culture of plant and animal cells which permits products to be obtained in commercially-significant quantities. Secondly, improved methods of fermentation of microbial cells have been brought into use which again allow larger yields to be obtained, and from a wider range of organisms.

Following on from such production processes, new and very specific means have been found to separate and purify the products required at a reasonable cost. Lastly, techniques have been developed which allow cells and enzymes to be immobilised, thus creating a means by which the bioprocessing can be carried done through a stationary bioprocessing matrix. Taken together, such developments are transforming what can be done and the yields, purity levels and rest- levels of production that can be achieved in such a manner that can only expand the applications of biotechnology in the future.

1. Obtain Mutant Myeloms Cells and Culture
2. Obtain Spleen Cells from Mouse and Fuse with Myeloma Cells
3. Culture in Medium where only Hybrid Myeloma- Spleen Cells (Hybridomas) Survive
4. Check for Antibody Production and Clone

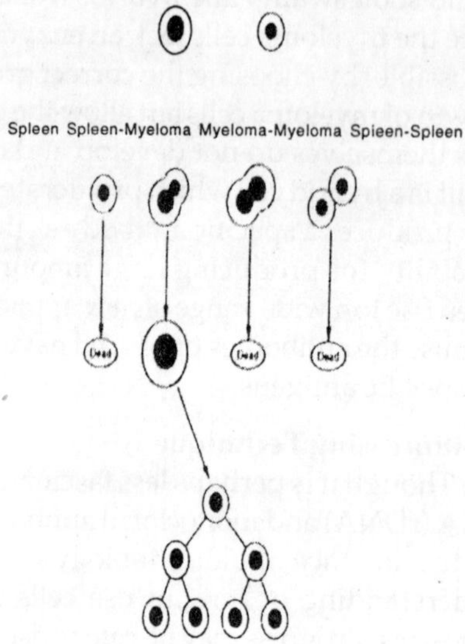

Fig. 2.5 Production of monoclonal antibodies*.

The New Biotechnology

It is necessary to understand the nature of the commercial driving forces behind the growth of biotechnology. This is not an industry of giant, mature companies like the chemical industry. Especially in the United States there are several small companies competing for vast commercial profits. An example is Amgen. Which was a struggling start-up company in 1980. In 1983 a molecular biologist with the company became successful in cloning erythropoietin (EPO), a substance which induces red blood cell production. After linking up with the giant Japanese company Kirin (a brewing company seeking to diversify) and jointly developing a second drug (granulocyte colony-stimulating factor, which raises white blood cell production) Amgen made more than $1bn profit in 1992. Given such opportunities, it appears likely that several small companies will be the driving force force change in biotechnology for some time to come. What we are dealing with then is first a drive for commercial profit through practical implementation of new product discoveries. This is associated with two other factors: methodological breakthroughs (such as recombinant DNA technology) and developments in theoretical understanding (such as the intron/exon structure of the genome of higher organisms).

Together, these factors interact in a mechanism that bring about extremely rapid scientific and technological change. Moreover, it is not at all easy to predict what changes will occur and what the shape of science, technology and commercial industry will be in a decade from now. The intention here is not to attempt an overview of current developments, but rather to show what is happening in the areas important for our consideration of possible new biological weapons. We shall therefore deal mainly with certain recent developments in medicine and agriculture.

We shall also limit our discussion to developments closely linked to our interest in micro-organisms. Thus most of what we read in news papers on new gene therapies and the sequencing of the human genome will not be covered. Nevertheless, it is necessary to briefly demonstrate the capabilities for intervention that are now possible, even for human beings. One example is the cure that now appear possible for adenosine deaminase deficiency (ADA). In this disease the victim lacks an enzyme that breaks down deoxyadenosine; the chemical builds up in the body and unluckily kills the T-lymphocytes of the immune system. The victim is therefore unable to fight off infections. The cure involves extracting some of the victim's bone-marrow cells and introducing the missing gene into these cells using a harmless virus. The properly functioning cells may then be returned to the victim's body where they continue to produce blood cells having atrility to manufacture the missing enzyme. The person is then able to lead a normal life. We concentrate here on biontechnology developments, particularly relating to infectious diseases: both new threats from old diseases, like the resurgence of tuberculosis in the developed world resulting from changes in our life- styles, and the potential evolution of new threats from previously unknown diseases:

We shall cover some features of biotechnology in relation to agriculture where, for instance, it seems there is a rising threat from a new form of the late blight fungus of potatoes which caused the Irish potato famine in the last century.

Somatostatin

Somatostatin a peptide that controls the release of insulin and human growth hormones from the pituitary gland. Somatostatin is known to be an amino acid chain of 14 components Fig. 2.6. From this sequence it has been possible to develop a synthetic human gene with the correct sequence of nucleotides by chemical methods. This gene was then inserted into the plasmid pBR322. The plasmid contains a control region for the *lac* operon of *E.coli*. It is recalled that genes in bacteria are found in groups called operons. The *lac* operon of *E. Coli* is associated with the production of lactase which splits the lactose of milk into monosaccharides.

However, it would be wasteful for a small bacterium to have this system in its operating state, directing the production of lactose, if no milk were available in the gut of its human host. The bacterium therefore has a group of regulatory genes to switch production on and off. The *lac* operon has three structural genes and two other

1. Determine Sequence of Amino Acids
2. Make Synthetic DNA to Match
3. Open up plasmid and Recombine with Somatostatin Gene
4. Transform into <u>E.coli</u>
5. Harvest Somatostatin

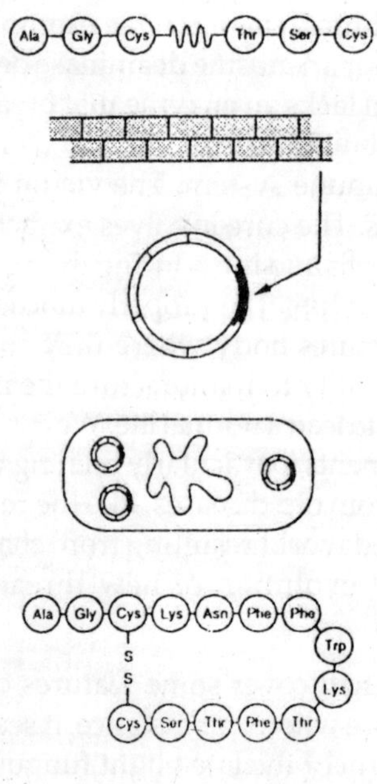

Fig. 2.6 Somatostatin production*.

signalling sequences know as the promoter and the operator. Nearby there is an associated regulator gene. If there is no lactose in the environment, the regulator gene produces a protein that binds to the operator site and overlaps the promoter.

Neither can operate when thus covered by the repressor protein. When eactose molecules become abundantly present, the repressor moves and instead binds to these molecules. This exposes the promoter and operator sites and allows RNA to be transcribed from the three structural genes. The three genes are transcribed as a set and only later they are translated into three different proteins.

To produce synthetic somatostatin, *E. Coli* having the plasmid pBR322 is cultured. If the synthetic somatostatin human gene is inserted correctly into the plasmid transcription, continues through the *lac* operon and the somatostatin gene. The somatostatin peptide can then be separated from the three structural proteins produced by the *lac* operon at a later stage. The resulting somatostatin is similar to the natural hormone. What is more, instead of a yield of one milligram of hormone from 500,000 sheep brains, the same amount can also be extracted from a four-litre culture of recombinant *E. Coli* cells.

Insulin

This hormone is secreted by the pancreas and regulates glucose concentration in the blood. It can be used to treat disorders of glucose regulation in the disease diabetes. The insulin molecule is built up by two chains of amino acids: 21 in the A chain and 30 in the B chain. A synthetic from of insulin is now available. Synthetic genes were again produced form a knowledge of the amino acid sequences.

The DNA sequences for each chain were inserted into separate pBR322 plasmids and the plasmids were then inserted into *E. Coli* cells. After the two amino acid chains had been separately developed are linked together after harvesting and purification. Before the production of insulin by this method, it had to be taken out of the pancreases of pigs and cows. Synthetic insulin was the first rDNA product to be approved for commercial use in 1982. Such practical outcomes depended on what was already known about the structure and function of bacterial cells and knowledge continues to accumulate rapidly.

Nevertheless, it is significant to know how bacteria operate when they are functioning in a victim's body, and not just in the more easily observable laboratory test-tube. Techniques are now being developed to allow such research. Whilst some of the factors involved in bacterial disease, such as the toxins of cholera and diptheria, were found by the examining proteins produced by the bacteria under laboratory conditions, researchers have sought ways of identifying genes which are switched on in the much more complex situation of the host body. Efforts started about a decade ago to approximate to such conditions by mixing host cells with bacteria, but recently more sophisticated means have been developed.

The technique called in vivo expression technology, was used with *Salmonella typhimurium,* which causes a typhoid- like disease in the mouse. The first step includes working with a bacterial strain which cannot develop in the mouse because it lacks the gene *pur* A that is needed for purine metabolism. Functional *pur* A genes were extracted from a related bacterial stain and linked to *lac* Z, a gene which makes an enzyme that is easily detectable by using colour assay technique. The entire *Salmonella* genome was then split up and pieces were inserted in front of the artificial two-gene combination that had been made. The researchers assumed that some of the pieces of *Salmonella* DNA would have genes that would switch on the inserted *pur* A and *lac* Z in the real host conditions. All the constructed lengths of DNA were then put into the straing of bacteria lacking *pur* A which were then used to infect mice. Bacteria that survived for three days were gathered from the infected mice. It was supposed that in order to survive in the mice, the bacteria would have had their inserted *pur* A switched on.

To discover whether these bacteria also had their *pur* A switched on in the laboratory they were grown on special agar which changed colour in response to the operation of *lac* Z. Of the bacteria that survived after three days in the mice 95 per cent were shown to be able to function in the laboratory as well as in the host. However, five per cent were found not to operate in the laboratory. These, logically, had to contain gene fragments which were switched on specifically in the mouse-host conditions alone. It was a fair assumption that such genes were necessary only for host infection.

The genes were therefore likely candidates as virulence genes. So far, genes necessary for growth of the bacteria in the host have been identified, but if genes necessary for the deadliness of the infection were to be found, they would be potential targets for mutation to make attenuated strains of the organism which could perhaps then be used in live vaccines. Another possible line of research that could be followed with such a technique would be to try to discover the factors needed switch on the deadly effects of bacteria which are particularly harmful when they migrate to a specific cell type in the host body.

Hepatitis B Virus (HBV)

This virus is a cause of a common type of liver disease and is also linked to the later development of liver cancer. World-wide, almost 300 million people are supposed to be chronically infected with HBV, three- quarters of them in Asia. Children are frequently infected via their mother at birth or soon afterwards. The population in some badly affected regions may have 10 per cent of chronic carriers of HBV. In poor areas of the world the disease primarily affects the young. In the rich world, there are far fewer carriers and they are mostly adults whose lifestyle brings them into contact with the virus. It seems that a chronic infection goes through a stage of active virus replication with minimal immune reaction from the host individual. After 20 to 30 years the virus appears to become less efficient and an immune response develops. The infected liver cells are destroyed where active virus replication is evident, but in other cells the virus becomes incorporated into the genome of the cell itself. People may suffer both declining liver function and liver cancer, although it does not seem that the virus is directly responsible for switching on oncogenes, potential inducers of cancer, in the cell in which it is incorporated. People infected with HBV develop an antibody in their bloodstream which can be used to detect the presence of the virus. This antibody is produced against the HBV surface antigen.

The immediate disease may take any one of many forms, ranging from acute hepatitis followed by recovery (with considerable immunity to reinfection), to a fatal disease caused by immune responses resulting from killer T-cells attacking infected liver cells. A proportion of victims recover, but become chronic carriers with about 100 times the normal risk of developing hepatocellular carcinoma. Modern biotechnology has been highly successful in understanding the HBV virus and the disease it causes and in finding ways of dealing with the disease.

Much of the initial work obviously concentrated on finding good vaccines. The HBV genome is packaged inside two coats. The inner of these, called the capsid, is made up of one protein. The outer coat has got three proteins and there the surface antigen in each of these proteins. The HBV genome is the smallest of known animal virus genomes, being a circular DNA molecule of about 3,200 nucleotide sub-units. Unusually, one strand of DNA is longer than the other. Using standard methods, the HBV genome was cloned in *E. Coli.* This allowed the production of large amounts of the virus and its components for detailed study. The entire sequence of bases was determined and the way in which its proteins are coded worked out.

There are only four potential genes and these overlap in an amazingly compact structure which also has the necessary regulatory sequences that control protein production. Gene S, for instance, codes for the major outer coat protein and the surface antigen. About 500 bases which precede the S gene are transcribed along with it. This sequence codes in part for the other two outer-coat proteins and is also involved in the penetration of the virus into liver cells. Using transgenic mice, which have had part or the complete HBV genome added to their DNA, it has been possible to illustrate that gene S is expressed at high levels only in lever cells and this expression is under the control of steroid hormones. This would reveal why men, who have higher circulating levels of steroids than women, are at a greater risk of HBV infection and disease. HBV is a member of a group of viruses which are similar, called hepadnaviruses which have an extraordinary mechanism of replication. Studies of how these viruses function in animals has elucidated this mechanism.

Instead of using their DNA as a template to create new DNA direct, these viruses replicate indirectly via an RNA intermediate. After entering the target cell, the hepadnavirus genome enters the cell nucleus where a long RNA molecule is transcribed from its DNA. This is called the pregenome. Pregenome and a viral DNA polymerase are put in a newly-formed capsid and move back into the cytorlasm of the cell. There the RNA is reverse-transcribed by the polymoase into a DNA strand; the RNA pregenome is destroyed and a second DNA strand is developed to complement the first. The capsid and the viral DNA are then enclosed in a new outer layer of protein protection periodic leaving the liver cell. With this level of knowledge, practical applications have been made possible. Diagnostic testes have been developed which rely on the affinity of short strands of cloned DNA for complementary DNA in blood serum having infectious viruses.

The method is so reliable and sensitive that it may be used to track the level of viruses in the blood following medical treatment. The sensitivity of the test. has also been improved by using the polymerase chain reaction to amplify the amount of DNA in the infected sample. Vaccines were originally produced by inactivating viruses obtained from the blood serum of chronic HBV carriers.

The problem was that, although the vaccine had been found to be reliable, the serum supply was limited, purification was complex and expensive, and all batches had to be tested for safety. Thus a genetically- engineer, vaccine was a high-priority goal for researchers. It was found that genetically-engineered bacteria could mass produce the surface antigen, but its chemical structure was not recreated accrarely enough in these organisms to be properly immunogonic. It was therefore necessary to produce the needed material in higher organisms.

One vaccine was produced and marketed after genetically engineered production in yeast, and mammalian cells have also been used to produce antigenic material. Vaccination of very young children against HBV has been shown to be highly effective. Forty-seven countries now have national vaccination campaigns. In one of the earliest of these, dating from 1984 in Taiwan, the percentage of children providing proof of the surface antigen, and therefore evidence of past exposure to HBV infection, has dropped dramatically. The HBV vaccination works by activating a person's immune system to deal with invading viruses. It has been noticed that viruses have evolved a variety of strategies to frustrate the immune system. One such was illustrated by workers researching tumour necrosis factor (TNF), a molecule used by the immune system to increase attack on tumours or virus- infected cells.

On searching DNA database for sequences akin to for the TNF receptor they found something very similar in a member of the poxvirus family. The viral gene was, however, different from the true TNF receptor gene. For the true gene the protein product is anchored in the membrane of the host cell. When TNF binds to the protein receptor in the correct response, an internal reaction is started in the cell. The viral gene seems to have lost the membrane-anchoring aspect, indicating that its role is to produce a soluble product that exists in the bloodstream rather than being attached to a cell membrane. The investigators guessed that this product would bind and deactivate the TNF. This turned out to be true. Virus- infected cells were found to secrete a protein that binds to TNF; TNF was bound to the soluble protein in fluids rather than on to the protein anchored in the surface of virus- infected cells. In brief, the virus has evolved a decoy system to disable the body's defence by mopping up TNF and preventing it binding to and activating, virus- infected cells. Other instances were quickly demonstrated of soluble products being used a similar way against other parts of the immune system. Another viral strategy includes a more direct interference with the operations of the immune system.

A group of plasma proteins called 'complement' is involved in immune responses to infections agents. When not in use, complement is kept under check by specific proteins called 'Complement' is involved in immune responses to infectious. Vaccinia virus perhaps produces a protein with a similar controlling function to help frustrate the host defensive system during infection. More complex strategies have also been described, but the general point is that with the level of understanding we now have magor new therapeutic applications are possible.

The Vaccinia Virus

Nearly two centuries after Jenner first used vaccination against smallpox this much-feared disease was eradicated. The vaccinia virus which has been used for safety in the modern era is an orthopoxvirus closely linked to variola, the cause of smallpox, with cross-reactive antigens sufficient to provide good cross- protection. Research on vaccinia did not cease after the elimination of smallpox in 1977; indeed, there has been major progress of particular interest in our opinion. One reason for continuing research on vaccinia was that, unlike most viruses, DNA replication takes place in the cytoplasm and not the nucleus of host cells. Instead of being able to use the host nuclear enzymes, the vaccinia virus must carry coding for several of the enzymes necessary to *make viral mRNA* and for DNA replication. The virus is therefore a good target in which to examine how processes such as transcription actually take place.

The other major reason for the continuing interest in vaccinia research is that it has proved likely to insert DNA into its genome, and to delete sections from its genome, without destroying its infectivity.

Thus it is possible to have genes derived from other organisms producing antigenic material when a recombinant virus is replicating in a host. This gives a new route for the production of vaccines in medicine or veterinary work. The vaccinia virus used in this way is called a vector. Other viruses have also now been used in the same manner, as live immunogens. These viruses, because they retain their infectivity, are self-replicating and are cheap to manufacture and administer, have many benefits for vaccine production. They also have good resistance to T-cell or hormonal attack by the host immune system. The orthopoxviruses are a genus of the Poxviridae family. Apart from vaccinia, this group includes variola, cowpox, and monkey pox.

Whilst all these viruses, and other genera of the Poxviridae, have a common strategy of replication, vaccinia is most known about the vaccinia virus particle, as mechanically isolated from cells, is a large oval structure about 200 by 300 nm (m-9). The exterior surface is covered by tubules. Antibodies directed against the protein of these tubules, or against a surface protein, can neutralise the infectivity of the virus. The core of the virus has a complex mechanism. Characteristically for this group of viruses, the core carries both the genome and several enzymes derived from its DNA. When naturally released from infected cells, and not mechanically isolated, the virus particle has a further envelope of proteins around it. The vaccinia genome is a linear, double-stranded DNA molecule of about 185,000 base pairs. The ends of the DNA have variable regions which can be removed or transposed to the opposite end of the genome without affecting virus replication in many cell cultures. This provides relatively large amounts of foreign DNA to be inserted into the genome, without corresponding deletions, in forming a recombinant virus. The vaccinia vector can therefore be used to construct potential vaccines against more than one pathogen. In contrast to the ends of the genome, which are so variable, the central portion of about 120,000 base pairs is required for the correct functioning of the virus.

This is typical of the orthopoxviruses and the central section is therefore said to be highly conserved. The central part of the genome has been examined with restriction enzymes and much of the DNA sequence has been determined. The genes deduced to be present from knowledge of the DNA sequence seems to be closely packed without intervening non-coding sequences. The viral mRNAs and protein amino acid sequences can thus be readily identified. From this information much has already become about how viruses in general are assembled and operate. Vaccinia recombinant viruses are formed in a two-stage process. The foreign DNA is first cloned into a plasmid downstream of a vaccinia promoter, the whole being surrounded by vaccinia DNA from a non-essential part of the genome. This plasmid is then transafected (introduced) into cells which are infected with vaccinia.

Within such cells recombinant viruses are made by transfers between the inserted vaccinia sequence in the plasmid and corresponding regions of the infecting vaccinia virus. Although some of the viruses so developed in the infected cells will gave recombinations resulting from transfers, most will not, so standard methods have been developed for marking and selecting those that do. Vaccinia already had major advantages which had favoured its use in the smallpox eradication campaign.

It was heat stable, and cheap to manufacture, and easy to administer in the field. Its considerable capacity for carrying foreign DNA and its broad range of potential host added to the attraction of this vector system. There is now a long list of instances of protective immunity being created in experimental animals by the use of altered vaccinia virus. Work continues: to improve the amount of antigen expressed to raise the degree of immune response to the antigens, and to improve the safety of the vaccines. Many genes have been detected in the vaccinia genome which are implicated in viral pathogenicity in a multicellular host. These can be grouped into genes aiding viral replication within cells; genes which promote cell proliferation and thereby provide host cells with greater activity in which the virus can operate; genes which help viral dissemination; and genes which help in the evasion of the host immune system. The protein earlier described, which interferes with the complement control process, is in this final group.

Breeding of Plants

Humankind has been involved in selectively breeding plants

for some 10,000 years. Whilst techniques have become more sophisticated during the twentieth century, it is only for about a decade that the techniques of genetic engineering have been employed. The first and still most widely-used techniques relied on the plant pathogen *Agrobacterium tumefaciens* which produces crown gall disease. This bacterium naturally transfers a portion of its DNA (called transfer or T-DNA) into the DNA of infected plants. There it induces the plant to produce elevated levels of plant hormones. These cause the plant to produce abnormal structures, such as galls, which gives suitable places and nutrients for the particular strain of *Agrobacterium* to thrive. Researchers first removed the disease-causing elements from the transfer DNA.

Such 'disarming' leaves the transfer mechanism intact without the complication of the disease. The first demonstration of the creation of a transgenic plant, in the early 1980s, involved the transfer of resistance against a plant inhibitory chemical by this techniques. Apart from demonstrating that genes could be transferred to plants in this way, the transferred resistance to the inhibitory chemical provided a useful way of distinguishing the cells affected by the treatment, an example of a marker method. Since whole plants can be regenerated from very small pieces of tissue, genetic engineering usually concentrates on small groups of cells cut away from plants.

The Agrobacterium method is now used routinely around the world and applied to such small groups of cells. Several thousands of plants have been modified by this technique, but a large plant species, including cereals, are not natural hosts for *Agrobacterium* and other technique of modification have therefore had to be developed. One method relies on removing the strong plant cell wall and then moving DNA across the exposed plasma membrane; but, again, this does not work well with the critically significante cereal grains. A different method involves very small metal particles coated with DNA being shot into the plant cells. The cell walls rapidly close over the small holes and the metal particles just remain in the cell. Some of the injected DNA can then be included into the plant's own DNA. A much cheaper and easier method of introducing foreign DNA to plant ceus has recently been announced. Microscopic crystals of silicon carbide are briefly agitated in water with the DNA to be inerted and the plant cells: the extremely hard crystals perforate the cells and allow the DNA to peneterate

Genes that will work in higher organisms need three regions, first the promoter sequences region, which is involved in the timing and location of the expression of the gene, then the structural gene, which specifies the protein to be produced and finally, the polyadenylation (or poly-A) region, which makes sure the correct termination of mRNA transcription from the DNA. In plant genetic engineering the structural gene can come from a wide range of various sources and the promoter can be designed to operate in specific plant organs, such as leaves or roots, or even inside special cell types within such organs. A major subject of economically significant research is obviously the transfer of resistance to viruses into plants.

If for instance, the coat protein of tobacco mosaic virus (TMV) is expressed in tobacco or tomato plants by the methods described, the plants are found to be strongly resistant to the virus. It has known long ago that infection of a plant with a mild form of a virus gives protection against subsequent infection by a virulent strain. There seems to be an interference with the subsequent infection caused by replication of the mild strain. This method has therefore been used to produce resistance in a number of different crop species. For more than thirty years now, farmers have used the bacterium *Bacillus thuringiensis* (Bt) to provide some protection against predation by moth and butterfly caterpillars. If the bacteria are sprayed on to crops the insecticidal proteins they cause disrupt caterpillar feeding. The chemicals do not seem to be toxic to mammals or even other insect species. Unfortunately, the bacteria are easily washed off plants by rain or watering. From the mid-1980s onwards efforts were made to transfer the bacterial genes for the insecticidal proteis into plants. The original efforts led to the B_t protein being poorly shown and only affecting very susceptible insects in the laboratory. However, the original bacterial gene was redesigned and then achieved much imported effects. For example, Bt genes in cotton plants have effectively controlled major pests. Careful screening of strains of the bacterium have uncovered some which attack other insect pests very good & results have been of late in protecting potato plants from Colorado beetle by the genetic engineering of a toxin gene from *Bacillus thuringiensis tenebronis into Agrobacterium* and thence into Russett Burbank potatoes, the most popular US variety. Other applications of plant genetic engineering have conferred better resistance to herbicides, delayed ripening and enhanced nutritional properties. While there are limits as to what can be done, biotechnology seems one of the few practical means by which the food needed by the world's rapidly expanding human population may be produced.

No where is this need for efficient food production more pressing than in China, where 20 per cent of the world's population has only seven per cent of the world's cultivable land. Not surprisingly great attempt have been made to develop plant biotechnology there. Following the successful work with tobacco mosaic rirus described above, Chinese scientists began to test coat protein genes from local pathogenic viruses. This is the most active field of plant biotechnology in China today, where coat proteins for TMV, cucumber mosaic virus (CMV), potato viruses and several others have been cloned and characterised. Some have been engineered into plants and tested for antiviral activity in field trials. Other genes from resistant local plants age also being analysed. Most work is understandably being carried done on rice . In August 1992 the Chinese Government announced a 15-year 'Rice Genome Project ' to sequence the whole rice genome.

Other research is aimed at increasing the nitrogen- fixing capabilities of the bacterium *Rhizobium* which is symbiotic with legume varieties, and to developing cloned genes, which produce heavy-metal-binding proteins, into weeds which can be used to help to clear contaminated land. The preceding sections are intended to convey the reality of a new mechanistic biology in operation all over the world. If the revolution in chemistry at the end of the last century allowed the development and use of chemical weapons in the First World War, and the revolution in nuclear physics earlier this century made possible the development and use of neclear weapons in the Second World War, the inevitable question that must be asked is 'Can we stop the development and use of new biological weapons in the inevitable conflicts in the near future.

3

Biological Weapons: Before 1969

Major nations like the USA, UK, Japan and Erstwhile Soviet Union all had biological weapons programme around the Second World War period. The United States continued its programme till late 1960. A considerable range of potential agents was available to the military.

Let us start by examining the official summaries of their offensive programmes from 1946 onwards provided by the UK and the USA as part of the enhanced confidence-building measures agreed at the third five-year Review Conference of the Biological Weapons Convention in 1991. We shall then be able to fill in more of the detail of these programmes, within that official framework, from some of the investigations conducted during the Cold War period. In a final section an effort is made to emphasise on the real meaning of this information. It is argued that in the early 1940s this was a very new area of military research. Great advances were supposed to be possible in all aspects of the production and use of these weapon systems at this early stage of scientific and technological development. Several advances were indeed produced by rational application of vast amounts of money and the employment of many talented people in these research programmes so that, by the end of the 1960s, many effective weapons systems had been developed.

Previous Programmes

The United Kingdom

The UK stated that it had a programme of offensive biological research and development from 1940 to the late 1950s. Concerns over the possible advent of biological warfare had been there before the Second World War and in 1940 a small unit had been established at Porton Down to investigate biological warfare and possible defensive measures, and to develop the methods to retaliate in kind if that became necessary. As is now well known, as part of the efforts to develop a retaliatory weapon, anthrax spores were released in tests conducted at Gruinard Island off the Scottish mainland, which led to its contamination for decades afterwards. The UK report stated that the success of these trials led to a joint project with the USA and Canada with the objective of the development of an anthrax cluster bomb. This was called the N-bomb project, but was not finished before the end of the war.

Instead, the report suggested, the retaliatory capability during the war was met by an aircraft-delivered system having cattle cakes filled with anthrax and directed against German livestock. The stockpile of five million cattle cakes was almost entirely destroyed after the war, and the remainder when the UK signed the Biological Weapons Convention in 1972. Whilst some research on offensive programmes went on after the war, the report concluded that by 1957 the UK had abandoned such work.

The United States

According to the US report, high-level official concern over biological weapons was first noticed in the autumn of 1941. During the war there were clearly links with the UK and Canada on offensive research. The report pointed out that, from 1946 to 1949: Most of the BW R & D programme concentrated on the antipersonnel aspects of BW such as highly infectious bacteria (*Brucella suis, Pasteurella Francisella tularensis*, Q-fever/rickettsia. Venezuelan Equine Encephalomyelitis (VEE), *Bacillus anthracis* and staphylococcus enterotoxin)....

There were also smaller programmes linked with anti-plant and anti-animal agents. However, from the end of the Second World War until 1950 no production was done 'for the purpose of operational readiness' and no facilities were available for such work.

Field-testing sites had been shut down at the end of the war and testing was therefore done during this period in closed laboratory-sized chambers. Some small-scale outdoor testing was done with what were considered harmless organisms. In 1949 a one million-litre test sphere was built at Camp Detrick and explosive munition tests of some pathogens were undertaken there. A change of policy occurred in mid-1950 when it was recommended that a biological weapons production facility should be setup and that the testing of agents and munitions should be done in the context of a general expansion of the whole programme.

Open-air sea trials using *Bacillus globigii* (BG) and Serratia marcescens (SM), considered to be effective stimulants, started with tests of the vulnerability and detection capabilities of US naval ships. The Army was instructed to produce *Brucella suits and Pasteurella [Francisella] tularensis* agents at a facility in Pine Bluff Arsenal, Arkansas, and an anti-crop bomb was produced, tested and put into production in 1951. Moreover, large-scale tests of the vulnerability of the San Francisco Bay area were done with BG and SM in September 1950.

The biological weapons programme continued to develop from 1954 to 1958. Vaccine research on.....tularemia, Rift Valley Fever, and Q fever at Fort Detrick was supplemented by a major contractual effort at Ohio State University Research Foundation. The program included the use of human volunteers.

Responding partly to changing Soviet statements, official policy was substantially changed again towards biological warfare in 1956 from 'retaliation only' to a policy in which the USA 'would be made to use BW or CW in a general war to enhance military effectiveness. Further enhancement of the offensive programme followed in the period from 1959 to 1962 and 'developmental work on Q fever and tularemia proceeded to their standardisation as BW agents'.

A test centre at Fort Douglas, Salt Lake City, Utah, was also maintained at this time. During the period from 1963 to 1968, the report stated, the primary work was aimed at producing the agents that had been found to be useful for military. A number of munitions were filled and stored at the Pine Bluff Arsenal. This offensive programme was then curtailed by President Nixon.

One might conclude that these reports are less than comprehensive (see below) and it can be argued that there is a fine distinction between some feature of the offensive programmes described and the defensive biological weapons programmes which have continued. It is evident nevertheless, that these official reports confirm the existence of offensive programmes both during and after the Second World War.

Some More Information

The United Kingdom

An account of 'Biological warfare and biological defence in the United Kingdom 1940-79' was published in the *Royal United Services Institute Journal* in December 1992. The author, Gordon Carter, was a senior staff member of the Chemical and Biological Defence Establishment at Porton Down. Carter revealed how British interest and concern about biological weapons predated the outbreak of the Second World War, indicating that it was perhaps triggered by allegations of German biological weapons research.

This concern was more at the beginning of the war and was acted on at the highest level, Lord Hankey writing a key paper pointing out 'the need for studies of BW to leave the realm of hypothesis and enter that of practical experiment'. The group was set up at Porton Down to do the necessary work. From considerations of the knowledge of gas warfare it had been decided that the most effective means of using biological weapons would be:...to disseminate an aerosol of lung-retention size particles from a liquid suspension of bacteria in a bursting munition such as a bomb, delivered so that effective concentrations would be inhaled by anyone in the target area....

Work was to focussed on the anthrax bacterium and to a lesser extent on botulinum toxin. By 1942 laboratory work at Porton had determined what inhalation doses of anthrax were required to infect and kill various animal species, and trials at the Porton ranges with *Bacillus subtilis* had determined how bombs might be used to spread spores effectively. It was then thought to be necessary to test the real agent at the secure site of Gruinard Island in Scotland. The trials included use of a modified 30-ib high explosive/chemical bomb with some three litres of anthrax spores suspended near the ground and fired electrically.

The trials in 1942 illustrated just how deadly the weapons could be. It was realised that the weapon was more potent than any chemical weapons agent or munition of like size examined by the British, and in 1943 attention turned to the study of 4-Ib bombs that might be more effectively used in clusters. Work on the anthrax weapon (N-bomb) was transferred to the United States and Canada as the early stage in a long association concerned with Biological weapons. Indeed, the leader of the British group had all the methodology data assembled and dispatched to the United States where it provided 'the foundations for the later US BW programme'. This was the programme which was to develop to such massive proportions in the Cold War period , and, as we shall see later, utilised data from another national programme of offensive biological weapons research. The War Cabinet's requirement for a biological retaliation-in- kind weapon was met by the production of the five million anthrax cakes at Porton. Carter commented: 'The possible impact of this weapon on the beef and dairy industry of Germany remains conjectural' but he pointed out its historical significance as 'possibly the first acknowledged biological weapon'. Carter argued that, despite the post-war development of nuclear weapons and the discovery of the improved capability of the chemical nerve agents developed by Germany during the war, there was still a perceived need to build a retaliatory biological weapons capability. A 'remarkable indicator' of the significance of biological weapons at this time, Carter suggested, was the construction of a new purpose-built laboratory at Porton. The building, believed to have been one of the largest brick buildings of modern times had, eventually, 210,000 square feet of floor area, and for decades was regarded as the best designed and equipped microbiology institute in the world....

At a time of severe post-war austerity measures in the UK £2.25m was spent only on this single element of the biological weapons programme. The armed services were particularly concerned to achieve a better understanding of the factors affecting the survival of pathogenic micro-organisms in aerosols. It was regarded that this could best be done safely at sea and in November 1948 tests were conducted off the Bahamas with munition effects being examined by sampling devices and animals in rubber dinghies upwind of the device.

By this means the factors affecting the physical fallout, viability and virulence of the weapon pathogens in real conditions were correlated with laboratory findings. Similar trials were conducted in 1952 and 1953 off Scotland and in 1954 and 1955 off the Bahamas. Carter conclude that the scale of resources devoted to biological weapons at the time stressed official concern to have a proper assessment of this potential threat. Thus, whatever current opinions of the seriousness of biological weapons prevail amongst both specialists and the general public, the history of the British biological weapons programme backs high-level interest, the allocation of large-scale resources, a perception of biological warfare as a threat , the perceived vulnerability of Britain to strategic attack and, finally, the production of offensive biological weapons.

The United States

The same themes are amply shown in detailed documentation produced in Congressional enquiries and obtained under the US Freedom of Information Act, In its 'Summary of Major Events and Problems' for 1959, for instance, the US Army Chemical Corps reported that ten years earlier, in its search for biological weapons agents, it had established a research project on tularemia. After analysing the life-history of the disease organism and its effect on human beings, the report continued, in conformity with the information presented in the last chapter: ...There are two forms of tularemia, the cutaneous and the typhoidal. The latter is much more dangerous, with the mortality rate in untreated cases about 30 percent. If pneumonia develops the mortality rate jumps to 40 percent. It is this typhoidal form which is of paramount importance as an agent...

The authors further explained that antibiotics could be used to arrest the progress of the disease, but not its debilitating results . This was considered significant because convalescence may take from six months to a year. Troops infected with the disease could therefore put a great strain on enemy hospital facilities. There are a number of stains of the organism and the one chosen by the Corps as an agent was a streptomycin-resistant strain'. Regarding a production of the agent, Fort Detrick procuced and maintained the stock culture and large quantities were developed by the Directorate of Biological Operations at Pine Bluff Arsenal. The bacteria were maintained at a temperature of 4°C, at which half would remain alive after 40 days. The weaponisation of the agent was also reported: The Corps CP-120 program, designed to evaluate the effectiveness of E120 bomblets loaded with B. [*Francisella] tularense*, had indicated that a single aircraft sortie would produce more than 50 percent casualties over an area of 16 square miles... Moreover:

While the munitions are capable of causing widespread outbreaks of tularemia, they can be transported, stored, and handled logistically with no more hazard than with regular explosive munitions.

The report concluded that, as the development of this agent 'had reached the point of uniform mass production in a form specified to produce optimum military effects', it was agreed as a standard- type, biological anti- personnel agent in August 1958. In a section devoted to yellow fever, the report observed that Fort Detrick had formed a project to study the use of arthropods for spreading anti personnel biological agents in 1953. One of the insects chosen for study was *Aedes aegypti*, the carrier of yellow fever virns. Some of its benefits as a vector were then set out, for example: since the mosquito injects the agent into the body, masks would provide little protection and since the insects survive for some time, a targeted population would remain under danger for that period. The life-cycle of the mosquito and its mode of transmitting the virus were then fiefly described. The report emphasised the dangerous nature of yellow fever, and its debilitating effects even amongst those who recover.

The authors added that there was no known therapy other than treating the symptoms and that, 'Of the clinical cases since 1900, one-third of the patients have died'. The fact that the disease has never occurred in Asia was taken to indicate that 'the populations of the USSR would be quite susceptible to the disease. It was indicated both that an attack using mosquitoes would not be easy to detect and confirm and that, although a yellow fever vaccine exists, it would be diffcult for the USSR to quickly mount a mass immunisation programme. Thus it was concluded that:

.... The difficulties that an enemy would face in detecting infected mosquitoes and protecting their population would make the *Aedes aegypti*- yellow fever combination an extremely effective BW agent.

Like the earlier commentators have noted, the US Army did not seem to have regarded that the yellow fever virus might have been transmitted to an animal reservoir population had it been used. Sources of reinfection could therefore always have been present as they are now in parts of Africa and Central and South America. The practicality of using the mosquito was tested by releasing uninfected females in a residential area of Savannah, Georgia, and checking how many of them had entered houses and bitten people. Also, in 1956,600,000 uninfected mosquitoes were released from a plane on a bombing range and within a day the insects had gone one or two miles further and bitten several people, Further tests revealed that the insects could be spread from helicopters, from devices dropped from planes, or from the ground. The method of breeding mosquitoes was summarised and it was noted that Fort Detrick's laboratories could produce half a million mosquitoes every month. The yellow fever virus used was acquired from a person infected in Trinidad in 1954 and was propagated by infecting monkeys. The mosquitoes were in turn infected with the virus by immersing their larvae in infectious Rhesus monkey serum.

The virulence of the infected mosquitoes was then checked by having them attack and infect mice. The Chemical Corps Technical Committee classified the yellow fever-*Aedes aegypti* mosquito as a standard-type biological weapon in June 1959. It was suggested to use an aircraft-delivered cluster bomb or missile warhead to disperse the mosquitoes over enemy territory. Tests of various munitions continued. A contract was led in December 1957 'to determine feasibility of conducting large-area warfare attacks by means of spray tanks carried on low flying aircraft'. The research was reported to have been highly successful.

The critical necessity was for the design of a nozzle that would spray out liquid particles of five micrometres in size orless in order that the drops would float in the air and spread over a large area and, crucially, be very effective in penetrating the lungs of victims. After the 275- gallon spray tank and nozzle had been tested in the laboratory, field tests were conducted at Dugway Proving Ground using an F-100A plane. This flew over a triangular area nearly 15 miled long and 12 miles wide. Sampling devices all over the area allowed the behaviour of the aerosol cloud to be examined. The results showed that spray attacks were feasible and that an area 10 miles or better downwind could be covered. Five of the trials were conducted using simulants, but on one flight the agent of Q- fever was used. The results suggested that 99 per cent of humans in the area would have been infected. Other 'important results' were said to reveal that the spray device was much more effective than bomb or shells for disseminating an aerosol of the biological agent and that the tank could hold a much larger amount of the agent relative to the weight of the spray system. The report concluded that it had been proved that airborne attacks could be carried out at low level and that the system could bring an area of 50,000 square miles under contamination one sortie. The importance of this finding, according to the report, lay in the efficiency of this type of attack. It stated: .... on a night when the wind were blowing ten miles per hour, *three large* aircraft, each carrying 4,000 gallons of liquid BW agent, and flying at a speed of 500 knots, *could stray an area of 150,000 square miles, causing more than half the people in the area to become ill.*

Presumably too given the low altitude of attack, the aircraft would probably not be picked up on radar and the attack would therefore not be come to notice before people became ill.

Information to the Public

Information on the biological weapons research done in the United States during the Second World War became available through articles in scientific journals and in more popular books written by former scientists and soldiers who had been associated with the programme. The turmoil of the Vietnam War and the US use of herbicides on a large scale there provoked renewed concern about chemical and biological warfare. Several books try to present the available information in the mid-to late 1960s before the publication of the major UN report in 1969 and the SIPRI studies of the early 1970s. Seymour Harsh, writing in 1968, correctly placed of the significant change of policy for use of biological weapons which had taken place in the 1950s:

In fact, by the mid-1950s official military policy toward the use of CBW agents had undergone a dramatic change, one that still remains secret... The change in policy was simple enough... the military was free to wage chemical and biological warfare on a first strike basis during conventional warfare...

He claimed support for his viewpoint in changes he recorded as occurring in Army field manuals in the 1950s.

Hersh's book tried to summarise much of the information from other sources and was supplemented by his own extensive interviews and research. He was highly critical of what had been done in the United States and emphasised that large increases in expenditure had occurred from the early 1960s to the time that he was writing. In his opinion, this allowed the Pentagon to make use of increasingly sophisticated scientific technology in its offensive biological weapons programme and the result was an inevitable series of spectacular advances across the whole spectrum of chemical and biological warfare. He argued indeed that behind a wall of secrecy a vast research programme had produced 'a massive array of killers'. Hersh tried to examine both the results of the research and the organisations involved. He discussed evidence given to Congress by military officers and what he had gleaned from papers published in the open literature by scientists working for the military, and from diseases contracted by them during the course of the work.

Regarding the research results, he noted for instance, the potential benefit of using dry powders rather than liquid sprays of biological organisms and of protecting the agents in better sub-packages.

As for anti- crop research, Hersh noted that: ...

The program has been emphasised in recent years. Research is now under way into various forms of bacteriological, viral, and fungal crop diseases, with two of the latter- rice blast and *puccinia graminis* (stem rust)-receiving special study.

Considering the time at which he was writing, Hersh was naturally mostly associated with the use of herbicides in Vietnam. His description of the bases at which biological research, development, testing and production were being conducted is useful in giving a snapshot of the final stages of the offensive biological weapons programme in the USA. Noting that Fort Detrick was based near the small town of Frederick and had been in operation 'since 1943 when the base-then a top secret operation comparable only to the Manhattan Project—was opened', he stated that it controlled the procurement, testing, research and development of biological munitions and vaccines and defence measures. But he argued that the stress was on 'the offense'.

The base had a budget of $38 million in 1966 and covered 1,300 acres. It employed '2,500 civilians and 500 military personnel.. Including 320 B.S., 110 M.S., 120 Ph.D, 14 M.D. degree holders and 34 veterinarians. Hersh made an estimate on the number of animals used for experiments at various times in Fort Detrick's history. He suggested that usage per month in the early 1960s could have been as high as 60,000 assorted mice, rats, guinea pigs, monkeys, etc. He also studied work on human volunteers, particularly ' Seventh Day Adventists serving noncombat Army duties as conscientious objectors [who] were exposed to airborne tularemia;. The organisation of the base, with its greenhouses for work on anti-crop agents and simulated rice paddy for work on rice blasts, was described exhaustively from Hersh's own visit there. He also argued that the heavy investment in Fort Detrick from the late 1950s had produced an organisation very expensively equipped for its intended research programme and especially for aerobiological experimentation.

Cloud chambers, which were used to study the dispersal of micro-organisms, were described as available in volumes of 6,200 litres 50,000 litres, 100,000 litres, 850,000 litres and a new 1 million litresphere constructed of steel $1^1/_4$ inches thick'.

Pine Bluff Arsenal, in Arkansas, was described by Hersh as the centre for the production of biological agents and their processing into munitions. Again based on research and a personal visit in 1967, a description of the site was given. Hersh noted that:..

The base's 1966 budget was $ 18.8 million; more than $5 million of this went directly for biological operations.

Initially, the Chemical Corps considered building the whole laboratory underground, but it finally settled for a 10- storey building with only three floors below ground level....

Hersh's attempts to see the highly secret X201 production laboratory were unccessful:

Dugway Proving Grounds with its one million acres in distant Utah was also described. Hersh describe that Dugway had six majro divisions, with the meteorologicl division being added in 1953 just before the first testing of biological agents and that 'the station was redesigned and vastly overhauled in 1962'. The biological test compound was kept under tight security and Hersh could get not much information on its operations. Finally he described the associated airforce and naval bases where biological warfare research was being done alongside the main army programme. In the United Kingdom, at the same time, Robin Clarke published his analysis of the prospects for chemical and biological warfare. He described in detail the problems of the aerosol dispersal of agents. He noted that the US Army had even sponsored two conferences on this subject and that research had illustrated the optimal size of aerosol particles to be between one and five micrometres.

The reason for this was explained. Such minute particles-a micrometre is one ten-thousandth of a centimetre- are small enough to pass down into the lung and penetrate its wall. Clarke gave examples of the effect size has on infectivity:...

The infective dose of Venezuelan equine encephalomyelitis virus increases by a factor of 14,000 if the particle's diameter is increased by a factor of ten.

Of course, even if the particle diameter is of the hight order the weapon system designed to carry it must not only achieve an even spread of the organism over the target area but also protect it from the environment. Clarke reviewed some of the problems in handling micro-organisms, including their sensitivity to the ultraviolet (UV) rays in sunlight. He also discussed how temperature and humidity can be significant in ensuing the survival time of the organism. Hence, as Clarke pointed out, Fort Detrick's interest in ways of protecting the organisms during dispersal. It is evident that there was sufficient information available even to the general public for the importance attached to biological weapons by the USA to be understood.

Yet it is unlikely that the full scale and importance of the programme was widely appreciated. More recently, Bernstein has given a detailed account of the origins of the US programme during the Second World War, and Susan Wright has reviewed the offensive programme from the end of the war until the late 1960s as part of her account of the entire post-war programme. According to Wright the whole of the offensive programme period was marked by reviews of the problem which continually led to increased flow of funds. She argued that the reviews were influential:

The role and status of CBW programs rose. Total suppport for the CBW programs increased from approximately $10 million in the early 1950s to $352 million in1969- an increase of over 2,000 percent, allowing for inflation...

Support for CBW (chemical and biological weapons) research and development also trebled in actual terms between the late 1950s and the mid-1960s. In summary, the results, according to Wright, were that eight anti-personnel and five anti- crop agents were brought in by the US military. There was one other important input to the US programme that we must now discuss-the work done by Japanese scientists and military before and during the Second World War.

Japan and the Offensive Biological Weapons Programme

The Russians indicted members of the Japanese army for crimes involving biological weapons in 1949 and found them guilty, as stressed by Hersh. The transcripts from the trial were published in English. The same information was examined by other authors but until recently was not given much general credence in the West. That position has altered as the entire story has been more widely reported. The detailed study by William and Wallace shows how the Japanese tried to research, develop and deploy biological weapons before and during the Second World War.

The main group involved was called Unit 731 and was based in Manchuria under the direction particularly of General Ishii. According to Williams and Wallace, Unit 731 had eight divisions. The first of these was associated with bacteriological research, the second with warfare research and field experiments, and the fourth with bacterial mass production and storage. They stated that: Unit 731's bacteriological research division was divided into more than a dozen squads, each investigating the warfare possibility of a wide variety of deseases.

The studies conducted were extensive. The authors continued: Plague, anthrax, dysentery, typhoid, paratyphoid, cholera and many other exotic and unknown diseases were studied. So too were vaccines and blood sera for the prevention and treatment of diseases. Various disease vectors, mainly insect, were investigated, as were new drugs, chemical toxins and frosbite.

They opined that Ishii was centrally interested indeveloping weapons for sabotage and clandestine use and for causing mass out breaks of disease through the aerial delivery to pathogens by plane. They thought that he had managed to 'solve' the latter problem. Extensive work was on the use of infected fleas to carry plague. A porcelain bomb was designed so that the fleas would more easily survive.

Named the *Uji*, the 25-kg bomb exploded in the air, cracking the porcelain like eggshell and spreading the fleas over the target area. Porcelain bombs were also considered useful for deploying tetanus, anthrax, typhoid and dysentery. Another kinds of bomb, the *Ha*, was a steel bomb containing 1,50 cylindrical shots immersed in anthrax or tetanus emulsion. It was designed for battlefield use against trops whereas the *Uji* bomb was thought more suitable for use against civilians. Clearly, what is being mentioned here is an intensive, expensive programme which must have had serious, high-level support. Besides anti-personnel weapons, research was also conducted on anti-animal and anti-plant diseases. The uniquely terrible feature of the work was that 'Ishii based his unit in remote northern Manchuria so he could experiment on human beings'. Williams and Wallace record that the human beings, called 'marutas' or 'logs':

...were ' used up' at the rate of two or three per day. Every now and then the number would be topped up from the holding posts in Harbin. Researchers would submit a requisition to the Unit's commander to gain charge over a new maruta...'There was no running away for anyone who entered the clutches of the unit. It was estimated that some 3,000 people got killed in all manner of horrifying ways in pursuit of improving the knowledge that was considered necessary for the success of the programme.

The Unit seems also to have used biological weapons. For instance. During the operation that followed, the germs of cholera, dysentery, typhoid, plague, anthrax and paratyphoid were all used. Flasks containing pure germs were poured by BW cadres into reservoirs, wells and rivers. Containers were also tossed into houses. Three planes from Nanking Unit under fighter escort dropped germs from the air....

The Chinese losses emanating from this 1942 Chekiang Campaign were said to be inestimate. "There were also high Japanese casualties when a unit overran a contaminated area inadvertently. All the results fromthis Japanese programme fell into US hands after the war when a deal was agreed granting immunity from prosecution in exchange for the information available from members of Unit 731.

Research Objectives and Results

Even on the scale of these research programmes, not all avenues of work would have led to successful outcomes, but it is evident that the programme directors considered significant advances would result if enough were pursued. This point was made very strongly in a report by the US Secretary of Defense's *Ad Hoc* Committee on Biological Warfare in 1949. It stated:

Biological warfare is in its infancy... Foreseeable improvements in the prduction and distribution of existing biological weapons would increase their effectiveness by a very large factor.

Towards the end of the 1940s, therefore, the United States felt that work in the area hand only just started but that enough was known to be sure that grent improvements in these weapons systems were assured. It is easy to envisage what te aims of the post- war US offensive research programme might have been. Work would surely have been directed, for instance to analysing whether other agent kinds were available, whether the efficiency of the prduction and storage of agents could be improved, and whether the release of agents from weapon systems could be achieved more effectively and the agent dispersed with better yield on to the target. There would surely also have been objecting linked to an understanding of how agents were taken up by victims and caused infection, and of how agents could be made more virulent and drug-resistant, and work would have been aimed at improving the available vaccines against potential agents. The significant point is that the US offensive biological weapons programme did deliver several of the expected advances by 1969. As Perry Robinson has noted the data: ....

Suggest in increase in BW efficiency of four orders of magnitude over the period 1940 to 1965.

In other words: if, for regular military purposes, an agent-production capacity of 5 tons per day was judged necessary in 1945... improvements in technology could have reduced the requirement to 0.5 kg per day 20 years later.

An imperial ton is equal to 1, 016 kg, so the required capacity had been brought down from 5,000 kg to 0.5 kg per day over just two decades. To move through four orders of magnitude- 5,000-500-50-5-0.5-in just 20 years implies a rapid rate of technological change in biological weapons systems. Some sense of perspective on the whole US programme, which has to be observed as the major driving force in the immediate post- war period of offensive research, can be gained from the information available now although it isundoubtedly true that much is still withheld from the general public. For instance, we referred earlier to arthropod vectors of diseases and studies made of mosquito carriers for yelow fever. A publication of the early 1980s, *An Evaluation of Entomological Warfare as a Potential Danger to the United States and European Nato Nations* has a section on the history of entomological (insect) field testing in the post-war US programme.

A summary of this information is set out in Table 3.1 . The first column of the table gives the name of the particular field test, the second column the year of the test and the final column a brief summary of what was done. It is clear that the field trials discussed earlier were part of an extended series which, at the least, carried on for almost a decade. Furthermore, the subsequent trials seems to have been building on and refining the information gained earlier. A similar general sequence of activity would surely have heppened concerned with potential weapons systems.

Table 3.1 Some Entomological Warfare Field Tests In the USA

Name of Test	*Date*	*Description*
Big Itch	1954	Tests of E-14 munition for distribution of fleas.
Big Buzz	1955	To demonstrate mass production and dissemination of msquitoes from aircraft and dertermine if they survived and took blood meals from humans.
May Day	1956	Tests of dispersal of mosquitoes from a ground surce carried out in an urban area of Sarannah Georgia.
Munition	1957	Report states: 'A minimum of Dissemination five infected mosquitoes, five Tests houseflies, and 30 fleas or ticks per person.. required for effective coverage of a target area.
Bellwether I	1959	To determine the effects of environmental factors'on the biting rate of starved, virgin female A. *aegypti* mosquitoes on troops in the open'.
Bellwether II	1960	Series of trials with up to 100 military personnel in each to determine effects of victim distance, movement etc. on mosquito biting
Bellwether IV	1962	To compare strains of A. *aegypti* for biting propensity, dispersal and building penetration.

Whilst the SIPRI study, CB *Weapons Today* was careful to point out that several of the biological munitions it provided data on in the early 1970s were experimental, the data reveals that a wide range of systems had been developed in the United State. Table 3.2 gives us some of the SIPRI information on biological munitions. These ranged from 'depositors' for small scale use by troops through free-fall cluster bombs in the 1950s, to missile warheads and spay tanks in the mid- to late 1960s.

Table 3.2 Some Munitions Developed by the USA for Biological Warfare

Type	*Mechanism*	*Note*
Generator E44R2	Depositor	Under development in 1965.
Warhead for guided missile M210	Bomblets in warhead [M143]	Under development in 1967.
Spray tank for liquid	Spray agent A/B45 y-1	Expendable for high-speed tactical aircraft. Under development in 1965.
Spray tank for dry agent	Dispenser A/B45Y-4	Tested with PG toxin agent Under development in1966.
Cluster bomb E 133	Bomblets [E61R4]	Under development in 1958.
Submunition E61R4	For E133	Under development in 1958.
Submunition M143	For M210	Entered inventory in mid-1960s.

The SIPRI data also included information on the agents for these munitions. It was indicated for example, that if enough of agent reached the target for each person to receive 20.000 anthrax spores, or 3,000 plague bacteria, or 25 organisms of VEE or tularemia, or 10 of Q- fever, about 50 per cent of those people would become ill. Much more detail was given, however, on production concentrations, half-life in storage and aerobiological decay rate after dispersal. These data are set out, partly in Table 3.3.

As a further example of the enhancement in capabilities derived from the research programme we may consider the dissemination of the agent from the munition. The *Joint CB Technical Data Source Book*, Volume VIII of 1973, was linked with anthrax. It was noted that: The dissemination component of the... model describes the transformaion of the biological agent (aqueous slurry or presized dry

Table 3.3 Characteristics of Agents used in US Munitions

Species	*Symbol*	*Production concentration (organisms/gm)*	*Half- life in store (weeks)*	*Aerobiological decay rate (min^{1})*
Bacillus anthracis	N (wet)	3.10^{10}	80 at 15°c	Insignificant
Coxiella burnetii	OU2 (wet)	$1\text{-}5.10^{10}$	>170 at -50°c	0.001 at any RH
VEE virus %RH	NU (wet)	$2\text{-}4.10^{10}$	>40 at-40°c	0.02 at 85 RH
Puccinia graminis	TX (dry)	$2\text{-}4.10^{8}$	100 at 4°c	Insignificant

particles) into a viable , infective, inhalable aerosol cloud of specified strength size, and location...

The source of strength of the early cloud of spores released by the munition is a function of the concentration of the agent in the munition and the dissemination efficiency of the weapon. The dissemination efficiency of the munition is defined as 'the ratio of the number of viable spores aerosolized in particles with ≤5 microns [micrometres] diameter to the number of viable spores in the agent fill'. As we have noticed the size of the particles had been found to be of critical importance, particularly in relation to penetration of the lungs.

It is known that the efficiency of the early munitions, even with anthrax as an agent, was not high. Regarding an anthrax agent (TR) the source book noted:

...Efficiencies of aerosolization of TR from the.... A/B45Y-1 and A/B 45Y-4 spray tanks are based on data obtained with a biological simulant and are... 17.2 per cent and 49.1 per cent rspectively.

Livewise the source book for agent PG(staphylococcal enterotoxin) stated that the dissemination efficiency for the A/ B45Y-4 munition was: ...63 per cent if all aerosolized particle sizes are considered; 26 per cent if less than 5 micron particles only are considered. Thus, although more fragile agents could not be used with such efficiency amount of the technical change in the period from the end of the Second World War is apparent in the enhanced capability to release agents effectively from munitions. Coming back to the kinds of question that might have been asked at the start of this period, it is obvious that the range of agent types had been substantially expanded.

In the case of tularemia a virulent strain had been selected and some drug resistance developed in it. As we have just seen, the engineering problems of releasing agents from munitions had been handled with some success and, probably most critically of all, great strides had been made in understanding the behaviour of agents in the air, during dispersal to the target and inhalation. Most of this knowledge had been subject to specific, systematic refinement that provides the development of relatively precise mathematical models on which weapons usage could be based. There can be no doubt that, since the termination of the US programe, another country undertaking an offensive biological weapons programme would be able to take advantage of US experience and expect to move along the same trajectory with greater ease. It has often been said that the fact that something has been done once is the crucial information a technologist or engineer needs. With that knowledge, a way to proceed is likely to be found. In addition, of course, much of the information necessary to help a country achieve success has become publicly available over time. The whole idea of using biological weapons is so repellent that it is difficult for most people to imagine anyone wishing to establish an offensive biological weapons programme even if it were feasible. It is perhaps as well to note that the conditions in which it might once have seemed reasonable and sensible were very differnt from those prevailing in relatively peaceful areas of the world today. It should be recalled that in the depths of the Second World War the British decided that it was necessary to carry out field trials with anthrax on the Scottish island of Gruinard, and only after 45 was it:....

Possible for the island to resume its rightful place as just one of the many islands which so enhance the beauty of the rugged coastal scenery of NW Scotland.

We may all agree with that opinion of the island's rightful place, but the pressures to procure and perhaps regard using such dread weapons will doubtless recur in the future. An example of what could possibly happen was put forward in a recent paper about the war in Rhodesia. It was argued that an unusual outbreak of anthrax, involving several cases above the normally low level, occurred between 1979 and 1980. The unusual geographical distribution of the disease at the height of a bitter war suggestion that it had resulted from deliberate use by the losing side ina futile attempt to stave off defeat. All such suggestions naturally need the most careful study, but the point that the presure of warfare or the threat of warfare may be used to justify behaviour of a desperate inhumanity has to be accepted. In the light of evidence presented in this chapter, it is not necessary to *raise questios* over the possible fall out of the misapplication of modern biotechnology to see the value of arms control and disarma-ment measures in this area of potential proliferation.

4
Dissemination of Biological Agents

Any Biological agent has to have a certain set of properties to make it an effective agent for biological warfare. In this chapter we shall focus on those properties that are sought out in the agent in order to get good results from them. Today's scientific developments make it possible to develop highly effective biological weapons.

The onward march of the science of microbiology, has ensured that today's biological warfare will clearly be a much more refined form of the primitive one. No doubt, it will be much more effective since the latest scientific discoveries will be technologically exploited in terms of warfare. If it is true that horses were inoculated with glanders, and cattle with anthrax by German saboteurs in World War I, the very choice of such agents and the method of application must certainly be considered as a step towards progress in biological warfare.

Selecting Suitable Agents[1-8].

A BW agent is not just another disease-producing germ but one having a particular set of properties, that conform more or less to certain criteria and has ability of meeting military needs. Even though an ideal selection of agents may not be feasible in practice, the potential value of an infective organism may be understood to a reasonable extent based on such criteria as potency, transmissibility, epidemicity, infectivity, resistivity, availability, means of protection (specific immunization and therapy), detectivity, retroactivity and rapidity of action. Each of these criteria is explained as follows:

1. **Potency.** This is measured basically by the degree and duration of the disability produced, the per centage of mortality

resulting from the infection and the incubation period. While the percentage mortality and duration factors affect the application—the particular tactical uses of the agent, the incubation period would influence both selection and application of the agent. Diseases with incubation periods of just a few days are usually preferred.

2. **Transmissibility**. This refers to the mode of transmission of the agents. The most preferred mode of transmission is the air route, so that the atmosphere over the target area can be easily contaminated. The next in order of choice but more difficult than air transmission is the dissemination through water or food. The use of those germs which require transmission by vectors of infection, such as insects and rodents, appear impracticable owing to the difficulty in controlling such such vectors and the uncertainty of results. Thus the use of agents of rickettsial diseases such as Rocky Mountain spotted fever, Q fever, etc. in BW may be of doubtful value, despite the high proportion of deadly infections which some of them cause and the ease of their production 7. Further, they need non-flying insect carriers which spread inefficiently, vaccines are easily prepared, and the clinical cases can be controlled by antibiotics. If, however, it could be possible to adapt rickettsiae to transmission by mosquitos, they would have sufficient possibilities as BW agents. On the other hand, those germs which are capable of transmission by multiple routes, such as air, water, food, vectors and direct contact and simultaneous fulfil the criteria of infectivity, potency and resistivity are apparently most suited as BW agents. Already some types of germs ordinarily vector-borne have been shown to be capable of dissemination by air and producing infection in laboratory animal 9. Regarding the significance of the aerosol method (6) it has been shown that particle size not above 1-5 microns in diameter can penetrate into the lungs to produce infection. Effectiveness of lower particle size has been illustrated with aerosols of anthrax, Venezuelan Equine Encephalomyelitis, etc. Smaller particles remain suspended in the air for a longer time and can travel over a long distance under suitable meteorological conditions. The aerosols diffuse through structures as if they were gaseous.

3. **Epidemicity.** It refers to the relative tendecy of germs to spread from one host to another. In order to be really effective as BW agents they should not only be infective but also be capable of producing

widespread epidemics. Diseases like bubonic and pneumonic plague and influenza fulfil this requirement.

4. **Infectivity.** It means the capacity of a particular kind of germ to produce infection or the number of germs needed to produce infection after entering the body of the victim. To be an effective BW agent, the pathogens should be highly infective. If a single germ is enough, infection is a much more certain event than when very large numbers are needed. Under approariate conditions, one pair of pneumococci or one bacillus of tularemia can kill a mouse whereas more than half a million of cholera germs are necessary to destory the same animal species. In experimental work, infectivity is defined as the number of any given kind of germ needed to infect (or to kill one- half of the exposed hosts.

For example, the 50 percent fatal dose (LD50) of the germ of melioidosis for mice when exposed to infection by inhalation is computed as 73.5 germs. To get precise infectivity data for man is practically impossible. What is known is based on single instancel of human infecton—accidental infections, and inferences drawn from epidemics.

5. **Resistivity**. It refers to the power of germs to brave adverse environmental stresses such as spraying during dissemination, drying and ultraviolet rays from the sun, oxidation by atmospheric oxygen, high temperatures, and shock when released from the bursting of bomb containing them, or the concentration of disinfectants in the target area. Those types of germs which cannot survive or retain their potency and infectivity for sufficent dutration will apparently be ruled out as BW agents. Resistivity is, however, a relative term. Those types of germs which are by nature quite resistant provide an edge. For example, the spores of anthrax which are very hard or the coccidioides fungus which is a little less resistant may remain alive in open terrain for long periods, and hence the more resistant types in general may be used to contaminate large parts of land. For the lesser resistant kinds used as BW agents, it is required to disseminate them in such way that they would more quickly reach the victim. While intending to use the most sensitive ones like the tularemia bacillus or the coccus of cerebrospinal meningitis, it will be necessary to depend on the mode of direct transmission from source to victim, for instance, through the air. Tularemia bacillus has in fact been stabilised by some means.

The spirochete of relapsing fever is ordinarily unstable but remains alive and virulent in ticks that have been starved for about five years—a case of rare resistance through the vector. Experimental data on the dispersion of pathogenic germs as related to their resistivity are not available. Some idea might, however, be obtained on the dispersion of harmless bacteria suspended in a fine vapour or aerosol 6. In one experiment 450 lbs. of a harmless substance released in an aerosol form contaminated 35,000 square miles and was carried 450 miles downwind. It has been noticed that much large areas could be covered under military conditions.

6. **Availability.** The question of using a specific kinds of germs as BW agent arises only when it is avalilable at hand, and its mass production is possible and practicable. Usually, most bacteria and fungi can be grown more easily while rickettsiae and viruses needed special methods or are dufficult to develop.

7. **Means of Protection.** It is clear that the value of a particular pathogen as BW agent is considerably reduced if the enemy against which this is employed is in possession of some means of protection. The small-pox virus against which effective vaccination is known, is a suitable BW agent even though the disease is highly epidemic. It may be used only against an unprotected population where vaccination is never practised. For this reason western countries seem to be probable targets of small pox in the even of its use in BW.

8. **Detectability.** An agent which is difficult to detect and identify is more effective against defence of the area attacked. The bacillus brucella is highly difficult to detect in comparison to the more potent anthrax bacteria and hence may be preferred to the latter. However, this does not always mean that organisms which are comparatively easy to identify will be excluded as BW agents. This criterion can charge the application rather than the selection of an agent.

9. **Retroactivity.** This means the capacity of an agent to backfire those using it as a weapon and hence it is required to know the potential retroactive power of each agent to be selected for BW.

10. **Rapidity of action**. It refers to the length of time required for a given kind of germ to produce its casualty effcts, and this generally depends upon the incubation period. The shorter the period needed to produce casualties, the more suitable is the organism for selection as a BW agent.

List of Likely BW Agents

Quantitative figures associated with these criteria are, however, to obtain. But from comparative epidemiological study of natural incidents of various infectious diseases and also from limited laboratory experiments, a list of likely BW agents may be made. In the 1942 report (I) mention was made of some 39 such agents against man, animal and plants and a more recent report includes more than fifty such agents for use against either humans or animals 4. These are described in Table 4.2

TABLE 4.1

human diseases and infective agents for BW

S. No.	*Type of infections and intoxications*	*Mode of transmission*	*Usual incubation period*	*Specific protection available against presently known strains*	*Strategic use*	*Tactical use*
1	2	3	4	5	6	7
Bacterial infections and intoxications:						
1.	*Anthrax	C,A, WF	1-4 days	+to?	+	+
2.	*Botulism	WF,C,(a)	12-36	+to?	+	+
3.	*Brucellosis (Z)	A,C, WF	6-60 days or longer	?	+	+
4.	Cholera	WF	Few hrs. to 5 days	?	-	+
5.	Dysentery (Bacillary)	WF	1-7days	-	-	+
6.	Erysipeloid (Z)	C		+	-	+
7.	Diphtheria	A, WF	2-5 days	+	-	
8.	*Glanders (Z)	V, (a)	1-5days	-	+	
9.	Hemophilus influenza	A		-	+	+
10.	Leptospirosis	V	6-15 days	?to-	+	+
11.	Listeriosis (Z)	WF,A		-	+	+
12.	*Melioidosis	V, (a)		-	+	+

1	2	3	4	5	6	7
13.	Meningococcal meningitis	A	2-10 days	+	+	+
14.	Pertussis	A	5-10 days	+	-	+
15.	*Plague (pneumonic) (Z)	V, (a)	2-12 days	+ to?	+	+
16.	Pnemococcal pneumonia	A	1-7 days	+	+	+
17.	Streptococcosis (antibiotic resistant)	A,WF,C		?	+	+
18.	Staphylococcosis (antibiotic resistant and enterotoxin producing)	WF		=	=	+
19.	Treponematoses	C		+	-	+
20.	*Tuberculosis (Z)	A,WF	Variable	?	-	+
21.	*Tularemia (Z)	A,WF,V,C, (a)	1-10 days	?	+	+
22.	Typhoid and other salmonelloses and shigellosis	WF	10-14 DAYS	?to-	?	+

Mycotic infectons

1	2	3	4	5	6	7
23.	Blastomycosis	A		-	?	+
24.	*Coccidioid-omycosis	A	7-21days	-	+	+
25.	Cryptococcosis	A		-	?	+
26.	Dermatomycoses (Various)	C		-	-	+
27.	Histoplasmosis	A		-	?	+
28.	Nocardiosis	A,C		-	+	+

Viral and Rickettsial Diseases

1	2	3	4	5	6	7
29.	*Adenoviruses of some strains: Types 4 and 7 producing acute respiratory disease (ARD)	A	5-6 days			
	Type 3 producing pharyngitis and pharyngoconjunctival fever	A	5-7 days	?	+	+

1	2	3	4	5	6	7
	Types 3 and 8 producing conjunctivitis and keratoconjunctivitis	A	2-7 days			
30.	*Arthropod-borne viruses (Z): Western equine encephalitis (WEE)	V (Culex tarsalis)	4-21 days			
	Eastern equine encephalitis	V (Aedes solli-) citans mosquitos)	Probably less than that for WEE			
	Venezuelan equine encephalitis	V(Culicine or Aedes mosquitos), A	2-5 days			
	St. Louis encephalitis	V (Culex mos) quitos)	4-21 days			
	Japanese B encephalitis	V (Culex mosquitos)	4-21 days	+to -(I)	+	+
	Russian spring summer encephalitis	V (Ixodidae ticks)	7-10 days			
	Dengue fever	V(Aedes aegyp-ti), (a)	3-15 days			
	Yellow fever	V(Aedes Haemagogus, (a)	3-6 days			
	Rift Valley fever	V (Aedes, Culexmos-quitos)	5 or 6 days			
31.	*B Virus	V	10-20 days	-	+	+
32.	*Coxsackie group (B)	V,WF	1-14 days	-	+	+
33.	ECHO (Enteric cypopathogenic human orphan) (Some strains)	WF		-	-	+
34.	Infectious hepatitis	WF, G	1-3 months	-	-	?
35.	*Influenza	A	7-14 days	+to?	+	+

1	2	3	4	5	6	7
36.	Lymphocytic choriomeningitis (Z)	C	8-14 days	-	+	+
37.	Mumps	A	7-26 dsys	+	-	?
38	Parainfluenza group	A		-	?	+
39.	Poliomyelitis	A, WF, V	7-21 days	+	?	+
40.	Phlebotomus fever	V	2-6 days	-(I)	-	+
41.	*Psittacosis (Z)	A	6-15 days	?	+	+
42.	*Q fever(Z)	V,A	2-4 weeks	? to-	+	+
43.	Rabies (Z)	C	10 days to 6 months	+ to?	-	+
44.	*Rocky Mountain spotted fever	V, (a)	2-12 days	?	+	+
45.	Rubella and Rubeola	C,A	14-23 days	? to-	-	+
46.	Scrub typhus (Z)	V	10-12 days	-(I)	-	+
47.	Small pox (z)	A,C	8-12 days	+	-	+
48.	*Typhus (epidemic)	V, (a)	8-14 days	+ to ? (I)	++	

Protozoal Infections:

1	2	3	4	5	6	7
49.	Bilharziasis	W		-to ?(I)		-
+						
50.	Dysentery (amoebic)	WF,V		-to ?	-	+
51.	Leishmaniasis	C,V	Weeks to 6 months-(1)		-	+
52.	Malaria	V	Variable	+(I)	-	+
53.	*Toxoplasmosis (Z)				-	+
+						
54.	Trypansosomiasis	V		?(I)	-	+

Mostly based Kaplan[4] except the coloums 3 and 4

A - Air-borne.
(a) - Artificially transmitted by air in the laboratory.
WF- Water and/or Food borne.
C - Direct contact borne.
V - Vector borne.
(Z) - Zoonoses (i.e. infectious diseases of animals that can be transmitted to man by any of the usual routes).
+ - Suitable.
— - Unsuitable.
? - Questionable, either because of the nature of the agent or insufficient knowledge.
• - Especially suitable agent.
(I) - Insecticle effective against usual carriers.

TABLE 4.2

Animal Diseases and Ainfective Agents for BW

Sl. No.	*Type of infections and intoxications*	*Strategic use*	*tactical use*	*Specific protection available against pre sently known strains*
1.	2	3	4	5
Bacterial infections and Intoxications:				
1	*Anthrax	+	+	+
2	*Blackleg and other clostridial diseases	+	+	+ to?
3	*Brucellosis	+	+	+ to?
4	*Botulism	+	+	?
5	Glanders	-	+	—
6	Leptospirosis	+	+	? to-
7	Listeriosis	-	+	-
8	Pasteurelloses	-	+	? to
9	Salmonelloses	-	+	-
10	Streptococcal and staphylococcal (antibiotic resistant) infections	-	+	-
11	Swine erysipelas	-	+	+ to ?
12	*Tubercuiosis	+	+	? to
Mycotic infections:				
13	Aspergillosis	-	+	-
14	Blastomycosis	-	+	-
15	*Coccidioidomycosis	+	+	-
16	Cryptococcosis	?	+	-
17	Dermatomycoses (various)	-	+	-
18	Epizootic lymphangitis	-	+	-
19	Histoplasmosis	?	+	-
Viral and Rickettsial Diseases:				
20	*African swine fever	-	+	-
21	*Arthropod-borne viruses (Eastern Western, Venezuelan, Japanese B, Louping ill, Rift Valley			

1.	2	3	4	5
	bluetongue, African horse sickness)	+	+	+ to ? (I)
22	Born disease	-	+	-
23	Bovine mucosal complex	-	+	-
24	*Bovine pleuropreumonia	+	+	+ to ?
25	Chronic respiratory disease (poultry)	-	+	-
26	Duck hepatitis	-	+	-
27	Equine infectious abortion	-	+	-
28	Equine influenza	-	+	-
29	*Foot and mouth disease	+	+	+ to ?
30	Fowl plague	-	+	+ to?
31	Fowl pox	-	+	+
32	Heartwater	-	+	?
33	Infectious laryngotracheitis (fowl)	-	+	+
34	Infectious bronchitis (fowl)	-	+	?
35	Leukosis complex (fowl)	-	+	-
36	Lumpy skin disease	-	+	-
37	Newcastle disease	-	+	+
38	Psittacosis	-	+	-
39	Q fever	-	+	? to -
40	*Rinderpest	+	+	+
41	*Sheep-pox	+	+	+
42	Swine fever (hog cholera)	+	+	+
43	Swine influenza	-	+	-
44	*Teschen disease	-	+	+ to ?
45	Rift Valley fever	-	+	+ to ?
46	*Vesicular exanthema	-	+	-
47	*Vesicular stomatits	-	+	-

Protozoal Diseases:

48	Anaplasmosis	-	+	-(I)
49	Babesiasis	-	+	? to -(I)

1.	2	3	4	5
50	Coccidiosis	-	+	-
51	Theileriasis	-	+	? to - (I)
52	Trypanosomiasis	-	+	? to - (I)

Some Human Diseases

It is intended to describe here a few promising infectious diseases and some common ones with a view to ascertain their importance in BW.

Bacterial Infections and Intoxications [3, 10]

1. **Anthrax** is a communicable disease caused by the Bacillus anthracis which infects both animals and men, but chiefly the former. Ulcerations of the skin, enlargement of the spleen, and general collapse are a few features of the disease which is usually fatal. The anthrax bacilli are prominently resistant and their spores can stay in the soil for years. It is quite possible that these organisms would withstand the adverse effects of dissemination from bombs and aircraft spray apparatus. Infection in men and animals may take place due to inhalation of contaminated air or dust and also through direct contact with soil and other contaminated objects. The spores are also dust-borne and can infect a host through the air. From centres of infection, the disease may spread rapidly over vast areas. In comparisons to some other kinds of pathogenic bacteria these organisms are not so highly infective and are rather easily detected and identified. Various kinds of anthrax vaccines are available for immunizing animals, and the success in developing an effective and satisfactory vaccine for man has been reported quite recently.

2. **Botulism**, a kind of food poisoning, is an acute, quick acting, and frequently fatal disease caused by a highly powerful poison (botulinum toxin) produced by the bacillus Clostridium botulinum outside the body of the victim. Particularly because of its unusual potency, this has been regarded as a highly potential biological warfare agent.

Brucellosis (undulant fever), also known as Bang's disease, is a highly infective disease caused by Brucella bacteria which are strict parasites. The disease is characterised by repeated attacks of fever which rises and falls but is rarely fatal. Its incapacitating effects last over a long period. It may also recur after many years. The disease attacks both man and domestic animals such as cattle, sheep, pigs and goats. Direct transmission from man to man or other animals is rare. The germs are transmissible by multiple routes, such as food and water, contact with the skin and inhalation, and are hard to detect. The usual source of infection in man is contaminated food and water, especially milk from infected animals. A satisfactory human vaccine against brucellosis is not yet developed. In point of infectivity, potency and epidemicity, the germs of brucellosis compare favourably with those of tularemia, a single germ being enough to cause infection. Also the brucella germs are more resistant then the tularemia bacteria and are transmissible via air more effectively.

3. **Cholera** (Asiatic) is an acute disease of the digestive tract caused by spirillum, cholerae, asiaticae germs and characterised by severe vomiting and purging, with gripings and cramps, and collapse. It needs more than half a million cholera germs to kill a mouse, whereas a single bacillus of tularemia or a pair of pneumococci will do the same. However, this low order of infectivity is not as important since cholera is a water borne disease and a few drops of contaminated water may contain the fatal dose. The disease can spread fast and produce large scale epidemics with high mortality rates. Although there is a vaccine against cholera to give immunity for six months, a serious out break of the disease will cause the problem of mass immunization.

Being primarily a water and food-borne disease, the use of cholera germs in war will depend primarily on their introduction into the water system in the target area. In case this is done, counter measures like the use of disinfectants in the water or the use of alternate sources of water supply will considerably reduce the danger.

4. **Dysentery** (bacillary) is an acute, malignant, and often fatal disease of the large intestine, caused by particular highly infective germs and is characterised by griping and discharge of mucus and blood. It is much more serious than either ordinary dysentery or the chronic amoebic dysentery endemic to tropical countries. In the past, dysentery was one of the diseases which caused more nonfatal casualties than weapons of the enemy. It is a strictly water and food borne disease like typhoid and spreads rapidly in an area with a low standard of hygiene. Strict sanitary measures are needed to check the out break. There is, however, a good vaccine against

bacillary dysentery which undoubtedly lowers its value as a probable bacterial warfare agent. Chemoprophylaxis has also been recommended. As BW agents, the germs of bacillary dysentery and typhoid probably fall in the same category.

5. **Glanders** is a very infective and highly fatal disease of horses, mules, and asses, caused by the Bacillus mallei and is transmissible to other domestic animals and men. The disease is characterised by fever, inflammation of the mucous membranes, especially the nose, with enlargement and induration of the glands of the lower jaw. Though commonly a vector borne disease, the germs can also be transmitted through air. They rank high in infectivity, potency, epidemicity, resistivity and availability, but are not so destructive to man.

6. **Influenza** is an acute, respiratory disease caused by Bacillus influenza and its symptoms include severe inflammation of the bronchi, often accompanied by high fever, great muscular prostration, and severe neuralgic pain. It is a rapidly spreading infectious desease, and in epidemic form has led to high percentages of mortality. However, recovery of survivors is rapid with little after effects. To prevent the spread of a fluepidemic still remains a problem. An effective vaccine against influenza is known and for treatment is certain sulpha drugs and antibiotics are used. Being an air- borne desease, the causative agents might probably be disseminated quite effectively by some artificial means. The use of germ proof face masks, air conditioning systems of buildings and public shelters equipped with special filters, and decontamination with disinfectants as envisaged against other air borne diseases would afford a considerable degree of protection also in this case. In point of infectivity, potency, and epidemicity influenza bacteria are considered at a lower level of effectiveness in comparison to, plague, anthrax and some other types of pathogenic germs.

7. **Melioidosis** is an uncommon malignant disease recently discovered in a limited area of south-eastern Asia. Of the 300 documented cases, which included several American soldiers of World War II, over 90 per cent proved fatal. This represents indeed one of the highest mortality percntages of any known disease. Both men and animals can be victims but horses are particularly susceptible. However, the disease can not be directly transmitted from horse to man. Like bubonic plague, the germs are carried by rat

fleas and the animals can be infected by inhalation. Like tularemia and brucella bacteria, melioidosis microbes though not naturally air borne can be successfully disseminated in air by spraying. They are not as highly infective as those of tularemia and brucella but are much more deadly, and there is no human vaccine available against this desease. Thus it seems to be one of the most potentially dangerous germs that may find use in bacterial warfare.

8. **Meningococcal** meningitis, caused by Neisseria meningitides, is a febrile disease which affects the central nervous system. The organisms are strict parasites of man. They gain entry to the body via the respiratory tract. Their resistance towards chemical and physical agents is relatively low. They are potent casualty producers and the resulting mortality is appreciable. Treatment is based on chemotherapy. The drugs of choice are the sulphonamides singly or in combination with penicillin. Cheoprophylaxis with the same drugs in an epidemic also gives good results.

9. **Plague,** the notorious Black Death of history, is cused by the Bacillus pestis in appears in several forms, of which the bubonic and pneumonic are the most common and fatal. Bubonic plague is syrnptomised by fever and chills, great prostration and inflammatory swelling of the lymphatic glands, especially in the groins (buboes). Pneumonic plague resembles the bubonic form in several ways but its most characteristic effect is on the pulmonary system, leading to some symptoms of pneumonia. In either form, the disease is highly infective and very quick in action causing death usually within 2 or 3 days after the onset of attack. It spreads very quickly over extensive areas and is a problem to eradicate once it breaks out in a community. The mortality rate is among the highest of any of the epidemic diseases known. *Chemotherapy* has displaced serum and bacteriophage therapy. The therapeutic value of sulphonamides, streptomycin, chlortetracycline and chloramphenicol in plague of both the forms has proved effective in India and Madagascar. The most effective means of preventing the outbreak and spreading of the disease is by a rigid control of rats, the fleas of which are the principal carriers.

Due to its high infectivity, great potency, epidemicity, and mortality, plague might be considered as one of the most dangerous threats of biological warfare. If the air route of transmission becomes a reality, plague bacilli will undoubtedly rank as one of the most effective biological warfare agents.

10. **Pneumonia** is yet another acute, respiratory disease which resembles influenza. Infections in man can be caused by any of the more than seventy five serologic types of pneumococcus. The virulent strains are capsular. They are normally treated as to two kinds: lobar pneumonia localising in the lobes of the lungs, and pleuropneumonia concentrating in the pleura of the lungs. Pleuropneumonia is a particularly virulent and deadly disease among cattle. In point of infectivity and potency, the pneumococcus ranks high, a single pair being enough to infect a man. It produces disease almost singularly through invasive properties. The incapacitating effect is quite severe and the recovery often takes many weeks. The sulphonamides, penicillin, the tetracycline compounds and chloramphenicol are the most effective curative agents. Though the pneumococci and the influenza bacteria seem to be in the same category as BW agents, the former of do not have the capacity of propagating epidemics.

11. **Tuberculosis** is caused by Mycobacterium tuberculosis. The fact that many individuals, young and old, are incapacitated for long periods of time by tuberculosis, although they may not die of it, makes it of a great social and economic significance. The decrease in mortality rate from tuberculosis has not been paralleled by an equal decline in morbidity and prevalence of infection. It appears likely that the present rate of decline in mortality will continue, as a result of chemotherapy; but morbidity will decline more slowly. In the Orient, in Central and South America, in Africa and in Asia, both morbidity and mortality rates are still very on the higher side. It is generally believed that malnutrition increases susceptibility to tuberculosis.

The incubation period is variable and generally quite long. Tubercle bacilli of human type are transmitted basically by droplet infection from person to person. Bacilli of the bovine type reach man usually by way of unpasteurized milk from the tuberculous cow; they also can be transmitted by the same route as the human type. The human strain is responsible for more 90 per cent of all cases.

A large number of cattle are infected with the bovine type of tubercle bacilli and several of them have progressive disease. The host range of tubercle bacili is almost unlimited. The mammalian types can infect wild animals in captivity especially primates, and domestic animals, including dogs and cats. Avian tubercle bacilli infect, apart from fowl, swine and rarely, cattle sheep and horses. The avian type is also not pathogenic for humans. In aquaria,fishes and turtles too, occasionally suffer from progressive tuberculosis caused by mycobacteria pathogenic for poikilothermic animals.

12. **Tularemia** (rabbit fever) is an acute, highly infective febrile disease, caused by Bacterium tularense. The clinical picture varies considerably depending on the mode of entry of the germ. The incapacitating effect continues for a cosiderable duration. The disease resembles typhoid but has also a tendency to pneumonic complications. It can spread by different routes, like the bites of many different kinds of insects, contaminated food and drinking water, direct contact, and inhalation. Tularemia is similar to bubonic plague in some respects but it does not have a definite cycle of infection like plague and is not communicated from man to man. Man may enter into the chain of infection accidentally or occupationally. Hence its spread would not be so wide as some other epidemic diseases. On the other hand, the germ of tularemia is one of the most highly infective of all known pathogenic bacteria, the injection of a single germ being enough to kill a mouse. An aerosol dose containing 25 to 50 micro-organisms has been shown to be enough to cause the disease. Though not a very resistant type, its effective transmission by air after stabilisation with glycerine or other similar protective material seems to be possible. A satisfactory vaccine for human use against tularemia has yet to be developed, though some success in this direction has been achieved. Owing to their high infectivity, multiple routes of infection, and prolonged incapacitating effects, the germs of tularemia are placed among the potentially dengerous germs for use in war. They may be used for producing wholesale nonfatal incapacitation of persons over smaller areas.

13. **Typhoid** fever, like cholera, is a strictly water and food borne disease. The causative agent, Bacillus typhosus, attacks the digestive system, particularly the intestines, and in severe cases, may cause death. There is a fairly effective vaccine available against typhoid infection. As BW agents, the germs of typhoid fever and cholera are probably in the same category.

Mycotic Infections (10)

Coccidioidomycosis is primarily an infection of the respiratory tract caused by Coccidioides immitis. The fungus is dust borne and also contaminates cotton, wool, etc It may be easily produced in the laboratory. The inculation period differs from one to three weeks. Flu, chills, fever, malaise, anorexia, cough, pleurisy, headache, backache and night sweats etc areits symptoms. About 2 to 5 per cent of such cases develop hypersensitivity. The infection in this form is not fatal and is known as San Joaquin fever (Valley fever, Desert Rheumatism when linked to allergic manifestation). Dissemination at the time of the primary infection gives symptoms akin to those of tuberculosois. Lesions may appear anywhere in the body- lungs, larynx, lymph nodes, bones, joints, central nervous system etc. This form of infection which is a secondary progressive disease is highly fatal and is known as coccidiodal granuloma. Infection from man to man or from animal to man is not recorded. Dust control of areas helps to limit infection rates.

Viral and Rickettsial Diseases [3, 11]

Adenoviruses: This is one of the recently discovered groups of viruses found primarily in the adenoids and tonsils of man, who is the only species readily susceptible to this infection. Occurrence of these infections is perhaps worldwide, 4 to 5 per cent of the respiratory illness being because of adenoviruses. The incubation period is on an average 2 to 7 days. About 18 types of adenoviruses have been isolated from human sources. The period of sickness ranges from 1 to 4 weeks. Types 4 and 7 cause the acute respiratory disease (ARD); Type 3 causes pharyngitis and pharyngocojuctival fever; and Types 3 and 8 produce conjunctivities and keratoconjunctivitis respectively.

There is considerable overlapping in the syndromes, so that one kind of virus may cause an illness that resembles acute respiratory disease in one patient and conjunctivitis or pharyngoconjunctivitis fever in another. Further these clinical entities may also be caused by other agents and so are not essentially specific for the adenovirus group. Thus difficulties might be encountered in an effort to make an etiologic diagnosis on clinical grounds. It required is, therefore, that non- bacterial pharygitis and ARD must especially be distinguished from undifferentiated acute respiratory diseases of unknown etiology, streptococcal pharyngitis, herpangina, influenza, primary a typical pneumonia, psittacosis and Q fever. Deaths as a result of the most common adenovirus infections have not been documented. Disability for a few days is the common effect of infection from these viruses.

Arthropod borne animal viruses (arbor): These are defined as viruses which have the capability to infect certain vertebrates- mammals and birds—and to multiply in the body of arthropods (e.g., mosquitos, lice, fleas, mites, ticks and sand flies). They can be disseminated by spreading virus carrying insects. This method, though crude makes the propagation of disease independent of the stability of the virus itself. Besides transmission by insects, they can cause infection by the respiratory route. A group of these viruses produces in man and other animals diseases symptomatised by brain inflammation (encephalitis). Examples are Western, Eastern and Venezuelan equine encephalitides, St. Louis, Japanese B and Russian spring summer encephalitides Clinical differences in the different virus encephalitides, have been noted, but all are characterised by fever, lethargy and visual disturbances. Many occur in epidemic form, some being most prevalent during the spring and summer months, and other are non-epidemic. With some forms of infection, the fatality rate may range from 30 to50 per cent in man. Often, the outcome of infection with one of these agents, from being symptom free, is unpredictable in terms of the severity of the clinical result.

Further, the clinical diagnosis of infection becomes very diffiicult when diiferent types of viruses cause the same clinical picture and the same virus causes different clinical pictures. Though the most common mode of transmission of these viruses to man (who is usually a secondary host, another animal being the primary host) is by insect vectors, in most cases this is not settled. Some cases may be food and water-borne and some may be air-borne. Not proplactic immunization methods have been developed and there is no specific treate enough ment for these infections. Control measures are generally directed towards attack on the carrier. The three other arthropod - borne viral diseases considered are dengue, yellow and Rift Valley fevers.

Rift Valley fever is an acute disease principally of sheep and cattle and is caused by a particular virus. In man the disease is characterised by a brief incubation period of 5 or 6 days, acute onset;

fever of several days' duration, prostration, pain in the extremities and the joints, abdominal discomfort and leukopenia. The disease usually lasts for a few days but the most significant complications are ocular. Man is usually infected secondarily during the course of an epizootic in domesticated animals. Some mosquitos (Aedes and Culex) act as carriers. The disease is not contagious. There is no specific treatment described. There is also no specific means of prevention of human infection at present, although vaccines have been developed for veterinary use. Control measures include the eradication of the arthropod vectors.

Dengu fever is an infectious, mosquito-transmitted disease (Aedes aegypti as carrier) of virus etiology having symptoms such as fever, pain in different parts of the body, prostration, rash, lymphadenopathy and leukopenia. The usual incubation period is 5 to 8 days. In one of the recent outbreaks, appearing in the form of haemorrhagic fever, the case fatality rate has been 15 percent. A single mosquito bite may be adequate to transmit the virus of dengue fever to volunteers, and a dose of 2 micrograms has been found reasonable in the course of studying the effective-ness of vaccines. Though much less fata than other epidemic deseases, dengue fever (and malaria which is a protozoal disease transmitted by anopheles) is perhaps the most incapacitating desease and some of the symptoms, like neualgic pains, weakness and mental depression may remaina for several months. Hence the dengue viruses (and malaria parasites) might presumably be effective warfare agents for producing non-fatal incapacitation of the population with some psychological effects. No specific therapy against this desease is available. Mosquito control is the usual measure to avoid the recurrence of epidemics,. Some success has been achieved in the development of vaccines against dengue with the modified type I and type 2 dengue viruses.

Yellow fever is an acute, highly infective and often fatal, febrile disease of viral origin. It is symptoms include jaundice,haemorrhages, vomiting and albuminuria. In severe cases the incubation period varies from 3 to 6 days. The causative agent can be transmitted not only by the bite of certain mosquitos (Aedes aegyptae), but also through air route when the cultivated virus is in dry powdered form. Owing to their high infectivity, potency and epidemicity, yellow fever germs might be regardes as one of the most potentially dangerous warfare agents, inspite of the fact that a very effective vaccine is available against this infection.

B Virus (Herpesvirus simiae) infection produces a clinical picture that reveals the same variability as expected in any central nervous system infection. Incubation period may be 10 to 20 days. The illness may lead to death after a course of 1 day to over 3 weeks from onset of symptoms. An occasional recovery has been recorded but with considerable residual edisability. Normal monkeys are the reservoir of the virus. Infection can be acquired through bites and apparently by contamination of normally orminionally traumatized skin by monkey saliva or tissues. No specific therapy is known. Naked skin's exposure to contact with any secretion or tissue of monkeys must be avoided. No vaccine is yet prepared.

The Coxsackie virus group: All over the world they are common enteric infections in man with a mean incubation period of 3 to 5 days. The viruses, types 1 to 5, are known to cause aseptic meningitis or nonparalytic poliomyelitis. These viruses are found in connection with pleurodynia. They may cause intra-uterine or neo-natal infection manifested as acute myocarditis in newborn infants. No kind of therapy is known. Control measures to infection by Coxsackie viruses have not been devised. These agents may be distributed through the oropharyngeal secretion and the faeces of infected persons, several of whom often remain undetected. Flies and cockroaches may harbour and transport Coxsackie viruses, but whether they are of importance in the transmission of Coxsackie-virus diseases from person to person has not yet been ascertained. Due to the unusual stability of Coxsackie viruses at ordinary temperatures and their resistance to alcohol and other substances commonly used as antiseptic solutions, decontamination of objects which cannot be boiled or autoclaved may not be achieved by conventional methods. However, Coxsackie viruses can be inactivated rapidly by 0.1 Nhydrochloric acid or 0.3 per cent formaldehyde. No reprorts have been received on the efficacy of vaccines in prophylaxis.

Respiratory viruses: Viruses of diseases like influenza, parainfluenza and the common cold are unsuitable for purposes of biological warfare since they produce only mild diseases, usually a certain degree of disability but rarely severe incapacitation or death. Further, owing to their wide distribution all over the world, a certain degree of immunity is prevalent in a given population at any time. These viruses can easily be grown in tissue cultures and are found to be very stable. However, all respiratory viruses are variable and that the sudden occurrence of a strain capable of causing severe illness through natural or artificially induced mutations cannot be excluded.

Influenza is an acute infectious respiratory disease of man, generally encountered in epidemic form, caused by one of the influenza viruses. Clinical symptoms include fever, myalgias, pharyngitis, cough, leukopenia; the course is usually self- limiting in 3 to 4 days . Constitutional manifestations ordinarily overshadow respiratory characteristic. Complications of bronchitis and bronchopneumonia are common. Epidemics are characterised by rapid dissemination, high morbidity (20 to 40 per cent in general population during extensive outbreaks) and low mortality; however, they may be world wide and of such severity as to acquire catastrophic proportions. Of the four distinct immunologic types of influenza virus recognised till now. Types A, B, C and D), influenza A and inflenza B are encountered most often and their clinical pictures are essentially the same. The incubation period of influenza is short, ordinarily 1 to 2 days. Experimental infection by direct inhalation of fine sprays of virus has at times revealed even shorter incubation periods. The patient experiences as sense of fatigue or weakness building rapidly to prostration. Ocular tenderness, conjunctival injection and watery eyes generally occur usually without photophobia. Although the pathologic picture of influenza virus infection in man is clouded by bacterial complications, epithelial degeneration does not happen with H. influenzae or pneumococcus unless influenza virus infection is also present.

Infection can be induced experimetally in man by intranasal instillation of virus that has been maintained in ferrets, mice or eggs. Sweine have been a common host for swine influenza virus. There is no specific therapy for influenza. All patients ill with influenza in whom it has been illustrated that secondary bacterial infections have developed should be treated with a sulphonamide or antibiotic of choice. Vaccination can be a practical effective prophylactic measure but the problem of strain variation has still to countered.

Enteric viruses: Viruses of diseases polio and infections hepatitis are also regarded in the same manner as the respiratory viruses.

These viruses are easily grown and relatively stable. While the enteric virses, particularly polio, can cause severe illness and death in a fairly high proportion of infections, the population at large has such a high level of immunity that the chance of producing epidemics by these agents is quite unlikely. Infectious hepatitis viruses, on the other hand, cannot at present by developed under laboratory conditions. It is not known if infections through aerial dissemination is possible by these viruses.

Poliomyelitis is an acute febrile infection which leads to an inflammatory reaction in the central nervous system. The disease is caused by a small virus which very commonly infects the human alimentary tract and is found throughout the world. Usually, this infection reveals no signs or symptoms of disease and in such instances, the virus grows harmlessly in the alimentary tract. The infection would be quite insignificant except that rarely, in relation to the total number of infected individuals, it invades the central nervous system by a route not yet perfectly known and causes paralytic desease as a result of destruction of motor neurons in the medulla and the spinal cord. Fatality is below 10 per cent of acute paralytic cases, but what is serious is thecrippling effect on survivors. The infection is considered transmittted through nose and throat discharges from acute or asymptomatic cases. The virus excreted in faeces of infected individuals may contaminate food, water, and milk or may be carried by flies. In essence, it may find entry through the respiratory or oral route. Convalescent serum or gamma globulin may alleviate symptoms and abort paralysis if given early in the disease. The Salk vaccine prepared from the virus grown on monkey-kidney tissue and killed with formalin seems to prevent the disease in some contacts and to prevent the incidence of paralysis in others.

Infectious hepatitis (epidemic jaundice) is a relatively common and widespread acute or subacute viral infection in which there is a diffuse involvement of the liver. It seems both endemic and in epidemic forms. In children the illness may be brief, but in adults it usually remains from 3 to 8 weeks. It is thought to be transmitted by the oral- enteric route and generally leads to homologous immunity. The incubation period ranges from 15 to 40 days, with an average of 25 days. Man is known to be the only source of this agent, and intestinal excretion is its main infective source. The transmission of the disease occurs through some kind of person to person contact, although water borne, food borne and milk borne epidemics may also occur. Control measures include proper sanitation and prompt administration of normal immune globulin to intimately exposed persons.

Psittacosis (parrot fever) is a severe and highly fatal form of pneumonia caused by an air-borne virus and in point of infectivity and potency, is as powerful as any other known pathogenic germs. The disease develops after an incubation period ranging from 1 to 2 weeks. It has been recorded that a quart of psittacosis virus preparation might contain enough virus to infect more than 7 billion human beings. The germs are more resistant as compared to those of tularemia and glanders and can be diseminated by air more effectively. There have been no widespread epidemics of psittacosis but severe epidemics might occur as a result of a sufficient number of initial cases. The tetracycline antibiotics are useful in the treatment of psittacosis and in eliminating the organisms from the body. Natural immunity to this infection is automatic from the disease. But a vaccine as a prophylactic measure needs to be developed. Due to their high infectivity, extreme potency, and considerable percentage of mortality, psittacosis germs are placed among the potentially dangerous biological warfare agents.

Q Fever is caused by the Rickettsia burneti which may be distributed in ticks, human body lice, small wild animals, cattle, sheep, goats, birds and man. The primary carrier is the tick which plays a significant role in the maintenance of the infection in nature. The manner in which it is transmitted to man is not know. Possibly it is contained in dust and gains entrance via the respiratory tract. The incubation period may vary from 2 to 4 weeks but its wide host range is significant. Its symptoms include fever, malaise and no rash, frequently cough and patolly peneumonia. Experiments have established that one microgram of infected chick embryo tissue can transmit this disease.

Rocky Mountain spotted fever is an acute, endemic, infectious disease which is recognized as being one of the severest of all infections. Its incubation period ranges from 2 to 10 days. It is essentially a generalized intracellular infection of the small peripheral blood vessels. One of the causative agents in the group is Rickettsia rickettsii. The only known mode of natural transmission to animals or man is through the medium of infected ticks. The nature of distribution of human vectors and of those shown experimentally to be capable of transmitting spotted fever serve to expose the wide dispersal of ticks and the threat they present to man. In several of its aspects, Rocky Mountain spotted fever resembles typhus, the chief differences being the duration of fever, the severity of the disease, and the time of appearance and the location of the rash. Attacks range from mild ambulatory and abortive forms to rapidly terminating fatal infections. The fatality rate in some outbreaks is shown to be of the order of 15-25 per cent. In vaccinated persons and young children, the attacks are often mild and atypical. In some patients the acute changes clear up with convalescence, but that in other the residual damage persists for more than a year and may be considered permanent. The problem of treatment of spotted fever as also of all other rickettsial diseases essentially has been solved, for now at least three antibiotics are available-chlortetracycline, chloramphenicol and oxytet racycline-which have been proved to be of great value. There are three possible means of preventing spotted- fever infection, namely, personal care, vaccination and use of tick-control methods.

The Small- pox virus is a dangerous agent with high proportion of lethal infections. Its cultivation under laboratory conditions and its stability are not well known.

The desease is endemic in certain areas of the world and hence a certain degree of immunity prevails in the population.. Small-pox vaccination is a highly effective prophylactic measure. Where vaccination is not used, this virus may prove an effective BW agent.

Typhus fever is a serious, highly infective disease, characterised by prolonged fever lasting many weeks, and attended by great prostration and cerebral dissorder, with copious eruption of red spots on the body. The incubation period lasts from one to two weeks. The disease tends to spread rapidly, especially in crowded areas with insanitary conditions, and the death rate from epidemics has frequently ranged from 10 to 40 percent. Typhus germs could be transmitted not only by the human body louse, but also via the air as dust. Inhalation of contaminated air will thus be dangerous. Owing to their capacity to spread via the air the causative organisms might be chosen as possible biological warfare agents. Effective vaccine against this infection is known. In point of infectivity, potency and epidemicity, these germs compare favourably with other potentially dangerous BW agents. The most important step for the rapid control of typhus is the application of insecticides with residual effect to all contacts.

Protozoal Infections.

Toxoplasmosis has been reported in a number of cases of encephalitis, chiefly in newborn infants and children and in a typhus-like pneumonitis of adults. Incidence in general population may be as high as up to 60 percent. Some opthalmological disorders may be expected with the results of infection. Many mammals and birds are susceptible, and infection has been produced by a number of routes, though the natural means of spread is still unknown.

Some Animal Diseases.

An idea about a few animal diseases like anthrax, glanders, brucellosis, Rift Valley fever, encephalomyelitis (equine), and botulism, which are also common to man has already been given. These are preferred although there are some infectious deseases, such as haemorrhagic septicemia (similar to plague in man), pleuropneumonia, hog cholera and fowl plague, known for their high infectivity and fatality. Now a few of the bacterial and viral diseases considered relatively more important will be described.

Bacterial Infections and Intoxications (13-16)

Blackeg known also as black quarter is an acute, infectious disease that affects mainly young cattle and also sheep. The causative micro-organism Clostridium chauvoei forms spores, which are highly resistant to destruction by heat, cold, drying and disinfectants. The spores survive in the soil of a pasture and retain their capacity to germinate and produce the disease for many years. It grows only in the absence of oxygen and hence minute puncture wounds that exclude the air favour the development of blackleg. It is believed that animals usually get the disease when food, water, and soil contaminated with the blackleg germs gain entrance to the body through small punctures of the mucous membrane of the digestive-tract or skin. Most affected animals die within 12 to 36 hours after the first symptoms are noticed. Vaccination is the only effective and reliable means known for protecting animals against blackleg. It usually produces in 10 or12 days a high degree of immunity, which lasts 9 to 12 months or longer. Antibiotics like aureomycin, terramycin and penicillin, have given good results in the treatment of cases exhibiting early symptoms of the disease. Recognised control measures in outbreaks of blackleg involves the isolation and treatment of all animals showing early symptoms of the disease and the cleaning and disinfection of contaminated stables.

Tetanus, also known as lock jaw, is a wound infection disease that is usually accompanied by a fatal toxemia. The causative organism, Clostridium tetani, produces an extremely potent toxin which acts on the nervous system. The organisms or their spores remain scattered in the top layers of soil and in street dust and hay. They are found in abundance manure. The disease is common in human beings and horses. It may also attack other warm blooded animals. Horses, mules and asses, which are highly susceptible may contract the disease from any type of wound but most frequently from wounds of the feet. Infections are also seen in sheep and cows especially under conditions of any bodily injury. Mortality is 55 to 90 percent in certain outbreaks. Animals that recover often remain sick for a month. Antitoxin and tetanus toxoids are the two immunizing agents. Routine preventive immunization of animals and immediate treatment of injured animals with tetanus antitoxin following wounds will materially lessen the chances of infection. Treatment of an established case of tetanus in animals that shows well-marked symptoms is futile.

Viral Diseases [13-16]

African swine fever (hog cholera) is a highly infectious desease of swine caused by the filterable virus, Tortor suis, and serious outbreaks occur in non-immune herds. It is pathogenic only for swine and produces a generalized infection. The transmission of the virus is thought to be through ingestion or inhalation. The disease get transmitted directly from one hog to another . Sources of contamination are infective pens, pastures and lots, stable fly and house fly, and pork scraps in garbage. Passive transmission takes place through by feet of men and animals and by carnivorous birds. The average incubation period is 6 to 8 days and the duration of the disease 3 to 4 days. Mortality is about 100 percent, with only an occasional animal surviving. Anti-hog cholera serum and vaccine have been of no use in the prevention of African swine fever.

Louping ill occurs in spring and autumn among lambs and yearlings and occasionally in older sheep. Mortality rate is quite high. It is not a serious cause of human disease. The virus is transmitted in nature by the bite of ticks (Ixodes ricinus). Diphasic febrile reaction is manifested in most cases. Preventive measure is based on tick control. Immunization is possible.

Blue tongue, showing symptoms like swollen and cyanotic appearance of the tongue or catarrhal fever, is a viral disease of sheep. Acute phase is somewhat short but recovery may take a long time. The mortality occasionally is high but usually does not exceed 15 percent of the affected animals in an outbreak. The indirect economic losses, because of inferior quality of wool from the so-called recovered animals, are considerably higher than those suffered directly in terms of actual deaths. It is a seasonal disease and mostly transmitted by nocturnal blood sucking insects (e.g., gnats of Culicoides species), which transfer the blood from diseased to susceptible sheep. The virus is also found in cattle, but in cattle the clinical manifestations of the disease are not found . The virus can remain viable in decomposed blood and tissues for long periods. In suitable storage it remains dorment for years together . It is not a contagious disease and the incubation period may be 6 to 9 days in a sheep. Though treatment is useless, the disease can be prevented by vaccination procedures.

African horse sickness is a reason for serious losses in horses and mules in Africa. Plurality of the virus has been established. It is not spread through contact but insect vectors probably mosquitos, have been suspected. It is an acute or subacute febrile disease, but may also occur in plumonary or cardiac forms. Death rates and complications are comparatively higher in the pulmonary type of the disease. In some outbreaks mortality may be 90 to 95 percent , while in others it may be only 25 percent. Vaccines are known. Animals which recover from the disease are immune to the homologous strains but may yet contract the disease due to exposure to a strain of different antigenic type.

Bovine pleuropneumonia has caused great losses of cattle in all countries where it has struck. The organism causing contagious bovine pleuropneumonia is known as Mycoplasma mycoides. It is highly infectious and is transmitted by direct contact and by water and feed recently contaminated by an infected animal. Apparently healthy animals may remain infected for 2 to 3 years. Under natural conditions this organism produces pleuropneumonia in cattle and other such animals—the buffalo, yak, reindeer and bison. Experimentally sheep and goats have been infected. Although in naturally occurring epizootics of the disease cattle become easilty infected, it has been found to be difficult produce the disease artificially. Antiserum is used for artificial immunization.

Rinderpest (cattle plague) is an acute, highly contagious general disease primarily found in the cattle, secondarily of sheep, goats, gazelles and deer, characterised by a rapidly fatal febrile course with inflammation and necrosis of the mucous membranes, especially those of the digestive tract. Transmission of the disease takes place through direct contact with diseased animals, or products such as flesh or hides and by ingestion of contaminated feed and water. Incubation poeriod from 2 to 6 days and the animal dies in 4 to 7 days. Mortality is 90 to 95 percent. No medicinal treatments have been successful so far. Immunization with tissue vaccine is effective against spread of disease. Proper sanitation helps to prevent outbreaks.

Sheep-pox is a more severe disease than cow pox or horse pox and is accompanied by fever and generalized sympotms in addition to eruptions of the skin. Mortality varies from 5 to 60 percent. Transmission is by contact and the virus is air-borne. Vaccination will give protection in enzootic areas.

Teschen disease (encephalomyelitis of swine) is propagated only by susceptible swine. The virus, Theilerella tescheni, is transmitted by contact and generally attacks young pigs. The incubation period is 4 to 28 days but may be a week if the dose is high. Death follows in 3 to 4 days in different cases after the symptoms are found. Mortality rate ranges from 50 to 70 percent but may reach 90 to 100 percent in some outbreaks. A live vaccine is known that prevents the disease. The virus is resistant to penicillin and streptomycin.

Vesicular exanthema (eruption of blisters on feet and snouts) is one of the diseases infecting baby pigs, though mature pigs are also affected. The disease spreads rapidly through a herd and causes a temporary setback to growing market hogs. Sows affected with it early in the gestation period may farrow undersized or runty pigs. Sows affected late in the gestation period may abort. Thus this disease of swine may become a national problem. The spread of vesicular exanthema takes place principally in three ways; the feeding of raw garbage containing infected raw pork scraps; direct contact with infected swine; and contact with mechanical carriers, including people's clothig and vehicles. Control and eradication measures include quarantine, speedy disposal of infected and exposed swine, cleaning and disinfection, etc.

Vesicular stomatitis (pseudo foot and mouth disease) is a viral disease principally of equines but occurs in cattle and swine as well, characterised by a superficial inflammation of the mucosa of the tongue and mouth and the formation of thin walled vesicles. The virus is spread usually by direct contact with the saliva or material contaminated by the saliva of infected animals. Insects are suspected as carriers. The disease is not essentially transmitted from animal to animal. Incubation period of the disease varies from 2 to 5 days. In comparison to foot and mouth disease this is more benign, is less contagious and does not cause mouth lesions in cattle. Prophylactic measures include strict quarantine, isolation and proper sanitation. Disinfectants used are the same as in case of foot and mouth disease. No practical immunizing procedure has so far developed.

Plant Pathogens as Possible Agents [1, 3, 8, 17]

Very few such agents are known. There are no palnt pathogens that cause disease in man or animals. But some plant pathogens cause food intoxications when consumed by man (e.g., ergotism) or animals. These are not, however, suitable for use in BW. Most of the plant pathogens that might cause damage to major crops are mostly weather-dependent and the results might be uncertain. Weather dependence is greater with air-borne than with soil-borne pathogens, but the former group is preferred in war since it is expected to produce results quicker. A huge amount of damage to various crops may be caused by introducing some viruses into regions where they do not now occur by dropping large numbers of infective insects. However, the carriers and the disease might be controlled to some extent by insecticides. It is more or less a common experience that producing plant disease in the field by infectious agents artificially is a difficult one and the results are delayed. Nevertheless mention may be made of three kinds of fungi which might prove under favourable conditions dangerous to food crops. Two of these cause blast diseases and brown spot in growing rice (or stem rust of cereals) and the third one causes late blight in Irish potatoes and tomatoes. If forms of fungus such as stem rust could be bred that attack all current wheat varieties, releasing their spores over a cultivated field, widespread outbreaks of rust might occur . The peculiarities of wheat stem rust are that the spores develop into fungus growths in only a few days. Brown postules are then produced on wheat leaves, stocks and stems. The fungus injures stems, prevents nourishment of grain which then shrivels. Once rust begin it spreads across the field, and then to other fields. Usually the crop is badly damaged and this disease has been the cause in recent years of considerable loss of wheat crop in some countries.

A family of compounds called "plant hormones" or "auxins", which stimulate broad leaved plants to overgrowth and resultant death are available as synthetic products. One of these, auxin, 2.4-D, can damage almost any crop of bread leaved plants when spread in overdose, at a rate of a couple of pounds per acre over the fields. Their efficiency when spread from aeroplanes has been proved. They may play a greater role since efforts to introduce plant pests and diseases have led to uncertain and limited results.

The means of Offence

A brief discussion on the means of production, assembly and dissemination of infective agents is made here, utilizing some limited material[1-3].

Production

To get quantity of bacteria is not a major problem. Under suitable conditions of cultivation bacteria grow profusely, and with the help of chemostat it is possible to keep a culture growing over an indefinite period of time, at a constant population size and at a controlled rate of growth. In most cases standard laboratory procedures are suitable on a small scale; however large scale applications are generally feasible in many cases.

For the sake of economy it is recommended to replace the costly standard nutrient media ordinarily used in laboratory practice. Cheaper resources, which might be used in the preparing necessary media, may be slaughter house wastes, food industries wastes, substitute foods like soya-bean extracts if available, milk industry by products like peptidose, corn steep liquor, cheap grades of casein and sugar, etc. Cheap grades of casein and glucose, and corn steep liquor may be used, for instance, in the making the botulinum toxin. Medium from an infusion of tomatoes and containing glycerine and no meat or meat products will give as good results meat medium for the germs of glanders or melioidosis. Peanut hulls, tomato waste, etc., may be used in the preparing of a medium for growing plant infesting fungi. For cultivation on a large scale all necessary installations may be built on engineering principles as employed in breweries, fermentation factories, penicillin production plants and vaccine laboratories. The fermenters may be of 50 cubic meters and higher capacity.

The culture of pathogenic viruses is more complicated, particularly in large quanitities, but this problem may be considerably solved by the use of birds' eggs and tissue culture. The more highly infective agents like the bacilli of plague or tularemia or the viruses of yellow fever or psittacosis may require that a totally isolated building of suitable size be devoted to the preparation of a single agent. It is hardly required to point out that the laboratory and plant equipments must ensure safety to the workers.

Following the production stage the infective agents need to be transferred to suitable containers, forming part of the weapon. Delicate organisms can be preserved alive and virulent for a considerable length of time by freezing and dryng. Several others like influenza virus can be kept alive over long periods by drying them rapidly from the frozen state and then storing them in sealed containers in a cool place. Ordinary refrigeration or rapid drying alone may serve in some instances. Use of suitable stabilizing agents such as glycerine, broth, dextrin, degraded proteins, etc., plus the application of the principles of preservation described above will go a long way. For glanders and melioidosis bacilli a mixture of glycerine and broth is satisfactory. A mixture of dextrin and a commercial protein decomposition product is appropriate for the bacillus of brucellosis. Some viruses of psittacosis group, psittacosis itself and some of its relatives do well in broth alone. Dilute glycerine serves the purpose to an extent in the case of the bacilli of tularemia.

Assembly

Container types for infective agents and the style of assembling or packing them depend on the nature and physical state of the agent and on the use to which it is to be put. The procedures suggested in this concern are as follows. Culture preparations of bacteria or viruses intended for either the water borne or the indirect contact routes might be dispensed, either in liquid suspension or in dry form as may be indicated, in large thin-walled glass ampules.

These might then be packed in sawdust in outer containers for safe handling, arranged so that the bottom can be taken out before discharging the ampule over the target. To make sure the breaking of such an ampule on contact with water, a gas-generating element like those used in fire extinguishers might be included in the ampule, which would then be weighted at the upper end and maintained upright until discharged.

An alternative container for water-borne agents in dry form, such as botulinum toxin, might be made of porous paper impregnated with a water soluble gum or pectin, perhaps protected for safety in handling by a metal frame sufficiently heavy to sink the container. For air-brone agents the problem of assembling them in suitable cotainers is part of the large problem of means for their dissemination, which is considered here. Containers for infected vector like flies, fleas, mosquitos, lice, rats, mice, certain birds, etc must be so constructed as to permit survial of the vectors inside for the required periods and to allow their safe landing from aircruft and insure tiberation as the vectors on the ground. along with the usual need for protection in handling up to the point of discharge. Adequate safety as welll as greater effectiveness would appear to require somewhat more elaborate measures. Pasteboard or other light containers, either small or with large surfaces to slow their descent, suitably perforated and screened if necessary, perhaps with one weighted and fragile point to assure breakage on landing might serve the need. Some vectors might possibly be used in frozen condition as well.

Dissemination

Aircrafts and helicopters seem most suitable means of dissemination of all agents, whether the agent itself is capable of spreading by the air-borne route or not. Parachutes may be used advantageously in some operations. The actual weapons for delivery will probably comprise appropriate kind of bombs (100 lbs. weight containing 50 lbs. of culture in liquid or powder form) sprays (like insecticide spray apparatus) and miscellaneous devices (portable containers like small flasks or bottles). Rockets may also be used suitably for dissemination of BW agents. On their use will probably depend much of the future development. For the dissemination of agents other than the air-borne group from aircraft no requirement suggests itself other than the simple discharge of the appropriate container over the target, with or without automatic devices to increase aiming precision as circumstances may suggest.

The dissemination of air-borne agents, on the other hand, is a special problem, particularly because of their dependence on meteorological conditions. Micro-ogranisms can be spread by creating an aerosol or cloud of the agent or by covert sabotage attempts. The pathological effect of inhaling aerosols depends strongly upon the size of the particles.(6). Very small particles, 1-5 microns in diameter, can enter into the lungs where infection takes place. In experiments where animals were exposed to anhrax aerosols, it was observed that particles a thousandth of a centimeter in size were 17 times as infectious as particles 12 times larger. even more striking results were achieved with other organisms. In the case of Venezuelan Equine Encephalomyelitis, increasing the particle diameter by a factor of 10 decrease the effectivity by a factor of 14,000. One of the less toxic smoke screen agents like titanium tetrachloride might possibly find use as a vehicle (the emulsion of bacteria in this reagent may remain stable for 24 hours), and if such a medium is feasible it might serve the dual purpose of disguising the nature of the attack and preventing speedy dissipation of the agent in the open air.

Another possible vehicle is glycerine which has the benefit of being an excellent preserving medium for many bacteria and viruses. It may also prove practicable to spray desiccated bacteria or virus preparations without any medium apart from the nutrients in which they were dried. If means can be sought to distribute dried infective agents so that the individual particle size approaches the order of magnitude of standard naval smoke (two ounces of crude oil can yield 1000 cu. ft. of such smoke), a cloud might be produced having similar dispersal properties but of much lower and perhaps negligible visibility.

A fine dust of lyophilized material might even scatter sufficiently if merely dropped in a glass vessel. Concerning the area of spread of a biological aerosol on a smaller scale, the following observations may be interesting (6). In a test, 130 gallons of a suspension of spores of bacillus globigii, a non-pathogenic organism, were distributed in the shape of particles 1-5 microns in diameter, on a two-mile offshore course while the breeze was blowing inland. An area upto 23 miles downwind and nearly 5 miles across was sampled and found sufficiently covered with the "fall-out". Dissemination of infective agents via contaminated projectiles, if feasible at all, will depend on the nature of the projectiles, whether they be aircraft bombs, artillery shells , or even small bombs of the hand grenade type. The agent should be incorporated in the projectile rather than applied to its surface, in order to provide reasonable quantity of the agent and for the safety of those handling the projectile before discharging or firing it.

Whether the last (small bombs) might be used at all is a question linked to that of the dissemination of infective agents by individual carriers or saboteurs. While such methods are undoubtedly practicable in appropriate circumstances, they are likely to be very limited in scale and call for no detailed comment. Though the question of utilising infected persons for spreading disease over enemy territory may be raised, it remains to be seen whether such a method can be of practical importance in BW. Finally, something may be said about the alleged BW activities by the Japan in World War II and by the America in the Korean war 18, in order to merely point out that the mothode mentioned for utilizing microbes were akin to those outlined above. For example , the Japanese were said to have utilized three principal methods of dissemination, namely, spraying bacteria form aircraft, dropping special bacterial bombs from aircraft, and contaminating water sources, pastuer and inhabited areas of land by methods of sabotage.

The microbic agent most prominently mentioned was that of plague. Hundreds of millions of fleas were bred in special chambers. Seven hundred victims of plague had been attributed to such attacks. The agents of cholera, tyhoid and paratyphoid fevers, and anthrax were also mentioned. The Americans were blamed to have used germs which caused an outbreak of plague, with 50 cases and 35 deaths in a human population of 600 , respiratory anthrax and heamorrhagic anthrax meningitis. Infected carriers like fleas, rodents and insects packed in containers were dropped from aeroplanes. An outbreak of acute encephalitis of viral origin with about 73 percent case mortality was reported The viral agents were disseminated by the air-borne route. Efforts were made to contaminate water reservoirs with cholera germs from the air. Becterial and fungal plant pathogens are also alleged to have been dropped by planes. Both the Japanese and Americans were alleged to have used similar BW containers or bombs for the purpose.

References

1. T. Rosebury et al. Jour. Immunology, 56:7 (1947).

2. T. Rosebury, Peace or Pestilence (McGraw-Hill, 1949).

3. A.M.Prentiss, Civil Defence in Modern War (Mc Graw-Hill, 1951).

4. M.M. Kaplan, Bull. Atomic scientists, 16:237 (1960).

5. A. Lwoff, Bull. Atomic Scientists, 16L243 (1960).

6. L.D. Fothergill, Bull. Atomic Scientists, 16:244 (1960).

7. H.S. Anker, Bull. Atomic Scientists, 16:246 (1960).

8. F.C.Bawden, Bull. Atomic Scientists, 16:247 (1960).

9. T.Rosebury et al. , Experimental Air-borne Infection (The Williams and Wilkins Company, 1947).

10. Bacterial and Mycotic Infections of Man, edited by R.J. Dubos, 3rd edition (Pitman Medical, 1958).

11. Viral and Rickettsial Infections of Man, edited by T.M. Rivers and F.L.Horsfall, Jr., 3rd edition (J.B. Lippincott Company, 1959).

12. W. Burrows, Textbook of Microbiology, 16th edition (Saunders, 1954).

13. I.A. Merchant, An Outline of the Infectious Diseases of Domestic Animals (Burgess Publishing Co., 1951).

14. Animal Diseases, the Yearbook of Agriculture, U.S.D.A., Washington 1956.

15. I.A. Merchant and R.A. packer , Veterinary Bacteriology and Virology , 5th edition (Iowa State College Press, 1956).

16. W.A.Hagan and D.W.Bruner, The Infectious Diseases of Domestic Animals, 3rd edition (Cornell University Press, 1957).

17. Plant Diseases, The Yearbook of Agriculture, U.S.D.A., Washington, 1953.

18. T. Rosebury, Bull, Atomic Scientists, 16:227 (1960).

5

Potential Biological Weapons Agents

Bacteria and viruses are used as the agents in biological weapons. This organisms have the ability to spread diseases on a large scale. There are other ability which are before to man and animals. In the course of evolution organisms have developed complex cooperative and competitive interactions. For instance, ruminants such as cows depend on micro-organisms in their gut in order to digest the cellulose they eat. Without these micro-organisms cows would not be able to digest grass as effictively as they do, and we would not have a dairy industry. We are more concerned here with the competitive interactions between organisms: particularly with the way in which bacteria, viruses and, to some extent, fungi, may be manipulated to cause harm to human beings and their economically important food producing animals and plants. The definition and classification of bacteria, viruses and fungi are complex issues, the details of which need not unduly worry us here. It is necessary, however, to scniember that higher organisms like ourselves are made up of minute cells. Each cell consists of cytoplasm and a nucleus where the genetic material is held.

Bacteria are simpler, single-celled organisms in which, for instance, the genetic material is not separated off from the cytoplasm in the same manner. Bacteria are visible with the light microscope, but are generally smaller than 10 micrometres (m^{-6}) in diameter. Viruses are much smaller in size and consist predominantly of genetic material. they can only reproduce by invading a suitable cell and taking over its operations. Viruses can be seen through use of more powerful electron microscopes. Fungi are widespread organisms in nature having greater importance they include the common edible mushroom, toadstools, smuts, rusts and powdery mildew. They are much different from green plants in lacking chlorophyll and thus must obtain their nutrients from parasitism or the decomposition of dead matter. Here we should deal, however, with bacteria and viruses. Given the unending threat of invasion from other organisms. Animals have evolved complex mechanisms of protection. We human beings keep out as many invaders as possible by means of our tough exterior called skin. Where we are more exposed, for example in our eyes and mouth, tears and saliva contain enzymes to attack invaders. Additionally, other bacteria which normally live with us harmlessly, in our digestive systems, help in different ways to make it difficult for harmful invaders to becomes established. If an invading organism breaches these outer defences it becomes much more difficult for the body to defend itself. However, a complex mechanism based on the white blood cell (leucocytes) has necessarily evolved to protect us. There is first a 'non-specific' internal defence system including cells which attack foreign invaders.

To do this the cells have to recognise the foreign meterial, which they do with the help of different mediators. However, this non-specific system is supplemented byt a highly sophisticated and very specific immune response system. The body's specific protective system depends on the class of white blood cells called lymphocytes. Two kinds of lymphocyte are of particular importance. These are the T-cells from the thymus gland and the B-cells from the bone marrow. The interactions between these two types of cell are complex, but it is evident that B-cells specialise in responding to foreign material in circulation whilst T-cells attack body cells showing evidence of having foreign material within their cytoplasm. B-lymphocytes have very specific receptors (antibodies) for foreign molecules (antigens) on their surfaces. When an antigen molecule comes across the B-cell is activated to divide and secrete its antibody protein. This then binds and neutralises the foreign material in a precise manner. T-lymphocytes are likewise highly specific. but they respond to pieces of foreign material brought to the surface from within cells. This system can clearly be overwhelmed, for instance, by a massive injection of a toxic chemical in a snake bite which takes effect before a suffcient response can be produced. Same way in an illness such as measles, there is a period of time required following initial infection for the body to produce enough antibody to destroy the invading organism. On the other hand, once specific initial invasion has taken place, some cells which can respond specifically will remain in a dormant state in the body. If a later attack by the same organism occurs, these cells and their reaction are more swiftly activated. We say that the person has become immune to the disease, and we make use of this mechanism when we vaccinate people against disease with harmless elements taken from threatening micro organisms.

Agents of Disease

Before the public anxiety over HIV and AIDS arose in the last decade most peope in the developed world had little concerns over infectious or contagious (communicable) diseases and agents of disease than for much of the past hundred years. Our medical concerns were linked more to illnesses such as heart disease and cancer which are not often caused by infectious agents. Of course, as the science of biology and its application to medicine and agriculture developed, for those of us in the rich world an unstated assumption had arisen that infectious diseases were not any more a serious problem.

Whilst AIDS and, to a lesser extent, Legionnaire's desease, Lassa fever, Marburg virus disease and Ebola virus disease have jolted that confident outlook, it is necessary to start by reminding ourselves of just how dangerous infectious diseases can be. While the classification of bacteria is complex, they do have standard biological (generic/species) double names. For viruses the nomenclature remains less standardised.

Thus, while bacteria are given standard names here, the scientific names of viruses are not always used, though family groups and genera within families will be mentioned where useful. One small fact that should be borne in mind is that some bacterial diseases, particularly rickettsial diseases such as typhus (agent *Rickettsia Prowazekii*), Q-fever (*Coxiella burnetii*) and Rocky Mountain spotted fever (Rickettsia rickettsii), are caused by bacteria which are obligatory intracellular parasites. Like viruses, they can only metabolise and multiply inside other living cells. A full account of the infectious diseases would need a medical taxtbook but, bearing in mind our concern with the military use of infectious agents, we may simply focus here on the questions of which agents cause which diseases and how the agents are transmitted (this will help us to get to grips with later discussions about which agents have been used to produce weapon systems). Thus if we regard AIDS, we know that acquired immunodeficiency syndrome-the name from which the acronym is derived- is caused by te action of a human immunodeficiency virus (HIV) and that its transmission between people is by sexual contact and the exchange of blood products (for example, in the re-use of needles for durg injections).

Not much interest has been shown in weaponising living agents more complex than bacteria for direct use against man. Thus we are not concerned here with vitally significant infectious diseases, such as malaria or African sleeping sickness as these are caused by more complex (protozoan) organisms. Amongst the fungi, only coccidioidomycosis, a respiratory infection caused by airborne spores on *Coccidioides immitis*, is considerd to have aroused much military interest. Thus other fungal infections will be discussed here only in relation to potential attacks on agriculture. Although we have tended to forget about the great danger infectious disease, we still protect ourselves against their harmful effects wherever possible.

We carefully vaccinate our children against those childhood diseases-diphtheria (*Corynebacterium diphtheriae*), mumps (virus), poliomyelitis (viruses), rubella (virus), rubeola (measles virus), whooping cough (*Bardetella Pertussis*)—from which previous generations suffered greatly. Caring people keep their own, and their childern's tetanus jabs (against *Clostridium tetani toxin*) up to date; they ensure that they and their children secure protection against typhoid fever (*Salmonella typhi*), yellow fever (virus), cholera etc. If they are visiting those areas where this is necessary. Similarly, anyone bitten by a rabid dog would avoid the fatal consequences by quickly obtaining the injections needed to halt the growth of the viral rabies infection. While we may not recognise the fact as directly, we are also the beneficiaries of the growing understanding of infectious diseases that forced new standards of public hygiene upon earth generations. Thus we know that cholera (*Vibrio cholerae*), viral hepatitis and typhoid fever can be greaty restricted if water and food supplies are clean.

We know that brucellosis (*Brucella abortus*, B. melitensis, and B. *suis*) can be effectively controlled, particularly by the pasteurisation of milk. Bacillary dysentery, gastroenteritis (many possible causative organisms) and botulism (poisoning by *Clostridium botulinum toxin*) also demand care in the making of food and drink if they are to be avoided. Due to the protection available to us through modern medicine and improved public health and hygiene measures we have predominantly lost contact with the grave conseomence of the great killer infectious diseases. We need to supplement the facts of everyday life in the West with a little history.

Some Prominent Infectious Diseases

To get a realistic picture of the issue we are discussing it is necessary to briefly examine what is known of diseases such as those already mentioned and others such as bubonic plague (*Yersinia pestis*), influenza (viruses), leprosy (*Mycobacterium leprae*), smallpox (*variola viruses*), tuberculosis (*Mycobacterium tuberculosis*) and yellow fever (*virus*). In his classic book, *Plagues and Peoples*, William McNeill presented an overview of how the interation of such diseases with the growing human population had often moulded historical events. His curiosity had been aroused by the ease with 600 Spaniards under Cortez had conquered the Aztec Empire. He concluded that the main reason was the Aztec susceptibility to smallpox and other diseases carried by the Europeans. Moreover, he opined that this was a specific example of a genreal feature of European expansion: that it was a disease-experienced society that, during the maritime voyages of recent centuries, frequently came across native populations with no resistance ot the diseases it carried. The tragic consequences are revealed by Mc Neill's account of the conquest of Mexico: ....

Population decay was catastrophic.....less than fifty years from the time Cortez inaugurated epidemiological as well as other exchanges between Amerindian and European populatios, the population of central Mexico had shrunk to about three million , i.e., to about one tenth of what had been there when Cortez landed.....

The population decay went on at s slower rate, for another 50 years. And, of course, such a devastating assault had profound psychological and social implication on the native peoples. Mc Neill attempted to explain how the gradual build-up of the human population and the increasing contacts between centres of population in Eurasia had produced the disease-experienced Europeans, and then to take the story forward to the present situation where the world's human population can be harmed by a new influenza virus. As he pointed out, and as biologists stress today, we are getting on with a radically new experiment with our massive population growth and the development of many megacities. Despite our medical technology, successful rapid conquest of opportunistic pathogens which might take advantage of these circumstances is not assured. To follow the outcome of the impact any disease organism may have on a human population needs data on the characteristics of the organism and its mode of action, and on the population's environment and characteristics.

With such data precise models of how diseases spread and are controlled may be obtained. It is clear, for instance, that the European population gone through similar devastation to the Aztecs when plague returned, after many centuries' absence, in the fourteenth century. Mc Neill estimated that one-third of Europe's population died between 1346 and 1350. Such huge setbacks undoubtedly severly hampered the build-up of the human population. Other diseases, such as smallpox, later became endemic amongst the European population.

Those who survived childhood were likely to have a degree of immunity as adults. It took the development of vaccination at the turn of the eithteenth century to minimise the impact of this dreaded disease on children. Other diseases, such as cholera, which started effectively the European populations more as contact with India increased and the rapid urbanisation of the last century provided conditions for its propagation, then triggered the changes in public health provisions needed for effective control. Also, towards the latter half of the nineteenth century medical experimentation and theoretical advances allowed the development of specific control measures. In recent times, of course, the use of antibiotic drugs against bacteria has been of great significance.

Bubonic Plague

If most of us were asked to name an infectious disease which had profound impact in history we would most probably think of bubonic plague or the Black Death. Plague is caused by the bacterium *Yersinia pestis*, which is a natural infection of rodents. It infects human beings by the bite of fleas which have earlier fed off infected rodents. As we have a very poor natural immune response to this particular organism, death rates are high in untreated cases. In the bubonic form a lump-or bubo-arises in a lymph node around the site of infection within six days. This indicates the immune system's effort to deal with the infection. After a week, typically about half of those infected in the great pandemics were dead.

In the septicaemic form of the disease the bacteria rapidly enter the blood and spread widely throughout the body. Death rates then approach 100 per cent in untreated cases. On some occastions after the bacteria reach the lungs of an infected person, there is a highly contagious spread of the deadly primary pneumonic form of the disease through the air from person to person. Death rates for pneumonic plague again approach 100 percent for untreated cases. Somtimes, after circulatory collapse, the surface of the victim's body blackens. 'Black Death' is the name given to the pandemic which razed Europe in the middle of the fourteenth century. This was the first devastating wave of the second great cycle of plague. The first occurred in late Greco-Roman times, but the second cycle went on until about 1800 . Since then a third cycle has spread through non-European parts of the world.

The black Death had a profound effect on European society. It swept over huge areas and the *Cambridge History of Human Disease* agrees with Mc Neill on its impact in numbers of deaths:....

historians generally agree that death rates most commonly ranged between about 30 to 50 percent in both Europe and the Middle East, with the best records indicating a mortality in the upper end of that range....and its unexpectedness:

The Black Death was in several ways a completely unprecedented experience for those who suffered through it. Plague had virtually vanished from the Middle East and Europe during the centuries between the end of the first pandemic in the eighth century and the beginning of the second pandemic....

Whilst vigorous attempts were made to combat the disease, given the suddenness of its onset, the intensity of its effect and the lack of medical understanding, the well-documented devastating impact of plague on the whole society is understandable.

Cholera

Cholera is a diarrhoeal disease caused by the bacterium *Vibrio cholerae*. The bacterium is transmitted from an infected person's faeces through a contaminated water system to another person. The bacterium does not have other regular animal hosts. Whilst some people seem to have a natural resistance to cholera, infection does not produce a strong lasting immunity. The bacteria adhere to the intestinal wall of human beings and secretes a toxin that causes very severe diarrhoea. Patients may lose 10-12 litres of fluid a day and death results as a fallout of such a catastrophic loss. Modern treatment aims to safely replace the lost water and salts. Thus cholera is treatable today. That was certainly not the case in the last century. Cholera seems to have long been endemic in the Ganges Delta of the Indian continent and since the early nineteenth century some seven pandemics are considered to have spread out from this source to several the world's major cities. Death rates often reached 50 percent during some of the epidemics, since medical knowledge was only gradually obtained and public health measures to prevent the spread to the disease were only gradually understood and implemented. Of course, proper understanding of the cholera toxin and its role in the disease was only achieved in the 1950s.

Influenza

Influenza is a disease to humans and various other mammal and bird species. It is a respiratory disease which may be worsened by other infections and which, though generally of low lethality, is always a threat to the young and old. Due to its highly infectious nature very large numbers of people are usually affected, and thus the total numbers of deaths caused by influenza are much higher that might generally be expected owing to its low lethality. Influenza is caused by three viruses classified as A, B and C of the Orthomyxoviridae family.

The most important influenza virus type is A and it exists in a number of sub-types which usually do not provoke cross-immunity to each other. Due to the normal airborne route of infection, influenza epidemics in temperate zones tend to occur in cold winter weather when people are huddled together in conditons of poor ventilation. Influenza A virus is genetically unstable. Between pandemics the proteins in the shell of the virus, which flanks the genetic material, undergo continuous change which progressively invalidates acquired immunity and many times a century the virus seems to undergo radical change which invalidates most people's immunity. There is no good evidence of influenza before its occurrence in Europe in the Middle Ages. Surely, there were pandemics in the sixteenth, the eghteenth and the nineteenth centuries. Yet, whilst the total numbers of deaths were probably much higher than for the obvious killer diseases like cholera, it took the pandemic of 1918-19 to really focus the society's attention to the disease. The Spanish 'flu' pandemic began in the spring and proceeded with standard low lethality rates. In August a second wave of infection arose. This had various immunological features and double or triple the death rates. The *Cambridge History* comments: .....It is possible that the 1918-19 pandemic was, in terms of absolute numbers, the greatest single demographic shock that the human species has ever received.....The ..... flu did most of its killing in a 6-month period and reached almost every human population on Earth....

More than 21 million people died world-wide and, since several were young adults, the impact on affected societies was more pronounced beyond that had only the very young and old died. Why the 1918-19 pandemic was so destructive remains unclear, but later pandemics have re-emphasised the threat. Not surprisingly, a lot of research has been done on the disease and the World Health Organisation has a world wide network of centres monitoring what is happening to the virus so as to detect new strains rapidly.

Leprosy

Leprosy is a disease that occurs naturally only in human beings. The cause is an infection by the bacterium *Mycobacterium leprae*. This bacterium multiplies very slowly *within* human cells. Thus antibodies circulating in the blood are of no use against it. Immunity mediated directly against cells is therfore the body's main defence mechanism. Transmission is through sustained exposure to affected individuals, with nasal secretions considered to be the most likely source of infectious material. The incubation period for the disease is normally three to five years. About three-quarters of those exhibiting early signs of leprosy recover spontaneously. A milder form of leprosy develops in those with a hypersensitive reaction to the bacterial antigens.

Severe progressive leprosy occurs in those who neither recover nor exhibit a hypersensitive response. In untreated cases the beacteria kill skin tissue, leading to loss of facial fearures, fingers, toes etc. There exists now, in fact, cheap and effective medication for leprosy, but according to a rough estimate there are still some 15 million lepers world-wide. These people are located predominantly in poor, rural parts of the world. From the historical incidence of the disease, in which leprosy seems to be replaced by tuberculosis as urbanisation proceeds, it has been suggested that there is some limited cross-immunity with *Mycobacterium tuberculosis*, the causative agent of tuberculosis. As population density rises up, it is argued that this favours the spread of tuberculosis and thus it could be that leprosy is replaced. Whether this explanation is correct, and, while accepting the fact that leprosy may have been difficult to diagnose in earlier centuries, there is no doubt that leprosy and the stigma it carries have been major factors within judaeo-Christian history.

Measles

Measles is caused by a virus of the *genus Morbillivirus* of the family paramyxoviridae. It infects only human beings. It is highly contagious and spreads through the air or direct contact. Infants have a passive immunity provided by maternal antibodies for up to 6-9 months after birth, and infection bestows lifelong immunity thereafter in almost all cases. The same is true for vaccination.

Given these features, in unvaccinated populations measles can be an endemic disease which causes epidemics every few years. Mortality is highest amongst the very young and very old and can reach 5 to 10 percent in poor conditions. Currently on an estimate that there are 50 million cases and 1.5 million deaths occur annually world-wide as a result of measles. Vaccination programmes are considered to be preventing a similar number of cases and fatalities, but much work needs to be done on understanding the measles virus and providing an effective vaccine for the developing world. It has been argued that measles probably arose from a related animal virus as the human population reached levels which would sustain the virus.

Some unidentified epidemics in Roman and Chinese history could have been because of measles. The disease was well characterised in the tenth century and was clearly present in Europe from the medieval period onwards. The most dramatic fallout of measles often occured when a population without immunity was brought into contact with the disease. This frequently occurred during the European expansion and led to high levels of death in several native populations.

Smallpox

Smallpox viruses (variola major and variola minor) of the Poxviridae family are now found only exist in laboratories. This viral disease was formerly transmitted primarily by airborne droplets being inhaled. It would infect almost all people at risk. The more dangerous variola major typically killed 25-30 percent of those infected, and variola minor about 1 percent. After an incubation period of some 12 days there was an abrupt onset of high fever and other symptoms. Most people survived for a further 2-5 days when the characteristic rash started appearing. After a few days the small pimples of the rash turned to pustules. If the person survived, the pustules dried up and the remaining scabs fell off after a few weeks. The person could be left much disfigured, but with long-lasting immunity.

Death rates could range between a quarter and a half of children affected. Although the disease may well have existed in antiquity it was only definitively described in the ninth century. It, however, became a major killer disease in the sixteenth and the seventeenth centuries. There are similar diseases such as cowpox, but smallpox seems to have only affected human beings. As it did not lie dormant within human beings and there was therefore no reservoir of symptomless carriers, it seems to have needed large populations-with numerous, new, non-immune, potential victims-to have persisted. This has led to speculation that the virus may have arisen from a related animal virus in Neolithic times as the human population began to increase.

It has been estimated that in the eighteenth century smallpox accounted for 10-15 percent of all deaths in some European countries, and that 80 percent of victims were below 10 years of age. Even more terrifying, as we have seen, was the impact of small pox on non-immune native peoples as they came into contact with the colonising Europeans. Gradually methods were developed to combat the disease. Variolation, the artificial infection of people with small amounts of smallpox material, was the first. This was a dangerous practice, but skilful practitioners did improve the technique to ensure only a very light pricking of the skin.

The great breakthrough was made when Edward Jenner noticed that those who had suffered cowpox did not catch smallpox. He then tested vaccination with cowpox as a defence against smallpox and wrote up his successful work in 1798. The practice of vaccination spread extremely rapidly. The *Cambridge History* comments:.....

England led the way in the new practice...... more than 100,000 were vaccinated there by 1801.... Within three years of the publication of jenner's *Inquiry* it was translated into German, Frech, Spanish, Dutch, Italian and Latin. In France 1.7 million were vaccinated between 1808 and 1811.... and so on across the world.

Towards the end of the century some European countries had paractically eliminated the disease , and by the middle of the twentieth century most wealthy countries became free of it. The final action was then taken by the World Health Organisation which, in a vaccination campaign in the developing world, put an end the disease in the 1970s.

Tuberculosis

Tuberculosis is an infectious disease caused by the bacterium *Mycobacterium tuberculosis*. It is generally a chronic desease which affects the lungs, but it may also affect almost any other part of the body. Given the right conditions tuberculosis may affect 100 percent of the population and thus, despite its non-acute nature, it has killed several millions of people.

About 30 species of *Mycobacterium* exist and many can cause disease in a wide variety of animals. Some cause diseases other than tuberculosis in human beings. Human tuberculosis is typically caused by *Mycobacterium tuberculosis*. There are three main types, I, A and B. These are distributed in various parts of the world and each seems to be strongly resistant to mutation.

The bovine species (*Mycobacterium bovis*) can be transmitted through contaminated milk, and this may be prevented by pasteurisation. Generally, tuberculosis is transmitted by airborne droplets inhaled into the lungs after release from an infected individual coughing, sneezing or spitting. Very small numbers of bacteria are enough to infect an individual and these can lie dormant for long periods of time and then cause active disease. Several environmental factors influence how the disease develops. In particular, the poor living conditions typical of early phases of industrialisation have repeatedly produced high rates of tubercolosis. Pulmonary tuberculosis starts when scavenging cells or macrophages engulf the bacteria in the lungs. The bacteria, however, are able to develop slowly within these cells. Thus only cell-mediated immunity is effective against the infection. T-cells and other activated scavenging cells or microphages move to the site and slowly form the characteristic tubercle. In most cases the bacteria become dormant within this structure. In about 10 per cent of untreated cases the disease keeps growth and the bacteria spread throughout the body. Dormant bacteria can also be activated in times of stress and in old age. There is also little acquired immunity from an infection. Tuberculosis seems to have been a human disease since the Neolithic period. Clear signs of the disease are found in archaeological specimens. It seem to have been described in many early texts and was certainly present in the medieval period in Europe. As the population grew, and urbanisation proceeded, tuberculosis became more severe. Towards the middle of the sixteenth century about 20 percent of deaths in England are estimated to have been caused by different forms of tuberculosis. The great epidemics of tuberculosis developed with industrialisation and urbanisation.

Whilst medical advances now make effective treatment possible, the improvement in living conditions in mature industrialised societies appears itself to have reduced the incidence of the disease dramatically. On the other hand, the disease is still very significant in the dveloping world and could clearly strike anywhere when social conditions deteriorate dramatically. There has also been increasing worries over the appearance of drug-resistant tuberculosis in some cities of the world in recent times an instance, of the worrying growth of microbial drug resistance.

Typhoid

Typhoid fever is caused due to infection with the bacterium *Salmonella typhi. This organism* attacks only human beings and should therefore be controllable by public health measures. However, there are a large number of related *Salmonella* bacteria which infect a very wide spectrum of hosts and which can cause milder salmonellosis in humans. A variant illness called paratyphoid fever, which is also caused by *Salmonella* other than *S . typhi*, can show similar symptoms to typhoid fever. Typhoid fever is spread when S. typhi bacteria in faeces shed by an infected person are ingested by another person, either by drinking untreated water or eating contaminated food on which the bacteria can multiply well. Many bacteria are destroyed by acid in the stomach, but once in the small intestine the bacteria enter its cellular lining and are then ingested by white blood cells.

Instead of being destroyed by these cells, *S. typhi* multiplies and then passes into the bloodstream. White blood cells in the liver and spleen then attack the bacteria, but, again, intracellular multiplication takes place and the organisms flood back into the bloodstream. Clinical symptoms of the disease-fever, weakness, etc. may develop at this stage. The bacteria load the lymph nodes of the small intestine particularly and intestinal haemorrhage and perforation are major causes of death. Over a period of some weeks the imrnune system in survivors develops enough response to destroy the infection. In untreated cases the mortality rate is between 10 and 20 percent. A particular charectristic of the disease is that some people who recover (about two percent) maintain an infection in the biliary tract and continue to shed *S.typhi* in their faeces without exhibiting signs of illness. Vaccination does produce immunity, but it is not 100 percent effective. Typhoid fever is thought to have long been a human disease. It first effectively became known in the early part of the last century and it was also the subject of some of the early study of how such diseases spread. *S. typhi* was one of the earliest of the bacterial agents to be identified.

Despite all this, mortality rates caused by the organism amongst American soldiers in the Spanish -American War of 1898 and British soldiers in the Boer War were very high. Vaccination and improved military sanitation standards drastically cut down the incidence of the disease in the American and British armies during the First World War. Indeed, in the developed world the disease is now of limited concern. In poorer parts of the world though, typhoid fever still ravages several lives. Crude estimates indicate that there are 15 million cases of typhoid each year and that one million people, mainly children, still die of the disease.

Typhus

Typhus is a natural infection found only in humans . It is caused by *Rickettsia prowazekii* and transmitted by the human body louse or sometimes the head louse. The rickettsial organisms are excreted in louse faeces and are transmitted to human beings mechanically through cuts in the skin. The louse is killed by the infection which is not passed on in its eggs.

The disease spreads when infected lice move to new human bodies. Obviously, typhus flourishes where people are crowded together in unhygienic conditions. Mortality rates in untreated cases could be between five and 25 percent, but can reach 40 percent, Whilst people of all ages are susceptible to the disease, those under

15 years are less affected. An attack of typhus confers long immunity, although the organism persists in the tissues of victims and may reappear later in periods of stress. Typhus is thought to have a long history. Accounts which seem credible date back to the wars of the fifteenth century. Napoleon's campaign in Russia in 1812, for instance, was severely disrupted by typhus. Although modern armies can be protected by vaccination and the destruction of lice, it is evident that wherever the appropriate conditions arise in famine, war, or other forms of social breakdown typhus could quickly return.

It may be noted that Howard Taylor Ricketts and Stanislaus von Prowazek, after whom the infectious agent of typhus is named, both died of the disease while working on it.

Yellow Fever

Yellow Fever is a natural disease found monkeys especially and of non-human primates. It is transmitted between animals by blood-sucking mosquitoes. When such mosquitoes, especially *Aedes aegypti*, feed off human beings the yellow fever virus can be transmitted to the human population.

In densely populated urban areas the disease can then be transmitted directly between humans by infected mosquitoes. In humans symptoms arise three to six days after infection. After another two or three days, those who eventually survive start feeling better. Others, however, experience a variety of symptoms as the remission is short-lived. Jaundice sets in if the liver is damaged and copious black vomit may be produced. Death follows between the seventh and tenth day of the sickness for those who do not survive. Reported mortality rates may be very high in urban-based epidemics, ranging between 20 and 70 percent. However, as many mild cases are not easy to distinguish from other diseases the overall mortality rate is probably much lower. An attack of yellow fever which is survived gives a lifelong immunity to the disease. With these characteristics and the fact that the disease appears to affect children less severely, populations could, in the past, build up effective immunity to the disease.

Epidemic outbreaks would then occur when large numbers of non-immune people arrived in an infected area or infected individuals encountered a non-immune community. Instances of such events abound in the history of the New World. *The Cambridge History* gives many illustrations:

During the first six decades of the nineteenth century, Savannah suffered from 15 epidemics, Charleston had 22, and New Orleans at least 33. The most notable of the New Orleans epidemics occurred in 1853 during which the city lost almost 8,000 individuals to the disease.....and, of course:

Chief among the victims of this and all other epidemics were Northerners and foreigners.... along with white Southerners from the interior. Permanent white residents, however, rarely suffered from fatal yellow fever...

The discovery that mosquitoes transmitted the disease led to it being quickly controlled in North America during the first decade of this century, and effective vaccination is now possible. The disease is still a threat. The virus remains within the monkey populations of Central and South America and there are cases of humans being infected each year. Severe outbreaks of yellow fever have been recorded in recent decades in Africa. Oddly, the disease is unknown in Asia. Some people have suggested that closely resembling natural diseases such as dengue and Japanese encephalitis in Asia have stopped the incursion of yellow fever there.

As may be seen from Table 5.1, the weapons designer would have a very wide range of choice even if consideration were limited to the foregoing ten diseases. Four are viral agents, six are bacterial agents. Transmission modes range from air-and water-borne through to a variety of insect vectors. The diseases also attack human beings in a wide veriety of different ways.

Table 5.1
Summary of Major Infections Diseases Described

Disease	*Agent*	*Transmission*
Bubonic plague	*Yersinia pestis*	Flea bite
Cholera	*Vibrio cholerae*	Faecal-oral
Influenza	Virus (Orthomyxoviridae)	Airborne
Leprosy	*Mycobacterium leprae*	Sustained contact
Measles	Morbillivirus (Paramyxoviridae)	Airborne
Smallpox	Variola major (Poxviridae)	Airborne
Tuberculosis	*Mycobacterium tuberculosis*	Airborne
Typhoid fever	*Salemonella typhi*	Faecal-oral
Typhus	*Rickettsia prowazekii*	Contact with lice faeces
Yellow fever	Virus (Flaviviridae)	Mosquito bite

The choice for a weapons designer, however, is much greater that these major killer diseases.

At a Royal United Services Institute lecture in 1981 Colonel Vicary and Wing-Commnader Wilson of the Defence NBC Centre stated that there were at least 30 known micro-organisms and toxins which are suitable for use in weapons. In its analysis, *Chemical and Bacteriological (Biological) Weapons and the Effects of Their Possible Use,* the United Nations in 1969 listed some 22 biological agents that might be used against human beings. These are listed in Table 5.2. It is easy to find by referring the table that the mortality rates (taken from epidemiological data and therefore not necessarily indicating the effects of deliberate use of high dosages delivered by the most dangerous route) do indicate a wide range of lethal and incapacitating agents. Moreover, the UN list does not include a number of the major infectious diseases that we have just discussed. Evidently, there are military considerations that have to be taken into consideration in selecting from the range of possible agents. Let us analyse such considerations now.

Military Considerations

The UN study provides some general information on the features of biological weapons that we need to take into account. First, of course, such weapons employ living organisms which multiply within the target organism, or extremely toxic chemicals which can be produced by living organisms. The high concentrations that can be easily acquired of these small living organisms or toxic chemicals imply that very large areas could be affected by the weapons.

Table 5.2
Some Possible Biological Agents for Use Against Man

Disease	*Mortality Rate*
Viral	
Chikungunya fever	Very low
Dengue fever	Very low
Eastern equine encephalitis	High (>60%)
Tick -borne encephalitis	Variable (up to 30%)
Venezuelan equine encephalitis (VEE)	Low
Influenza	Usually low
Yellow fever	High (up to 40%)
Smallpox	Variable (but usually up to 30%)
Rickettsial	
Q-fever	Low
Psittacosis	Moderately high
Rocky Mountain spotted fever	Usually high(up to 80%)
Epidemic typhus	Variable (but usually up to 70%)
Bacterial	
Anthrax (pulmonary)	Almost invariably fatal
Brucellosis	Low
Cholera	Usually high (up to 80%)
Glanders	Almost invariably fatal
Melioidosis	Almost 100% fatal
Plague (pneumonic)	Almost 100 % fatal
Tularemia	Usually low (can be up to 60%)
Typhoid fever	Moderately high
Dysentery	Low to moderately high
Fungal	
Coccidioidomycosis	Low

The SIPRI study, *CB Weapons Today*, studied a number of other considerations which allow a rough classification, from a military point of view, of the available biological agents. Some of these are shown in Table 5.3. Some agents are clearly much more infectious to victims than others. The potentially infectious agents could therefore spread rapidly and uncontrollably. This makes such agents of limited attraction to military planners. Within the two categories, of potentially infectious and not, there is also a division between highly lethal and just incapacitating agents. From a military point of view one might not wish to use a lethal agent, for instance against enemy troops in an area where there were also civilians.

Table 5.3
Military Classification of Biological Agents

Principal characteristics	*Examples*	*Militarily significant features*
Potentially infectious from first victim		
Incapacitating	Influenza virus	Military attraction imited by
Lethal	*Yersinia pestis* (plague)	Potential uncontrollability
Not infectious from first victim		
Incapacitating	*Coxiella burnetii* (Q-fever)	Dacay rate in air, incubation period;
Lethal	Bacillus anthracis (anthrax)	length of illness; etc.

The SIPRI study examines other military considerations, for instance, the rate at which the agent's infectivity would decay when disseminated by a weapon system, the length of the incubation period for the illness caused, and the type and duration of the illness.

Some of the complexities may be demonstrated by considering the potential use of an agent which had an arthropod carrier (fly, mosquito, etc.) in an area where such a potential carrier was part of the local fauna. If such an agent were used it might be difficult to forecast the fall outs even if the disease were not directly infectious from person to person. The militarily-desirable characteristics of biological agents have been discussed in numerous open sources. Some of these are summarised in Table 5.4. Evidently , the weapons designer would need an agent which would produce a given effect at low dose in a predictable time and was easy to produce and use. Against this background we can now analyse some of the weapon systems known to have been standardised prior to the agreement of the Biological Weapons Convention in the early 1970s.

Table 5.4 : Some Militarily-desirable Characteristics of Biological Agents.

1. *An agent should produce a certain effect consistently.*
2. *The dose needed to produce the effect should be low.*
3. *The target population should have little or no immunity.*
4. *There should be a short and predictable incubation period.*
5. *Treatment for the disease should not be available to the target population.*
6. *It should be possible to mass-produce the agent.*
7. *The user should have the means to protect troops and civilians.*
8. *The agent should be stable in storage and transportation in munitions.*
9. *It should be possible to disseminate the agent efficiently.*

The SIPRI study focussed what was then known of the agents developed in the major post-war US biological weapons programme. The information on anti-personnel agents is summarised here in Table 5.5. We have already discussed yellow fever. We need now to briefly review the other agents and diseases mentioned in order to complete our overview of the biological possibilities that were there before the development of the new method of genetic engineering and other kinds of modern biotechnology.

Table 5.5
Some Anti-personnel Biological Agents Standardised by the USA[1]

Species	*Agent Category*	*Incubation Period (days)*	*Duration of Incapacity of survivors (weeks)*	*Mortality rate (%)*
Bacillus anthracis	Lethal	2-3	4-5	95-100
Yellow fever virus	Lethal	3-6	1-2	4-100
Francisella tularensis	Lethal	2-10	1-3	30-40
Brucella suis	Incapacitating	7-60	8-12	1-2
Coxiella burnetii	Incapacitating	15-18	1-2	0-1
VEE virus	Incapacitating	3-4	1/2-1	0-2

[1]Modified from reference 14.

Anthrax

Anthrax is a natural disease of herbivorous animals which is trasmittable to human beings. Although it has only been specifically characterised in recent centuries, there are several historical accounts which are almost certainly descriptions of outbreaks of this disease. The causative agent, *Bacillus anthracis*, can form spores which are extremely hardy and can remain alive for extraordinarily long periods after dissemination. The bacterium can enter the body through the skin and cause cutaneous anthrax or through ingestion of contaminated material.

Infection through the lungs is particularly dangerous and untreated pulmonary anthrax has a mortality rate approaching 100 percent. Fortunately, rather large numbers of bacteria are required to cause the disease in human beings through this route. After inhalation of a heavy dose of anthrax spores, however, the onset of the disease may occur within a day and death may rapidly follow after a couple of more days. The pathological responses to the organism are caused by toxins that its produces. Vaccination is available but its effectiveness against massive doses is uncertain. Given these characteristics, it is not surprising that anthrax has been a choice agent for the designer of biological weapons. We shall return to its use in biological weapons programmes in more detail later.

Brucellosis

Three main infectious agents found in domestic animals cause brucellosis in human beings. These are *Brucella melitensis* which attacks goats, B. *abortus* (cattle) and B. *suis* (pigs). Although the disease docs not often result death in human beings, it is very debilitating. The initial period of intermittent waves of fever (undulant fever) often lasts up to a month, but it can last a year and relapses may continue over a period of many years. The usual means of transmission to human beings is from the ingestion of contaminated meat or mild products. Direct entry through skin cuts is also possible. The persistent nature of the disease results from the failure of the immune system to deal effectively with the bacterial invasion. Descriptions of this type of fever in the Mediterranean region date from classical times. Success in understanding the agent of the disease in goats and its transmission to human beings in milk dates from investigations in Malta at the turn of the last century.

There are several other diseases which have symptoms resembling to those of brucellosis and this obviously complicates diagnosis. Infection and recovery confer strong immunity, but no vaccine is presently availabe for human beings.

Q-Fever

Q-Fever is caused when human beings become infected by *Coxiella burnetii*. This is a natural infection of several animal species, and, unlike other rickettsaial infections, is not necessarily transmitted to man by an arthropod. Transmission can occur by inhalation of the organism. The illness starts two to four weeks after exposure and involves symptoms such as fever, pains, headache and so on. If untreated, these may last for one or two weeks and longer-lasting complications are possible. Infected animals develop large numbers of disease organisms, and these rickettsiae are extremely resistant to adverse environmental conditions. Furthermore, very low doses are sufficient to cause infection in human beings. With such features, the organism can cause sudden, localised outbreaks of disease.

There were several cases, well-documented, amongst military personnel during the Second World War. Laboratory-acquired infections were also a serious problem in dealing with this organism and vaccines were first developed to protect laboratory workers. Military interest would certainly have been aroused due to the infectivity and environmental hardiness of this organism.

Furthermore, it is easily grown in high concentrations. The effects of Q-fever in combination with those of other incapacitating agents such as tularemia or VEE virus have been studied.

Tularemia

This is a natural disease of rodents, rabbits and hares. The causative agent *Francisella tularensis*, however, has been found in a large variety of other mammal, bird and insect species. It also can infect human beings. Two variants (biovars) of the disease are known. The one found naturally in North America is F. *tularensis biovar tularensis* (type A) and is much the more virulent in human beings. Infection can come about in various ways: through an insect bite, through contaminated water or food, or through direct contact with infected material and passage through the skin or lungs. The incubation period is two to ten days and the debilitating disease lasts for about a month. Convalescence needs a further two to three months. Good immunity follows an attack and an effective vaccine is now available for laboratory workers. There seems to be reasonable proof of the presence of tularemia in the northern hemisphere in the eighteenth and the nineteenth centuries. Its wide distribution and adaptation to a range of hosts indicates that it is an ancient disease. It was the subject of detailed study in the United States during the early part of this century. Given the complexity of the agent's natural ecology, eradication of the disease seems unlikely. For the weapons designer the evidence that the bacterium can remain alive in the soil for weeks would suggest that it is a hardy agent. When given to human volunteers by aerosol (airborne into the lungs) in heavy doses the incubation period could be reduced to two to three days and the standard US BW agent was capable of causing 30-40 percent mortality rates.

It was also found that very small numbers of bacteria dilivered by aerosol could cause infection with great reliability. Though, as noted earlier, recovery from an attack confers long-lasting immunity and a vaccine is available, it has proved possible to develop strains of the organism resistant to specific drugs, such as the streptomycin-resistant strain used as the standard US agent.

Venezuelan Equine Encephalitis

Venezualan Equine Encephalitis (VEE) is one of a large group of arboviruses. These are arthropod-borne viruses which need multiplication in their vectors for transmission, other examples are yellow fever and dengue. VEE has a wide variety of hosts. It causes a fatal disease of the central nervous system in horses and mules and an incapacitating influenza-like disease in humans. In natural occurrences in humans, VEE takes nearly two to five days to produce the symptoms of fever, nausea etc. The illness ususally lasts between one and four days, and recovery time is a week or longer. An effective vaccine is available.

Whilst the lethality of VEE for humans is very low, the virus is stable in aerosol dissemination and highly infective to human beings when administered by the respiratory route. This obviously would be useful in a weapons agent. Even on the basis of such a brief review it becomes clear that some of the potential agents discussed satisfy well many of the requirements for biological weapons agents set out in Table 2.4. As an instance, we might note that yellow fever is not known to have occurred in Asia. The weaponisation of this agent by the United States during the Cold War would therefore have resulted in a system which could potentially have been used against a target area with little or no natural immunity. We need now to turn to the question of attacks on plants and animals of economic significance.

Diseases of Plants

We depent on plants for our staple crops (wheat, rice, corn, for example), for fibres (cotton, flax, for example, for wood and several other materials with industrial uses, and for vegetables, fruits and luxury items such as tea, coffee and tobacco. All these economically important types of plants are open to attack by plant diseases. Well-known examples that can readily be called to mind are the Irish Famine of 1845-46 resulting from blight of the potato crop, and Dutch elm disease which has destroyed so many trees in Europe and America in recent times. Plants may be damaged by a number of organisms but, as Table 5.6 shows, military interest, as with human pathogens, centres on viruses, bacteria and fungi, the most significant of the plant pathogens, are organisms which differ-from plants particularly in lacking conductive elements, and chlorophyll in their cells.

The vegetative body or mycelium of a typical fungus is made up of individual branches or hyphae which may or may not have septa or cross-walls. Some lower fungi (slime-moulds) do not have a true mycelium. Fungi reproduce by means of spores, specified cells or small cell groups produced by asexual or sexual processes. In higher fungi asexual spores or conidia are produced from specialised hyphae.

Table 5.6
IIlustrative Examples of Potential Anti-plant Biological Agents

Disease	*Agent*	*Note*
Viruses		
Tobacco mosaic	TMV	Natural airborne transmission
sugar-beet curly top	CTV	Natural leafhopper transmission
Bacteria		
Rice blight	*Xanthomonas cryzae*	Many modes of transmission
Corn blight	*Pseudomonas alboprecipitans*	
Fungi		
Late blight of potato	*Phytophthora infestans*	Caused Irish potatato famine
Black stem rust of cereals	*Puccinia graminis*	P.*graminis tritici* was a standardised agent
Rice blast	*Pyricularia oryzae*	Standardised agent

Of the 100,000 species of fungi known so far, or 50 cause disease in human beings but some 8,000 are known to cause disease in plants. About 200 of the 1,600 known species of bacteria are plant pathogens but there exists a complication a species may often have a number of pathovars, each of which is confined to one particular host. Nearly 500 viruses are known to cause diseases in plants. These viruses come from a wide range of different taxonomic groups. We shall consider some demonstration examples of plant pathogens, again concentrating particularly on those known to have been standardised in the US offensive biological warfare programme.

Sugar Beet Curly Top

An example of a viral disease which has been analysed as a potential agent is sugar beet curly top. Curly top occurs in the United States, Turkey and South America. The curly top virus (CTV) infects some 150 species of herbaceous plants, but is very destructive of sugar beet, bean and tomato. The virus kills young plants and leads to stunting and lower yields in older plants. Losses of sugar beet and tomatoes have been so severe as to cause cultication of these plants to be abandoned over wide areas. CTV is transmitted from plant to plant by the leafhopper *Circulifer tenellus*. The virus overwinters in infected weeds and other plants.

The leafhopper feeds on these plants in the winter and spring and then carries the virus to cultivated crops in late spring and summer, transmitting the virus from crop plant to crop plant as it feeds. The insect feeds by inserting its stylet mouthpart into the phloem or sap vessels of the plant; the virus enters by this route and then quickly spreads in the whole the plant and harms the phloem elements. The disease can be controlled by the use of insecticides against the leafhopper, but resistant varieties of sugar beet, tomato, bean and other crops have been developed.

Bacterial Blight of Rice

Rice is perhaps the most important crop for human beings. The large and growing populations of Asia are highly dependent on continued improvements in its productivity. Bacterial blight is widely prevalent in Asia and can devastate crops. Yield losses in severely infected fields usually range from 20-30 percent and many occasonally go even higher.

Bacterial blight was first observed in Japan in the latter part of the last century and the bacterial nature of the disease was identified there in the early part of this one. The causative organism is *Xanthomonas oryzae*. This bacterium can enter the growing plant in various different ways, ranging from mechanical injury through to entry via natural stomata. It also overwinters in a number of ways, either in a dry dormant form or in an active growing form in other plants. It is carried to the host plant by wind, rain insects, etc. On infection, spots start appearing on leaves, and infected leaves turn yellow, dry rapidly and then wither as the spots grow. Enormous attempts have been put into the development of resistant varieties of rice, work which began in Japan in the 1920s .

At the International Rice Research Institute more than 100 cultivars have been developed as sources of resistance to bacterial blight. Mechanisms for forecasting blight attacks, for instance by monitoring of the bacteriophage population (which increases in advance of the disease), are also widely used.

Black Stem Rust of Cereals

Wheat bears diverse environmental stresses -erratic rainfall and poor soil amongst others—and still produces stable, satisfactory yields. Epidemics of rust diseases can, however, cause severe crop losses. There are three forms of wheat rust disease-black (stem) rust, brown (leaf) rust and yellow (stripe) rust. The fungus *Puccinia graminis tritici* is the causative agent of black stem rust in wheat and also causes black rust in barley. Other *Puccinia* species cause concerned diseases in cereals such as oats and rye. The fungus has a complex life history which includes overwintering and alternation of hosts.

The chief characteristic, however, is the massive production of uredospores on the wheat plant: one estimate for a moderate infection of black rust was $4x10^{12}$ uredospores/day/hectare. These can travel extremely long distances on the wind and then be deposited, for instance by rain, to infect distant areas. It is known that there are occasional exchanges of spores between the very distant eastern and western wheat-growing areas of Australia, and there is regular infection of crops in New Xealand from Australia, 2,000 km away.

In the United States there is regular movement of uredospores over 4,000 km northwards to infect the growing crop and then a movement back to the southern wintering areas. In order to reduce crop losses large numbers of various cultivars are used in the United States. With the movement of spores over such vast distances, mathematical models, and even computer programs, have been developed so as to assist farmers in dealing with the arrival of clouds of potential infective agents. Much work has also been carried on resistance and the genetics of resistance in wheat. Other steps like the destruction of alternate hosts and chemical control regimes have also been employed.

Rice Blast

Rice blast disease has been documented for perhaps 200-300 years. It is known to occur in about 85 different countries. Yield losses during epidemics can go up to as much as 50-60 percent. The causative agent of rice blast disease is the fungus *Pyricularia oryzae*. The typical symptoms of infection are small, bluish, water-soaked flecks on leaves which rapidly enlarge. The lesions may join up to destroy entire leaves in susceptible varieties. The disease minimises the number of panicles and therefore grains that mature, and the total yield of the crop. Several toxins have been isolated from the pathogen and studies made of their role in the disease. The fungus overwinters in a number of different ways depending to an extent on climatic conditions. In the tropics conidia are present throughout the year, whereas in temperate regions the fungus can overwinter as a mycelium on straw.

Mature conidia become airborne and lodge mainly on the leaves of plants where they germinate in the thin film of water provided by rain or dew. The fungus then goes through a cycle of further conidia production on the rice plant and the conidia travel through the air to infect other plants. Again, mathematical models have been developed to assist in the prediction and control of infections. Great attempts have also been made to understand the different races of the fungus, and resistant strains and resistance genetics of rice itself. Breeding of resistance strains of rice has been under way for some years in various countries. Chemical control methods are also available to combat the fungus. As with the human diseases analysed previously, it is clear that some features, particularly of the two plant diseases that were weaponised in the US, fitted well with military requirements.

Both black stem rust and rice blast disease are caused by agents which are very well suited for widespread distribution and damage vital staple crops severely.

Animal Diseases

Whilst no animal diseases were weaponised in the US post-war offensive biological weapons programme, intensive studies were conducted on a number of diseases. Some of the available information is summarised in Table 5.7. It should also be observed that , as we shall see in a later section, the British developed a crude capability to retaliate with an anti-cattle anthrax weapon during the Second World War. It is therefore necessary, as with the human and plant diseases, to give a brief illustrative accounts of some of the more serious animal diseases in order to have a biological background for the discussion of the offensive weapons programmes conducted by major states.

Table 5.7
Illustrative Examples of Potential Anti-animal Agents

Disease	*Agent*	*Note*
Viruses		
Foot-and-mouth disease of cattle	FMD virus	
Rinderpest or cattle plague		Intensively studied in World War II
Newcastle disease of poultry	NDV	Intensively studied in World War II
Rickettsiae (Bacteria)		
Heart -water of sheep and goats	*Cowdria ruminanantium*	Tick carrier
Fungi		
Aspergillosis poultry	Aspergillus fumigatus	

Foot-and -Mouth Disease

Foot-and-mouth desease (FMD) is a highly contagious disease of cloven-hoofed animals (cattle, pigs, sheep, goats, etc.). It is caused by the FMD virus of the *Aphthovirus* genus of the Picomaviridae family. There are seven serotypes of the virus and no cross-immunity between the various kinds . Although the disease is of low lethality to adult animals, it does cause serious production losses and can have 50 percent lethality rates in young calves. Major regions of the world, especially North and Central America, and Australia, are free of the disease: Islands such as Japan and the UK are also free of the disease and it is on the decline in Europe. It is, however, enzootic in South America, the Middle East, Asia and Africa. Most wild cloven-hoofed animals, as also some other animal species, are susceptible. FMD is highly contagious. It is in fact one of the most contagious animal diseases known. Infected animals produce viruses from various sources, for example, exhaled air, saliva, milk, faeces and urine. Virus excretion starts one to five days before vesicles are found on the tongue, lips and feet. As antibodies build up the levels of virus excretion decline, but it can persist for weeks and some animals which recover may become long-termcarriers. Cattle appear to be most susceptible to airborne infection and pigs are thought to be major amplifires of the disease because they produce high concentrations of the virus in exhaled air.

There are, however, many other potential modes of transmission: from direct contact between animals, and since the virus can survive for many weeks in the environment, indirectly from contact with contaminated straw and manure. The virus is also known to have survived airborne transmission of at least tens of kilometres and to have begun infecting thereafter. It is hardly surprising that countries free of the disease take tough measure to keep it out and to deal with outbreaks vigorously if they do occur. In natural infections the incubation period is two to eight days, but it can be induced experimentally in a shorter time.

The first symptoms of the disease are fever, loss of appetite and cessation of milk production. Vesicles then develop, particularly areas around the mouth and the feet. The vesicles quickly rupture eading to painful ulcers. In cases without complications the ulcers heal over about ten days and the animal starts to eat a few days after the vesicles rupture. The lesions on the feet make the animal reluctant to move and may result in long-term damage. Foot-and -Mouth disease may be difficult to separate from a number of other infections. Collection and study of samples has also to be carried out with great care because of the readily transmissible nature of the virus.

Newcastle Disease

This disease infects both domestic and wild birds and causes gastrointestinal, respiratory and nervous problems. It is caused due to a virus of the Paramyxoviridae family and genus *Paramyxovirus*. Paramyxoviruses affecting birds have nine serogroups, of which Newcastle disease virus is A/PMV 1. The various strains of the disease virus vary widely in virulence and affect domestic fowls, turkeys, pheasants, etc. Ducks and geese are susceptible, but the disease is not much severe in these species. Newcastle disease is highly contagious with the virus being chiefly spread by direct or indirect contact. It is excreted in faeces and in exhaled air. Windborne transmission of the virus is possible and in affected areas there are important reservoirs of infection in wild birds. The incubation period can range from 2 to 15 days , but is generally five to six days. The effect of the disease is variable, depending for example on the virulence of the virus, the age of the bird and its immunological and health status.

In its most virulent form, viscerotropic velogenic (VVND), there is a sudden arrival and spread of the disease. Birds lose appetite and egg production drops sharply. Profuse bright green diarrhoea is common and rapid dehydration takes place. Many birds die within a day or two and mortality rates can exceed 90 percent. At death severe lesions are noticed in many internal organs.

Heartwater

This is a tick-borne rickettsial disease of ruminants. It is caused by *Cowdria ruminantium*, an obligate, intracellular, rickettsial parasite. Cattle, water buffalo, sheep, goats, and several species of wild ruminants are its natural hosts. The disease occurs mainly in Africa, south of the Sahara. It is transmitted by ticks of the genus *Amblyomma* which prefer wooded or bushy country to the open plain areas. The ticks pick up the *Cowdria* when they are larvae or nymphs and then transmit them to other animals. The incubation period for heartwater is between two weeks and a month. Sudden onset of high fever, followed by death within one to two days is possible. Mortality rates range from 10 to 100 percent. Animals affected many circle and charge objects. In acute cases death occurs within a week. Dead animals exhibit lung and other areas of oedema, and spleen and lymph nodes enlarged and congested. Again, as with human and plant diseases, a minimal acquaintance with the wide variety of possibilities indicates that any weapons designer intent on attacking animal production would have a wide range of choice.

Toxins

Though toxins are chemicals and not living organisms, it is important to review the possible use of toxins derived from living organisms as means of attack. Botulinal toxins, shellfish poison (saxitoxin) and staphylococcal enterotoxin are mentioned seriously in the literature.

Botulinal Toxins

The toxins developed by the bacterium *Clostridium botulinum* are much more poisonous than even nerve gases. They cause the food poisoning termed botulism and have been well-studied as potential warfare agents.

There are six types of toxin of which type has been the most seriously investigated. It is very easy to culture and harvest and can be stored in the form of a dry white powder without great loss of activity. However, the toxin does decay in air and is threfore not much more lethal when released as an aerosol than nerue gas. Other likely uses are for sabotage or as contamiinant for small arms munitions. Botulin poisoning rusults from interference with the normal transmission of impulses from nerves to muscles. Recovery from the poisoning provides some immunity and some protection by vaccination is possible, yet the lethal dose for the toxin is very small.

Shellfish Poison (Saxitoxin)

The planktonic dinoflagellate *Gonyaulax catanella* produces a toxin which can be accumulated by shellfish which feed on this source. If such shellfish are then eaten by human beings a severe form of poisoning results. During the 1950s procedures were developed for growing the toxin-producing organism and extracting the toxin at high yields. As a contaminant of small arms munitions, it was found to act much faster than botulin toxin.

Staphylococcal Enterotoxin

This is the causative toxin of the food poisoning which results from consumption of food contaminated with *Staphylococcus* bacteria. Again, simple methods have been developed to produce large amounts of toxin from strains of *Staphylococcus aureus*. This was designed to be used in a number of incapacitating weapons systems. Whilst toxins such as those described above are not biological warfare agents per se, there has been increasing interest in novel biological products in recent years. It is therefore necessary to include such products when condsidering future weapons systems and arms control measures.

Based on this outline of possible biological and toxin agents, we may now consider the major offensive biological weapons programmes which were in place before the signing of the Biological Weapons Convention.

6

Biological Warfare Agents

The destructive power of an effective biological warfare agents are extremely high Effectively employed, these agents are capable of wiping out a vast city in just one stroke. There lethal strength is far in excess of nuclear or chemical weapons .

'Anthrax, sprayed from the back of an aircraft on a cool, calm night, could take out all of Washington DC. This could cause up to three million fatalities compared to two million from a hydrogen bomb. This is how Dr Graham Pearson, former Director of the UK's biological defence establishment at Porton Down, reveals the destructive potential of biological versus nuclear weapons. In this chapter, we take a look at the agents of biological warfare, and how they are used as weapons. First of all, we should find out about just how dangerous they are.

Weapons of Mass Destruction (WMDs)

Biological weapons are, pound for pound, far more lethal than either nuclear or chemical weapons. Their killing potential is only exceeded by the most powerful nuclear weapons, i.e. H-bombs. An official American study made a comparison amongs the numbers of dead that would result from an attack with a nuclear weapon the size of the Hiroshima bomb (i.e. an explosive power equivalent to 12.5 kilotons of TNT, 300 kg of sarin nerve gas or 30 kg of anthrax spores. The Bomb would kill between 23,000 and 80,000 people; the nerv gas, 60 to 200; He anhrax, 30,000 to 100,000. These estimates were made based on a neither best nor worst case scenario. The study points out that if conditions were more favourable to chemical and biological warfare, those weapons are capable of killing even more. The difference between the lethality of biological and chemical weapons is large. According to Dr Jonathan Tucker, then of the US

Arms Control and Disarmament Agency: 'Inhalation of only about eight thousand spores of anthrax bacteria, weighing slightly less than a hundredth of a microgram [and a microgram is a millionth of a gram], results in an illness that is about 100 percet fatal within five days. This compares with an inhaled lethal dose for the nerve agent sarin of about milligram, or about one hundred thousand times greater. As a result, ten grams of anthrax spores, efficiently disseminated, could theoretically be as destructive as metric ton of sarin.

Biological weapons are also inexpensive. The cost of the casualties they cause is a tiny fraction of those from conventional or nuclear weapons or nerve gases. Anthrax is one of the most useful agents for biological weapons. However, there are at least 20 to 30 agents that are suitable to be used against human beings. They are caused by many types of micro-organisms.

Causative Micro-Organisms

Viruses are the simplest sort of micro- organisms. They are not able to reproduce by themselves but they colonise other cells, reprogramming them to produce more viruses. Some viruses spread when we cough or sneeze; and others are carried in blood or other body fluids. In people, viruses cause colds , AIDS herpes, chicken pox, flu, polio, hepatitis , yellow fever, smallpox, dengue fever and different of encephalitis.

In animals, they can cause foot-and- mouth desease in cattle, sheep and pigs, canine distemper, rabies, African swine fever, Newcastle disease in poultry, Rift Valley fever in cattle , sheep and goats, and vesicular stomatitis in cattle, horses and pigs. In plants they cause mosaic diseases in tobacco, tomatoes and soybeans, and sugar-beet curly top.

Bacteria are free-living organisms. Made up of only one cell, they are the smallest. Organisms that can reproduce themselves. Some kinds of bacteria can transfrom themselves into sporesa form which offers more resistence than usual to heat, cold and other environmental stresses. In general, bacteria cause illness in two ways: either by invading tissues or by producing toxins. Some do both. Bacteria can be killed by antibiotics. Bacterial toxins include botulinum, ricin, tetanus, diptheria shiga, which causes dysentery, and staphy lococcus enterotoxin (food poisoning). Bacterial diseases include anthrax, brucellosis cholera, glanders, melioidosis, pneumonic plague, tularemia and typhoid.

These diseases have been considered to be anti-personnel rather than anti-animal biological weapons, although the British also developed anthrax to attack cattle during World War Two. In plants, bacteria can cause rice and corn blight.

Rickettsia are a kind of mid-way between viruses and bacteria. They are bacteria but can only live inside host cells as viruses do. Insects such as lice, ticks, mice and leas carry them. Like bacteria, they are sensitive to antibiotics. In people, rickettsia cause typhus, Q fever, psittacosis and Rocky Mountain spotted fever. In animals, rickettsia cause heart-water in sheep and goats.

Fungi are larger and more complex organism than bacteria. They reproduce by forming spores. In people, fungi cause a lung infection known as coccidioidomycosis. In animals: fungi produce a mycotoxin (aflatoxin) which leads to the respiratory disease aspergillosis in poultry. In plants, fungi cause late blight in potato (which was responsible for the Irish potato famine), black stem rust in cereals, and rice blast.

These lists of diseases are not the only ones caused by the various micro-organisms. They are the ones found most suitable as biological warfare agents. But not all of them are equally suitable for weapons.

Suitability Factor

For a micro -organism to be suitable for use in biological war, a low dose of it should consistently produce a certain effect with a predictable incubation period. On dissemination it must be able to survive long enough to reach its target. The target population should have little or no immunity, and no access to treatment. The user should be able to safeguard their own troops and civilians. And the agents must be capable of mass production, stable storage and efficient dissemination. What then are the agents most commonly cited as suitable for biological warfare, and what influences would they probably they have? Further scientific developments will increase the numbers of agents suitable for use as biological weapons. While this is a worrying prospect, the traditional agents are quite enough to cause alarm. The following ones do not depend on any new science. They exist in nature and have been either weaponised or researched for biological weapons for as long as programmes have existed. They could be used to target people, animals and plants.

Targeting Mankind

The first five agents listed below were weaponised and stockpiled by the US before negotiation of the Biological Weapons Convention took place in1972. Anthrax is a disease which affects herbivorous animals but which can also infect people. The bacteria (*Bacillus anthacis*) can be introduced through the skin (in a cut, for instance), or through eating infected meat, or can be inhaled into the lungs. The cutaneous (skin) form huge black blisters and, if untreated with antibiotics, will result in death in 20 per cent of cases. Pulmonary anthrax is far more serious but requires a higher dose to develop. it results in toxaemia and septicaemia and death within 48 hours in almost100 per cent of cases. A vaccine has been developed but its efficacy against a heavy dose of pulmonary anthrax is not known. Antibiotics can be effective if the patient has earlier been vaccinated, but must be given inside a few hours of the onset of symptoms. The bacteria, which are easily produced in bulk, form spores which are resistant to heat and light and remain in the environment for decades. These spores would be sprayed in an aerosol if anthrax were to be used most effectively as a weapon.

(ii) **Tularemia** is found in rodents rabbits and hares. The causative agent (*Francisella tularensis*) can infect people through insect bites, contaminated water or food or by being breathed into the lungs. It is highly contagious: one bacterium is enough. After an incubation period of two to three days the symptoms are as that of pneumonia, and mortality varies according to the type of bacteria. It is highest-up to 40 per cent -in the USA vaccine is available, and recovery provides life-long immunity. The bacteria are easily produced and persist in the environment.

(iii) **Brucellosis** is an incapacitating disease which humans can catch from goats, cattle and pigs, usually by eating contaminated meat or milk. The patient is feverish for between a month and a year, and relapses can occur for many years. Mortality is low: between two and five per cent. There is no human vaccine.

(iv) **Q-fever** is also incapacitating. It is caused in humans by a bacterium called *Coxiella burnetii*, which is carried by various animals. After an incubation period of two to three weeks the patient develops a high temperature, intense headache and pneumonia. The mortality rate is low-one to four percent of cases- but the agent is hardy and very little of it is needed to cause the disease. Vaccination is available.

(v) ***Venezuelan*** *equine encephalomyelitis* is mainly a disease of horses, but insects can transfer it to human beings. After an incubation period of 4-20 days, it causes an influenza-type illness which lasts for up to a week. Mortality is low, but the causative virus is stable in an aerosol and highly infectious to humans when delivered through this route. A vaccine is available.

These agents were stockpiled by the US military before being destroyed between 1971 and 1973. Another agent analysed by the US in the 1950s is *Yersinia pestis*, the rod-shaped bacterium which is responsible for bubonic or pneumonic plague. Fleas carried by rats transmit the bubonic form. The pneumonic form from breathing the organisms in, and as they would almost certainly be delivered inaerosol form, pneumonic plague would most likely result from a biological warfare attack. After an incubation period of two or three days, victims develop symptoms like cough and develop pneumonia with high temperatures, chills and muscle pain. Harsh laboured breathing and death quickly follows. The condition is almost always fatal if antibiotics are not given within 24 hours of the onset of symptoms. There is no effective remedy or vaccine against pneumonic plague.

(vi) **Yellow fever** is caused by a virus normally spread through mosquitoes. It is highly infectious in aerosol form. Afther an incubation period of three to six days, the desease beings with fever, muscle aches, headache and nausea, and progresses through jaundice and black vomit to death for victims ranging between 20 and 70 per cent. Vaccination is widely available. People who survive are immune, but epidemics occur in populations who lack immunity.

Targeting Animals

These agents have not produced as much military interest as those effective against mankind, but the Americans studied all the following ones intensively during World War Two. This was also when the British readied for attacks against German cattle, although with anthrax rather than the agents listed below.

(i) **Foot- and -mouth** is an extremely contagious disease of cloven-hoofed animals (cattle, pigs, sheep etc). After an incubation period of two to eight days, infected animals develop painful ulcers that last for about ten days on the tongue, lips and feet. The disease causes large production losses and may kill up to 50 per cent of calves infected. The virus which causes it is hardy and can persist in hay for weeks or months together.

(ii) **Newcastle disease** affects birds and is also highly contagious. The incubation period is generally five to six days, after which various symptoms like loss of appetite, plummeting egg production, green diarrhoea and dehydration appear. Mortality can exceed 90 per cent.

(iii) **Heart-water** affects ruminants (cattle, water buffalo, sheep, goats etc) and is carried by ticks. It occurs mainly in Africa, south of the Sahara. The incubation period is two to four weeks, after which infected animals develop high fever and can die in about a week. Mortality can be as high as 100 per cent.

Targeting Plants

Staple crops form major targets for economic warfare. The first two of the following agents were stockpiled but not weaponised by the US. All have been analysed as potential BW agents.

(i) **Rice blast** is caused by a fungus (*Pyricularia oryzae*) which survives in a number of ways, depending on climate, and can be widely disseminated. It causes small, bluish flecks on the leaves, which rapidly enlarge and may kill entire leaves. The number or rice grains that mature goes down, and yield loss go up to as high as 60 per cent

(ii) **Black stem rust** attacksreals—wheat, barley, oats and rye- and causes croplosses of up of to 90 per cent. The fungus (*Puccinia graminis tritici*) that causes it in wheat forms huge amounts of spores, which can be blown for enormous distances: for instance 4,000 km from the west to the east of Australia. Both for black stem rust and for rice blast, computer programmes have been developed to try to foretell the spreal of the disease, to help farmers combat it. Understanding the genetics of resistance in rice and wheat has been another line of defence against it and the rice blast.

(iii) **Sugar beet curly top** is a disease of herbaceous plants which devastates sugar beet, bean tomato. It is spread by a leafhopper, which transmits the causative virus while feeding. Resistant varieties of sugar beet, bean and tomato have been developed.

(iv) **Bacterial blight of rice** is widespread in Asia where it causes yied up to 30 per cent. It is carried by wind, rain or insects, and causes infected leaves to turn yellow and wither. In this case also, resistant strains of rice have been developed.

TOXINS

The first two toxins of those listed below were weaponised by the US after the Second World War, the third was produced there in developmental quantities during the War.

(i) Botulinum toxins are the most toxic compounds known. A mere thousandth of a millionth of a gram per kilogram of body weight of the type called strain A is enough to kill a human being. That makes it 15,000 times more toxic than the nerve gas VX and 100,000 times more toxic than the nerve gas sarin. Produced by the bacterium *Clostridium botulinum,* the toxin is a white crystalline substance that easily dissolves in water when finely powdered. It could be used in an aerosol attack (although it decays in air and loses much of its toxicity very fast), or to contaminate food in which it causes the poisoning known as botulism. Symptoms begin with nausea, diarrhoea, dizziness and weakness, and progress through double vision, choking mucus and laboured breathing to convulsions and death. An antitoxin, if given before the onset of symptoms (i.e. before 24 hours has elapsed), is effective against inhaled botulinum.

(ii) Staphylococcal enterotoxin B is a highly toxic incapacitant, low doses of which cause poisoning which lasts for one to two weeks. Most patients would recover, but the toxin can be lethal for some. It is relatively stable in aerosol form and could also be ingested in food, or freeze-dried to produce a white, fluffy material that dissolves easily in water-making it sutable for poisoning small volume water supplies. Three to twelve hours after inhaling the toxin, victims suddenly develop symptoms like fever, headache, chills, a cough, nausea, vomiting and diarrhoea. There is no human vaccination against *SEB* but various candidates are in development stage.

(iii) **Shellfish poison**, also known as saxitoxin, is made by certain algae including some types of plankton. Shellfish that feed on them are highly poisonous. People who eat the shellfish develop symptoms ten minutes-four hours afterwards: tingling numbness in the mouth, muscular weakness, decreasing muscular co-ordination, paralysis and death. The toxin is readly produced and is soluble in water. Estimates of the lethal dose via ingestion range from 0.2 mg to 4 mg; but only one-tenth of this is required to cause death by injection. In that case-say on a rifle-fired flechette, which can penetrate the skin with a hardly noticeable sting-death can occur in 15 minutes.

(iv) **Ricin** is made from castor beans. In its crystalline form its toxicity is similar to that of saxitoxin. Its effect is delayed by 12-24 hours, but it produces fever, collapse in blood pressure and death.

Making Agents into Weapons

All of the agents considered above have to be made into weapons before they can be employed in biological warfare. The kinds of weapons used depend on the way the disease is spread.

Spreading of Disease

As the lists above shows there are various ways of spreading these agents of disease. They may be dispersed in the atmosphere, added to food or water, or injected by objects or by insects. Whatever the method used they must first be stabilised in liquid suspensions or alternatively freeze dried and kept in powdered form. When biological weapons were first being developed, they were dispersed into the air in an aerosol produced when a bomb exploded. This is still an option-for example, Iraq had such weapons ready to fire in the 1991 Gulf War. Aerosols can also be produced by spray units, which can be fitted to aircraft if a large area is to be covered or can be as small as paint or even scent sprayers for a localised attack. As Dr Graham Pearson has observed : "We need to always remember that effective dissemination can be achieved through relatively simple spray systems. A simple paint sprayer can produce particles of the right size very effectively.

The effect actually obtained depends on many factors. To start with, the particles of agent have to survive their journey to the lung. Different particles have different sensitivities, but some will be killed in the explosion if they are dispersed from a bomb, or in a sprayer. A number of factors affect their survival: temperature, light, humidity and air pollutants. Unsuitable weather can lessen the effect of aerosolised agents to great extent.Clear nights with little wind are reckoned to be best: they allow the aerosol cloud to remain reasonably concentrated. There is then more chance that anyone caught in it will breathe in the required dose.

For this is another factor that has to be taken into consideration: the agent will only cause the condition if enough of it is taken in. Different diseases need different doses because biological agents differ in their ability to cause illness or death. Half of one ounce of botulinal toxin would in principle be enough to kill 350 million people, although in practice its loss of toxicity in an aerosol would reduce its lethality. The lethal dose of anthrax spores nearly eight thousand-would easily fit on the full stop at the end of this sentence. One gram of anthrax could, if distributed effectively, kill more than 100 million people. In practice, however, it would not be distributed optimally and would not kill as many. Other diseases need fewer bacteria: one single bacterium can cause tularemia. Agents will inevitably die or lose their virulence when they are released into the atmosphere.

World Health Organisation experts have estimated different decay rates for different agents in an aerosol cloud. If the agents have been produced in a particular manner to protect them from environmental conditions, experts tell us that the agents that cause Q-fever will decay at a rate of ten percent per minute; those that cause yellow fever at 30 per cent per minute; tularemia and plague, 2 percent per minute; and anthrax, 0.1 percent per minute. The particles also have to be of the optimumn size to be breathed in and kept in the lungs: between 1 and 5 microns (1-5 millionths of a metre) is most efficient. Aerosolisation is the most difficult (if also the most dangerous) process of spreading agent; but the difficulties are not always considered insuperable.

Contaminating Food and Water

The other means of administering biological agents is by the way of contaminating food or water. The virus which causes foot-and -mouth disease in cattle, say, could be fed to them on hay. People's food can be poisoned with micro-organisms which attack the digestive organs (e.g. *Salmonella*). A phial of these agents could be added to food during production, distribution or during other moments of the consumer chain. Nearly all micro-organisms are destroyed by heat, but if they are added later in the production process the food provides a good environment for them to survive and for some to even produce toxins. Food poisoning can be immediately incapacitating-attested to by airline crews having to eat different meals-and even fatal. In 1996, the bacterium E.coli 0157 was blamed for outbreaks of food poisoning in Japan, where it killed eleven people and caused illness to other 10,000 and Scotland, where it killed 17 people and made more than 100 ill.

Urban water supplies in developed countries are less vulnerable than might be considered to contamination. Although reservoirs contaminated with disease-causing agents could theoretically poison large sections of populations, they are protected not only with chlorine and filters, but also by the sheer volume of water they supply. Any agent added would be so diluted as to probably cause little harm. Smaller volume supplies, as also untreated supplies and wells, are more vulnerable.

Trasmission of Disease

Some infections are transmited by insescts: bubonic plague by fleas, spotted typhus by fleas and lice, malaria by mosquitoes. These then is another possible ways of dispersing biological agents. In this case the weapon is a container for the insects plus a delivery system for taking them to the target area. The difficulties of making sure that the insects find their targets made this an unreliable method, but it could still have large effects.

A computer simulation imagines a fishing boat with a crew of three men saving some refugees, who die from exposure before the boat reaches port. Unknown to the crew, the refugees have been infected with bubonic plague but have not yet revealed the symptoms. The crew, who are bitten by the plague-carrying fleas, carry the infection back to their village of 400 people. In six days, 250 villagers have come down with the disease. An agent will infect the largest number of people if it is aerosolised, and national programmes have focussed on this method of dispersion. So far, non-national groups have not been able to straddle the hurdles that aerosolisation sets up, and they have found it most effective in order to introduce the agent to the victim directly, either injecting it or contaminating food. But this state of affairs is not expected to last. This is why the terrorist threat is becoming so real.

7

Toxin Weapons: Changing Status

Toxin agents have the features like high toxicity, availability and stability. They are posisonous substances produced by living organism. Antibiotic are needed by making use of toxins. These are various living organisms which produce toxing.

The Renewed Military Interest

Toxins have heen considered as poisonous substances produced by living organisms. This definition applies independent of whether the toxin in question is in fact produced by an organism or by chemical synthesis. Toxins which inhibit the growth of and/or kill bacteria are usually designated as antibiotics, even if they are also toxic for animal cells.

Toxins are produced by various different living organisms.

Table 7.1 Classification of Selected Toxins According to their Producing Organisms

Producer	*Toxin*
Bacteria (Including their episomes, plasmids, and viruses)	
Bacillus anthracis	Anthrax toxin[a]
Clastridium botulinum	Botulin A,B,C,D,E
C. tetani	Tetanus toxin
Corynebacterium diphtheria	Diphtheria toxin[b]
Escherichia coli	heat-labile enterotoxin LT[a]
	heat-stable enterotoxin ST.[a]
Pseudomonas aeruginosa	Exotoxin A
Shigella dysenteriae	*Sh. dysenteriae toxin*
Staphylococcus aureus	*Staph.* enterotoxin A,B,C,D,E
Streptococcus pyogenes	Erythrogenic toxin[a]
Vibrio cholerae	Cholera toxin
Anabacna flos aquac[d]	Anabaena toxin

Producer	Toxin
Aphanizomenon flos-aquae[d]	Aphanizomenon toxin
Microcystis (Anacystis) cyaned[d]	Microcystin
PROTOZOA (Dinoflagellida)	
Gonyaulax catanella[d]	Saxitoxin ('shellfish poison')
Gymnodinium brevi	Red tide toxin (Gbt X)
FUNGI	MYCOTOXINS
Aspergillus flavus	Aflatoxin B_1, B_2, G_1, G_2 , etc.
A. parasiticus	
Fusarium spec.	Trichothecenes
F. episphaeria	Fusarenon-X
	Nivalenol
F. lateritium	T_2 toxin
F. nivale	Diacetylnivalenol
	Fusarenon-X
	Nivalenol
F. oxysporum	Diacetylnivalenol
	Fusarenon-X
	T_2 toxin
F. ridiusculum	Neosolaniol
	T_2 toxin
F. roseum	Diacetoxyscirpenol
	Diacetylnivalenol
	Fusarenon-X
	HT_2 toxin
	Neosolaniol
	Nivalenol
	T_2 toxin
F. solani	HT_2 toxin
	Neosolaniol
	T_2 toxin
F. tricinctum	*HT_2 toxin*
	Neosolaniol
	T_2 toxin
F. viride	*T_2 toxin*
PLANTS	
Abrus precatorius	*Abrin*
Adenia digitata	*Modeccin*
Ricinus (castor bean)	*Ricin*

Producer	Toxin
COELENTERATA	
Seawasp, box jellyfish *(Chironex fleckeri)*	Seawasp toxin
Soft corals *(Palythoa)*	Palytoxin
MOLLUSCA	
Mytilis californianus[e]	
Mytilis edulis[e]	
Saxidomus giganteus[e]	Saxitoxin (shellfish poison)
Spisula solidissima[e]	
and other mussels[e]	
Fish-hunting cone snails	
(Conus geographus, C. magus)	a-Conotoxins and other
Conotoxins	
AMPHIBIA	
Californian newt *(Taricha torosa)*	Tarichatoxin
Columbian frog *(Phyllobates aurotaenia)*	Batrachotoxin
REPTILIA	
Chinese cobra *(Naja naja atra)*	Cobrotoxin
South-American rattle snake *(Crotalus durissus terrificus)*	Crotoxin
Formosan snake *(Bungarus multicinctus)*	alpha-bungarotoxin beta-bungarotoxin
FISHES	
Deadly death pufferfish *(Arothron hispidus)*	Tetrodotoxin
White-spotted pufferfish *(Arothron meleagris)*	Tetrodotoxin

[a] plasmid-coded
[b] phage-coded.
[c] resides on a transposon.
[d] cyanobacteria, formerly designated as blue-green algae.
[e] mussels, i.e. shellfish, become poisonous and cause 'shellfish poisoning' by ingestion of Gonyaulax catanella.
[f] said to be identical to tetrodotoxin.

Owing to such features as their toxicity Table 7.2, availability and stability toxins are known and/or suspected to be of military interest as toxin warfare (TW) agents or toxin weapons Table 7.3. As toxins act faster than biological agents, they have potentially greater military utility. If biological weapons were used in combat, said Theodore Gold (who until recently headed the Pentagon's chemical programmes), toxins would be their probable form. Moreover, toxins are considered to be sabotage weapons, and the fear is often expressed tnat some toxins might be used by terrorists. The degree of toxicity (in terms of LD_{50}) is not always the deciding factor for the military use of toxins, however. For instance, staphylococcal enterotoxin B (the type of staphylococcal enterotoxin easiest of many to obtain in large amounts), is only moderately toxic.

Nevertheless it is of great military interest (and was weaponized by the US Army, Anderson & King , 1983,) as it is supposed to be a powerful incapacitating agent, Staphylococcal enterotoxins induce symptoms of food poisoning which are extremely debilitating. Therefore, in cases of staphylococcal enterotoxins and other incapacitating toxins, the mean illness dose for 50 per cent of subjects (the ID_{50}) is a more relevant military factor than the LD_{50} value (Table 7.2) various quite different toxins have been analysed by the US Army even though they are of little importance for military.

Table 7.2. Selected Toxins Classified as to LD_{50}

Toxin	*More-sensitive species*	*Less-sensitive species* LD_{50} *(ng/kg)*
Botulin	0.6 (guinea pig)[a]	10 (man)[a]
Shigella dysenteriae toxin	0.9 (rabbit)[a]	>9000 (guinea pig)[a]
Tetanus toxin	<2.5 (man)[a]	7 (Mouse)[a]
Abrin	40 (mouse)[b]	
Staphylococcus a toxin	50 (mouse)[g]	1300 (rabbit)[a]
Batrachotoxin A	100 (mouse)[c]	
Ricin	100 (mouse)[b]	
Diphtheria toxin	≤100 (man)[a]	200000 (mouse)[a]
Palytoxin	150 (mouse)[c]	
Saxitoxin	200 (mouse)[c]	
Staphylococcus enterotoxin A(SEA)[k]	1300 (rabbit)[a]	60000 (mouse)[a]
Staphylococcus enterotoxin B(SEB)[7]	6000 (rabbit)[d]	
Tetrodotoxin	8000 (mouse)[1]	
Scorpion toxins III.IV[m]	20000 (chicken)[c]	
Anthrax toxin (LF+PA)	<114000 (rat)[a]	
Aflatoxin B_1	300000 (rabbit)[a]	40000000 (mouse)[i]
Diacetoxyscirpenol	376000 (swine)[h]	23000000 (mouse)[h]

Toxin	More-sensitive species	Less-sensitive species LD_{50} (ng/kg)
T_2 toxin	1210000 (swine)[h]	10,500000 (mouse)[h]
Fusarenon X (4-acetyl In ivalenol)	3400 000 (mouse)[t]	4600 000 (rat)[h]
Nivalenol	4100 000 (mouse)[h]	
HT_2 toxin	7200 000 (chicken)[h]	9000 000 (mouse)[h]
Diacetyenivalenol	9600 000 (mouse)[h]	
Neosolaniol	14500 000 (mouse)[h]	24 900000 (chicken)[h]

*Further data are compiled by Gill (1982) and USA (1982c).

[a]USA. 1982_C.

[b]Olsnes *et al.* 1974

[c]Franke, 1977.

[d]Notermans & Dufrenne, 1982.

[c]Watt & Simard. 1984.

[i]Hayes, 1981.

[g]Bornheimer & Schwartz. 1963.

[h]USA, 1983 a.

[i]Busby & wogan. 1981a.

[i]ID_{50} (mean illness dose for 50% of subjects) of *Sh. dysenteriae* toxin for monkeys and presumably humans -2 ng/kg (Olsnes & Eiklid 1984).

ID_{50} of SEA for man 130 ng/kg (Beisel, 1976).

ID_{50} of SEA for man 150 ng/(Beisel, 1976).

[m]Isolated from scoron (*Centruroides sculpturatus*) venom.

little importance for military. Thus the US Department of Defense supports studies on *Pseudomonas exotoxin* A. According to a spokesman for the US Army Medical Research Institute of Infectious Diseases, *Pseudomonas exotoxin* A was never regarded seriously as a biological warfare agent. Nevertheless, such toxins can be used as models to analysis the action mechanisms of more potent toxins. Some substances produced by living organisms act as algogens, that is substances that carry pain.

Algogens of military importance are found among quite differrent groups of chemical substances. Among algogens of plant and animal origin, some polypetides (such as substance P, uradikinine, collidin, histamine-releasing factors) are of special singificance.

Table 7.3. Putative TW Agents Having the Highest for Operational Use

Toxin	*1940*[a]	*1956*[b]	*1969*[c]	*1983-5*[d]
Abrin			+[e]	
Aflatoxin				+
Algal toxin with low molecular weight[f]				+
Batrachotoxin				
Botulin (A)	+	+	+	+
Coral toxins with low molecular weight[i]				+
Ricin				+[g]
Saxitoxin				+
Seawasp (box jellyfish) toxin				+
Stapylococcus entrotoxin (B)		+	+	+
Tetanus toxine[i]				
Tetrodotoxin	+			
Trichothecene mycotoxins e.g.				+
Diacetoxyscirpenol (DAS)				+
Diacetylnivalenol				+
Fusarenon-X (4-acetylnivalnialenol)				+
HT_2 toxin				+
Neosolaniol				+
Nivalenol				+
Rc toxin				+
Rd toxin				+
T_2 toxin				+

[a]Japanese BW resarch activities during 1935-45 (USA,1947b).

[b]USA, 1956.

[c]USA, 1969,p. 42; WHO, 1970.

[d]Anderson & King, 1983 ; if no other reference is given.

[e]SIPRI, 1971a, p. 126. Abrin acts like ricin (Olsnes & Pihl, 1982[a])

In an advertisement , the US Army refers to blue-green algae toxins (i.e. toxins produced by organisms now designated as 'cyanobacteria') (USA, 1984b). Microcystin (Zoler, 1985) and other potent cyanobactlrial toxins are produced by Microcysits(Anacystis), cyanea, Anadbaena flos aquae and Aphanizomenon flos-aquae (Encyclopaedia, 1985b, p.902).

[g]USA, 1984b.

[h]Perera, 1985. seawasp toxin might be indentical coral toxins'.

[u]Franke, 1977.

[i]Soft corals of the genus *Palythoa* produce palytoxin, a non- proteinaceous neurotoxin (Dubis & Cohen, 1977).

Some algogens may be so potent that exposure to them can cause death. Nevertheless they are discussed mainly in the context of sabotage weapons or agents that might be used by terrorists. Concomitantly with the renewed military interest in conventional weapons and in CBW agents dealt with elsewhere, TW agents have grown in importance during the last decade.

A comparison of the data from the open literature reveals a dramatic increase of interest in TW agents by the military (see table 7.3) . Whereas both Japanese and US CBW research workers considered only two toxins as putative TW agents during 1940-60 , in the 1980s some 20 toxins were considered as such. This change, which parallels the marked increase of interest in viruses as BW agents seems to have been caused by various factors:

Several toxins have been found to be more than organophosphorus compounds and other chemical poisons Table 7.4. One molecule of the A chain of ricin in its cytoplasm is sufficient to kill a cell. Because of their high potency, the weight of toxic munitions required to cover a given area would be lower than the corresponding need for standard chemical munitions;Toxins are of particular concern; held the Chemical Warfare Review Commission convened by US President Ronald Reagan, 'becaause they can be developed to be hundreds of times more lethal than agents in existing munitions. For instance, this is the case for staphylococcal enterotoxins, which were described by the US Army as 'particulary attractive as agents because much less enterotoxin is needed to produce incapacitation as compared to standard CW agents.

(ii) Growth achieved in the field of micro-encapsulation might make aerosol distribution of TW agents more feasible technically. Numerous toxins, such as botulinum toxin, are said to be even more effective in aerosol form than if the same dose were taken orally.

Thus, distribution of toxins by aerosolized micro-capsules is well understood.

(iii) A large number of new toxins possessing high levels of toxicity have been discovered among them are more than 300 different mycotoxins Table 7.2.

Table 7.4
Comparison of the Lethality of Selected CW and TW Agents

Poisons	LD_{50} *(ng /kg)*[a,b]	*Toxins*
	2[c]	*Sh. dysenteriae* toxin
	<2.5[c]	Tetanus toxin
	10[c]	Botulin
	40	Abrin
	≤100[e]	Batrachotixin
	<100	Diphtheria toxin
	100	Ricin
	130[d]	*Staphylococcus* alpha toxin
	150	Palytoxin
	200	Saxitoxin
Dioxin	600[t]	
	8,000	Tetrodotoxin
VX	20000 / 30 000[g]	
Soman	100000 /- 700 000[f]	
Sarin	200000[f] /-1500 000[g]	
	300 000	Aflatoxin B_1
	376 000	Diacetoxyscirpenol
Tabun	400 000 /-3000 000[g]	
	1210 000	T_2 toxin
	3400 000	Fusarenon-X

[a]In animals, if no other information is given.

[b]See table 7.2.

[c]In man.

[d]ID_{50}

[e]Schwetz *et al* , 1973.

[f]In mice (Perry Robinson, 1985b).

[g]Estimated value in man, lower dose (Vojvodic, 1982).

4. Since toxins are produced by livzing organisms, their synthesis is controlled by genes directly (proteinaceous toxins) or indirectly (low-molecular weight toxins). Such genes, designated as tox genes, are accessible to technique of genetic engineering just as other genetic deteriminants are. Modern methods of genetic engineering cell procedures, protein engineering and immune techniques make it possible to produce large amounts of toxins and to develop derivatives therefrom.

5. The different methods make it possible to develop protective

and prophylactic means decreasing an aggressor's risk of being known as harmed by his own TW agents. The growing interest in research on TW agents, ostensibly for peaceful purposes, which is not for bidden by the Biological weapons. Convention but which might lead to results that can also be used for offensive purposes, is alarming various authors mention that at least in the USA new military interests in research on TW agents have been seen in recent years. For instance the US Army sought investigators interested in using genetic engineering to study acetylcho linesterase, the target not only of organophosphorus compounds but also of some neurotoxins. A minimum of six research projects introducing the gene encoding acetylcholinesterase into bacteria were funded by the US Department of Defense. Moreover, in advertisements the US Army has asked for 'proposals for research in low molecular weight toxins of military importance like' (a) trichothecene mycotoxins (T-2, DAS, nivalenol) and their metabolites, (b) sodium channel blocker agents (saxitoxin and tetrodotoxin), (c) other toxins of marine origin, (d) blue-green algae toxins, and (e) other low-molecular-weight oxins of plant and animal origin (such as ricin) which are of military importance in biological warfare defence' (USA, 1984b). Simultaneously US Secretary of Defense, Caspar Weinberger, and *The Wall Street Journal* in a series which later came to be-heavily criticized, repeatedly alleged that the USSR and other socialist states had developed and employed a chemical warfare agent[1] yellow[2] rain containing mycotoxins of the trichothecene type[3]. These charges were not only opposed to declarations by the USSR (UN, 1982), but could not be independently substantiated. A detailed investigaion done by a multidisciplinary group of researchers concluded it was highly probable that 'the origin of the alleged chemical agent... the yellow rain...is a phenomenon of nature, not of man (Seeley *et al*, 1985). These allegations have lead to increased interest by military researchers in trichothecenes and in other mycotoxins.

Mycotoxins

Mycotoxins are low-molecular-weight-non proteinaceous compounds produced by moulds. They are capable of causing illness or death upon ingestion, skin contact Dr inhalation. The disease caused by them are mycotoxicoses which differ form mycoses in as much as fungal growth in the host organism is not necessary for expression of the symptoms. Mycotoxicoses first came to light in the early 1960s when the acute liver disease among poultry in the UK, the turkey 'X' disease, could be attributed to aflatoxin. Mycotoxins are increasingly discussed as potential TW agents. They exhibit great stability and heat resistance. Mycotoxins are not easy to detect, to identify, and to decontaminate. Deseases caused by them are difficult to diagnose and to treat. There are two major groups of myctotoxins: *aflatoxins* and *trichothecenes*.

Aflatoxins

Aflatoxins are low-molecular-weight, non-proteinaceous compounds (highly substituted coumarins containing a fused dihydrofurofuran moiety). These are produced by *Aspergillus flavus and A. parasiticus* Forur major aflatoxins (AFs) are known: aflatoxins B_1, B_2, G_1 and G_2 and G_2, AFB_1 is the most potentt toxin, being acutely toxic to numerous organisms. The toxic dose for humans has not been established, but the levels of aflatoxin found in food suspected of causing reported toxic outbreaks in humans are known. AFB_1 is the most potent hepatocarcinogen cincl one of the most potent mytagens known AFB_1 and also the other aflatoxins, seem to act predominantly via inhibition of DNA and RNA synthesis, thus inhibiting protein synthesis as well Table 7.5. Other cell structurres and functions are targets of aflatoxins as well.

Trichothecenes

Trichothecenes, are chemically related low-molecular-weight mycotoxins produced by difference species of *Fusarium* and several othe moulds. In addition, synthesis of trichothecenes with some other organisms cannot be ruled out. At least one trichothecene compound, baccharin, is produced by a higher plant *Baccharis megapotamica* (Asteraceae).

Table 7.5

Mechanisms of Action and Targets of Selected Toxins

Cardiotoxin	Sea wasp toxin
Dermatoxins	Diacetoxyscirpenol Fusarenon-X Nivalenol T_2 toxin
Hepatotoxins	Aflatoxin B_1 G_1
Neurotoxins	Batrachotoxin Botulin Alpha- Bungarotoxin Conotoxins Microcystin and other cyanobacteiral toxins Palytoxin Red tide toxin (GbTx) Saxitoxin (*Shigella dysenteria toxin*)[a] Tetanus toxins Tetrodotoxin
Inhibition of nucleic acid synthesis	Aflatoxins
Inhibition of protein synthesis	Abrin Diptheria toxin Modeccin *Pseudomonas aeruginosa* exotoxin A Ricin *Shigella dysenteria toxin* Trichothecenes
Interference with regulation	Anthrax toxin Cholera toxin *Escherichia coli* enterotoxins LT,ST Seaphyloco enterotoxins A,B
Membrane-damaging	Staphylococcal haemolytic taxins.

Note:

[a] The neurologial symptoms caused by *Shigella dysenteria toxin,* which is often designated as '*Shigella dysenteria neurotoxin*', appear to be secondary to toxic effects on endothelial cells in the spinal cord.

Inexcess of 50 different trichothecenes have been identified so far which fall into five structural categories:

(i) Hydroxyl-or acyl-subsitituted trichothecenes;

(ii) 8-keto trichothecenes;

(iii) 7,8-epoxytrichothecenes;

(iv) Verrucarins and roridins; and

(v) 7,8-epoxyroridins.

Several of the trichothecenes are acutely potent toxins in mammals. Some of them also several antifungal and phytotoxic properties. Their primary effect is considered to be the inhibition of protein synthesis by interference with several steps of this process.

Neurotoxic Substances

In relation to their action mechanisms and to their targets in susceptible cells and organisms, toxins can be subdivided into various classes. Militarily important toxins are either neurotoxins interacting with structures and /or functions of the nervous system, such as organophosphorus compounds hepatotoxins, cardiotoxins, or dermatoxins table 7.5. Most toxins interfere with macromolecular synthesis either by inhibition of replication or expression of the genetic material.

Gene expression is inhibited by interference with either transcription of DNA (messenger-RNA production] or with protein synthesis. Trichothecenes are some of the highly potent inhibitors of protein synthesis. Other substances (anthrax toxin, cholera toxin) disturb regulation of gene expression and activity of gene products by altering regulatory proteins (e.g. adenylate cyclase and guanylate cyclase).

Owing to the existence of several different targets, combinations of differently acting toxins might exhibit synergistic effects. Almost nothing has been published with respect to this. There is only one report of synergistic lethal effect in mice when aflatoxin B_1 and T_2 trichothecene toxin were applied jointly in acute toxicity trials. These experiments were conducted with a rather small number of animals, however, and the results are yet to be confirmed. *Staphylococcus aureus* exotoxins have also been reported to enhance the toxicity of *Escherichia coli*. In this connection it should be mentioned that anthrax toxin consists of three protein components which act in binary combinations (sic) to produce two distinct toxic effects, oedema in skin and lethality.

One could wonder, therefore, whether this and possibly other similar toxins might be developed into 'binary TW agents like the binary chemical weapons known so far.

Neurotoxic agents are generally said to act as inhibitors of *acetylcholinesterase*. In fact, just small number of neurotoxins interact directly with this particular enzyme. Instead, as the results of molecular- neurobiological studies suggest, there are various different specific targets for neurotoxins. Examination of the structure and functions of the nervous system are therefore supported by military agencies, because knowledge of the nervous system might help one realize such projects as: (a) tailor-making new neurotoxic agents; (b) a target- directed search for agents reacting with pre-selected structures and or functions; or (c) the development of effective antidotes and protective and prophylactic procedures.

Genetic Engineering and Research

Toxins are generated by living organisms and their production is encoded, directly or indirectly in specific genes. Some toxins are peptides or polypeptides table directly encoded in *tox* genes. Some oligomeric or compound proteinaceos toxins having different polypeptide subunits are encoot in a single gene, whose single polypeptide product is cleaved after synthesis into two or more different parts (e.g. botulinum toxin, tetanus toxin). Other oligomeric toxins are encoded in various *tox* genes, whose products are assembled after synthesis. Non-proteinaceous, low-molecular-weight toxins are usually products of the cell's intermediary metabolism. They are synthesized by the tandem action of several enzymes, that is by geve products not encoded in *tox* genes. *Tox* genes, as well as genes coding for enzymes responsible for the synthesis of low-molecular-weight toxins, and/or their products are subject to manipulation by genetic engineering and/or by protein engineering.Genetic engineering allows for the identification of such genes, their separation from othe (tox) genes, their multiplication (cloning) and their transfer into other host cells.

Recipients for tox gene transfer might be cells lacking the proteolytic enzymes found in different pathogenic bacteria. Such enzymes are responsible for degradation of toxins, and their presence in cells that poduce toxins has made detailed investigations of toxins highly difficult in the past. Thus, genetic engineering can facillitate analyses of the structures and functions of toxins.

Moreover, *tox* genes and other genes of TW interest may be transferred to other sites within he genome of one and the same cell to achieve higher and or unregulated gene expression. These genes, on the other hands, may be transferred to other host cells either to enhance toxin production or to establish a toxin mass production system which can be more easily handled by industrial microbiologists. For instance, *spe*A gene encoding type A streptococcal exotoxin (erythrogenic toxin) has been transferred to E. *coli* and to *Streptococcus sanguis* (Challis). This resulted in *Str. sanguis* transformants that secreted the type A exotoxin. Heterologous transfer of such geve should be especially easier if they are already located on extrachromosomal genetic elements which then can be used [1]as natural gene vectors.

Table 7.6
Composition of Elected Toxins

Toxin	Molecular weight	Remarks	Reference
LOW MOLECULAR- WEIGHT SUBSTANCES			
Aflatoxins	310-330		
1			
Batrachotoxin	399	Chemical synthesis possible	2
Saxitoxin	370	Chemical synthesis possible	2
Tetrodotoxin	319	Chemical synthesis possible	2
Trichothecenes	250-550	Some analogues synthesized	3
PEPTIDES AND POLYPEPTIDES			
Conotoxins	1500-3000	Some have been synthesized chemically	25
Alpha- Bungarotoxin	8000		4
Anthrax toxin (PA, LF,EF)	8500; 83000; 89000	PA and LF genes cloned PA+LF, andPA+EF act together without being covalently bound	5
Cobrotoxin	6800		2
Botulinum neurotoxin type E	150 000	Sequence analysed in part	
Diphtheria toxin	62000	Becomes activated by cleavage into fragments A+B toxgene cloned and sequenced	7, 8, 23
Escherichia coli enterotoxin ST	8000	Gene cloned and sequenced	9
Pseudomonas aeruginosa exotoxin A	60000		8
Staphylococcus enterotoxins	27500(SEL)	ent A gene cloned and sequenced in a part ent B gene cloned and Sequenced Enterotoxin C_1 sequencced	22

Staphylococcus haemolytic toxin	26000-39000	a- toxin gene cloned and sequenced	20
Streptococcus exotoxin A	spe A gene cloned		11
MULTIMERIC PROTEINS			
Abrin	65000	2 different chains	12
Botulinum neurotoxin type A	H: 100 000; L:50 000	I polypeptide split into 2 chains; sequences analysed in part	13,14
Cholera toxin	A_1: 23 500; A_2 5 500 B : 11 600 84000	one single ctx opern, cloned and sequenced A polypepude split in 1 A1 +A2	15
Escherichia coli enterotoxin LT	A: 25 500; B: 11 500	2 genes of I operon, cloned and sequenced !A +5B chians	16
Ricin	6200	2 different chains sequenced	17-18
Shigella dysenteriae toxin	55 000-60 000	1A+6-7 B chains	
Tetanus toxin	H: 100 000; L: 50 000	1 polypeptide split into 2 chains; sequence - analyseed in part	19

1. IARC,1972.
2. UN,1980b
3. USA, 1983a.
4. Editorial, 1971.
5. Leppla *et al*, 1985.
6. Schmidt *et al*. 1983.
7. Kaczorek et al, 1983.
8. Uchida, 1982,pp. 1-31.
9. So & McCarthy, 1980.
10. Betley *et al*, 1984.
11. Weeks & Ferretti, 1984.
12. Olsnes & Pihl, 1982a.
13. Sakaguchi, 1983; schmidt *et al*, 1984.
14. Van Heyningen, 1982.
15. Mekalanos et al, 1983; Lockman & Kaper, 1983.
16. Dallas & Falkow, 1979; Yamamoto *et al*, 1984.
17. Olsnes & Sandvig, 1985.
18. Beiel, 1976.
19. Robinson & Hash, 1982.
20. Gray & Kehoe, 1984.
21. Ranelli *et al*, 1985.
22. Schmidt & Spero, 1983,
23. Murphy *et al* , 1974.
24. Lofdahl *et al*, 1983.
25. Olivera *et al*, 1985.

The tox genes coding for diphtheria toxin (Murphy *et al*, 1974), for the erythrogenic toxin of *Streptococcus pyogenes*, for staphylococcal enterotixin A and for Shiga-like toxin are all located on the genomes of specific bacteriophages also as genes responsible for the synthesis of botulinum toxins C_1 and D Furthumore, the genes coding for a protective antigen, a part of anthrax toxin, tetanus toxin (Finn *et al*, 1984) and for *E. coli* enterotoxins LT and ST are located on plasmids (i.e. on extrachromosomal genetic elements). The *ent* B gene, coding for staphylococcal enterotoxin B, may be carried by a large movable genetic element as well. Cloning of *tox* genes, isolation of their messenger RNA and/or purification of their products permits sequence analysis.

Knowledge of the related nucleotide and amino acid sequence, respectively, permits synthesis of the corresponding gene by oligonucleotide synthesis and of the gene product by polypeptide synthesis. Knowledge of the sequence is also a neccessary requirement for manipulating these genes and/or their products by genetic engineering and protein engineering. In the meantime various examples of the application of these techniques in the study of potential TW agents and of other toxins, as well as of their targets, have been reported. Some of the results published in the open literature follow.

Anthrax Toxin

A project of the US Army Medical Research Institute of Infectious Diseases deals with cloning and exhibiting genes for anthrax toxin. The anthrax toxin includes of three protein components: protective antigen (PA), *lethal factor* (LF_4), and oedema factor (*EF*). They are secreted by *Bacillus anthracis* in ratios of approximately 15:3:1. Individually they are non-toxic. They act in binary combinations to produce two distinct toxic response: oedema in skin. (PA + EF) and lethality (PA +LF), respectively (Leppla *et al* , 1985). The genes for PA (Vodkin & Leppla, 1983) and LF (Robinson & Leppla, in preparation, quoted by Leppla *et al*, 1985) have been cloned ; at least the structural gene for PA is located on a plasmid (Vodkin & Leppla, 1983). After transfer, the PA gene is expressed in *Escherichia coli* (vodkin & Leppla, 1983). The PA protein has been crystallized and its structure has been studied with the help of X-ray analysis (Allured et al, 1985).

Botulinum Toxin

The two polypeptide chains of botulinum type A toxin, produced by proteolytic cleavage of one single gene product of the *tox* gene, have been sequenced partly (Schmidt *et al*, 1984), as well as the single polypeptide chain of botulinum type E toxin (Schmidt et al, 1983).

Cholera Toxin

Cholera toxin genes, which consist of a single cholera toxin operon (*ctx*) have been cloned and sequenced (Mekalanos *et al*, 1983).

Diphtheria Toxin

It has long been known that the diphtheria *tox* gene is located on the genome of several interlinked corynebacteriophages (Leong *et al*, 1983). The *tox* gene has been cloned and sequencel cleong *et.al 1083; Greenfield et al., 1983) and* changed by site-directed mutagenesis (Collier& Kaplan, 1984). Frangments of the *tox* gene are fused with both a synthetic gene sequence coding for a human hormone (alpha-melanocyte stimulating hormone) and for interleukin-2; and the hybrid genes are cloned by Murphy.

Escherichia Coli Enterotoxins

The US Department of Defense funds the cloning of *E. coli* enterotoxin genes done at Tulane University. The Shiga-like toxin genes from *E. coli* have been cloned at the Uniformed Services University of the Health Services, Bethesda, Maryland (Newland *et al*, 1985) Additionally, the genes coding for enterotoxins Lt (heat laible) and ST (heat stable) have been cloned (So *et al*. 1976, 1978). Their DNA sequences have been studied and the corresponding amino acid sequences have been deduced (Holmgren, 1985).

Ricin

The primary structures of ricim A and B have been determined (Funatsu *et al* 1978, 1979). Work has been conducted in many laboratoriesto produce hybrid toxins comprising the A-chain of a toxic protein and an alternative protein instead of the B-chain (Olsnes & Pihl 1982). The gene encoding the A-chain has been cloned and expressed by Cetus, a company located in California (Olsnes, personal communication, 1986). Experiments aimed at cloning and expression of the ricin A-chain genes are also being done (Vitetta & Uhr, 1985).

Shigella Dysenteriae Toxin

The gene encoding shigella toxin has been cloned by a group at the Uniformed Services University of the Health Services, Bethesda, Maryland, USA (Olsnes, personal communication, 1986).

Staphylococcus Aureus Alpha-Toxin

The alpha -toxin gene has been cloned and sequenced (Kehoe *et al*, 1983; Gray & Kehoe, 1984).

Staphylococcus Aureus Enterotoxin

The *ent* A gene coding for enterotoxin A has been cloned (Betley *et al*, 1984). Also, the *ent* B gene has been cloned and sequenced (*Ranelli et al*, 1985). The amino acid sequence of staphylococcal enterotoxin C_1 has also been expressed. (Schmidt & Spero, 1983).

Shuttle Hybrid Plasmids

Shuttle hybrid plasmids are recombinant plasmids capable of replication in various host cells. Such recombinants have been developed which encode toxin genes (e.g. *Staphylococcus aureus* alpha-toxin gene) and which are able to multiply both in *E coli* and S. *aureus* (Kehoe *et al*. 1984).

Snake Venom

Snake venom genes are cloned at the US Army Medical Research Institute for Infectious Diseases (USA, 1985b). Tamiya *et al* (1985) describe cloning and sequencing a snake neurotoxin precursor gene.

Tetanus Toxin (Tetanospasmin)

The amino acid sequence of tetanus toxin has been studied in part (Robinson & Hash, 1982) and sequences of the corresponding gene have been synthesized in part in *vitro*. These gene fragments have been used to localize the gene (Finn *et al*. 1984).

Monoclonal Antibodies

The possibility to develop and produce monoclonal antibodies, that is homogenous preparations of antibodies reacting with a single determinant, should also be mentioned in this regard (Kohler & Milstein, 1975; Milstein, 1980). Monoclonal antibodies are highly useful for purification of proteins and for quantitative determination of unidentified substances. Monoclonal antibodies have been developed against various toxins, among them all three anthrax toxin components (Leppla *et al*, 1985), cholera toxin (Lindholm *et al*, 1983). diphtheria toxin (Hayakawa *et al*, 1983; Yoshimori et al 1983), and *trichothecenes* (USA , 1983a).

Targets of Toxins

Genetic engineering and other new techniques permit study of other the targets of toxins and their action mechanisms. The results of such research might be useful in developing unconventional antidotes to neurotoxins and other neurotoxic CW agents (Anonymous, 1984a). Use of these methods have already led to :-

(a) synthesis of an antibody against acetylcholine and its use as a specific marker for cholinergic neurons pertaining to rat central nervous system (Geffard *et al* 1985);

(b) elucidation of structure and function of the acetylcholine receptor (including binding studies of alpha bungaro toxin) (cf. Chageux *et al*, 1984; Mishina *et al* 1985 ; Boulter *et al* 1986). Cloning of genes for receptor sites is party funded by the US Department of Defense (USA, 1985 b);

(c) cloning of the genes for major neurotransmitters of the brain (cf. Snyder, 1984);

(d) cloning and sequlncing of the gene encoding acetylcholinesterase of the ray *Torpedo california*. (The electric organ from the fish *Torpedo* is exceptionally rich in a single class of cholinergic synapse and is therefore a major neuro-biological study object). From the gene sequence the entire sequence of the 575 amino-acid residues of acetylcholinesterase has been inferred (schumacher *et al*., 1986). This work was obvisous not found by the Department of Defense, although the US Army had already in the early 1980s solicited proposals to clone the acetylcholinesterase gene (USA, 1980a) and, in addition, asked various research groups to do so (wright & Shinsheimer, 1983). At least $1.3 million has been spent on such contracts (*Yanchinski, 1984*). Cloning of this gene will allow its expression in foreign host cells or host organisms to make vast quantities of acetylcholinesterase. This in turn will lead to detailed studies of the function of this special enzyme, but also the development of specifically targeted neurotoxins and of effective acting antidotes, as well;

(e) selection and use of monoclonal antibodies specific for neurotransmitter receptors, ion-selective channels and pumps, and for other neuron-specific proteins and protein complexes (cf. Reichardt, 1984);

(f) cloning and identification of brain specific genes (cf. Sutcliffe et al 1984).

Artificial Toxins

The work described above might be done with different aims. It might be undertaken to get knowledge about fundamental living structures and functions. Neurotoxins, for example, have been found to be specific, high affinity probes for distinct regions of receptors, ion channels, and other highly specialized structures of the nervous system (C. Cold Spring Harbor Laboratory, 1984). Research of toxins and/or their targets might also be conducted to develop new drugs. Thus, some richothecenes are studied as candidate chemotherapeutic agents for the treatment of human malignancies (USA, 1983a) The same holds true for the construction of fusion proteins including subunits of ricin or other toxins.

Such research does not contravene the language of the Biological Weapons Convention. Even work on toxins and/ or on their targets done with military support to develop antitoxins, antidotes, and diagnostic tools, is not forbidden by the Biological Weapons Convention, because work for 'prophylactic protective, and other peaceful purposes' is permitted. It must be borne in mind, however, 'that almost any type of BW research could be justified as defensive-for instance developing and investiganting novel agents so as to prepare vaccines against them' (Anonymous, 1984a,), not to mention that defensive reserarch within this very field is highly problematical. New methods, of course, could also permit the production of proteinaceous toxins destined to be used as TW agents by genetically engineered bacteria or other host cells. They could be produced either by their natural producers after insertion of regulatory signals or after other manipulations raising the synthesis of the on toxic gene products or by cells normally not expressig the products of tox genes. This kind of work would contravene the Biological Weapons Convention, however, because its language forbids the development and/or production of BW and TW agents 'whatever their origin or method of production. Combined use of DNA recombinant techniques and protein engineering, however, could result not only in making toxic gene products more efficient by alterig their catalytic properties, thermostability, temperature optimum, substrate and reaction specificity, cofactor requirement, resistance to enzymatic degradation, antigenicity, and capability to be absorbed and taken up by target cels (Ulmer, 1983; Perutz, 1985), but could also lead to totally new types of toxic molecule not found in nature.

These compounds, which might be called artificial toxins' (Olsnes & Pihl, 1982a), could vary from their natural models by gross changes in the sequence and/or number of amino acid residues and composition of multimeric proteins. Even molecular cannibalism' is envisaged by protein engineers (Vines, 1985), namely grafting potentially toxic groups onto the framework of an exisiting protein that would work advantageously as a potential TW agent. Toxicity of toxins differs considerably from one cell line to another and from one species to another. The main causes for this seem to be the different binding affinities of the toxins to receptor sites and the differences in the efficiency of toxin penetration of the target cells (Olsnes *et al.* 1985). Enhanced knowledge of the structure of proteinaceous toxins reveals that specific domains of single polypeptide toxins (e.g. the C-terminal part of diphtheria toxin) or speific submits of oligomeroc toxins (e.g. the B-chains of abrim and ricin are responsible for adsorption of the toxins while other parts of the proteins are the toxic components.

By means of protein engineering it should be possible to extend the host range and/or to increase toxicity. Work on ricin and related toxins has revealed the importance of the subunits of bipartite and/ or oligomeric toxins responsible for adsorption to and penetration through the membranes of target cells . As already pointed out work has been carried out to produce hybrid toxins consisting of the effector chain of a toxic protein, for example the A-chain of ricin, and an alternative binding protein as haptomer, instead of the B-chain of ricin (Olsnes *et al.* 1974; Olsnes & Pihl, 1982a), These artificial toxins gained by polypeptide hybridization may have diffierent activities.

Some hybrids of ricin A-chain and abrin B-chain were found to be as toxic as the native toxins. Although in most cases the hybrid toxins proved to be much less toxic (Clsnes & Pihl, 1982a), one cannot exclude that some hybrid toxins might be more toxic than the parental molecules, especially if the effector chains are coupled to haptomers specially tailored for this purpose. In discussing their successful cloning of the frangment of the *tox* gene encoding the enzymatic active N-terminal part of diphtheria toxin, Leong *et al*, (1983) point out that 'hybrid toxin genes can be developed in which the enzymatic active fragment A and hydrophobic domain of fragment B are fused to various eukaryotic cell receptor-specific ligands.

The expression and secretion of these defined chimeric toxins will advance...the development of targeted chimeric toxins... Leong *et al.*, are obviously thinking in terms of new drugs as does Murphy when fusing *tox* gene fragments to other gene sequences-Like wise, Olsnes and Pihl (1982b) are developing possible new types of anti tumour agent or compound useful for target- specific cell destruction of medical importance ('toxosurgery'). Naturally, one can also think in terms of chimeric artificial toxins to be used as potential TW agents.

Techniques needed for the *in vitro* synthesis not only of low-molecular-weight toxins (batrachotoxin, convallotoxin, saxitoxin, and tetrodotoxin; UN, 1980b) but also of proteinaceous high molecular - weight toxins are provided by current biotechnology. In some of the cases it should be sufficient to synthesize only those fragments of a toxin, the toxophores' in which the toxic activity resides, as is now done with immunogenic peptides. When more knowledge becomes available about the target stuctures and their functions, which information is now appearing during the emergence of molecular neurobiology (Cold Spring Harbor Laboratory, 1984), it should even be possible to tailor specific artificial toxins. These might be more effecient than their genuine prototype molecules. Moreover, they might be different enough in structure from the prototypes. Work on eserine, for example, led to the preparation of hundreds of new pharmacologically active carbamates (some of which are powerful competitve inhibitors of acetylcholinesterase binding) already long before the emergence of genetic and protein engineering SIPRI, 1971a, p. 64; 1973, p. 56). Whether low molecular-weight toxins and other non-proteinaceous toxins will some day be produced by engineered bacteria, cells or organisms and converted into artificial toxins is an open question.

All the same, one can imagine that it should be possible to introduce genes coding for some relevant enzymes into toxin-producing modifying cells in order to add one or more steps to existing biosynthetic pathways so that more efficient artificial toxins can be obtained. It should be mentioned in this regrard that the multiplicity of trichothecenes presumably arises, in part, from the ability of certain *Fusarium* strains to acetylate or deacetylate toxins (Busby & Wogan, 1981b, p. 30). The preparation of synthetic analogues of trichothecenes is also underway USA, 1983a, p. 53). A non-toxic synthetic analogue of T-2 toxin, deoxyverrucarol has been synthesized. However, synthetic analogues of trichothecenes might be developed which are more toxic than the natural.

Thus, the members of an expert 'Committee on Protection Against Mycotoxins' convened by the National Research Council at the request of the US Army, mentioning that trichothecenes have relatively low binding constants for their cellular targets (ribosomes), discussed the possibility that more toxic derivatives with higher binding constants possibly be synthesized (USA, 1983a, p. 160). 'In time it will probably be possible to synthesize any toxin, no matter how large or complex; as the depositary governments of the Biological Weapons Convention pointed out in their background paper submitted before the first review Conference and added that 'the ability to synthesize toxins also implies the ability to synthesize compounds which are closely related and possess greater toxicity but are not found in nature' (UN, 1980B,). The eventual emegence of artificial toxins was thus already envisioned without, however, drawing explicit conclusions. Unfortunately the Biological Weapons Convention includes no definitions and 'does not make clear what poisons are or are not to be regarded as toxins" (Perry Robinson, 1981).

Accoding to Goldblat, however, the language of the convention is meant to avoid ambiguity and to make sure that the concept of toxins is understood broadly: both biological and synthetically produced or modified compounds that can be used as warfare agents are covered by the prohibition " whatever their origin or method of production" (Goldblat, 1982,). Nevertheless, one can question whether the language of the Convention also encompasses artificial toxins. Regarding to such 'artificial toxins' the assumption of the first Review Conference no longer seems valid, 'that Article I has proved reasonably comprehensive to have covered recent scientific and technological developments relevant to the Convention' (UN, 1980d,). This also holds true for the assessment of the depositary governments that 'scientific and technological developments have not caused ambiguities or fundamentally new possibilities which could be exploited violate covertly or bypass the Convention' (UN,

1980 b, to). In this regard there are numerous uncertainties regarding the definition of the term 'toxin'. One must question whether the US Army would still define true toxins' as 'poisonous substances chemically allied to proteins' (USA, 1964) . In this case the non-proteinaceous toxins that the US. Army plans to study like trichothecenes, saxitoxin and tetrodotoxin might not be considered true toxins' and might therefore be interpreted as not being covered by the Biological Weapons Convention: Moreover, it must be noted that the1925 Geneva Protocol is weakened not only by reservations made by various states parties, but also by problems raised by interpretations in the absence of definitions. The United States, for example, has given the Geneva Protocol a narrow interpretation and contends that the use of irritants, such as tear gas, and anti-plant chemicals (herbicides) are not covered by the Protocol (see USA 1974).

This again raises the question of whether the Biological weapons conventions is also open to narrow interpretation for instance defining artifivial toxins as not being covered by it. To avoid such a weakening of the Convention, for the purposes of the Biological Weapons Convention all poisonous chemicals which are originally produced by living organisms should be regarded as toxins. For the puproses of the Convention these poisonous substances should also be regarded as toxins—which (after chemical synthesis or after chemical or biological modification) differ to some extent from their natural model—if they have been derived from natural origins or if they reveal the same-mechanism of action (including adsorption to and penetration into the target cells) as the model toxin.

Conclusion

Toxins are likely to become more and more important in a military context. A large number of toxins are far more effective as lethal or incapacitating agents than chemical poisons are. Genetic engineering and other methods of bitechnology provide new and / or more efficient ways to produce and/or develop toxins. Increasing knowledge of structures and functions of organisms permits tailor-making or more effective toxin and other chemical weapons. Development and production of toxin weapons by classical methods and by making use of genetic engineering are forbidden as per the language of the Biological Weapons Convention:

As the Biological Weapons Convention does not define toxins, it cannot be excluded, however, that 'artificial toxins' might be declared to be not toxins but synthetic poisons which later might be regrarded as not being covered by the Convention.

References

1. It does not matter in this connection that Gold (as numerous other US sources, see page 5) condidered TW agents to be biological weapons.

2 Besides staphylococal enterotoxins, the US Army had considered some biological agents such as the agents causing Q fever and VEE as possible incapacitating BW agents, but these 'were not as desirable as toxins because of the concern about possible spread, the predictability of effects on the target population, and on available knowledge about their long term effects on the environment (USA, 1977b, pp.50-1).

3. The United State has also claimed repeatedl that an out break of anthrax in Sverdlovsk in April 1979 resulted form the accidental release of Bacillus anthracis or its spore from an alleged Soviet BW centre (cf.UN 1980f. p.3; USA, 1984 a p.73) The Soviet Union has vigorously denied these allegations. As early as 1980 (in fact, during the first Review Conference of the Biological Weapons Convention) ambassador Issraelyan explained tha the Soviet Union had always scrupulously observd the Convention's provision...The incident in 1978 referred to by the United States delegation has in fact resulted from an epidemic caused by consumption of infected meat which had not been subjected to normal inspection before sale' (UN, 1980f, p.5; see also Bezdenezhnzkh & Nikoforov, 1980). Huan cases of anthrax occur normally as a result of exposure to infected meat or other animal products (Poretx, 1979), for instance during the recent outbreak in Zimbabwe, where more than 30000 cases were ecored (Davies. 1982). Several careful evaluations of the US allegaitions do not in fact. lend support th the US chargexs (cf.Zilinskas, 1983a; Twinning, 1981; Wade 1980b).

4. Luria (1965, pp. 123-4) was speculating two decades ago about whether multi- component biological weapons might be conceivable. he wondered whetherr in humans, as in frui flies. there exists a virus that causes a treendus sensitivity to carbon dioxide. For fruit flies that carry

this virus, carbon dioxide becoes a deadly poison. It would in man, too. What would be the chance , if such a possibiility sudenly arose in man, of avoiding such an infection and the resulting calamity? Someone could gain a tremendous control over humanity by spreading such a terrible object, therby holding the power of life and death over a large number of human beings.

Fortunatly, such systems have not been discovered (or, at least, have not been reported) so far More realistic, however, are ideas expressed about the same time by Bring. Gen. Blount, the then Commanding General of the US Army Medical Research and Developing Command, and by Col. Crozier, the then commanding officer of the US Army Medical Unit stationed at Fort Detrick, which was the major US BW installation at the time, with respect to tandem diseases' designed to confuse medical workers. Some of those becoming ill would exhibit the signs and sympoms produced by one organism, some, those of the second agent, while still others might prsent some of the features of each. A viral agent showing no response to speific therapy in combination with a bacterial agent which produces a desease with a high mortality rate if untreated, and with an incubation period which would allow the onset of symptoms to correspond to the beginning of the recovery phase of the viral disease could result i considrable delay in the institution of proper therapy for the secnd disease... (Blount & crozier, 1963, p.131).

5. In this connection it is not the organ attacked or the structure or function damaged which is decisive. Both botulinum toxin and organophosphates are neurotoxic. However organophosphates cannot be designaed as toxins or even as derivatives of botulinum toxin (or of any other neurotoxin, infact), because they act by different mechanisms: and they act on diferent cellular targets (see table A6.1).

However, a poisonous synthetic oligopeptide or polypeptide shose mechanism of toxic action results from the inteactionof a group of amino acids with a target molecule similar to the interaction of an active centre (a toxophore) of a ton , should be regarded , within ithe scope of the biological Wepons convention, to be a toxin, even if theamno acid sequence of the synthetic sequence analyses of ezymes have revealed, for instance, that- although within a limited range amino acids can be substituted by isopolar exchanges without ignificant loss of physiologicalactivity).

Likewise,a toxic compound consisting of the A- chain of a dimeric toxin (which, for instance in the case of ricin, is responsibe for the toxicity of the dimer; see page53) and a pllypeptide synthesized de novo and diffent from all known B- chains (which are responsible for adsorption to and penetratin of the compound; see page 53), should be regarded as a toxin for the purposes of the biological weapons convention similar to an artificila toxin consisiting of a B- chain of natural origin combined with an unnatural, synthetic poisonous moleccule.

8

Vaccines Against Toxin and Biological Weapons

Vaccines are the inculations which make a person safe against particular desease over a certain period of time. These are prepared from the virulent bacteria or Viruses using their inactivated pathogem. Vaccines against toxims and BWs hour a numberal uses. These are discussed here. Vaccines are prepared from living bacteria and viruses, of killed (inactivated) pathogens, or of immunogenic structures isolated from such organisms ('split vaccines') which are administered to humans or animals to induce, or raise immunity against particular infectious disease. Toxoids are non-toxic derivatives of toxins prepared by chemical modification; they resemble vaccines in that are administered to induce immunity to the toxims in question. Antitoxins are antibodies directed against toxins and toxoids. From a military point of view, vaccines (an to toxoids) are important for three different reasons. First, vaccines an be used to protect the armed forces and the civilian population against BW agents and TW agents used by an aggressor. In fact, effective vaccines and antitoxins were declared to be an he 'an absolute neccessity' for defence against BW and TW agents (Anderson & King, 1983. p. 33). Second, vaccines can be used to safeguard the aggressor's own armed forces against an intended BW or TW agent. Third, they can be used to protect the troops against the natural outbreak of exotic diseases. Vaccines studied by the US Army prior to he date of ratification of the Biological Weapons Convention are listed in Table 8.1.

Since then, there has been a major break through in the design, development and production of new vaccines (see chanock Lerner, 1984; Lerner *et al*, 1985). In addition to the conventional approaches to the development of vaccines, several alternative strategies are provided by genetic engineering, protein engineering, and immunological methods.

(a) Synthesis of protective antigens by mass culture of prokaryotic or eukaryotic host cells carrying cloned gnes encoding these antigens. The development of a new variety of split vaccine is possible, being no longer dependent on the dissociation of pathogenic organisms or viruses but on the synthesis of single proteins or even of smaller fragments (polypeptides and oligopeptides) thereof.

(b) Development and production of immunogenic polypeptides and peptides by chemical synthesis after prior elucidation of the primary structure of the corresponding antigens. Again, smaller fragments of the immunogenic substances might be created.

Table 8.1
Vaccines Analysis by the US Army Prior to 1977[a]

Vaccine	*Research Period*	*Status*
Anthrax	1959-1968	Development completed
Venezuelan equine encephalitis	1960-1974	Development completed
Tularemia	1960-1969	Development completed
Plague	1965-1974	Development completed
Q fever	1960-1974	Development completed
Rocky Mountain spotted fever	1972-1974	Final stage
Chikungunya	1969-1974	Final
Rift Valley fever	1963-1974	Final
Western equine encephalitis	1968-1974	Intermediate
Eastern equine encephalitis	1967-1974	Intermediate
Staphylococcal enterotoxin B	1964-1974	Intermediate toxoid
California encephalitis	1968-1974	Early stage
St. Louis encephalitis	1969-1974	Early stage
O' NyongNyong	1969-1974	Early stage
Mayaro	1970-1974	Early stage
Sindbis	1971-1974	Early stage
Langat	1972-1974	Early stage

[a]USA, 1977c, p. 216.

(c) Modification by protein engineering, of immunogenic polypeptides or oligopeptides synthesized in invitro or vivo. By using this method, the immunogens would become resistant to enzymatic degradation and to other defence factors, thereby allowing oral or aerosol administration of the antigen.

(d) Development of attenuated non-virulent mutants of pathogens by site directed mutagenesis and other techniques of genetic engineering as well as by use of neutralizing monoclonal antibodies.

(e) use of vaccinia virus (or other suitable viruses) as viral vectors to introduce and multiply heterologous genes coding for protective antigens in a host organism.

There are methods now available that should lead to the production of vaccines which would be capable or providing long-lasting immunity, would not induce side effects, could be produced cheaply in large quantities, and would satisfy the World Health Organization and national requirements by simple control procedures (relyved, 1984). Moreover, these mothods allow for the development of vaccines against some pathogens for which, because of technical reasons, no safeguard was possible in the past. New possibilities of developing split vaccines by genetically engineered bacteria or cells and by chemical synthesis are especially promising with respect to reducing side effects.

These methods might provide protective antiges free from the impurities associated with the antigens obtained by classical means. Adverse reactions following immunization with toxoids result from the presence of extraneous antigens present in crude or partially purified toxins or in toxoids derived from them (Relyveld, 1984). The new developments offer means to produce toxin preparations of higher purity.

Military Interest

Vaccines and toxoids might thus be developed against a large number of pathogens and toxins. An expert Committee on Issues and Priorities for New Vaccine Development' concluded in 1984 that, based on health benefits only, the main candidate vaccines are against: *Hemophilus influenza* type B bacteria (a cause of meningitis in young children), hepatitis B virus, respiratory syncytial virus influenza viruses A and B, and *Herpes* virus *varicellae* (Leeper, 1984 /85). In contrast, vaccine development funded by military institutions, for example by the US Department of Defense (according to a list released on 17 April 1985), deals mainly with pathogens and toxins which are likely candidates for possible use as BW and

TW agents(Table 8.2). The US Army is also studying the effectiveness of aerosol immunization, in which the vaccine distributed by an aerosol is inhaled rather than swallowed or taken by injection (piller, 1983).

According to a congressional report (USA 1980b), these studies are targeted on stimulating protective immunity on mucosal surfaces throughout the respiratory tract. Aerosol vaccines are of low medical importance for the civilian population except for the protection of newborn babies against measles viruses, (Aerosol vaccines are, however, important in protecting farm animals). But aerosol vaccines are of interest for the militaty because they can be used clandestinely protect not only the attacker's armed forces, and the civilian population.

SENATOR KENNEDY: But the military does not have the responsibility, as you understand it, other than the protection of the military forces; in terms of crops and animal, that responsibility is the department of Agriculture's. As I understand it, in terms of rest of the population, it is the public Health Service?

Mr MILLER: I believe that is right. (USA, 1977a, pp. 8-9).

Table 8.2
Genes of Putative BW and TW Agents Cloned for Vaccine Development

Agent	*Institution*
POXVIRUSES	
Vaccinia virus as vector-carrying antigenic determinants	USAMRDC[c]
ALPHAVIRUSES	
Chikungunya, immunogenic protein genes	USAMRIID
Mayaro, immunogenic protein genes	USAMRIID
O'nyong- nyong, immunogenic protein genes	USAMRIID
Ross River, immunogenic protein genes	USAMRIID
FLAVIVIRUSES	
Dengue-1 surface protein gene	USAMRDC[c]
Dengue-2 surface protein gene	USAMRDC[c]
Dengue-3 genome	URAIR[w]
Japanese encephalitis surface protein gene	USAMRDC[c]
ARENAVIRUSES	
Lassa virus N gene	Porton Down[d]
Lymphocytic choriomeningitis	USAMRDC[c]
BUNVAVIRUSES	
Hantaan viral surface protein	USAMRIID[c]

Agent	Institution
Phlebotomus fever	USAMRDC[c]
Punta Toro phlebovirus, M gene	USAMRIID[f]
Rift Valley fever	USAMRDC
Rift Valley fever, M gene	USAMRIID[e-g]
PICORNAVIRUSES	
Hepatitis A	USAMRDC[C]
BACTERIA	
Coxiella burnetti	USAMRIID
TOXINS	
Anthrax toxin genes (PA,LF)	USAMRIID[h]
Pseudomonas toxin	USAMRIID
Snake venom genes	USAMRIID

[a] Anonymous, 1985a.
[b] USAMRIID= US Army Medical Research Institute of Infectious Diseases. WRAIR = Walter Reed Army Institute of Research. USAMRDC= US Army Medical Institute of Research and Development Command.
[c] Under contract with.
[d] Centre for Applied Microbiology and Research, Porton Down, UK. Reference: clegg & Oram, 1985.
[e] Additional reference: Dasey, 1984.
[f] Additional reference: Leppla *et al* , 1985.
[g] Additional eference; Collett *et al* , 1985.
[h] Additional refrence:Ihara et al, 1985; Leppla et al, 1985.
[i] Additional reference: Southern & Oldstone, 1984.

Table 8.3
Current US Army Stockpiles of Vaccines, Antitoxins and Toxoids

Agent	Stockpile	Remarks
Smallpox virus	+(L)	
Chikungunya virus	0	Under study[c]
Eastern encephlitis virus	+(K)	
Venezuelan encephalitis virus	+(L)[g]	
Western encephalitis virus	+(K)	
Dengue virus	0	Under study[f]
Yellow fever virus	+(L)	
Tick-borne encephalitis virus	0	other source:Austria
Junin-Machupo virus	0	Under study[c]
Lassa fever virus	0	Under studey[c]
Lymphocytic choriomeningitis virus	0	Under study[c]
Crimean-Congo haemorrhagic fever virus	0	Under study[c]

Agent	*Stockpile*	*Remarks*
Hantaan virus	0	
Rift valley fever virus	+(K)	
Ebola- Marburg virus	0	
Coxiella burnetti	+(K,L)	
Bacillus anthracis	+(K)	Under study[d]
Francisella tularemia	+(L)	
Botulinum toxin	+[c]	
Staphylococcal enterotoxin	0	
Aflatoxin	0	
Trichothecenes	0	Under study[c]
Saxitoxin	0	Under study[c]

[a] Anderson & King , 1983.
[b] K= inactivated vaccine, Llive vaccine.
[c] USAMRIID.
[d] In addition live vaccine under development at USAMRIID.
[e] Both antitoxin and toxoid available.
[e] Is said to be available now (Zoler, 1985).
[g] A killed vaccine is said to be available as well (Zoler, 1985).

The following additional observations may be made in relation to vaccine development against the possible candidates for operational us as BW and TW agents Table 8.2,:

(a) Many vaccines, antitoxins and toxoids are already stockpiled Table (8.3).

(b) The current immunization needs of the US Army provides not only protection against respiratory disease (caused by adenovirus) and meningitis but include protecting against possible biological warfare agents (USA, 1985a). Thus, all recruits are protected against smallpox, although mass vaccination of the general population against smallpox is no longer practised. Smallpox virus has been considered as an ideal BW agent since the 1930s (Wade, 1978; Schopp. 1985). In addition, the US Armed Forces are vaccinated against, among other diseases, typhoid, plague 'when required', and yellow fever. Moreover, contractors of the US Army Medical Research and Development Command produce limited quantities of some vaccines which has no public health applications, especially those of BW interest '(USA, 1985A)'.

(c). The use of viral vectors to transfer heterologous protective antigen genes appears to be a promising means of protecting the armed forces and the civilian population against BW andTW agents used by an aggressor. Vaccinia virus is one of the most-promising viral vectors (Brown *et. al* 1986).

Vaccinia virus has been used for about 200 years to vaccinate against smallpox, and its use made eradication of that disease possible. Consequently, almost all countries have followed the proposal of the World Health Organization to restrict smallpox vaccination to 'investigators at special risk' (Fenner, 1985). Some countries also vaccinate military personnel against smallpox. Vaccinia virus has turned out to be an effective vector for the transfer of heterologous gens into animal cells and organisms. Genes from various pathogens have been imcorporated into the genome of vaccinia virus. Organisms infected by these recombinant viruses react as if they are infected not only by vaccinia virus but also, for example, by influenza virus.

Recombinant vaccinia viruses have been constructed that provide immunity against various viral antigens as well as a malarial parasite antigen. It was even possible to construct vaccinia virus recombinants harbouring at least three antigenic determinants and providing immunity against three different pathogens in experimental animals (Perkus *et al,* 1985). The investigators concluded that one can readily think of polyvalent vaccinia virus vaccines genetically engineered to exhibit foreign genetic information encoding several dozen antigens' (Perkus *et al.,* 1985, p. 983). Whether genes encoding immunologic determinants of putative BW and TW agents have been used in such vacinia virus recombinants is not know. One of the most active groups involved in the development of vaccinia virus vactors and headed by E. Paoletti is funded by the US Army Medical Research and Development Command (Anonymous, 1985a).

(d) Immunological protection against trichothecenes and other low molecular-weight toxins might also be possible. Serious limitations regarding the effectiveness of such procedures, including the issue of immunologic specificity. The Committee on Protection Against Mycotoxin's found it conceivable that antibodies might be formed against a common determinant on all trichothecenes (USA, 1983a, p.160). Since then, trichothecenes are said to 'get top billing in the [US] Army's antitoxin program' (Zoler, 1985).

(e) Whether studies on vaccines to against organophosphorus poisoning (strenberger *et al.*, 1972) will lead to practical results is still open to debate question. Currently the (U.S.) Army funds a modest-sized program... Work going on by a competent group of scientists at Edgewood Arsenal is modest in size relative to the nature of the questions that must be answered to learn how practical it will be to produce vaccines effective against chemical warfare agents' (Anonymous, 1981).

Finally, one could speculate on the use of monoclonal antibodies for passive immunization against some diseases, including those caused by BW and TW agents. Conventional antisera contain mixtures of many diffrent anti-bodies which react more or less - specifically with various antigenic sites of viruses, bacteria, or other immunogenic structures. In comparison, monoclonal antibodies are preparations of identical antibodies able to react with one and the same antigenic determinant. They are called 'monoclonal' because they are identical and because they are produced by single clones of engineered antibody- producing cells. Being identical, they react much more specifically and hence more effectively with a given antigen. They are believed to be superior to conventional antisera for passive immunization ('serum therapy'). Passive immunization using monoclona antibodies might be especially important with respect to viral diseases.

Viruses have become significant as putative BW agents. Currently, there is no specific therapy available for the treatment of most viral infections. Regarding passive immunization for protection against them, one must, however, take into account that, because of the high mutation frequency of viruses, variants might arise which can replicate also in the presence of neutralizing monoclonal antibodies. Nevertheless, farm animals, which are also potential BW and TW targets, seem to profit from a passive immunization programme employing monoclonal antibodies (Faras *et al.*, 1983). The same holds true for the therapy of diseases caused 1by toxins. Thus, antitoxin is the only specific therapeutic agent available for the treatment of botulism (Lamanna & Carr,1967). The U.S. Army at its Fort Detrick laboratories has been the leader in the study of botulinal anatoxins (toxoids, e.g.) for use in humans' (Lamanna & Carr, 1967, p. 306) already in the 1960s. Here again, monoclonal antitoxic antibodies should be more effective than classical antitoxin preparations.

Useful for Aggressors

Development, production and stockpiling of vaccines and toxoids including the development, production and stockpiling of BW and TW agents in quantities necessary for development and testing of vaccines and toxoids is not prohibition by the Biological Weapons Convention because there is 'justification' for prophylactic, protective or other peaceful purposes. However, effective defensive protection of the armed forces (not to mention protection of the entire civilian population) against a BW or TW agent that an aggressor might be planning to use is almost impossible. First of all, immunological prophylaxis is highly specific. Protection is only provided for a particular kind of pathogen. Subtle changes in the primary structure of some proteins of the pathogen may entirely overcome the protection provided by vaccination. The limitations of immunological protection are exemplified most dramatically by the incomplete immunity provided by previous infections with influenza viruses and by the incomplete effciency of vaccienes directed against influenza viruses.

Considering this and the fact that so many variations of BW and TW agents are possible, reliable intelligence data would have to be abailable to the defender regarding the particular type of BW and TW weapon to be used by the aggressor. But even if these data were available, effective mass vaccination would cause formidable problems both with respets to the time neccessary to develop effective protection after vaccination to the availability of the quantities of vaccine necessary—not to mention the need for development of an effective type of vaccine in the first place. In the case of an anticipated attack with eastern encephalitis virus (EEV) according to an estimate only about half a division (i.e. about 8000 men) could be immunized with EEV vaccine stockpiled by the US Army. It would need about three months to produce enough vaccine to protect the rest of the division, and about one year's production would be needed to immunize an independent five-division corps (i.e. about 190,000 men) Anderson & King, 1983. In addition, it would take many weeks or months before the vaccinated individuals would develop an adequate level of immunity. Hence, protection of significant portions of the civilian population would be impossible.

Additional problems would be created if an aggressor were to disseminate a BW or TW agent in aerosol form, as the resultant exposure to them would be far greater (at least in certain locations) than that which would be encountered by natural exposure. Vaccines considered to be effective under normal conditions might not provide sufficient protection under such circumstances (Anderson & King, 1983). However, as more and better vaccines are developed, the prospects of some state choosing to use BW and TW agents might increase. An expert panel asked by the US Department of state to assess the impact of genetic engineering, observed that 'an increased protection capability may be an inducement to use biological warfare, since the instigator has a decreased risk of being harmed by his own actions' (USA, 1981b, p.4). Therefore, increased protection capabilities may be an inducement for some countries to use biological agents against others' (USA, 1981a ,p. 2), especially if the aggressor's armed forces and its civilian population can be protected clandestinely, for example by aerosol immunization. Thus one of the requirments of effective BW (and TW) agents could be fulfilled.

Uses of Vaccine Development

New techniques are now available for the developent of new and /more efficient vaccines. Military institutions have great interest using genetic engineering and other techniques for the development of new vaccines. Vaccine development funded by the US Army is directed mainly at providing protection against pathogens and toxins that are putative BW and TW agents. Vaccine development is not forbidden by the Biological Weapons Convention. Vaccine development might need the development and production of BW and TW agents in quantities also useful for conducting hostile activities (at least on a limited scale). By protecting the aggressor's armed forces, vaccines might lessen the risks in using BW and TW agents and lower the barriers against their use.

Development and Production

A great influence of the new methods provided by genetic engineering, protein engineering and immune techniques looks to be on the development and production of vaccines, especially of viral vaccines. The progress that may be expected in the development of vaccines is described in Table 8.1 Numerous conventional vaccines are already available, both for civilian and military use Table 8.4. Some of these are inactivated or killed vaccines consisting of bacteria or viruses inactivated or killed by heat or by treatment with formalin or phenol. One special class of inactivated vaccines consists of toxoids. Toxoids are toxins which have lost their toxic properties due to treatment with formalin or other agents, but which have retained their immunogenic properties.

Another class of inactivated vaccines comprises split vaccines which comprise immunogenic sub-fractions derived from pathogens.Other conventional vaccines are live vaccines. Live vaccines are prepared from attenuated pathogens that produce asymptomatic infections in their natural hosts. Attenuated pathogens are descendents of natural occurring.

Table 8.4 Progess Pattern in Vaccine Development[a]

Stage	Type of vaccine	Basis
I	Conventional vaccines	Empirical knowledge Living attenuated and crude killed vaccines
II	Improved vaccines	Large-scale culture including mammalian cell culture Purification of antigens Gennetic Basis for Virulence Immunologica understanding
III	Single-protein vaccines	Monoclonal antibodies Pure antigens Gene cloning and sequencing Improved adjuvants
IV	Simple synthetic peptide vaccines	Immunochemistry Computer chemistry understanding of basis of adjuvanticity
V	Simple synthetic peptide vaccines active orally	Medicinal chemistry.

A slightly modified From vane of cuatrescas, 1984. Variants that were identified by their lack of virulence. In most of the cases, however, attenuated bacteira or viruses were selected by multiple passages under unnatural conditions. During these passages, the pathogens may gather numerous mutations in different genes. 'In a sense (the) satisfactorily attenuated mutants are the product of a process of genetic roulette followed by selection of mutants with the desired properties of attenuation and immunogenicity (Murphy & Chanock, 1985, p.357) In most cases the genetic basis of attenuation of live vaccines has not yet been clearly understood, although sequence analysis and other methods made available by genetic engineering (will) now provide insights into the molecular basis of attenuation. Both live and inactivated vaccines have various disadvantages, for example with respect to contamination with live adventitious pathogenic agents and with retaining certain levels of residual virulence (Dick ,1966; Murphy & Chanock, 1985).

Therefore, methods of genetic engineering, protein engineering and immune methods are increasingly used to develop new types of vaccine (Hilleman, 1985). These methods, in contrast to past ones ,even allow development of vaccines against pathogens that cannot be multiplied in the laboratory. In the development of vaccines, we are according to vane & Cuatrecasas (1984) through stages I and II and into stage III (table A7.1). Genetic engineering, protein engineering and immune techniques, however, still contribute greatly in improving conventional vaccines according to stage II: induction of attenuation by site-directed mutagenesis and by recombination including *in vitro*, recombination berween different strains of viruses and other pathogens. Besides, techniques are being developed to use vaccinia virus or other suitable viruses as vectors for antigenic determinants. Some current viral vaccine biotechnology projects are described in table A7.2. Several viral proteins or immunogenic peptides or polypeptides derived there from have already been produced. The US Army funds cloning of a large number of viral genes for vaccine development Table 7.2 . Subunit vaccines from genetically engineered bacteria have not been encouraging, however. He patitis B antigen, for example, can be effectively produced only in yeasts (where it is, however, not well glycosylated) or in animal cell culture (Collins, 1986). Further progress towards peptide split vaccines, consist of major antigenic determinants of the pathogen only, depends, among other things, on the undrstanding of protein chemistry.

Now it is evident that immunity can be elicited by small peptides corresponding to a region of the antigen involved (Shinnick *et al*, 1983). (The immunogenic peptides are identified either by sequence analysis or by expression of immunogenic fragments of genes in genetically engineered bacteria or cells). In comparison to earlier assumptions, it does not seem to be necessary to construct synthetic peptides (or corresponing fragments of polypeptides) in such a way as to reproduce the tertiary conformation of an antigenic site of the intact protein. (They need the addition of appropriate adjuvants, however. Selection of proper, safe and efficient adjuvants is a remaining major problem which must be solved before synthetic

Table 8.5
Viral Some on going Vaccine Biotechnology Projects

Viral disease	*Company*	*Project Description*
Influenza virus	Numerous investigators	Improved attenuated strains
	Numerous investigators	Modification of viral genome through rDNA
	Scripps (USA)	Synthesis of short peptides corresponding to fragments of viral surfce proteins
	Scripps (USA)	Attachment of viral subunit to larger carrirer to evoke broader immune response
Polio virus	Numerous investigators	Modification of viral gnome through rDNA
Hepatitis B from	Merck (USA) VirusInstitut Pasteur Production	Purification of viral particles blood
	Chiron Corp (USA)/ Merck/ University of Washington/UCSF Takeda/Osaka and Hiroshima Universities (Japan) Amgen (USA) Biogen/Green Cross (Japan) University of Edinburgh Intergrated Genetics (USA)/Connaught (Canada)	Production of viral surface protein through rDNA in yeast
Herpes Viruses	Merck	Purification of surface glycoprotein from herpes simplex viruses
	Molecular Genetics (USA)/ Lederle Labs (USA) Institut Merieux (France)/ University of Chicago	Production of viral proteins in bacteria through rDNA Production of non- pathogenic viruses by the deletion of specific genes

rDNA = recombinant DNA research (genetic engineering).

Source: USA 1984, p. 137.

peptide immunogens can be used (vaccines).Thus entire synthesis of a diphtheria vaccine based on fewer than 20 amino acid residues has been achieved (Audibert *et al.*,1981), as well as induction of an immune response to foot-and-mouth disease virus using peptide fragments of the antigenic protein consisting of 14, 16 ad 21 amino acid residues, respectively (Bittle *et al.* 1982; Pfaff *et al.*, 1982, 1985).

Besides a 14 amino acid immunogen has been identified and synthesized which provides immunity to feline leukemia virus (Nunberg *et al.*, 1985). Some kinds of results were obtained with syntheitic immuno genic peptides of other viruses (cf. Lerner *et al.* 1985). Using methods of protein engineering, it is possible, through the insertion of 'unnatural' substituents that provide resistance to enzymatic degradation, to develop synthetic peptides carrying activity into the body via oral and/or nasal routes (Vane & Cuatrecasas, 1984). In this manner, peptide vaccines might be developed which may possibly be applied not only with a nasal spray but which might even be distributed by aerosol. Aerosol vaccines are of high priority among the military as they allow covert application. It is even possible to construct hemisynthetic polyvalent vaccines capable of inducing high antibody titres against the different antigenic specificities present in the immunity preparation (Audibert *et al.*1985). Split vaccines can also be produced by genetically engineered bacteria or cells. The basic protocol for development of genetically engineered split vaccines includes, first, indentification of the major surface antigen, which will induce antibodies having ability the infectious organism, and identification of its gene, and, second, isolation of the corresponding gene and its transfer to and expression in a suitable host cell or host organism (Faras *et al.*,1983). Split vaccine technology against bacterial infections has not yet been widely analysed.

Increasingly, bacterial proteins are recognized, however, which perform functions essential to the disease mechanism. Some of these proteins may provide targets for subunit vaccines in not so distance future. Among other projects, the genes that specify five highly antigenic proteins of leprosy bacclilli (*Mycobacterium leprae*) have been cloned and expressed in E. Colis (Young et al., 1985a). The method used has also been applied to *Mycobacterium tuberculosis* (Young *et al.*,1985). So as to elucidate whether the traditional BCG vaccine can be substituted by new ones that are even more efficient and safer. Other progress in this field is described by Lerner *et al.* (1985).

Much progress is being made, at the same, in developing malaria vaccines using by biotechnological means (Lerner *et al.*,1985). However, synthetic peptide vaccines are considered superior not only to inactivated or attenuated vaccines but also to split vaccines produced by genetically engineered becteria or cells(Newmark,1983).

Rcombinant Live Vaccines

The potential for the use of vaccinia virus as a vector for the development of recombinant live vaccines appears to be overwhelming (Brown *et al.*,1986). Animal tests are highly encouraging. The basic protocol for development of vaccinia virus recombinant vaccines includes marker rescue (Nakano *et al.*, 1982) in order to insert foreign genes into the large, fragile genome of the vaccinia virus. (Marker rescue is integration of undamaged genes from fragmented or otherwise inactivated viruses into the genome of viable helper viruses in mixed infected cells). Therefore a cloned subgenomic fragment of vaccinia virus is employed. The foreign genetic element is inserted at a site of the cloned vaccinia virus DNA fragment which is known either to contain no genetic information or information not essential for replication of the vaccinia virus. Simultaneously provision has to be made that the foreign DNA insert can be expressed in a suitable host. The recombinant DNA comprising a vaccinia genome fragment including a foreign gene is then introduced in suitable host cells. Additionally, these cells are infected with wild type vaccinia virus. When the genome of the wild-type virus is replicated, chance recombinant events may take place between vaccinia DNA sequences flanking the foreign gene and homologous DNA sequences on the vaccinia genome. Thus the foreign genetic element may eventually become integrated into a complete vaccinia virus DNA molecule by *in vivo* recombination. This novel recombinant DNA molecule is replicated in the infected cell, along with the DNA molecules that have not participated in the recombinant process; it participates in the subsequent muaturtion steps; and is packaged into novel live recombinant vaccinia virus particles which, then , can be identified basedon of expression of the foreign virus gene(s) (Paoletti *et al.*,1986).

Recombinant vaccinia viruses have been constructed that produce immunity to Hepatitis B virus surface antigen (HBsAg) Smith *et al.*, 1983a: (Paoletti *et al.*,1984), Herps simplex virus glycoprotein D (HSVgpD) (Paoletti *et al.*, 1984). influenza virus hemaglutinin (FluHA) (Panicali *et al.*, 1983; Smith *et al.*, (1983), rabies virus glycoprotein (Klieny *et al*, 1984: Wiktor *et al.*, 1984), vesicular stomatits virus G protein (Mackett *et al.*, 1985) and a malarial parasite antigen, the sporozite antigen of *Plasmodium knowlesi* (Smith *et al.*, 1984). It was even possible to develop vaccinia virus recombinants harbouring at least three antigenic determinants (HBs Ag , HSVgpD, Flu HA) and providing immunity to three different pathogens in experimental animals (Perkus *et al.*,1985).

The investigators concluded, as already mentioned, that 'one can readily think of polyvalent vaccinia virus vaccines genetically, engineered to express foreign genetic information encoding numerous antigens. Whether the immunological system could respond reasonably to such an intrusion remains to be established (Perkus *et al.*, 1985, p. 983). A further question is, whether the immunological system can be saturated. Moreover, it is not known whether the expresssion of one antigen results in suppression of the immunological reactivity to other antigens (Paoletti *et al.*, 1986). An accidental human infection with an infectious vaccinia virus recombinant showed that this recombinant can prduce specific antibodies to a non- vaccinia virus protein, not only in experimental animals but in humans (Jones *et al.*,1986). The use of other viral vectors for the development of such vaccines seems un necessary, especially if the incidence of post-immunization vaccinia encephalitis Dick, 1966) can be reduced. Such a reduction can be achieved (at least in experimental animals) by splitting or deleting the gene coding for vaccinia virus thymidine kinase (Buller *et al.*, 1985). This very gene, for example, might be used as the recipient DNA sequence selected for insertion of foreign gene(s).

References

1. The US Army had carried out at least 239 (Editorial, 1979) top-secret open - air disseminations of micro-organisms during the 1950s and 1960s. Target areas were, among others, the Bay region of San Francisco, the New York subway system. Washington's National Airport, the Kittatinny and Tuscarora Tunnels on the Pennsylvania Turnpike and along Pennsylvania State Highway 16 (USA, 1977 a Cole, 1982; 1985; Anonymous, 1984c; Wines, 1984). The public was never told about these test which were revealed only in the mid- 1970s by journalists (Anonymous, 1976). In 1984 it was revealed that the US Army sprayed several germs also over Hawaii during 1960s (Oshiro,1984). Many of these tests involved live biological organisms which we know can affect human beings, particularly those in a weakened state. The Defence Department continued to use a certain organism, which they appaently believed to be harmless, long after some medical experts had published reports describing human illness, and even death, resulting from infection with the same type of orgainsm (Senator Schweiker in USA, 1977a, p. 262). The main objective of some of these tests is still classified (Oshiro, 1984). They demonstrate., at least, that completely covert aerosol immunization can be carried out.

2. The activities of the US Army for vaccine development are not aimed protection of the civilian population, however as it was revealed during a hearing.;

Mr. MILLER (Assistant Secretary of the Army for Research and Development): We feel that without appropriate protective mechanisms- our ground forces would indeed be vulnerable. We are lookig I think aggressively, we are working at the pace that satisfies us so we are overcoming those problems with respect to the Known agents. SENATOR (EDWARD M.) KENNEDY: As I understad from your answer, your responsibility is related to the military, is that correct?

Mr. MILLER: Yes, sir

SENATOR KENNEDY: who is protecting the general public?

GENERAL AUGERSON (Assistant Surgeon General for Research and Development): The overall responsibility for plants and animals resides with the Department of Agriculture. SENATOR KENNEDY: Department of Agriculture?

GENERAL AUGERSON: Yes, sir That is my understanding.

Bibliography

Chanock, R.M. and Lerner, R.A. (eds), *Modern Approaches to Vaccines, Molecular and Chemical Basis of Virus Virulence and Immunogenicity* (Cold Spring Harbor Laboratory: cold Spring Harbor, NY, 1984).

Lener, R.A., Chanock, R.M. and Brown, F. (eds). *Vaccines 85, Molecular and Chemical Basis of Resistance to Parasitic, Bacterial, and Viral Diseases* (Cold Spring Harbor Laboratory: Cold Spring Harbor, NY, 1985)

Norrby, E., 'Toward new viral vaccines for man', *Advances in Virus Research*

(Academic Press: Orlando, FL., 1986, in press).

Relyveld, E.H., Recent development with vaccines against bacterial protein toxins, in Alout et al. (184), pp. 217-26.

Chanoc R.M. and Lerner R.A. (eds), *Modern Approaches to Vaccines. Molecular and Chemical Basis of virus Virulence and Immunogenicity* (Cold Spring Harbor Laboratory: Cold Spring Harbor NY, 1984).

Laver w.g. and Air, G.M. (eds) *Immune Recognition of Protein Antigens , current Communications in Molecular Biology* (Cold Spring Harbor Laboratory: Cold Spring Harbor NY, 1985).

Lerner R.A.Chanock, R.M. and Brown, F. (eds), Vaccines 85. *Molecular and Chemical Basis of Resistane to Parasitic Bacterial ,and Viral Diseases* (Cold Spring Harbor Laboratory: Cold Spring Harbor , NY, 1985).

Relyveld, E.H., 'Recent developments with vaccines against bacterial protein toxins, in Alouf, J.E. Fehrenbach, F.J., Freer, J.H. and Jeljaszewicz, J. (*eds*), *Bacterial Protein Toxins* (Academic Press Inc: London, 1984), pp. 217-26.

Tickhonenko T.I, 'Virion proteins and the perspectives of gene manipulations in vaccine preparations', Acta Virologica , **29** (1985), pp. 254-65.

9

New Techniques and Weapons

With the development of science and technology new weapons are on the way to be developed having great destructive capacities. These weapons spell down for the mankind. Yet we cannot help stop their production. In the future, we may see weapons having capacity to end the existence of man on the planet. Eminent scholars across the political spectrum in the West have warned of the dangers of new biological weapons, during the recent past. Examples include Susan Wright and Robert Sinsheimer's article in the *Bulletin of the Atomic Scientists* in 1983, 'Recombinant DNA and biological warfare', in 1986, Joseph Finder's article in *The Wshington Quarterly* entitled 'Biological warfare, genetic engineering, and the treaty that failed, and, in 1992, the article by Joseph Douglass Jr. asking Who's holding the psychotoxins and DNA- altering compounds? in *Armed Forces Journal International*. Various other articles could be pointed out where this issue has been discussed, and particular viewpoints argued, in both the specialist and the general open literature. Fortunately also, official government estimates of the problem have been given in papers concerned with the Review Conferencs of the BWC. Before trying out further detailed analysis, it therefore appears sensible to summarise how governments have seen the problem.

Governmental View Points

The depository governments were asked to prepare a background paper on new scientific and technological developments for the first review in 1980. This paper forms a good baseline against which to set more recent estimates for the 1991 third Review Conference.

The Period 1980—1991 The paper produced for the first review had five major sections in addition to general introduction and final summary.

The major central section dealt with recombinant DNA techniques, new infectious disases, chemical synthesis of toxins the industrial use of fermentation techniques, and the microbial control of pests.

The conclusion of the document was quite sanguine. The paper ended thus: From a scientific technological standpoint, the developments discussed in this paper, which are directed to peaceful purposes, do not appear to alter substantially capabilities or incentives for the development or production of biological or toxin weapons.

The same viewpoint is closely reflected in the individual sections of the paper, for example in connection with recombinant DNA techniques. While these are clearly set out, the possible relevance to biologcal weapons stated, and the necessity for continued monitoring noted, the techniques were said to be, similar in principle' to classical genetics, and it was concluded that any agents produced would be:

....unlikely to have advantage over known agents sufficient to provide compelling new motives for illegal production or military use in the foreseeable future.....small so the argument can be made that a separate paper from Sweden had a slightly different tone in stating, for instance 'that the new genetic techniques imply a potential' to change existing biological weapon agents and that the possibility of the construction of new agents could not be excluded. On the chemical synthesis of toxins, the paper from the depository governments noted that in the future it would probably be possible to sythesise anything, however large or complex, but at the time the synthesise were very difficult. It seemed unlikely that production of militarily-significant quantities of toxins would be achieved by such a route. Likewise, whilst the rapid expansion of capabilities in fermentation technology were described, it was concluded thus :

...From a scientific and technological standpoint, growing industrial use of fermentation techniques does not appear to substantially alter capabilities or incentives for biological or toxin warfare.

In regard to the microbial control of pests, although it was agreed that there were some similarities to biological warfare in such activities, it was concluded that the risks were outweighed by the advantages to the peaceful purposes of such work.

As Sims has remarked, there was little consideration of scientific and technical issues at the first Review Conference. He got the impression that participants were optimistic, if not complacent. Even the Swedish paper, he felt, did not factually dissent from the depositories reassuring assessment. He also observed that, perhaps to avoid the sensationalism and crudity of some popular presentations, the papers prepared by the depositories and other governments for the second review in 1986 were sober and measured.

There is no doubt, however, that the assessment of the impact of biotechnology, as brought out by the papers for the second review, was changing.

Sims pointed out that the Swedish paper for this review referred to frequently-voiced concerns over the introduction of resistance to antibiotics, microencapsulation of agents, production of toxins on a large scale, and insertion of genetic material coding for the production of a potent toxin into a virulent organism that can infect human beings. He had the feeling that the British paper qualified the judgement made by the depositories in 1980 by suggesting that the pace of change indicated a greater potential to change capabilities an incentives in regard to biological weapon developments that was evident earlier. A study prepared in the USA for the Office of the Defense Secretary in March 1986, during the run-up to the second review, detailed some of the reasons for the increasing concerns.

Arguing that the earlier times had witnessed impressive advances, and that the distinction between biology and chemistry was becoming blurred, it listed seven technologies which were having an impact in areas of concern. These are listed in Table 9.1.

Table 9.1
Specific Technologies Influencing the Biological Agent Preparation Production and Use

1. Recombinant DNA (genetic engineering).
2. Protein engineering.
3. Computer-aided orthomolecular drug design.
4. Fermentation engineering.
5. Mammalian cell culture.
6. Peptide synthesis.
7. Biolphysics of cell memberanes.

Within the first topic of genetic engineering, the text went on to discuss plasmid stabilisation by which, instead of bacterial strains tending to lose their drug resistance during fermentation, all the cells would retain the genes for drug resistance. Other aspects of genetic engineering included were the production of plant toxins, enhancement of the lethality of bacteria and new viral pathogens. Even though protein engineering was considered some years away from realisation, computer-aided orthomolecular drug design applied to short sections of proteins (peptides) was reported to have been used.

Considerable attention was given in the report to progress in fermentation engineering. Particular note was taken of the rise in productivity that could be achieved by the use of computers in process control. This is significant which has continued to be a focus of attention. We shall deal with the important issue of mammalian cell culture later in regard to documents prepared for the third review of the BWC in 1991, but in this 1986 document particular attention was paid to peptide synthesis. Peptides were seen as important substances, active at very low concentrations, which could have startling effects on animals after what seemed to be slight changes of chemical a structure. It was brought to notice that new means of transferring peptid from the environment into the human bloodstream were being discovered (biophyics of cell membranes) and that these substances could have effects ranging from controlling mood, sleep or emotions, to mental processes and consciousness. Summarising some of the implications of all such technological changes, it was suggested that one outcome might be new, improved strains of drug-resistant bacteria with more poisonous toxins, a reduced lethal dose because of plasmid stability, and a higher production yield through computer control of the process. Of course, as a further result of such improvements, the size of the production plant needed might be 10 to 50 times smaller, with some pieces of equipment 1,000-fold smaller. Concerns about the fallouts of scientific and technical changes were seen in the background document prepared for the third Review Conference in 1991, to which a number of countries contributed. The Australian contribution was brief and to the point.

A brief introduction stated that there had been major advances in biotechnology since the last review, national capabilities had spread and, whilst this had positive sides, it also had the potential for misuse. The remainder of the contribution was divided into five sections dealing with production cell culture, fermentation technology, harvesting, dissemination and delivery, and genetic engineering.

Several biological compounds of commercial interest cannot be produced by fermentation using bacteria, even by means of genetic engineering, since bacteria lack the capabilities of more complex cells to modify products after translation from RNA. Such products, for instance some ehormones, must be produced in animal cells. As viruses are necessarily parasitic, they must also be grown in appropriate cell systems. It is hardly surprising, therefore, that various, new ways were sought and found to improve animal cell growth systems. The old system was to have a monolayer of cells on a solid surface in roller bottles. The Australian text analysed the development of new means of growing cells on the surface of beads and then the use of hollow-fibre perfusion systems where the cells remain within the fibres and nutrients pass to them through press in the fibres. This allows very high density of cells and in the case of soluble products provides a simultaneous separation of product from cells. The section concluded that :

These new techniques simplify virus production and allow large yields from relatively small facilities.

The idea of improvement in production technology was emphasised strongly in the next section of the Australian contribution. Automation of process control, in-plant cleaning systems and continuous flow fermenters were cited as examples of important developments. Improved harvesting methods also have been necessitated by the improvement of fermenter technology. In the section on dissemination and delivery it was suggested that reaction against the overuse of chemical pesticides had caused increased interest in biological control method. Unfortunately, Various problems in applying such methods are akin to those encountered in biological warfare. Agents in both cases are affected by UV light or desiccation. Means developed to microencapsulate agents for peaceful pest control could clearly also be used to protect warfare agents, and the lessons learnt in developing effective spraying systems for agriculture could also be applied to biological warfare. In regard to genetic engineering the crucial impact was seen to be the possibility of the large-scale production of toxins:

... Most potent toxins have formerly been available only in very small quantities, and then only upon isolation from vast amounts of biological material. The cloning of the genes coding for production of toxins into micro-organisms has enabled production of kilogram quantities of these toxins.

It was also found that the advances in fermenter technology referred to previously made it possible to conduct such production in small facilities. Concern over the use of genetic engineering to develop bacterial strains resistant to antibiotics was repeated. The contribution from the UK started by explaining that the term genetic modification (GM) would be used in place of recombinant DNA techniques or genetic engineering in order to reflect current practice in the European Commission Directives.

The term biotechnology was defined as 'the application of scientific and technological principles to the processing of materials by micro-organisms' The text explained that this covered GM techniques, fermentation and downstream (later) processing of products. The UK argued that there had been no significant innovations in GM techniques since the last review, but rather steady refinement and ever- widening application. Trends similar to those covered in the Australian document were mentioned; for example, it was stated that modification of the characteristics of any microbial species had become increasingly possible. Two specific examples were quoted:

...Modification (increase) of virulence has been reported for several pathogens; thus , an increase in the virulence of *Yersinia pseudotu berculosis* after a double mutation has been described.. and

.. baculovirus modified by insertion of the gene for the neurotoxin of the North african scorpion showed increased virulence for some species of insect. The same illustrative approach was them employed to illlustrate that capabilities for vaccine production were spreading:

.... several vaccines now at the field trials stage have been developed outside developed nations, including vaccines for leprosy (Venezuela and India), leishmaniasis (Venezuela and Brazil) and dengue haemorrhagic fever (Thailand).... and to reveral that GM techniques were being used for advanced developments:

... Use of GM produce a live vaccine is one idea being considered for the development of an oral vaccine against anthrax for use with livestock or wildlife, by introducing the gene for the Protective Antigen into a non-anthrax bacterial species

... We shall go into studies of anthrax in more detail later in this chapter. The 1991 UK text also made a mention of GM techniques being used to produce a potein from *Brucella* in E. *coli* and the development in the UK of an animal vaccine that used fowl pox virus as a vector for Newcastle disease viral antigens. The UK paper also covered protein engineering and other techniques using labelled antibodies and the polymerase chain reaction. It was noted that the latter developments could have a positive impact by enhancing capabilities for indentification and diagnosis of possible biological warfare agents.

On the other hand, the rising capabilities for the large-scale production of toxins and agents were considered potentially open to abuse, and the UK argued that further advances in these capabilities were to be expected. In line with assessments made by the depository states in 1986, the UK concluded that newly-recognised diseases like Marbug, Ebola and Lassa had no special relevance in relation to the BWC. However, the point was made that, as knowledge of these new diseases and new arboviruses went up there was an associated increased potential for its misuse. Accordingly attention was then sufficient to toxins and their production. It was argued that since 1986 more toxins had been isolated they could be more readily produced and much more was understood about the molecular bases of their toxicity. Such understanding allowed the development of novel toxins not found in nature :

.... For example, the A and B sub units of Shiga toxin and Shiga-like toxins have been combined. Such toxins may have altered toxicological or immunological properties...

The higher potential for the production of toxins by microbial cloning was recongnised, though chemical synthesis was seen as remaining difficult to scale up. Whilst some particlar problem were felt to remain is using micro - organisms to produe some compounds,the possibility of cloning cassettes' of genes to produce non- protein toxins was pointed out. As in the Australian submission, special attention was paid by the UK to industrial microbiology.

Similar points were made, for example, relating to the necessity of using higher organisms to produce some proteins, and the gains in productivity that had come from the use of real-time sensors, feedback loops and microprocessor control. The UK concluded that:

> There can thus be no doubt that the proliferation of legitimate civilian industrial microbiology activities and the continuing development of the underlying theory and equipment, has increased the potential world-wide for developing and producing biological weapons in contravention of the BWC...

The paper added that the increasing focus on environmental risks, and thus the use of better containment means, actually made it easier for the necessary equipment and expertise to be acquired by countries around the world. In regard to the microbial conrol of pests, *Bacillus thuringiensis* was still seen as the most widely used entomopathogen (insect pathogen), but it was noted that some 20 of the several hundred fungal species of entomopathogens were also being analysed in great detail. Work was also mentioned on making these control methods more efficient, for example by the use of UV protectants. Again the conclusion was significant:

> ... There has been increased study of factors relevant to effective disemination. Such knowledge could in principle be misused by an aggressor intending to attack crops... Some aspects of the dissemination technology would also be relevant to the deliberate release of organisms or toxins harmful to humans or animals.

The UK concluded saying that the enhanced potential for the misuse of biotechnology noted in the 1986 review was further evident in 1991. In 1986, it was recognised, there was an increased potential for large- scale production of possible agents with enhanced military utility. In 1991 the world-wide increase in knowledge of pathogenic micro-organisms, toxins and other possible agents had further improved this potential, as had the continuing pace of developments in civil technology. The continuing evolution of biotechnology, the expansion of industrial activity and of the microbial control of pests, in had :

> further increased the capability world- wide for the production

and dissemination of micro-organisms, of their prodducts,and of other types of biological agents.

...This capability could clearly be misused in an offensive biological weapons programme. The paper produced by the USA went through the similar ground, with sections on altered organisms, toxins peptides advances in production, mammalian cell culture, regular flow fermenters, safety and environmental standards, and hollow fibre technology. The general conclusion of the USA was that:

...The ease and rapidity of genetic manipulation, the ready availability of a variety of production equipment, the proliferation of safety and environmental equipment and health procedures to numerous laboratories and production facilities throughout the world, are *signs of the growing role of biotechnology in the world's economy..*

The paper concluded emphasising once again that these same signs point to the possibility of misuse Canada contributed only by way of a short note of two paragraphs to the back ground document, which referred to a study, *Novel Toxins and Bioregulators: the Emerging Scientific and Technologic Issues Relating to Verification and the Biological and Toxin Weapons Convention* which it had circulated to state parties. The Canadian contribution observed that although the study, prepared by a contract organisation, carried a traditional disclaimer, this 'should be understood to apply only to... policy issues', That means the disclaimer did not apparently apply to the scientific and technical content which, in effect, was therefore endorsed by the government. The study, in addition to an introduction and a general conclusion, had three sections dealing with technological changes, the novel toxins and bioregulators, and the potential dangers caused due to changes to the technology in this general area. The introduction made clear that before 1975 production of militarily-significant quantities of peptides (a peptide was defined as a molecule linking up a chain of between two and 50 amino acids) was not possible.

Since 1986, it was stated, progress had been such that various commercial companies could offer for sale 'quantities of peptides that could have military significance. There had been progress across the board in identification, synthesis, modification and large-scale production. Large-scale production was stated to be possible through recombinant DNA techniques, enzymatic synthesis or solidphase synthesis. The introduction also clarified that toxins inanimate chemicals as they are, became incorporated in the BWC largely by historical accident. At the time when the convention was agreed, it we still required to extract toxins from biological material, and production methods were therefore similar to those for biological weapons agents. Thus they became grouped together.

Toxins, though inanimate, generally have a higher specificity for their living target receptors than do man-made chemicals like nerve agents. Bioregulators were defined as small peptides that often control the release of hormones and 'could be regarded master switches of life. The technological changes in this regard between 1975 and 1990 were felt to have been dramatic, with a thousand-fold rise in capabilities for the synthesis and purification of peptides. The study also briefly reviewed several toxins and bioreguators. Examples were conotoxins from marine snails, which are relatively small peptide of 13 to 29 amino acids, and the 14 amino acid- chain somatostatin. It was argued that, although the available evidence showed that the lethality of toxins could not be increased by manipulation of their structure, considerable effects could be produced by changes in the structure of biorgulators, furthermore, the under standing of the structure and function of bioregulators was regarded tobe at an early but rapidly developing stage. The study suggested that there were military to fallout these developments that needed monitoring. In regard to toxins was suggested that new agents might be developed and produced which had novel sites of action, rapid and specific effects, the ability to penetrate protective filters in masks or the ability to the incapacitate. The question of the production of militarily-effective incapacitating agents was discussed also in relation to bioregulators.

Given that these substances can affect many different functions, and can be selectively modified by changing their amino acid sequences, it was suggested that:

This gives rise to the possibility of selectively affecting mental processes and many aspects of health such as control of mood... Even a small imbalance in these natural substances could have serious consequences inducing fear, fatigne, depression...

Not surprisingly, the study ended with the remanx that the possibility of new warfare agents had gone up.

It is evident from these official reports that a significant change had been detected between 1980 and 1991. There are several aspects of modern biotechnology that give rise to conerns over its misuse in offensive biological weapons programmes. There is not space here to review in detail all the aspects mentioned in these studies, but what may be more useful is to try to demonstrate the present state of knowledge, and ideas, of future developments, in a few key areas which well covered in the open literature. We shall focus here mainly on agents and toxins in our discussion.

The Objectives

In the late 1980s Professor Harry Smith, published two articles in which he reviewed the development of studies on bacterial and bacterial and viral pathogenicity. He stated that the objective of studies of pathogenicity was to explain in molecular terms the various biological aspects of this multifactorial property.This level of molecular explanation, he argued, needed the acccomplishemen of a series of logical steps which are set out in Table 9.2. Clearly if it hence possible to establish that only a virulent strain produced a certain toxin and that this toxin, because of its chemical structure and its target in a host, damaged the host in a very specific way, the kind of explanation needed would be achievable.

Table 9.2 Steps Needed in the Molecular-level Explanation of Pathogenicity

1	Comparison of virulence of strains in the host or relevant model.
2	Identification of strains of high and low virulence.
3	Strains compared in biological tests related to the key requirements for pathogenicity: infection and penetration of mucous surfaces; multiplication *in vivo.* interference with host defences; and causation of damage to the host.
4	Identification of the determinants that cause these biological properties.
5.	The relevance of a property and its determinant to infection *in vivo* must be proved.
6.	The chemical structure of the determinant must be related to its biological action.

Smith opines that there have been two period of rapi development of knowledge in this field of scientific research, first during the 'golden, age of medical bacteriology' between the 1870s and the First World War and then again since the 1960s. According to him

... However only for a few bacterial toxins and for certain aspects of viral replication have all these steps been achieved....

Smith's view, studies of bacteiral pathogenicity were essentially moribund in the late 1940s and studies on the pathogenicity of viruses begun Smith's opinion on the impact of genetic manipulation must be seen against that background. As he puts it: To sum up, genetic manipulation has transformed the study of pathogenicity. Difficulties may arise in using a particular method, but now there is such a variety of powerful techniques that if one does not work, another will probalebly substitute.

Though the study of the effects of mutagens on pathogens has been pursued for decades, the present ability to remove a virulence property from a stain to add it to a non-virulent strain by removing or inserting specific genes is exteremely powerful. Moreover, the gene porducts causing a particular effect can now be effectively altered down even to the change of single amino acids by altering the nucleotide sequence of the gene. In this the steps manner the nucleotide for amolecular- level explanation can be undertaken As Smith noted:

...Site-directed mutagenesis is even more specific.. Two examples among many are single amino acid substitutions in diphtheria toxin fragment A and in the exotoxin of P. *aeruginosa*, which showed that glutamic acid residues at positions 148 and 553, respectively, are crucial for... toxicity.

Still yet a great deal remains unkown. Smith argued in 1989 that future work should both try to achieve a molecular level of explanation in more examples than those at present under study, and certain areas that have been neglected should receive more attention. For bacteria, Smith identified areas needing more work, such as how small numbers of bacteria initiate the first stage of infection and how long-term survival in the host is assured, in both cases against the forces of the host defence mechanism. However, in his view.

... The major gap in our understanding of bacterial pathogenicity is lack of knowledge of the nutrients and metabolism that underlie growth *in vivo*.

... Concerning the virus virulence Smith's view was that it had not been analysed in anything like the depth achieved for bacteria. He opined that whilst viral replication had been well studied:

... Mucosal invasion, mucosal penetration, and interference with host defence mechanisms have been neglected, and damage to host issue has been understudied..

He held that such omissions required remedying. The lag between bacterial and viral research had another consequence, however, which we must analyse before turning to the current state of the art in some specific areas of research.

Defensive Research Programmes

Here we shall discuss a particular characteristic of defensive research programmes which is srelevant to the direction of current developments. David Huxsoll, who was formerly commander of the US Army Medical Research Institute for Infectious Diseases (USAMRIID) at Fort Detrick, pointed out that the technology needed for manufacturing large amounts of viral agents in cell culture only became available at the end of the offensive biological research programme in the USA. Had the programme not been terminated, he would have expected to see viral agents which were in the research and development stage in the late 1960s moved forward being to classified as standard agent types in the 1970s, to join the predominantly bacterial agents already standardised. This view fits well with Smith's assessment that studies of bacteria were further advanced than studies of viruses all through the cold War period .

It would follow that dangerous new advances are now even more likely in regard to potential viral agents than possible bacterial agents. This point was strongly brought out by for Erhard Geissler in his assessment of new biological weapons carried out as part of the SIPRI study of biological and toxin weapons in the mid-1980s. Geissler listed publicly-available information on military in terest in different viral, fungal and bacterial pathogens for different years. He concluded that in 1969 most potential agents (20 out of 31) were bacterial or fungal (19 out of 22) were viral. Whilst this measure may have been relatively crude, Geissler then gave four good reasons to support his observation. He suggested that the advent of genetic engineering techniques had made it possible for agents previously very dangerous to handle in the laboratory to be manipulated with relative safety

An example cited was the study of the function of various genes within. E. *coli.* Viral diseases were often more attractive to the military planner, Geissler suggested, because they were even more difficult to treat than bacterial diseases. Such viral diseases were quite to much more difficult to diagnose. Finally, he argued that the rising number of anti-viral vaccines were being developed which would allow the potection of an aggressor's own military forces before the agents being used. Geissler covered many of the points made by Smith concering the lack of knowledge about the mechanisms underliying viral virulence. He indicated that genetic engineering raised advancesim the new possibility of increasing such virulence by adding toxin- encoding genes to the viruses. He noted that vacccinia virus had been used to develop vaccines by the addition of genes or antigens and that the same techniques had been applied to other viruses. Thus:

... The same techniques might possibly be used to develop viral vectors carrying genes coding for highly toxic molecules.. It may be noted that the British paper for the 1991 review had mentioned just such an example of a toxin being added to a baculovirus thereby improving its virulence against insects. In a later study Geissler himself expaded on the same theme, stating that:

Recombinant on virus expression vectors have been created as novel vaccination agents, carrying and expressing , for example, genes derived from dengue virus, Hantaan virus, Lassa virus, Rift alley fever virus, and Russian tick-borne encephalitis virus. These viruses have been considered as putative BW agents...

Considering that work is also underway to develop means of targeting such viruses, say against cancer cells, very powerful new lethal agents could become available. Improving knowledge of, and the ability to manipulate, viral genomes are obviously two of the major specific developments that need to look to in considering the current state of the art.

Current Research: Some Examples

It will be worthwhile to deal first with some recent examples of work on bacteria and bacterial toxins, then to look at peptides and finally recent studies of viruses.

Bacteria

Recent reviews clearly reveal that studies of bacterial pathogensis have various moved beyond investigations of single genetic factors with in species or even of various different genetic factors within a single species. It is now possible to make factually-based broad generalisations about how regulator genes control the operation of various lethal factors in a pathogen and about how evolutionary developments of different pathogens have arisen. Additionally, the complex interactions between hosts and pathogens are becoming evident and molecular-level explanations are being advanced of how pathogens operate within micro-environments created by the interactions.

Discussions of individual cases have to be seen against that broader background of developing knowledge. One example described recently related to the species of *yersinia* which are pathogenic for humans *Y enterocolitia and Y Pseudotuber culosis* are acquired by ingestion and are not particularly dangerous Yersinia pidaestis, which is transmitted by the bite of rodent, fleas, is the cause of plague. It seems that these species are very closely related; indeed, *Y. pestis* has been classfied as a sub-species of *Y. pseudotuber* culosis. The most evident difference in evident the genetics of the latter two species is that *Y. pestis* possesses two large plasmids. The smaller of these has been shown to have a sure link to causation of plague. If mice are infected with *Y.pestis* deeply, by intravenous means, it does not matter whether this plasmid is present or not for plague results because the bacterium is free to multiply all over the body.

However, if the bacteria are injected just subcutaneously (as in a flea-bite) and the smaller plasmid is absent, the median lethal dose needed to cause infection increases by more than a million- fold because the bacteria are unable to break out of the localised area and reproduce massively. Thus it appears that the acquisition of the smaller plasmid was the crucial factor which led to the evolution of *Y. Pestis* from the *Y. Pseudotuber culosis* line. The smaller plasmid is needed to make sure that the initial flea-bite turns into a widespread massive infection and then uninfected fleas will be infected on biting such an infected animal. As death in humans seems to be caused by over-reaction to coating of the bacteria if they are present in large numbers rather than to a specific toxin they produce, it would appear that the plasmid is also responsible for the virulence of the species in humans. In the *Y. pestis* strain KIM -10, isolated from a human plague victim in Iran in the early 1960s, the small plasmid was designated p PCPI . A series of strains containing mutants or cloned fragments of p PCPI was by developed investigators and it was shown that if the gene for a particular one of the three products known to be produced by the plasmid was missing or inactivated, virulence dropped in the dramatic manner just described for mice. Likewise, if this gene was present, even in the absence of any other gene on the plasmid, the virulence was restored. This plasmid gene, *pla,* encodes for a surface protease. The operation of this enzyme was investigated by increasing large amounts of it in *E. coli* after genetic engineering.

The investigators regarded that the most likely mode of operation of the enzyme was in breaching the barriers put around the site of the initial infection by the host body's defence mechanisms. Such an action would then allow the bacteria to spread throughout the body. Genes with strong similarities to pla have been found in other bacteria and are regarded to probably play a similar role in such species and their pathogenesis. Another well-understood host-pathogen example is that of anthrax.There seem to be two principle virulence factors which operate in man and animals. *Bacillus anthracis* produces a capsule which protects it from phagocytosis and is there fore crucial in allowing an infection to become established, and a three-component toxin which causes tissue oedema and is the major cause of mortality.

The virulent stains of the bacterium have two large plasmids designated pXO1 and pXO2. The genes for the toxin are on pXOI and those for the capsule are on pXO2. Virulence requires both genes. Strains without pXO1 do not produce toxin and are therefore not virulent. Stains without pxO2 but with pXO1 are at least 10 times less virluent than the original wild strain because the bacteria lack the protective capsule and are more effectively destroyed by the host. Although the organism has been found to secrete other substances, none has been found to be involved in pathogenesis. The anthrax toxin components are individually not toxic.

The three proteins involved are called the protective antigen (PA) the lethal factor (LF) and the oedema factor (EF). It seems that there are two distinct toxic activities. Combinations of LF and PA are called lethal toxin and combinations EF and PA are called oedema toxin. The PA protein seems to bond to receptors on suitable cells and promote the entry of LF and EF. PA is the main immunogen for the production of vaccines against anthrax. Early work between 1940 and 1965 led to techniques which allowed the production of anthrax toxin in milligram amounts. However, the genes have now been sequenced and cloned into therelated species B. *subtilis.*

The PA gene has also been sub-cloned into baculovirus-derived vectros and expressed in insect cells, an also into vaccinia virus. The mechnism of action of the toxin has been thoroughly studied as has the evolution of its component parts. Clearly, the role of PA in promoting the entry of LF and EF into cells might be improved by the use of other proteins. The damage caused within cells would thereby be increased.

Toxins

Botulinal neurotoxins produced by *Clostridium botulinum* have been the subject of intense research for a long time. There are seven different types of botulinal neurotoxin, four of which (A, B, E and F) have been discovered through outbreaks of botulism in human beings. There is only one type of tetanus toxin, produced by a related bacterium of the *Clostridia* group. Tetanus is safely prevented by immunisation with a formaldehyde treated toxin. This is the most extensively used vaccine all over the world. But there are still large numbers of people needlessly affected by tetanus in poor countries of the world. Tetanus is initiated through a wound; botulinal toxins are usually ingested and therefore have to survive through the gut. Both toxins, however, then have particular effects on the nervous system. As both toxins rapidly kill, infection causes an animal corpse of enormous potential infectivity containing vast numbers of infective spores. For *Clostridium tetani* it was shown in the mid-1970s that toxigenic strains always contained a large plasmid, loss of which correlated with loss of the toxic effect.

The complete sequence of nucleotides of the gene for the toxin was worked out in the mid-1980s. Much is also known about the genetics of the botulinal toxins and the gene for the A toxin, although not on a plasmid, was recently entirely sequenced. The amino acid sequences of the tetanus and some of the batulinal toxins have been worked out and detailed comparisions have been made between them and other bacterial toxins. The mecanisms of action of these toxins on the nervous system are still being throughly studied and genetic engineering methods are being increasingly used. A recent reviewer concluded that it looks to be just a matter of time before the parts of the molecules involved in their binding to nerve cells, entry into nerve cells and toxic effevt would be characterised. Then it would be possible to undertake a genetic redesign of the toxins. Similar under standing of the genetics, structure and function of staphy to lococal and other several bacterial toxins is also being achieved. Some toxins (e.g. Saxitoxin) have recently been brought under the direct control of the Chemical Weapons Convention.

However, concerns have been expressed about a very wide range of possible new agents such as trichothecenes in yellow rain and new incapacitating agents. While less stress has been placed on the likely misuse of trichothecenes in recent times it may be that new chemical incapacitating agents, the US Advanced Riot Control Agent, could escape control if developments are not monitored carefully. Generally, it appears that toxicologists are increasingly seeking molecular explanations for the phenomena they study and, within the larger field of research, neutoxicology is more important. An example of what can be done was the response to a disorder which affected some people in Nova Scotia who ate contaminated mussels in 1987. The usual symptoms of food poisoning were followed by continuing problems with short- term memory. The cause was found to a substance called demoic acid, and research groups are now engaged in analysing how it interferes with the formation and storage of memory.

Viruses

The classification of viruses is still under development stage and several new ones are being discovered. Standard classifications rely on the morphology, structure, site of replication, mode of transmission and so on of the viruses. One system of classification, put borth by the Nobel Prize winner David Baltimore, focuses on the mode of replication and expression of the viral genes. This classification is helpful to our present concern with current research on viral diseases at the molecular level. As protein synthesis takes place in the same way in all cells, messenger RNA (mRNA) is central to the scheme.

All viruses are grouped according to the pathway of mRNA synthesis in Baltimore's classification. In order to maintain the unity of the scheme, all mRNA is designated as plus (+) and strands of viral RNA or DNA which are complementary to the mRNA are designated as minus (-). Those which have the same sequence as mRNA are also designated as plus. The scheme logically leads to seven classes of virus type. These are listed in Table 9.3 Class 2 is split as the Class 2b group of viruses was discovered after Baltimore produced his classification and therefore had to be made a sub-set rather than having a class of their own in the scheme. It is evident that yellow fever virus was investigated as a potential biological, warfare agent. Current research on this, and related flaviviruses, can give us a picture of the current state of research on such organisms. It will be recalled that yellow fever was recognised as a disease from the seventeenth century on wards and that fit had been a reason for great misery until the role of mosquitoes as vectors for transmission of the virus was discovered at the start of the century. A safe vaccine. Was eventually also devloped, but the disease

Table 9.3 The Baltimore Classification

1. Viruses with double-stranded DNA genome.
2a. Viruses with single-stranded DNA genome of the same sequence as mRNA.
2b. Viruses with DNA complementary to mRAN. Before synthesis of mRNA the DNA must be converted to double-stranded form.
3. Viruses with double-stranded RNA genome. Known viruses of this type have a segmented genome, but mRNA is only synthesised on one strand of each segment.
4. Viruses with single-stranded RNA genome of the same sequence as mRNA. Synthesis of the complementary strand needed prior to production of mRNA.
5. Viruses with single-stranded RNA genome of base sequence complementary to mRNA.
6. Viruses that have a single-stranded RNA genome a which have a DNA intermediate during replication.

cannot easily be eradicated as it also infects monkeys. The complete genome of yellow fever virus was sequenced in the mid-1980s and the relationship between the genome and the key viral proteins was deduced. A review of what was known of the flaviherus genome in the early 1990s an provides overview of what was known of this group of viruses as a whole. The Flaviviridac family of viruses takes its name from yellow fever, the Latin for yellow being 'flavus'. The group had 68 known viruses in 1990, the majority of which are transmitted to vertebrates through mosquitoes or ticks. The life-cycles of the viruses between their very different hosts are therefore complex.

The infective virus particles or virions are small, being about 40-70 nm (m^{-9}) in diameter. The single stranded positive RNA in the genome (Baltimore Class 4) is immediately enclosed by a protein capsid to form the nucleocapsid. This structure is enclosed by another envelope of lipoprotein. Representative examples of the apart from group yellow fever, are tick borne encephalitis, *St. Louis encephalitis* and *dengue*. Yellow fever, dengue and Japanese encephalitis are major world diseases; a number of the other viruses in the group are of regional concern. The genome RNA is approximately 11,000 bases in length. It is infectious and can thus be used for translation of vilar proteins. Following translation, the +mRNA replication involves the production of complementary minus strands of RNA which are then used as templates to produce more plus stands. These + mRNA strands can then be used for the direct production of protiens, synthesis of more minus strands, or encapsulation into new virus. The most important of charatecristic of the genome is that it has one open-reading frame of over 10,000 bases. That is to say, only one polyprotein is produced which is then cut in various paces to produce the virus structural and non-structural proteins.

At least ten proteins are produced: three of these are structural and seven are non- structural . Much is known about these proteins throughout the flaviviruses group. Fig. 9.1 shows the genome of yellow fever virus and the relationship of major protein products to the coding regions of the RNA. The capsid structural protein (C) is small. It forms the structural part of the capsid which together with the genome of the virus constitutes the nucleocapsid. The amino acid sequence of this protein, and thus the RNA sequence coding for it, is quite variable amongst different flaviviruses. The prM protein is a precursor to the M glycoprotein which along with E protein forms part of the lipid bilayer of the envelope surroundig the nucleocapsid.

Fig. 9.1 Organisation of the Yellow Fever genome and the Processing of Proteins

Yellow Fever 17D Genome

total 10,862 nucleotides

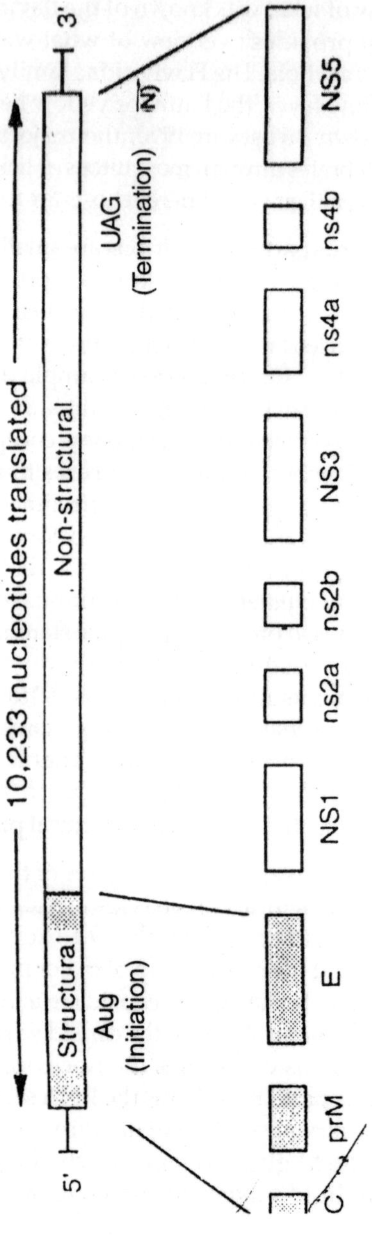

It seems that inside the infected cell the prM protein is the only from of this protein, but out side the cell the M part predominates as the or segment is removed. The E protein is the major structural protein of the complete virus particle or virion and is assumed to be significance in key activities such as binding to cells and fusing with membranes. It is the main target for antibodies. The protein has been subject of a detailed study and a model of its structure proposed. This is based on studies of the tick-borne encephalitis virus. The NS3 non-structural protein is the second largest produced and is very similar (highly conserved) throughout the flavivirus group. NS5 is the largest of the proteins and is again highly conserved . It is regarded that the conservation of the NS3 and the NS5 proteins throughout the group indicates that they play a role as enzymes in RNA replication.

The strong similarities between the genetics of the group of viruses is thought to be because of the selective pressures exerted by their need to adapt to both their arthropod and mammalian hosts. More importantly, in our opinion the complete genome of virulent yellow fever and the avirulent YF 17D vaccine strain have been compared. These differ at 67 nucleotide positions and in 32 amino acids (because of the redundancy of the nucleotide code, not all substitutions change amino- acids). As it is now possible to produce complementary DNA and clone it to make infectious RNA rapid growth in understanding the biological basis of virulence should be possible. As the authors of the 1990 review concluded.

Molecular studes on flaviviruses have etered an explosive phase. The past several years have seen an amazing accumulation of structural information and common as well as distinct features of flavivirus genome RNAs and proteins have begun to emerge ...

The review ended with hopes that such advances would lead to the discovery of means to control these important pathogens on the other hand, clearly, is that the same knowledge could so easily be misused. The pace of research continues to be rapid, as was seen at the IXth.

Table 9.4 Examples of Current Studies of Flaviviruses

Paper No.	*Institution*	*Topic*	*Virus*
W77-2	Faculty of Medicine Mahidol University Bangkok, Thailand	Japanese encephalitis in Asia, Description of current incidence of disease, causes and prevention measures	Japanese encephalitis
W77-1	Medical departments in Japan and Pakistan	Detection of viral sequences in Japanese cerebrospinal fluid from encephalitis cases using reverse transcripta-sepolymerase chain reaction	West Nile and encephalitis
W10-5	Department of Microbiology Emory University Atlanta, USA	Proteins involved inflavivirus virion assembly investigated by expression of gene cassettes in a vaccinia virus expression system	West Nile and Dengue
P10-6	John Curtin School of Medical Research Australian National University, Canberra	Investigation of prM protein cleavage and spike secretion by NS3 proteinase using vaccinia virus recombinants	Murray Valley encephalitis
P10-9	Microbiology Molecular and cell Biology Departments Singapore	Investigation of NS2 a and NS2b proteins expressed in E. coli	Dengue1
P10-16	Institute of Virology University of Vienna Austria	Molecular basis of virulence studied by comparison of genomes of virulent and non-virulent strains	Tick- borne encephalistis strains
W51-4	Dept. of Molecular Microbiology Washington Univer. St Louis, USA	Highly neuro-virulent strain for mice compared with less virulent strain in terms of C pMr-E NS1 nucleotide sequences	Yellow fever

P51-6	Australian National Univesity Canberra	Variants of the E protein tested encephalitis for cell fusion and virulence in mice. A specific single amino-acid substitution found to increase median lethal dose needed by 10^6-fold	Murray Valley
P30-7	Institute Pasteur Paris, France	Investigation of the immunogenicity of E protein expressed in insect cells via baculovirus vector	Dengue 2
W30-5	Army Medical Research Institute of Infectious Diseases; National institutes of Allergy and Infectious Diseases, USA	Evaluation of alternative vaccines produced via recombinant vaccinia virus baculovirus expression and construction of a chimeric dengue	Tick- horne encephalitis
P-18	Centre for Applied Microbiology, Porton Down, UK and Ivanovsky institute, Moscow	Investigation of antigenic variation in viruses from different sources in Russia by means of mooclonal antibodies against both E and NSI proteins	Tick- borne encephalitis
W30-6	Institute of Molecular Biology, Novosibirsk Region, Russia	Vaccinia virus containing multiple foreign genome pieces responsible for immune responses produced and tested in preclinical trials	Tick- borne enclphalitis (Hepatitis B Venezuelan equine encephalitis)

International Congress of Virology held in Glasgow during August 1993. More than 50 papers on flaviviruses were presented at the Congress. Some representative examples have been briefly summarised from the abstracts and are listed in Table 9.4. It will be observed that investigators are spread all over the world; studies of the structure and function of the genome and its immediate protein products are advancing on various fronts numerous vector and expression systems are in use; and the research is clearly going to pay increasing dividends in medical applications. From our point of view perhaps the most important of the papers was by the group at Washington University, St. Louis, some of whom were individually responsile for the earlier papers on yellow fever virus that have been cited here. Paper W51-4, on the genetic analysis of yellow fever neurovirulence in mice, states that for a strain highly nuroviralence in mice, states that for a strain highly neurovirulent in mice '3 amino- acid changes were onsistently observed in the E protein relative to the less virulent [strain]'. These minor looking changes are now being investigated in greater detail in recombinant viruses. Of course, ths example of the detaile knowledge being generated in present studies is not an isoloated one.

The paper on the E protein of Murray Valley encephalitis (P51-6) severals how a single specific amino acid change can have a dramatic impact on virulence. Again, such a specific change can be subjected to further effective research. Similar advances in knowledge are being achieved with various viral groups other than just the Flaviviridae, as papers at the Congress demonstrated. Table 9.5 provides examples of current work on some viruses known to be of potential interest to planners of biological warfare programmes.

The papers of outstanding interest are obviously those concerned with the elucidation of the nucleotide sequences of the samll pox (variola major) strains (W 20-1, W20-2). The Congress included a round-table discussion of the current proposals for the final elimination of small pox stocks. The research on recently discovered viruses like Marburg, Lassa and Ebola is also advancing as full nucleotide sequences become available. In general terms, the papers listed in Table 9.8 again demonstrate the widespreadability to manipulate a large number of vector and expression systems for these viral genomes. It is instructive compare such recent research with the requirements for a molecular level of understanding of viral pathogenicity set out in Table 9.1. In an article at the end of 1993 on the French research which produced a map of the human genome, the London Financial Times indicated that it had been a 'golden year for genetics.' What the year had produced is more significant than any since 1953 when Watson and Crick discovered the structure of DNA and the prcise genetic cause behind many inherited diseases

Table 9.5
Examples of Current Studies of Potential Viral Agents[1]

Paper No. Groups	*Institution*	*Topic*	*Virus/*
W6-2	Medical Virology University of Heidelberg, Germany	Viral proteins expressed in yeast cells after cloning with a shuttle vector	Hantavirus (Bunyavirus)
W6-3	Virology Division, Army Medical Research Institute for Infectious Diseases, and Chemical Engineering Johns Hopkins University USA	Viral proteins expressed in a recombinant baculovirus and in recombinant vaccinia virus studied for assembly of virus-like particles and induction of immunity	Hantaan (Bunyavirus)
W20-1	Centre for Disease Control and Prevention, Atlanta, Institute for Genomic Research, Gaithersberg, USA	Complete nucleotide sequence of virulent strain compare with vaccinia virus	Variola major (Strain Bangladesh 1975) (Poxvirus)
W20-2	Institute for Molecular Biology, Novosibirsk Region, Russia	Complete nucleotide sequence of virulent strain compared with that of variola minor sequences	Variola major (Strain India 1967) (poxvirus)
W32-6	Virus Reference Division Colindale, and Centre for Applied Microbiology Porton Down , UK	Use of reverse transcriptase and polymerase chain reaction for a fast and safe diagnostic tenchnique	Lassa fever (Arenavirus)
W38-4	Kenya Agricultural Research Institute, Nairobi ; US Universities	Expression of proteins in a recombinant capripoxvirus and determination of immunogenicity for domestic ruminants	Rift Valley (Bunyavirus)
W52-4	Institute for Molecular Biology, Novosibirsk Region, Russia	Complete nucleotide sequence obtained and compared with Ebola virus sequence	Marburg (Popp strain) (Filovirus)
P38-3	Institute for Plant Protection and university departments in Tel- Aviv and Jerusalem, Israel	Lqhal T neurotoxin cDNA cloned into AcMPV insect baculovirus and expressed in extracts of insect cells. Toxin tested effectively on live insects	Yellow scorpion inseo-specific neurotoxin

P44-7	Institute fur Virologie, Marburg, Germany	Expression of the L gene multifunctional protein enzyme in insect cells	Marburg (Filovirus)
P51-16	Institute for Molecular Biology, Novosibirsk Region, Russia	Computer analysis of complete genome sequence compared with protein data banks to identify clusters of genes important in pathogenicity	Variola major (strain India 1967) (Poxvirus)
P52-2	Institute for Molecular Biology, Novosibirsk Region, Russia	Full nucleotide sequence of genome determined	Ebola (Filovirus)
P65- 23	Botanical Institute, Munich	The Tm-2^2 resistance gene used in most commercial cultivars shown to be overcome by a ToMV mutant with two specific amino acid substitutions in the movement protein.	Tomato mosaic virus (To MV).

1. Papers are included in this list only in order to illustrate the range of topics covered in the Congress which could be of interest to military planners.

had been found Dr. Cohen leader of the French team, was quoted as saying:

... In 10 to 20 years most of the diseases caused by single gene defects like cystic fibrosis will be cured...

Concerning the diseases of Western society which have much more complex causes, involving multiple gene interaction and the environment. Cohen added that in half a century most of these serious diseases will also be cured. That may provide us an approproate time scale to consider for the issues we are discussing. It appears most probable that a nation wishing to begin offensive biological weapons programme today would make effort to produce well known agents such as anthrax or botulinal toxins. This was what Iraq attempted. To go beyond that would need country to have a strong background in biotechnology and the ability to organise a talented research group from currently limited resources. We cannot expect that situation to last long.

Maybe for the next decade or two the capabilities we have just discussed will remain predominantly in the hands of western countries but it does not appear likely to be true 20 years from now. Centainly in 50 years' time, the ability produce many different kinds of new biological weaponry will surely become widespread. What today would need the ingenuity of a Nobel Prize- winner will by then be commonplace.

10

Iraq and Biological Weapons

The war in the gulf in 1990s brought Iraq and its biological weapons Programme in. limelight. Later discoveries revealed that Iraq had much more developed BW programme that was anticipated. This became known though the UN inspections in the Iraq.On 11 December 1998, US President Clinton and UK Prime Minister Tony Blair agreed to bomb Iraq. the United Nations was reporting that Iraqi President Saddam Hussein was continuing to break the agreement he had signed in 1991 at the end of Gulf War under which he promised to reveal the stock of his biological weapons. For seven years the United Nations had been making efforts. With some ssuceess, to outwit the Iraqis attempts duck this obligation. The UN report of yet more Iraqi non Compliance helped bring US frustration- possibly stoked by Clinton's domestic political difficulties-to thc boil. On16 December the attack started. For four nights, cruise missiles and other bombs struck at Iraq's weapons installations, air defence facilities, state security apparatus and the Republican guard- the elite force close to Saddam.

One of the targets of British bombs was an airbase at Itali in south-east Iraq, which the British said housed unmanned aircraft, with facilities to fit aerosols to spray biological weapons. Under the circumstances seems highly unlikely that Iraq ill allow any more inspectores from the United Nations Special Commissin on Iraq (UNSCOM) to continue their efforts touncover any remaining preparations for biological war.

Birth of UNSCOM

The United Nations established UNSCOM in 1991, following Iraq's invasion of Kuwait and the subsequent Gulf War. The ceasefire arragements at the end of the war were aimed at reducing the threat posed by Iraq's weapons. The UN Security Council demanded that the defeated state should not try to develop nuclear weapons, and it made the International Atomic Energy Agency responsible for preventing this. It also laid down that Iraq must accept the destruction, removal or rendering harmless of missiles with a range beyond 150 kilometres, and all chemical and biological weapons. This disarmament should be spervised by an international body, which would have unrestricted access to Iraqi facilities.

Thus UNSCOM was born. The idea was that Iraq would make a clean breast a its chemical. Biological and missile capabilities to the UN. As far as its biological weapons programme was concerned, it would provide details of the locations in which it had to make research, development, support and manufacturing. It would specify the types of agents it had worked on and the amount it had stockpiled. Working on leads provided Iraq's declarations, UNSCOM would inspect the facilities to check that its activities tallied with its declarations. Obviously Iraq was less than enthusiastic about the plan. For the first two years of UNSCOM's life it refused, in effect, to co-operate. The task facing the inspetors was daunting.There was no evidence that Iraq had developed biological weapons. There had been rumours, but no proof. And the nature of biological weapons made their job even tougher. It is rather easy to detect whether a state is developing and deploying nuclear weapons. The production of the fissile materials for a militarily-significant number of nuclear weapons, for example, needs quite large plants which are extremely easy to detect by, say, reconnaissance satellites. But biological weapons are entirely different. The bacteria and viruses they depend on are produced in exactly the same way as those used for legitimate health-care: for vaccines and antibiotics.

Micro-organisms for biological weapons are developed in the same equipment that can be found in pharmaceutical companies, university biological laboratories, breweries, distilleries, dairies, diagnostic laboratories, and vaccine- producing facilities. Once upon a time it was hard to produce micro- organisms on a large scale. But these days, modern biotechnology makes it easy; and the know-how as well as the equipment is commonplace. The Equipment that can be used for both military and civilan purposes is called 'dual-use'; and it poses a problem that lies at the heart of controlling the development of biological weapons. It presented the U N S C O M team with an uphill task . They were charged with monitring Iraq's dual-use equipment to ensure that it was only being used for inocent purposes. But they needed Iraq to tell them about its past clandestine programmes and its current legitimate ones, to form a baseline from which ongoing activities could be monitored. And Iraq refused. It took pressure for it admit in May 1992 that it had a very small defensive biological research programme- but no weapons. On paper, the inspectors had formidable power. They could inspect anything- site, activity, material unannounced, as often as they liked; they could fly overwhatever they wanted for surveillance purposes using their own aircraft. They could install sensors and video recorders sensitive locations; they could take pictures; they could gather inormation from other countries about what pieces of dual-use equipment they had exported to Iraq. But it was not until January 1994 that Iraq gave UNSCOM enough information for them to conduct meaningful inspections for biological capabilities. The first such inspection, which was to establish the baseline against which others would be judged, was conducted in April that year.

Tough Task

Rod Barton, then of the Australian Department of Defence, was sent to Baghdad in September 1994 to form part of an UNSCOM team. It was not his first taste of Iraqi methods: before that also he had tried, again with UNSCOM. To uncover the full extent of Iraq's chemical weapons programme, when he joined the effort to discover whether Iraq had developed biological weapons as weapons as well, he was in for altough but exciting time. As Barton recalls in the journal Pacific Research, things did not look rosy. The Iraqi government persistently denied that it had developed biological weapons, saying that UNSCOM had free re in for three years to go anywhere, look anywhere, and had found nothing. He goes on:

Iraq had admitted to having the research programme. They said this facility was at Salman Pak, which had been heavily bombed during the war, so there was not much left of it. Iraq also had another facility, at al- Hakam that was not known to coalition governments before Gulf War, and therefore was not bombed. The inspectors were told that it was a biological facility for producing yeast for animal feed. Inspection teams had visited it frequently, as it an odd place, which didn't make technical sense, but were not able to gather any hard evidence that it was anything other than what the Iraqis claimed.

'We decided to ask supporting countries for information about imports into Iraq. The lists we got were quite comprehensive, but most items were dual-use in nature, so it was not easy to sort out what was legitimate from, what was not.

In addition, the team decided to interview Iraqi officials who had been involved. All ten people from Salman Pak that we asked to interview turned out to be now at al- Hakam far from driving taxis or doing whatever jobs they could find, as Iraqi officials had told us. This gave us a link between Salman Pak and al Hakam. It was clear to the inspection team as they interviewed the ten that all had been coached,and our suspicions were raised. Every single one said they knew nothing about anyone else, not even about people who had worked in the room next door, which the inspectors found unbelievable. But we were not able to get much more out of them.

Two wild cards proved very useful-the names of indviduals who had signed import orders. These, it turned out, were not scientists but clerks. One had been working or the Technical Scientific Materials Import Division (TSMID), and import organisation apparently connected with the Ministry of Trade. A breakthrough came when one of the clerks confessed that. TSMID had been importing only for Salman Pak, nowhere else. This turned out to be vital information.

The subjects interviewed in November 1994 were, on the whole, fairly arrogant and dismissive of the UNSCOM inspectors, as were Iraqi officials. They were confident that we would not be able to find out anything. Later, some officials became scared and nervous in the presence of the UNSCOM inspectors, and evinced signs of feding threatened. Some were even threatened by Iraqi offcials in our presence. One gave a story that technically and scientifically could not have been true. He asked for a break, then gave a new story, which was equally illogical. He produced a third story, a couple of days later. This chapter told us later he was so nervous at this time that he could not keep any food down. The ones who were scared had good reason to be so.

'We had one other breakthrough, from the information on imports provided by other governments. In1988 TSMID had imported many tons of bacterial growth media- stuff to grow bacteria on consisting of case in from milk, with other proteins and glucose). It was legitimate to grow bacteria for research, but you would need only, may be, one kilogram for research. If Salman Pak was using so much, then it could not be just for defence research. It must have been for something more aggressive.

The Iraqis denied that they had imported large quantities of growth media, but the UNSCOM inspectors quoted letter-of- credit numbers as proof that they had. The Iraqis then said the media had been used for the Ministry of Health for hospital use. The inspectors were suspicion. We checked with hospitals in different places, recalls Rod Barton, and found out, for example, that one big New York hospital might use a few kilos a year. We found that one whole country in the Middle East had used only a few tons over five years. By this stage we had discovered that TSMID had imported over 40 tons of growth media. The Iraqis told us the minister of Health had made a mistake and ordered much more than was needed. But the types of growth media were wrong, the quantities were wrong and they were in the wrong containers for hospital use. Some was in 25 kg containers, and some in 100 kg drums. This was not believable as quantities for hospital use, where you would need only a few grams at a time. Because, like milk powder, it cakes if you take the lid off and don't use it quickly, and you would expect it to be in small jars.'

The inspectors tried to track down the media using documentation. Iraq produced 22 documents receipts transfer documents and store —inventrey cards- which fornsic analysis revealed to be recently created. The originals, said the Iraqis, had been the only documents in a filing cabinet, which had been destroyed in a fire barton comments: The story was patently absurd. We asked for a report from the fire brigade. Was the office burnt down? No, it was just the filing cabinet. What was the cabinet made of? Steel. Was anything else burnt? No, there was nothing else in the cabinet. We asked for originals of the transfer receipts, and were told these had fallen off the back of a truck during a transfer from one store to another. With the third set of documents, the store inventory cards, the storeman got to the point where it was obvious his stories were absurd and there was no believable explanation for how the originals had been destroyed. We interviewed this poor storeman for hours.

The inspectors' interview were continuing against a background of UN sanctions against Iraq. These had been imposed in August 1990, after Iraq had invaded Kuwait as part of an attempt to force its withdrawal. When UNSCOM was set up, in 1991, the UN declared that sanctions would not be lifted until Iraq had cooperated fully with its activities. By 1994, the sanctions had crushing impact on the country and were causing appalling hardship to its people: poverty and prevailed allover and an almost total breakdown of medical services. In April 1995, the team reported to the UN Security Council that although they found no proof that Iraq had biological weapons, they did have circumstantial evidence. Back in Iraq, in May and June, officials refused to cooperate the inspectors. They said we were responsible for sanctions not being lifted; we were responsible for children dying,' remembers Rod Barton. 'On one occasion they actually brought dying children to our hotel, and there was a demonstration by doctors and nurses against UNSCOM. In July, the Iraqis changed their statement yet again. 'In a half-hour presentation, the head of the defensive research programme admitted that Iraq had developed a biological weapons programme, that it had started at Salman Pak and then gone to Al Hakam. The plants produced bacterial agents for anthrax and botulinurm toxin, about half a milloion litres. This would account for about 17 tons of the missing growth media. We asked if weapons hd been made, and got the answer, 'There were no weapons , we just produced and stored agent.'

On 7 August 1995, Saddam Hussein's son-in-law, General Hussein Kamal Hassan Majeed, fled Baghdad to seek asylum in Jordan. He had been looking after Iraq's entire nuclear, chemical and iological weapons programmes. The Iraqis initially tried to persuade him to return, and when this failed they apparently tried to assassinate him. This also failed and so the Iraqis finally, admitted, that they had made and deployed biological weapons. 'In the circumstance of potential disclosures by the most well-informed defector possible, the Iraqi government decided to pre-empt that eventuality by making them itself, writes Milton Leitenberg, of the Center for International and Security Studies at the University of Maryland.

'They admitted' recounts Rod Barton, 'that Iraq had made gas gangrene, anthrax, botulinum toxin , viral and fungal agents (including aflatoxin), agents against crops (such as wheat smut), and ricin (a deadly poison made from castor beans). These agents had been made not only at Al Hakam but at other plants as well.

There was a vast organisation, which employed many people.

UNSCOM was surprised-we hadn 'texpected the biological weapons programme to have been so big.

One of the more bizarre events of the saga occurred regarding these admissions. When General Hussein Kamel Hassan Majeed fled from Baghdad, the Iraqi gobvernment informed UNSCOM's Chairman, Ambassador Rolf Ekeus, that it had more information to add to its earlier disclosures. It was to Ekeus that the Iraqis made their admissions. Ekeus complained that he had not been provided with any documentation to support the new disclosures. As he was about to go to the airport to leave the country, he was contacted by an Iraqi General asking him to call at a farm on his way to the airport.

It was General Hussien Kamel Hassan Majeed's farm, and in a locked chicken house at the farm, Ekeus found 150 'metal and wooden boxes which were packed with documentation, together with microfiches , computer diskettes videotapes, photographs and prohibited hardware components. In all, there were more than half a million pages of documentation, much of it about UNSCOM's areas of interest. The Iraqis later admitted that, in the summer of 1991, the directors of the sites associated with the biological weapons programme had been ordered to pack up important documents quickly, and hand them over to the secrurity organisations. The documents recoved from the chicken coop were a major breakthrough for UNSCOM, but by no means do they provide an entire record of Iraq's biological weapons programme. Much is still missing, Ambassador Ekeus is far from convinced that Iraq divulged the full scope of its biological weapons programme. He opnines that Iraq wanted the UN to lift its sanctions without ever having to reveal its biological programme. 'They kept biology as the prize he concludes. 'The suspicion that Iraq is still concealing a great deal cannot be dismissed lightly. If you had seen the officers, who had denied everything until recently. Admit the existence of biological weapons without blushing, without feeling any remorse, you would understand why many in the United Nations still have doubts about Iraq's credibility.

Had Iraq's weapons been used, says Ekeus, they 'would have killed millions of people. What shocks me in retrospect is the realisation that the world was facing an enormous catastrophe, of which we did not even have a clue.'

How much do we know at present about Iraq's BW programme? The information it has released leads the UNSCOM inspectors to draw the following and probably incomplete) picture:

The programme began in 1975, achieved little and was closed down in 1978. It was re-started in 1985, at the Muthanna State Establishment, Iraq's main facility for chemical weapons research and development. In April 1986, bacterial strains were made available at Muthanna. It has been reported that the anthrax culture was bought by mail order from the US, and sent by overnight mail. Work on anthrax and botulinum toxin, thus began. In May 1987, the programme moved to al-Salman, where the agents were tested on sheep, donkeys, monkeys and dogs. A former biotechnology plant at Taji was also taken over for the purpose weapons production in mid-987. At the end of that year it was decided to step the programme up, and in 1988 a new weapons production facility was created and equipped at Al Hakam. It included space for studies of genetic engineering and work on viruses.

Meanwhile, at Al Salman, work began on the agent that produces gas gangrene (*Clostridium perfringens*) and aflatoxin (a poison which induces liver cancer many years after exposure. Researchers at the Stockholm International Peace Research have speculated that it may have been intended as a genocidal weapon against the Kurds. By the time symptoms became known, there would be no way of proving that they had been the Victims of biological warefare. Aflatoxinmay also have been intended as an immune. suppressant, to make other agents act more effectively. Later research was also conducted on toxins that produce nausea, vomiting, diarrhoea and skin irritation; on ricin, a lethal toxin; on haemorrhagic conjunctivitis virus which leads to acute pain and temporary blindness; and on rotavirus which causes diarrhoea. UNSCOM uncovered circumstantial evidence that tests of some of these agents may have been on human subjects. The programme was not confined to agents that would harm people. It also worked on camel pox which results in fever and skin rash in camels, and black stem rust of wheat which causes severe crop losses. The programme was drastically intensified after Iraq invaded Kuwait in August 1990. By December of that year, the Iraqis had manufactured 166 R400 aerial bombs filled with biological agents: 100 with botulinum, 50 with anthrax and 16 with aflatoxin. They had also made a specail BW warhead for the Al Husayn ('Super- Scud') missile: 25 of them; 13 filled with botulinum toxin ten with anthrax and two with aflatoxin. Just before the start of the Gulf War, in January 1991, these weapons were dispersed to four locations throughout the country where they remained during the war.

During the war, Iraq pre-delegated authority to launch the weapons in the even that Baghdad suffered nuclear attack. Comments UNSCOM: 'This pre-delegation does not exclude the alternative use of such a capability and therefore does not constitute proof of only intentions concerning second use.

Professor Paul Rogers, of the University of Bradford's Department of Peace studies remarks: 'If BW or chemical warfare agents had been used in the conflict on a substantial scale, and if the attack had been successfully undertaken against civilian targets such as Riyadh, Dhahran or Tel Aviv, casualties would have been broadly similar to those caused by nuclear weapons. A recent US Department of defense simulation exercise of a future Gulf crisis ended with a BW attack on Dhahran killing one million people, followed by a US nuclear retaliation against Baghdad.

Iraq claimed that it destroyed most of its BW facilities after the war, but reports of this destruction have been inconsistent and no proof had been offered to back them up. Meanwhile, UNSCOM got engaged in physically demolishing the Al Hakam site. Explains Rod Barton: 'Nothing will remain of the facility'. The equipment will be crushed ad the scrap buried in pits back-filed with concrete. The building will be blown up and the foundations removed. Even the power lines will be pulled down and the access roads bulldozed. Essentially the site will be returned to the desert so that Nothing will remain that can be used for biological weapons purposes again. Perhaps then this chapter on Iraq will be closed.

Microbiologist Raymond Zilinskas, of the University of Maryland Biotechnology Institute, was also seconded to UNSCOM and participated in two inspections in Iraq in 1994. His experience tells us different things... as far as is known, none of the persons who staffed Iraq's former BW former programe were harmed or killed during Desert Storm. We may assume that all of them would be available to staff a resurgent BW program, should the Iraqi leadership so decide. Likewise the same Iraqi leadership that decided to acquire biological weapons—and therfore launched Iraq's former BW program—remains intact and incharge. Thus the political will and the intellectual knowledge remain in place. A briefing paper written for UK Members of Parliament also notes stores of freeze-dried organisms could be easy to keep and hide, allowing a BW programme to be sewiftly reinstated.. [T] he concerns are that production of militarily significant quantities could resume in as little as six months.

Iraq's clandestine efforts to develop biological weapons are certainly not the first. Since the 1920s, the Western allies, Japan and the former Soviet Union have all done extensive work on agents and weapons.

The American Help

There no 18 doubt that the Americans helped the Iraqis develop biological weapons. American organisations supplied microbes to the Iraqis for 20 years- during the 1970s and 1980s.

The American Type Culture Collection (ATCC) is a non-profit firm based in Rockville, Maryland. It has the nation's leading collection of cultured diseases, and acts as a library of nearly 1,000 microbes for institutions all over the world. It sells approximately 130,000 cultures annually and ships orders to 60 nations- including Iraq. ATCC supplied 17 shipments to Iraq between 1986 and 1991: Director Robert Stevenson declined to reveal exactly what he had sold to the Iraqis, but tularemia is known to have been among the samples. The shipments, having attenuated strains of various toxins and bacteria, went to Iraq's Atomic Energy Commission, which is believed to have procured components for biological weapons.

Although the exports were not vetted by Pentagon or intelligence analysts, they had the approval of the Department of Commerce. Robert Stevenson is also the head of the Commerce Department's Advisory Committee on biological exports. Although Stevenson admitted that he did not really know who in Iraq was using his microbes, he stressed that there was nothing to worry about. He claimed that the materials he sent would be of no use for biological warfare- although he conceded that ATCC cultures would be 'useful' in a biological warfare program as 'reference points to determine if the deadly strain under was the real thing. The Commerce Committee believed him. ATCC was not the only us organisation to export micro organisms to Iraq.

In April 1990, NBC television reported that during the 1980' the Public Health service's Centers for Disease Control shipped deadly viruses via Express Mail to researchers in Iraq, South being engaged in. Africa, Cuba, the Soviet Union and China- all nations suspected of in biological warfare research-ostensibly for public health reasons. Acoording to NBC producer Robert Windrum and reporter Eric Nadler, 'the virus requested by, and supplied to, an Iraqi researcher in Basra was an Israeli strain of West Nile encepwhalitis. The virus had been the subject of a long-term vaccine research project in Israel supported by the US army because of its potential as a bio-warfare agent. The same virus was a cause of concern inside the Israeli defense forces medical corps due to outbreaks in Negev desert posts in the early 1980s. When NBC asked the CDC to provide documentation of these exports under the Freedom of Information act, the center said it had no records, since such transfers are handled 'informally'.

Remarkably, CDC staffers revealed no fear that the exported agents (all Biohazard level 3 and 4 materials the deadliest classification) would be used for germ warfare, 'because we know these people', as CDC spokesperson Gayle LIoyd breezily put it. She called any biological war scenario 'far- fetched.'

The NBC report brought an end to CDC biological shipments to Iraq. (*Source:* Eric Nadler and Robert Windrem, San Diego Union-Tribune, 26 January 1991, pb-11.)

Help from UK

The UK also helped Saddam Hussein develop his biological arsenal- by providing training to one of the Iraqi scientists in charge of the germ warfare unit.

Dr Taha Rihab received her PhD in Plant pathology at the University of East Anglia in 1984. She had come to the University from one in Iraq. Her PhD work was focused on a disease of tobacco plants. 'She really was an outstanding student', recalls one of her lecturers, Dr John turner. 'Hard working, very dedicated and absolutely charming. Not in my wildest dreams would I have thought of her in [weapons] work.'

The revelation provides an ironic twist to the fears of scientists afraid that their work could be used for aggressive purposes. It reveals how easy it is for people educated in good faith to use their skills for offensive ends, and how difficult would be to prevent the spread of knowledge needed for biological warfare in such a scenario.

Gulf War Syndrome

Major Hillary Jones returned to the UK from the gulf with a flu-like illness that she could not shake off. She had a persistent cough and developed chronic fatigue syndrome; whose exact cause is unknown but which is believe to be caused by prolonged exposure to viruses. Major Jones was forced to give up her work as a nurse lecturer. She is one of the ex-service personnel claiming her health was damaged due to service in the Gulf, and suffering what has come to be called Gulf War Syndrome. Other ex-Gulf personnel have suffered from skin rashes, headaches, nausea, musculoskeletal problems and depression.

There have been claims that children born to men who served in the Gulf have shown-higher- than a normal incidence of birth defects. More than 1,000 veterans have issued the Ministry of Defence with writs claiming compensation for the syndrome and its effects.

After years of refusal that there was any problem, the British Government finally agreed in December 1996 to conduct two epidemiological studies to see whether Gulf War veterans have suffered as a result of their service. One study, based at the University of Manchester, was to compare the health of 3,000 veterans with 3,000 matched service personnel who did not go to the Gulf. The other one, at the London School of Hygiene and Tropical Medicine, intended compare the reproductive health of Gulf and non-Gulf personnel, as also the health of their children. Both studies began in January 1997 and will take three years to complete. However, the MoD failed to keep proper records about which personnel were given which drugs.

These failings may scupper the reliability of the studies. They also point to the requirement for better administration, and raise yet again the question of whether secrecy does not inevitably lead to carelessness, sloppiness and reluctance to admit mistakes. As well as the usual jabs against hepatitis B typhoid, tetanus, polio, yellow fever, and meningitis, service personnel sent to the Gulf were vaccinated with a pertusis/ anthrax combination, a US- made vaccine against bubonic plague, and a botulism vaccine. Since the war, the UK government has acknowledged that one of these was unlicensed. Chemistry in Britain reports that the National Institute of Biological Standards and Control (NIBSC) 'had tested two of the vaccines on animals and had forewarned the Ministry of Defence (MoD) in a fax in December 1990 that they were unsafe when used in combination. The MoD logged receipt of the fax, but then lost it and no action, followed. In the fax, NIBSC had warned against administering pertussis (whooping cough) vaccine to accelerate the onset of immunity conferred by anthrax vaccine. In laboratory tests, animals given this combination had shown illness Pertussis is not licensed for use on adults in the UK. The trops also received tablets to protect against nerve gas poisoning which were not licensed until two years after the war. The fact that a medication is unlicensed does always not mean that it is dangerous. But the effects of using so many vaccines in combination are not well known.

As Dr Graham Pearson, formerly director of the chemical and biological defence establishment at Porton Down, told a House of Commons Defence Committee, most of the research is concerned with the of a particular vaccine and is not particularly looking into how that will be administered in war [or the] particular circumstance that need them all to be done together two days before you deploy.

Another suggested the health problems were caused by nerve gas, which blew over Allied troops after they blew up an ammunition depot where it was stored. Another cause of the troops' illnesses may be organophosphate pesticides, used to prevent troops contracting flyborne diseases. The Ministry of Defence misled Parliament about the actual amount used, dramaticlly underestimating it for more than two years. The American government also faces problems intrying to investigate their personnel' exposure to hazards, as their records are also.

After repeated refusals to allow access to a crucial chemical warfare log kept for American commanders, the Pentagon admitted that more than three-quarters of the log was missng.

In January 1999, a US- funded study of UK Gulf War veterans found that they are more likely than those who served in Bosnia to develop symptoms of what has been termed as gulf War Syndrome. 'Our study provides the first clear proof that going to the Gulf has affected the health of our soldiers', said one of the project's leaders, Professor Simon Wessley from the School of Medicine, King's College London. The study also revealed that the Syndrome itself is not peculiar to Gulf War veterans. Bosnian veterans also reported headache, fatigue , chest pain, poor concentration, asthma, arthritis, dermatitis, although less than Gulf veterans. Bosnian veterans also reported chronic fatigue and post-traumatic stress, although only half as often as gulf veterans. The only factor that caused health effects in the Gulf veterans and not in the Bosnian veterans was the multiple vaccinations. The study thus indicates that there is no such thing as 'Gulf War Syndrome—although this does not mean that sick veterans do not have a genuine illness. It is probably impossible to stop all ill health after active combat duties, but we must do a better job in preparation, support and follow up monitoring, said the study's other leader, Professor Anthony David of King's College London.

11

Defensive Biological Weapons Programmes

A defensive biological weapons programmes needs as much research and resources as does an offensive programme. Since needs for both the programmes are somewhat similar it can be easy to run a offensive programme under the garb of defensive programme. The blur in these two makes it clear that one cannot be very sure about the intent of the programme. Organisms dangerous to human health and welfare, like influenza virus dengue virus, *Bacillus anthracis* and the fungi that produce aflatoxins, already plague human society. There is no doubt, given the fiscal resources made available to the military establishments of major industrial nations and the new developments in biotechnology, that new variants of these and several other harmful organisms can be generated. Despite their developmet in the name of national security, the existence of such organisms is likely to rise enormously the risk of their use and decrease national and international security.

Article I of the Biological Weapons Convention of 1972 pledges singnatory nations never to develop, produce, stockpile or otherwise acquire or retain ... microbial or other biological agents, or toxins whatever their method of production, of types or in quantities that have no justification for prophylactic, protective or other peaceful purposes. However the Convention neither prescribes biological weapon researcch nor the possession of quantities (not otherwise specified) of biological agents for prophylactic, protective or peace purposes. This has been conveniently interpreted as allowing research for defensive purposes.

Within both national and international sphere, the legitimacy of the development of a ' defensive' biological weapon programme lies on two major assumption to that the content of a 'defensive' programme differs fundamentally from the content of an offensive programme; and it that it would infact be possible to defend populations of humans, plants, and animals from an adversary bent on utilizing biological (king , 1985). Below we outline the arguments which suggest that both of these assumptions are unfounded and fundamentally incorrect.

Needs for Offensive and Defensive BW Programmes

The transformation of an infectious agent into a biological weapon is a complex, multi- step process. Some of these steps are summarized in table 11.1. Several of the individual measures are needed for it should be observed that the blurring of defensive and

Table 11.1
Needs for the Transformation of an Infectious Agent into a Biological. weapon

---

MICRO-ORGANISM
high infectivity
high virulence
low persistence in the environment
able to be grown in large quantities
stable for storage and dispersal
resistan to routine medical countermeasures

MANUFACTURING FACILITIES
highly contained
sufficient capacity

TEST FACILITIES
highly contained
dispersal capabilities
access totarget species

STORAGE FACILITIES
highly contained scure

DELIVERY VEHICLES
arthopod
aerosol
bomb, missile
waterborne

ABILITY TO PROTECT OWN TROOPS AND POPULATION
vaccines, antibiotics ofr other prophylactic measures
building, protective clothing or other physical barriers therapeutic measures
well-trained personnel for detection and protection
decontaminaton procedures

METHOD (S) DETECTION
in the field
laboratory confimation
alarms

COMMAND AND CONROL
experience personnel for decision making

Source U.N. 1969. both defensive and offensive programmes; the distinction at the research stage is only in the stated intent.

offensive programmes is not limited to research, but extends beyond to development, testing, production and training. Although it may be possible to use the scale of the project as an indicator or the intent at the development stage and beyond, there is a large grey area where offensive and defensive needs will become distinguishable.

As an example, consider the case of vaccine development. In a hypothetical offensive programme to develop variant (non-naturally occurring) viral pathogens, a first step would involve developing vaccines against them, for protecting ones's own personnel. Both the agents and the vaccines have to be tested for efficacy. Now let us consider a 'defensive' vaccine programme. Such vaccines would only be useful against viral agents that an adversary is likely to choose or develop. The development of the vaccine will in general involve the isolation, identification, modification, and growth of the potential BW agent. Studies of the vaccine's efficacy would have to be conducted requiring exposing test animals and perhaps humans to the agent. These—steps the generation of a potential BW agent, development of a vaccine against it, testing of the—efficacy of the vaccine— are all components that would be linked an offensive BW programme.

It is not that the programmes' appear similar; it is that they share similar components. An infectious organism must possess various characteristics to make possible its conversion into an effective biological weapon. These include: *(a)* high infectivity; *(b)* high virulence; *(c)* low environmental persistence; *(d)* capability of being grown in large quantities; *(e)* stability under conditions of storage and of dispersal; and *(f)* resistance to routine medical countermeasures. The study and manipulation of factors that lead to these traits can thus clearly be interpreted as offensive in nature. A research and development programme designed to protect against such putative BW agents would need similar studies often, the argument presented is as follows: In order to defend against a pathogenic organism, it is necessary to: *(a)* understand the underlying mechanisms of pathogenesis especially those pertaining to infectivity and virulence; *(b)* study of the mechanisms by which infectious organisms evade the immune systems or develop resistance to common antibiotics; *(c)* develop effective medical and non- medical counter measures; *(d)* know by which routes different organisms may be dispersed and the infectiity of the organism by each route; *(e)* develop appropriate methods of detection; and *(f)* develop effective decontamination procedures (this would need an understanding of an organism's ecology, mode of transmission and the potential reservoirs that will contribute to its persistence.

Again we see that offensive and defensive biological weapon programmes share the same components one has to rely basically on the stated interest of the programmes to distinguish between them. In order to analyse adequately the pathogenic organisms that have weapon potential, it would be necessary to have sufficient quantities of the organism. This would be especially true for studies of means of dispersal, such as aerosolization. Thus a by-product of the 'defensive' research would be knowledge of how to grow the organism in significant quantities and the facilities in which to grow it. Similarly, the study of means of dispersal and the development of effective counter measures, such as protective clothing, would require special facilities. It may be possible to discern the difference between offensive and defensive intent by size of the manufacturing and, or dispersal facilities, but often there will be a large grey area where claims of either intent will be equally convincing. Discerning the intent of research is further complicated by the fact that much of the basic research needed to alter an organism for weapon purposes contributes to important, non- weapon-related areas. These include infectious disease toxicology, and the commercial development of micro-organisms destined for evironmental release for use in agriculture, mining, pollution control, and so on. For instance, the study of mechanisms of pathogenesis and disease immunity has long been a central focus for researchers interested in the infections diseases of humans, animals and plants.

Likewise, research into effective medical counter measures to diseases, including vaccines and antibiotics, has long been a focus of many health scientist. The development of micro-organisms for use in the environment has given a push to research about the persistence of micro-organisms the environment and how stabilize them for storage and dispersal . Although the micro-organisms being developed for commercial use are much different from those being examined for their weapon potential, the basic mechanisms and methods for decreasing persistence in the environment while raising stability for storage and dispersal purposes are likely to be similar. In addition to the BW agent itself and protective vaccines, various other processes and associated equipment are important for both offensive and defensive purposes. These include: *(a)* methods of detection; *(b)* methods of decontamination; and *(c)* command and control structures. For example, the development of protective clothing and masks oils necessary for battlefield protection no matter who initiates and atack.

Such protection is necessary for defensive purposes as vaccines and the rapeutic drugs are not likely to be effectives. It may also be important following an offensive attack with a known strain of weapon if a protective vaccine is not totally effective. Methods of detection and decontamination also serve both offensive and defensive need. Reliable, sensitive and specific methods of detection are critical to a defence against attacks with biological weapons (UN, 1969); SIPRI, 1975). A technique must be reliable and sensitive in order to determine that an attack has occurred. It must be specific in order to identify the organism and decide upon appropriate counter measures. (Multiple methods of detection in the field followed by identification of the specific organism in a laboratory might be required in order to fulfill these needs.) Reliable and sensitive methods of detection are important to the aggressor in order to determine the extent of spread of the biological agent and when an area is safe for the occupation of a non-protected population. Methods of decontamination are significant to rid an area of the harmful organism so it canbe reoccupied by a non- protected population. Effective decontamination procedures are also important during the research and development stages of weapon programmes in order to clean up after accidental releases of harmful organisms. A command and control structure for decision making with respect to biological weapons is also important for both offensive and defensive weapon programmes (UN, 1969).

For both programmes, predictions have to be made about the spread of a biological agent, its persistence and its likely effects on the target population. Furthermore, appropriate medical and non-medical protective measures must be decided upon and carried out for both the aggressors and the target population. Well-trained personnel and knowledgeable officers are needed to man a suitable command and control structure.

Difficulties of Defending against BW

While discussing the possibility of defence against biological agents, we take as the starting point the current inability to stop the spread of many infectious diseases in both industrialized and developing societies. There are three major strategies for preventing or alleviating the effects of an infectious disease: *(a)* preventing exposure to the agent; *(b)* rendering the population resistant; and *(c)* alleviating the effects of the disease by drugs or other therapeutic methods. Our ability to control exposure to many infectious diseases in humans is quite limited (Westwood, 1980); recent world pandemics of influenza, the growing international problem of AIDS, and our everyday experience with the common cold are proof enough. Given the inability to control the spread of known agents, even during times of international co-operation, we have to assume that the control of agents introduced intentionally into local environments and ecosystems would also spread. Thus 'defences' would have to be at the level of rendering the target population resistant or adopting effective therapeutic measures.

Targets biological weapons can be people, livestock or plants (king 1982; UN, 1969). For each of these targets, there is a large collection of viruses, bacteria, fungi and other biological agents known to cause disease. For instance, there are more than 200 obligate human viruses having of virulence (kilbourne 1975; Rotuschild, et al., 1978) and & species of different degrees rickettsia that cause human disease (Murray, 1975). This does not include the various variants associated with several of these species, the large number of human bacterial pathogens and their many variants, and the agents that cause disease in plants and animal populations. This enormous diversity of potential biological weapons can now be raised, virtually without limit, by the use of recombinant DNA techniques and some of the other new biotechnologies. Safeguard from biological safeguard agents may be possible if the specific agents is known beforehand. For humans and livestock, the means of protection include vaccination in the case of viruses and the use of antibiotics in the case of sensitive bacteria. For plants crops or cultivars resistant to the specific disease would have to be planteder an appropriate fungicide or other pesticide must be available. However, the early knowledge the exact nature of a biological agent will in general available to a nation planning the use of the agent in an offensive mode.

From the point of view of a target population, the notion of an effective defence against such agents is misleading. It is not possible to vaccines all individuals against all possible naturally existing strains and variants of viruses that might be used as weapons. The use of recombinant DNA technologies to alter viruses limits the possibilities of vaccination even against specific strains. For example, using recombinant DNA technologies, it is possible to identify and the alter the factors that affect whether or not a virus is recognized by the human immune system. This has been the case for influenza where epede ics have been linked to the occurrence of virus variants that have altered surface proteins. Immunity developed against a previous strain is not effective against new strains (Webster *et al.*,1983). It is now possible to generate variant of influenza and other viruses in the laboratory. Again, immunization against earlier out breaks would not confer resistance against the new strain. Those producing the new strain could, of course produce a vaccine initialy protective against it (Chanock & Lerner, 1984). Those defending against an altered viral strain would have to know the genetic alteration so as to generate an effective vaccine. However, if the exact strain of the biological weapon were known, either by good intelligence or rapid detection and identification techniques, it is not possible to have sufficient doses of the appropriate vaccine could be delivered in timely manner.

A similar problem exisits with antibiotics. Bacterial strains can usually be generated that are resistant to most antibiotics in common use (Stuttard & Rozee, 1980). Though one could certainly find an antibiotic to which a BW bacterial agent was sensitive, the change are that this would be in mass production or widely available at the time of the challenges is vanishingly small.

Plants are far more susceptible to biological agents because they do not have an immune system. In general, it would not be possible to protect food crops from intentional exposure to infectious agents. Plants are a particularly vulnerable target due to the extensive use of mono cultivation in modern agriculture (Doyle,1985). Often all of the cultivators planted across a vast area are quite uniform. Once planted, the crop cannot usually be rapidly ploughed under or replanted because of limits on the growing season. In addition, rapidly changing the cultivar in use to one resistant to a specific disease would be difficult because of the amount of seed that would have to be produced assuming that such a resistant strain could even be identified). In summary, although it may be possible to vaccinate a population against one or at most a few agents, or to develop crop strains resistant to particular plant pathogens, it is totally unrealistic to expect to protect a population from the great variety of agents that might be developed as potential weapons.

Thus the implicit assumption that defensive biological weapon programmes can provide reliable defences of civilian populations against biological weapons is unrealistic.

Health and Environmental Risks of BW

Programmes

The development of 'defensive' biological weapon programmes may constitute a substantial environmental and health risk to the nation carrying out the research. As noted above, such programmes generally need growing and testing agents thought to be related to potential BW agents. Several of these will be pathogenes or relatives of them. Even in the absence of an accident, it will be extremely difficult to develop and test the effects of such agents on organisms without substantial risk of their escape into the ecosystem (Harrison & Hattis 1985). Once a pathogen has entered the ecosystem, it may persist for long period of time, causing major disruption to the economy and / or public health of the area (Strauss *et al.*, 1985, pp.

53-55). For example, Bacillus anthracis, the bacterium responsible for anthrax, appears to be capable of establishing itself in a wide range of climates.

This could lead to the creation of new and permanent reservoirs of the disease (Westing, 1977, p. 42). A pathogen that has escaped into the environment has the potential to disperse by natural forces Liva wind, water or insect vectors. The survival and dispersal properties of such micro-organisms are difficult to predict or control (strauss *et, al.*,1985).

Biomedical Research: Military and Civilian

Sectors

Over past few years, there has been a disturbing shift in resources and funding in the biomedical sciences from the civilian to the military sectors. During 1980-84, in the United States the total federal support for research in the life sciences went down by 2 per cent, while Department of Defense funding rose by 26 per cent. This implies a net transfer of $50 million for life sciences research from the civilian to the military sector (Wright, 1985). Even within the US military, there has been a shift in funding from general biomedical to biological weapon programmes. In 1985, the US Armyzays it spent $ 39 million on defensive biological weapon programmes Zoler, 1985). Owing to he present level of international distrust and the inability to distinguish between defensive and offensive weapon programmes, this shift in resources is likely to be viewed by opposing intelligence agencies as offensive, in intent. It is likely to lead to continued accusations of treaty violations and demands for increased funding for biological weapon programmes The end result may well be a biological weapons arms race. As an effort to dispel some of the distrust of intentions, we suggest that all funding for biomedical and agricultural research be transferred to civilian funding agencies. Since much of the research applicable to weapons programmes has important civilian uses, the were should be no classification of any biomedical research or of any research pertaining to genetically engineered micro-organisms. This demilitarization of basic research will not eliminate any of the basic science programmes, but it may serve to refocus applicatins on non-weapon-related areas. in addition, civilian funding of all biomedical research may serve to allay fears that classified research is being conducted covertly. By limiting the biomedical research in military facilities, and the military funding of research in civilian facilities, there would be less likelihood for activities that violate the letter or the spirit of the Biological Weapons Convention.

Bibliography

Doyle, J., 'Inviting disaster', chapter 10 in *Altered Harvest* (Viking Press:New York, 1985).

(*Note* : This chapter provides insight into the vulnerability of world agriculture to new diseases (and biological weapons) because of the lack of genetic deversity and large-scale monoculture).

King, J. 'New diseases in new niches' *Nature* 276 (5683): 47; (1978).

Strauss, H. Hattis, D., Page G. *et al.*, Direct release of Genetically-Engineered Micro organisms: A Preliminary Framework for Risk Evaluation under TSCA. Report No. CTPID 85-3 (Center for Technology, Policy and Industrial Development, Massachusetts Institute of Technology: Cambridge, MA,1985) (Also partially published in the *Recombinant* DNA *Technical Bulletin* 9 (1) , *March 1986*, and *in press for 9 (2) and (3).*

(*Note:* This report describes the types of information needed to asess the risks of releasing genetically engineered micro-organisms into the environment. Among others, it contains chapters on the transport of micro-organisms through the environment, and on monitoring, containment and control).

Westwood, J., *The Hazard from Dangerous Exotic Diseass* (Macmillan Press Ltd: London (1980) (Also available from theFranklin Institute Press, Philadelphia, PA).

(*Note:* This book discusses the problems associated with mounting effective medical countermeasures to epidemic human disease.

Wright, S. The military and the new biology, *Bulletin of the Atomic Scientists* (September 1985), pp. 10-6.

(*Note:* This article contains a discussion of the funding and some of the objectives of the US biological weapons programme).

12
Warfare and Technology

Various technologies cab be employed in a warfare of these, biotechnology is not only cheaper but also the most lethal. The other technologies are gallium arsenide technology, micromachining technonology, information technology etc.

William Mc Neill, in his classic work, The Pursuit of Power : Technology, Armed Force and Society since A. D. 1000 Lattributed the rise of the West in part to the relationship between technology, public finance, war and political power. Since there was no central power established in Europe, different political groups were able to use superior military technology to secure and extend their own power. Mc Neill's book is part of recent rich and diverse developments in the historical study of technology and war, but what is of particular interest here is that it brings out that there are clearly historical periods when the technology of warfare develops very rapidly. We are living in such a period of rapid change now: the technology of war is changing and with it the nature of modern warfare. To bring home the point we may refer to work by Captain J.W. Bodnar who has a doctorate in biochemistry and is a member of the Chemistry Department at the US Naval Academy. He suggested in a paper titled, 'The military technical revolution: from hardware to information', that there has been a three-phased change in military technology since the Second World War. First there was an engineering revolution which steadily transformed weapons and platforms. This started during the last war and had practically ended by the 1980s. Then there was a reolutionary change in the capabilites of military sensors which began in the early 1970s and greatly enhanced the ability of individual platforms (e.g., ships) to analyse data and use weapon systems effectively.

Bodnar believed this second phase of the military technical revolution would end in the 1990s. The third phase, according to him, began in the late 1970s and is concerned with the enhancement of command, control, communications and intelligence as applied to military forces. This phase was evident in the DESERT STORM operation against Iraq in 1991 but is far from complete. A decade down the line, from now the effectiveness of military forces will therefore be very different again from what it was there. A similar but more general argument was put forward by two analysts from the US RAND orgainsation in a paper entitled 'Cyberwar is coming'. They argued that industrialisation caused the development of mass armies and attrition warfare, as in the First World War, mechanisation then allowed manoeuvre warfare with tanks, as in the Second World War, but now:

...The information revolution implies the rise of cyberwar, in which neither mass nor mobility will decide outcomes; instead, the side that knows more, that can disperse the fog of war yet enshroud an versary in it, will enjoy decisive advantages.

Whilst the information tecnnology revolution, which has influenced so many spheres of civilian life, lies at the heart of this analysis, the authors were evident that enormous consequential changes would occur in military organisations and forces. The argument was taken step agead by an engineer, Flt. Lt. P.C. Emmett, of the Royal Air Force, in a paper entitled 'Software warfare: the emerging future'. He observed that the software used in the new information technology is of crucial importance: any effective modern force must understand its features and production and integrate them, not just into weapon systems, but into the very preparations for war. He envisaged a two-way influence whereby the process of software reduction would affect the character of war which would thenf feed back to accelerate the process of software production. Such interest in new military technology and its consequences obviously stems in part from the dramatic events of Operation DESERT STORM.

A few brief illustrations of the practical application of the new technology in the 1991 war against Iraq are discuss as below. Marshall Ogarkov of the Soviet Union, whose writings were closely followed by some observers in the West, had anticipated much of what happened. We shall therefore also briefly consider Ogarkov's views.

Technology's Influence on Warfare

Operation Desert Storm

Bodnar listed some of the examples where the communications capabilities of the coalition forces permitted operations of a new character against Iraq. He referred, for instance, to the way in which individual buildings or bridges were bombed by laser-guided weapons: the weapons were fired from planes which were co-ordinated by airborne AWACS and which had struck the target area through the use of precision navigation. But most significantly, he observed that the information required to guide the planes was derived from satellite reconnaissance systems: the data passed first to rear-area analysts berore being used to guide the attack squadrons. Bodnar also recalled the remarkable long-range bombing operation whereby B-52s flew from bases in the United States to bomb Kuwait and were then able to fly on to land in Diego Garcia. Bodnar also remarked on the ground attack which concluded the war so rapidly through a co-ordinated, multinational operation in the desert.

Much has been written about that operation and one of the most interesting comments was made by Rear Admiral Sir Peter Anson, Chairman of Matra Marconi Space Limited, and his co-author, in a paper entitled 'The first space war. 'According to them, the coalition serviceman: ...

> ... was able to move with confidence over difficult desert; terrain, avoiding enemy defences, assured of resupply and able to pinpoint and target enemy arms and installations with remarkable precision, thanks to the technological 'discovery' of the war-Global Positioning System (GPS).

Whilst the military receivers for GPS were being provided as fast as possible, $3,000 hand-held models were on the commercial market and some US troops asked their relatives to buy units for them. Although it is needed to exercise a of certain amount caution over some of the claims made about the nuture of the Gulf War, this image of coolition Boldier being able up to pinpoint his exact position with a hand-held instrument surely shows the superior information-processing capability of the coalition vis-a vis that of Iraq.

Soviet View Point

Like their Western counterparts, Soviet military analysts studied the 1991 war in the Gulf with great deal of care. Also, as might be expected, Westren analysts of Soviet military affairs were scrutinising Soviet conclusions about the war. One such analyst, Mary FitzGerald, of the Hudson Institute, wrote a long artical in the US *Naval War College Review* in the autumn of 1991. What is striking in FitzGerald's analysis is her argument that the Gulf War essentially proved what the Soviet military had already concluded about the form that warfare would increasingly take. She argued that, while the soviet military had undergone profound change during the Gorbachev period, the mainstream military view still reflected the view that Marshal Ogarkov had put on 'emerging technologies' from the early 1980s onwards. She suggested that the civilian leadership had not attempted to block the development of technologies perceived to be at the heart of future military capabilities, such as advanced conventional munitions and space-based systems. Moreover, they considered the developments as inevitable, as she put it, the soviet military had developed a comprehensive and revolutionary vision of future war much before the Persian Gulf conflict'. In another paper she put forth the point even more strongly, suggesting that for Soviet military analysts 'the Gulf War is said to have confirmed Marshall Oharkov's forecasts on the nature of future war'.

If that was so, then Ogarkov's views are important for anyone trying to understand the current relationship between science, technology and warfare. Marshall Ogarkov's ideas, in fact, been the subject of Western analysis for most of the 1980s. Dale Herspring, a Foreign Service officer in the US Department of State, had written on the state of the Soviet military in the aftermath of the 27th Party Congress. His paper of 1986 provided a good insight into Ogarkov's importance. He opined that current events and them had to be situdied against the backdrop of the period from 1977 to 1984 during which Ogarkov had dominated military politics due to his position as Deputy Defence Minister and Chief of the General Staff. Ogarkov had not been reticent in openly axpressing his disagreement with politicians.

Herspring argued that though this led to his dismissal in the uncertain times of 1984 Ogarkov was not disgraced: he had a major book published in 1985 and was, in fact, transferred to head the critical Western Theatre of Military Operations. In another article, Herspring tried to further explain Ogarkov's importance. In his view, the impact of the scientific-technical revolution in military affairs was a matter of concern to all Soviet military officers, but Ogarkov devoted more time and passion than anyone else to the subject. He argued throughout his period as Chief of the General Staff that it was important for the Soviet military to understand and adapt to the major scientific-technical advances being made. Herspring thought that Ogarkov was awarded the top post precisely to drag a force dominated by the large scale manoeuvre warfare of the previous war into the modern age of computers and information technology. As a Foreign Service officer, Herspring's analysis was naturally largely related to the political aspects of Ogarkov's work. More detail on the technical issues is available from a study published by FitzGerald in 1987. She argued that Ogarkov's views fitted well into the evolution of Soviet views on nuclear warfare. From 1966 to 1976, she suggested, a segment of the Soviet military held the view that a defence against nuclear weapons would be found.

This idea was firmly countered by Brezhnev's address in Tula in 1977. Thus after 1977 it was accepted that offence would always predominate in the balance between nuclear offence and defence and that there was a stalemate between East and West at the nuclear level. There was little sense in developing further offensive systems since both sides would have the capability for retaliation whatever the other did. However, the implication then was that beneath this nuclear 'umbrella' conventional systems would become more pertinent.

Ogarkov's views were well known to the military in the West. For example, two officers serving in the Intelligence Division at Headquarters Allied Forces Central Europe (AFCENT), one British, one American, contributed an article entitled 'Ogarkov's revolution' to the journal *International Defense Review* in 1987. They emphasised the revolutionary nature of his thinking, its technological basis and its link to the nuclear stalemate. As they saw it, Ogakrov's view was that nuclear war becomes unnecessary if coventional technology is exploited.

... Wars can remain conventional, according to Ogarkov, because new technologies guided by new highly accurate delivery systems, will 'make it possible to conduct military operations with the use of conventional means of qualitatively new and incomparably more destructive forms than before.....

It is hardly surprising, given the changes taking place in Western military technology at that point time, that Soviet writings were replete with accusations that the West of might attack the Soviet Unioni on in precisely this manner. Fitzgerald's 1987 article set out Soviet views on some of the main feature envisaged in the new form of warfare. First she noted the extended range of operations and Soviet fears that the West's Air Land Battle operation could involve conventional strikes against the entire strategic depth of the War se Pact. She then emphasised that the targets of the conventional attack were seen to be equivalent to the standard targets for nuclear weapons, for example, command-and-control points, communication networks and nuclear missiles. To to it, there was the element of surprise:.

... Soviet military figures have repeatedly stressed that the new conventional means will be used to deliver 'surprise' or 'pre-emptive' strikes against the opponents' most important........targets......Ogarkov wrote that Air Land Battle envisions simultaneous, surprise strikes with the latest conventional means by air, naval and ground forces........

Against that background one can see the force of the later argument that the form of the DESERT STORM attack on Iraq came as no great surprise. Writing in 1991, Fitzgerald added further technical detail on what the new form of warfare was expected to be . She noted that since the early 1980s military theorists in the Soviet Union had concentrated their attention on technologies related to automated decision-support systems, microelectronics, and so on. He laid emphasis that the potential for continued evolution of technology and warfare was recognised and that two period of change were suggested by the Soviet theorists.

In the first, up to the turn of the century, there would be a continued development of enhanced types of current systems, for instance, for surveillance and target acquisition; in the first two decades of the next century it was hoped that very different systems, such as directed energy weapons and advanced robotics would come into play. Future war was seen as potentially global, with the control of space systems being of particular importance. The integration of means of reconnaissance, decision-making and action through new technology was to be at the core of the new warfare. The significance attatched to high-technology capabilities in Soviet military writing during the 1980s is beyond doubt, but the erstwhile Soviet Union lacked the industrial strength to put the ideas fully into effect.

Although the USA was able to *implement* similar ideas, they were similarly concerned about their industrial capabilities and the long-term health of their defence industrial base. In order to pursue the issue further we need to consider the debate in the USA.

Industry and Warfare

From the Second World War the United States emerged as the dominant world industrial power. Following the war it is undoubtedly true that investment in military systems led to spin-on advances of use to the civil sector. Areas which reaped benefits of military-related investment in the USA included aviation and computing. Yet it is now widely acknowledged that, as the information technology revolution has progressed, the speed of technological advance in the civil sector has overtaken that in the military. More fundamentally, new developments are occurring less often in the United States and more often elsewhere.

It is now evident that the modern world economy is essentially a single market. This has well-defined featured, like its division into three tiers of states: core, periphery and semi-periphery. However, the position of states in these tiers can change over time, and the whole system has gone through a cyclic pattern of growth and recession. Periods of growth over the last two hundred years get welll with major periods of innovation in core technologies: smelting iron with coal, and the mechanisation of textile manufacture in the original 'industrial revolution'; steam engines and railways in the mid-to late nineteenth century; electrical and heavy engineering in the late nineteenth and the early twentieth centuries; Mass production of vehicles likes cars, trucks, etc. from the 1930s to the 1980s; and electronics and information technology in our own times. What is more, the innovatory changes occur not just in technology, but in what has been termed the whole techno-economic paradigm:

The new key factor does not appear as an isolated input, but rather at the core of a rapidly growing system of technical, social and managerial innovations, some related to the production of the key factor itself and others to its utilisation.....

At the centre of the current pattern of growth is Japan and its commercial industry and the rate of change is extremely rapid, with flexibly-organised firms able to rapidly alter their mix of goods in the core electronics and information technology sector. Moreover, this commercial capability is increasingly allowing Japan to raise its military potential. As the revolution in technology has progressed, a wide - ranging debate has developed in the USA on the implications for its continued military dominance. The debate has covered such aspects as strategy, foreign dependence and the technological base, and industrial policy.

From our present perspective, the aspect of the debate associated with 'critical technologies' is of particular interest. The efforts within the US Department of Defense to define what technologies are crucial for future military needs, and to put plans in place to ensure their development, has been subjecct to extensive Congressional scrutiny. One point came out very clearly in the first report of the National Critical Technologies Panel to Congress in April 1991. As may be seen from Table 12.1, the panel found that there was large overlap

Table 12.1
Some Critical Technologies Identified in the USA

National critical technology panel	*Commerce emerging technologies*	*Defence critical technologies*
Materials		
e.g., Electronic and photonic materials	Advanced semiconductor devices	Semiconductor material and microëlectronic circuits
Manufacturing		
e.g., Intelligent processing equipment	Artificial intelligence	Machine intelligence and robotics
Information and communications		
e.g., Software	High-performance computing	Software producibility
Biotechnology and life sciences		
e.g., Applied molecular meterials biology	Biotechnology	Biotechnology and processes

between its own identifications and previous Department of Defense analyses of critical technologies, and those considered to be important commercially. The table demonstrates the overlap of interest in new materials, advanced manufacturing and computer software. It is somewhat difficult to grasp what is really involved in these newly-developed technologies. Two examples may reveal the level of sophistication involved.

Gallium Arsenide Technology

The core technology driving both economic growth and the revolution in military operations of the late twentieth century is information technology (IT) based on electronics. This technology is based on scientific discoveries in physics which were made at least a century ago. An example was the discovery by Thomas Alva Edison that electricity flows through space from a heated metal. By the early years of this century it has come to light that the electrons (negatively-charged particles which are constituents of all atoms) released from such a heated metal flow only to a positively-charged anode. Thus an alternating current which switches from positive to negative could be changed or rectified to direct current through the Edison effect. Later developments revealed that the Edison effect was much stronger in a vacuum (tube or valve), and that other processes such as amplification could be achieved. The practical applications developed clearly depended not just on the flow of electricity (as in, motors) but also on the control of the behaviour of electrons: hence electronics.

It became known that similar effects could be produced in crystals of some materials but, while valve technology predominated, not much interest was shown in such solid-state devices. This all changed when Shockley, Bardeen and Brattain, working at the Bell Laboratories in the 1940s, discovered how to make crystals which could rectify as efficiently as valves, and which could amplify. The new crystals were called 'semiconductors' and for a long time silicon was the preferred material.

A semiconductor is a crystalline material whose electrical conductivity lies between that of a conductor and that of an insulator. Addition of small amounts of different impurities allows a rise in the number of negative-charge carriers (electrons) in n-type semiconductors, and the number of positive-charge carries (holes) in p-type semiconductors. The introduction of such impurities is called 'doping'. The creation of solid-state devices like transistors (the basic elements of modern amplifiers and logic circuits) and thus integrated circuits (many connected elements) depend on the properties of junctions between p-type and n-type regions within the same piece of semiconductor crystal. There are two main types of transistor. Bipolar transistors are the basic elements in a computer's central processing unit, and field- effect transistors (FETs) are commonly used in a computer's memory and increasingly in the logic operations of smaller computers. Both types, in effect, are switches which may be either turned 'on' or 'off' by the application of an electric charge to particular regions of the transistor.

The performance of both types of transistor depends crucially on the quality of the silicon crystal. Relatively uniform and defect-free crystals are grown to a size of nearly six inches in diameter in a complex process involving dipping and then slowly removing a small seed crystal from molten silicon. The large crystal thus produced is then sliced and polished to produce thin wafers of material. Integrated circuits are etched on to the surface of the wafers in another complex process, and doping is done to generate regions which have different electronic properties. Finally, the wafer is cut into a number of small chips, each of which may have as many as a million transistors. The possibility of using gallium arsenide (GaAs) instead of silicon became known about three decades aslo. Gallium arsenide has distinct advantages: owing to the speed with which electrons move through it; in weak-signal operations; and in the generation and detection of light. Thus GaAs chips are well-suited for use in computing, television reception and the opto-electronic transmission of data (photonics). Gallium arsenide light-emitting diodes and lasers, used in visual displays and audio-disc players, are widely used ; domestic satellite-receiver dishes use gallium arsenide detectors. Gallium arsenide is also superior to silicon due to the ease with which its electronic characteristics may be manipulated, for example in alloys of aluminium gallium arsenide.

Very thin layers of two or more alloys may also be alternated on a chip to create so-called heterojunctions in which the precise electrical properties vary from layer to layer. Given these advantages, why has gallium arsenide not superseded silicon as the preferred semiconductor redium? The answer to that question lies in the difficulties faced in manufacture high-quality, low-cost gallium arsenide chips. One of the most serious problems in manufacturing is the lack of a native oxide. Silicon oxide readily forms on heating silicon in air. It has an electronic and mechanical seal and can thus be used as the insulator between adjacent transistors on a chip or as a protective mask through which 'windows' can be cut and chemicals allowed to react in etching and doping processes. Much more difficult approaches are required in gallium arsenide chip manufacture. A further disadvantage is that gallium arsenide is a compound. Defects in the element silicon may be annealed by heating the crystal, but heating gallium arsenide causes selective loss of arsenic . Again this greatly complicates manufacture since defects caused at various stages of the production process are difficult to correct. Applications of gallium arsenide technology, not surprisingly therefore, have been resticted to devices where specific, desirable features compensate for the relatively high cost of production. The most familiar example in everyday use is at the focus of satellite receiver-dish antennae, since communications satellites use microwaves for which gallium arsenide's speed characteristics are eminently suitable.

Additionally, it can amplify the weak signals practically without distortion (noise). Gallium arsenide is therefore also specifically important in many current defence systems which rely on microwave technology.

Almost certainly, gallium arsenide's most important future applications will be seen in the photonic transmission of information. Light propagation in fibres (fibre optics) allows transmission of more information further and faster than the transmission of electrical signals in conventional metal wires is capable of. As optical fibres are increasingly, gallium arsenide usage is also likely to rise due to advantageous optical properties. Furthermore, the advantage that gallium arsenide has in speed of operation could ultimately lead to its increasing incorporation into the central functions of computers by the displacement of slower-acting, silicon-based systems.

Micromachining Technology

Micromachining is the process of fabricating miniature objects and structures, generally on the surface of a silicon chip. It is akin to the technology for etchinig electronic circuits on to silicon chips, but varies in that mechanical structures, not electrical circuits, are created.

Micromachining technology is important because it provides a direct means of linking inforamtion on other aspects of the physical world, like pressure or acceleration, with modern electronic systems. This combination allows the development of highly powerful and economically important new devices. Such devices already have important commercial applications, but technical developments in the 1980s have opened up a huge range of potential new applications. Some of these are already coming on stream, but several other possibilities look likely to emerge. The oldest micromachining technology is called bulk micromachining because the entire mass of the chip is used: areas of silicon are marked (burned) by light shining through a patterned template (photolithographic mask). The marked areas are then etched away using by alkaline chemicals. Micromachining work in the 1960s produced the sillicon-diaphragm pressure sensor. In such a device a silicon chip is modified so that it has a very thin layer in one part of its surface. This layer or diaphragm distorts slightly under pressure, the distortion causing stress in the crystal which, in turn, generates electrical signals (a piezo-electric effect.)

By this means, changes in pressure may be detected through the electrical signals generated, and this information may then be processed in an electronic system. However, this technology is quite different from that used to make standard chips and thus, although successful and subject to refinements which allow greater control, is not easily integrated into standard chip manufacturing technologies. A second process known as surface micromachining is much closer to the standard chip technology. For example, a small structural projection or 'beam' can be constructed on a silicon chip in four stages. First, ultraviolet light passed through a photolithographic mask is used to define an area on the surface which is susceptible to etching in the next stage. The defined area is then partially etched out by hydrofluoric acid and depression is formed. A layer of new silicon can then be deposited on the whole surface from silicon vapour. A supporting base in the depression and a projecting 'beam' lying on top of the *original* silicon outside the depression can be made out of the newly-deposited silicon. Finally, the 'beam' is released by etching away some of the original sillicon beneath it. However, even this newer technique has its limitations because the structures so built are extremely thin. Another technique, LIGA)

Lithographie, Galvanoformung, Abformung), eliminates this problem to some extent.

Again, lithographic patterning is used, but instead of ultraviolet light patterning and chemicals etching into silicon, high-energy X-rays are used to cut directly into X-ray-sensitive polymers laid over the surface of the chip. the shorter wavelengths of X-rays allow more detailed features to be built and deeper cutting into the polymers allows wider and thicker structures. Unwanted surface polymer is removed by chemicals, leaving a mould which can be filled to make the microstructure, or used as the template for a further moulding process. The United States probably remains the leading actor, at least in academic research on micromachining, and its Defense Advanced Research Projects Agency (DARPA) is funding a programme at the level of $20 million over three years. In Japan, the Ministry of International Trade and Industry (MITI) has begun to support an integrated research programme which is planned to run over 10 years.

Reports indicate that future developments will need a much greater understanding of the materials used in micromachining technology. One particular problem with silicon-based devices is that they tend to have high levels of residual stress which cause difficulties in moving parts . Some researchers are investigaing non-semiconductor materials with magnetic properties; others are investigating combinations of silicon chips and biological enzymes or antibodies. Formidable technical problems will obviously be encountered in such new applications, but the commercial rewards for success could be considerable. Table 12.2 reveals comparisons made in the USA in 1991 for Defence technologies. It is evident that the main competitors in these advanced industrial systems are the USA, Europe and Japan and that most Third World countries have very little chance of competing at such levels of sophistication even though the capabilities are spreading across the globe.

Biotechnology

Biotechnology was considered important in the US assessments of critical technologies (Table 12.2). This is reflected in Europe where the life sciences find a prominent place in the Fourth Framework Programme. In the UK a new Biotechnology and Biological Sciences Reasearch Council has been recently set up which again serves to stress upon the growing importance of this aspect of technological development. The stark fact is that biotechnology is cheaper and simpler to master than the advanced information technologies we have just discussed, but the biological weapon systems that could result wouldnevertheless be extremely powerful.

Table 12.2
Illustrative Comparative Technological Capabilites

Critical technology	Dual-use	USSR	NATO allies	Japan	Others
Semiconductor materials and microelectronic circuits	√	***	****	****	** Israel
Machine intelligence and robotics	√	***	****	****	**Finland, Israel, Sweden
Software engineering	√	*	**	**	**Various countries
Biotechnology materials and processes		**	***	***	**Various countries

Others relative to USA
**** Broad technical achievement, capable of major contributions.

*** Moderate technical achievement, capable of important contributions.

** Generally lagging.

* Lagging in all important aspects.

Not surprisingly, therefore, the American literature contains frequent references to the likely development of biological weapons by other states as a relatively inexpensive means of countering sophisticated Western conventional military technology. The nature of this new biotechnology requires careful study, for it would be almost inconceivable were such a new and powerful technological capability not at least *considered* for application in the military areas.

13

Weapons of Mass Destruction: Counter Measures

Weapons of mass destruction include Nuclear, chemical and biological weapons.

Now-a-days several countries possess nuclear weapon capability. Also the number of countries possessing chemical and biological weapons. This situation calls for effective counter measures.

The proliferation of Weapons of Mass Destruction (WMD) has, in the mid-1990s, posed a serious threat to the United States. This threat is multidimensional, for WMD include Nuclear, Biological, and Chemical (NBC) weapons. Moreover, the threat has been further increased by the proliferation of ballistic and cruise missiles, which make longer-range delivery systems available to nations possessing WMD. (For a fuller treatment, see *Strategic Assessment* 1995.) The United States is responding to this threat by pursuing policies and initiatives designed both to prevent proliferation or check it, and to minimize the strategic and tactical consequences should prevention fail.

Nuclear weapons. At the end of 20 succeeding, the number of countries that have nuclear, weapons, have the capability to produce nuclear weapons, or are seeking the capacity to produce and deliver nuclear weapons stood at about two dozen. In addition to the five declared nuclear powers, some states are judged to have either fully developed nuclear weapons (e.g., Israel) or the ability to assembble ad deliver such weapons rapidly (e.g., India and Pakistan). Several states are attempting to obtain, or have the facilities to produce, weapons-grade fissile material (e.g., Iraq, Iran, and North Korea). A rising number of states possess the requisite scientific and industrial infrastructure to initiate a weapons program, while others seem to be in the early stages of acquiring the expertise and infrastructure required for a nuclear-weapons program, often through the acquisition of nuclear reactors for ostensibly peaceful purposes (e.g., Algeria and Syria). Lastly, there is increasing concern that terrorist groups and organized crime syndicates could come into the possession of nuclear weapons-including crude radiological devices. These fears are further fueled in part by concerns about a possible loss of control over stocks of weapons-grade nuclear material in the former Soviet Union.

Chemical and Biological Weapons. The number of countries with chemical and biological weapons is on the rise, and experience has shown that once states have made the decision to acquire a WMD capability, biological weapons (BW) and chemical weapons (CW) are generally pursued simultaneously.

Many experts trust that Iran, Iraq, Libya, Syria, Cuba, China, and North Korea, among others, have on going biological-weapons programs. In the early 1990s, Russia admitted it had a BW program in the past, and concerns are in place that this program still exists in some form and that Russia may be maintaining illegal capability to manufacture biological warfare agents. Other countries that may be pursuing BW include Argentina, Brazil, South Africa, India, pakistan, and Laos. Thus, the problem, though global, is concentrated in regions of instability-some of which, like the Middle East and North-east Asia, are quite significant to the West. The cost of develoing a stockpile of chemical or biological weapons is very small when compared with the cost of achieving nuclear capability. Biological and chemical weapons are relatively easy to acquire because almost all the technologies associated with them are widely available and used for legitimate commercial activities. In additon, defensive biological and chemical programs can provide cover for covert offensive BW and CW programs.

For all these reasons, the production of BW and CW weapons is difficult to detect, and offenders can often plausibly deny that they are producing such weapons. Alarmingly, states are building BW capability and CW not just for deterrence but because they are perceived as operationally useful. Iraq used CW effectively against

Iran throughout their nearly decade-long war, and Iraq also used chemical weapons against its own people. In addition, CW and / or BW are believed to have been used in conflicts in Afghanistan, Vietnam, Laos, and Cambodia. And the 1995 sarin gas attacks in Tokyo's subway revealed the feasibility of terrorist attacks using CW.

Countering Instruments

Non-proliferation (Prevention)

The global proliferation of NBC weapons, their concentration in unstable regions vital to U.S. interests, the perception of their increasing military and political utility, and the greater likelihood of their use-in war, as a tool for political blackmail, or by terrorists-all serve to increase the threat to U.S. and allied forces. Instruments that aim at preventing or limiting the spread of such weapons are known as instruments of non-proliferation.

The proliferation process starts a state first considers acquiring WMD and tries to develop or acquire the technical and manufacturing expertise to do so. Prevention measures are most effective at these early stages and fall within a number of categories.

Dissuasion. Convincing non-WMD states that their security interests are best served by not obtaining WMD.

Denial. attempting to restrict a state's ability to obtain WMD technologies or devices.

Arms Control seeking to set limits on or eliminate WMD through bilateral or multilateral agreements and the building of international norms against proliferation.

International pressure punishing states who pursue acquistion of WMD through trade or economic sanctions, publicizing companies and countries that assist in the acquisition of WMD, and sharing intelligence.

While prevention efforts are generally diplomatic in nature, defense-related agencies play an important supporting role. Their involvement may include providing inspection, verification, and inforcement support for non-prolieration treaties and control regimes; helping to identify states that might obtain, or are obtaining, NBC capabilities; and conducting interdiction missions.

The central tool of prevention traditionally has been arms control, which remain in the focus of the world community's attempts to create norms against proliferation and to limit the spread of WMD. The primary international mechanism for controlling nuclear proliferation is the Treaty on the Non-Proliferation of Nuclear Weapons (NPT) and its associated monitoring arm, the International Atomic Energy Agency (IAEA). The Chemical Weapons Convention (CWC), not yet in force as of late 1995. Prevents the production, use, possession, and transportation of chemical weapons. The Biological Weapons Convention (BWC) which has been in force since 1972, prohibits the development, production, stockpiling, or acquistion of in biological or toxin agents and weapons. In addittion to formal treaties, many multilateral regimes exist to prevent potential proliferators from gaining access to critical technologies and material.

Arms control and other prevention tools have had some significant successes. In 1989-1990, South Africa reversed its policy on nuclear weapons, and Argentina abandoned the Condor missile program. But despite efforts an arms-control, the diffusion of WMD technologies has proven exceptionally difficult to control. In this regard, the Iraqi experience is starting. While export controls did succeed in delaying and increasing the cost of Iraq's nuclear program, post-Gulf War discoveries found that it is much more advanced than most analysts had suspected. Thus, while arms-control and export-control regimes can be helpful in stouring and raising the cost of obtaining NBC weapons, states that are reasonably motivated and possess adequate resources will probably succeed if they persist. If increasing numbers of states do acquire WMD, other tools to enhance security must be employed, in particular, tools that afford some protectyion-against these weapons.

The remaining four instruments examined here are military instruments used to counter the threat of NBC weapons after an enemy has obtained them. Such instruments are often known as instruments of counter-proliferation. Deterrence remains the first line of defense, and counter-proliferation instruments can strengthen deterrence. Should deterrence fail, however, the instruments of counter-proliferation provide a measure of safeguard.

Role of Nuclear Deterrence

During the Cold War, when strategic nuclear war was the central threat to U.S. national security, nuclear deterrence was the main instrument of response. However, the last year of the Cold War saw in dramatic drawdown—partly negotiated, partly by unilateral choice—a the size and number of the United States's theater nuclear arsenal. And the Cold War's end has resulted in a change in the entire nuclear environment, as well as questions on the utility of both strategic and theater nuclear weapons. Two issues stand out: (1) what role nuclear weapons have in the post-Cold War age; and (2) how effective nuclear deterrence will prove in regional conflicts where an adversary as NBC weapons.

In its 1994 Nuclear Posture Review (NPR) and later affirmations, the Clinton administration reaffirmed the United states requirement for a nuclear deterrent. Concretely, the administration identified a requirement to, among other things: maintain 3,500 strategic warheads; keep ICBMs and modernize the Minuteman III; complete the D-5 Trident missile purchase and maintain fourteen Trident boats armed with D-5s; adopt a stockpile stewardship program to make sure a reliable, safe, and secure stockpile without nuclear testing; and commit the resources required to verify START compliance and monitor Russia's stategic offensive modernization program.

Strategically, the document seeks to hedge against the possibility of a reversal of democratization in Russia; to allow for the possibility of armed confrontation with a regional power that has obtained WMD; to continue to extend the U.S. nuclear deterrent to major allies; and to discourage or even reverse nuclear proliferation. A key element in the rejection of nuclear disarmament is the realization that nuclear weapons cannot be disinvented; that is, the knowledge of how to make them is widerspread and the most demanding part of the process (acquiring fissile material) is extremely difficult to prevent. Even if the world's political processes sustain arms-control efforts and achieve related measures, like a comprehensive nuclear test ban and cessation of the production of plutonium for weapons purposes, the problem of so-called virtual nuclear arsenals-the technical and industrial capability ot create a nuclear arsenal quickly remains. Moreover, despite whatever arms pacts may be signed, reliable and effective verification measures do not yet exist. Thus, without the capacity to verify universal nuclear disarmament, the United states would run a tremendous risk in eliminating its own nuclear deterrent.

Many wary policy-makers emphasize that, though diplomatic relations between Washington and Moscow have considerable since 1989, Russia has gone on to produce nuclear weapons while the United States has ceased its production. Other great powers, too, may someday build large nuclear arsenals. Furthermore, a number of policymakers argue that the elimination of the U.S. arsenal would inspire other nuclear states to build up their arsenals in order to challenge U.S. power and deter U.S. conventional military forces.

Further, some observers have pointed out that if the United states were to do away with its nuclear capability, many non-nuclear states that rely upon U.S. security assurances for their protection would have an incentive to find their own nuclear deterrent capabilities. Thus, the supposition one must take into consideration when developing a long-term vision of nuclear forces is that future challenges may again require a response of significant proportions. Whether the laws, rules, and institutions of the international system will be sufficient to contain those challenges without the backing of proportionate force is doubtful. Whether nuclear weapons might be needed to provide such force is at least an open question. Underneath the level of greatpower challenges lies the question of nuclear deterrence against regional power having NBC weapons. The Concern is that U.S. conventional capabilities may not serve as an effective deterrent against BW and CW use in limited or regional military engagements.

Should Washington drop the option of retaliating in kind to CW (as it already has done with BW), nuclear weapons will then provide the only non-conventional military deterrent to the use of WMD against U.S. or allied forces. In late 1995, Iraqi officials gave U.N. envoys the first authoritative, even though incomplete, account of why they did not use biological and chemical arms against coalition forces. Though Iraq had embarked on a much accelerated nuclear-weapons program after the invasion of Kuwait, and had reportedly loaded nearly two hundred bombs and missile warheads with biological agents, Iraqi officials claim that they did not use them as they interpreted a storng warning delivered by Secreary of State James Baker as implying that the United States would use nuclear weapons if Iraq used CW or BW against the coalition. Such revelations bolster the need for continued credible nuclear capabilities as well as the need to resist efforts to delegitimize U.S. possession of nuclear weapons. Nonetheless, while apparently successful in deterring NBC use against U.S. and allied forces in the Gulf, the effectiveness of nuclear deterrence cannot be relied on exclusively. Several factors might lessen the credibility of a U.S. nuclear response in certain situations that are not difficult to imagine. First, asymmetrical interests are present in some of, if not all, regional conflicts. A regional regime might be convinced that its survival is at stake, while the U.S. interest in the conflict might will fall far short of that.

A regime making such an assumption might gamble that Washington's stakes in the conflict would not be high enough to warrant a U.S. nuclear response to the regime's NBC use (especially if limited), with all the inevitable international political repercussions. Secondly, a desperate regime might reason that a limited U.S. nuclear response would cause less damage to its military capabilities than a continued, unrelenting conventional attack. Thirdly, an enemy's use of NBC-perhaps even at the outset of hostilities, and not as an act of desperation-might be carefully measured to inflict enough casualities to make the U.S. leadership reconsider the price of its intervention, yet not be of magnitude high that enough it would be likely to provoke a nuclear resopnse. Scenarios such as these- and others can easily be envisioned - suggest that while the United States must maintain a credible nuclear deterrent against NBC use, the efficacy of that deterrent cannot be depended on absolutely. That said, deterring NBC armed regional aggressors will remain the United States's preferred and first line of defense. An integral element of Such deterrence will be maintaining a credible capability across the spectrum of forces, from conventional superiority-including the ability to operate in an NBC environment supported by active and passive defenses and adequate counterforce capabilities - to a reliable and effective nuclear deterrent. However, it is also needed to go beyond capabilities and reanalysis how to think about and plan for deterrence in a regional conflict. For example, some of the assumptions on which U.S., Soviet deterrence was founded (such as a basic and shared rationality) may not hold in regional conflicts. Articulating a regional deterrence and defense strategy (or strategies) will be a difficult but a significant challenge. Understanding deterrence and defense in a regional context will need a better appreciation of the military/cultural/political dynamics, as well a better understanding of possible employment doctrines of regional states with NBC weapons. Another issue is the continued role for so-called tactical nuclear weapons, that is, weapons to be used on or near the battlefield against enemy military forces in comparison to weapons that hold at risk deeper, "strategic" tragets. By the end of the Cold War, the technical distinctions between tactical and strategic systems had become blurred.

Continuing the trend in the last years of the Cold War of reducing dramatically the U.S. tactical nuclear arsenal, the Nuclear Posture Review endorsed a non-strategic nuclear force structure comprising only of Air Force dual-capable aircraft and Navy Tomhawk missiles, which could in an emergency be deployed on submarines.

Use of Counterforce

Counterforce is the ability to strike an enemy's forces before they can be used. It has always been a central objective of military operations. In a WMD scenario, counterforce capabilities include the ability to target, deny, interdict, or destroy hostile NBC forces and infrastructure supporting them. Counterforce principles operate at all levels of military conflict and engagement. At the tactical level, for instance, destruction of an enemy's artillery and supply capabilities is a prime method of suppressing that enemy's ability to deliver chemical or nuclear weapons in the field. Even under the doctrine of mutual assured destruction, the ability to destroy an enemy's residual nuclear forces after an early strike was seen as the most effective way of limiting damage should deterrence fail. In the post-Cold War world, strong counterforce capabilities serve not only to reduce or eliminate existing NBC threats but to deter their creation in the first place. The acquistion of offensive counterforce capabilities was partly a consequence of improved technological capabilities.

Nonetheless, despite the push from technology, the progress of strategic counterforce capabilities was declined during the Cold War, largely because counterforce capabilities sufficient to achieve a first-strike capability were considered destabilizing. In a regional setting there would various special political and operational aspects associated with trying to destroy NBC associated weapons and facilities. Missions of this kind would impose unique considerations on all involved in the planning, decision, and execution, from the National Command authorities to the local commander. The character and symbolism of weapons of mass destruction would make striking NBC related targets as much a political act as a military one. Political authorities would no doubt scrutinize closely any recommendation to destroy NBC related targets. The needs for success would also tend to be more stringent that for non NBC counterforce strikes. Because collateral damage from the destroyed weapons can be so great, the effects of such damage would have to be known in advance and held to a minimum. These needs would have to be taken into consideration during planning and might require unique technical capabilities. Taken together, these considerations would impose special burdens on the intelligence units and military forces if they were to undertake counterforce missions against NBC targets. One lesson that potential adversaries learned from the Gulf War is that in order to survive in the face of U.S. conventional superiority, an enemy needs to go underground. In 1994, a Senate Armed Services Committee report acknowledged, "While Operation Desert Storm revealed the accuracy of U.S. precision guided missiles, it also revealed serious shortcomings in their lethality against buried, deep underground, or otherwise hardened facilities." Increasingly, regional powers are taking this lesson to heart, hiding their WMD facilities and stockpiles in underground bunkers in order to reduce the possibility of detection and the effectiveness of conventional weapons directed against them if they are detected. Such action places greater demands on both intelligency and counterforce resources, as capabilities must be improved to identify underground NBC targets and develop technologies to destroy them.

Active Defense

Active defenses—the ability to prevent weapons from reaching their intended targets—can increase deterrence by denying an enemy the ability effectively to employ NBC-armed missiles and aircraft. Such defenses may become necessary to ensure that the United States or its allies are not deterred by an NBC threat, or do not have to suffer massive casualties unnecessarily. The pursuit of active defenses against the greastest Cold War WMD threat-nuclear armed Soviet ballistic missiles—was carefully circumscribed and formally limited by the Anti-Ballistic Missile (ABM) Treaty.

In 1972, at a time when the number of offensive missiles and nuclear warheads numbered in the tense of thousands the ABM treaty was adopted assuming that in light of these great numbers, active defenses imply not capable of defending against the full magnitude of the threat; mutual assured destruction was considered to be the most stable policy. Further, policymakers hoped that a limit on active defenses would encourage greater restraint in the production of offensive weapons and, conversally, feared that the pursuit of active defenses would lead to even greater offensive efforts. They also hoped that the ABM Treaty might provide a political foundation for reductions in the offensive nuclear stockpiles of the United States and Soviet Union. If the end of the Cold War was accompanied by a diminished perception of the Russian threat, it also resulted in an increased perception of the threat posed by regional powers. Indeed, as ballistic and cruise missiles become readily available to emerging powers, the need for active defenses to protect U.S. forces in regions where NBC proliferation is taking place becomes clearer.

Additionally, the evolution of missiles that are both longer range and mobile decreases the likelihood that counterforce options will be completely successful. The difficulties in location and destroying mobile missiles were vividly demonstrated during the Gulf War. While not designed primarily to intercept SCUD-type missiles, the Patriot missile deployed to the Gulf did provide significant psychological and political benefits in the prosecution of the war. From that experience, it became more apparent that effective active defenses against nuclear, biological, or chemical weapons would be an important consideration in future regional conflicts, for both military and political reasons. Longer-range active-defense missiles, such like the Theater High-Altitude Area Defense (THAAD), will enable warheads to be intercepted at ever greater ranges. This is more important for defense against NBC warheads, because destoying them close to the intended target may not significantly reduce exposure to the agents they carry. The farther from the target that active missile defense systems can intercept an incoming warhead, the less the chance that the agent will affect friendly troops or territory. A nearness with an NBC warhead might still cause a damage to U.S. or coalition forces, or to civilian populations.

Passive Defense

Passive defense seeks to provide protection for U.S. and allied forces against an NBC attack. It can take many shapes, from protective uniforms and masks to equipment incorporated into larger systems (such as entire naval vessels or air-base command centers) that enable them to operate in chemical, biological, and , in limited aspects, some nuclear environments. Passive defense involves detection and identification of NBC agents, medical response to NBC effects, and decontamination of equipment and facilities. Many experts believe that a strong passive-defense capability serves as a deterrent, discouraging use of WMD by an-adversary who knows that U.S. forces are able to operate in chemical and biological environments.

Following the Cold War such circumstances have arisen as underscore the need for effective passive-defense equipment, including protective masks and suits. First, the spread of biological and chemical capabilities means that U.S. forces must be ready to operate in a WMD environment worldwide. Secondly, since the threat is no longer localized in the relatively benign operating climate of Europe, the possibility of having to operate in chemical gear under harsher climatological conditions has increased . Thirdly, the CWC's need that all chemical stockpiles be destroyed within a decade of the treaty's ratification will, if ratified by the United States, preclude any possibility of Washingtons's theatening and in-kind response to the use of chemical weapons against U.S. forces. In the face of a proliferator armed with chemical or biological weapons, this inability to threaten response in kind may weaken deterrence and, in doing, so raise the chances that an adversary will use chemical weapons. Robust passive-defense capabilities are key to operating without a significant loss in effectiveness in a BW or CW environment.

Actions by the Department of Defense to improve chemical- and biological-defense capabilities include the integration of separate service programs into a consolidated DOD Chemical/Biological defense Program. The objective of this program is to enhance the ability of U.S. forces to defend against BW and CW agents by developing and procuring the capabilities to avoid contamination (through a reasonable detection and warning/reconnaissance), protect forces (through individual and collective protective gear and adequate medical support), and improve decontamination measures. In the future, U.S. forces must be ready to operate in the presence of chemical and biological agents in an ever widening variety of contingencies. The ease with which chemical and biological agents cab be produced and delivered means that these threats may be present even in peacekeeping operations. Despite advances, operating in chemical gear continues to place great physical and psychological stress on individual soldiers and units. The possibility that U.S. forces will be called upon to operate in the presence of an NBC threat means that continued improvements in individual protection equipment are required.

The likelihood that U.S. forces will often operate as part of a coalition brings up questions about the possible potitical and military impact of NBC weapons on coalition cohesion. In the event of an NBC threat, it will not be adequnate for U.S. forces alone to have ensufficit protective equipment. An adversary might exploit gaps in the passive-defense capabilities of coalition partners, thereby undermining coalition cohesion and posing acute problems for political leaders and military commanders alike. Furthermore, in some situations, the issue of protection for civilians could become vital not just politically but also operationally. In many instances, for example, a largely civilian work force will be required to maintain capabilities at ports and airfields. The absence of adequate personal protection for civilian workers will result in a degradation of operational capabilities.

Conclusion

An ideal tool for national-security strategy is a combination of two attributes. First, it should contribute to the deterrence of war. Deterrence remains the first line of defense against the use of nuclear, biological, and chemical weapons. Secondly, should deterrence fail, a useful military instrument must lead to the successful prosecution of war by denying the enemy the ability to achieve its objectives—even if that enemy does resort to the use of NBC weapons. The counterproliferation tools described above hold the promise of fulfilling these two needs. To the extent that an enemy realizes the United States maintains the abilities to neutralize (or at least minimize the damage inflicted by) NBC weapojns and to effectively respond to their use, counterproliferation tools may deter an enemy from aggression. This is termed "deterrence by denial." If an adversary knows that possession or even use of NBC weapons will not intimidate or beat U.S. forces, the chances of that adversary's employing N B C Weapons—or, indeed engaging U.S. forces in the first place—will be reduced. However, if deterrence fails, the ability of U.S. forces to operate in an NBC environment and respond decisively to NBC use will be crucial to success.

The United States must aim to make deterrence as credible as possible. Achieving credible deterrence of NBC use in regional conflicts is a complex and uncertain task; nuclear weapons are necessary but not sufficient. Establishing and maintaining a credible deterrent against NBC use in regional conflicts will also need the ability to operate and prevail with conventional forces in an NBC environment. Achieving deterrence by denial will require continued attention to gaps in operational capabilities. The armed services will increasingly need to pay close attention to the fall out of WMD use against U.S. and coalition forces in regional conflicts, and to the imperatives of operating in an NBC environment. The use, or threat of use, of such weapons will have far-reaching impacts on both the tactical and strategic character of the conflict. Coalition warfare may be particularly affected by the use or threatened use of NBC weapons. A coalition will not be politically sustainable if some members are significantly more vulnerable to NBC attack than others.

In addition, a coalition might not be sustainable if it cannot protect the citizens of a coalition country from NBC attack. Proliferation will place additional strains on intelligence needs. The potentially severe effects of NBC use against U.S. forces will need that increased intelligence resources be devoted to identifying and analyzing the NBC capabilities of potential adversaries on a realtime basis. The consequences of failing to identify NBC targets could impose a heavy penalty on U.S. forces operating in the region. The demand for timely and a accurate intelligence on enemy NBC capabilities and readiness will only increase in the years ahead.

14
International Concern: Protocol and Conventions

In order to control the menace of biological weapons, several international efforts are made since early times. Starting with the 1925 Geneva Protocol to the BWC (1972) and its review every five years, there have been some serious attempts in this direction. Let us know these:

I. The 1925 Geneva Protocol

Protocol for the prohibition of the use in war of Asphyxiating, poisonous or other gases, and of bacteriological methods of warefare

Signed at Geneva on 17 June 1925 Entered into force on 8 February 1928 Depositary: French government.

The Undersigned plenipotentiaries, in the name of the respective Governments:

Whereas the use in war of Asphyxiating, poisonous or other gases, and of all analogous liquids materials or devices, has been justly condemned by the general opinion of the civilized world; and

Whereas the prohibition of such use has been declared in Treaties to which the majority of Powers of the world are Parties; and

To the end that this prohibition shall be universally accepted as a part of International Law, binding alike the conscience and the practice of nations;

Declare

That the High Contracting Parties, so far as they are not already

Parties to Treaties prohibiting such use, accept this prohibition, agree to extend this prohibition to the use of bacteriological methods of warfare and agree to be bound as between themselves according to the terms of this declaration.

The High Contracting Parties will exert every effort to induce other States to accede to the present Protocol. Such accession will be notified to the Government of the French Republic, and by the latter to all signatory and acceding Powers, and will take effect on the date of the notification by the Government of the French Republic.

The present Protocol, of which the French and English texts are both authentic, shall be ratified as soon as possible. It shall bear today's date.

The ratifications of the present Protocol shall be addressed to the Government of the French Republic, which will at once notify the deposit of such ratification to each of the signatory and acceding Powers.

The instruments of ratification of and accession to the present Protocol will remain deposited in the archives of the Government of the French Republic.

The present Protocol will come into force for each signatory Power as from the date of deposit of its ratification, and, from that moment, eact Power will be bound as regards other Powers which has already deposited their ratifications.

II. The 1948 Genocide Convention

Convention on the prevention and Punishment of the Crime of Genocide

Adopted at Paris by the UN General Assembly on 9 December 1948
Entered into force on 12 January 1951
Depositary : UN Secretary-General

The Contracting Parties,

Having considered the declaration made by the General Assembly of the United Nations in its resolution 96 (I) dated 11 December 1946 that genocide is a crime under international

---

Source: League of Natio[illegible] Treaty Series, Vol. 94 (1929).

law, contrary to the spirit and aims of the United Nations and condemned by the civilized world;

Recognizing that at all periods of history genocide has inflicted great losses on humanity; and

Being convinced that , in order to liberate mankind from such an odious scourge, international co-opertion is required.

Hereby agree as hereinafter provided:

Article I

The Contracting Parties confirm that genocide, whether committed in time of peace or in time of war, is a crime under international law which they undertake to prevent and to punish.

Article II

In the present Convention, genocide means any of the following acts committed with intent to destroy, in whole or in part, a national, ethnical, racial or religious group, as such:

(a) Killing members of the group;

(b) Causing serious bodily or mental harm to members of the group;

(c) Deliberately inflicting on the group conditions of life calculated to bring about its physical destruction in whole or in part;

(d) Imposing measures intended to prevent births within the group;

(e) Forcibly transferring children of the group to another group.

Article III

The following acts shall be punishable:

(a) Genocide;

(b) Conspiracy to commit genocide;

(c) Direct and public incitement to commit genocide;

(d) Attempt to commit genocide;

(e) Complicity in genocide.

Article IV

Persons committing genocide or any of the other acts enumerated in article III shall be punished, whether they are constitutionally responsible rulers, public officials or private individuals.

Article V

The Contracting Parties undertake to enact, in accordance with their respective Constitutions, the necessary legislation to give effect to the provisions of the present Convention and in particular, to provide effective penalties for persons guilty of genocide or of any of the other acts enumerated in article III.

Article VI

Persons charged with genocide or any of the other acts enumerated in article III shall be tried by a competent tribunal of the State in the territory of which the act was committed, or by such international penal tribunal as may have jurisdiction with respect to those Contracting Parties which shall have accepted its jurisdiction.

Article VII

Genocide and the other acts enumerated in article III shall not be considered as political crimes for the purpose of extradition.

The Contracting Parties pledge themselves in such cases to grant extradition in accordance with their laws and treaties in force.

Article VIII

Any Contracting Party may call upon the competent organs of the United Nations to take such action under the Charter of the United Nations as they consider appropriate for the prevention and suppression of acts of genocide or any of the other acts enumerated in article III.

Article IX

Disputes between the Contracting Parties relating to the interpretation, application or fulfilment of the present Convention, including those relating to the responsibility of a State for genocide or for any of the other acts enumerated in article III, shall be submitted to the International Court of Justice at the request of any of the parties to the dispute.

Article X

The present Convention of which the Chinese, English, French, Russian and Spanish texts are equally authentic, shall bear the date of 9 December 1948.

Article XI

The present Convention shall be open until 31 December 1949 for signature on behalf of any Member of the Unted Nations and of any non-member State to which an invitation to sign has been addressed by the General Assembly.

The present Convention shall be ratified, and the instruments of ratification shall be deposited with the Secretary-General of the Untied Nations.

After 1 January 1950 the present Convention may be acceded to on behalf of any Member of the United Nations and of any non-member State which has received an invitation as aforesaid.

Instruments of assession shall be deposited with the Secretary-General of the United Nations.

Article XII

Any Contracting Party may at any time, by notification addressed to the Secretary-General of the United Nations, extend the application of the present Convention to all or any of the territories for the conduct of whose foreign relations that Contracting Party is responsible.

Article XIII

On the day when the first twenty instruments of ratification or accession have been deposited, the Secretary-General shall draw up a *process-verbal* and transmit a copy thereof to each Member of the United Nations and to each of the non-member States contemplated in article XI.

The present Convention shall come into force on the ninetieth day following the date of deposit of the twenhtiety instrument of ratification or accession.

Any ratification or accession effected busequent to the latter date shall become effective on the ninetieth day following the deposit of the instrument of ratification or accession.

Article XIV

The present Convention shall remain in effect for a period of ten years as from the date of its coming into force.

It shal! thereafter remain in force for successive periods of five years for such Contracting parties as have not denounced it at least six months before the expiration of the current period.

Denunciation shall be effected by a written notification addressed to the Secretary-General of the United Nations.

Article XV

If, as a result of denunciations, the number of Parties to the present Convention should become less than sixteen, the Convention shall cease to be in force as from the date on which the last of these denunciations shall become effective.

Article XVI

A request for the revision of the present Convention may be made at any time by any Contracting Party by means of a notification in writing addressed to the Secretary-General.

The General Assembly shall decide upon the steps, if any, to be taken in respect of such request.

Article XVII

The Secretary-General of the United Nations shall notify all Members of the United Nations and the nine-member States contemplated in article XI of the following:

(a) Signatures, ratifications and accessions received in accordance with article XI;

(b) Notifications received in accordance with article XII;

(c) The date upon which the present Convention comes into force in accordance with article XIII.

(d) Denunciations received in accordance with article XIV.

(e) The abrogation of the Convention in accordance with article XV;

(f) Notifications received in accordance with article XVI.

Article XVIII

The original of the present Convention shall be deposited in the archicves of the United Nations.

A certified copy of the Convention shall be transmitted to each Member of the United Nations and to each of the non-member States contemplated in article XI.

Article XIX

The present Convention shall be registered by the Secretary-General of the United Nations on the date of its coming into force.

Article XII

Five years after the entry into force of this Convention , or earlier if it is requested by a majority of Parties to the Convention by submitting a proposal to this effect to the Depositary Governments, a conference of States Parties to the Convention shall be held at Geneva, Switzerland, to review the operation of the Convention, with a view to assuring that the purposes of the preamble and the provisons of the convention, including the proussions converning negotiations on chemical weapons, are being realized. Such review shall take into account any new scientific and technological developments relevant to the Convention.

Article XIII

1. This convention shall be of unlimited duration.

2. Each State Party to this Convention shall in exercising its national sovereignty have the right to withdraw from the Convention if it decides that extraordinary events, related to the subject matter of the Convention, have jeopardized the supreme interests of its country. It shall give notice of such withdrawal to all other States Parties to the Convention and to the United Nations Security Council three months in advance. Such notice shall include a statement of the extraordinary events it regards as having jeopardized its supreme interests.

Article XIV

1. This Convention shall be open to all States for signature. Any State which does not sign the Convention before its entry into force

---

Source: Treaty Series, Vol. 78 (United Nations, New York).

in accordance with paragraph (3) of this Article may accede to it at any time.

2. This Convention shall be subject to ratification by signatory States. Instruments of ratification and instruments of accession shall be deposited with the Governments of the United States of America, the United Kingdom of Great Britain and Nothern Ireland and the Union of Soviet Socialist Republic, now Russia which are hereby designated the Depositary Governments.

3. This Convention shall enter into force after the deposit of instruments of ratification by twenty-two Governments, including the Governments designated as Depositaries of the Convention.

4. For States whose instruments of ratification or accession are deposited subsequent to the entry into force of this Convention, it shall enter into force on the date of the deposit of their instruments of ratification or accession.

5. The Depositary Governments shall promptly inform all signatory and acceding States of the date of each signature, the date of deposit of each instrument of ratification or of accession and the date of the entry into force of this Convention, and of the receipt of other notices.

6. This convention shall be registered by the Depositary Governments pursuant to Article 102 of the Charter of the United Nations.

Article XV

This Convention, the English, Russian, French, Spanish and Chinese texts of which are equally authentic, shall be deposited in the archives of the Depositary Governments . Duly certified copies of the Convention shall be transmitted by the Depositary Governments to the Governments of the signatory and acceding States.

Source: Treaties and Other International Act, Series 8060 (US Department of State, Washington, D.C. 1975)

IV Convention : Review of Negotiations

1. Introduction

1. The question of the regulation of biological weapons was for many years considered jointly with chemical means of warfare. The interest in and the concern over these weapons was expressed by the international community already in the first resolution of the General Assembly of the United Nations. Resolution 1 (I) of 24 January 1946 envisaged not only the elimination of atomic weapons, but also "of all other major weapons adaptable to mass destruction", and of which chemical and biological weapons were one important Category. Thereafter, after frequent references were made to the need of the Climination of "all weapons of mass destruction", and chemical and biological weapons were explicity included in various proposals put forward at the time. However, no specific negotiations took place on the subject. It was only towards the end of the 1960 that this question moved to the forefront of disarmament negotiations.

2. The move occurred during the 1968 session of the Eighteen-Nation Committee on Disarmament (ENDC) which, under the heading "non-nuclear measures" of its provisional agenda. Envisaged the consideration of the question of chemical and bacteriological warfare. This was followed by a number of specific proposals on the subject submitted during the session. One of them was a working paper on microbiological warfare submitted by the United Kingdom on 6 August 1968[1] which was of particular importance for two reasons: first, it was based on the assertion tat, for a number of reasons, the Geneva Protocol for the Prohibition of the Use in War of Asphyxiating. Poisonous or Other Gases, and of Bacteriological Methods of Warfare of 1925 was not an entirely satisfactory instrument to deal with the questions of chemical and microbiological warfare and, second, it suggested that the problem could become more manageable by considering chemical and microbiological methods of warfare separately. In view of this, the United Kingdom proposed the early conclusion of a convention for the prohibition of microbiological methods of warfare, which would "supplement but not supersede" the Geneva Protocol. Such a convention would ban the use for hostile purposes of microbiological agents causing death or disease by infection in man, other animals, or crops, and it would also include a ban on the production of microbiological agents "which was so worded as to take account of

the fact that most of the microbiological agents that could be used in hostilities are also needed for peaceful purposes".

3. The reaction to this proposal varied considerably. Basically, Western countries were sympathetic to it and found the British arguments convincing, while the non-aligned and socialist countries viewed this approach with serious misgivings. They believed that the adoption of that approach would inevitably result in the reopening of issues which had long been solved. In their opinion, the Geneva Protocol was not obsolete since its provisions covered not only methods and agents of warfare which existed at the time the Protocol had been concluded, but also the new methods and agents of warfare that had emerged since then.

4. The consideration of the question led to the adoption on 20 December 1968 by the General Assembly of resolution 2454 A (XXIII) requestiong the Secretary-General to prepare, with the assistance of a group of experts, a report on the effects of the possible use of chemical and bacteriological means of warfare. After the submission of the report in 1969[2], ENDC devoted considerable attention to the question of chemical and bacteriological (biological) weapons.

2. **Negotiations in the Conference of the Committee on Disarmament (CCD)***

2.1 Scope

5. The negotiations on the subject-matter which started in the course of the 1969 session of the Committee predictably centred on the question of the scope. In this regard two distinctly different approaches were proposed. A draft convention of 10 July 1969 submitted by the United Kingdom of Great Britain and Northern Ireland was limited in scope to the prohibition of biological methods of warfare[3]. In contrast, a draft convention of 19 September 1969, submitted by the Union of Soviet Socialist Republics together with Bulgaria, the Byelorussian Soviet Socialist Republic, Czechoslovakia, Hungary, Mongolia, Poland, Romania and the Ukrainian Soviet Socialist Republic, dealt with the prohibition of the development, production, stockpiling and the destruction of both chemical and bacteriological (biological) weapons[4]. Both draft conventions received support from a number of States. The United States of America, for instance, in supporting the British proposal stressed the difference between the two types of weapons. It pointed

out that chemical weapons, unlike biological weapons, had actually been used in warfare and that, therefore, many States would be reluctant to give up the possession of chemical weapons without reliable assurances that other States were not developing, producing and stockpiling chemical weapons. It held further that biological weapons presented less intractable problems and that an agreement on banning them should not be delayed until agreement on a reliable prohibition of chemical weapons could be reached. Those States which favoured a comprehensive prohibiton, in supporting the Soviet draft, pointed out that chemical and biological weapons had been treated together in the Geneva Protocol and in the General Assembly resolutions, as wellusion the report of the Secretary-General and, therefore, should continue to be dealt with in one instrument. In their opinion, a separate convention covering only biological weapons, might serve to intensify the chemical arms race. A number of them, however, while supporting the comprehensive approach, considered that it would be acceptable only with an adequate control system.

6. The course of further negotiations on the scope was influenced by outside developments. Thus, on 25 November 1969, the United States announced a unilateral renunciation of the first use of lethal or incapacitating chemical agents and weapons and an unconditional renunciation of all methods of biological warfare. On 14 February 1970, the ban was extended to cover toxins. Similar announcements were made by other States. For instance, Canada, Sweden and the United Kingdom announced that they had no biological weapons nor the intention of producing them. These declarations were generally welcomed and also contributed towards creating an atmospher conductive to undertaking the commitment in the form of abandoning international instrument. In response to these developments, the USSR, together with Bulgaria, Czechoslovakia, Hungary, Mongolia, Poland and Romania, submitted to the Conference of the Committeee on Disarmament on 30 March 1971 a new draft convention confined in scope to biological weapons and toxins. Its pertinent provisions read as follows:

Article I

Each State Party to this Convention undertakes not to develop, produce, stockpile or otherwise acquire:

(1) Microbioligical or other biological agents or toxins of such types and in such quantities as are not designed for the prevention of disease or for other peaceful purposes;

(2) Auxiliary equipment or means of delivery designed to facilitate the use of such agents or toxins for hostile purposes.

Article II

Each State Party to this Convention undertakes to destroy within a period of three months after the entry into force of the Convention-observing all the necessary precautions—or to divert to peaceful uses all previously accumulated weapons in its possession as well as the equipment and means of delivery mentioned in article I of the Convention.

Article III

Each State Party to the Convention undertakes not to assist, encourage or induce any particular State, group of States or international organizations to take action contrary to the provisions of this Convention.

7. A number of States, in particular the non-aligned, while welcoming the draft in general, reiterated their preference for a comprehensive prohibition of both chemical and biological weapons. Concern was also expressed that the scope, even if it were to remain confined to biological weapons, was not exhaustive enough since, the proposed ban in article I did not, for instance, cover research work. In view of this, Egypt submmitted a proposal to include research work among the activities to be prohibited.

8. Those States which had advocated a separate regulation of biological weapons welcomed the draft convention as an acceptable basis for further negotiations. They also made it clear that it was the only possible way of approachihg this issue if unneccessary delay was to be avoided.

9. On 5 August 1971, following further negotiations and exchanges of views, the sponsors of the 30 March draft and the United States submitted separate but identical texts of a new draft convention on bacteriological (biological) and toxin weapons. The

---

*ENDC had its name changed to the Conference of the Committee on Disarmament (CCD) in 1970. Following its enlargement by the addition of new Member States.

scope of the draft convention, in comparison with the previous one, was somewhat widened. in article I, for example, the scope was strengthened first by adding to the undertaking "not to develop, produce, stockpile or otherwise acquire" the words" or retain", and , secondly, by specifying that the ban on the use of those weapons applied not only to hostile purposes in general but also to armed conflicts. Further, in article II, the undertaking to destroy, or to divert to peaceful purposes the agents, toxins, weapons, equipment and means of delivery, as specified in article I, in the possession of the Parties was extended to cover those under their "jurisdiction or control as well. Similarly, the undertaking in article III was broadened to include a ban on the transfer. The provisions of the draft pertaining to the scope read as follows:

Article I

Each State Party to this Convention undertakes not to develop, produce, stockpile or otherwise acquire or retain:

(1) Microbial or other biological agents or toxins of types and in quanitities that have no justification for prophylactic or other peaceful purposes;

(2) Weapons, equipment or means of delivery designed to use such agents or toxins for hostile purposes or in armed conflict.

Article II

Each State Party to this Convention undertakes to destroy, or to divert to peaceful purposes, as soon as possible but not later than— months after the entry into force of the Convention all agents, toxins, weapons, equipment and means of delivery specified in article I of the Convention, which are in its possession or under its jurisdiction or control. In implementing the provisions of this article all necessary safety precautions shall be observed to protect the population and the environment.

Article III

Each State Party to this Convention undertakes not to transfer to any recipient whatsoever, directly, or indirectly, and not in any way to assist, encourage, or induce any State, group of States or international organizations to manufacture or otherwise acquire any agent, toxin, weapon, equipment or means of delivery specified in article I of the Convention.

10. The main objections to the identical drafts related again to the question of the prohibition of research work. Many States reiterated their view that a ban on research work would considerably strengthen the convention. Others, however, argued that research work was indispensable for the use of biological agents or toxins for prophylactic and other peaceful purposes. No agreement was reached on this issue, nor with regard to a ban on research work on weapons, equipment or means of delivery designed to use as agents and toxins. Some States argued that, in view of the proposed total destruction of those weapons and the prohibition of their production, such a provision would be redundant.

11. However, some changes were made in the draft in the course of its consideration. Thus in article I phrase "never in any circumstances" was inserted after the word "undertakes", but its impact was the strenghthening of the undertaking rather than the broadening of the scope. But the insertion in the same article of the phrase "whatever their origin or method of production" after the words "microbial or other biological agents, or toxins" closed any loopholes that might have existed with regard to the scope as proposed in the draft. On 28 September 1971, a revised draft convention was submitted by Bulgaria, Canada, Czechoslovakia, Hungary, Italy, Mongolia, the Netherlands, Poland, Romania, the USSR, the United Kingdom and the United States reflecting these changes. The draft was transmitted to the General Assembly for its consideration.

12. On 16 December 1971, by resolution 2826 (XXVI), the Assembly commended the Convention. The relevant articles read as follows:

Article I

Each State Party to this Convention undertakes never in any circumstances to develop, produce, stockpile or otherwise acquire or retain:

(1) Microbial or other biological agents, or toxins whatever their origin or method production, of types and in quantities that have no justification for prophylactic, protective or other peaceful purposes.

(2) Weapons, equipment or means of delivery designed to use such agents or toxins for hostile purposes or in armed conflict.

Article II

Each State Party to this Convention undertakes to destroy, or to divert to peaceful purposes, as soon as possible but not later than nine months after the entry into force of the Convention, all agents, toxins, weapons, equipment and means of delivery specified in article I of the Convention, which are in its possession or under its jurisdiction or control. In implementing the provisions of this article all necessary safety precautions shall be observed to protect populations and the environment.

Article III

Each State Party to this Convention undertakes not to transfer to any recipient whatsoever, directly or indirectly, and not in any way to assist, encourage, or induce any State, group of States or international organizations to manufacture or otherwise acquire any of the agents, toxins, weapons, equipment or means of delivery specified in article I of the Convention.

2.2 Measures Regarding Chemical Weapons

13. The negotiations on other provisions of the Convention proved equally important, particularly those concerning further measure for broadening the scope to cover chemical weapons. As soon as it became clear that a joint regulation of chemical and biological weapons was not possible at the time and that the efforts would concentrate first on biological weapons, a number of States, particularly the non-aligned, pointed out that their acceptance of the limited approach would depend on the solution of the follow-up regarding negotiations on chemical weapons.

14. In recognition of that concern, the draft convention of 30 March 1971, submitted by the Soviet Union and other sponsors, dealt with the matter in the preamble as well as in two separate articles of the draft convention. Thus, preambular paragraphs 8 and 12 respectively recognized the significance of the 1925 Geneva Protocol and expressed the conviction that the proposed convention would facilitate progress towards complete prohibition of chemical weapons on which negotiations would continue . Article VIII reaffirmed the obligations assumed by States Parties to the Geneva Protocol, while article IX provided for an undertaking by States Parties to conduct negotiations in good faith for effective measures for the regulation of chemical weapons.

15. The identical drafts of 5 August 1971, submitted by the Soviet Union and a group of other sponsors, on the one hand , and the United States, on the other, with minor drafting changes included the same text of the 30 March 1971 draft convention of which the provision on negotiations on chemical weapons read as follows:

Article VIII

Each State Party to this Convention undertakes to conduct negotiations in good faith on effective measures for prohibiting the development, production and stockpiling of chemical weapons and for their destruction and on appropriate measures concerning the equipment and means of delivery specifically designed for the production or use of chemical weapons for warfare.

These provisions were generally welcomed. However, a number of suggestions were made with a view to givinng practical effect to the proposed undertaking. Mexico, for instance, proposed the inclusion of an additional article in the draft which read[8]:

"Pending the agreement referred to in article VIII, the States Parties to ths Convention undertake to refrain from any further development, production or stockpiling of those chemical agents for weapons purposes which because of their degree of toxicity have the highest lethal effects. The agents in question are listed in the Protocol annexed to this Convention.

16. A similar proposal was made by Morocco, which stated that it would be highly desirable to reach agreement immediately after the entry into force of the biological convention, on the cessation of the production of chemical weapons[9]. Although supported by a number of delegations, both proposals proved unacceptable to a number of other delegations which left that such an undertaking must be, *inter alia*, based on adequate verification.

17. The negotiations which followed resulted[IX], however, in the improvement of the proposed text. Changes were made in the preambular paragraphs and in article VIII, which now became articleIX, strengthening the link between biological and chemical disarmament. The relevant provisions of the Convention in its final form read:

(Preambular paragraph 2)

"Recognizing the important significance of the Protocol for the

Prohibition of the Use in War of Asphyxiating. Poisonous or Other Gases, and of Bacteriological. Methods of Warfare, signed at Geneva on June 17, 1925, and conscious also of the contribution which the said Protocol has already made, and continues to make , to mitigating the horrors of war.

(Preambular paragraph 8)

"Recognizing that an agreement on the prohibition of bacteriological (biological) and toxin weapons represents a first possible step towards the achievement of agreement on effective measures also for the prohibition of the development, production and stockpiling of chemical weapons, and determined to continue negotiations to that end."

Article VIII

Nothing in this Convention shall be interpreted as in any way limiting or detracting from the obligations assumed by any State under the Protocol for the Prohibition of the Use in War of Asphyxiating, Poisonous or Other Gases, and of Bacteriological Methods of Warfare signed at Geneva on June 17, 1925.

Article IX

Each State Party to this Convention affirms the recognized objective of effective prohibition of chemical weapons and, to this end, undertakes to continue negotiations in good faith with a view to reachning early agreement on effective measures for the prohibition of their development, production and stockpiling and for their destruction, and on appropriate measures concerning equipment and means of delivery specifically designed for the production or use of chemical agents for weapons purposes.

2.3 Compliance

18. The provisions on compliance did not give rise to any particular difficulty. The draft convention of 30 march 1971 dealt with this matter in two articles. Article IV stated that States Parties should be internationally responsible for compliance with the provisions by their legal or physical persons while article V committed States Parties to undertake as soon as possible, in accordance with their constitutional prcedures, the necessary legislative and administrative measures for giving effect to the undertakings provided for in articles I-III. The identical drafts of 5 August 1971 incorporated the same idea but the language was

brought more into line with the revised articles dealing with the scope, and the commitment on compliance was further strengthened. Thus, for example, the request to States Parties to undertake "the necessary legislative and administrative measures" was replaced by the phrase "to take any necessary measures". The provision was also strengthened by adding to the words "within the territory of such States" the phrase "under its jurisdiction or under its control anywhere" (Art. IV). With this new formulation the provision referring to international responsibility for compliance was considered redundant and was consequently dropped. Instead, a new article was included in the draft dealing with the consultations between States Parties in solving problems connected with the application of the Convention (Art. V). No further changes were made in the wording of these articles and they were included in the Convention as they appeared in the draft of 5 August. They read as follows:

Article IV

Each State Party to this Convention shall, in accordance with its constitutional processes, take any necessary measures to prohibit and prevent the development, production, stockpiling, acquisition or retention of the agents, toxins, weapons, equipment and means of delivery specified in article I of the Convention, within the territory of such State, under its Jurisdiction or under its control anywhere.

Article V

The States Parties to this Convention undertake to consult one another and to cooperate in solving any problems which may arise in relation to the objective of, or in the application of the provisions of the Convention. Consultation and cooperation pursuant to this article may also be undertaken through approproate international procedures within the framework of the United Nations and in accordance with its Charter.

2.4 Breach of the Obligations

19. The question of a breach of the obligations to be assumed under the proposed convention was dealt with in close conjunction with the problem of compliance. It was of particular importance in view of the fact that it was understood from the very beginning that the convention would be based on national rather than on

international means of verification. This necesitated the elaboration of specific and effective procedures to which States Parties could easily resort in case of any problem regarding the compliance with the provisions of the convention. Although there was general agreement in this regard, the initial proposals for the resolution of this problem were based on somewhat different approaches. The British draft of 10 July 1969 basically entrusted the Secretary-General of the United Nations with receiving any complaint, investigating it and reporting on the results of the investigation to the Security Council (Art.III), In contrast, the draft of 30 March 1971, submitted by the Soviet Union and a group of sponsors, accorded the central role in these matters to the Security Council of the United Nations rather than to the Secretary-General (Art. VII). Both approaches had their supporters and critics, as well. Thus, it was argued that the British proposal offered greater advantages to a complaining Party since it was designed to circumvent any delays in the investigation that otherwise might occur as a consequence of political deadlock in the Security Council surrounding any particular complaint. Those States which favoured the other approach did so because they believed that matters pertaining to a breach of obligations had a direct bearing on the security of States Parties and therefore it was only logical to entrust investigation procedures to the Security Council which was primarily responsible for the maintenance of international peace and security. The latter approach eventually prevailed. The identical drafts of 5 August 1971 provided that a complaint in connection with a breach would be lodged with the Security Council and committed States Parties to co-operate in carrying out any investigation which the Council might undertake (Art. VI). With the exception of the transposition of the last sentence from paragraph 1 to paragraph 2, this provision was, without any further changes, included in the text of the final draft of 28 September 1971. This draft, however, contained an important additional article committing States Parties to provide or support assistance to a Party in danger as a result of violation of the Convention. These two articles as included in the Convention read:

Article VI

(1) Any State Party to this Convention which finds that any other State Party is acting in breach of obligations deriving from the provisions of the Convention may lodge a complaint with the Security Council of the United Nations. Such a complaint should include all

possible evidence confirming its validity, as well as request for its consideration by the Security Council.

(2) Each State Party to this Convention undertakes to co-operate in carrying out any investigation which the Security Council may initiate, in accordance with the provisions of the Charter of the United Nations, on the basis of the complaint received by the Council. The Security Council shall inform the States Parties to the Convention of the results of the investigation.

Article VII

Each State Party to this Convention undertakes to provide or support assistance, in accordance with the United Nations Charter, to any Party to the Convention which so requests, if the Security Council decides that such Party has been exposed to danger as a result of violation of the Convention.

2.5 Peaceful Bacteriological (biological) Activities

20. The question of peaceful bacteriological (biological) activities was one of the central issues in the negotiations on the convention on biological means of warfare. When the United Kingdom first suggested separate regulation of this category of weapons it made it clear that the wording of the scope would have to reflect the fact that "most of the microbiological agents that could be used in hostilities are also needed for peaceful purposes". All the subsequent drafts in defining the scope of the proposed convention took into account this fact by specifying that the prohibition covered those types and quantities that had no justification for prophylactic or other peaceful purposes. Although there was no objection in principle to the concept of peaceful application of biological and toxin agents, a number of States, particularly the non-aligned, expressed serious concern that these provisions might provide some loop holes for activities contrary to the purposes of the proposed that the article dealing with the scope exempted from the ban certain types and quantities of those agents and toxins without specifying what, in fact, they were. Other States argued that the provision barring development, production, stockpiling or acquistion of equipment or means of delivery designed to use such agents or toxins for hostile purpose or in armed conflict was more that sufficient to guarantee against a possible misuse of the provision on peaceful uses. Although mixed feelings on the wording of the article on the scope remained even after the

Convention had been adopted , no one challenged the need for peaceful bacteriological (biological) activities. In order to strengthen this notion the draft of 30 March 1971, submitted by the Soviet Union and a group of sponsors, included a separate article on the right of States Parties to participate in international exchange of relevant material for peaceful purposes (Art. X). The identical drafts of 5 August 1971 incorporated this article without any changes (art. IX). In the course of the subsequent negotiations paragraph 1 was expanded to include the commitment of Parties to contribute to the development and application of scientific discoveries for prevention of disease or for other peaceful purposes. This addition was reflected in the final draft of 28 September 1971 (Art. X) and read:

Article X

(1) The States Parties to this Convention undertake to facilitate and have the right to participate in, the fullest possible exchange of equipment, materials and scientific and technological information for the use of bacteriological (biological) agents and toxins for peaceful purposes. Parties to the Convention in a position to do so shall also co-operate in contributing individually or together with other States or international organizations to the further development and application of scientific discoveries in the field of bacteriology (biology) for prevention of disease, or for other peaceful purposes.

(2) This Convention shall be implemented in a manner designed to avoid hampering the economic or technological development of States parties to the Convention or intenational co-operation in the field of peaceful bacteriological (biological) activities , including the international exchange of bacteriological (biological) agents and toxins and equipment for the processing, use or production of becteriological (biological) agents and toxins for peaceful purposes in accordance with the provisions of the Convention.

2.6 Amendments

21. The question of amendments, being one of the standard clauses in international agreements, was very little discussed. Those States which referred to it noted only that the provision should ensure the right of each State Party to propose amendments and that they should be accepted by a sufficient number of States before entering into force. The draft of 30 March 1971 fully reflected these requirements (Art. XI). Without any changes it was included in

subsequent drafts and eventually in the Convention as article XI which read:

Article XI

Any State Party may propose amendments to this Convention. Amendments shall enter into force for each State Party accepting the amendments upon their acceptance by a majority of the States Parties to the Convention and thereafter for each remaining State Party on the date of acceptance by it.

2.7 Review Mechanism

22. The question of the review of the operation of the proposed convention was dealt with in close conjunction with the provisions concerning compliance and further negotiations on chemical weapons. It was widely felt that a provision permitting periodic reviews would greatly enhance credibility of the undertakings since it would enable Parties not only to consider the operation of the convention but also to determining whether or not it might be necessary to amend it in view of possible scientific and technological developments relevant to the convention. This provision was particularly important for those States which felt that the proposed scope was unduly limited and that it should in due course be enlarged to cover chemical weapons as well. They emphasized the need for a review mechanism that would place under periodic scrutiny the implementation of the undertaking regarding further negotiations on chemical weapons.

23. The text of the article on the review procedure, contained in the draft of 30 March 1971 (Art. XII), took this concern into account by mentioning in particular the implementation of the provisions concerning chemical weapons. The formulation of the article was generally welcomed, nevertheless suggestions for its improvement were made. Some non-aligned States, while not objecting to the proposed five year period after which a review conference would be convened, felt that a provision should be made to enable the convening of this conference, in case of need, even earlier than that. In addition, these States expressed preference for the formulation which would provide for regular periodic reviews rather than for only one review after five years.

24. The identical drafts of 5 August 1971 reflected only the first suggestion (art. XI). As regards the second one, it was pointed out,

on the one hand, that the provision on amendments was sufficient to take care of any further improvements of the convention required as a result of new scientific and technological developments and, on the other, that negotiations on chemical weapons would be conducted separately and at their own pace. It was also noted that a conference to be convened for the purpose of reviewing the operation of the convention five years after its entry into force could decide itself if and when to meet again. With this understanding and without further changes this article was included in the final draft of 28 September 1971 as article XII. It read:

Article XII

Five years after the entry into force of this Convention, or earlier if it is requested by a majority of Parties to the Convention by submiting a proposal to this effect to the Depositary Governments, a conference of States Parties to the Convention shall be held at Geneva, Switzerland, to review the operation of the Convention, with a view to assuring that the purpose of the preamble and the provisions of the Convention, including the provisions concerning negotiations on chemical weapons, are being realized. Such review shall take into account any new scientific and technological developments relevant to the Convention.

2.8 Duration and Withdrawal

25. From the outset of the negotiations there was a widely held view that one way of underlining the utmost importance of the prevention of the arms race in the field of biological methods of warfare would be to make the proposed convention of unlimited duration. Already the British proposal of 10 July 1969 contained a provision to this effect and so did all subsequent drafts. Although there was no objection to this rule as such, it was also widely held that some provision should be made for the withdrawal from the convention under certain strictly specified circumstances so as to enable States Parties to protect their supreme interests. This notion was reinforced by the fact that other arms regulation agreements, such as the Treaty on the Non-Proliferation of Nuclear Weapons of 1968 and the Sea-Bed Treaty on which the negotiations were about to be completed, contained such a provision. Consequently the British draft used the wording from those previous agreements (art. IX). The draft of 30 March 1971 did not make reference to the right to withdraw but the identical drafts of 5 August 1971 reintroduced the whole

provision (art . XII). Without any further changes it was included in the final text of the Convention as article XIII which read:

Article XIII

(1) This Convention shall be of unlimited duration.

(2) Each State Party to this Convention shall in exercising its national sovereignty have the right to withdraw from the Convention if it decides that extraordinary events, related to the subject matter of the Convention, have jeopardized the supreme interests of its country. It shall give notice of such withdrawal to all other States Parties to the Convention and to the United Nations, Security Council three months in advance. Such notice shall include a statement of the extraordinary events it regards as having jeopardized its supreme interests.

2.9 Final Clauses

26. The final clauses of the draft convention, providing for signature, ratification, entry into force, registration and authenticity of the text, were very little discussed. It was generally felt that the proviously concluded arms regulation ageements had set an acceptable pattern in this respect which could be used in subsequent cases as well. Statements made in this regard stressed the view that the proposed convention should enter into force upon a reasonable number of ratifications-neither too few nor too many-including certain major military Powers. Both the drafts of 30 March and of 5 August, 1971, used the language of corresponding articles of the Sea-Bed Treaty of 1971 but did not specify the required number of ratifications. However, the final draft of 28 September 1971 included also the Sea-Bed Treaty formula concerning the number of ratifications. Thus, in their final form these provisions were identical to the provisions of the Sea-Bed Treaty, and they read as follows:

Article XIV

(1) This Convention shall be open to all States for signature. Any State which does not sign the Convention before its entry into force in accordance with paragraph (3) of this article may accede to it at any time.

(2) This Convention shall be subject to ratification by Signatory States. Instruments of ratification and instruments of accession shalll be deposited with the Governments of the United States of America,

the United Kingdom of Great Britain and Northern Ireland and the Union of Soviet Socialist Republics, which are hereby designated the Depositary Governments.

(3) This Convention shall enter into force after the deposit of instruments of ratification by twenty-two Governments, including the Governments designated as Depositaries of the Convention.

(4) For States whose instruments of ratification or accession are deposited subsequent to the entry into force of this Convention, it shall enter into force on the date of the deposit of their instruments of ratification or accession.

(5) The Depositary Governments shall promptly inform all signatory and acceding States of the date of each signature, the date of deposit of each instrument of ratification or of accession and the date of the entry into force of this Convention, and of the receipt of other notices.

(6) This Convention shall be registered by the depositary Governments pursuant to Article 102 of the Charter of the United Nations.

Article XV

This Convention, the English, Russian, French, Spanish and Chinese texts of which are equally authentic, shall be deposited in the archives of the Depositary Governments. Duly certified copies of the Convention shall be transmitted by the Depositary Governments to the Governments of the signatory and acceding States.

3. Status of the Convention

27. The Convention was opened for signature on 10 April 1972 in the capitals of the USSR, the United Kingdom and the United States which had been designated by article XIV. paragraph 2, as Depositary Governments. It entered into force on 26 March 1975, upon the deposit of the twenty-second instrument of ratification, including the instruments of the three Depositary Governments, as stipulated in paragraph 2 of article IV. Lists of States that have signed and ratified or acceded to the Convention are maintained by the

---

Source : UN, 1980a.

Depositary Governments.

V. Biological Weapons Convention : The Review Conference

The States Parties to the Convention on the Prohibition of the Development. Production and Stockpiling of Bactreiological (Biological) and Toxin Weapons and on their destruction, having met in Geneva 3-2 March 1980 under the provisions of Article XII to review the operation of the Convention with a view to assuring that the purposes of the preamble and the provisions of the Convention are being realized:

Reaffirming their determination to act with a view to achieving effective progress towards general and complete disarmament including the prohibition and elimination of all types of weapons of mass destruction and biconvinced that the prohiition of the development, production and stockpiling of chemical and bacteriological (biological) weapons and their elimination, through effective measures, will facilitate the achievement of gereral and complete disarmament under strict and effective international control.

Recognizing the continuing importance of the Convention and its objectives and the common interest of mankind in the elimination of bacteriological (biological) and toxin weapons.

Affirming their belief that universal adherence to the Convention would enhance international peace and security, would not hamper economic or technological development, and further, would facilitate the wider exchange of information for the use of bacteriological (biological) agents for peaceful purposes,

Reaffirming their adherence to the principle and objectives of the Geneva Protocol of 17 June 1925 and calling upon all States to comply stricly with them,

Realling that the General Assembly of the United Nations has repeatedly condemned all actions contrary to the said principles and objectives,

Recognizing the importance of achieving international agreement on effective measures for the prohibition of the development, production and stockpi!'ng of chemical weapons and for their destruction as a matter of high priority,

Noting the relevant provisions of the Final Document of the Tenth Special Session of the General Assembly devoted to Disarmament,

Appealing to all States to refrain from any action which might place the Convention or any of its provisions in jeopardy,

Declare as follows:

The States Parties to the Convention reaffirm their strong determination for the sake of all mankind, to exclude completely the possibility of bacteriological (biological) agents and toxins being used as weapons. They reaffirm their strong support for the Convention, their continued dedication to its principles and objectives and their commitment to implement effectively its provisions.

Article I

The Conference notes the importance of Article I as the Article which defines the scope of the Convention and reaffirms its support for the provisions of this Article.

The Conference believes that Article I has proved sufficiently comprehensive to have covered recent scientific and technological developments relevant to the Convention.

Article II

The Conference noted the importance of Article II and emphasizes that States which become Parties to the Convention, in implementing the provisions of this Article, shall observe all necessary safety precautions to protect populations and the environment.

The Conference welcomes the declarations of several States Parties to the effect either that they do not possess and have never possessed agents, toxins, weapons, equipment or means of delivery specified in Article I of the Convention, or that having possessed them they have destroyed them ordiverted them to peaceful purposes. The Conference believes that such voluntary declarations contribute to increased confidence in the Convention and believes that States not having made such voluntary declarations should do so.

Article III

The Conference notes the importance of the provisions of Article III which proscribes the transfer of agents, toxins, weapons, equipment or means of delivery specified in Article I of the Convention to any recipient whatsoever and the furnishing of assistance, encouragement or inducement to any State, group of States or international organizations to manufacture or otherwise acquire them.

Article IV

The conference notes the provisions of Artice IV, which requires each state Party to take any necessary measures to prohibit and prevent the development, production, stockpiling, acquisition or retention of the agents, toxings, weapons, equipment and means of delivery specified in Article I of the Convention, within its territory, under its jurisdiction or under its control anywhere, and calls upon all States Parties which have not yet taken any necessary measures in accordance with their constitutional processes to do so immediately.

The Conference invites States Parties which have found it necessary to enact specific legislation or take other regulatory measures relevant to this Article to make available the appropriate texts to the United Nations Centre for Disarmament, for the purposes of consultation.

Article V

The Conference notes the importance of Article V which contains the undertaking of States Parties to consult one another and to co-operate in solving any problems which may arise in relation to the objective of, or in the application of the provisions of, the Convention.

The Conference considers that the flexibility of the provisions concerning consultations and co-operation on any problems which may arise in relation to the objective, or in the application of the provisions of, the Convention, enables interested States Parties to use various international procedures which would make it possible to ensure effectively and adequately the implementation of the Convention provisions taking into account the concern expressed by the Conference participants to this effect.

These procedures include, *inter alia*, the right of any State Party subsequently to request that a consultative meeting open to all States Parties be convinced at expert level.

The Conference, noting the concerns and differing views

expressed on the adequacy of Article V, believes that this question should be further considered at an appropriate time.

Article VI

The Conference also notes the importance of Article VI, which in addition to the procedures contained in Article V, provides for any State Party, which finds that any other State Party is acting in breach of its obligations under the Convention, to lodge a complaint with the United Nations Security Council, and under which each State Party undertakes to co-operate in carrying out any investigation which the Security Council may initiate.

The Conference further notes that no State Party has invoked these provisions.

Article VII

The Conference notes with satisfaction that it has not proved necessary to invoke the provisions of Article VII.

Article VIII

The conference reaffirms that nothing contained in the Convention shall be interpreted as in any way limiting or detracting from the obligations assumed by any State under the Protocol for the prohibition of the use in war of asphyxiating, poisonous or other gases and of bacteriological methods of warfare, signed at Geneva on 17 June 1925. The Conference calls on those States Parties to the Convention which are parties to the Protocol to comply strictly with its provisions and those States not yet Parties to the said Protocol to ratify or accede to it at the earliest possible date.

Article IX

The Conference notes the importance of the provisions of Ariticle IX and of the preambular paragraphs concerning the commitment of States Parties to continue negotiations in good faith with a view to reaching early agreement on effective measures for the prohibition of the development, production and stockpiling of chemical weapons and for their destruction. The Conference deeply regrets that such agreement has not yet become a reality despite the fact that eight years have already elapsed since the Convention was opened for signature.

The Conference urges the Committee on Disarmament to undertake negotiations on an agreement on the complete and effective prohibitioon of the development, production and stockpiling of all chemical weapons and on their destruction, as a matter of high priority, taking into account all existing proposals and future initiatives. To this end, the Conference welcomes the establishment, by the Committee on Disarmament, of an *ad hoc* working group on chemical weapons and urged all the members of the Committee to contribute towards the fulfilment of its mandate.

The Conference takes note of the bilateral USA-USSR report (CD/48) presented to the Committee on Disarmament on the progress of their negotiations undertaken with a view to presenting a joint initiative to that Committee and notes their stated intention to continue intensive negotiations to this end.

The Conference reaffirms the obligation assumed by States Parties to the Convention to continue negotiations in good faith towards the recognized objective of an early agreement on complete, effective ad adequately verifiable measures for the prohibition of the development, production and stockpiling of chemical weapons and for their destruction.

Article X

The Conference notes that since the entry into force of the Convention, increasing importance has been attached by the International community to the principle that the disarmament process should help promote economic and social development, particularly in the developing countries. Accordingly, the Coference calls upon States Parties, especially developed countries, to increase, individually, or together with other States or international organizations, their scientific and technological co-operation, particularly with developing countries, in the peaceful uses of bacteriological (biological) agents and toxins. Such co-operation should include, *inter alia*, the transfer and exchange of information, training of personnel and transfer of materials and equipment on a more systematic and long-term basis.

Furthermore, the Conference notes with satisfaction that the implementation of the Convention has not hampered the economic or technological development of States Parties.

The Conference requests the United Nations secretariat to include in the background materials prepared for the second Review Conference of the Parties to the Convention on the Prohibition of the development, Production and Stockpiling of Bacteriological (Biological) and Toxin Weapons and on Their Destruction, information on the implementation of Article X by States Parties.

Article XI

The Conference notes the importance of the provisions of Article XI and that during the first five years of the operation of the Convention these provisions have not been invoked.

Article XII

The Conference welcomes the spirit of co-operation in which this Review Conference was conducted, and believes that such conferences constitute an effective method of reviewing the operation of the Convention with a view to ensuring that its purposes and provisions are being realized, in particular with respect to any new scientific and technological developments relevant to the Convention.

The Conference decides that a second Review Conference shall be held in Geneva at the request of a majority of States Parties not earlier than 1985 and , in any case, not later than 1990.

Any information provided by States Parties on scientific and technological developments relevant to the Convention, and on its implementation, shall be made available periodically to States Parties, in particular through the United Nations Centre for Disarmament.

Article XIII

The Conference notes the provisions of Article III and expresses its satisfaction that no State Party to the Convention has exercised its right to withdraw from the Covention.

Article XIV

The Conference notes with satisfaction that 81 States have ratified the Convention, 6 States have acceded to the Convention and a further 37 States have signed but have yet to ratify the Convention. the Conference calls upon all signatory States which have not ratified the Convention to do so without delay and upon those States which have not signed the Convention to join the States Parties thereto in their efforts to eliminate the risk of biological warfare.

Article XV

The Conference notes the provisions of Article XV.

VI. States Parties to Protocol and Conventions

Number of parties as on 31 December 1985	
1925 Geneva Protocol (GP)	108
1948 Genocide Convention (GC)	95
1972 Biological Weapons Convention (BWC)	103

	GP	*GC*	*BWC*		*GP*	*GC*	*BWC*
Afghanistan		1956	1975	Fiji	1973	1973	1973
Albania		1955		Finland	1929	1959	1974
Algeria		1963		France	1926	1950	1984
Argentina	1969	1956	1979	Gabon		1983	S
Australia	1930	1949	1977	Gambia	1966	1978	S
Austria	1928	1958	1973	German Democratic			
Bahamas		1975		Republic	1929	1973	1972
Bangladesh			1985	FR Germany	1929	1954	1983
Barbados	1976	1980	1973	Ghana	1967	1958	1975
Belgium	1928	1951	1979	Greece	1931	1954	1975
Benin			1975	Guatemala	1983	1950	1973
Bhutan	1978		1978	Guinea-Bissau			1976
Bolivia	1985	S	1975	Guyana			S
Botswana			S	Haiti		1950	S
Brazil	1970	1952	1973	Holy See (Vatican	1966		
Bulgaria	1934	1950	1972	City)			
Burkina Faso (formerly Upper Volta	1971	1965		Honduras		1952	1979
				Hungary	1952	1952	1972
Burma		1956	S	Iceland	1967	1949	1973
Burundi			S	India	1930	1959	1974
Byelorussia	1970	1954	1975	Indonesia	1971		S
Canada	1930	1952	1972	Iran	1929	1956	1973
Cape Verde			1977	Iraq	1939	1959	S
Central African	1970		S	Ireland	1930	1976	1972

Country			
Republic			
Chile	1935	1953	1980
China	1929	1983	1984
Colombia		1959	1983
Congo			1978
Costa Rica		1950	1973
Cuba	1966	1953	1976
Cyprus	1966	1982	1973
Czechoslovakia	1938	1950	1973
Denmark	1930	1951	1973
Dominican Republic	1970	S	1973
Ecuador	1970	1949	1975
Egypt	1928	1952	S
EI Salvador	S	1950	S
Ethiopia	1935	1949	1975
Liberia	1927	1950	S
Libya	1971		1982
Luxembourg	1936	1981	1976
Madagascar	1967		S
Malawi	1970		S
Malaysia	1970		S
Maldives	1966	1984	
Mali		1974	S
Malta	1970		1975
Mauritius	1970		1972
Mexico	1932	1952	1974
Monaco	1967	1950	
Monogolia	1968	1967	1972
Morocco	1970	1958	S

Country			
Israel	1969	1950	
Italy	1928	1952	1975
Ivory Coast	1970		S
Jamaica	1970	1968	1975
Japan	1970		1982
Jordan	1977	1950	1975
Kampuchea	1983	1950	1983
Kenya	1970		1976
Korea, Republic of (South)		1950	S
Kuwait	1971		1972
Lao People's Democratic Republic	1950	1973	
Lebanon	1969	1953	1975
Lesotho	1972	1974	1977
Saudi Arabia	1971	1950	1972
Senegal	1977	1983	1975
Seychelles			1979
Sierra Leone	1967		1976
Singapore			1975
Solomon Islands			1981
Somalia			S
South Africa	1930		1975
Spain	1929	1968	1979
Sri Lanka	1954	1950	S
Sudan	1980		
Sweden	1930	1952	1976
Switzerland	1932		1976
Syria	1968	1955	S

Nepal	1969	1969	S	Taiwan	x	+	1973
Netherlands	1930	1966	1981	Tanzania	1963	1984	S
New Zealand	1930	1978	1972	Thailand	1931		1975
Nicaragua	S	1952	1975	Togo	1971	1984	1976
Niger	1967		1972	Tonga	1971	1972	1976
Nigeria	1968		1973	Trinidad and Tobago	1970		
Norway	1932	1949	1973	Tunisia	1967	1956	1973
Pakistan	1960	1957	1974	Turkey	1929	1950	1974
Panama	1970	1950	1974	Uganda	1965		
Papua New Guinea	1981	1982	1980	UK	1930	1970	1975
Paraguay	1933	S	1976	Ukraine		1954	1975
Peru	1985	1960	1985	United Arab Emirates			S
Philippines	1973	1950	1973	Uruguay	1977	1967	1981
Poland	1929	1950	1973	USA	1975	1986	1975
Portugal	1930		1975	USSR	1928	1954	1975
Qatar	1976		1975	Venezuela	1928	1960	1978
Romania	1929	1950	1979	Viet Nam	1980	1981	1980
Rwanda	1964	1975	1975	Yemen Arab Republic	1971		S
Saint Vincent and the Grenadines		1981		Yemen, People's Democratic Republic			1979
San Marino			1975	of			
Sao Tome and				Yugoslavia	1929	1950	1973
Principe			1979	Zaire		1962	1977

Notes :

S= signed treaty.

*The Geneva Protocol, signed in1929 in the name of China, is valid for Taiwan which is part of China.

+The Genocide Convention was ratified in 1951 by Taiwan in the name of China. the People's Republic of China consider this ratification as null and void.

++The United States ratified the Genocide convention in Februrary 1986.

Source : SIPRI, 1986

Index